Canadian Sport Marketing

THIRD EDITION

Norm O'Reilly, PhD, MBA, CPA
University of Maine

Benoit Séguin, PhD
University of Ottawa

Gashaw Abeza, PhD
Towson University

Michael L. Naraine, PhD
Brock University

Library of Congress Cataloging-in-Publication Data

Names: O'Reilly, Norm, 1973- author. | Séguin, Benoit, 1963- author. | Abeza, Gashaw, author. | Naraine, Michael L., 1987- author.
Title: Canadian sport marketing / Norm O'Reilly, Benoit Séguin, Gashaw Abeza, Michael L. Naraine.
Description: Third edition. | Champaign, IL : Human Kinetics, Inc., 2022. | "This book is a revised edition of Sport Marketing: A Canadian Perspective, published in 2012 by Nelson Education Limited"—Title page verso. | Includes bibliographical references and index. | Summary: "This book focuses on sport marketing concepts, theories, applications and cases/expert perspectives on the Canadian marketplace. It covers essential topics including the Canadian sport system, market research, consumer behavior, digital marketing, and provides an example of a marketing plan for students to use and build from. In the Know sidebars and Executive Perspective sidebars provide practical application to the material and follow successful programs and individuals"—Provided by publisher.
Identifiers: LCCN 2021032868 (print) | LCCN 2021032869 (ebook) | ISBN 9781718200944 (paperback) | ISBN 9781718200951 (epub) | ISBN 9781718200968 (pdf)
Subjects: LCSH: Sports—Canada—Marketing
Classification: LCC GV716 .O739 2022 (print) | LCC GV716 (ebook) | DDC 796.06/9—dc23
LC record available at https://lccn.loc.gov/2021032868
LC ebook record available at https://lccn.loc.gov/2021032869

ISBN: 978-1-7182-0094-4 (print)

Copyright © 2022 by Norm O'Reilly, Benoit Séguin, Gashaw Abeza, and Michael L. Naraine
Copyright © 2009, 2012 by Nelson Education Limited

Human Kinetics supports copyright. Copyright fuels scientific and artistic endeavor, encourages authors to create new works, and promotes free speech. Thank you for buying an authorized edition of this work and for complying with copyright laws by not reproducing, scanning, or distributing any part of it in any form without written permission from the publisher. You are supporting authors and allowing Human Kinetics to continue to publish works that increase the knowledge, enhance the performance, and improve the lives of people all over the world.

The online learning content that accompanies this product is delivered on HK*Propel*, HKPropel.HumanKinetics.com. You agree that you will not use HK*Propel* if you do not accept the site's Privacy Policy and Terms and Conditions, which detail approved uses of the online content.

To report suspected copyright infringement of content published by Human Kinetics, contact us at **permissions@hkusa.com**. To request permission to legally reuse content published by Human Kinetics, please refer to the information at **https://US.HumanKinetics.com/pages/permissions-information**.

This book is a revised edition of *Sport Marketing: A Canadian Perspective*, published in 2012 by Nelson Education Limited.

The web addresses cited in this text were current as of 09/2021, unless otherwise noted.

Acquisitions Editor: Diana L. Vincer; **Developmental Editor:** Melissa Feld; **Permissions Manager:** Dalene Reeder; **Indexer:** Ferreira Indexing; **Graphic Designer:** Julie L. Denzer; **Cover Designer:** Keri Evans; **Cover Design Specialist:** Susan Rothermel Allen; **Photograph (cover):** Grant Faint /The Image Bank/Getty Images and Roberto Machado Noa/LightRocket via Getty Images; **Photo Production Manager:** Jason Allen; **Senior Art Manager:** Kelly Hendren; **Illustrations:** © Human Kinetics; **Production:** Westchester Publishing Services

Logo Credits

p. 4: Courtesy of T1 Agency; p. 7: Courtesy of National Lacrosse League; p. 10: Courtesy of UNB; p. 28: Courtesy of Curling Canada; p. 30: Courtesy of University of Guelph; p. 46: Courtesy of iSPARK Consulting; p. 50: Courtesy of Canadian Football League; p. 65: Courtesy of T1 Agency; p. 71: Courtesy of University of Waterloo; p. 103: Courtesy of Canadian Tire; p. 107: Courtesy of University of Windsor; p. 118: Courtesy of Canadian Olympic Committee; p. 133: Courtesy of ParticipACTION; p. 138: Courtesy of Hockey Canada; p. 142: Courtesy of NBA Canada; p. 147: Courtesy of York University; p. 154: Courtesy of University of Guelph; p. 161: Courtesy of Simon Fraser University; p. 162: Courtesy of Hamilton Tiger-Cats; p. 168: Courtesy of Guelph Nighthawks Basketball Club; p. 179: Courtesy of Canada Games Council; p. 211: Courtesy of True North Sports & Entertainment—Winnipeg Jets; p. 213: Courtesy of Brock University; p. 222: Courtesy of VISA; p. 242: Courtesy of Roth + Associates Revenue Consultants, Inc.; p. 250: Courtesy of Canada Paralympic Committee; p. 287: Courtesy of FSL; p. 294: Courtesy of Canadian Women & Sport; p. 300: Courtesy of Mount Royal University; p. 310: Courtesy of SPAD; p. 312: Courtesy of Ontario Soccer; p. 318: Courtesy of Canadian Olympic Committee; p. 331: Courtesy of CSIO; p. 338: Courtesy of Canadian Hockey League.

Printer: Versa Press
Printed in the United States of America   10 9 8 7 6 5 4 3 2 1

Human Kinetics
1607 N. Market Street
Champaign, IL 61820
USA

United States and International
Website: **US.HumanKinetics.com**
Email: info@hkusa.com
Phone: 1-800-747-4457

Canada
Website: **Canada.HumanKinetics.com**
Email: info@hkcanada.com

E8221

Tell us what you think!
Human Kinetics would love to hear what we can do to improve the customer experience.
Use this QR code to take our brief survey.

As a group of authors, we sincerely thank our families, colleagues, and former students, all of whom have shaped our paths and careers in the wonderful world of sport.

We would like to dedicate this book to the many Canadian sports business professionals who persevered during the COVID-19 global health pandemic, and who continue to innovate and pave a path for the next generation of leaders in the great sporting nation of Canada.

CONTENTS

Foreword   xi

Preface   xiii

Acknowledgments   xv

Introduction by Bob Wanzel, Founding Director, Institute for Sport Marketing,
Laurentian University   xvii

PART I   INTRODUCING CANADIAN SPORT MARKETING

CHAPTER 1   An Introduction to Sport Marketing   3

What Is Marketing? 4 • Key Marketing Concepts 6• The Uniqueness of Sport
Marketing 12 • Chapter Summary 13 • Test Your Knowledge 13 • Key Terms 14

Executive Perspective: Mark Harrison, President and CEO, The T1 Agency 4
Athlete Perspective: Curtis Knight, National Lacrosse League (NLL) Player and
Marketing Professional 7
Expert Perspective: Jonathon Edwards, University of New Brunswick,
Faculty of Kinesiology 10

CHAPTER 2   The Canadian Sport Industry   15

A Brief Introduction to Canada 16 • Sport Organizations in Canada 17 • Sport
Events in Canada 18 • Sport Facilities in Canada 19 • Professional Sport 20 •
University and College Sport 27 • Olympic Sport 33 • Grassroots and Amateur
Sport 39 • Chapter Summary 41 • Test Your Knowledge 42 • Key Terms 42

Executive Perspective: Katherine Henderson, Chief Executive Officer,
Curling Canada 28
Executive Perspective: Scott McRoberts, Director of Athletics,
University of Guelph 30

CHAPTER 3   Sport Market Research   43

Time as a Key Element in Marketing Research 44 • The Uses of Marketing
Research 44 • Types of Market Research 46 • Types of Data Sources 48 • The
Market Research Process 49 • Chapter Summary 60 • Test Your Knowledge
60 • Key Terms 60

Executive Perspective: Krista Benoit, President and CEO, iSPARK Consulting 46
Executive Perspective: Indivar Kushari, COO, Q.i. Value Systems Inc., and
former Chief Data and Information Officer, Canadian Football League 50

CHAPTER 4   The Canadian Sport Consumer   61

Understanding Sport Consumption 62 • Sport Consumption as Spectators 64 •
Sport Consumption as Participants 72 • Chapter Summary 76 • Test Your
Knowledge 76 • Key Terms 76

Executive Perspective: Rebecca Shanks, Vice-President, The T1 Agency 65
Expert Perspective: Luke R. Potwarka, Director, Spectator Experience and
Technology (SEAT) Laboratory and Associate Professor, Department
of Recreation and Leisure Studies, University of Waterloo 71

vi   Contents

PART II SEGMENTATION, TARGETING, AND POSITIONING AND THE CANADIAN SPORT MARKETING MIX

CHAPTER 5 Segmentation, Targeting, and Positioning in Canadian Sport   79

Segmentation, Targeting, and Positioning (STP) as Economic Advantage 80 • STP as the Bridge to Marketing Strategy 80 • Market Selection 83 • Targeting 90 • Positioning 93 • Common Target Markets in Canadian Sport 96 • Chapter Summary 98 • Test Your Knowledge 98 • Key Terms 99

Executive Perspective: Dale Hooper, Former Chief Brand Officer, Rogers, and Past Vice-President, Marketing and Consumer Insights, PepsiCo 80

Expert Perspective: Katie Sveinson, Assistant Professor, School of Sport, Tourism and Hospitality Management, Temple University and Larena Hoeber, Professor and Associate Dean for Graduate Studies, Research, and Special Projects, Faculty of Kinesiology and Health Studies, University of Regina 84

CHAPTER 6 The Sport Product   101

What Is the Sport Product? 102 • Sport Product Forms 107 • Sport Brands 112 • Packaging Elements of the Sport Product 113 • Chapter Summary 114 • Test Your Knowledge 114 • Key Terms 114

Executive Perspective: Darryl Boynton, Former Associate Vice-President Partnerships, Canadian Tire Corporation 103

Expert Perspective: Terry Eddy, Assistant Professor of Sport Management, University of Windsor 107

CHAPTER 7 The Digital Sport Product   115

What Makes a Sport Product Digital? 117 • Why Is the Digital Sport Product Special? 120 • What Are the Two Types of Digital Sport Products? 124 • Chapter Summary 135 • Test Your Knowledge 135 • Key Terms 135

Executive Perspective: David Thomson, Vice-President, Managing Director, NFL Canada 116

Executive Perspective: Mark Nadolny, Canadian Olympic Committee, Product Manager, Digital and Data 118

Executive Perspective: Alanna Harman, Assistant Professor in the Kinesiology and Physical Education Department, Laurier University 122

Executive Perspective: Elio Antunes, President and CEO, ParticipACTION 133

CHAPTER 8 Branding in Sport   137

Branding and Sport 138 • Building Brand Equity 141 • The Branding Process 146 • Real-Life Brand Management 147 • Chapter Summary 150 • Test Your Knowledge 150 • Key Terms 150

Executive Perspective: Scott Smith, President and CEO, Hockey Canada 138

Executive Perspective: Leah MacNab, Managing Director, National Basketball Association (NBA) Canada 142

Executive Perspective: Vijay Setlur, Sport Marketing Instructor, Schulich School of Business, York University 147

Contents vii

CHAPTER 9 Pricing in Sport Marketing 151

Price: What Is It? 152 • Price and the Four Ps 152 • Price and Value 156 • Ethics and Pricing 156 • Setting Price 157 • Break-Even Analysis 158 • Controlling Costs 158 • Key Pricing Issues 160 • Chapter Summary 165 • Test Your Knowledge 165 • Key Terms 166

Expert Perspective: Mike Alcorn, Researcher, International Institute for Sport Business and Leadership 154
Expert Perspective: Peter Tingling, Associate Dean, Undergraduate Program, and Associate Professor, Management Information Systems, Beedie School of Business, Simon Fraser University 161
Executive Perspective: Matt Afinec, President and COO, Hamilton Tiger-Cats Football Club, 2021 Grey Cup Festival, and Forge FC Hamilton Soccer Club 162

CHAPTER 10 Sport Promotion 167

Promotion 168 • Promotional Mix 170 • Executional Elements of Promotions 176 • Chapter Summary 182 • Test Your Knowledge 182 • Key Terms 182

Executive Perspective: Cameron Kusch, President, Guelph Nighthawks Basketball Club 168
Executive Perspective: Erin Mathany, Vice-President, Marketing and Partnerships, Canada Games Council 179

CHAPTER 11 Media and Distribution in Sport 183

A Brief History of the Sport Media Business 184 • Overview of Media Rights Revenue 186 • Models of Delivering Sport Content 188 • Key Players in the Sport Media Business in Canada 188 • Media-Relations Management 189 • Distribution of Tangible Sport Products and Events 192 • Chapter Summary 194 • Test Your Knowledge 195 • Key Terms 195

CHAPTER 12 Social Media and Distribution in Sport 197

Social Media and Its Distinguishing Features 198 • Dimensions of Social Media Use in Sport Marketing 201 • Practical Guide: Managing Social Media Platforms 207 • Return on Investment from Social Media in Sport 213 • Chapter Summary 217 • Test Your Knowledge 217 • Key Terms 217

Executive Perspective: John Delaney, Manager, Social Media, True North Sports + Entertainment—Winnipeg Jets 211
Expert Perspective: Olan Scott, Assistant Professor of Sport Management, Brock University 213

PART III IMPORTANT STRATEGIC ELEMENTS OF SPORT MARKETING IN CANADA

CHAPTER 13 Sport Sponsorship 221

Market Trends in Canadian Sponsorship 224 • Sponsorship and Activation 225 • History of Sponsorship 226 • Sponsorship and Its Roots in Philanthropy 227 • Relationship of Sponsorship to Marketing 227 • Relationship between Sponsorship and Advertising 228 • Corporate Objectives and Sponsorship 230 • Reaching the Target Market 233 • Sponsorship and Olympic and Paralympic Sport Properties 239 • Chapter Summary 240 • Test Your Knowledge 240 • Key Terms 240

viii   Contents

Executive Perspective: Brenda Woods, Vice-President of Marketing, Visa Canada 222

Executive Perspective: Don Mayo, Global Managing Partner, IMI International 237

CHAPTER 14 Building Successful Sport Sponsorships   241

Sponsorship Stakeholders 244 • Sponsorship in Canada: A Model for Sport Sponsorship Success 245 • Step 1: Presponsorship Practices 246 • Step 2: Negotiation Stage 253 • Step 3: Sponsorship Life 255 • Step 4: Sponsorship Termination 259 • Best Practices in Canadian Sport Sponsorship 259 • Chapter Summary 261 • Test Your Knowledge 261 • Key Terms 261

Executive Perspective:Gavin Roth, Founder and Managing Partner, Gavin Roth+Associates Revenue Consultants Inc. 242

Executive Perspective: François Robert, Executive Director, Partnerships, Canadian Paralympic Committee 250

CHAPTER 15 Ambush Marketing   263

The Business Impact of Ambush Marketing 264 • What Does Ambush Marketing Look Like? 264 • Ambush Marketing: An Alternative to Traditional Sponsorship Strategies? 265 • Research on Ambush Marketing 266 • Strategies of Ambush Marketing 267 • Counter-ambushing Strategies 271 • Ambush Marketing and Clutter 273 • Chapter Summary 274 • Test Your Knowledge 274 • Key Terms 275

CHAPTER 16 Technology in Sport Marketing   277

Information Technology and Information Systems 278 • Information Systems in the Marketing Cycle 283 • Chapter Summary 291 • Test Your Knowledge 291 • Key Terms 291

Expert Perspective: Cheri Bradish, Ryerson University 287

CHAPTER 17 Social Marketing in Sport   293

What Is Social Marketing? 295 • When Is Social Marketing Appropriate? 296 • Understanding Social Marketing and the Company and Consumer 298 • Segmentation, Targeting, and Positioning for Social Marketers 299 • Social-Marketing Strategy 301 • Target Market: High-Performance Sport 303 • Chapter Summary 303 • Test Your Knowledge 303 • Key Terms 304

Executive Perspective: Allison Sandmeyer-Graves, CEO, Canadian Women & Sport 294

Expert Perspective: David Legg, Professor, Mount Royal University 300

CHAPTER 18 Sport Marketing Strategy Implementation and Evaluation   305

Marketing Strategy Implementation in Sport 306 • Marketing-Strategy Evaluation in Sport 309 • Chapter Summary 314 • Test Your Knowledge 314 • Key Terms 315

Executive Perspective: Paul Ausman, Manager, Event Services, Ottawa Sports and Entertainment Group 308

Expert Perspective: Dana Lee Ellis, Associate Professor, School of Sports Administration Management, Laurentian University 310

Executive Perspective: Johnny Misley, CEO, Ontario Soccer, and Board of Directors, League1 Ontario 312

CHAPTER 19 Olympic Marketing 317

History of Olympic Sponsorship: 1896 to 1976 319 • IOC's Sponsorship Expansion: 1976 to the Present 323 • Olympic Broadcasting 325 • The Olympic Partner (TOP) Sponsorship Program 328 • The Olympic Brand 329 • Olympic Marketing in Canada 330 • Chapter Summary 335 • Test Your Knowledge 336 • Key Terms 336

Executive Perspective: Andrew Baker, Vice-President, International Relations and Public Affairs, Canadian Olympic Committee 318

Executive Perspective: Debbie Low, CEO, Canadian Sport Institute Ontario 331

Executive Perspective: David Bedford, CEO, Athletics Canada 333

CHAPTER 20 Marketing Plan Example 337

The Desert Dry Rack: A Product by Desert Sports Limited 337 • Executive Summary 337 • Market Research 339 • Situation Analysis 341 • Competition Analysis 343 • Marketing Strategy 345 • Financials 351 • Chapter Summary 353

Executive Perspective: Dan MacKenzie, President, Canadian Hockey League 338

Glossary   354
References   361
Index   371
About the Authors   381

FOREWORD

As this third edition is going to press, the world is facing an existential crisis—the COVID-19 pandemic—that has affected every continent and has not yet been contained. Political and policy leadership with respect to the pandemic has been well short of impressive. World economies have been devastated, and efforts to stimulate them by throwing money into hastily conceived short-term measures will have long-term tax and other implications. Reliable vaccines have not been available, and even if available shortly, will not have been sufficiently researched by reference to normal standards of effectiveness and a study of side effects. It is indeed a strange new world.

If not as strange, the new world of sport that has emerged in the past decade is decidedly different from that which existed at the time of the second edition, close to a decade ago. Interestingly enough, the Canadian sport landscape provides a perspective that is reflective of many developments that have also occurred elsewhere.

It is easy to admire the enormous success of the 2010 Olympic Winter Games in Vancouver-Whistler and their impact on the whole of Canada and Canadian sport. As was the case in the two previous Canadian editions of the Olympics in 1976 and 1988, we demonstrated organizational competence and a warm reception for the world. Vancouver was also the occasion for Canadian athletes to enjoy a previously unmatched success on the Olympic field of play. A measure of the impact of the Vancouver Olympics is that, even 11 years later, a significant percentage of the all-time Canadian television viewing audiences remain Vancouver 2010 experiences, led by the gold medal hockey games and opening and closing ceremonies.

The organizational skills and special topographical features available in Canada led the International Olympic Committee (IOC) to all but offer the 2026 Winter Games to Calgary. Unfortunately, indifferent city and provincial leadership led to a fumbling of that opportunity. The Canadian Olympic Committee has, however, begun a review of possibilities for bidding to host subsequent editions of both summer and winter games under the more accessible host selection process developed by the IOC.

As the effective headquarters of the World Anti-Doping Agency (WADA), Canada has been central to developments in the fight against doping in sport. Canadians were at the centre of the two WADA investigations of the doping system in Russia that led to suspension of the Russian athletics federation, the WADA recommendation that Russia be suspended from international competition and hosting of sports events for four years, which is currently before the Court of Arbitration for Sport. The same investigations led to successful French criminal prosecutions of officials of the International Association of Athletics Federations (now World Athletics), with sanctions that included prison terms for several of the accused. A substantially revised World Anti-Doping Code was to come into effect on January 1, 2021.

On the sport marketing front, including broadcasting, there have been unusual challenges resulting from the postponement of the Tokyo 2020 Olympics to 2021, the full impact of which is not yet clear, including any possible knockoff impact on the 2022 Olympic Winter Games in Beijing. Both Japanese and Chinese organizers are committed to proceeding with organizing and holding the Games, but they can only control their own efforts, not the pandemic.

The growth of social media has led to a better understanding of digital marketing, including ambush marketing in the post-2020 Vancouver era. Developments in the sport landscape have seen the emergence of extraordinary advancements in digital sports, esports, and fantasy sports, turning them from mere curiosities into significant "players" that cannot be ignored. The interplay between these developments and traditional sports is a work in progress as 19th- and 21st-century paradigms attempt to understand each other and find ways to coexist.

In Canada the past decade has been noteworthy for its lack of "big" events. Apart from planning to share the 2026 FIFA World Cup with the United States and Mexico and hosting the 2015 Pan American Games and the 2015 FIFA Women's World Cup, Canada has held no major events. In the pro sport world, a women's hockey league has foundered, but other leagues in basketball and soccer have managed to launch and survive in the relatively small Canadian market.

A special feature of this edition is its increased focus on the Canadian scene, providing insight that does not occur in works dedicated to world-level market analysis. In addition, it now facilitates access to senior high school and junior college students as well as to the usual university-level students.

The principal authors have added to their bench strength with Gashaw Abeza and Michael Naraine, recent Canadian doctoral graduates and now professors, which will bring added value to an already comprehensive sport marketing resource.

Richard W. Pound
October 2020

PREFACE

Thank you for selecting sport marketing as a potential career or a topic of interest. This third edition of this book is very special for the lead two authors, as we are being joined by two of our colleagues and former graduate students, to bring our author team to four. As a group, it is a privilege for us to share our passion for sport marketing and the knowledge, contacts, and concepts we have built up over a combined 100 years—yes, a century—in sport as athletes, coaches, event operators, administrators, volunteers, heads of delegations, professors, board members, technical officials, and in many other roles. Further, as a team, we all have deep ties to Canada but have also spent significant parts of our lives internationally, which allows us to bring a global view to Canadian sport.

This book comes out of our many years as students of sport marketing, ever learning, ever experiencing, and ever building our knowledge base. As former athletes, coaches, officials, and sport administrators, we put forward our first two editions of this book in times of growth and excitement in sport, while this edition is written under the shadow of COVID-19, a global pandemic that has deeply affected our industry at home and abroad. Even in this time, however, we agree unanimously that marketing in Canadian sport has a bright future and an important role to play in our society.

The book is organized in three sections. The first introduces sport marketing and sport marketing research, and describes both the Canadian industry and the Canadian sport consumer. The second section builds out the strategic elements of the Canadian sport marketing mix, namely product, price, promotion, and place-related strategic elements. The third and final section goes in depth into a series of key areas of sport marketing, including sponsorship, ambush marketing, services, technology, and social media. Two new chapters in this edition are "The Digital Sport Product" and "Social Media and Distribution in Sport." Each chapter includes exercises, "In the Know" sections that describe an important aspect of the content in detail, applied examples, and mini case studies, which are available in HK*Propel*.

As we reflect on this third edition, we are especially proud that more than 40 colleagues and experts in marketing and in sport have also shared their views in this book in the form of executive or expert perspectives or case studies. We all strongly support the concepts of applied learning and believe that this book will provide you with the tools necessary to begin or enhance a career in sport marketing in both good times and bad.

Some might ask, given our small market, why a Canadian book? Our answer is simple. We have always said that marketing is strategic and strategy is driven by its environment; therefore, material specific to the Canadian environment is important, perhaps vitally important, to any Canadian student of sport marketing.

Thank you, and we hope you enjoy the read.

ACKNOWLEDGMENTS

The authors acknowledge the significant contributions to this book of the many industry experts and academic colleagues who provided their point of views and insights on the industry for the purposes of improved learning. This is wonderful and appreciated. The backgrounds of these nearly 40 contributors are included throughout the book, along with their bios.

We also sincerely thank Lance Warwick, research associate, for his contribution, which helped make this book a reality.

As with the first two editions, we view this book as an ongoing work in progress and welcome any comments or feedback you may have as you work your way through its pages.

INTRODUCTION

Baseball game today 2:00 p.m. Wanzel Field.

A can of peas—on special.

The previous two notices are related—and therein lies the development of the field of sport marketing. Historically, a sporting contest such as a baseball game was simply "announced" and a packaged goods item was noted at a special price at the local store. The proliferation of packaged goods products (and other grocery and nongrocery items) available to the public through the development of super-store distribution brought sophisticated product marketing to the industry. The advent of the Internet brought digital sponsorship activations and online access to sport products. Social media has turned athletes from stars in their sports to global celebrities who transcend industries and borders and rival movie stars for attention. Most recently, we have seen sport take to being a digital product itself, esports.

Looking back, at each of these stages, the development of sport marketing lagged behind most other industry marketing thrusts for many years. This has been well written about. Now we're being hit again, making us lag behind most industries, as our live events and participation programs are grounded by the global pandemic known as COVID-19.

But we always catch up eventually. Following the turn of the millennium, as media platforms developed, sport diversified, event growth surged, and sponsorship expanded, sophisticated sport marketing became essential and developed into a major industry in which thousands of professionals made a living. The convergence of product, entertainment, and sport marketing became the norm. Because sport can now deliver an audience or target market, the "Wanzel Field" (or venue) has itself become sponsored, now being named as a business marketing tool (e.g., Scotiabank Centre).

As the founding director (1974) of Canada's first university (and business) degree program in sports administration (which the Laurentian University senate approved in 1972), I discovered a dearth of information on sport marketing. At that time, only three universities in the United States had sport management programs (and none offered a business degree). To build a curriculum meant importing articles from the sport and business sections of newspapers and extrapolating from textbooks on business marketing. Slowly the development of sport and event marketing led to specific information being written about the field. This information was, for the most part, focused on the development of the field in the United States. Today this trend continues, but Canada is an important player, home to leading professional clubs and host of three Olympic Games and the upcoming FIFA 2026 World Cup, to be hosted jointly with the United States and Mexico.

This text by Professors O'Reilly, Séguin, Abeza, and Naraine is important: It has information and case examples drawn from Canadian experiences, which are essential, not only for Canadian students, but also for students and practitioners worldwide in this field. The authors' background experiences in sport and event marketing bring a very interesting perspective to the information conveyed. The text offers a broad insight into the field, with an introduction to the sport marketing landscape, the sport marketing mix, and strategic elements in a number of areas. The executive perspectives adds to the in-depth knowledge presented for all components of the text.

Since my time at Laurentian, which included founding Canada's first research centre in sport business, the Institute for Sport Marketing (ISM) at the School of Sports Administration at Laurentian University, Canadian universities and colleges have expanded their offerings and programs enormously, providing valuable human resources to sport organizations across the country and beyond. Whether at Laurentian, Brock, New Brunswick, Ottawa, Waterloo,

Alberta, Simon Fraser, McMaster, or Guelph, many in our field have worked to improve private-sector sponsorship and investment in the Canadian sport system, a key content area in this book and, in my view, a very important contribution to the sport marketing field.

Bob Wanzel

Professor Emeritus Laurentian University and Founding Director Institute for Sport Marketing

Advisory Board Member, International Institute for Sport Business and Leadership, University of Guelph

October 2020

PART I
INTRODUCING CANADIAN SPORT MARKETING

CHAPTER 1

An Introduction to Sport Marketing

LEARNING OBJECTIVES

After studying this chapter, you will be able to do the following:

- Define a market, marketing, and sport marketing
- Understand the role of marketing in sports
- Distinguish marketing of sport from marketing through sport
- Understand the importance of target markets; market research; segmentation, targeting, positioning (STP); fan loyalty; the marketing mix; digital marketing; social media marketing; and sponsorship

Every day we are hit by thousands of messages about products, ideas, activities, services, and entertainment. Many of these make sense; many do not. Some catch our attention; others do not. Some make us think, "I should get one of those." And sometimes we even stop what we are doing and impulsively make an immediate purchase, whether online or offline. At the same time, in the marketing offices of organizations across Canada, marketers plan how they can get their product offerings to attract our attention and, ideally, lead to a purchase.

This is **marketing**. Marketing involves an **exchange** between two parties that provides a win–win benefit to both. This is typically an exchange of some product—some tangible good, service, idea, or behaviour—in return for money. Ideally, this exchange is the building block for multiple exchanges, or a long-term **relationship**, between the marketer and the **consumer**. This process is supported by a **marketing mix** composed of the strategic elements of **product**, **price**, **promotion**, and **place**, commonly referred to as the four Ps of marketing, which are developed to support and ultimately achieve an exchange.

Although sport had been "sold" since the days of the ancient Olympics in Greece and the gladiators in Rome, it is only in the past 40 years that the marriage between sport and marketing became a formal arrangement worth multiple billions of dollars annually. Regardless of the industry in which the marketer works (e.g., retail, banking, high technology), sport has the ability to provide marketing benefit beyond that of other properties (e.g., festivals, arts, community events). It is the mission of this book to describe this advantage and provide tools that allow marketers to apply it.

What Is Marketing?

The American Marketing Association (AMA) updated its definition of marketing in 2017 as follows:

> *Marketing is the activity, set of institutions, and processes for creating, communicating, delivering, and exchanging offerings that have value for customers, clients, partners, and society at large. (American Marketing Association, 2017)*

This definition clearly describes marketing as not only an organizational function but also a set of processes that enable the creation of

---

EXECUTIVE PERSPECTIVE
The Power of Sports

MARK HARRISON, President and CEO, The T1 Agency

I refer to sport marketing as a subset of marketing that presents a unique opportunity to marketers to activate their brands. With the power of sports, a marketer can conduct strategic initiatives using any of the key marketing tactics—public relations, celebrity spokespeople, sampling, advertising, corporate hosting, contesting, and so on.

So what makes sport marketing unique? Powerful? Dynamic? Why is it that sport marketing is more studied and practised than, say, entertainment marketing or cause-related marketing? The answer lies in the fact that it is different from those other areas of marketing.

I propose, and I am not the first person to do so, that sport has a unique attribute, unseen in all other properties in marketing, that drives its appeal. That attribute is the power of uncertainty in sport. Sport has no predetermined outcome. It has no set conclusion. There is no confirmed ending. Think about it. A concert has a start and an end, with very few surprises. A play or a movie may be new, but it is driven by a script, and you can find the outcome ahead of attending (by the way, she dumps the good-looking guy for the nice guy in the end!). A fundraiser marches to a particular drummer: We listen to the speeches, we eat the food, we bid on the auction items, we dance, we go home feeling worthwhile. These examples are from the more dynamic forms of marketing, not even the more traditional forms such as TV advertising, in-store displays, or billboards.

Sport has no script. It has no screenwriter. It has no predetermined plot. Yet it does have a stage. It does have directors. It does have performers. But best of all, it has circumstance. It is affected by the weather. It hinges on the physical and mental well-being of the competitors. It has uncontrollable variables, such as officiating and coaching. It is unpredictable due to momentum and how it changes within the game or competition, when spontaneous reactions erupting from the athletes add to the pressure of the moment.

Coupled with the unpredictability of sport are the overpowering emotions associated with it. But what drives these emotions? Surely uncertainty on its own cannot be enough to excite spectators or make them clasp their hands in prayer, to encourage fans to act like children, to lead the media to debate mundane stats till sunset, and to drive commentators to act like Elvis had been spotted in the building. Beyond the "Go Team Go," beyond the cheering for an individual elite athlete in an international competition, beyond the "She's my favourite player" is something more fundamental, more personal, more involved. That is the connection between the athlete and the team and the individual fan.

That team or athlete represents not just my country or my region or my city or my school. They represent me. And because they represent me, the team in black represents the other guys. Not the other city or the other country or the other school. They represent everybody I want to be better than. If my team or my hero conquers all, not only are they more powerful, smarter, stronger, and better looking, but magically I am as well. Magically I can deal with my boss, my neighbour, my family, my annoying cable installer, with a bit more authority, a little more confidence, and a touch more swagger. Why? Because I'm a winner.

I worked just as hard as my team or favourite athlete did in training. I endured the same late nights and early mornings, strict diets and intense workouts, demanding coaches and intimidating trainers. I sacrificed, and I won. I bled for this. Now I am more than a fan. I am the coach, the quarterback, the boxer, the race car driver. I made that 11-foot putt on the 18th. Or at least I believe deep down inside that if I had been taught to golf when I was three and had had 72,000 hours of range time, I could have made that putt!

In the end, the sports arena provides an unparalleled opportunity for fans to transpose themselves to another place, to ride every emotion possible upward and downward until the outcome is determined, and then to be encased by the resulting emotion. As a marketer, you have a unique opportunity to become part of this experience, to demonstrate that your brand is just as involved in this modern-day tragedy as the fan is, and to communicate that your brand is helping the consumer's team to win, to play better, and to overcome all odds. And if the brand is doing that for my heroes, it must also be doing that for me.

MARK HARRISON is the founder of the T1 Agency and SponsorshipX. He is a sought-after speaker, holds an MBA in entrepreneurship and strategic marketing, and has 25 years of cutting-edge experience in sponsorship, event marketing, and promotions. He has worked with blue chip brands including Mattel, Coca-Cola, Canadian Tire, the Canadian Football League (CFL), BMW, Esso, HBC, and Johnson & Johnson.

relationships (multiple exchanges) between an organization and its stakeholders, both internal (e.g., employees, consultants) and external (e.g., suppliers, customers). Value is a key construct in the definition, which explicitly appreciates that the benefits provided to both parties in the exchange result from the delivery of value to customers. A recent development in marketing is also emphasized in the AMA definition—the move to include the impact on society at large of a marketer's activities and decisions is also emphasized.

Marketing has been around a very long time. In older times, barter was often at the heart of the exchange between two entities. For example, a corn farmer would exchange five bushels of corn for a quarter side of beef from a nearby beef farmer. Some marketers have even traced the roots of marketing as far back as 3,000 years, to the Lydians, who were known to be the first to use coins as a form of value (Dewan et al., 2005). Bartels (1976) suggests that the term *marketing* was coined around 1910. Following World War II, we begin to see in the literature and in practise the early developments of the field as a management discipline. Often described as "marketing management," the field has evolved considerably, and today we know that business is most profitable when both parties in an exchange (i.e., the selling organization and the buying customer) are satisfied and happy.

Key Marketing Concepts

This book assumes that the reader has only a limited understanding of marketing. Therefore, we will now highlight some key concepts of marketing.

The Marketing Exchange

The marketing exchange, which is a key concept of marketing theory, articulates that both sides must receive value from the transaction that they perceive to be greater than what the exchange is costing them. For example, if Susan is considering spending $139 on a ticket to a Calgary Flames hockey game, she will only make the exchange if she believes that the value she will receive back (e.g., entertainment, seat location, team, associated activities, telling her friends she went to the game) is worth to her more than $139. This concept of value varies from one individual to the other and from one group to the next.

Value and Utility

A set of marketing concepts that aid marketers in their activities are the four well-established utilities (values provided from satisfying a need or want) of marketing. When achieved, these four utilities—**form**, **time**, place, and **possession**—are what provide value to the customer.

- *Form* refers to the tangible properties of the product. For example, the form properties of a running shoe include comfort, durability, look, colour, ease of use, and packaging.
- *Time* describes the consumer's ability to access the product at the right time. From the organization's end, this includes such considerations as inventory, delivery, and warehousing. An example is the concession stands (i.e., the food and beverage vendors onsite) at the 2016 IIHF Women's World Ice Hockey Championships in Kamloops, which were placed where fans who wanted to be able to purchase cold beer, warm hot dogs, and salted popcorn could do so without missing any of the action on the ice.
- *Place* is the **utility** of being able to purchase or receive the product at a convenient and accessible location. Buying tickets for a sporting event is a good example, because those that are easily accessible (available through Ticketmaster, StubHub, VividSeats, in person, online from the club/event, retail outlets, etc.) are more likely to sell than those sold by limited outlets. The location of the concession, or the "place" of purchase, is the important aspect of this utility, whereby the marketer wants to facilitate access and purchase by a potential consumer.
- *Possession* is the value created by giving the consumer the ability to actually take ownership of the product immediately. Possession becomes more important in a high-involvement decision such as purchasing a Montreal Canadiens season ticket package. The rationale for this utility for a consumer is best explained via the (nonsport) purchase of a house or automobile. The "wait" to move in or get your new car is a negative for many consumers, which makes possession an attractive utility.

Needs and Wants

A key idea in marketing is the satisfaction of consumer needs and wants. Indeed, this is what marketing seeks to do: to respond to needs and wants of consumers and potential consumers. At a most basic level, people have needs (e.g., shelter, food, drink) and wants (e.g., ego, self-actualization) that organizations in capitalist societies seek to meet. In the Western world, where technology, disposable income, and free time have led to a consumer-based society, one could argue that many wants have become needs. For example, an individual who golfs five times a year does not require a set of high-end Tiger Woods–endorsed clubs to play a round; however, given the advances of our materialistic culture, for some this may be considered a necessity. Right or wrong, this is a reality.

ATHLETE PERSPECTIVE
Sport Marketing: A Pro Athlete's Perspective

CURTIS KNIGHT, National Lacrosse League (NLL) Player and Marketing Professional

So, you want to work in sport marketing?

I would like to share my experiences with sport marketing from two perspectives. I am guessing that many of you who are reading this book share a passion for athletics or have been an athlete at some point in your lives. For me, I have been very fortunate to have become a professional athlete in the sport I love, lacrosse. I just finished my seventh year in the National Lacrosse League (NLL). This was my first year with the Rochester Knighthawks, following six years with the Saskatchewan/Edmonton Rush. So far, I have played 111 games and have 353 points to my name. Combined with being an athlete, I have had the opportunity to work in sport while I am playing or in the off-season, so I want to share my perspective of being both a professional athlete and an industry professional.

Since you are reading this book, I am sure many of you aspire to work in the sport industry, specifically sport marketing. As a professional athlete, I have the good fortune to have insider knowledge of how the industry works. If you are an athlete, leverage your insider knowledge, because you have many skills that carry over directly to the workforce. If you are not an athlete, find ways to learn through volunteering, coaching, refereeing, or interning. Leverage these experiences, which will come in handy when entering the industry.

Working in sport marketing requires a knowledge both of sport and marketing. Your experience as an athlete, a coach, an official, or an administrator, has allowed you to build foundational skills such as teamwork, a work ethic, sportsmanship, and strategy, among others. Years of coaching, being a coach, or observing coaching will have taught you how to receive feedback, which has made you "coachable." All these foundations can be applied to sport marketing.

In my case, when I got my first sport marketing job at an agency in Toronto, I treated my first few months on the job similarly to how I would treat a tryout for a new team: I put my head down and worked as hard as I could. Eventually people noticed the value I provided.

The second perspective I will share is my experience working as an industry professional in sport marketing at that same agency. I was lucky enough to start as an intern and work my way up to an analyst role before deciding to go back to school and get my master's degree. I would recommend, if you can, starting from any entry level, co-op, or internship position in order to get your foot in the door at an agency or a brand or sport organization. I worked specifically in sponsorship consulting. However, it does not matter whether you choose the agency route or work for a sport organization; getting your foot in the door is invaluable. I would argue that I learned five times as much working at the agency within a few months than I did throughout my entire undergraduate degree. Any practical experience you can get early on is priceless. With that said, start early! I recommend trying to work for a provincial sport organization (PSO) or national sport organization (NSO). It is not the most glamorous or financially rewarding work, but organizations like Rugby Canada, Lacrosse Canada, and Swimming Ontario truly need you, and you will get high-level experience as a result. You will learn, gain experience, and begin to build a network. Everyone wins.

> *continued*

> Sport Marketing: A Pro Athlete's Perspective > *continued*

Expand Your Thinking

One more thing I would suggest to you is to expand your horizons and work in different places. It is very common in our field and in Canada to be too focused on the big sports (for example, the seven clubs in the National Hockey League [NHL], the Toronto Raptors, or the Toronto Blue Jays) when there are so many other organizations and leagues with great potential to launch or build your career. Oftentimes many young professionals only seek the most prestigious jobs in sport; however, this is not always the best route (or, in many cases, no door opens at one of these jobs and the individual moves out of sport). As noted, my sport is lacrosse. I grew up playing in Whitby, Ontario, before making it to the Junior ranks and eventually to the top indoor lacrosse league in the world, the NLL. I am looking forward to my eighth season, and from what I have witnessed, there is so much room for growth in leagues like the NLL and many others such as the Canadian Football League (CFL), Canadian Premier League (CPL), and Canadian Elite Basketball League (CEBL). Similar to the PSOs and NSOs, these organizations and leagues are in need of young, dynamic thinkers. I encourage you to keep your mind open to the possibility of working for these types of organizations and not just the "name-brand" ones. There are many options available to sport marketers here.

CURTIS KNIGHT is a professional lacrosse player for the Rochester Knighthawks of the National Lacrosse League (NLL). In the past, he's worked for the T1 Agency in downtown Toronto, where he specialized in sponsorship consulting and worked with brands and properties such as Dairy Farmers of Canada, Nestlé, Canadian Interuniversity Sport (now U Sports), and Tennis Canada. At the time of writing, he is working toward an MSc degree in Management at the University of Guelph. His research is focused on how professional sports teams make decisions about athlete compensation.

In practice, marketers' work is a two-stage process—discovering customer needs and wants and then satisfying them. The first task is driven by discovery through market research; the second is driven by strategy development and implementation through the application of marketing concepts.

Applied Sociology

Some people view marketing as the application of sociology. As marketers, we seek to understand society and how it functions and then work within it. Our understanding of how society is structured, how people live, and what people need and want allows us to help our organizations be successful. On this point, it is important to note that marketers do not critique society; rather, they work within it.

Relationship Marketing

Relationship marketing—also known as 1:1 Marketing—is based on the notion that organizations use communication to market to individual consumers through databases, online ordering, social media, and direct phone or Internet communication to create one-to-one relationships without the necessity of individual in-person interaction. Quite simply, technology has enabled mass-market offerings to be customized. Although this is impossible with certain products and in certain industries, it is widely viewed as the ideal form of marketing—providing an offering that is designed to meet the needs of specific customers.

Understanding the Internal Environment: The Three Cs

When looking internally at their own organization and offerings, marketers focus on the three Cs—**company**, **competition**, and **consumers**. To be successful, they must understand their internal reality just as much as their external environment, and knowing each of the three Cs is a way to do this.

IN THE KNOW

Wants Are the Secret to Marketing in an Advanced Society

Although many of us focus on the idea of "needs" in our purchases and our life, the reality is that in most developed societies in the world, most purchases are made at the level of "wants." To borrow from Abraham Maslow's concept of the hierarchy of needs, this refers to the idea of "self-actualization," or the interest in a purchase reflecting who we are or perhaps suggesting who we might want to be. A front-row seat to a Montreal Canadiens game is a "want," as are most merchandise purchases or the support of a club sponsor by purchasing their product or service. We urge you to focus on wants when building marketing programs and activities.

• The company (the first C) is the firm or organization of the marketer and it is described based on its assets (e.g., skilled employees, physical structures, patents) and competencies, or things it is good at (e.g., software development, supply chain management, social media). The things the company does better than its competition are called competitive advantages, and those that can endure are known as sustainable competitive advantages.

• Competition (the second C) involves understanding who the company is competing against for customers. It takes three forms: direct competitors, **substitutes**, and future competition. For example, in seeking to increase ticket sales, the marketing director of the Toronto Argos CFL team would consider nearby professional football clubs (e.g., Buffalo Bills and Hamilton Tiger-Cats) as direct competition; any entertainment activity that could replace going to the game (e.g., other sport events, going to a movie, going on a date, watching television) as a substitute; and a possible National Football League (NFL), Arena Football League team (again), or entrant from a new football league setting up shop in Toronto as future competition.

• For consumers (the third C), the marketer uses various concepts of consumer behaviour to understand the individuals in the market and why, for example, these people might attend an Argos game. The term *consumers* in this context refers to both existing ones (i.e., they have already made a purchase from us in the past) and potential ones (i.e., people in our potential target market whom we'd like to convince to make a purchase). Later chapters in the book are devoted to market research (to learn about our current and potential consumers) and to understanding Canadian sport consumers by identifying who they are and what they need and want.

Understanding the External Environment: PEST

Marketers must understand their organization's external environment to develop and implement effective strategy. PEST—which stands for political, economic, social (demographic), and technological—is a useful tool to describe and organize the forces whose opportunities and threats the marketer must consider. The importance of PEST (or any external tool for marketing analysis) is to allow marketers to understand the market in which they operate and plan for the potential external (and noncontrollable) factors that will affect their activities in the future. This could include things such as

1. an election leading to a new prime minister with a different political philosophy,

2. a rise in interest rates, meaning the cost of borrowing money to finance activities increases,

3. the impact of an aging population, and

4. the development of new technologies.

Tools for external environment analysis are shared in detail in chapters 2 through 5 in the book.

EXPERT PERSPECTIVE

Marketing for Survival: A Case Study of Private Hockey Schools in Canada

Kinesiology
Fredericton

JONATHON EDWARDS, University of New Brunswick, Faculty of Kinesiology

Marketing does not exist in a vacuum, and the focus, for most organizations, is to market a product (also called a *good*) or service for the intention of gaining profit and competitive advantage over organizations operating in the same or similar environments. The term *profit* is understood in different ways when discussing it within the context of sport. For example, professional sports franchises (e.g., Toronto Maple Leafs, Los Angeles Lakers, and Toronto Blue Jays) seek profit in the form of revenue through the marketing of merchandise, tickets, athletes, teams, and leagues. Conversely, in amateur sports, marketing for profit can mean that the nonprofit organizations are using marketing techniques to attract athletes, sustain the organization, increase membership, and attract sponsors.

Drawing on the work of Fullerton and Merz (2008), sports marketing can be understood in one of two ways: marketing through sports and the marketing of sports. Marketing through sports "is using sport as a promotional vehicle or sponsorship platform for companies that market consumer to a lesser extent, industrial products," while the marketing of sports is "the application of marketing principles and processes to market goods and services directly to sports participants and spectators" (Gray & McEvoy, 2005, p. 229). As such, the core product or service can centre around an individual athlete, team, or league.

An example showing how marketing plays a critical role in the sports industry is the competition for talent between the private sports schools (also identified as prep schools) and public club sports at the amateur sports level. This is particularly the case in the Canadian hockey industry: These private schools (e.g., Notre Dame School) are looking to gain a competitive advantage for the most talented hockey players over the club hockey system (e.g., Canadian Athletic Club). Washington and Edwards (2016) indicated that prep schools have existed in Canada since the 1800s: "Stanstead College (1872); St. Andrews College (1899); Bishops College (1836); and Ridley College (1889)" (p. 2). Some examples of elite prep schools are Notre Dame, Edge Hockey School, Rothesay Netherwood School, and Ridley College. Prep schools often require the player to leave home and live on campus at the school, similar to that of an individual leaving home to attend a university or college. According to Washington and Edwards (2016), "There are approximately 100 prep schools with elite-level hockey programs in North America with approximately 17 to 20 schools located within Canada. These programs are available for players between grades 6 and 12" (p. 4).

A fundamental difference between prep schools and the club system is that in the former, there is a higher level of commitment, and the cost to play and attend school is significantly more. On average, the cost for playing hockey at prep school is between 25,000 and 45,000 CAD per year, whereas the cost of playing Triple-A hockey (the highest competitive level at the youth level) is between $5,000 and $12,000 per season. From a marketing perspective, prep schools are not inclusive but rather exclusive, because the customer base (i.e., players and parents) consists of those players of elite status who can afford to attend a prep school.

Prep schools have the reputation of producing elite players that have gone on to compete at the highest level possible in hockey: the National Hockey League (NHL). For example, players who have graduated from a prep school and played in the NHL include Sidney Crosby, Jordan Eberle, Curtis Lazar, Sean Couturier, Tyler Myers, Mike Iggulden, Brad Richards, Joe Hicketts, Vincent Lecavalier, Justin Schultz, David Pope, and Mathew Dumba (Washington

& Edwards, 2016, p. 4). Ultimately, prep schools create an attractive and marketable reputation by having players reach higher levels of competition, whether in the Canadian Hockey League or a team in Division I of the National Collegiate Athletic Association (NCAA).

In the case of prep hockey schools, the focus is on the marketing of sport as a means of attracting the most talented hockey players to enhance the school's reputation and give it a competitive advantage over the club hockey system. The focus of the marketing strategy is on attracting the most talented players by creating a reputation around player selection processes, player development practices (holistic training, access to facilities, the time allotted to training, expert coaches and staff, and access to player resources), and the player experience, as indicated by Washington and Edwards (2016). By enhancing their reputation, prep schools can acquire resources in the form of sponsorship, be recognized as an opportunity for elite hockey training, and gain a competitive advantage over club hockey organizations. The development of a strong reputation plays a critical role for organizations in gaining a competitive advantage and gaining profit.

> JONATHON EDWARDS is an associate professor in the faculty of kinesiology at the University of New Brunswick (UNB), Canada. He teaches courses in sports marketing and sponsorship, human resource management in sport and recreation, and sport and recreation delivery systems for the undergraduate and MBA in sport and recreation management programs at UNB. He takes on an applied qualitative research approach to explore sport and recreation delivery systems through institutional theory, and he has published in a variety of journals, spoken at several conferences, and conducted research on behalf of national, provincial, and community-based sport and recreation organizations.

Segmentation, Targeting, Positioning (STP)

Segmentation, targeting, positioning (STP) is the process of building from the background research (PEST and the three Cs) to (i) aggregate or group potential buyers with common needs into similar segments, (ii) define the target market(s) by identifying the most attractive segments (targeting), and (iii) demonstrate how the offering will be positioned vis-à-vis the competition (positioning). The STP provides the basis for developing the marketing strategy. An entire chapter (chapter 5) in the book is devoted to explaining this process and sharing the tools a marketer can use to undertake an STP.

The Marketing Mix

Also known as marketing strategy, the marketing mix involves the well-known four () Ps—product (what is offered to the consumer), price (what the consumer must pay to take ownership), promotion (communicating to or with the consumer about an offering), and place (how

to get the product from production to the consumer). Any marketing plan needs to consider these four elements to develop a strategy based on the product attributes desired by the target market or markets, a price point that leads to perceived value, promotional techniques that will reach the target markets, and making sure that distribution plans are set up so that the product can get into the hands of consumers.

Figure 1.1 illustrates the sport marketing process and how all the key elements of sport marketing (e.g., the four Ps, STP, PEST, and the three Cs) and the content of this book fit together as parts of the process of sport marketing. Note that the Cs that are listed under internal analysis refer to the assessment of the company, the competition, the climate (i.e., internal culture), and the consumers from an internal perspective and from internal data and other information. The external work on these items is captured in that bucket and elaborated on in chapter 3.

As reported in figure 1.1, the process of sport marketing is driven by market research (chapter 3) that is both internal and external in nature. Upon building this understanding, the

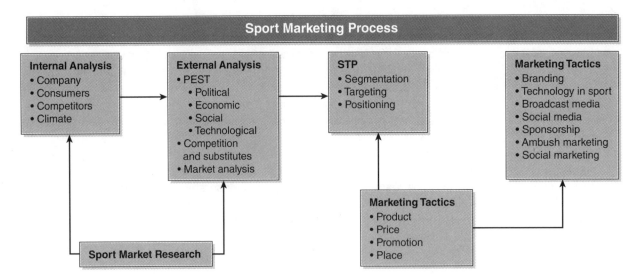

FIGURE 1.1 The process of sport marketing.

steps of segmentation, targeting, and positioning (chapter 5) lead to the building of marketing strategy and the many tactics therein, which is covered in detail in the remainder of the book.

Marketing as a Revenue Generator

Marketing scholars and practitioners stress that marketing is the only revenue-generating activity in an organization. This is a very important point when you consider an organization in full (i.e., from the perspective of the chief executive officer [CEO] or executive director): There are many activities and roles taken but only one brings in the resources to allow the organization to operate, grow, pay staff, and reward investors. That is marketing.

The Uniqueness of Sport Marketing

Marketing principles are applied in most industries, if not all. Sport marketing, however, is one of a few industry-based subfields of marketing that has developed its own body of literature and methods of common practice. Why is sport marketing different? Why does it merit its own text and its own courses? By definition, "sport marketing is the specific application of marketing principles and processes to sport products and to the marketing of non-sports products associated with a sport" (Shank & Lyberger, 2014, p. 5).

Simply put, sport marketing provides organizations—both those marketing sport directly (e.g., learn-to-swim programs selling lessons to children) and those marketing it indirectly through sport (e.g., Ford selling more cars through its sponsorship of the Montreal Canadiens)—with access to properties where people have unbridled passion for their team, their sport, their favourite players, their favourite coaches, their favourite equipment, or their favourite ball cap. For example, the strong attachment fans have to the Toronto Maple Leafs is rarely found with other products. Sport marketing is thus about more than just the needs and wants; it is about connecting to emotions, building passion, and leveraging images.

A number of factors further elevate the importance of sport marketing.

- The ability of sport organizations to provide means by which a nonsport organization can associate itself with attractive sports and sports heroes is on the rise.
- Sport is increasingly accessible through such media technologies as social media, streaming, television, radio, web, and satellite phone.
- Sport has been shown to generate considerable excitement and emotional attach-

ment on the part of its consumers, which may render them more susceptible to product-based messages and other marketing initiatives (Foster et al., 2020).

- Sport and its events have the ability to provide significant leveraging opportunities (e.g., merchandise, cross-promotions, brand extensions, licensing, dealer incentives) to nonsport sport marketing: activities that provide organizations—both those marketing sport and those marketing through sport—with access to properties where people have unbridled passion for their team, their sport, their favourite players, their favourite coaches, their favourite equipment, their favourite ball cap, and so forth (O'Reilly et al., 2015).

- Interest in leisure-type events and properties has been increasing for many years, and today it is very difficult to find a sporting event that is not sponsored.

- Sport spectators—both in person and via media—are exposed to messages in favourable conditions, where there is enthusiasm, excitement, and enjoyment and where they are relaxed and receptive to sponsors' messages.

- A sport can be adopted to reach specific target market segments of narrow demographics in a more diverse and cost-efficient manner.

CHAPTER SUMMARY

This chapter introduces marketing and sport marketing. It assumes that the reader has little experience or background in marketing and, therefore, provides a brief overview of marketing and its key concepts. Three industry contributors—an agency CEO, a professor of sport marketing, and a professional athlete—provide their perspectives, describing the importance of sport marketing and emphasizing how effective it can be if done right. The goal of marketing is to satisfy the needs and wants of consumers by engaging them in an exchange process to build long-term relationships. While sport marketers also aim to satisfy needs and wants, they seek to connect emotions and build passion with consumers. Sport marketing happens in two distinct ways: the marketing of sport products and services directly to consumers of sport (e.g., Speedo swim suits, Wilson tennis racquets) and marketing through sport, or using sport to market other consumer and industrial products through promotions (e.g., BMO using its jersey sponsorship of the Montreal Impact of Major League Soccer to market their bank and financial products).

TEST YOUR KNOWLEDGE

1. What do the letters in STP stand for? Describe each term and explain how it fits into marketing theory.
2. Analyze the 2017 AMA definition of marketing. From your review, list at least four key points of that definition that marketers should adhere to.
3. A smart marketer considers which element first: product, positioning, segmentation, price, place, targeting, or distribution?
4. In fewer than 50 of your own words, describe what marketing is.
5. What is the competition for each of the following?
   a. Toronto Blue Jays
   b. Callaway Golf
   c. Sport Canada
   d. Jim's Bike Store in Kelowna, British Columbia

e. the Ottawa 67s Junior A Hockey Club

f. Alpine Canada

g. a player's agent

h. any coach

6. What makes sport marketing unique? Are there any reasons you can think of that are not in this text?

7. Define and give examples of the following concepts:

a. marketing

b. exchange

c. consumer

d. competition

e. substitute

f. product

g. price

h. promotion

i. place

KEY TERMS

company	place	segmentation
competition	positioning	substitute
consumer	possession	targeting
exchange	price	time
form	product	utility
marketing	promotion	
marketing mix	relationship	

CASE STUDIES

Visit HK*Propel* for case studies organized by chapter.

CHAPTER 2

The Canadian Sport Industry

LEARNING OBJECTIVES

After studying this chapter, you will be able to do the following:

- Understand the complexity, scope, and variation of Canadian sport
- Speak knowledgeably about and understand the differences among professional, Olympic, university and college, and grassroots sport
- Explain the organizations, facilities, events, and policies driving sport in Canada
- Understand the role of governments in Canadian sport
- Understand the role of corporate Canada in sport
- Understand the roles of coaches, athletes, and administrators in sport in Canada

From a child playing hockey on a frozen pond to a sprinter at the starting line of the Olympics or a professional athlete hoisting a championship trophy, sport engages and fascinates people on individual, national, and international scales. In Canada, sport is deeply rooted in our past, present, and future and, as such, it plays an important role in the lives of millions of Canadians. However, despite its importance, many Canadians are unaware of the potential impact sport has on strengthening communities, generating economic growth, and shaping the cultural identity of the nation (Sam, 2011). Sport in Canada does bear this incredible power. However, to gain a greater understanding of this impact, it is important to examine the pieces that compose Canadian sport landscape. In this chapter, a comprehensive overview of the sport landscape in Canada is presented, with the intention of familiarizing the reader with the Canadian context that frames the remainder of the book.

The Canadian sport system can be broken down into four distinct yet interconnected facets:

- *Professional sport* refers to leagues and athletes that represent private enterprise and/or who compete in exchange for economic gain.
- *University and collegiate sport* pertains to competitions that involve student-athletes competing on behalf of the postsecondary institution in which they are enrolled.
- *Olympic sport* covers high-performance athletic competition in which athletes typically compete more for personal than economic gain, although many Olympic athletes do experience significant financial benefit from their athletic careers.
- *Grassroots sport* refers to sport that is based in local communities and participation by the general public, and which may or may not be designated as an Olympic discipline.

In addition to the four facets of our sport system, this chapter discusses **sport events** and facilities in a Canadian context to provide a comprehensive view of sport in Canada.

A Brief Introduction to Canada

To explain sport in Canada, it is important to describe the country. Canada is widely known as a nation of vast distances, natural resources, and peacekeeping. Diversity prevails in everything from population to climate and topography. As a member of the British Commonwealth, Canada is both a constitutional monarchy and a parliamentary democracy. However, despite our tie to Britain, Canada's closest ally is the United States, with which it shares its southern border. Canada is also bordered by three oceans: the Atlantic to the east, the Pacific to the west, and the Arctic to the north. Measuring 9,984,670 square kilometres, Canada is the second largest country in the world. Its vast expanse comprises a wide diversity of topography, with mountains in

the west, prairies in central Canada, tundra to the north, and lowlands in the southeast. The climate is similarly diverse and varies between arctic and subarctic in the north and temperate in the south (Central Intelligence Agency, 2019).

The population of Canada is estimated at almost 38 million people (Statistics Canada, 2019e). The majority (66 percent) are between the ages of 15 and 64, with a median age of 40.8 years (Statistics Canada, 2019c). Canada also maintains a low population density of about 4 people per square kilometre, whereas the United States has 35.8 people per square kilometre and the Netherlands 511.5 (Statista, 2020a, 2020c, 2020e). Despite its vast size, four out of every five Canadians live in a metropolitan area, with three cities in particular—Toronto, Montreal, and Vancouver—accounting for over a third of the entire population (Statistics Canada, 2019d). However, other metropolitan areas are experiencing population increases in the Canadian market, due in large part to record numbers of international migration (Statistics Canada, 2019a).

Canada is a highly developed nation with a long life expectancy. On average, citizens live into their late 70s or early 80s (Statistics Canada, 2019c). Language plays a major role in Canadian society, as the country recognizes two official languages, English and French. About 68 percent of the population speaks English and no French, 12 percent speaks French and no English, 18 percent speaks both languages, and 1.9 percent speaks neither language (Statistics Canada, 2019b). Canada also has a diverse ethnic population, with many Canadians being foreign-born. In 2019, about 313,000 immigrants arrived in Canada, nearly a 40 percent increase from the number of immigrants entering the country two decades earlier (Statista, 2020d). The multicultural nature of Canadian society is a major facet of Canada's identity and plays a large role in the generally diversified character of the country.

An economically affluent country, Canada operates in a market-oriented economic system that represents about 2 percent of the world's economy. The gross domestic product (GDP) in 2019 was 1.640 trillion CAD, with an annual growth rate of roughly 1.75 percent (Statista, 2020f). Canada's closest neighbour, the United

States, is also its largest trading partner, with combined trade figures totalling 606 billion CAD (Tremblay, 2014). Beyond the convenient geographic proximity, Canada possesses vast natural resources, including iron ore, zinc, copper, nickel, gold, lead, diamonds, silver, fish, timber, wildlife, coal, petroleum, natural gas, and hydroelectric power, which makes it a valuable trading partner with the United States and other countries around the world. Its demographics, diversified nature, and economic situation have a large impact on how other elements develop within the Canadian market, so the information presented in this section helps contribute to a better understanding of sport in this context.

Sport Organizations in Canada

This chapter describes four main sectors of sport in Canada: professional, university and college, Olympic, and grassroots. Each of the four plays an integral role in shaping Canadian sport, and without any one aspect, holes would appear and the system would be drastically weakened. Each sector is interconnected with the others, and it is the strengths and weaknesses of these connections that will help or hinder the progress of the overall system. For example, a strong university and college sport sector can produce an excellent feeder system for future Olympic or professional athletes. For Canadian sport to reach its full potential, cooperation, communication, and interaction between all these elements are essential. Figure 2.1 describes sport in Canada.

Connected to these sectors are two additional elements of sport in Canada: events and facilities. These features provide the context and place in which sport is set or housed across the nation. Furthermore, there are reoccurring, high-profile events that are significant to sport in Canada, as well as facilities that are used often and are home to multiple teams, leagues, or sport offerings.

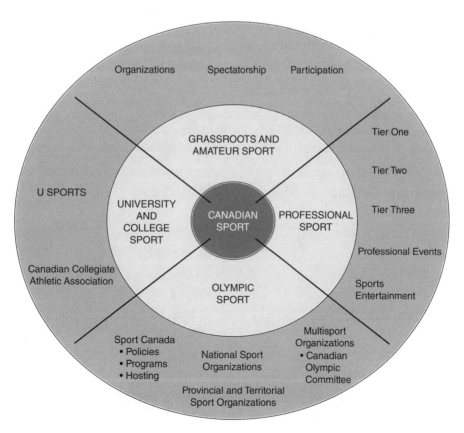

FIGURE 2.1 The Canadian sport landscape.

Sport Events in Canada

Through the creation of its hosting policy, the Canadian government has shown that it recognizes the contribution of international events. In addition to international events, numerous national and local events, as well as annual professional championships, also take place.

Table 2.1 lists some of the events that have been hosted in Canadian cities since 2010 (or will be in the near future). This list includes international multisport events, international single sport events, national multi- and single sport events, and specialty games. The list gives a general overview of the Canadian **sport event** landscape. As reported in table 2.1, a number of these events

TABLE 2.1 Selection of Major Events in Canada

Major Sport Events	Location	Year/Time
Winter Olympic Games	Vancouver	2010
IIHF World Junior Ice Hockey Championships	Saskatchewan	2010
World Women's Curling Championship	Swift Current	2010
World Men's Curling Championship	Regina	2011
World Women's Curling Championship	Lethbridge	2012
IIHF World Junior Ice Hockey Championships	Calgary-Edmonton	2012
World Men's Curling Championship	Victoria	2013
IIHF World Women's Ice Hockey Championships	Ottawa	2013
World Women's Curling Championship	Saint John	2014
Pan American Games	Toronto	2015
IIHF World Junior Ice Hockey Championships	Toronto-Montreal	2015
World Men's Curling Championship	Halifax	2015
FIFA Women's World Cup	Various	2015
World Women's Curling Championship	Swift Current	2016
IIHF World Women's Ice Hockey Championships	Kamloops	2016
World Men's Curling Championship	Edmonton	2017
IIHF World Junior Ice Hockey Championships	Montreal-Toronto	2017
World Women's Curling Championship	North Bay	2018
IIHF World Junior Ice Hockey Championships	Vancouver-Victoria	2019
IIHF World Women's Ice Hockey Championships	Halifax-Truro	2021
IIHF World Junior Ice Hockey Championships	Edmonton-Red Deer	2021
World Men's Curling Championship	Ottawa	2021
FIFA World Cup	Various	2026
Tim Hortons Brier (Curling)	Various	March
Calgary Stampede	Calgary	July
Canada Summer/Winter Games	Various	Biennial
Grey Cup (CFL championship)	Various	November
Memorial Cup (CHL championship)	Various	May
Provincial Summer/Winter Games	Various	Biennial
Rogers Cup (Tennis)	Toronto/Montreal	August
Scotties Tournament of Hearts (Curling)	Various	March
Vanier Cup (U SPORTS Canadian football)	Various	November

are sanctioned by the International Ice Hockey Federation (IIHF), Canadian Hockey League (CHL), and Canadian Football League (CFL).

Sport Facilities in Canada

A wide variety of sport facilities can be found across Canada, ranging from local ice hockey rinks and soccer fields to Olympic-calibre training and competition venues to stadiums that seat thousands of spectators. Tables 2.2 and 2.3 list major Canadian sport facilities that cater to **professional sport, Olympic sport,** and sometimes recreation. These lists are not intended to be comprehensive but rather to provide a sample of the extent of facility offerings in Canadian sport.

Canadian Sport Centres, which are high-performance training centres in cities across the country, represent a joint effort between Sport Canada, the Canadian Olympic Committee (COC), Own the Podium (OTP), and the Coaching Association of Canada and offer athletes a wide range of training facilities and sport services.

While the lists in tables 2.2 and 2.3 cover the majority of major sport facilities across the country, numerous smaller facilities cater to third-tier professional and semiprofessional leagues and teams. In addition, the Vancouver 2010 Winter Olympic and Paralympic Games and the Toronto 2015 Pan American and Parapan American Games created a new set of world-class winter and summer sport facilities to match

TABLE 2.2 Tier One and Tier Two Professional Facilities

Facility Name	City	Sport Usage	*Capacity	Year Built
BC Place	Vancouver	Canadian football, global football	59,841	1983
Centre Bell	Montreal	Ice hockey	21,273	1996
Bell MTS Place	Winnipeg	Ice hockey	15,321	2004
BMO Field	Toronto	Canadian football, global football	30,000	2007
CAA Arena	Belleville	Ice hockey	4,365	1978
Canadian Tire Centre	Kanata	Ice hockey	19,153	1996
Coca-Cola Coliseum	Toronto	Ice hockey	7,851	1921
The Brick Field	Edmonton	Canadian football	55,819	1978
IG Field	Winnipeg	Canadian football	33,500	2013
McMahon Stadium	Calgary	Canadian football	35,650	1960
Mosaic Stadium	Regina	Canadian football	33,350	2017
Stade Percival-Molson	Montreal	Canadian football	23,420	1915
Place Bell	Laval	Ice hockey	10,000	2017
Rogers Arena	Vancouver	Ice hockey, lacrosse	18,910	1995
Rogers Centre	Toronto	Baseball	49,282	1989
Rogers Place	Edmonton	Ice hockey	18,347	2016
SaskTel Centre	Saskatoon	Lacrosse	15,195	1988
Scotiabank Arena	Toronto	Basketball, ice hockey, lacrosse	19,800	1999
Scotiabank Centre	Halifax	Lacrosse	10,595	1978
Scotiabank Saddledome	Calgary	Ice hockey, lacrosse	19,289	1994
Stade Saputo	Montreal	Global football	19,619	2008
TD Place	Ottawa	Canadian football	24,000	1908
Tim Hortons Field	Hamilton	Canadian football	23,218	2014

* The number refers to largest possible sport-based capacity.

TABLE 2.3 Canadian Sport Centres and Other Sport Facilities

Facility Name	City	Sport Purpose
Canadian Sport Centre Atlantic	Halifax, Fredericton, St. John's, Charlottetown	Multisport
Canadian Sport Centre Calgary	Calgary	Multisport
Canadian Sport Centre Ontario	Toronto	Multisport
Canadian Sport Centre Saskatchewan	Regina	Multisport
Canadian Sport Centre Winnipeg	Winnipeg	Multisport
National Multisport Centre	Montreal	Multisport
Pacific Sport Victoria	Victoria	Multisport
Pacific Sport Vancouver	Vancouver	Multisport
Olympic Park	Calgary	Multisport
Calgary Oval	Calgary	Speedskating
Stade Olympique	Montreal	Baseball
Spruce Meadows	Calgary	Equestrian
Mattamy National Cycling Centre	Milton	Cycling
Aviva Centre	Toronto	Tennis
Whistler/Blackcomb	Vancouver	Alpine Skiing

those remaining after Calgary. For instance, the Mattamy National Cycling Centre in Milton, Ontario, 50 kilometres southwest of Toronto, opened in 2015 for the purpose of hosting track cycling events for the 2015 Pan American Games.

The following sections and the remainder of the chapter provide an overview of the Canadian sport system that provides an outline at the levels of professional sport, university and college sport, Olympic sport, grassroots and amateur sport, and sport events in Canada.

Professional Sport

Professional sport in Canada can be divided into five categories:

1. Tier one professional sport
2. Tier two professional sport
3. Tier three professional sport
4. Professional sport events
5. Sport entertainment

This section looks at each of these categories and discusses the challenges facing professional sport in Canada. This nomenclature of categories was developed by the authors in the first edition of this book.

Tier One Professional Sport

Tier one professional leagues are considered the highest level of professional sport competition in North America and usually considered the highest level of professional competition globally as well. Canadians have been an increasing presence in all professional leagues; in 2019, six Canadians athletes were selected in the National Basketball Association (NBA) draft, while there are increasing numbers across Major League Baseball (MLB) and even the National Football League (NFL). In fact, Laurent Duvernay-Tardiff, a graduate of McGill University, was a standout for the Super Bowl LIV victors, the Kansas City Chiefs. However, the professional league with the greatest number of Canadian athletes is the National Hockey League (NHL).

National Hockey League

As of 2021, seven Canadian teams compete in the NHL. From 1992 to 1995, there were eight Canadian teams; however, in 1995 the Quebec Nordiques moved to Denver and the Winnipeg Jets moved to Phoenix, leaving the Vancouver Canucks, Calgary Flames, Edmonton Oilers, Toronto Maple Leafs, Ottawa Senators, and

Montreal Canadiens. In 2011, after years of financial loss, the Atlanta Thrashers were sold to a Canadian investment consortium that moved the franchise to Winnipeg and renamed them team the Jets (Brunt, 2011). Despite being home to only 7 of the league's 32 teams (with the addition of Seattle in 2021), Canada's influence on the league is unmatched. For instance, during the 2019-2020 season, nearly half of all NHL players were Canadian. Additionally, two franchises, the Toronto Maple Leafs and Montreal Canadiens, were ranked second and third as most valuable, with both estimated to be worth over 1 billion USD (Ozanian, 2019). Despite these positives, other Canadian teams are susceptible to financial or political difficulties, including the Ottawa Senators and even the Calgary Flames, the latter of whom have struggled to secure financing for their aging facility (Chin, 2017).

The COVID-19 global pandemic resulted in a significant loss in revenue for all NHL teams and in particular the Canadian Teams who were not allowed to sell tickets and therefore played in empty or sparsely filled stadiums. The long-term financial impact of COVID-19 on Canadian franchises remains unknown. However, the financial shortfall resulting from it created a need for the league to increase its creativity on the marketing front and allow the teams to look for other sources of revenues, such as providing the marketing departments of teams with the green light to place sponsored logos on helmets and large ads to cover the empty seating in arenas (Simpson, 2021). While this was initially to be for only one year, the NHL has agreed to make helmet advertising a permanent part of the revenue streams and recently announced that small jersey advertising will be allowed for the 2022-2023 season. How will this be received in Canada? For traditionalists, this is most likely not a welcomed development, as they believe that this advertising will pollute the "hallowed hockey sweater, enshrined in Canadian culture with the classic short story, The Hockey Sweater, and held up as sacred by those who insist, 'It's not a jersey, it's a hockey sweater'" (Wagner, 2021).

Major League Baseball

As of 2021, there was only one MLB team operating in Canada: the Toronto Blue Jays. However, from 1977 to 2005, there were two teams. In addition to the Toronto Blue Jays, the Expos made their home in Montreal until 2004, when the team permanently relocated to Washington under a new moniker, the Nationals. While the Expos only reached postseason play once, making and subsequently losing the National League Championship Series in 1981, the Blue Jays have experienced more success in that regard. Affectionately known as just the "Jays," Toronto's MLB team competed in postseason play in 1985, 1989, 1991, 1992, 1993, 2015, 2016, and 2020, and won the World Series in 1992 and 1993. The Jays, who play their home games at Rogers Centre in downtown Toronto, experienced fluctuations in their attendance, given the large gap in playoff appearances from 1993 to 2015. In 2019, the Blue Jays averaged 21,606 fans during their 81 home games, ranking 22nd out of all 30 MLB clubs (Rush, 2019). Prior to the Expos departing Montreal, the team played their home games at Olympic Stadium, a facility also used by the Jays since 2013 for exhibition series (Brudnicki, 2019). The 2020 MLB season was shortened by COVID-19 to 60 games, and the Toronto Blue Jays played out of Buffalo, New York, for the season due to travel restrictions.

National Basketball Association

Similar to MLB, there is only one Canadian team in the NBA, the Toronto Raptors. Similarly, Canada did not begin with just one team; in 1995, both the Raptors and the Vancouver Grizzlies were established. As the latter experienced low attendance figures, they were eventually sold and relocated to Memphis, Tennessee; they are still known as the Grizzlies. Meanwhile, as the lone Canadian team, the Raptors began to expand their fan base nationwide, particularly among younger generations and new Canadians, with whom basketball has become an increasingly popular sport. In 2019, after a string of playoff appearances that were cut short, the Raptors hoisted the Larry O'Brien trophy as NBA champions.

The Raptors championship was a culmination of multiple victories, including a successful rebranding and working with music superstar and fellow Torontonian Drake as the team's global ambassador. The Raptors also call downtown Toronto home, playing their games at Scotiabank Arena, formerly known as the Air Canada Centre. The Raptors have consistently sold out tickets for their games at Scotiabank Arena and were now valued at 2.1 billion USD following their championship season (Settimi, 2020). The 2020 NBA season was shortened to 72 games due to the COVID-19 pandemic, and the Raptors played out of Tampa, Florida, due to cross-border travel restrictions.

Tier Two Professional Sport

Tier two professional leagues include leagues that represent a high level of professional sport in Canada or North America, but not the world.

Canadian Football League

The CFL is a professional football league made up entirely of Canadian teams. There are eight teams in two divisions: The East Division consists of the Hamilton Tiger-Cats, Montreal Alouettes, Toronto Argonauts, and Winnipeg Blue Bombers; the West Division consists of the BC Lions, Calgary Stampeders, Edmonton Eskimos, and Saskatchewan Roughriders. In 2021, the league was to expand to nine teams, adding the Atlantic Schooners, which will be based in Halifax, Nova Scotia. Founded in 1958, the league has seen its fair share of franchises come and go, including six now defunct teams in American cities. The league championship, called the Grey Cup, takes place each November, and the all-Canadian nature of the league has led the event to become a powerful symbol of Canadian sport. The numerous differences between the football of the CFL and that of the NFL include the size of the field (the Canadian field is 110 by 65 yards and the American field is 100 by 53.5 yards) and the number of downs (to advance the ball 10 yards, Canadian football allows three downs and American football allows four downs). Recent years have seen an increase in attendance levels for most of the CFL teams. The average attendance hovers near 23,000, with franchises in smaller markets like Hamilton and Saskatchewan enjoying larger attendance figures than those in big markets like Toronto and Vancouver, the latter of which serves as home base for the BC Lions (Ralph, 2019). The 2020 CFL season was cancelled due to the COVID-19 pandemic.

American Hockey League

The AHL is composed of the minor league affiliate teams of the NHL. Four Canadian teams in the AHL are affiliates of Canadian NHL teams: The Manitoba Moose are affiliated with the Winnipeg Jets, the Laval Rocket with the Montreal Canadiens, the Belleville Senators with the Ottawa Senators, and the Toronto Marlies with the Toronto Maple Leafs. In all four cases, the AHL team is not too far, geographically speaking, from their NHL affiliation, easing the logistics of player mobility for organizations. However, these AHL teams suffer from lower attendance figures relative to tier one sports, with averages well below the 10,000 mark per season. The 2019-2020 and 2020-2021 AHL seasons were impacted significantly by the COVID-19 global pandemic, with both seasons shortened and no champion crowned each of the two seasons.

Major League Soccer

The top Canadian and U.S. global football (also known as soccer in the North American context) teams compete in the MLS. With its first season in 1996, the MLS did not originally have any Canadian teams. However, the league expanded north over 10 years later, as Toronto FC began play in 2007. That same year, the league encountered some more international exposure as global football star David Beckham joined the Los Angeles Galaxy. As a result of Beckham's fame, the league expanded to Vancouver (Whitecaps FC) in 2011 and Montreal (the Impact) in 2012, in addition to other U.S. markets such as Miami and Nashville. Its expansive pace and increased exposure have also led to more athletes and coaches from Europe migrating to MLS, including Italian national Sebastian Giovinco playing for Toronto FC and French national Thierry Henry coaching the

Montreal Impact. Although neither Vancouver nor Montreal have reached an MLS Cup final, Toronto FC has made the finals three times, winning in 2017. Despite its growth, MLS does not compare to leagues such as the English Premier League or Spanish La Liga in terms of status, support, or financial capability. For example, average attendances in 2019 for Toronto FC (25,048), Vancouver Whitecaps FC (19,514), and Montreal Impact (16,171) are well below those of teams in the English Premier League, many of whom have average attendances north of 50,000 (Statista, 2020b). Toronto FC play their home games at BMO Field, on the grounds of the Canadian National Exhibition (CNE); Vancouver Whitecaps FC play their home games at BC Place; and Montreal Impact play their games at Stade Saputo. The 2020 MLS season was interrupted by the COVID-19 pandemic and, at times, the three Canadian clubs had to play their home games in the United States due to travel restrictions.

National Lacrosse League

The NLL consists of 13 teams, 5 of which are located in Canadian cites. The Vancouver Warriors, Calgary Roughnecks, and Saskatchewan Rush compete in the West Division, while the Toronto Rock and Halifax Thunderbirds compete in the North Division. However, the league has experienced a high degree of team mobility and relocation, and teams have also existed in other Canadian markets including Edmonton (Rush), Ottawa (Rebel), and Montreal (Express). The Rock is the most successful team in the history of the league, having won the championship six times, a distinction shared with the Philadelphia Wings. The average attendance for the Canadian teams is just under 10,000, which is 2,000 higher than the league's average attendance figure. The 2020 NLL season was cancelled due to the COVID-19 pandemic.

Tier Three Professional Leagues

Tier three professional leagues represent a lower level of professional competition in a spe-

cific sport. Often there are also leagues that are in a stage of growth and have yet to establish themselves as major sport entities. Recently, there has been an expansion of the number of tier three professional leagues specifically based in Canada coming to the fore.

Canadian Premier League

In 2017, the CPL was established as a Canadian global football (soccer) league. The league features seven teams located from coast to coast, including Pacific FC in British Columbia, Cavalry FC and FC Edmonton in Alberta, Valour FC in Manitoba, Forge FC and York9 FC in Ontario, and HFX Wanderers in Nova Scotia. The league requires that teams have the majority of their athletes from Canada, thus ensuring the development of talent within the country. In 2019, Forge FC, who play their home games at Tim Hortons Field in Hamilton, were the inaugural champions of the CPL. The league is set for future expansion, and it has added a new team in Ottawa, owned by the La Liga club, Atletico Madrid.

National Basketball League of Canada

The NBL was founded in 2011 in an attempt to create a minor basketball league in Canada. Originally, the league started with seven teams: Halifax Rainmen, London Lightning, Moncton Miracles, Saint John Mill Rats, Oshawa Power, Summerside Storm, and the Quebec Kebs. However, since its inaugural season, teams have moved and experienced name changes. For instance, teams have also played in Mississauga, Orangeville, Niagara, Ottawa, and Montreal. At present, there are eight active teams: Halifax Hurricanes, Island Storm, Moncton Magic, St. John's Edge, Kitchener-Waterloo Titans, London Lightning, Sudbury Five, and Windsor Express. The Lightning own the most NBL championships, with four.

Canadian Elite Basketball League

The CEBL was founded in 2017 as a competitor to the National Basketball League of Canada. In the league's first season in 2019, there were six teams: Edmonton Stingers, Fraser Valley

Bandits, Guelph Nighthawks, Hamilton Honey Badgers, Niagara River Lions, and the inaugural champion, Saskatchewan Rattlers. The CEBL is part of Canada Basketball's overall development framework, which focuses on expansion possibilities in other markets. For instance, the league has established a new team in Ottawa, the Blackjacks, to begin play in 2020.

Women's Professional Leagues

Even at the highest levels of professional competition available for women in sports, the women's professional leagues in Canada are considered third tier. They simply do not have the status or visibility of the comparable men's leagues, and in most cases, the women are not full-time athletes. One example of this lack of status is the Canadian Women's Hockey League (CWHL). The CWHL was founded in 2007, but its clubs were not well distributed across the country, with teams located mostly in the Greater Toronto Area and Greater Montreal Area. Over time, the league began to stabilize and expanded into the United States with teams in Minnesota and Boston, and China, with two teams from Shenzhen. However, due to the fragmentation of corporate sponsorship across the women's ice hockey space, the CWHL ceased operations in 2019 (though there have been discussions about NHL support in the women's ice hockey space, including adding more Canadian teams). However, in 2020, the National Women's Hockey League (NWHL) announced a new team that would be located in Canada, the first outside the United States. The new team was to be known as the Toronto Six, a play on the fact that this franchise is the sixth team in the NWHL and that there are six boroughs in the City of Toronto. There are also other examples of women's professional sport in Canada such as the Queen City United SC in United Women's Soccer.

NASCAR Pinty's Series

Previously called the CASCAR Super Series, this Canadian professional stock car racing series was relaunched as the Canadian Tire NASCAR Series for the 2007 season. However, after eight years as title sponsor, Canadian Tire did not renew their title sponsorship of the event in 2015, and Pinty's, a packaged foods company, agreed to sponsor the series until 2021. The series consists of 10 to 12 races a year and targets a Canadian NASCAR fan base of about 5.8 million people.

Global T20 Canada

The Global T20 Canada is a professional cricket league comprised of six teams: Brampton Wolves, Edmonton Royals, Montreal Tigers, Toronto Nationals, Vancouver Knights, and Winnipeg Hawks. While these teams are associated with a Canadian city, all matches are played at the CAA Centre, a multipurpose arena and field complex, in Brampton, Ontario. The league is set on the widely popular "T20" format of cricket, whereby there are 20 overs per team, essentially lasting as a long as a traditional nine-inning baseball game. While cricket has not been popular in the Canadian sport landscape for some time, it has deep, historical roots. Canada competed against the United States in the world's first international cricket match back in 1844, and cricket remained popular in the nation until the turn of the 20th century when the emergence of baseball in the United States spread north of the border, coupled with waves of immigration from non–cricket playing countries in Europe (e.g., Italy, Poland, Germany). However, more recent waves of immigration from cricket hotspots such as the Caribbean and South Asia have sparked a resurgence in the sport in Canada. The emergence of the Global T20 Canada league in 2018 brought some of the game's best players to the Greater Toronto Area, including the likes of Steve Smith and David Warner from Australia, Chris Gayle and Darren Sammy from the West Indies, and Yuvraj Singh from India. The league has also served as an important training ground for Canadian talent, including former Canadian national team captain Nitish Kumar. While the CAA Centre has a capacity of only 5,000, the league has garnered significant attention from abroad, with over 150 million viewers worldwide. However, given its lean structure and operations and its location in the global cricket landscape, the league remains a tier three professional sport opportunity in Canada.

East Coast Hockey League

The ECHL is another minor ice hockey league, sitting a tier below the AHL. However, like the AHL, ECHL teams may have some affiliation with NHL teams. Two of the league's 27 teams are based in Canada: Trois-Rivières Lions and Newfoundland Growlers. The Lions are affiliated with the Montreal Canadiens of the NHL and the Laval Rockety of the AHL. They play out of the Colisée Vidéotron, a new venue completed in 2021, the same year the club began play. The Newfoundland Growlers began play in 2018, based out of St. John's, Newfoundland, and Labrador. Sharing the same facility as the St. John's Edge of the NBL, the Growlers are affiliated with the Toronto Marlies in the AHL and the Toronto Maple Leafs in the NHL.

Major League Rugby

The MLR commenced its first season in 2018 with its first and only Canadian team, Toronto Arrows, entering in 2019. The MLR is a rugby union league, featuring the 15 versus 15 style of rugby. The Arrows play their games at Lamport Stadium in Toronto, as well as some games at York University's Alumni Field.

Betfred Super League (Rugby)

The Super League, known through its title sponsorship as the Betfred Super League (BSL), began play in 1996. While the league is based in England with 10 teams, one team is based in France, and another in Canada. The Toronto Wolfpack entered the BSL in 2017, and also play their home games at Lamport Stadium in Toronto, which the team affectionately refers to as "The Den."

U.S. League One (USL1)

Beneath MLS lies a tier of global football (soccer) leagues known as the United Soccer League. The second tier, the USL1, has teams predominantly in the United States but one located in Canada: Toronto FC II. The team exists as a reserve to the Toronto MLS team, Toronto FC, thus acting as a de facto minor league affiliate. The team is also owned and managed by Maple Leaf Sports and Entertainment and has a brand identity similar to that of its MLS counterpart. The team plays its home games at the BMO Training Ground, in the north end of Toronto.

American Ultimate Disc League (AUDL)

The AUDL is a professional ultimate frisbee league that held its first season in 2012. Another primarily U.S.-based league, AUDL has three teams in Canada: Toronto Rush, Ottawa Outlaws, and Montreal Royal. The Rush, who play their home games at Varsity Stadium at the University of Toronto, have the designation of being the only AUDL team to win the league championship, which also coincidentally happened to be their first season of play, in 2013. The Montreal Royal, which entered league play in 2014, play their home games at the Claude-Robillard Sports Complex, a facility built for the 1976 Montreal Summer Olympic Games. Finally, the Ottawa Outlaws, which entered the league in 2015, play their home games at MNP Park, on the grounds of Carleton University.

Professional Sport Events

Professional events represent those sport properties that have no major professional league or tour operating exclusively in Canada but rather have specific professional events on their world tours that take place in Canada.

- *Tennis:* The Rogers Cup is the annual Canadian stop on the Men's Association of Tennis Professionals (ATP) Tour and the Women's Tennis Association (WTA) Tour. The men's and women's events alternate between Montreal and Toronto each year.
- *Golf:* The RBC Canadian Open is the annual Canadian stop in the Professional Golf Association (PGA) Tour, while the CN Canadian Women's Open is the annual Canadian stop for the Ladies Professional Golf Association (LPGA).
- *Car racing:* Several Canadian cities host annual races. The Canadian Grand Prix on the Formula One calendar is held at Circuit Gilles Villeneuve in Montreal. The Honda Indy is an annual race part of the IndyCar Series that runs through the Canadian National Exposition (CNE) in Toronto.

- *Combat:* Canada has emerged as a popular destination for combat sport, namely, mixed martial arts (MMA) and boxing. The Ultimate Fighting Championship (UFC), the preeminent MMA promotion, has had several events in Canada. Montreal and Toronto have both hosted six UFC pay-per-view events, with Vancouver, Edmonton, Calgary, and Winnipeg hosting multiple UFC events as well. Additionally, smaller UFC events known as "Fight Nights," which are televised on traditional sports networks and not pay-per-view, have been hosted in other cities, such as Halifax, Saskatoon, Ottawa, and Moncton.
- *Other.* Many other professional competitions take place regularly in the Canadian market, including ironman competitions, running marathons, figure skating, equestrian events, and extreme sports.

Besides the UFC, there are Canadian-focused MMA promotions that are lesser known, such as the Prospect Fight Championship and the BTC Fight promotion, the latter of which operates out of Burlington, Ontario. While boxing has taken a backseat to MMA in Canada, there are still several boxing promotions in operation. For instance, the United Boxing Promotion often holds events at the CAA Centre in Brampton, Ontario, while CCC Promotions holds events at the Memorial Centre in Peterborough, Ontario. Other boxing promotions operating in Canada include:

- Three Lions Promotions
- Classic Boxing Co.

- Fallsboys Promotions
- Liveco Promotions
- Lee Baxter Promotions

Sport Entertainment

Sport entertainment represents sports that do not fit the mould of traditional professional sports but whose popularity has made them an important aspect of Canadian professional sport culture. Most notably, professional wrestling has become a huge business dominated by World Wrestling Entertainment, Inc. (WWE). While its matches are staged and the outcomes predetermined, the athletic ability of the performers is unquestionable. The WWE makes frequent visits to Canadian cities for live performances, including some pay-per-view events held in large Canadian stadiums and arenas. Canada also has a strong history of producing high-profiled WWE performers, including Bret Hart, Owen Hart, Edge, Christian, Kevin Owens, and Trish Stratus. WWE content airs regularly on Canadian sports television broadcasters. There are other examples of sport that have been glamorized for entertainment purposes, including rodeo, poker, and strongman competitions. The latter, in particular, has resonated with audiences in Quebec, thus cheering in local athletes like Hugo Girard and Jessen Paulin.

Challenges for Canadian Professional Sport

Many factors work together to challenge the Canadian professional sport community. The

---

IN THE KNOW

Canadian UFC Fighters

The most high-profiled UFC fighter from Canada, Georges St-Pierre, is a three-time champion, who held the UFC Middleweight and Welterweight championships. In 2020, St-Pierre was elected to the UFC Hall of Fame's Modern Wing. Other notable Canadian UFC fighters include Rory MacDonald, Patrick Côté, Sam Stout, Felicia Spencer, Trish Stratus, Valérie Létourneau, and Alexis Davis, just to name a few. Davis should be particularly highlighted for defeating Amanda Nunes—widely considered as the best female fighter of all time—in 2011.

first is the *value of the Canadian dollar* in comparison with the American dollar. With the constant fluctuations in the economic environment, there are often long periods where the Canadian dollar is worth significantly less than the American dollar. While this can assist industries in Canada that wish to export south, it poses a problem for Canadian teams in professional leagues based primarily in the United States. For example, while most Canadian team revenues are collected in Canadian dollars, players are typically paid in American dollars, and to attract and retain players in a competitive marketplace, Canadian teams must pay similar salaries to those offered in the United States.

Taxation policies are a second challenge facing Canadian professional teams. The high salaries of leading professional athletes are typically taxed at a higher level in Canada than the United States, depending on the province or state. This can vary considerably as income tax rates vary by province or state, with many states having tax rates much lower than Canadian provinces. This poses a problem for Canadian teams competing to attract the best players, since many players do not want to come to Canada and have a larger portion of their salaries taxed.

The level of public subsidy is a third challenge to Canadian professional teams. American taxpayer dollars compose the majority of finances used to build new professional sports complexes and facilities. Public subsidies in Canada are much lower and make Canadian cities much less attractive for new franchises or existing ones looking to remain in their locale. However, some Canadian communities have started to shift this narrative, contributing public funds to new sport facilities. Recently, the Calgary Flames secured millions of funding from the public coffers, while Quebec City has also built stadiums with the hopes of attracting an expansion or relocated NHL franchise.

University and College Sport

In Canada, university and college sport comprise a critical element of the sport system. **Collegiate sport** represents an important pipeline or feeder system into the professional sport organizations that operate in this country. At this level, athletics is narrowed even further than grassroots or secondary school sport; athletes train with a high-performance focus and learn to balance competition, training, and nutritional habits, as well as the camaraderie of being with teammates for elongated periods, similar to the situations that might occur at the professional level and the opposite of the situations at the grassroots level. There are also many universities and colleges with athletic programs spread throughout Canada, making them important anchors for sport in their communities. So, while a smaller city or town may not have a professional sports team, the local community can rally behind their university or college teams and instill a sense of pride and identity in their area. For Canadian sport marketers, there are two key organizations at the collegiate level: U SPORTS and the Canadian Colleges Athletic Association (CCAA).

U SPORTS

U SPORTS is the governing body for university athletics in Canada. The first Canadian university sport organization, the Canadian Interuniversity Athletic Union (CIAU) Central, was founded in 1906 and represented only universities from Ontario and Quebec. Over the years, the organization grew, developed, and changed names many times. In June 2001, CIAU became Canadian Interuniversity Sport. The organization felt that this name better represented its mission and function, as the word "athletics" is typically used when discussing only track and field events and "union" typically applies to labour organizations. In October 2016, the organization was rebranded to U SPORTS, resulting in a unified, bilingual brand.

U SPORTS currently offers programming to over 10,000 student-athletes at 56 member institutions across the country. It offers championships in 11 sport disciplines: swimming, wrestling, track and field, basketball, hockey, volleyball, curling, rugby, cross country, field hockey, and soccer. In total, university sport recognizes a schedule of about 3,000 events during each school year.

EXECUTIVE PERSPECTIVE
Curling Canada: At a Crossroads

KATHERINE HENDERSON, Chief Executive Officer, Curling Canada

Amateur sport in Canada is a complicated and, at times, confusing system that covers playground to podium sport activities. This system is a web of oversight of everything from sport introduction to grassroots participants to the identification, training support, and team selection of those athletes who represent us internationally in pursuit of the podium.

In Canada we have decentralized system management; differing governance structures of organizations that oversee various parts of a sport; a complexity of local, regional, and national funding and compliance agreements; a pool of high-performance athletes who seamlessly move between amateur competition and professional-style events; and layers of multisport organizations who support the system; each of these contributes to a complex ecosystem of sport management and delivery.

Additionally, Canadians see sport as a delivery vehicle for social development. This results in the Canadian sport system being required to deliver programs and services, beyond sport, that assist with human and social initiatives that deliver equity, empowerment, and leadership opportunities for marginalized communities.

Curling in Canada, like most sports in the Canadian amateur sport system, exists as a federated model. From a vertical perspective, local curling clubs affiliate with province or territory curling sport organizations (PTSOs), which represent the club's needs and, in turn, these PTSOs are the members of the national organization (Curling Canada is the NSO). Curling Canada, then, is a member of an international federation (World Curling Federation) and represents Canadian curling and curlers on a global level.

In Canada in 2021, there were about 1,000 curling clubs, 14 PTSOs, and a single NSO. Each one of these curling entities is distinctly managed with different funders, different governance structures, different missions, and different areas of responsibility. The net result is a system that has significant opportunity to improve its alignment and efficiency.

The symptoms of system misalignment include role confusion and struggles between organizations on decision-making responsibility, lack of consistent national data to understand participant needs and programming outcomes, variations in program delivery and participant experience based on geography, and obstacles in delivering important national mandates through a system where clubs or PTSOs in the system are not accountable to the national body to deliver on mandates such as helmet use, safe-sport policies, or data collection. Much work has happened over the past years in order to recognize barriers to alignment and to correct these but like in most ecosystems, a change in one relationship creates significant ripple effects and requires ongoing dialogue and calibration of goals between multiple organizations. Change is an enormous endeavour.

Curling Canada, like most sports, is provided base funding for sport administration and support for high-performance programs through government (Sport Canada administrates). The PTSOs also have separate funding relationships with their local governments. Curling Canada does not have a direct relationship with clubs, but instead works through the PTSO to provides services that are enjoyed by individual clubs and delivered through their PTSO.

Curling Canada also works with many multisport organizations. From a horizontal perspective, Curling Canada delivers on pan-sport requirements, initiatives, and issues through these subject matter experts. Curling Canada works with partner organizations that manage antidoping and drug testing (Canadian Centre for Ethics in Sport), team selection, jurisdiction, sport-mediation matters (Sport Dispute Resolution Centre), athlete rights (AthletesCan), medical science, and daily training environment supports (Canadian Sport Institutes).

Other, related aspects include Olympic and Paralympic medal delivery preparation and readiness (Own the Podium), Team Canada management at the Olympic and Paralympic Games (Canadian Olympic and Paralympic Committees), school programs, recreation programs, programs for special groups—and the list goes on.

Curling Canada is a sport organization whose funding is a combination of directed government and sport agency monies and self-generated funding through corporate marketing partnerships and television broadcast agreements. Curling Canada, with its partner The Sports Network (TSN), delivers over 320 hours of television broadcast hours of the sport each year, which is regularly seen by about 40 percent of Canada's population. Its marketing partners are some of Canada's best-known brands and companies and its television audiences are among the highest in Canada.

Given its status as a registered amateur athletic association and as a Canadian not-for-profit corporation, Curling Canada then must invest any surplus in the amateur curling system. The organization uses event-driven revenue through tickets, marketing partnerships and broadcast agreements to fund grassroots and junior curling, long-term athlete development, education and certification programs, and club development initiatives. The organization funds 19 multifaceted and inclusive national competitions from bantam to seniors; provides educational programs for ice technicians, umpires, coaches, and officials; and delivers support and advocacy services that keep the curling system healthy and viable from the gym floor (Rocks and Rings introduces curling to about 225,000 school children each year) to significant incremental investments in Curling Canada's high-performance national team athletes and programs.

Given the size of the curling population in Canada (about 1.9 million Canadians claim to have curled in the past year), and the size of the business of curling (about 584 million CAD a year) there can be no argument as to how much the sport contributes to the physical, mental, community, and economic health of the country. Curling clubs are major community hubs, the sport is played for life in every province and territory, curling events create enormous economic effects as well as grassroots investment in curling in the communities that host them, and curling athletes have found tremendous success at world, Olympic, and Paralympic games and inspire both young and old.

Curling Canada exists in a sports system that requires change. Efficient sport delivery, greater asset utilization, deeper capacity, more revenue, and profound learning are available to the amateur sport system where resources are scarce and demands are increasing. A concentrated effort by Curling Canada to understand themselves and the system that they are a part of was studied in a partnership with the Canadian Olympic Committee and delivered by Deloitte-Monitor Consulting. Curling Canada, along with its member associations, is now considering the findings and taking action to ensure that curling remains a healthy, vibrant sport for life that all Canadians can enjoy now and in future.

KATHERINE HENDERSON began a career in brand marketing and has managed some of the world's most beloved sports properties as a rights holder including the NHL, the NBA, MLB, and LPGA, as well as many professional teams and athletes. She was one of the longest-serving employees of the Toronto 2015 Pan and Parapan Am Games, serving as senior vice president of marketing and revenue. Under her watch, the games delivered the largest non-Olympic sponsorship portfolio in Canadian history, which included a who's who of Canadian brands. She and her team delivered record-breaking ticket sales, attendance, broadcast audiences, and merchandise sales. She is now the CEO of Curling Canada. She graduated from Western in 1986 with a BSc (Hons) in nutrition, has an MBA (marketing and public policy) from the Schulich School of Business at York University, and has an MTS from the University of Toronto.

University sport in Canada is divided into four regional associations:

1. Ontario University Athletics (OUA) represents 20 institutions.
2. Atlantic University Sport (AUS) represents 11 universities in New Brunswick, Nova Scotia, Newfoundland and Labrador, and Prince Edward Island.
3. Quebec Student Sport Federation (QSSF) represents Quebec's eight universities.
4. Canada West represents 17 universities in British Columbia, Alberta, Saskatchewan, and Manitoba.

Champions from each of these regions meet every year in national championships sanctioned by U SPORTS. The largest of these are the Vanier Cup (national football final) and the University Cup (national men's and women's ice hockey final).

U SPORTS seeks "to provide exceptional experiences which empower today's student-athletes to be tomorrow's leaders" (U SPORTS, 2018). It has five core values:

1. Students first
2. Excellence
3. Equity
4. Competitive balance
5. Integrity and transparency

U SPORTS seeks to ensure that student-athletes who have attained a high level of success both in academics and athletics are recognized for their achievements through the Academic All-Canadians Program. To be named an Academic All-Canadian, student-athletes must maintain a grade point average of 80 percent or better during the school year while competing for a varsity team. In addition, U SPORTS also names the top eight Academic

EXECUTIVE PERSPECTIVE
Marketing to Our Community While Growing Our Youth

SCOTT McROBERTS, Director of Athletics, University of Guelph

The Canadian university landscape provides over 14,000 student-athletes with an opportunity to compete for their institution in their chosen sport. Our four conferences are divided geographically; they include Canada West, Ontario University Athletics (OUA), Réseau du Sport Étudiant de Québec (RSEQ), and Atlantic University Sport (AUS).

Our member schools affiliate with both their conference (which sets the rules of league play and scheduling, deals with officiating, etc.) and our national governing body (which runs our national championships and sets eligibility rules). They are vital in the support they give as they allow our schools to collectively determine how their competitions will be regulated. Without our governing bodies, we wouldn't have any experiences to provide to our student-athletes!

We're funded through several different revenue streams. Student athletic fees fund a large portion of our department, from varsity athletics to the facilities and programming that are accessible to our student body. We also receive financial help from donations. Whether communicating with alumni or surrounding businesses, our key is to portray how their donations go to work in our community. A major part of this equation is how these donors see our student-athletes. Our student-athletes are fantastic role models, and we hold them to the highest standard to ensure they are seen in the best light.

At Guelph, we break our target market into two distinct groups: the student body and the community at-large. A challenge that many athletic departments in Canada face involves the marketing to student-athletes. We have a great product, and, in many sports, we provide the best amateur competition in Canada. However, our challenge comes in exposing our student bodies to the product. Through events such as "Stuff the Seats" for our volleyball teams or "Res Floods the Rink" for hockey, we strive to make our games "the place to be" for our student body. Once the speed and skill of the Gryphons are seen, we can usually get the students to come back.

Marketing a U Sports institution is quite different from marketing larger sporting brands (such as professional teams) because of the extra effort that is needed to get brand exposure. The adage "if you build it, they will come" does not apply to U Sports—significant effort is needed to push the product to target markets.

One way in which we conduct outreach with our community at the University of Guelph is through partnering with our minor sporting organizations. Starting in 2013, we began tapping into that brand exposure by growing relationships with these organizations, thus helping to provide a better sport experience for our Junior Gryphons.

Today, over 6,000 Junior Gryphons wear the red, black, and gold while playing soccer, hockey, football, basketball, volleyball, rugby, and lacrosse or playing as our Special Olympians. These organizations partner strongly with our department, playing at our on-campus facilities, receiving special training from our coaches, and allowing University of Guelph student-athletes to serve as role models for our Junior Gryphons. They want to see their new favourite teams play and watch their role models excel. They come, they bring their parents and siblings, and we create Gryphon fans (and revenue streams) in the process. We have so fully embraced this strategy that no Canadian university has its logo on the jersey of more youth athletes.

Our brand receives fantastic exposure from this program: As our Junior Gryphons travel, so does our brand, as opposing teams across the country become aware of our department. Other universities across the country are beginning to see the benefit and are starting to sponsor their youth athletic programs. As a bonus, this helps with our recruiting: Young, elite athletes from Guelph grow up dreaming of becoming Gryphons.

Personally, I witness both sides of the coin. I have two boys, aged 7 and 9, who are Junior Gryphons themselves, playing hockey, soccer and lacrosse (and perhaps you have Junior Gryphons in your house as well).

As director of athletics at the University of Guelph, Scott McRoberts has spent more than 12 years in strategic management and fundraising with universities, national sport organizations, and municipalities throughout North America. Previously, he worked with Stanford University, the University of San Francisco, San Jose State, and the City of San Francisco and was executive director of the Niagara Sport Commission.

All-Canadians by selecting the top male and female from each conference. There are also honours for All-Canadians who are the top athletes in each sport, selection of U SPORTS Male and Female Athletes of the Year, community service awards for deserving student-athletes, and numerous other sport- and championship-specific awards.

Historically, Canada has been behind the United States in the number and size of athletic scholarships that are distributed annually to student-athletes. This led to large numbers of talented Canadian athletes choosing to attend college or university in the United States, where they receive large athletic scholarships. More recently, the regulations concerning Canadian athletic scholarships have begun to reflect the desire of Canadian institutions to keep the best athletes in Canada by increasing maximum award amounts. Current U SPORTS regulations state that the maximum amount a student-athlete can receive annually covers their tuition and compulsory fees for the academic year. However, as athletic scholarships are the responsibility of each university and also subject to regulations from each of the four conferences, the number and value of scholarships vary widely from one university to another across Canada. It has been reported that the average sport scholarship within the Canadian system is 1,060 CAD (Lucas, 2019).

To receive any funding, student-athletes must meet the minimum academic requirements. U SPORTS regulations state that first-year student-athletes must have a minimum 80 percent entering average. After their first year of eligibility, student-athletes must have maintained a minimum 65 percent average in the preceding year's academic courses to be eligible for an athletic financial award in the next season.

It is important to recognize that tuition at U SPORTS member institutions is often much lower than U.S. institutions, making the former more appealing to both Canadian and U.S. talent. Concurrently, though U.S. scholarships might be higher than Canadian university scholarships, growing numbers of talented Canadian scholar-athletes go stateside and return to a U SPORTS institution; U.S. institutions offer increased access to coaches, high-performance resources, and U.S. national visibility, but Canadian athletes who get injured and lose their scholarship may look at U SPORTS as a very affordable, viable option. Furthermore, there have been increased media and word-of-mouth promotion about the rising quality in U SPORTS facilities, high-performance training, and coaching, leading many athletes outside North America, especially Europe (e.g., France, Spain) to choose university sport in Canada instead of the United States. Thus, while there remains a sizable difference in both award quantity and value between Canadian universities and larger universities in the United States, U SPORTS has become the first choice of many Canadian and U.S. athletes, and that trend is likely to continue.

Canadian Colleges Athletic Association (CCAA)

The Canadian Collegiate Athletic Association (CCAA) was founded in 1974, and the first national championship competitions were held for hockey and basketball in 1975. As the solitary governing body for college sport in Canada, its primary objectives are as follows:

- To provide a framework through which interprovincial, national, and international college athletic competitions may be conducted, developed, and promoted.
- To seek full and effective representation on committees, boards, study groups, and other like bodies, which make decisions concerning the development of college athletics in Canada.
- To provide for the recognition and achievement of intercollegiate athletic excellence on a national level.

The CCAA represents 94 member institutions that provide services to 9,000 student-athletes, about 700 coaches, and over 150 sport administrators. Its membership comprises community colleges, universities, university-colleges, Quebec-based CEGEPs, and technical institutions, making it the largest postsecondary sport organization in the country. The member institutions are organized into five regional conferences:

1. Atlantic Colleges Athletic Association (ACAA), comprising 10 colleges and universities in New Brunswick and Nova Scotia

2. Ontario Colleges Athletic Association (OCAA), representing 27 institutions across the province

3. Alberta Colleges Athletic Conference (ACAC), made up of 18 colleges throughout Alberta and Saskatchewan

4. Pacific Western Athletic Association, also referred to as the PACWEST, which includes 9 institutions in British Columbia

5. QSSF, made up of 37 universities, colleges, and CEGEPs in Quebec

Every year, the CCAA organizes national championship tournaments for golf, soccer, cross-country running, badminton, volleyball, basketball, and curling. Like U SPORTS, CCAA also sponsors several academic- and athletic-based excellence awards. They also recognize individuals as Academic All-Canadians. To receive this honour, student-athletes must demonstrate excellence in both academics and athletics at their institution. Specifically, they must be named to their regional conference all-star team in a CCAA-recognized sport and maintain a GPA standing of 3.5 (on a scale of 4) or equivalent. The institution with the most CCAA Academic All-Canadians in each year is presented with a CCAA Academic All-Canadian Recognition Award.

Olympic Sport

The Olympic movement is one of the most well-known parts of the sport industry. Every two years, millions of people in Canada and around the world tune in to watch the best elite athletes from each nation compete in summer and winter disciplines. In order to get athletes to that level requires an intricate sport system. In Canada, that system includes organizational bodies and policies that exist to govern, administer, and allocate resources to develop the next generation of Olympic athletes.

Sport Canada

Sport in Canada is governed at a federal level under the Ministry of Canadian Heritage, although previously it was shifted under various portfolios, including Health and Intergovernmental Affairs. At times in recent decades, Canada has had a minister responsible for sport, but this role is currently under the portfolio of the minister for Canadian Heritage. Within the ministry, sport sits alongside other cultural industries including media, diversity, indigenous affairs, museums, and the arts. Sport Canada's mission is "to enhance opportunities for Canadians to participate and excel in sport" (Sport Canada, 2020b). Additionally, Sport Canada has the following strategic directives:

- Strengthen sport leadership
- Provide strategic support for high-performance programming
- Promote technically sound sport development
- Enhance opportunities for sport participation
- Maximize the benefits of hosting
- Promote linguistic duality in the Canadian sport system
- Strengthen the ethical foundation of sport
- Expand the body of knowledge about sport
- Harmonize the Canadian sport system

Sport Canada Programs

The programs unit of Sport Canada is responsible for distributing funding for national sport organizations, multisport organizations, athletes, and events through three funding programs: the Sport Support Program, Hosting Program, and Athlete Assistance Program. In 2019-2020, Sport Canada contributed 233.4 million CAD in grants and contributions to these programs (Sport Canada, 2020b).

- *Sport Support Program:* In 2019-2020, the Sport Support Program allocated 178.8 million CAD in funding from Sport Canada, which was divided among the 58 national sport organizations (NSOs), 20 multisport and service organizations (MSOs), and 9 Canadian sport centres. From that amount, $64 million was earmarked for targeted funding toward sports and athletes with medal potential at the Olympic and Paralympic Games. The body responsible for recommending and funding sports and athletes with medal potential is Own the Podium (OTP), a third-party (i.e., nongovernmental) sport organization originally launched in 2005 to support Canada's success at the 2010 Vancouver Winter Olympic Games. OTP is also responsible for administering another $5 million from the Sport Support Program toward identifying next generation talent with the potential for medal success at future Olympic and Paralympic Games.

- *Hosting Program*: Sport Canada provided 21.6 million CAD of funding in 2019-2020 to assist with hosting sport events in Canada such as an international championship or a mega multisport event (Sport Canada, 2020c). Additionally, these funds are used to support the hosting of the Canada Games, the nation's largest multisport event held biennially with athletes representing each of the country's 10 provinces and three territories (for more on the Canada Games, see chapter 10). Hosting program funds are also used to support the travel costs for athletes from across Canada to compete at the Canada Games.

- *Athlete Assistance Program*: The third and final program that the Government of Canada finances through Sport Canada is known as the Athlete Assistance Program (AAP). The purpose of this program is to provide direct financial assistance to Canada's top high-performance athletes who compete at major international sporting events such as the Olympic Games, Commonwealth Games, Pam Am Games, Paralympic Games, and World Championships. The Olympic Games are considered the most important for this program. In 2019-2020, Sport Canada reported funding for the AAP in the amount of 33 million CAD and covering about 1,900 athletes (Sport Canada, 2020b). To qualify for this assistance, which is administered through the NSOs, athletes must be identified as among the top 16 in the world in their sport, or they must show the potential to be among the top 16. Further athlete eligibility requirements include their availability to compete for Canada in international competition. Assistance is provided to athletes to cover living and training expenses, tuition, and identified special needs. The amount given for living and training expenses depends on the "carding" status of the athlete and is paid directly to the athlete by Sport Canada. As of 2019, those athletes who hold a senior card for at least one year receive a monthly living and training allowance of $1,765, paid two months in advance. First-year senior carded athletes and development athletes receive $1,060 per month. Athletes who are attending a public postsecondary institution at a Canadian university of college at the same time as meeting the requirements for their carded status are also eligible to receive tuition support. Courses that are part of the National Coaching Certification Program (NCCP) are also eligible for support. Athletes may also defer this support and use it when they have retired from competition. Full-time and part-time study are both allowed. A lifetime maximum of $27,500 was set in the 2019 guidelines from Sport Canada. Subsidized special needs include relocation expenses and child-care assistance.

To identify which Canadian sport organizations (and athletes) are eligible for funding, Sport Canada uses the Sport Funding and Accountability Framework (SFAF), which was first introduced in 1995. Funding is divided into the NSO component, the multisport organization component, and the project stream component (referring to such projects as ethics strategies, events, and research). To determine the funding entitlement of each NSO and MSO applicant, the SFAF looks at eligibility, assessment, funding, and accountability.

- Eligibility: The organization or project ensures that they meet specific criteria set out by the government.
- Assessment: The organization is evaluated based on a range of qualitative criteria across key performance indicators of governance, programs, and engagement (Sport Canada, 2020c).
- Funding: Eligible NSOs and MSOs (multisport organizations) are required to provide a complete funding application.
- Accountability: Sport Canada provides specific guidelines on policy, which the sport organizations must incorporate to ensure that their funding will be granted and sustained. Created in accordance with the goals of the Canadian Sport Policy, these guidelines consider such issues as official languages, women in sport, harassment and abuse, and Aboriginal sport.

Sport Policy

The second main area of Sport Canada's work concerns sport policy. To understand the current policies, it is important to examine the evolution of the federal government's involvement in sport in Canada.

The first significant government sport policy is considered to be the Fitness and Amateur Sport Act. The legislation was created to "encourage, promote, and develop fitness and amateur sport in Canada" (Fitness and Amateur Sport Act, 1961, s. 3), as a response to concern over the health of Canada's population as well as the declining status of Canadian athletes in international competition. By most standards, the act had almost no major impact on sport and very little change occurred.

The issue of the government's involvement in sport was raised again in 1968, when Prime Minister Pierre Trudeau commissioned the Task Force on Sport for Canadians. This report had a significant impact on NSOs as it led to an era of direct promotion of high-performance sport by the federal government (Macintosh & Whitson, 1994). However, this impact was both positive and negative. While the increased funding to the organizations improved professionalism, it also led to greater complexity and a decrease in their established autonomy.

The next 20 years saw numerous other government papers and sport-funding plans, some of which were considered a success and others that were not (see Thibault & Harvey, 2013, for a more in-depth review of Canada's sport policy). These include *Game Plan* (1976) and *Partners in Pursuit of Excellence: A National Policy on Amateur Sport* (1979). The Ben Johnson doping scandal at the 1988 Seoul Summer Olympic Games was the catalyst for the creation of another important government sport report: The *Report of the Commission of Inquiry into the Use of Drugs and Banned Practices Intended to Increase Athletic Performance*. Also known as the Dubin Inquiry, the report was released in June 1990 and provided a critical evaluation of the government's emphasis on high performance and excellence over participation in sport (Semotiuk, 1994). The recommendations of the report forced the sport community to re-evaluate its priorities and responsibilities and eventually led to three phases of implementation: The first two phases dealt directly with the issue of doping, while the third focused on the structure of sport in Canada and led to the creation of *Sport: The Way Ahead: The Minister's Task Force on Federal Sport Policy* in 1992. This report recommended a decreased role for the federal government and an increased role for NSOs to create future Canadian sport policy (Thibault & Babiak, 2005).

The next major report on Canadian sport was *Sport: Everybody's Business*, also known as the Mills Report, which was released in 1999 and widely supported by the sport community (Athletes CAN, 2006). Its purpose was to examine the Canadian sport industry by analyzing various sport sectors, identifying challenges in those sectors, and providing recommendations for future improvements.

The next major government policy project was a Canada-wide consultation in 2000-2001 of sport organizations and athletes at six regional conferences regarding their vision and views on sport in Canada. The outcome of these consultations led to the National Summit on Sport in 2001 and, eventually, to the development and adoption of *The Canadian Sport Policy* in 2002, the framework that guides Sport Canada and the Canadian sport community. For the first time, the federal government and all 13 provincial and territorial governments agreed on a far-reaching sport policy and adapted their organizations accordingly. The mission of the policy was to have a dynamic, leading-edge sport environment that enables all Canadians to experience and enjoy sport and to achieve successful results in elite competition levels by the year 2012. The policy is built on the following four goals, or pillars, of achievement:

1. Enhanced participation, ensuring that Canadians from all segments of society are getting involved with sports at all levels and in all forms.

2. Enhanced excellence, expanding the pool of talented Canadian athletes and teams and ensuring they are ethical and fair in their success at international competitions.

3. Enhanced capacity, making certain those ethically based, athlete-centred development systems are modernized and continually refined as necessary.

4. Enhanced interaction, ensuring that the sport system is connected through committed stakeholder communication and coordination.

The realization of these goals is at the heart of any new Canadian sport policy and program. In addition, eligibility requirements for previously created programs such as the SFAF have been adjusted to reflect the overall vision of *The Canadian Sport Policy*.

In 2011, the provinces and territories gathered to renew the policy with contemporary updates addressing maltreatment, concussions, gender equity, reconciliation with First Nations, and inclusion for persons with a disability, among others (Sport Information Resource Centre, 2019). Consequently, while the initial policy was in place for a 10-year period spanning 2002-2012, the current policy has been in effect from 2012 and will cease in 2022, although it is likely to be followed by a third iteration.

This section highlights some of the most important sport policies and reports commissioned by the Canadian government, but numerous other policies and reports also exist, including those that focus on specific issues in the sport system, such as the Federal Government Policy on Tobacco Sponsorship of National Sport Organizations (1985), Women in Sport Policy (1986), Canadian Strategy for Ethical Conduct in Sport (2002), the Canadian Policy against Doping in Sport (2004), Sport Canada's Policy on Aboriginal People's Participation in Sport (2005), and the Policy on Sport for Persons with a Disability (2006). Each of these policies deals with issues in Canadian sport, and to receive funding from Sport Canada, sport organizations must adhere to each to be considered under the SFAF (see Thibault & Harvey, 2013).

Major Games and Hosting

In the mid-1990s, the Canadian government realized that hosting international sporting events presented an opportunity for numerous social, economic, and cultural benefits, including facility legacies, job creation, and volunteer development (Sport Canada, 2020a). At the same time, it recognized the need to ensure that those events receiving government funding provided a return of the positive benefits they were seeking. This led to the creation of the Federal Policy for Hosting International Sport Events in 2000 (modified in 2008), to provide a framework determining the level of federal involvement in the hosting of international sport events. The policy clarifies the federal government's role in hosting and provides a transparent, decision-making tool for the government to assess proposals against strict criteria. The federal government has identified eight tenets that must be examined for an event to receive government funding:

1. Potential to accrue net benefits
2. Fiscal reality
3. Proactive partnerships
4. Provision of legacies
5. No deficit guarantees
6. Compliance with federal standards (e.g., languages, environmental law)
7. Demonstrable community support
8. Sound management

By ensuring that these requirements are in place before providing funding, the government reduces its risk in making a safe investment from which it can expect a positive contribution toward Sport Canada's objectives.

National Sport Organizations

National sport organizations (NSOs) are the individual nonprofit sport governing bodies for all Olympic and non-Olympic sports in Canada. There are 58 NSOs that are funded by the federal government as listed on the Sport Canada website (Taks et al., 2020), including large organizations like Canada Soccer and smaller ones such as Ringette Canada. There are also numerous NSOs not funded by the government, such as the Canadian Handball Association and Quidditch Canada. To be funded by the government, the organizations must meet the requirements of the SFAF (discussed earlier in this chapter). While funding for NSOs changes from cycle to cycle, there are some organizations that are consistently at the top for overall Sport Support Program, Athlete Assistance Program, and

Hosting Program funding, including swimming, athletics, ice hockey, rugby, and basketball.

The operating budgets of Canadian NSOs widely vary from a few thousand dollars to millions of dollars. Besides government funding, NSOs typically rely on sponsorship, fundraising, merchandising, event hosting, and membership fees to make up the remainder of their budgets. However, this varies considerably with some NSOs (e.g., Hockey Canada, Golf Canada) having built a diverse revenue mix where government support comprises only a small proportion of total revenues, while others (e.g., Table Tennis Canada, Triathlon Canada) rely much more heavily on government support. Heavy reliance on government funding is not ideal from a financial perspective and may hinder the NSO's autonomy as they are increasingly required to meet government regulations under the threat of having their funding pulled (Macintosh & Whitson, 1994).

The responsibilities of NSOs include policy development, program development, national team selection, and national and international event hosting. NSOs also maintain membership in their sport's international federation. To compete at an internationally sanctioned event, athletes are required by the international federation to be a member of their sport's NSO. The majority of Canada's NSOs are headquartered in Ottawa; however, some are strategically located elsewhere, such as Bobsleigh Canada Skeleton, which is situated in Calgary, where the Olympic bobsleigh facilities are located.

Provincial and Territorial Sport

Each of Canada's 13 provincial and territorial governments plays a large and important role in sport in the country. While the organizations responsible for sport in each province vary in size and capability, they all seek to accomplish similar goals. It is the provincial or territorial government's responsibility to promote and develop sport in its jurisdiction and ensure that sport services are delivered on a provincial and territorial scale. While Canada's NSO tend to focus more on high-performance sport, the provincial and territorial governments focus on developing young athletes, **grassroots sport**, and sports participation and recreation.

The structure of sport at a provincial or territorial level is similar to that at the national level. In each province or territory, sport is a division of a larger government department. Each province and territory then has a provincial sport body whose membership includes the sport-specific organizations. For example, sport in Alberta falls under the Ministry of Culture, Multiculturalism and Status of Women and the Sport and Recreation branch of that ministry, and it is administered by Sport Alberta, which is tied to over 75 provincial sport organizations. Table 2.4 lists the sport body in each provincial and territorial government.

The major contributions and responsibilities of the provincial and territorial governments to sport are funding, hosting policies, high-performance and amateur sport development, provincial team selection, and award recognition. Each provincial/territorial sport organization is a member of their NSO (e.g., Basketball Ontario is connected to Basketball Canada), and they work together to support the development of their sport.

Multisport organizations (MSO) in Canada represent a diversity of interests and provide a variety of services to the Canadian sport community. There are MSOs responsible for such things as athlete interests (Athletes CAN), doping control (WADA), ethics (CCES), Aboriginal sport (ASC), wheelchair sport (CWSA), coaching (CAC), and women in sport (CAAWS), among others. Table 2.5 lists Canada's MSOs. Like NSOs, many of these MSOs receive funding from the federal government as long as they meet the requirements set out in the SFAF. Other sources of funding for these organizations include sponsorship, fundraising, and corporate philanthropy.

Canadian Olympic Committee

The Canadian Olympic Committee (COC) is arguably the most influential of all Canadian MSOs. Headquartered in Montreal and with a second office in Toronto, the COC focuses on high-performance sport and is responsible for all facets of Canada's participation in the Olympic movement. This includes managing Canada's involvement in the Olympic and Pan

TABLE 2.4 Provincial and Territorial Government Sport Departments

Province/Territory	Government Department/Ministry	Government Division/Branch	Provincial Sport Body
Alberta	Culture, Multiculturalism and Status of Women	Recreation and Sport	Sport Alberta
British Columbia	Ministry of Tourism, Arts, and Culture	Sport	Sport BC
Manitoba	Sport, Culture, and Heritage	Sport Secretariat	Sport Manitoba
Newfoundland and Labrador	Children, Seniors, and Social Development	Recreation and Sport	Sport NL
New Brunswick	Tourism, Heritage, and Culture	Sport and Recreation	Sport NB
Northwest Territories	Municipal and Community Affairs	Sport, Recreation and Youth	Sport North Federation
Nova Scotia	Communities, Culture, and Heritage	Sport and Recreation	Sport Nova Scotia
Nunavut	Community and Government Services	Sport and Recreation	Sport Nunavut
Ontario	Heritage, Sport, Tourism, and Culture Industries	Sport and Recreation	Sport Alliance of Ontario*
Prince Edward Island	Health and Wellness	Sports, Recreation and Physical Activity	Sport PEI
Quebec	Éducation et de l'Enseignement Supérieur	Recreation and Sports	Sports Quebec
Saskatchewan	Parks, Culture and Sport	Sports and Recreation	Sask Sport
Yukon	Community Services	Sport and Recreation	Yukon Sport

*This body declared bankruptcy in 2015 and, at the time of publication, it was unclear if a new provincial sport body would take its place.

American Games and numerous cultural and educational programs that seek to advance the Olympic Movement in Canada, selecting and supporting Canadian cities in bidding for Olympic and Pan American Games, and providing athletes with services that assist them in sport and in life (Canadian Olympic Committee, 2020a). The mission of the COC is "to lead the achievement of the Canadian Olympic Team's podium success and to advance the Olympic values in Canada" (Canadian Olympic Committee, 2020b). In 2018, the COC reported spending of over 55 million CAD in program and operating expenses, much of which supports athletes, coaches, NSOs, and other MSOs in the Canadian sport system (Canadian Olympic Committee, 2020c).

All of the COC's programs are created to push the organization toward the achievements set out in this mission statement. It also seeks to promote seven values to the Canadian sport community: excellence, fun, fairness, respect, human development, leadership, and peace.

The COC is a national, nonprofit organization that seeks revenue from various sources to fund its programs and promote its values. Matching the timing of the Olympic Games, the financial activities of the organization follow a quadrennial planning cycle. The most recent completed cycle began January 1, 2016, and continued until December 31, 2020. The cycle almost always ends on the last day of the year in which the Summer Olympics are held, though recent events like the COVID-19 global pandemic may affect quadrennial planning for the COC. During the last cycle, the COC committed to investing 16 million CAD into next-generation talent, $5 million in new coaching-enhancement pro-

TABLE 2.5 Selection of Canadian Multisport Organizations

Organization Name
Aboriginal Sport Circle (ASC)
Athletes CAN
Arctic Winter Games
Calgary Olympic Development Association (CODA)
Canada Games Council (CGC)
Canadian Centre for Ethics in Sport (CCES)
Canadian Olympic Committee (COC)
Canadian Paralympic Committee (CPC)
(Canadian) Sport Information Resource Centre (SIRC)
Canadian Sport Tourism Alliance (CSTA)
Canadian Women in Sport (formerly known as CAAWS)
Coaching Association of Canada (CAC)
Commonwealth Games Canada (CGC)
Sport Dispute Resolution Centre
Sport Matters Group

grams, and $1 million for Game Plan, its athlete transition program (Strong, 2017).

Grassroots and Amateur Sport

Every Olympic medalist's and professional star's first experience with sport was at the community level. Across Canada, hockey rinks, soccer fields, baseball diamonds, pools, and more are filled with the young Canadians, the next generation of superstars alongside those just out to stay healthy and have fun. The grassroots sport movement, however, is not just about playing the game; it is about being a part of the whole experience. Coaches, referees, administrators, parents, and athletes are all part of grassroots sport, and without the contribution of any one of these groups, it would not be possible. The grassroots movement can also be connected to **spectatorship**. Cities and towns all over the country support teams in various sports at various levels, and in many cases, those teams come to be a defining presence in the community.

In Canada, grassroots sport (or **amateur sport**) is fast becoming one of the most important pursuits for governments, researchers, and practitioners. It is a common topic at conferences and is on the agenda of government meetings. Recognizing the importance of grassroots sport to both high-performance sport and the health of all Canadians drives this increased interest. Specific to high-performance sport, an effective grassroots sport system

- increases talent identification opportunities,
- provides for the development of athletes, officials, and coaches, and
- enhances sport–community linkages.

With respect to the general health of Canadians, grassroots sport systems provide opportunities and incentives for people of all ages to participate in an active lifestyle.

We define grassroots sport as sport that is based around local communities and participation by the general public. This section outlines three aspects of Canadian grassroots sport: participation, spectatorship, and organizations.

Participation

At the grassroots level, **participation** in sport is not limited by age or ability and can arguably provide numerous social, economic, cultural, and physical benefits for the participants and the community. Donnelly and Kidd (2003) described the individual highlights of grassroots participation as "the joys of effort, the emotional drama of competition, the satisfactions of self-mastery and accomplishment, the lifelong friendships, and the adventures and learning of travel" (p. 25). In 2016, a Statistics Canada general social survey declared that 27 percent of adults over the age of 15 participated in sport on a regular basis (Statistics Canada, 2019f). This statistic is roughly on par with the United States and Australia, as there has been an overall decline in sport participation levels in the Western world due to several issues including economic uncertainty, austerity measures, and rising obesity rates.

In Canada, the five most popular sports for participants were ice hockey, golf, global football, running, and basketball. Hockey Canada, the NSO in charge of ice hockey in Canada, boasts more than 600,000 registrants across the country (Hockey Canada, 2017). However, with 72 percent of foreign-born Canadian males indicating that they participate in sport regularly (Statistics Canada, 2019f), sports that have more global appeal like global football (soccer) and basketball have experienced greater participation rates. Global football (soccer) registration rates have climbed for several years and have between 200,000 and 300,000 more registrants than ice hockey. However, other sports, such as badminton and cricket, are also experiencing increases in grassroots participation due to increased immigration to Canada. It is important to remember that grassroots participation is not just about the athletes; it is also about those who keep programs running.

Volunteering is an important aspect of grassroots sport, as community leagues are run almost entirely by volunteers, without whom the programs would cease to exist. In fact, 18 percent of all volunteers in Canada volunteer with organized sport, and they contribute a total of 167 million hours to sport alone (Doherty, 2005). While large numbers of Canadians are able to enjoy sport at a community level, many do not have the opportunity. Numerous barriers to participation exist in community sport, including access to facilities, access to coaching, parental support, gender, and household wealth; this should be of concern to Canadians.

Spectatorship

The second key aspect of grassroots sport is spectatorship. While most people associate this solely with professional sport, opportunities exist in communities all over the country for people to get out and support local teams. For example, it is not unusual in Canadian towns for the population to come out and enjoy a midget or juvenile ice hockey game or to get spectators out to a local curling bonspiel of golf club championship. Even the smallest towns have sports pages in their community newspapers and websites, which report the achievements of local athletes and the scores of all minor sport games from the previous week. The star of the local baseball team might live next door and walk your dog while the star quarterback serves coffee at the local Tim Hortons coffee shop.

The professional sports world has ties to grassroots sport. For instance, for the CFL and the Grey Cup, it is essentially the "Canadianness"

IN THE KNOW

BIRGing and CORFing: Fan Identity Conceptualized

Why is it that when Team Canada won double ice hockey Olympic gold (men's and women's) at the 2014 Winter Olympic Games in Sochi, Russia, did sales of Hockey Canada merchandise skyrocket to unprecedented highs? And why is it that after a big win against the Maple Leafs, formerly "lost" Montreal Canadiens fans are quick to jump back on the bandwagon, take their old jerseys out of the closet, and refer to "our big win" when talking about the game? On the other hand, why is it that these same people are nowhere to be found following an important loss for the Leafs?

These phenomena have been labelled BIRGing and CORFing. BIRGing, or basking in reflected glory, is the enhancement or maintenance of self-esteem through associating with winning teams, while CORFing, or cutting off reflected failure, refers to fans disassociating themselves from losing teams because it negatively affects their self-esteem (Wann & Branscombe, 1990). An interesting aspect of BIRGing is the tendency of people to publicize their connection with successful others (e.g., the team) when they have not contributed to the (team's) success, where they are really basking in reflected glory, not earned success. CORFing fans distance themselves physically, mentally, or emotionally, with the intent of avoiding negative relationships with the unsuccessful entity (the team).

of the league that distinguishes it and pulls its support mainly from a grassroots level, where Canadians can claim that the CFL is "league of our own." The league thrives in smaller cities and creates a sense of pride and identity in those communities (Brunt, 2011). Three CFL franchises (Edmonton, Saskatchewan, and Winnipeg) are community owned, and salaries in the CFL are comparable to average Canadian salaries, so the players are not far from the realities of the fans.

Organizations

Numerous grassroots organizations look to develop, protect, and advance the cause of community sport. The majority of these organizations are nonprofit, volunteer-directed, and funded by all levels of government and through sponsorship and donations. Grassroots organizations exist on the national, provincial, and local levels; some even have international connections.

Local

The Edmonton Sport Council is a grassroots support organization working at a local level. Its purpose is to serve and represent the local Edmonton sport community, and specifically to advocate for sport and promote sport development in Edmonton; advocate and support the development of stable and ongoing funding for sport in Edmonton; facilitate effective communication among Edmonton sport organizations and other key organizations, including all levels of government; and assist sport organizations and individuals by linking them to, or providing them with, sport-related education and sport services.

Provincial

KidSport Ontario represents the Ontario chapter of the National KidSport initiative. Operated in each province as an independent organization, the program follows the outline provided by KidSport Canada. Its mission is to assist children who are disadvantaged and help them overcome social and economic barriers that could prevent or negatively affect their participation in sport. The organization does this by offsetting registration fees and providing grants for equipment. With this in mind, KidSport Ontario has four main objectives: raising funds, gathering resources, and building program partnerships; establishing local chapters throughout the province; partnering with other charitable and community-based programs; and identifying and alleviating social and economic barriers to help children participate in sport.

National

True Sport is a national initiative that involves parents, teachers, athletes, officials, coaches, organizers, and community leaders working together to ensure that sport participation lives up to its potential for benefits. The organization works to mobilize communities and groups across Canada to ensure a positive and meaningful experience for everyone participating in sport.

International Connections

Play Soccer is an Ontario-based community sport program that works to enhance family fun and learning through global football in Ontario. The program has developed international connections with the Everton Football Club of the English Premiership League in a deal that benefits both parties. Everton provides coaches and coaching systems and commercial expertise to Play Soccer; in exchange, it looks for exposure in the Canadian marketplace to help in its pursuit of a more global brand.

CHAPTER SUMMARY

This chapter provides an extensive review of the landscape that is Canadian sport. The four major facets of Canadian sport are professional sport, university and college sport, Olympic sport, and grassroots or amateur sport. Each has its own set of organizations, events, and participants. Professional sport includes leagues (e.g., NHL) and athletes (e.g., Connor McDavid) that provide entertainment for an economic gain across five categories: tier one, tier two, tier three, professional sport competitions, and sports entertainment. Supported by the Canadian government through NSOs, Olympic sport covers high-performance athletic competition in which athletes compete, for the most part, for personal rather than direct economic gain, although indirect financial benefits (e.g., sponsorship, government funding, etc.) certainly accrue to elite Olympic athletes. The 13 provincial and territorial governments play a large role in sport in the country by promoting and developing sport in their own jurisdictions and ensuring that sport services are being delivered on a provincial and territorial scale. Grassroots (amateur) sport is based around local communities and participation by the general public. The three aspects of Canadian grassroots sport are participation, spectatorship, and organizations. Finally, sport events facilities are shown to be paramount to all four facets of sport in Canada. These sectors and characteristics of sport in Canada are vital knowledge pieces for sport marketers. Regardless of where in the system a marketer is working, a knowledge of its landscape and all stakeholders is key.

TEST YOUR KNOWLEDGE

1. What is the role of the Canadian government in sport in this country?
2. What is the role of the provinces of Ontario, Quebec, British Columbia, Alberta, and Nova Scotia in sport in this country?
3. Provide an example for each of the elements noted in figure 2.1.
4. How do each of the following groups fit into figure 2.1?
   a. coaches
   b. elite athletes
   c. developing athletes
5. Describe the size of the sport industry in Canada.
6. Distinguish between professional, Olympic, and grassroots sport.
7. What role do universities and colleges play in Canada's sport system?
8. In your opinion, what are the 10 most important sport organizations in Canada? Describe each and support your selection.
9. What types of sport events are most frequently held in Canada? Why do you think that is the case?
10. Is corporate Canada involved in sport? If so, explain how and why.

KEY TERMS

amateur sport	Olympic sport	spectatorship
collegiate sport	participation	sport events
grassroots sport	professional sport	

CASE STUDIES

Visit HK*Propel* for case studies organized by chapter.

CHAPTER 3

Sport Market Research

LEARNING OBJECTIVES

After studying this chapter, you will be able to do the following:

- Appreciate the importance of market research in business decisions
- Identify the role of market research in the marketing process
- Recognize the different types of research and techniques available
- Learn the different stages in the market research process
- Recognize the different data mining and analytics software programs
- Understand the importance of data in market research

A sport marketer must always consider the value of market research information, weighing its cost against the economic benefits (i.e., information that leads to improved marketing that results in increased revenues) it may provide. Although this research work can be delegated to a market research firm (or even a unit of a larger organization's marketing department), it can also be executed by an individual intern or staff member, a group, or a team. Numerous publications present techniques and options for performing market research that can be followed to enable the acquisition of quality data with which to make decisions. In simple terms, market research is a highly developed field of practice.

The market research process is centred around accumulating data, which is arguably the most important part of the process in any industry, including sport. This chapter discusses the types of data required and how to accumulate them. We discuss the three main types of research—exploratory, descriptive, and explanatory—and the two types of data—primary and secondary. We will also describe the marketing research process in detail, including several techniques. The objective of this chapter is, therefore, to discuss the importance of market research and its uses. You will also learn the various research methods and data sources that are most commonly used in sport marketing. As you go through this chapter, you will learn that marketing research is not only used in academic inquiry but also widely practiced in the sport business.

Time as a Key Element in Marketing Research

Time is a very important aspect in market research and in the resulting decision-making process. Marketers attempt to gather research to make better business decisions so they can gain a competitive advantage. Many times firms require the information quickly to be a first mover in the industry; in other cases, evidence is needed as to how to react to a competitor's new marketing strategy. These types of situations provide examples demonstrating that time can mean the difference between success and loss. A successful sport market researcher, thus, will understand, acquire, and present research findings in a timely manner. Simply put, a well-planned and properly implemented market research program will reduce the business risk of an organization by eliminating potential errors and saving both financial resources and, what is often more important, time.

The Uses of Marketing Research

It is important that sport marketers be familiar with the basic types of market research and the research process. Such familiarity will benefit day-to-day marketing efforts. Particularly, in view of today's competitive sport market environment and ever-changing customer expectations, sport organizations of any size rely on data-driven marketing research to make informed decisions and design adaptive strategies on an ongoing basis. Marketing research, which is defined as a systematic and objective collection and analysis of data about a particular target market, competition, or environment

(Arora & Mahankale, 2012), is mainly intended to provide supporting information to management so that they can make educated and timely decisions.

Marketing research can be conducted for different benefits and outcomes, which can range from finding what went wrong, to identifying needs of customers (e.g., the Toronto Raptors of the NBA testing a new in-stadium seat upgrade app to determine if users are satisfied), to finding new opportunities for existing products (e.g., assessing if Canada Basketball's "Mad Love" program, which was launched in May 2021, will have an impact on adolescent girls' participation in basketball). The Toronto Blue Jays of the MLB, for example, used telephone interviews to small-business clients and potential clients to determine what kind of business package (e.g., suite, tickets, game times) would be of interest to its target market. With this information, the Jays could alter their marketing mix to cater to these needs and wants.

Decision making is the act of choosing among several alternative possibilities (Foster et al., 2020). Decision making in sport marketing always involves making choices when something of value is at stake. A decision maker's degree of certainty about alternative choices and the outcome of any of the chosen options involves a certain level of risk. In such circumstances, marketing research enables managers to make informed decisions, which minimizes uncertainty.

In fact, not all types of decisions require marketing research. For example, a marketing manager who needs to assign a specific type of task to one of their marketing staff does not need to conduct marketing research to make that decision. Decisions that managers make can be categorized as routine or strategic decisions. Routine decisions are customary decisions that are based on structured, well-informed, and clearly presented organizational procedures and policies (Slack & Parent, 2006). These types of decisions are often used in routine operating decisions on a daily basis and are relatively straightforward. Strategic decisions in the sport business are often complex and made at the senior level of an organization, often without any established guidelines and procedures (Foster et al., 2020). Therefore, while marketing research helps produce evidence to make educated decisions in both routine and strategic decision making, it is not needed for all types of routine decisions, whereas it is an integral part of strategic decision making.

As discussed in chapter 1, before sport marketers make decisions and formulate strategies on the different elements of the sport marketing mix (the four Ps), they need to gather evidence-based information on their customers, company, competitors (the three Cs), and PEST (see table 3.1). Such information enables the sport marketer to do the following:

- To know and understand existing and new consumers on an ongoing basis. To fulfil this need, data is commonly gathered on factors such as consumers' demography (e.g., age, sex), psychography (e.g., attitude, opinion), geography (e.g., area, region, country), and behaviour (e.g., purchase behaviour, brand usage rate, brand loyalty).

- To assess and understand their own company. For this purpose, data is gathered on factors such as market share (e.g., fans outside the city of the team), financial resources (e.g., sponsorship, naming

TABLE 3.1 Areas of Data Needed Before the Development of the Four Ps of Marketing

Areas of Marketing	Purpose	Data needs
Customer	To know and understand existing and new consumers on an ongoing basis.	• Demography (e.g., age, sex) • Psychography (e.g., attitude, opinion) • Geography (e.g., area, region, country) • Behaviour (e.g., purchase behaviour, brand loyalty)
Company	To assess and understand their own company.	• Market share (e.g., fans outside the city of the team) • Financial resources (e.g., sponsorship, naming right) • Human resources (e.g., presence of famous player) • Competitive advantage (e.g., customers' purchasing power)
Competitors	To understand what others in their industry category are doing and capable of doing, so that an organization change existing or develop new strategies.	• Marketplace (e.g., number of professional teams in a city) • Competitors' data (e.g., ticket price of other teams) • Brand strength (e.g., Toronto Maple Leafs and their fan base) • Competitive advantage (e.g., Sidney Crosby in a team)
PEST	To assess the current situational factors that affect the sport business.	• Economic (e.g., the Calgary Flames and change in oil prices) • Legal (e.g., suspending players and scandal) • Social and cultural (e.g., sexual orientation of athletes) • Political (e.g., players' lockout) • Technological (e.g., first mover in technology adoption)

right), human resources (e.g., presence of famous player in a team), and competitive advantage (e.g., customers purchasing power).

- To understand their competitors and assess what others in their industry category are doing and are capable of doing, so that an organization can change existing or develop new strategies. For this, data is gathered on factors such as the marketplace (e.g., number of professional teams in a city), competitors' data (e.g., ticket price of other teams), brand strength (e.g., the Toronto Maple Leafs and their fan base), and competitive advantage (e.g., Sidney Crosby in a team).
- To assess the current situational factors that affect the sport business. For this, data can be gathered on factors such as economic (e.g., the Calgary Flames and the impact of oil prices on ticket sales), legal (e.g., suspending players and scandal), social and cultural (e.g., sexual orientation of athletes), political (e.g., players' lockout), and technological (e.g., first mover in technology adoption).

After information has been collected about the Three Cs, the next step is making decisions and formulating strategies about the marketing mix that allow an organization to identify customers' wants and needs and satisfy them while achieving the company's objectives. This involves the gathering of data that informs the creation of a product that appeals to customers, the development of an objectively based price that can be attached to a product, the designing of a distribution mechanism that gets the product to customers, and the designing of creative and objectively based promotional tools to communicate a product to consumers.

Types of Market Research

The three principal types of market research are exploratory, descriptive, and explanatory (Creswell & Creswell, 2017).

EXECUTIVE PERSPECTIVE
Why Market Research Is Everywhere

KRISTA BENOIT, President and CEO, iSPARK Consulting

You are likely aware of the prevalence of research, but have you thought much about its importance? You have probably made a retail purchase and been prompted to go online to complete a survey to get 10 percent off your next purchase. You may visit a website and be prompted to take a poll. You go to watch a video on YouTube but have to answer a survey before it plays. During or after attending an event, you have undoubtedly been asked to answer some survey questions about yourself and your experience. Online, in person, and by phone, market research is being conducted all around us. There is a good reason for that: It is critically important.

Embracing the Data

At my event-marketing firm, iSPARK, research and data are critical to the strategies we create and the decisions we make for our clients. Our specialization is event production and marketing, sponsorship strategy, sport tourism, marketing and communications, and coaching and training. Our data-driven approach generally involves three primary types of research:

- Postevent Attendee Feedback. We ask event attendees to tell us what they liked and didn't like about the event, to rate speakers or entertainers, to rank the food, and to weigh in on what they would like to see at next year's event. This information is a critical element of our post-mortem event debriefs.

- Audience Data. We collect information about event attendees, ranging from demographic info to buying habits, and more. This data helps us create powerful event-marketing campaigns and is critical in the development and design of event sponsorship programs.

    Pro Tip: Event sponsors care about who is in the room, not who is organizing or hosting the event. Sponsorship decisions are based on the audience an event attracts, so audience data is the key to attracting sponsors to your property.

- Economic Impact Data. We collect spending data from event attendees and combine it with event organizers' budget spends, both event operational and capital expenditures. This enables us to measure the economic impact of an event on a specific community in Canada. This data has many uses for event organizers, sponsors and funding agencies, as well as event suppliers and destination partners.

Being Data-Driven

Regardless of the type of research activities you may engage in, the purpose is the same: to mine the data for information and use it to formulate a plan, justify a decision, and take your event, sponsorship program, or sport marketing initiative to a new level. In this chapter, you will learn about various types of market-research techniques, methodology, data analysis, and more. I believe the chosen research technique (focus group, survey, interview, etc.) is the least important element. Most crucial is how the research is used and applied.

The Secret about Research

Many organizations, particularly in amateur sport, operate on gut feel. They make decisions about marketing, events, and sponsorship programs based on the seven most expensive words in business: "Because we've always done it that way." Many want to skip the research part and get right to the "doing"—they see research as onerous and desire a shortcut. These are usually the same organizations that see little growth (or none at all), have trouble staying relevant, or are slow to adopt new trends or adapt to a changing landscape. The secret about research is this: the data is the shortcut. Data makes the "doing" part easy. Research helps zero in with laser focus on the what, the where, the why, the when, and the whom. The data points us in the right direction. Without it, we are as good as stumbling around in a half-lit room and likely to fall back on "what worked before" rather than what's needed now.

If you remember only one thing from this chapter, make it this: Market research is the most important tool you have to make smart business decisions.

KRISTA BENOIT has an Honours Bachelor of Commerce in sports administration from Laurentian University and a Bachelor of Arts in French from Carleton University. Since 2000, she has led iSPARK Consulting Inc., a leader in leveraging sport as a catalyst for business and economic activity. Krista leads a team that transforms events, sponsorship, marketing, and sport tourism initiatives with creative genius and flawless execution.

Exploratory research is often used when the type of problem or issue faced by the marketer is vague. Therefore, marketers often use it to define the initial issue for a larger marketing-research project. For example, a manufacturer like Nike is unsure whether it should size the potential market for a new product or find a new product for its existing markets. Exploratory research helps to clarify problems by gathering ideas, details, explanations, and insights to form hypothetical solutions that can be further researched. During the process, it can unexpectedly discover new ideas, opportunities, and problems faced by the company. Exploratory research is usually relatively inexpensive and is rarely used to draw conclusions. Techniques include observation (such as ethnography), interviews, expert interviews, focus groups, and secondary sources. For example, exploratory research can be used to determine the change in consumer purchase behaviour as more consumers rely on the Internet to gather information: Interviewing 50 potential clients will enable researchers to determine where, when, and how they acquired their information.

Descriptive research is typically used after the exploratory research is complete and the problem faced by the marketer has been better defined. It generally asks specific questions about the who, what, where, when, and how; and it accurately answers them. The most common techniques of descriptive research are surveys, secondary data searches, expert interviews, and observation. For example, a marketer observes patrons at a local tennis club to determine where to best locate vending machines for beverages and snacks.

Explanatory research is used when the problem faced by the marketer is well understood and clearly defined. It is used primarily to discover the cause-and-effect relationships between two known variables. The researchers attempt to discover the relationships that predict future events. The most common technique in explanatory research is the experiment, where one variable's relationship to another is tested. For example, the relationship between gender and spending habits on Hockey Canada merchandise at Christmas could be determined using follow-up mail surveys.

Types of Data Sources

Marketers have two main sources of data: data collected through **primary research** and data collected through **secondary research**. While primary research is information gathered through self-conducted research methods (e.g., fans' satisfaction survey), secondary research is information gathered for some other purpose other than for the purpose at hand (e.g., ticket sales data from the previous year). Primary and secondary research types are discussed next.

Primary Research

Primary research involves accumulating data specifically for the purpose of the research through such means as surveys, observations, questionnaires, and focus groups. Researchers use it to find solutions and answers when secondary data is inadequate or inappropriate. It is a systematic process of collecting and logically analyzing information, and researchers need to follow steps in their effort to acquire trustworthy knowledge that is reliable and valid. The primary research process includes planning a research design, **sampling**, and collecting specific data and information on the topic of interest. Compared to secondary research, primary research is typically more costly and takes longer to complete since it is more labour intensive.

Secondary Research

Secondary research is typically used in marketing research to quickly and inexpensively find data about the research topic. Secondary data is data collected for other uses that contains information pertinent to the current marketing research project. Secondary data can be obtained from internal and external sources.

Internal sources are data that can be gathered within an organization. They can include data such as accounting information, sales information, merchandise sales records, and customer complaints. For example, a ticket sales manager uses ticket sales data for designing sales strategy and servicing fans. A sales manager needs an understanding of fans' frequency of attendance (single game, mini plans, and season ticketholder), sales by type of seats (regular seats, club seats, and luxury suites), and form of purchase (individual game tickets, group tickets). Data on various buying patterns of fans can be obtained from ticket sales data. Moreover, in today's digitized world, most of these types of data are available in structured and semistructured form, which make a speedy analysis possible for managers making timely decisions.

External sources are data that will be gathered from sources outside an organization. A common source of external data is **census** information collected by Statistics Canada, which has information available on a range of topics including agriculture, arts, culture, recreation, business enterprises, communications, manufacturing, population, demography, personal finance, social conditions, and travel and tourism.

Other examples of external sources include government reports and documents, marketing data suppliers (e.g., A.C. Nielsen), industry associations, researchers' compiled data (e.g., Rodney Fort's Sports Economics), and annual reports (e.g., Canadian University Sport annual report). Sometimes these sources of secondary data can fully answer the marketing problem at a fraction of the cost of primary research; however, they often do not have enough detailed information to be of use and are merely a convenient steppingstone in the market-research process. This is often the case because competing organizations do not share detailed information, and industry data (associations or libraries) is often dated and developed for other purposes.

In the discussion of external data, it should be noted that there are marketing companies that conduct research projects for interested sport organizations. Some companies may focus on specific industries such as automotive, medical, or financial services; some may concentrate on ethnic research, online research, international research, or other specialized areas. Here are a few examples of market research consultants that specialize, or have a component of their business, in the sport industry:

- YouGov Sports Canada (formerly Charlton Insights) (U.S., with an office in Toronto): Retail advertising, branding, strategy, political, and so on.

- IEG (U.S., with offices in Toronto and Vancouver): Sport sponsorship marketing
- IMI International (global, with a head office in Toronto): Consultancy and market research
- Ipsos Canada (international, with an office in Toronto): Advertising, marketing, and public affairs research
- iSPARK (Canada): Sport-management research

These companies provide public and private industries with strategic information by successfully acquiring the data, analyzing it, and communicating the results to the recipients, who use it to support their business decisions. Two marketing research firms, A.C. Nielsen and Ipsos Reid, are profiled in the In the Know sidebar.

The Market Research Process

The marketing-research process usually consists of six steps (Mullin, Hardy, & Sutton, 2000, p. 88):

Step 1: Define the marketing issue

Step 2: Set objectives and budget

Step 3: Designing research

Step 4: Collect data

Step 5: Organize and analyze data

Step 6: Prepare and present market research findings

IN THE KNOW

A.C. Nielsen and Ipsos Reid Profiles

The global leader in tracking television ratings, A.C. Nielsen collects data for television and streaming and publishes those ratings widely as a means to determine the success of individual television programs. Ipsos Reid, a leading research agency, is recognized for offering survey-based market research in Canada for many industries. The analysts at Ipsos Reid "use the best of science, technology and know-how and apply the principles of security, simplicity, speed and substance to everything [they] do" (Ipsos Reid, 2020). Ipsos Reid also specializes in market research for certain industries, including automotive, energy, financial services, health care, retail, sponsorship, and sport.

EXECUTIVE PERSPECTIVE
The Value of Data in Sport Marketing

INDIVAR KUSHARI, COO, Q.i. Value Systems Inc., and former Chief Data and Information Officer, Canadian Football League

Data plays an invaluable role in the world of sports. As sports teams and leagues are being increasingly seen as businesses that generate revenues, the role of data is increasing exponentially.

At the Canadian Football League, consumer data is used to understand fan segments and profiles to help sell season and casual tickets, sell appropriate merchandise and concessions, enhance the fan experience, attract new sponsors, and keep fans engaged through the year with the teams and the league as a whole. The smart analysis of this data has many benefits for professional sport organizations, including revenues, satisfied fans, new fans, and more efficient operations.

Specific to the on-the-field offering, player and game statistics are used to help teams be competitive on-field, as well as providing the data being used for informed broadcast commentary. An important future trend to keep in mind is that conventional and advanced game statistics will play an increasing role in the emerging world of sports betting, which is identified as a large future source of revenue.

Big data has become one of the most important elements of research in many industries, and it is now starting to be used in sport. Yes, professional sport leagues and clubs, sport networks, agencies, and amateur sport organizations are all starting to use big data sets to better understand their fans, their participants, their streaming audiences, their potential draft picks, their sponsors, and really any key stakeholder they need to market to. In my view, this pattern will continue to grow as team and league owners demand higher effectiveness and return on their investments. Big data provides the opportunity for real-time targeted messaging and customized communication. There will be a demand for talent who not only understand the sport but how to effectively use data and data tools to generate higher engagement and ultimately higher revenues and profitability for the clubs and leagues.

Finally, as a student of sport marketing, I would recommend that you prepare to work in or enhance a culture of data-driven decisions. Whether you are in the data department or a user of data, being able to back up your decisions with sound data will go a long way toward your success and the success of the sports organization you work for. I would encourage you to learn the basics of data management as a student so that you can hit the ground running when you join your first sports organization.

INDIVAR (INDY) KUSHARI is chief operating officer at Q.i. Value Systems Inc. Previously, he was the chief data and information officer and head of team services at the Canadian Football League. In this position, he oversaw the data and technology pillars of the league supporting the strategy and execution of revenue and fan engagement for league initiatives, as well as consulting with individual CFL teams to mine and manage their data. Prior to working with the CFL, he worked in various data and insights roles at Rogers Communications, Coca-Cola (global), Ipsos, and Nielsen. He currently runs Ark Strategy, his own insights and strategy consultancy.

The actual number of steps and each one's importance depends on the project's needs. For example, secondary data may sufficiently answer the issue, so steps 3 and 4 would not be required, or time and budget constraints may affect the shape and direction of the final process. The following section discusses the six steps in detail.

Step 1: Define the Marketing Issue

The initial stage of designing a market research project is defining the marketing issue—a problem or an opportunity facing the marketer. It should be noted that the dangerous part of many marketing problems is neither visible to nor understood by managers. As the **Iceberg Principle** states, in many cases only a very small amount (the "tip") of information is available or visible about a situation, whereas the "real" information or bulk of data is either unavailable or hidden. Therefore, this step is crucial: Failure to properly define the issue will result in unusable data. The marketer and researchers must ascertain the proper direction for further analysis.

Properly defining the issue, or cause, without confusing it with the symptoms can be difficult. At this stage, exploratory research is often used (e.g., interviews, focus groups, secondary source), not to draw final conclusions, but merely to confirm the issue's definition. By gathering ideas, details, explanations, and insights to form hypothetical solutions, the researcher can clarify problems and make further decisions in the market research process. At the end of this stage, the researcher should have a sufficiently precise definition of the issue to set objectives and a budget.

For example, a marketing manager of the Blue Jays notices that game attendance is decreasing and asks "Why?" The manager may think of a number of possible reasons:

- Are fans finding new and more exciting sports or entertainment venues?
- Are attendance prices too high?
- Is access to the stadium problematic?

Then, the manager should ask follow-up questions:

- How much is already known?
- Is additional information necessary?
- What is to be measured?
- How (e.g., ticket price, accessibility, competition—all of them)?
- What data is available (e.g., can we access attendance data from competitors? Do we have our own internal databases and, if so, can we access/use the data?)?
- Should research be conducted (i.e., is it worthwhile)?

In answering these and other, similar questions, if the manager establishes the need for research and defined the problem, the next step will be establishing the research objective and budget.

Step 2: Set Objectives and Budget

At this stage, a market researcher must formulate specific objectives for the research project based on the issue definition. These objectives must state the type of information required and several potential hypotheses to help answer the issue—the researcher must make educated guesses as to methods and direction that could acquire the necessary information. The objectives must limit the scope of the research project to control its size and costs. For example, if a midget boys soccer team in Red Deer, Alberta, needs to find sponsors for its annual tournament in Vancouver, an extensive and costly market research program to identify and describe all potential sources is beyond the team's resources.

Once the limits of the project have been defined, the market researcher can calculate the probable costs to proceed with the research. The cost for the marketing research process should not exceed any expected benefits that the information could deliver. For example, it is not cost-effective to spend $10,000 on a research project that could not result in increased revenues of at least the same amount. Therefore, the market researcher must find a new balance between the type of research (and its costs) and the relative importance of the data, or else cancel the research project.

Step 3: Determine the Research Design

The next step in the marketing research process is to determine the appropriate research design type(s). The research design could also be called the master research plan because it directs data collection and analysis. In designing your research, you should have a clear understanding of the following four components of a research plan. Figure 3.1 summarizes the process involved in designing a research plan.

As noted in Figure 3.1, there are four major steps in the market research process, each with a selection of methods that the researcher can use. The questions that each phase seeks to answer are listed here.

- *Research purpose.* What are you planning to accomplish (explore, describe or explain)?
- *Research approach.* What would answer your questions, numbers or words?
- *Research strategy.* What is the best way of obtaining data to answer your research questions?
- *Data-collection method.* What data-collection method best answers your research questions?

Additional questions to be asked at the onset of implementing this process that will help the researcher decide which methods and approaches to use for each phase include the following:

- What is the best way to collect this data?
- Will I need to collect primary or secondary data?
- What methods, for example, interviews, questionnaire surveys, and so on, will be best to collect the primary data?
- Who should participate in the research?
- How will I gain access to them?
- What are the exact procedures that I should adopt in my data collection to ensure reliability and validity?
- Are there any ethical issues associated with the research?

Research Purpose or Type

The three common research types or purposes are exploratory, descriptive, and explanatory. The choice of one (or more) of these types for any study is based on the clarity of the problem. Exploratory research is used initially

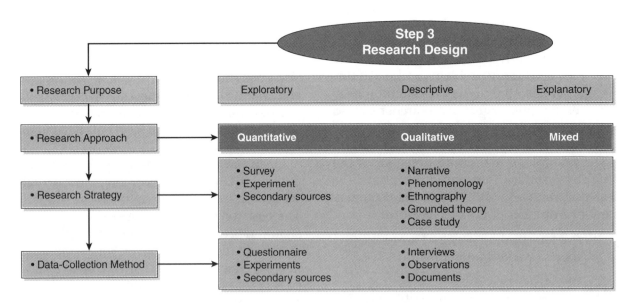

FIGURE 3.1 The process steps of research design.

to determine the real problem or issue (e.g., how do sport managers see the value of social media in sport marketing?). Its purpose is to gain an understanding of an area that has not been studied and in which a researcher wants to develop initial ideas and more focused research questions. Descriptive research is used to determine the answer to a specific problem (e.g., what are the values of social media in sport marketing?). The purpose is to "paint a picture" with words and numbers that presents a profile, outlines stages, or classifies types. *Explanatory* or *causal research* is used to determine causes and effects of relationships between known variables (e.g., why do managers see social media as a valuable marketing tool?).

Research Approach

In discussing the different types of research purpose, it will be important to differentiate qualitative and quantitative research approaches. The difference between the two would be, for example, a fan of Montreal Canadiens rating a game experience on a scale of 1 to 10 (quantitative) versus describing the experience in a one-page written report (qualitative). Quantitative research is a systematic investigation of marketing problems and opportunities via statistical, mathematical, or numerical data. Quantitative data is any data that is in numerical form, such as statistics, percentages, and so forth. Measurement is central to quantitative research, whereas qualitative research is concerned primarily with words and images rather than numbers.

Data Collection

The researcher then chooses a technique for gathering the required data. The choice will be influenced by the technique's limitations and effectiveness, as well as budget and time constraints. The researcher's experience is an asset in determining the proper technique: A seasoned researcher will have been exposed to a variety of research questions, methodologies, and protocols. Figure 3.2 presents some of the research techniques available in a qualitative study, and the text that follows provides additional explanation about some of those techniques.

Observation Observation typically requires no interaction between the researcher and the subject. Yet, the qualitative or quantitative data can easily be acquired by the observer (Babin & Zikmund, 2015). This method is widely used when subjects, such as children or animals, are not capable of expressing their opinion because it allows the observer to note their behaviour. A sport marketing research example of observation would be a researcher sitting in the stands of the Sudbury Arena to record and assess the behaviours of the spectators attending a Canadian Hockey League game involving

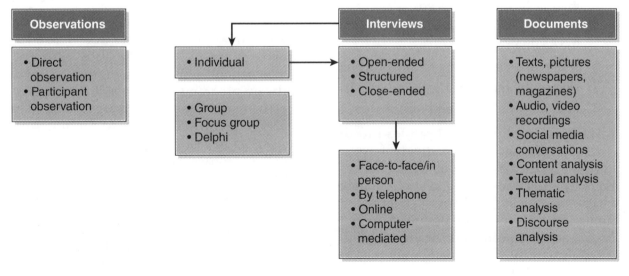

FIGURE 3.2 Qualitative research techniques.

the Sudbury Wolves. In such a situation, the researcher would observe and anonymously record behaviours undertaken by the people in the venue.

Interview and Expert Interview Interviews can be an expensive method for collecting data since they are labour intensive: the larger the sample size, the larger the number of interviewers required. Training and experience are critical factors in selecting interviewers. The interviews are done primarily in person or by telephone to allow the interviewer to elaborate when a respondent encounters some difficulty. By allowing the interviewer to probe for further clarification, this interactive technique enables new ideas to arise from the replies. Technique limitations include interviewer prejudice and time and budget constraints.

Focus Group The focus group is a research method that involves a small-group, facilitated, informal discussion "focused" on a particular topic or set of issues. Abeza and colleagues (2019) discussed the practical details of planning, designing, and conducting focus groups:

1. Select and recruit homogenous participants.
2. Determine the length of focus group discussion (typically 1 to 2 hours).
3. Establish the number of focus groups (normally three to five per project).
4. Define group size (a range of 4 to fewer than 12 is often suggested).
5. Articulate the discussion questions for the facilitator.
6. Settle on a relaxed and friendly setting.
7. Decree the moderator's (guiding) role.
8. Plan for note taking and recording.

The focus group method can lead to the generation of new ideas, as individuals reflect and build on each other's comments. This technique typically leads to a stimulating dialogue, which can result in a wide array of information. Limitations of focus group usefulness include the size and composition of the group and the experience of the facilitator. Simply put, the effectiveness of the focus group can be undermined if the discussion wanders off topic or if any of the participants fails to contribute—both of which are possible if the group is not cohesive or the facilitator is unable to manage it.

Questionnaire The questionnaire is considered one of the most economical methods of collecting data (Wong et al., 2005, p. 230). Researchers prepare a list of questions, which can be delivered to any size sample by hand, mail, fax, or Internet. It permits a certain flexibility because its confidential and anonymous nature allows for specific questions on opinions, satisfaction, and demographics. The final design of the questionnaire must take into consideration these limitations:

- Does the respondent fully understand the questions?
- Should it be kept simple?
- Should it ask the respondent to elaborate?
- Is the respondent motivated to return the questionnaire?

The greatest challenge with questionnaires is achieving a good response rate.

Experiment One of the best methods for carrying out explanatory research, the experiment allows the researcher to vary one factor while controlling all others to prove cause and effect (Aaker, Kumar, & Day, 2008). As this method can be costly and complex, it must be subject to stringent guidelines. It is important that any experiment be designed and executed by experienced researchers.

Data-Mining and Analytics Software Programs In today's technologically advanced world, a number of data mining and analytics software programs are available to researchers. These software programs are user-friendly tools that allow researchers to capture, sort, and analyze a vast volume of data. There are a number of software programs that can be used for data gathering (e.g., NCapture, DiscoverText, sitesucker, Netlytic), for social network analysis (e.g., Radian6 software, Socilyzer, NodeXL, R), or as content analytical tools (e.g., Leximancer, NCapture). Table 3.2 presents some of the data-mining and analytics software programs along with a brief description.

TABLE 3.2 Social Media Data-Collection and Analytics Tools and Software Programs

Social media collection and analytics tools	Purpose
NCapture	Helps to quickly and easily capture content such as web pages, online PDFs, and social media for analysis in NVivo 10
DiscoverText	Collects, cleans, and analyzes text and social data streams
DataSift	Collects live data as well as a comprehensive cache of past contributions from a variety of social media sites
NodeXL	Collects data from a variety of sites about organizations that are connected to your accounts
33Across	Helps analyze how audiences interact with the brand's social media interactions and helps to get insight into how people view, consume, and share content across devices.
Brandwatch	Monitors conversations across various social networks; helps conduct sentiment analysis
Google Analytics	Can be used to determine the conversion value of visitors from social sites as well as see how visitors from different social sites behave on an organizations' site
Moz Analytics	Helps visualize data; collects data, and offers insights into how one measures up to the competition
Salesforce Analytics	Helps to gather and analyze social media chatter
Social Mention	Aggregates user-generated content from across social media sites

Sampling

After deciding on the appropriate data-collection method, the researcher determines the sample. Since it is not cost-effective to obtain the data from every individual in a target population, we choose to obtain the data from a subset. Sampling enables a researcher to obtain information about a large group by examining a smaller selection (sample) of the group members. If the sampling is conducted correctly, the results will be representative of the whole group (Creswell & Creswell, 2017). There are two methods to choose a sample: probability sampling and nonprobability sampling.

- *Probability sampling* includes simple random sampling, stratified random sampling, and cluster sampling. Every member of the population has the same chance of being chosen for the sample. This method typically gives the most accurate representation of the actual population but may not be possible in all circumstances (Babin & Zikmund, 2015).
- *Nonprobability sampling* includes convenience sampling, judgment sampling, quota sampling, and snowball sampling. The sample is chosen for a particular criterion determined by the researcher. Although this method carries a higher risk of error, it is acceptable for certain research projects (Babin & Zikmund, 2015).

A researcher can usually judge the most appropriate method for sampling based on recommendations, experience, required degree of accuracy, budget, and time constraints. The final sample size will be determined by common statistical concepts or the researcher's experience and budget constraints.

It is worth mentioning that sampling applies to quantitative research. However, it is also important to mention that in qualitative research, for example for interviews, you will not interview everybody in your target population. Therefore, qualitative researchers use a concept known as **data saturation**. Data saturation occurs when a researcher tends to find no new information or starts to get the same information repeatedly from any additional interviewee (Faulkner & Trotter, 2017). The redundancy signals to researchers that further data collection will not be needed and the researcher can be reasonably assured that additional data would yield similar results and serve to confirm emerging themes and conclusions.

Step 4: Collect Data

Following the design plan, researchers initiate the chosen data-collection method while trying to minimize errors by maintaining consistency and accuracy. They ensure that the data gatherers are properly trained in the methodology. Researchers need to address the following questions at this stage of a research design:

- Who will gather the data?
- How long will data gathering take?
- How much supervision is needed?
- What operational procedures need to be followed?

Researchers will also need to do a test run to identify potential problems in the technique. Fatigue and even boredom of both researchers and participants must be addressed when designing the plan to minimize their effects in the data-collection process.

Step 5: Organize and Analyze Data

Once the data has been collected, the researcher must organize it into a usable format. Responses or observations can be tabulated by computer programs that can rapidly calculate percentage, frequency distributions, mean, median, mode, range, variance, and standard deviation. The needs of the research study determine the selection of metrics and methods and how the data will be displayed. There are a number of ways to display data:

- Bar graphs
- Contingency tables
- Displays box plot
- Histograms
- Line charts
- Ogives
- Pie charts
- Scatter diagrams
- Stem and leaf
- Tables

Similar to the other stages of a research design, researchers at this stage need to address several questions:

- Will standardized editing and coding procedures be used?
- How will the data be categorized?
- What statistical software will be used?
- What is the nature of the data?
- What questions need to be answered?
- How many variables are to be investigated simultaneously?

Further analysis of the data depends on the type of information that was collected and the potential requirements of the methodology. Numerous tools for statistical analysis are available to marketers, including frequency distributions, probabilities, proportions, measures of central tendency (mean, median, mode), measures of dispersion (range, variance, standard deviation), normal distribution, sampling distribution, central limit theorem, hypothesis testing, structural equation modelling, regression analysis, and chi-square tests for goodness of fit. Any market research textbook will contain information on these techniques and others. Students of marketing are encouraged to study market research.

Step 6: Prepare and Present Market Research Findings

At this stage, the researcher prepares a report on the market-research project and summarizes the conclusions. It is often left to the professional market researcher to explain the results to their clients or management. If the research was properly designed and executed, the data should answer the marketer's questions. The research findings may prove or disprove hypotheses, locate new segments, identify customer needs, or answer any number of other questions.

RESEARCH METHOD EXAMPLE

Netnography

Background

People wear many different hats. In addition to a sport marketer, you might also blossom to become a civic volunteer, an astute fan, or an expert cook. Becoming any of these things often requires that you be schooled by veterans in the trade. An effective way to do this is to become a member of a community organized around your chosen activity, like a fan club or recipe swap group. These clubs and groups used to meet personally, perhaps in a community centre or even casually on the street. The Internet has allowed many of these communities to become virtual entities, congregating in online forums, sometimes in lieu of physical meetings. These virtual communities have implications not only for community members, but also for organizations that market products to them. This research example outlines how netnography—a qualitative observation research method using the Internet—helps marketers learn about these communities and their cultures in a boundless and timeless online environment. Netnography is an ethnographic approach applied to the study of social interaction in online environments (Kozinets, 2006). In practice, understanding how to research online communities will help you make better decisions about your products, brand, and organization.

The Importance of Culture

Culture is not a difficult concept to understand, although it may be a relatively difficult term to define. Basically, culture describes the particulars of a distinct population. These particulars might include shared beliefs, meanings, customs, norms, patterns, or other nuances that both shape and are shaped by people's behaviours and attitudes. For example, Canadians understand that when people say "Canada's game," they are referring to hockey; and as do other countries with other sports, we exuberantly celebrate on the streets after significant major league feats (e.g., Canadian team wins the Stanley Cup). It is also common for people to wear hockey jerseys (known in general cultural jargon as cultural artifacts) while consuming games. Underlying these practices and meanings is a shared belief that the game of ice hockey is important in Canada, certainly over and above other sports, and possibly many other entertainment options as well. Collectively, these points could serve as a preliminary description of Canada's "ice hockey culture."

Members of Canada's ice hockey culture do another thing: They congregate online on social media. In this virtual arena there are many strata of fandom, from Toronto Maple Leafs fans to collectors of legendary hockey cards. These groups, or subcultures, enforce certain standards of attitudes, online conduct, or consumption decisions for their members. In a netnography of European football (soccer) fans, for example, Richardson (2011) found that one of the truest signs of a "real" fan, from the perspective of the subculture, was the choice to attend away games. Since only the real fans attended these games, this was a way one could "climb the ladder" in the subculture. Subcultural standards were also developed on which teams should be ostracized and how to do it. For example, in European football, the City Cork FC fans often referred to the Shamrock Rovers as the scum. Through this example, we see that peering into this window of subculture can help marketers gain insights into the tastes and desires of specific segments, especially where intense consumption is concerned. But before we can arrive at findings of our own, we have to learn how to carry out a netnography.

The Methodology

Netnography (Kozinets, 2006) emerged as an adaptation of some premises of the ethnographic method that was originally designed to investigate offline culture (Abeza et al., 2017). While traditional ethnography is concerned with observing people (Abeza, et al., 2017), netnography

> continued

Netnography > *continued*

studies "conversational acts," including "the act, type and content of the posting, the medium, and so on" (Kozinets, 2002, p. 7). Accordingly, the unit of analysis is the exchanged information online rather than the person. As Kozinets (1998) underscored, "a good netnography is built on the same foundation as a good ethnography, such as persistent observation, gaining rapport and trust, and researcher introspection" (p. 7).

Kozinets (2006) identified three types of netnography in terms of the extent of research participation in an online community, which vary from a distanced participation to one that is highly involved. The levels of participation are observational (no participation and unobtrusive), participant-observational, and autonetnographic (active participation).

Similar to their physical counterparts, ethnographers, netnographers become "flies on the wall," watching their subjects as they go about their routine interactions in online forums. In doing this, the researcher also becomes part of the virtual subculture, sometimes participating in the peripheral activities associated with being a bona fide member. From a research design perspective, this makes netnography contextualized, fast, simple, and unobtrusive, a combination that is absent in many other options.

Kozinets (2002) outlines four key aspects of a netnography:

1. Cultural entrée
2. Data collection and analysis
3. Research ethics
4. Member checks

Cultural Entrée

All good researchers need questions to investigate. As a sport-market researcher, you will find your questions undoubtedly shaped by the sport organization carrying out the research initiative. They might be to find out what functionalities or benefits are sought after in the next product line, what fans thought about your last acquisition, or what the current perception of your brand is compared to those of your regional competitors. In any case, solidifying your objectives through a list of questions of interest is a basic step in carrying out a netnography.

Once you have decided on the questions, the next step is to find online forums (e.g., different social media platforms) that can help you to answer them. No matter what their form or structure, as long as consumers can interact online (e.g., blogs), there is opportunity for netnography to take place. In selecting appropriate sources of data, Kozinets (2002) recommends that researchers consider four variables:

1. *Relevance to the research questions:* "Is the data in this forum going to help me answer my questions?"
2. *Traffic and homogeneity of posters:* "How many different people actually visit or post on the forum?"
3. *Detail and richness of data:* "How descriptive are the data on the forum? Do people just post questions and have them answered, or do posters often talk about feelings, try to influence others, or share in symbolic exchanges with other members?"
4. *Amount of social interaction:* "How many posts are there?"

Data Collection and Analysis

There are three potential sources of data in netnography.

1. First is mining content (i.e., text, audio files, video, and photo) from the online forum. Because of the overwhelming amount of content from this source, you may have to filter out irrelevant items, chunk together similar posts, or add notes and comments to sentences just to keep it organized.

2. The second source of data is your written "field notes," which may include shared meanings (recall "Canada's game" equals hockey), names or pseudonyms of key members, and things that would otherwise go undocumented such as details from your physical participation in events. The depth and amount of note taking would depend on your involvement in the community. In fact, a healthy netnography can be conducted without any field notes at all.

3. As the third source of data, online forum members can be interviewed via email, instant messaging, or private messaging.

Data analysis techniques used in netnography include symbolic, interpretive, and metaphoric methods. In much of the literature, netnographies are grouped thematically, profiling the subculture through select quotations and descriptions of cultural characteristics. Content analysis, in which posts are classified into groups based on factors the researcher wishes to study (e.g., counting posts including product feedback), is certainly welcome in a netnography study but should be used to supplement other types of culturally penetrating methods and not be generalized beyond the online culture of which the subjects are a part. Ultimately, Kozinets (2002) suggests, the choice of method(s) depends on both the researcher s strengths and the questions the researcher wants to answer.

Research Ethics

Kozinets (2002) raises two concerns in the use of netnography—the public or private nature of the online forums and the nature of consent from online forum members. Researchers should pay close attention to the individuals whose lives they prod and should err on the side of conservatism. It is our view that consent from members is *essential* when using direct quotations, regardless of whether the online forum is private or public. Pseudonyms and actual names of the members should be disguised in the final report. If there is a clear "owner" of the online forum, specific permission should also be solicited to conduct the study.

Member Checks

In this final stage, a researcher presents select online forum members with a copy of some or all of the report's findings. While this is useful for gaining additional insights into their culture, it can also work as an ethical control to give members a say in how they are presented to the outside world. As with interviewing procedures, member checks can be conducted via electronic means.

Summary: Relevance of Netnography to Sport Marketers

It is helpful to understand what research questions a new methodology can answer and hence why it should be used at all. Netnography offers sport-market researchers a way to gauge reactions to elements of the marketing mix. Consider, for example, some hypothetical utterances by forum members (e.g., Twitter followers' replies):

- *Product:* "Trust me, our team is going to trade for a marquee player, it is in their best interests!" "How come my soccer ball doesn't stay inflated as long as the other ones on the market?"

- *Place:* "Where do I get tickets to the game and how come they're not even posted on the team website?" "Does anybody know where I can get these golf clubs? I live in a really small town and can't find them anywhere."

- *Price:* "If you were a true hardcore fan, you wouldn't care about the price! Show some loyalty!" "I don't know, but I don't think you should really invest a ton of cash in those pads just because that brand makes skates. Why don't you shop around a bit more?"

- *Promotion:* "Lol did you see that commercial they just aired? I could have taken better shots with my cell phone." "The stick looks like a pretty good buy, but I doubt that player who sponsors it even uses it on the ice."

> *continued*

> Netnography > *continued*

More generally, examining macro-issues relating to culture can show sport market researchers how patterns of consumption work. You may, for example, be able to discover the following:

- Unknown purchases and attitudes shaped by the subculture that precede purchases of your product
- What types of purchases characterize the avid or astute subculture member versus the newbie
- How subculture members can change each other's attitudes about your brand, organization, or products

Although your first few netnographies will likely be constrained by a deadline, they can (and should) extend as long as new insights are being found. It is not often that market researchers can find primary data literally at their fingertips.

CHAPTER SUMMARY

Market research provides information that helps sport marketers make appropriate decisions about the type of product, price, place, and appropriate ways to communicate (promote) to consumers. The marketer may design research programs (exploratory research, descriptive research, explanatory research) to collect primary data or look for information from available sources (secondary research) such as Statistics Canada or internal data such as ticket sales report. The decision to use primary or secondary research or both depends on the kinds of information needed and available budget and time. Marketers go through six steps in conducting research—defining the marketing issue; setting objectives and budget; designing a research; collecting data; organizing and analyzing data; and preparing and presenting market research findings. Data-collection methods include questionnaires (quantitative) and focus groups and interviews (qualitative). With the increased importance of the Internet in consumers' lives, a number of data-mining and analytics software programs are becoming available to researchers.

TEST YOUR KNOWLEDGE

1. Name and describe the three different types of research purpose.
2. Describe the differences between primary and secondary research.
3. List the steps involved in the marketing research process.
4. Name and describe five different marketing-research techniques.
5. Name three statistical techniques used in market research.

KEY TERMS

census	explanatory research	primary research
data saturation	exploratory research	sampling
descriptive research	Iceberg Principle	secondary research

CASE STUDIES

Visit HK*Propel* for case studies organized by chapter.

CHAPTER 4

The Canadian Sport Consumer

LEARNING OBJECTIVES

After studying this chapter, you will be able to do the following:

- Understand the different forms of sport consumption
- Understand the different classifications of sport consumer in Canada
- Identify the factors that influence game attendance and fandom
- Identify the reasons that may contribute to declining stadium attendance
- Identify the factors that influence sport participation
- Describe the two popular types of mediated sport participation

Suppose that you got an internship this coming summer for two months at an organization that raises funds for cancer research. You have been told that your responsibility is to organize a 5K run in your town that helps raise funds for research. What type of factors would you examine to understand your potential consumers, and why? Who should be your potential consumers (e.g., the runners, sponsors, media), and why? What needs and desires do you think your event fulfills? What factors do you consider to break down the population composition so that you can focus on selected target markets? Your success depends on how

accurately you would answer these questions. Please attempt to answer these questions before reading this chapter. Write down your answers, and when you finish going through the chapter, come back and try to answer these same questions and compare your answers.

This chapter addresses questions such as what is sport **consumption**? Who are sport consumers? What is the consumption of sport as a **spectator** and as a **participant**? What motivates the consumption of sport both as participant and as spectator? How different are the spectator and participant consumer markets? Given that consumption in sport is a complex and multidimensional topic, this chapter discusses the consumption of sport by looking at the two major types of consumption: consumption of sport as a participant and consumption of sport as a spectator. The examination of sport consumption as spectators is core to this chapter, including recognizing the difference between sport consumers and **sport fans**, the classification of sport consumers, and the different factors that influence stadium attendance. Sport consumption as participants is also a key element of the chapter, in exploring participation in physical sport and the factors that motivates participants to take part directly in sport.

Understanding Sport Consumption

In the mainstream marketing literature, the act of purchasing and using a product or service is referred to as consumption and the people who purchase the goods and services are referred to as consumers. In the sport literature, the terms *consumption* and *consumer* have a similar interpretation to that of the mainstream marketing but also involve some distinctive features. For example, sport consumers are commonly referred to as spectators or sport fans. However, there is a subtle difference between spectators and fans, and not all consumers are sport fans.

Also, not all fans are the same. These distinct features will be discussed in this chapter. Similarly, as opposed to the interpretation of *consumption* in the mainstream business such as banks, airlines, or grocery stores, conception of the term *consumption* in sport has its own unique features, which is the other topic that will be discussed in this chapter.

With the understanding that the product (and service) that is offered to sport consumers being the performance segment (e.g., game, working out) of the sport industry (the other two being the production segment, such as Nike's products, and the promotion segment, such as Canadian Tire sponsorship), the consumers of sport can be classified into two groups: as spectators and as participants (Abeza, O'Reilly, & Séguin, 2019). The different sport consumption types that fall under these two major types of sport consumption—consumers as spectators and consumers as participants—are discussed next. As shown in figure 4.1, sport consumption as a spectator involves stadium attendance, media viewership, and the purchase of licensed merchandise. Similarly, sport consumption as a participant involves consumption of sport by physically participating in physical activity or participating in mediated games such as **esports** and **fantasy sport**.

It is important to note that, at the level of the Canadian sport consumer, for the vast major-

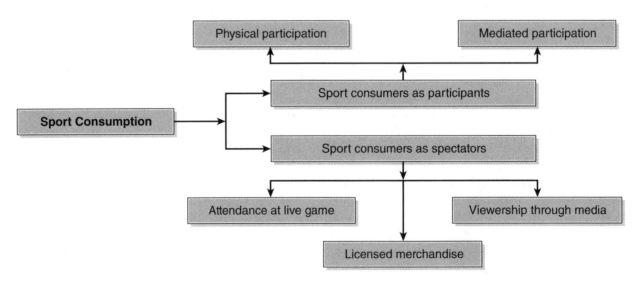

FIGURE 4.1 Sport consumption types.

Adapted by permission from G. Abeza and B. Séguin, "International Sport Marketing," in *International Sport Management*, 2nd ed., edited by E. MacIntosh, G. Bravo, and M. Li (Champaign, IL: Human Kinetics, 2019), 308.

ity, spectating and participating are mutually exclusive. Think, for instance, of the National Football League (NFL), the most popular (by far) spectator sport in North America. Of the millions who watch or stream games each weekend of the NFL season, only a few ever played competitive tackle football (certainly less than 1 percent). Similarly, if you went to the start line of the 2019 Montreal Marathon and surveyed the 18,000 runners who ran the race that year, our bet is that only a very few could name the 2016 Olympic or Paralympic marathon champion, either male or female. Thus, in marketing to consumers, these need to be two different strategies for sport marketers.

Although at the consumer level, spectatorship and participation are completely different decisions, from a sport property perspective, they are often not mutually exclusive, as a sport property may have both participants and spectators. For example, in running sports such as the Toronto Waterfront Marathon, while so many people take part in the event to consume the sport as participants, the event is also broadcasted live on CBC every year and people watch it on TV, a large number of people come to the marathon course to watch the race and cheer for the runners, and people buy the marathon's licensed merchandise. Hence, all types of sports may fall under both types of sport consumption, although in a given sport the consumers can be heavily participants (e.g., running sports) or heavily spectators (e.g., car racing). Accordingly, a sport marketer will be required to understand the predominant form of consumption in the consumer market of interest.

While people consume sport to stay active and healthy (as participants) or to be entertained (as a spectators), the consumption of any form of sport costs money and the cost is rising over time. For example, ticket prices for games, sport channels subscription fees, merchandise costs, race entry fees, gym membership fees, and other costs of sport consumption are rising. Hence, with the ever-changing customer expectations in competitive markets, a clear understanding of the different forms of sport consumption is essential for the success of any sport marketing effort. Moreover, the consumption of sport needs to be looked at from a broader perspective. Differentiating the two major types of sport consumption—as spectator and as participant—helps marketers design a customized marketing strategy relevant to the sport in focus. For example, for the sport of running, the number of people who take part in the sport (the participants) is far greater than the number of people who watch the running sport via media or at a racecourse (spectators). On the other hand, the number of people who watch the sport of car racing via media or at racetracks (spectators) is far greater than the number of people who take part in the sport (participating as drivers). Hence, understanding the consumer type of the consumers of the sport that you work in helps you better identify the motives for their consumption and thereby the framing of your offering in the way that fulfills their needs and desires. Equally, the socioeconomic status and the media consumption habits of those who consume, for example, the sport of running (largely active participants) are different from those who consume car racing (largely spectators). Hence, understanding the different types of consumption and the consumers' type is essential for successful execution of any sport marketing strategy. These include understanding consumers in terms of variables including the demographic, geographic, social-economic, behavioural, and psychographic, which are briefly discussed next.

Bases for Segmenting Consumer Market

Sport consumers are not alike, and different factors affect people's consumption of sport. These factors include the demographic, geographic, social-economic, behavioural, and psychographic. Consumer data on these different factors helps group consumers based on common needs, break a large market into smaller manageable groups, and understand the unique preferences of an identified group. While each of these factors is discussed in detail in chapter 5, it will be relevant to briefly describe each in relation to understanding sport consumers.

Demography

Demographic variables refers to age (e.g., who is more likely to take part in the extreme sport such as Ice Diving in Banff and whom you should market it to?), gender (e.g., who is more likely to watch Bare Knuckle Fighting or Pillow Fight League?), ethnic background (e.g., Toronto is a city known for its diversity and strong ethnic ties, and its soccer team, Toronto FC, has a number of supporters of different ethnic backgrounds). It is worth noting here that marketers need to avoid any assumption and stereotyping and must base their use of demographic data only on empirical evidence. Please note that demographic variables are simple but delicate variables that need careful handling. Otherwise, they have a potential to mislead marketing decisions. Particularly, demographic variables are related to attitudes and behaviours such as game attendance, merchandise purchasing, and TV subscription and watching. Therefore, arming oneself with evidence-based demographic data can facilitate the achievement of an efficient and effective marketing strategy.

Geography

Geographic data refers to where your consumers live, such as in the town or city, in the region, in the province, or in different parts of the country. While location data is straightforward and easy to understand, it can also be complex. For example, most of Vancouver Canucks fans might be those consumers who live in and around British Colombia, but the Toronto Maple Leafs may have fans all over the country due to the team's history. Therefore, if a marketing manager of the Leafs wants to air a radio commercial, it will be difficult to pinpoint one radio station that can reach all the fans, whereas it is a relatively easy decision to make for Canucks marketing managers.

Socioeconomic

Socioeconomic refers to consumers' level of income, educational background, and occupation. Data on these variables serves as a good indicator of consumers' behaviour. For example, the socioeconomic status of people who are drawn to the sport of polo or the Calgary Stampede are different from those drawn to the sport of figure skating or diving. Equally, hockey is one of the most expensive sports to play in Canada, whereas swimming is the most popular and affordable activity. Affordability, for example, can affect children's participation in a given sport. If parents find a given sport expensive, they tend to involve their children in a more affordable one.

Psychography

Psychographic variables are measures of consumers' beliefs, values, attitudes, interests, lifestyles, and other similar factors. In fact, psychographic data are difficult to get. One way to understand demographic variables would be to see your own spending pattern. For example, you can check your credit card statement and see if your bank may provide your spending data. Some banks show the summary of areas on which consumers spent their money, such as food, merchandise, flights, and so forth. Those types of spending summary show a customer's area of interest and lifestyle. Simply put, psychographic data helps you understand why your consumers are doing what they do.

Sport Consumption as Spectators

The consumption of sport as a spectator is the common form of sport consumption in sports such as hockey, soccer, basketball, tennis, and so forth. People consume sporting games either by going to a stadium to watch games live (attendance) or by watching live games through media (viewership) such as TV, streaming services, radio, or social media updates. For example, people may go to Scotiabank Arena to watch the Toronto Raptors playing one of the teams in the NBA Eastern Conference in the regular seasons or watch a Toronto Raptors game live on TV surrounded by family and friends at home or with friends and fans on big screen at Jurassic Forest in Alberta or at a bar. In either form of spectatorship (attendance or viewership), people also consume sport by purchasing merchandise

EXECUTIVE PERSPECTIVE
Women and Girls in Sport in Canada

REBECCA SHANKS, Vice-President, The T1 Agency

With more than 20 years of working in sport marketing in Canada under my belt, I am very fortunate to have had the opportunity to work in a variety of different roles, all of which I continue to draw learning from and apply on a daily basis as a vice-president at a leading Canadian agency.

Specific to women and girls in sport, I am a strong believer in placing a deep focus on how sponsorship can help create more equity for women in sport. It is well known that women's sport is underfunded in Canada. This has been in the headlines more often than I like to see, but the upside is that it is now recognized as fact. There are also more challenges than just funding, such as equity issues ranging from prizing to broadcast coverage to the treatment of women athletes relatively to their male counterparts. Of course, these equity challenges are not unique to sport, but sponsorship is one important way that we can help balance the sport landscape. Some of the ways sponsorship can help include the following:

- Building brands (i.e., helping Canadian brands reach female consumers in an authentic way)
- Developing properties (i.e., bringing resources to female sport properties to help them grow and expand—Saputo sponsoring Fitspirit)
- Driving awareness of women's sport (i.e., using multiple media platforms to drive awareness of different women's sports)
- Funding events (i.e., funding events focused on women's sport such as CP Rail and LPGA)
- Funding broadcasts (i.e., brands can fund additional broadcast production for increased reach of women's sport)
- Highlighting existing role models (e.g., featuring female athletes as spokespeople and influencers such as Adidas and Billie Jean King or Coca-Cola and Christine Sinclair)
- Research (e.g., funding new research to provide data to back up the need for support—Canadian Tire Jump Start and Canadian Women and Sport Rally Report)
- Content development (e.g., long-form storytelling content featuring unique athlete stories that provide inspiration to the next generation such as Dairy Farmers of Canada and TSN athlete stories)
- Content promotion (e.g., providing media dollars to promote inspirational content on multiple media platforms)

All this being said, brands will need to go in with a different approach and consider the right metrics to measure success. If you measure women's sports the same way as men's in the current landscape, there will be differences. It is not a fair comparison. We need to look at things differently such as the fact that women's sport can be more accessible and produce great content. We need to set benchmarks and measures specific to women's sport and not relative to men's sport.

In my decade at Coke, one of the biggest brands in the world, I was able to learn not only about the power of taking on different roles and positions within the organization in order to better understand Coke's complex system from sales to marketing to operations. I also learned how to sell internally and how to manage multiple stakeholders. It is not easy

> *continued*

Women and Girls in Sport in Canada > *continued*

to get decisions made when there are multiple stakeholders and learning how to involve them in the process in order to drive faster decisions that they were comfortable with, is a skill that I have taken to other clients I have worked with since on the agency side. Working in multiple different departments and roles at Coca-Cola also taught me how to better understand the motivations of different groups, from sales to marketing to operations. In a sponsorship management role at Coca-Cola, I learned the importance of negotiating for mutual value. Importantly, I learned not to wait for a proposal from a property looking for sponsorship, but to go back to them with the marketing value that the brand can provide and develop programs collaboratively that were valuable to both parties. This drove better engagement for the brand, property, and consumers. I would encourage you to do the same in your careers.

Finally, as a student of sport marketing, I would recommend that you get to know the industry and the people in the industry, both within Canada and globally. Attend events, go to conferences, watch webinars, read the trade publications, join industry communities, and network. Immersing yourself in this incredible industry will help spark new ideas on how we can all drive change so consumers, brands, properties and even the next generation of athletes can benefit.

REBECCA SHANKS is vice-president at The T1 Agency, where she leads internal teams and client programs in sponsorship strategy, integrated marketing, and various consulting initiatives, as well as sitting on the agency leadership team. Rebecca also volunteers with the Sponsorship Marketing Council of Canada. Formerly, at Coca-Cola Canada, she held roles in sponsorships and marketing capability, brand and customer marketing, integrated marketing, and commercial strategy. In her role on the board of Canadian Woman in Sport, she is the chair of the Nominations Committee and on the Marketing, Revenue Generation and Strategy committees, as well as a speaker on Women and Sport. Canadian Women in Sport seeks to harness the power of sport so that girls and women everywhere can benefit, and to build a stronger, more equitable sport system for all Canadians.

---

licensed by players, teams, or leagues. For example, a spectator may purchase and use the "We The North" tee-shirts, hats, scarves, water bottles, key holders, or Fred VanVleet's jersey.

Understanding Sport Consumption as Spectators and Fans

As spectators, consumers experience sport in different ways (e.g., regular versus occasional game attendance, following games on media, merchandise purchase), and they usually identify themselves with a sport or sport object to meet a diverse range of personal needs. However, as some may too easily assume, sport fans are not identical and cannot be viewed as a singular crowd (Abeza, O'Reilly, & Séguin, 2019). The perception that all sport fans are

loyal customers of a sport team is unrealistic, and sport fans vary in their commitment and allegiance to a team (Foster et al., 2020). In this regard, early research works discussed the difference between an ordinary spectator and a fan. According to Wann (1995), an ordinary spectator is an individual who is observing a sporting event and a fan is someone who is enthusiastic about a particular sport. The differences in someone's interest in sport as either an ordinary sport spectator or a sport fan is also captured by Pooley (1978), who touched on the enthusiasm aspect noted by Wann (1995, p. 14): "Whereas a spectator of sport will observe a spectacle and forget it quickly, the fan continues [their] interest until the intensity of feeling toward the team becomes so great that parts of every day are devoted to either [their] team or in some instances, to the broad realm of sport itself" (p. 14).

The difference between a fan and an ordinary spectator, by implication, is the difference in the degree of devotion to a sport object (e.g., team, player, coach). A sport fan can be defined as an ardent devotee of sport (Anderson, 1979). In other words, a sport fan can be described as an enthusiastic consumer of organized sports or a consumer who is motivated to engage in behaviour related to sports and has some level of attachment to a sport object (Hunt et al., 1999). Since there are differences among and between ordinary spectators and fans (e.g., the difference from fan to fan in terms of the level of attachment to a sport object, namely, the underlying motivation for consumption of sports, and actual sports-related behaviour), several authors have attempted to construct typologies or classifications of sport fans. Simply put, if 15,000 people are gathered at Bell MTS Place in Winnipeg to watch the Winnipeg Jets playing one of the NHL teams, all the 15,000 fans do not have the same level of affinity to the team. The attendees' affinity level may range from die-hard fans to those who might have attended the game just to get out of their daily routine for the day and be entertained. Therefore, the next section discusses the different classifications of sport consumers.

Classifications of Sport Fan

Several classifications of sport fans have been proposed by a number of different studies that based their classifications on factors such as psychological, economic, social, and other, similar factors. One important early study (Stewart et al., 2003) assembled most of the studies and synthesized the various classifications. The synthesis identified three types of sport consumers' classifications, namely, **dualistic typology, tiered typology**, and **multidimensional typology**. Dualistic typology argues that sport consumers can be classified into two categories: consumers who identify themselves with a team and those who only consume sport for entertainment purposes. The dualistic classification offers some insight regarding sport consumer typologies; however, it conflates the range of behavioural differences among sport consumers.

Building on the dualistic approach, studies classified sport consumers into different tiered typologies. Tiered typologies take into account the different levels or intensities of sport consumers' attachment to a team: top tier (vested or highly committed), middle tier (expressive and focused), and bottom tier (social and camaraderie) consumers. The tiered typologies indicate that consumers approach their sport consumptions in different ways, such as emotional commitment, reading and talking about sport, social interaction, camaraderie, and so on. In the same, but much better, way as the dualistic classification, the tiered typologies offer some insight regarding the different types of sport consumers. However, the tiered typologies themselves do not provide the full picture regarding the underlying beliefs and motives that drive an individual's loyalty and attachment to sport and their sport consumption behaviour. Such argument led some researchers to propose multidimensional typologies of sport consumers.

Multidimensional typologies of sport consumers are proposed based on the different ways in which consumers display their level of devotion, which, in turn, impact game attendance, television viewing, and the purchase of team merchandise. As Abeza, O'Reilly, & Séguin (2019) noted, multidimensional typologies for sport consumers are proposed based on classification factors such as the following:

- Frequency of game attendance (frequent, moderate, and low)
- Primary point of connection a team, a player, or a sport)
- Economic interest (strong, moderate, and weak financial interest)
- Emotional commitment (strong, conditional, and fragile)
- Consumption motives (escape, eustress, social interaction)
- Level of identification—as an extension of self-identity (civic and community pride, and/or social and cultural identity)
- Loyalty display (through game attendance, displaying team colours, chatter, and conversation)

An example of a consumer typology that is based on some of these multidimensional factors was proposed by Rein and colleagues (2006), who argue that sport marketers need to move sport consumers up on the fan ladder by applying different marketing strategies and progress them, at least, to the top three higher rewarding levels of fan groups, namely, ensnared, insiders, and attachers. The different fan types identified by the authors are presented in table 4.1.

While the three major synthesized typologies (i.e., dual, tiered, and multidimensional) gave us insight into the multifaceted nature of sport consumption, it should be noted that there is no single best typology because all the classifications have both strengths and limitations. This led Stewart and colleagues (2003) to argue that sport consumption is a self-defining phenomenon.

Factors Influencing Spectator Attendance

There are a variety of factors that influence consumers' decisions to attend sporting events, and sport marketers need to understand these factors to respond to them appropriately. In this regard, Shank and Lyberger (2014) identified nine critical drivers that influence game attendance. These include game attractiveness, economic factors, competitive factors, demographic factors, stadium factors, value of sport to the community, sport involvement, fan identification, and fan motivation factors. Each of these factors are described briefly in the following list. One of the factors, fan motivation (the last factor), being the prime element that requires sport marketers' attention, is discussed in some detail.

1. Game attractiveness: One of the factors that attracts fans to attend a sporting game is the attractiveness of the game. This could be NHL Winter Classic, the Raptors playing in NBA playoffs, a super-star hockey player coming to town to play with your home hockey team, the opening ceremony of the Olympic games, the All-Star games, and so on. These and other similar games, including regular games, may have a perceived value of attractiveness to a consumer and may motivate consumers to attend live games at a venue.

2. Economic factors: Clearly, ticket prices impact game attendance. For example, the highest average ticket price in 2018-2019 for a Canadian NHL club was Toronto Maple Leafs, at around 120.00 CAD, and the lowest was the Calgary Flames, at around 60.00 CAD. While a number of variables are factored into setting a ticket price, the size and economy of a city is an important one. A larger city could mean

TABLE 4.1 Sport Spectators Fan Ladder

Fan Type	Description
Ensnared	Unconditional supporters who associate their identity with the team's identity
Insiders	Supporters who often participate in the inner circle of sport, such as people who work in the sport; for example, buying season tickets, donating to the college team, buying a team share (i.e., purchasing a share to own part of a publicly traded club)
Attachers	Supporters who wish to receive communication from teams and heroes; for example, tired of being one in the crowd, these group may form a fan club
Collectors	Supporters who are willing to pay for merchandise that reminds them of the sport; for example, to remind their family, remember a rare visit, and so on
Wallets	Consumers who spend money to experience a game—the most sought out sports fan—for example, travelling to the Olympic Games
Eyeballs	Consumers who are counted as the primary audience by watching on television or web streaming
Indifferent Fans	Consumers who care little about sports

Adapted from Rein et al., 2006.

more potential buyers and a relatively higher demand than small cities.

3. Competitive factors: Cities such as Toronto have all the five major league sport teams, namely, the NHL, NBA, MLB, MLS, and CFL. All these teams are going after the same consumer market and can be considered to be in direct competition. Equally, the availability of entertainment options in a town or city, such as movies, concerts, restaurants, amusement parks, cultural centres, art exhibitions, and so on, provide options to consumers and can compete indirectly with sporting events. These options impact consumers' attendance at games.

4. Demographic factors: Factors such as age, gender, education, occupation, ethnic background, and so on relate to game attendance. These factors affect different sports differently. For example, older people might not be interested in extreme sports such as Ice Diving in Banff National Park, Alberta. At the same time, sport marketers likely will not invest their resources promoting extreme sports to older people.

5. Stadium factors: The access and aesthetics of a venue affect consumers' attendance at games. If an arena does not have enough parking and parking is difficult, people will be discouraged from making repeat purchases. Similarly, the comfort of seats, restroom availability, and cleanliness of the stadium impact attendance. Some stadiums are far from the areas where the majority of the people in the host city live, which affects consumers' attendance. Consumers factor in driving time and time spent in traffic when they decide purchasing tickets to games.

6. Value of sport to the community: Consumers' decision to attend a sporting game can be influenced by the value of the sport to the community. For example, if a high school organizes a charity hockey game, residents of the area can be drawn to the game and encouraged to buy tickets because they appreciate the intent of the game.

7. Sport involvement: Involvement is a vital factor in influencing, not only people's attendance at sporting games but also their inclination to like a given sport. Involvement is the perceived interest in and personal importance of sports to a consumer. Those who have not grown up playing or watching a certain type of sport are less likely to be drawn to that sport at a later age. In other words, a consumer who has grown up playing hockey will likely show interest in the sport. Similarly, if someone has not played lacrosse, the chance of that consumer showing interest in lacrosse is likely to be low.

8. Fan identification: Fan identification is the personal commitment and emotional involvement a customer has to a sport entity (e.g., an athlete, team, or coach). For example, customers who identify closely with the Montreal Canadiens will begin to define themselves in terms of the team. You may hear them calling the Canadiens "my team," but you rarely hear people referring to an airline or a bank as "my airline" or "my bank." In particular, die-hard fans continue to identify themselves with a team regardless of wins or losses.

9. Fan motivation factors: As consumers of any other industry, sport consumers have needs, desires, and wants to satisfy. Those needs, desires, and wants will motivate or stimulate a consumer to act to fulfill them. In this regard, since sport marketers' ultimate job is creating demand and satisfying needs, it is vital to have a clear understanding of the factors that motivate spectators to attend a sporting game. An early seminal analysis by Wann (1995) discussed eight of the common underlying reasons why people attend a sport game:

   a. Escape: Attending games allows people to escape from their daily routine and diverts their attention from any difficult situation they may have encountered.

   b. Economic (e.g., gambling): People may attend a sporting game because they play fantasy sports or are involved in sports betting and they want to stay informed on the performance of an athlete to help them make money or win.

   c. Eustress (positive level of arousal): This refers to the ups and downs of emotion that people experience while watching games. It involves both the euphoria one feels when a team shows a chance of winning and the stress one can experience when there's a chance of a favourite team losing a game.

d. Self-esteem: Attending games and witnessing a favourite team's win gives a sense of accomplishment and that enhances a sense of self-achievement.

e. Group affiliation: Attending games allows people to feel part of a group and gives a sense of group affiliation, which can involve cheering along others for a favourite team.

f. Entertainment: The unpredictable nature of a sport competition (the drama and excitement) attracts people to attend a sporting game and witness the outcome in person.

g. Family: Sport brings people together, especially family members. Watching games as a family creates excitement, entertains, and may strengthen their bonds.

h. Aesthetics qualities (i.e., artistic): People follow some sports because they have some inherent beauty such as the game of figure skating and gymnastics.

Emerging Technological Developments in Sport Consumption by Spectators

It is also worth mentioning here that in the past few years, the consumption of sport has been influenced by a number of emerging technologies such as **virtual reality** (VR) and **augmented reality** (AR). Virtual reality (VR) is "the computer-generated simulation of a three-dimensional image or environment that can be interacted with in a seemingly real or physical way by a person using special electronic equipment, such as a helmet with a screen inside or gloves fitted with sensors" (Merriam-Webster, 2020). Augmented reality (AR) is "a technology that superimposes a computer-generated image on a user's view of the real world, thus providing a composite view" (Merriam-Webster, 2020). The main difference between the two is that while VR immerses an individual in a new reality, AR supplements an existing reality. An example of VR would be when Toronto Raptors fans who cannot go and check seats at the Scotiabank

Arena can pick their premium seats using the 3D seating app of Scotiabank Arena. The app gives consumers a vantage point from which to see the stadium themselves. An example of AR is PuttView, an AR technology for putting practice. It enables the visualization on the putting green and provides everything from feedback on all the important parameters of a putt to entertaining games. There are a number of AR and VR tools implemented by different sports over the years to enhance fans' viewing experience of live games. These and other technological advancements will be discussed in chapter 16 of this book.

Contributing Factors for Stadium Attendance Decline

Although many critical drivers play a role in encouraging people to attend sporting games, there are also a number of factors that discourage consumers' stadium attendance. Some of the possible reasons that contribute to the declining fans' stadium attendance (per Abeza et al., 2018) include lack of Internet (Wi-Fi) access in the stadiums, quality of broadcast offerings, demographic shifts, higher ticket prices, the quality of opponents, issues with the comfort of stadium seats, and increasing number of competing entertainment options. The reasons identified by the authors can be organized into four different, but interrelated, categories: television, the Internet, cost of attendance, and other competing entertainment offerings. Table 4.2 presents a summary of these factors.

In today's fast-paced, technologically driven world, the TV viewing experience is changing all the time, and many fans today, particularly the younger generation, may watch sporting games on streaming services and TV rather than attending them. This is partly because of the experience of watching games on high-quality, big-screen TVs with replays and commentators' detailed commentary. The experience becomes much more comfortable and appealing because people can watch surrounded by family and friends. Watching sporting games on TV or streaming services also demands less effort and can be much more economical than attending a live game in a

EXPERT PERSPECTIVE

Neuroscience Approaches to Understanding Sport Consumers: Insights from the Spectator Experience and Technology (SEAT) Laboratory at the University of Waterloo

LUKE R. POTWARKA, Director, Spectator Experience and Technology (SEAT) Laboratory and Associate Professor, Department of Recreation and Leisure Studies, University of Waterloo

Social and technological forces are changing the way spectators experience sport events. People are increasingly choosing to use immersive technologies (e.g., virtual reality, augmented reality, and virtual fandom) to engage with elite sport event stimuli. Understanding these sport consumer experiences is of critical importance to both researchers and sport organizations. What people think about and how they feel while immersed in a spectator experience can predict postevent consumer behaviours (e.g., sponsorship patronage, purchasing tickets to future event, purchasing apparel, social media engagement, sport participation, etc.) that are of value to event stakeholders (Potwarka et al., 2017).

To date, however, sport consumer research has almost exclusively relied on self-report measures to assess the extent to which people are psychologically engaged (i.e., flow experiences characterized by intense absorption and focused attention) or involved (i.e., the degree which watching is a central component in a person's life) with the particular sports they consume (e.g., Csikszentmihalyi, 1997; Funk & James, 2001; Madrigal, 2006). Sport researchers and organizations are beginning to question the efficacy of solely conducting traditional survey-based research to understand sport consumer experiences. Can we fully understand the complexity and nuances of sport consumer experiences simply asking people to remember and describe what they were thinking about or how they felt after consuming a sport event?

The international team of researchers working in the Spectator Experience and Technology Laboratory (SEAT) at the University of Waterloo are beginning to address this question. The SEAT lab employs various technologies as both a methodology (e.g., social neuroscience, eye-tracking, second screens, etc.) and a means of experiencing sport events (e.g., virtual reality, augmented reality, virtual fandom, mobile devices). SEAT lab researchers are examining how biological and physiological measures might play an important role in understanding sport consumer experiences and behaviours. In particular, SEAT researchers are beginning to see evidence of the promising role neuroscience methods might play in understanding the cognitive and affective nature of sport consumer experiences. Currently, the SEAT lab is mobilizing a series of studies that investigate sport consumer experiences using functional neuroimaging methods, including electroencephalography (EEG), functional near-infrared spectroscopy (fNIR), and functional magnetic resonance (fMRI). These neuroimaging methods allow SEAT researchers to observe particular brain systems, which become activated as participants consume sport stimuli in real time. Knowledge of these brain systems might predict the behaviour of sport consumers above and beyond what can be gleaned solely from asking sport consumers to describe or self-report their experiences.

These studies may shed important insights into brain networks involved in affective and cognitive aspects of sport consumer experiences. The SEAT lab hopes that knowledge of these brain networks will help us better understand the role of sport consumption in the promotion of brain health and well-being. From a practical perspective, SEAT lab research might also provide biological answers to the question of whether more allegiant and loyal fans cognitively process sport events differently than people who are less interested in and engaged with a sport.

LUKE POTWARKA is the director of the Spectator Experience and Technology (SEAT) Laboratory and an associate professor in the Department of Recreation and Leisure Studies at the University of Waterloo. His research focuses on consumer behaviour related to sport events. It addresses the overarching question: Under what conditions do sport events have positive impacts for individuals and organizations in host communities? To this end, Luke's research falls within two broad themes: (i) Examining the role of elite sport events in the promotion of physical activity and sport participation; and (ii) examining commercial and tourism-related responses to elite sport events.

TABLE 4.2 Possible Reasons for Fans' Declining Stadium Attendance

Possible Reasons	Description
Television	• Viewing experience: Watching on big-screen TV in the comfort of home with friends, in a college dorm, or at a bar. • TV times: Some argue that TV times are catered more to TV networks, at the expense of fans' convenience.
Cost	• Cost of attendance: Attending games can be expensive in terms of money and time. Fans may find watching a game on TV much cheaper, easier, and more convenient.
Internet	• Live streaming: Fans are now able to live stream games on their phones, tablets, and laptops at any time, from anywhere, and at their convenience. • Entertainment technology: Electronic entertainment options such as video games, streaming services such as Netflix, and on-demand music can be more engaging and appealing to the younger generation.
Competing entertainments offerings	• Other entertainment offerings: A few other entertainment options are available to fans that compete for the same discretionary spending, such as concerts and movies. • The rise of other sports.

stadium. For example, drinks and snacks are sold at higher prices than what one can buy to consume at home. Also, not to be confined on a seat and the ability to be mobile as many times as one wishes, including visiting a restroom, may lead people to prefer watching games on TV than attending them. In contrast, some may also argue that TV times cater to TV networks at the expense of fans' convenience, so some screening times and primetime midweek games are not ideal for everyone.

In terms of an enhanced viewing experience, fans today can follow live games and game highlights right after games are completed on different social media platforms. In this regard, streaming services, both "on demand" (recordable) or "live" (available one time only), play a major role in streaming services. Streaming services provide the ability to watch content on a television, laptop, personal computer, tablet, or smartphone. Examples of streaming services include WatchESPN, Facebook Watch, and Fox Go. The factors that have played a major role in the increasing popularity of streaming services include the prevalence of portable devices, wider and stronger Internet reach, and the availability of bigger digital storage devices than before.

The time it takes driving to and from sporting games (time spent driving and in traffic) and costs (parking and gas) play a factor in a consumer's decision to attend. Many more traditional entertainment options, such as concerts, art shows, movies, and dining out, are available to fans who compete for the same discretionary spending they would normally allocate to tickets to sporting games. During the COVID-19 pandemic, when most spectator sport was cancelled or played in front of empty (or limited-capacity) venues, marketing moved entirely to the digital environment, which is the focus of chapters 7, 11, and 12.

Sport Consumption as Participants

Great numbers of people consume sport as spectators, but the consumption of sport as participants is also significant in sports such as running, swimming, and cycling. Playing hockey at a nearby neighbourhood hockey rink, working out at a local YMCA, taking part in the Calgary Marathon, or participating in the Iron Girl Canada Triathlon are all considered the consumption of sport. However, it is a different form of consumption because it involves participation or taking part in the sport. Similarly, with the advancement of technology in the sport industry in recent days, people are consuming mediated sport online. People spend a lot of time participating in or playing esports. For example, in the FIFA video game produced by EA Sports hundreds of thousands of Canadians engage in the sport of soccer via their avatars. In playing these mediated sports, people are consuming sport as participants.

Sport consumption as participants involves the consumption of sport by physically participating in sporting activities (e.g., working out in a gym, taking part in a 10k running road race) or participating in mediated games (e.g., esport, fantasy sport, sport betting). The consumption of sport as participants in both physical and mediated forms requires sport marketers' attention to the nature of sport consumption as a participant and the motives for participation. In this section, the consumption of sport as physical participation will be discussed first, followed by a discussion of mediated participation.

Participation in Physical Sport

Understanding what motivates consumers to participate in sport is particularly important for the development of informed marketing strategies in participant sport. People participate in both individual or team sports and informal or organized sports for the purpose of improving physical fitness and mental well-being or for competitive purposes. Motivations to participate in sport include to improve health and physical appearance, to have fun and relax, to improve physical performance and fitness, and to experience the spirit of competition (Downward et al., 2014). After conducting a review of the relevant literature, Eakins (2018) identified a list of socioeconomic factors that influence sport participation, which include the following.

- *Gender and age:* Research generally reported that males participate in sport more than females and that younger age groups and people with higher education levels tend to have higher sport participation rates.
- *Household income:* Studies reported that participants with adequate financial resources are more likely to participate in sport in formal surroundings than participants with insufficient financial resources.
- *Sport clubs and facilities:* Research generally reported that being a member of a sports club or a volunteer in a sport is positively associated with increased participation and time spent on sports and that the greater the number of sporting facilities, the higher the level of organized forms of sporting activity.
- *Location:* Studies showed that people located in rural, isolated areas lack access to certain types of sports infrastructure as compared to people living in suburbs or cities.

Participation in Mediated Sports

This section examines two of the most popular forms of mediated sport consumption as

---

IN THE KNOW

NBA2KL

The NBA was the first major professional sport league to launch an esports league on their own gaming platform. NBA2KL was announced in 2017 and launched in 2018. Throughout its first three seasons, the league saw its number of streamers on Twitch increase to more than 170,000 as of May 2021. The league is comprised of 22 clubs, including one in Canada, known as the Raptors Uprising GC. The other clubs are in the United States (20) and China (1). In addition to Twitch, NBA2KL content is streamed on YouTube, ESPN2, and TSN.

participants: fantasy sport and esports. While mediated sports such as esports and fantasy sport are heavily consumed by participants of the sport, they can also be consumed by spectators. For example, more than 100 million people watched the League of Legends World Championship. In this case too, the consumers of mediated sports are predominately participants than spectators.

Participation in Fantasy Sport

Fantasy sport participation is one of the fastest-growing consumption of sport. Fantasy sport is a type of online prediction game that allows users to build an imaginary sport team composed of real-life sports players and play against other users for a chosen amount of time, whether a single day (commonly referred to as daily fantasy) or for the entire season. Participation in fantasy sport involves selecting players, assembling a virtual team, and competing in games. The performance of a fantasy sport participant in a fantasy game depends on the performance of the real players in real games. For example, in the NBA Fantasy Basketball league, if, for example, a fantasy player drafted Fred VanVleet from the Toronto Raptors, whenever VanVleet scores and executes, the fantasy player is assigned a point value developed by the fantasy sport service provider to represent the scoring and the executing. The scoring includes three-point field goals, two-point field goals, and free throws made, and the executing includes rebounds, assists, blocked shots, steals, and turnovers. Thus, the better a player performs in the real-life sport, the higher the points a fantasy participant will gain who drafted that player for their virtual team. Therefore, like the team coaches and team managers in the real-world team, fantasy sport participants can manage the roster of their virtual teams by drafting, adding or dropping, trading, and starting or reserving players.

Participants can play fantasy games (e.g., fantasy hockey) using one of the many fantasy sport business providers' websites or mobile apps (e.g., DraftKings, FanDuel), league-owned fantasy sport websites and apps (e.g., Major League Soccer's MLS Fantasy), or media company–owned fantasy sport websites or mobile apps (e.g., CBS, ESPN, Yahoo). Participants can play fantasy games in private leagues with friends or compete against strangers in public contests. According to the Fantasy Sports and Gaming Association (2020), in the year 2019 in Canada and the United States, 19 percent of fantasy sport users were female, 50 percent of the users were between the ages of 18 and 34, 67 percent were employed full time, and 47 percent of total users earned more than USD\$75,000 a year. The association reported that in 2017 a total of 59.3 million people in Canada or the United States played fantasy sports, up from 32 million in 2010 (see table 4.3).

Motives of Fantasy Sport Participation

A number of studies have investigated the motives of fantasy sport participants. Tacon and Vainker (2017) synthesized these studies and reported that early studies drew primarily on motives associated with sport spectatorship, whereas later studies have also drawn on motives associated with online sport consumption, gambling, sport video gaming, and participation. According to Tacon and Vainker (2017), their systematic review of the fields literature revealed that the Fantasy Sport Motivation Inventory (FanSMI), developed by Lee and colleagues (2013), is the most comprehensive study in identifying the factors that motivate fantasy sport participants. Lee and colleagues' (2013) inventory identified 12 motives, which are listed next.

TABLE 4.3 Number of Fantasy Sport Participants in Canada and the United States (2010-2017)

Year	Estimated Number of Players
2010	32.0 Million
2011	35.9 Million
2014	41.5 Million
2015	56.8 Million
2016	57.4 Million
2017	59.3 Million

Data from Fantasy Sports and Gaming Association (2020).

1. Becoming a general manager or head coach: Fantasy sport helps participants compare themselves to real-world general managers and head coaches.
2. Knowledge application: Fantasy sport helps participants test their knowledge of the players and the sport they play.
3. Competition: Fantasy sport provides participants with a platform to compete with other people.
4. Prize: Fantasy sport provides a chance to win prizes, which helps keep participants involved.
5. Entertainment value: Fantasy sport is an inexpensive form of entertainment.
6. Bonding with friends or family: Fantasy sport allows participants to bond with friends or family.
7. Social interaction with other fantasy players: Fantasy sport allows participants to enjoy interacting with other participants.
8. Love for the sport: Fantasy sport participants play the games because it is about all the sport, not just about their favourite team or player.
9. Game interest: Fantasy sport stimulate participants' interest in live games.
10. Hedonic experience: Fantasy sport participants who play the game experience enjoyment.
11. Escape: Fantasy sport provides a means to escape from many burdensome tasks.
12. Substitute for a losing team: Fantasy sport gives participants who cheer for a losing team a chance to have, at least, a virtual winning team.

Participation in Esports

Esports, or electronic sport, is an organized competition in which individuals or teams compete (in leagues or tournaments) for money or prizes and that is open to spectators (in person or online). Today, there are an estimated 110 million esports participants (Finch et al., 2019). In esports, the casual fans and professional players compete on the same platform, unlike in the traditional sports. In esports, an individual can be both a fan and a participant, an opportunity that facilitates social bonding between ordinary and professional gamers. It is worth noting here that while esports and gaming are often used interchangeably, competitive electronic sport (esports) is actually a subset of gaming.

Esports takes on many different forms, including strategy games, multiplayer online battle arena, role-playing, fighting, racing, collectible card games and puzzles. According to Finch and colleagues (2019), there are four main genres in esport:

1. Real-time strategy (RTS) games, such as StarCraft
2. First-person shooter (FPS) games, such as Counter Strike Go and Dota 2
3. Simulated professional sports (SPS) games, which are virtual versions of the traditional professional sports such as the 2K league
4. Fighting games, such as Street Fighter, King of Fighters, Mortal Kombat, and Super Smash Bros.

According to Finch and colleagues (2019), the two most dominant genres are real-time strategy games and first-person shooter games. Examples of popular esports in 2020 include Fornite, NBA 2K, Dota 2, Apex Legends, Valorant, Call of Duty, Madden, CS-GO, Overwatch, FIFA, Rocket League, League of Legends, and StarCraft.

Unlike in traditional sport, to take part in esports, gamers do not necessarily need to have specialized facilities and equipment. An esports participant can take part in esports competition using devices such as a smartphone, laptop, tablet, or personal computer (PC). Participants need a gaming console, which is an electronic or computer device that outputs a video signal or visual image to display a video game that one or more people can play through some type of game controller. Other equipment that enhances gaming includes a controller, headset, mechanical keyboard, and mouse.

CHAPTER SUMMARY

The ultimate job of a sport marketer is creating demand and satisfying needs, so sport marketers need to have a clear understanding of what sport consumption is, who the sport consumers are, what motivates the consumption of sport both as participant and as spectator, and the differences between the spectator and participant consumer markets. All these are issues discussed in this chapter.

In sport consumption, there are two major types of consumption, namely, consumption as a participant and consumption as a spectator. Sport marketers need to understand the different forms of consumption that fall under these two major types of consumption: consuming sport by attending live games in a stadium (attendance), watching games through media (viewership), buying licensed merchandises (which falls under consumption as spectators), and mediated participation and physical participation (which fall under consumption as participants). Along with the different forms of sport consumption, the chapter presented the attempts made by different scholars to classify sport consumers, which showed the multifaceted nature of sport consumption. Having discussed the different types of sport consumers, the chapter looked at the factors that influence stadium attendance as well as those factors that can deter fans from attending live games in a stadium. This was followed by a discussion on sport consumption by participants and an examination of the different motives of participants in physical sport and in participants in the two popular mediated-participation sports, namely, esports and fantasy sport.

TEST YOUR KNOWLEDGE

1. Suppose that you are doing your internship at one of the NHL teams, and your manager asks you to bring fans who follow the team on Facebook but have not attended a home game in the past two years to a stadium. Whom would you target? Why?
2. Briefly discuss the different forms of sport consumption
3. What factors can be used to segment the consumer market based on common needs?
4. What are the three typologies of sport consumers? Briefly describe each.
5. Think for a moment about your recent decision to attend sporting events. What factors influenced your decision?
6. What is your favourite sport? Identify one or more of the motives discussed in this chapter that was the reason for attending your favourite team's game at a stadium.
7. What are some of the factors that dissuade consumers from attending live games?
8. What are the differences between sport consumption as participant and as spectator?
9. What are the key motives for sport participation?

KEY TERMS

augmented reality	fantasy sport	sport fan
consumption	multidimensional typology	tiered typology
dualistic typology	participant	virtual reality
esports	spectator	

CASE STUDIES

Visit HK*Propel* for case studies organized by chapter.

PART II

SEGMENTATION, TARGETING, AND POSITIONING AND THE CANADIAN SPORT MARKETING MIX

CHAPTER 5

Segmentation, Targeting, and Positioning in Canadian Sport

LEARNING OBJECTIVES

After studying this chapter, you will be able to do the following:

- Know the importance and advantages of effectively identifying target markets
- Understand the role of segmentation, targeting, and positioning (STP) in the marketing process
- Understand segmentation, targeting, and positioning and be able to apply each to any market of interest
- Be aware of the many potential bases of segmentation to divide markets into homogeneous groupings

An effective sport marketer understands that the "field of play" is in the minds, or perceptions, of consumers, whose worldview is coloured by their own background, experiences, and cultural makeup. The phrase "different strokes for different folks" is important to keep in mind here. Since each sport marketer is an "N of 1" (i.e., a single person with your own single view of the world), when trying to understand how hundreds, thousands, millions, or even billions of people think, it is vital to put our own views aside and use the **segmentation, targeting and positioning (STP)** process to objectively analyze and position an offering to markets and potential markets.

As sport marketers, we must realize that the total market can be subdivided into homogeneous subgroups consisting of people who are similar in some characteristic: their wants, needs, desires, interests, attitudes, hobbies, behaviours, pastimes, passions, and so on. And it is usually advantageous for an organization to selectively serve one or more specific subgroups, or market segments, as opposed to the entire population.

As consumers, we view the world through our own "lens" of personal experiences, needs, wants, and desire: Our worldviews are often similar to others', but nevertheless they are unique. As marketers, we must understand this phenomenon and adopt a scientific approach to **targeting** our marketing efforts to those consumer groups that are interested in making the exchange we seek. Using (STP) tactics enables marketers to use marketing resources effectively and efficiently.

Segmentation, Targeting, and Positioning (STP) as Economic Advantage

The field of economics supports STP, as it enables the marketer to relate supply to demand. The use of STP tools allows the marketer to uncover specific unsatisfied needs and wants (demand) in specific markets and, in turn, develop an offering (supply) that will meet such demand. For example, offerings of athletic apparel have grown over the years to a point where numerous manufacturers, labels, and retailers offer numerous lines of clothing and brands specific to target markets—items such as sneaker/rollerblade combos, running skirts, fast marathon shoes, and triathlon shorts that target specific market groups of people of similar age, fashion consciousness, occupation, level of competition, gender, style, usage, sport interest, and so on.

STP as the Bridge to Marketing Strategy

We refer to STP as the bridge to marketing strategy. STP enables the marketer to make sense of all of the background research and data so that the resulting marketing strategy and tactics

EXECUTIVE PERSPECTIVE
STP: The Key to Sport Marketing Partnerships

DALE HOOPER, Former Chief Brand Officer, Rogers, and Past Vice-President, Marketing and Consumer Insights, PepsiCo

Segmentation, Targeting, and Positioning

Every marketer who has led a major consumer brand has completed this exercise at least once for their brand. In a world of proliferation of new products, fragmentation of media, and time-starved consumers, having a clear concise understanding of your brand's positioning and the consumer group that will drive growth is more important than ever.

The key to successful "partnerships" between property owners looking for sponsors and consumer brands is a clear understanding of both brands' key segments and core targets, informed by data. Once there is consistency between the targets, then they can determine if the partnership will be successful. The property brand must allow the consumer brand to communicate/demonstrate its positioning to its consumers or capture data that can be leveraged to improve targeting or increase conversion of its advertising. If it only allows for a placement of a logo or some form of ad, it is not fully exploiting the opportunity, and success will be limited.

Three Types of Property–Consumer Brand Partnerships

In my mind, three types of partnerships are possible between properties and brands: philanthropy, building awareness, and positioning enhancing. In my professional life, I seek to develop partnerships of all three types.

1. *Philanthropy:* This typically involves supporting nonprofit organizations with cash, product in kind, or resources in return for logo as a gold or silver brand supporter.

Although some promotional value is achieved, there is no real ability to connect with the brand's audience to demonstrate the brand's core positioning or drive sales. However, in a world of scarce resources, it is critical for brands to find "causes" that support their brands positioning to ensure brand consistency at all touch points.

2. *Building Awareness (Brand Awareness/Product Distribution/Hospitality):* These partnerships involve relationships where a consumer brand sponsors an event/team/charity/entertainment property to build awareness and capture consumer data. The support comes with cash and/or in kind product support. Product may be available for sale, but the brand is rarely able to directly influence consumer buying behaviour.

3. *Positioning Enhancing:* In these partnerships, the property and the consumer brand share common targets and have positioning objectives that are consistent with each other. The property also enables the brand to not only drive awareness, distribution, and capture consumer data but to have the brand reinforce its position with its target. This is often accomplished by demonstrating a desired behaviour, encouraging trial, or reinforcing a brand truth. In these situations, participants can use the product but without any accompanying communication, which may work to reinforce a positioning of "authentic" or "for the experts."

Some Great Examples of Positioning Partnerships

One of the really great things about marketing is that every day we can see examples of how to do things all around us. In considering STP, I have seen successful positioning partnerships in the following examples:

- AMJ Campbell: To enhance their positioning as a dependable mover, it sponsors the AMJ Campbell Move of the Game, an in-stadium promotion that enables two fans in the nosebleed seats to move to platinum-level seats. AMJ Campbell executes this at many different events in different locations.
- Nicorette: The company sponsors no smoking areas at the Bell Centre. To enhance positioning as the number 1 smoking cessation product, Nicorette brands all the "no smoking signs" in the building.
- Gatorade: Gatorade has a presence at "point of sweat" at all key sporting events. It enhances its positioning as the hydration expert by sponsoring "sweat tests" with teams. Networks use this as content in their broadcasts as it demonstrates the athletes' game preparation.

My Advice to You

In considering STP, I recommend that, as a brand marketer, you spend time with your key internal and external partners, speak to consumers, acquire and review relevant data, and take the time to clearly determine your brand's key growth segments, its core consumer, and what positioning will promote brand growth. If you are a property manager, you must clearly understand what type of opportunities and data you can offer to potential sponsors. Once you know that, you can work closely to develop positioning-enhancing programs.

DALE HOOPER holds a Bachelor of Commerce in sports administration from Laurentian University's SPAD (Sports Administration) program. An accomplished industry executive, he has spent time at a number of major brands in leadership positions including Rogers (7 years), Pepsi (13 years), and Cadbury (7 years).

IN THE KNOW

Types of Property/Brand Partnerships and STP

As described by Dale Hooper, partnerships that seek to position or reposition a consumer facing brand linked to a sport property can do so in a number of ways. In terms of partnership between the brand and the sport property, we have learned that brand managers believe that there are three common options are available to marketers.

The first is philanthropy, which typically involves supporting nonprofit sport organizations with cash, product in kind, or resources in return for logo placements and status as some level of sponsor or supporter. Although some promotional value may be gained by the brand, there is limited ability to really drive return of investment (ROI) and connect in a deep way to the brand's target markets or to showcase the brand's positioning in a meaningful way.

In the second, which is often called brand awareness or product distribution or hospitality, the brand partners with a sport property with a goal of building awareness of their offering in target markets of interest. In these cases, direct links to sales of the brand's products are difficult to measure.

Third, and finally, would be what industry brand managers sometimes call positioning enhancing. These are the sport marketing partnerships where the brand and the sport property have common targets or followers and are aligned on the objectives of the partnership and how the brand and the sport property will be positioned. In these cases, activities such as trial, product sampling, utility demonstrations, and use to differentiate from the competition are often included and have the ability to position or reposition the brand or its products in the minds of those potential consumers associated with the sport property. The most important element here is that the consumer have the chance to use the products.

(the four Ps) are more likely to succeed since the strategy is customized both to the target markets of interest and to how the marketer's offering is positioned in the minds of the target markets compared to competitive offerings.

The bridge analogy emphasizes the role that STP can play in taking the large "mainland" of information and data—for example, external analysis; political, economic, social, and technological factors (PEST); competitive analyses—to a focused, customized "island" of market strategy, which enables the marketer to effectively and efficiently pursue their objectives. By linking the information mainland to the strategy island, STP acts as a bridge. The efficiency of the STP approach is also reflected in the bridge analogy in that it provides for the cost-effective use of resources in marketing. Figure 5.1 provides a graphical representation of STP as the bridge from analysis (market research) to marketing strategy (the four Ps).

Reflected in figure 5.1 is the STP bridge analogy, which describes the timing in developing marketing strategy: STP must always occur *after* fully understanding the external and internal environments and *before* developing marketing strategy. The importance of this timing is intuitive. How can a marketer determine their targets and position an offering without knowing the market, the competition, and their own competencies and capabilities? The necessity of completing marketing strategy

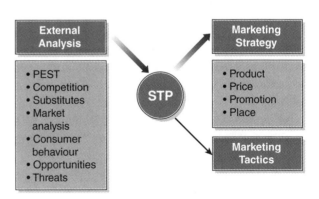

FIGURE 5.1 STP: The bridge to marketing strategy.

after STP is equally evident: Without knowing the specifics of our target markets and how we plan to position ourselves against competing offerings in those markets, how can we develop a successful marketing strategy?

Market Selection

With the possible exception of the world's largest global firms and their mass-market products (e.g., Coca-Cola, PepsiCo, Apple, Sony, Samsung, etc.), few organizations are able to fund marketing programs that involve some presence in all major international channels and markets. However, even the global organizations no longer diffuse the same message to all: Sophisticated marketing that selects market segments and tailors specific marketing programs to them has become commonplace. Furthermore, many other organizations that could afford to reach the vast majority of global markets choose not to since only certain parts of certain markets are interested in their offerings.

This move toward customized marketing messages forces organizations to determine which markets to pursue. They do not want to invest resources in marketing to segments where they have little or no competitive advantage or where there is limited opportunity for success. Success in for-profit organizations involves grouping consumers by similar needs or wants in order to increase profitability (e.g., Nike's line of running shoes), and success for nonprofit organizations involves achieving their own particular goals (e.g., the World Anti-Doping Agency seeking to eliminate doping from sport). In both cases, important decisions about which markets to enter are vital to success. The market selection decisions are one of the most important parts of the marketing process since they are what determine the elements of the development of the marketing mix—or marketing strategy—that will follow. STP decisions are based on the answers to these questions:

S—How can we break our market down into homogeneous, reachable groups?

T—Which of these groups should we target when committing our resources?

P—How do we want the selected target or targets to perceive our offering versus the offerings of our competition?

To answer these questions, we must remember that the three steps of STP occur in progression—segmentation, then targeting, then **positioning**—and build on each other to reduce a full market to manageable, reachable, and profitable chunks. This process is straightforward. First, segmentation involves identifying relevant bases and using them to segment the market and develop profiles for each identified segment. Second, targeting involves evaluating the attractiveness of all the identified segments to select the target market or markets to pursue. Third, and finally, the offering is positioned against the competition in the minds of those target markets. If more than one target market is selected in the targeting stage, then the positioning step must be carried out for each one.

What Is Market Segmentation?

Different customers want different things (products), are able to pay different prices, have different information sources (promotion), and buy at different places (geographic, demographic). Marketers, in turn, seek to understand their target consumers in order to develop a targeted, tailored marketing strategy (the four Ps), which is more likely to be successful than an unsophisticated blanket approach. The ideal scenario is a specific marketing strategy implemented for each consumer: Although advancements in technology have virtually made this possible in certain scenarios, it is generally very expensive and thus inefficient. This is where **market segmentation** provides support to a sport marketer and allows for the organization of people who behave similarly into groups, whether they be customers, fans, participants, sponsors, or suppliers. An easily observable example is a professional sport team that has developed specific marketing programs for various segments of spectators, including season-ticket holders (diehard local fans), partial season-ticket holders (diehard fans who are unable to commit or afford an entire season of seats), suite holders

EXPERT PERSPECTIVE
Reaching Women as Sport Fans

KATIE SVEINSON, Assistant Professor, School of Sport, Tourism and Hospitality Management, Temple University

LARENA HOEBER, Professor and Associate Dean for Graduate Studies, Research, and Special Projects, Faculty of Kinesiology and Health Studies, University of Regina

Women have been sport fans for decades, but marketers continue to have difficulty understanding their needs and wants. In fact, one study showed that 91 percent of women feel that advertisers do not understand them (Coffee, 2014). This particular group of fans has been steadily increasing over the years, with Nielsen Sport (2015) reporting that 46 percent of women from 24 countries stated they were either interested or very interested in sports.

One issue facing marketers is assuming that market segmentation based on gender is enough. In reality, women are heterogenous and have differences in preferences, needs, attitudes, and wants. When choosing women sport fans as a target market, it is important to segment them based on psychographics and behavioural characteristics that represent their heterogeneity. Further, it is important to consider the modern woman; the days of only offering sport fan clothing to women in the "shrink it, pink it, bling it" style is over because they do not resonate with all women. In this way, the positioning of products should move beyond concepts of feminization.

In our research that examines women sport fans, we have recognized their diverse experiences. The following are some aspects to consider when marketing to and reaching women as sport fans:

- *Motivations.* As a target market, there are variations among women as sport fans, based on social class, marital status, sexuality, age, and so forth. What unites them? They like sport! Like men, women are sport fans for a variety of reasons: it provides an opportunity to socialize with friends and family, support their community, support gender equality (as a fan of women's sport), and because they love the sport. Unfortunately, women have been viewed as less legitimate as fans and accused of other motivations, in particular, an interest in socializing or attraction to male players.
- *Knowledge.* Women are often asked to prove their knowledge of sport in order to be viewed as authentic or "true" fans. There are many women who are knowledgeable about sport, and marketers would benefit from recognizing their status as fans. For example, marketers could target women to join or create their own fantasy league. Additionally, marketers can showcase women as socializing agents for sport fandom, recognizing that they share their knowledge with friends and family. In some cases, events have been created specifically for women to gain knowledge, such as "Football 101." These events can be problematic when they overemphasize the feminine aspects (e.g., serving wine only) and assume that women are not interested in learning the details of the game. Additionally, these types of events do not need to be just targeted toward women, but rather can target anyone who wants to gain knowledge, such as new Canadians or men who are new to the sport.
- *Clothing.* Sport fan clothing is an important organization artifact that allows fans to demonstrate their identity with a team, league, athlete, or sport. One concern with women's sport fan clothing is how some merchandisers continue to follow the "pink

it, shrink it, bling it" viewpoint. While some women might want these elements in their clothing, many others want clothing that fits their varying body sizes in the official team colours. In other situations, retailers and merchandisers do not even offer women's versions of sport fan clothing, such as when away jersey of the Matildas (the Australian women's national soccer team) was initially only sold in men's sizes. If clothing for women sport fans is made available in styles and sizes that they want, they will buy it. There are lost opportunities for sport organizations to partner with brand-name women's clothing and shoe companies and designers. One good example of a partnership focused on women sport fans is Hillberg & Berk's relationship with the Canadian Football League to offer jewellery in official team colours.

- *Marketing.* While a significant number of women identify as sport fans, they continue to be tokenized by marketing campaigns occasionally including one woman as a fan. The illustration of men as sport fans in sport- and nonsport-related advertising reinforces the idea that sport fandom is for men only. Women need and want to see themselves represented in these ads to demonstrate the awareness of their role as sport fans. In fact, the Association of National Advertisers created the "See Her" movement, with the goal of creating gender equality in marketing practices.

All this information suggests that though women have specific needs and wants, they do not always seek to be identified by their gender. Instead, they want the opportunity to demonstrate and express their fan identities based on individuality. When targeting women, it is important to ensure they are authentically represented, respected, and recognized as fans. Remember, they are fans first and women second.

KATIE SVEINSON is an Assistant Professor in the School of Sport, Tourism and Hospitality Management at Temple University. Her work combines sport management and sociology of sport, with a focus on sport consumer behaviour. She investigates sport fandom from gender-, culture-, behaviour-, and identity-based perspectives using a variety of qualitative research methodologies and methods.

LARENA HOEBER is a Professor and the Associate Dean for graduate studies, research, and special projects in the faculty of kinesiology and health studies at the University of Regina. Her research interests are in women's roles and involvement in sport, contemporary qualitative research methods, and innovation and change in amateur sport organizations.

(corporate hospitality seekers), family game-zone single-game tickets (families), multigame ticket holders (non-local diehard fans, interested fans), and so on.

Formally, we define sport marketing segmentation as the delineation of a customer, fan, spectator, participant, or business-to-business (e.g., sponsor, media partner) group or groups with homogeneous needs or wants that the marketing function of the sport organization has the ability to successfully satisfy. This definition demonstrates five important aspects of segmentation in sport marketing:

1. *Wide product application:* Segmentation is beneficial to the sport marketer for a wide range of products, from tangible goods (Adidas segmenting the market of Canadian women for new product development) to services (Sport Canada and Own the Podium understanding Canadian high-performance sport and supporting the development of Olympic athletes when designing their athlete funding programs) and ideas (the Vancouver Bid Committee for the 2010 Winter Olympic Games understanding local citizens prior to launching their marketing efforts, leading up to a referendum on whether they should bid for the games) and behaviours (the World Anti-Doping Agency understanding athletes prior to developing a social-marketing campaign to encourage antidoping behaviour).

2. *Broad reach:* Segmentation in sport can be applied to any number of potential markets—spectators, participants, business partners, and others—where tailored marketing strategies will enable more successful marketing. For example, the organizing committee for a high-profile 10-kilometre run will use segmentation to best reach spectators (both in-stadium and via media), participants (both professional and participation), sponsors, suppliers, and media partners.

3. *Efficient reach:* If an organization understands its market properly, it can reach various segments with the same offering. For example, airline firms reach more than one segment with their flights (e.g., business travellers and well-to-do personal travellers in business-class seats; frequent flyers with point program benefits; and students, tourists, and lower-income travellers in economy). A sport example would be an airline seeking to reach upper-class consumers by taking out an advertisement in a yachting, sailing, or equestrian magazine.

4. *Timing:* A wide variety of stimuli, both internal and external, can quickly change the benefits that individuals are looking for at any particular time, thus moving them into another segment. For example, a casual fan who attends a few Major League Soccer games each year may have become a season-ticket holder following the Toronto FC winning the MLS Cup for the first time in 2017.

5. *Segment boundaries:* Only segmentations that yield segments that are both homogeneous and mutually exclusive are acceptable. Within each segment, homogeneous consumers possess similar needs and wants. Segments are mutually exclusive, each having different needs and desires with no cross-over between them. For example, a segmentation for a brand of golf clubs identifies a key target market as upper-class, retired women 60 years of age and older, where the analysis has found that women within that segment have very similar needs vis-à-vis golf clubs and are not members of any other segment (e.g., men, under 60, lower or middle class).

A sport marketer undertakes segmentation only when it makes financial sense. That is when a greater return is worth the cost in time, human resources, and financial resources committed to do the segmentation. Thus, deciding to sell tee-shirts to parents of a youth soccer team to raise funds for a tournament would not justify segmentation because the revenues would not offset the research costs involved, whereas selling tickets for the World Under-17 Soccer Championships in Toronto would justify segmentation because the market and potential revenues are significantly higher.

Practically speaking, market segmentation involves the aggregation of potential customers into groups, or market segments, that have similar needs or wants and will respond similarly to marketing action, thus helping the organization achieve its objectives.

The segmentation process typically yields one of three scenarios.

- In the "one product, multiple market segments" scenario, the same product is marketed in different ways to different market segments. A non-port example is the Harry Potter books, which are marketed in a completely different fashion to two segments—youth and adults—through different promotional strategies. A sporting example would be Toronto Blue Jays ticket sales: The same seat is marketed in very different ways to a number of very different markets—single game (e.g., online, mass-market promotions), corporate (e.g., phone sales to build relationships), season tickets (e.g., preseason promotions targeted to a previous season-ticket holders), and group (e.g., reduced pricing for volume purchases).

- The "multiple product, multiple segments" scenario involves different products for different segments. Marketers in general typically cite the example of Gap Jeans, which offers different brands of jeans to different markets through its three brand stores, Gap, Banana Republic, and Old Navy. In sport, a good example is when Maple Leaf Sports and Entertainment of Toronto targets different sport market segments through its four professional sport franchises: Toronto Maple Leafs, Toronto Raptors, Toronto Argos, and Toronto FC.

- In the "segment of one" scenario, the organization uses technology (e.g., online ordering, databases) or custom products (e.g., custom jewellery, custom home products) to develop marketing programs specific to each customer. In the example of Dell Computers, customers can build a custom computer with the specific options they want rather than select from a limited number of offerings, unlike most of Dell's competitors. A sport example would be a triathlon coach who customizes training programs for individual athletes.

Market Segmentation in Sport

In sport, like other industries, segmentation is a process: It is dynamic, as people's needs, wants, drivers, makeup, and interests change over time. This chapter presents a process for effective segmentation and describes how to use it.

Market segmentation is a straightforward process. It involves considering every potential consumer who might purchase your product—the total market—and determining how best to divide the total market into segments of individuals with similar needs and wants. This allows the marketer to invest resources in marketing to those groups that are most likely to be profitable over the long term and are reachable through existing marketing channels.

Thus, as a process that aggregates prospective buyers into groups, or market segments, with common needs or wants who will respond similarly to marketing action, segmentation enables organizations to market more efficiently. Important criteria for identifying market segments are **responsiveness** and **measurability**.

Marketers segment markets when it makes sense, when return on investment (ROI) is greater than its cost. Reaching a mass market is very costly, so an organization that can segment its market can reach it much more efficiently: A marketing program developed to target a specific market will cost less to implement than one targeted at the mass market. However, the marketer must be careful to not oversegment, since the segments must be large enough to make them worthwhile for the organization. There are four key criteria for effective segmentation:

1. Responsiveness: Does each identified segment respond to marketing action differently from the others?

2. Measurability: Can each segment's boundaries be identified and its size measured?

3. Accessibility: Is each member of each segment reachable by the marketer?

4. Substantiality: Is the segment large enough to warrant developing, implementing, and evaluating a unique marketing mix?

Thus, we know the key criteria for effective segmentation. But how do we do the segmentation? The next section explains our six-question segmentation process and its steps.

The Six-Question Segmentation Process

Although other segmentation processes, such as the product-market grid, are discussed in the sport marketing literature, we suggest the six-question segmentation process as it allows for a more comprehensive market analysis on three levels. There are three reasons why we prefer this approach. First, it enables in-depth analysis of each segment through the six-question process. Second, it is applicable to new product development as well as existing products. And third, it enables considerable feedback throughout the process, thereby yielding better results.

The process comprises three steps: (1) the identification of the total market of interest, (2) the iterative identification of the most relevant bases of segmentation, and (3) the six-question analysis of each identified segment.

Step 1: Identification of Total Market

The first step of the segmentation involves the articulation of the total market of interest. Very little if any research is required, as the marketer considers every person who could, even in what might be considered unlikely situations, be interested in the product offering, whether existing or planned. For example, the marketing director of a Canadian running series that offers 5-kilometre runs across Canada would consider all Canadian residents capable of doing a 5-kilometre run as the total market. To be more limited in defining the total market would risk missing a key market or potential niche market in later steps in the segmentation process.

Step 2: Bases of Segmentation

The second and most important step of the segmentation process involves identifying its bases. To start, the total market identified in Step 1 is divided into smaller, homogeneous, mutually exclusive groups using the most relevant characteristics that tell us why groups, or segments, differ. These differences could be in their needs, preferences, decision processes, or wants.

In terms of implementation, the marketer considers each of the potential bases of segmentation to the total market and selects those that are most relevant and will most appropriately divide the total market into segments. At least two bases of segmentation are selected (e.g., age and gender); theoretically, there is no maximum. In our consulting experiences, we have seen segmentations on over 50 bases.

In addition to selecting bases, the marketer also determines the **sensitivity** of each base, or its number of categories. For example, income can be used as a base with low sensitivity, where the market is divided by low and high income; or it could be used as a high-sensitivity base, where the market is divided into those earning under $40,000, $40,000 to $80,000, $80,001 to $120,000, $120,001 to $160,000, $160,001 to $200,000, and over $200,000. The determination of sensitivity is based on the market and the marketer's determination of which level of sophistication is required for effective segmentation.

How do we select the appropriate bases of segmentation? We do market research and pick the bases that make the most sense (e.g., gender and age for beer, social class, and disposable income for racehorses). And we typically include as many as we can that make sense (e.g., gender, age, culture, religion, sexual orientation, marital status, lifestyle). Table 5.1 lists many consumer market (**B2C**) and business market (**B2B**) bases of segmentation from which a marketer can select those that are most appropriate and relevant to their market.

There are a few important points to note in table 5.1. The B2C segmentation bases can be grouped into three general categories:

1. The market's state of being, or market bases, which includes all the demographic, geographic, and customer definition bases.
2. The market's state of mind, or psychology bases, including personality, activities, interests, opinions, and other similar bases.
3. Product-related bases, like volume of use and loyalty to brands.

There are no psychological bases on the B2B side because organizations do not think—rather, they work on policy. For example, a buyer for Nike purchasing toilet paper for the employee bathrooms considers price and firm policy, not personal associations with certain brands.

Once the bases of segmentation have been determined, the marketer decides on a level of sensitivity for each, given the results of their market research and the understanding of the particular segment's size and composition. Although it would seem desirable to have high sensitivity and many bases to define precise segments, this could lead to an untenable situation. For example, two bases of segmentation with two levels of sensitivity each yields a 2×2 matrix, or four groups to analyze. However, five bases with four, five, two, five, and three levels of sensitivity each yield a $4\times5\times2\times5\times3$ matrix, or 600 segments. Thus, unless one is running a complex database or is prepared for many hours of work, this decision needs to be taken carefully. Further, the marketer must also consider the size of each segment in the analysis. Segments that are too large may pose problems later on, during strategy implementation, and segments that are too small may not be worth pursuing.

Step 3: Segment-by-Segment Analysis

Once the appropriate bases of segmentation and their sensitivities have been selected, the marketer analyzes each segment by determining the following the process (outlined next) for each permutation of the bases, or sensitivities, that have been identified.

This process involves two steps: First, the bases, or levels of sensitivity, are organized

TABLE 5.1 Bases of Segmentation

Consumer Market (B2C) Bases of Segmentation	Business Market (B2B) Bases of Segmentation
Customer definition or category it belongs to (e.g., government, industry)	Industry
Geography (region, city, census metropolitan area [CMA], population, density, neighbourhood, climate)	Size
Culture	Location
Race	Organizational structure
Age	Head office location
Income	Region
Education	Store location
Lifestyle (activities, interests, opinions)	Industry classification
Media habits	Number of employees
Profession	Sales
Personality traits	Revenue
Volume of product use	Price
Customer loyalty, relationship	Benefits sought (organization)
Benefits sought	Usage rate (organization)
Consumer motivation	User status (organization)
Consumer behaviours	Loyalty status (organization)
Frequency of contact (i.e., number of visits)	Purchase method
Sensory factors (e.g., comfort, smell, etc.)	Centralization of buying process (central, de-centralized)
Social factors (e.g., fashionable look)	Buying decision process (individual, group)
Price sensitivity	Type of buy (new, modified rebuy, straight rebuy)
Usage rate	
User status	
Family size	
Stage of family life cycle	
Home ownership	
Values	
Attitudes	
Social class	

in table format; and second, six basic but thought-provoking questions are asked about each group, or segment. Table 5.2 reminds us of two important points described earlier: There is mutual exclusivity between segments and homogeneity within segments. Although it is quite likely that bases of segmentations have more than two levels of sensitivity with more sophisticated breakdowns, for simplicity in our example, we have kept the levels of sensitivity for each base to two simple groupings. The bases of segmentation in this example are:

Base 1: Income (high or low)

Base 2: Age (young or old)

Base 3: Personality (type A or type B)

Base 4: Geography (urban or rural)

TABLE 5.2 Mutual Exclusivity in Market Segmentation

Income	High				Low			
Age	Y		O		Y		O	
Personality	A	B	A	B	A	B	A	B
Geography	U	R	U	R	U	R	U	R	U	R	U	R	U	R	U	R

The breakdown clearly shows the $2 \times 2 \times 2 \times 2$ segmentation results in 16 segments, which are mutually exclusive: No individual in the total market appears more than once in the segmentation. The 16 segments can be counted in the bottom row of table 5.2, where the fourth base of segmentation (geography) is applied. From left to right, the first segment is "high income, young, Type A, urban"; the second is "high income, young, Type A, rural"; and so on.

From this point, we consider six specific questions for consumers within each of the identified potential market segments:

1. Who are they?
2. What do they want or need?
3. When do they want or need it?
4. Where do they get it?
5. Why do they want or need it?
6. How do they go about getting it?

These questions are important as they force the marketer to consider what is happening in the minds of the consumers in each potential target market. Through this, the marketer hopes to achieve a complete understanding of each segment prior to selecting among them, or targeting.

Using this same example, we end up with the segmentation grid shown in table 5.3. As the table clearly shows, for a 16-group segmentation, this process becomes very complex very quickly, and database-assisted organization is recommended for all but the simplest segmentation. In larger segmentations, a database program with queries would be ideal.

To help clarify the process, we present an example of a segmentation from a consulting project on the market for ice hockey nets. This involves a relatively simple 2×2 format with levels of sensitivity for Type of Hockey (ice or road) and Product Use (personal or institutional), which leads to table 5.4.

Table 5.4 and this section in general underline the fact that good segments are both homogeneous and mutually exclusive. The example of the hockey nets shows that each of the groups is different from one another while individuals within each group are similar. Further, no consumer would fall into more than one spot in the grid, and each member of the total market would fall there only once. In the case of a consumer who plays ice hockey in the winter and road hockey in the summer, they would be considered two different consumers as they would be using two different hockey net products.

Feedback as an Advantage of Segmentation

An important advantage of segmentation using the six-question grid is that it provides for double-checking of the work. Following completion of the grid, the marketer can double-check their work by comparing responses in each column. If the chart is identical under certain rows, then we have chosen bases of segmentation that are not relevant to our market. For example, in the hockey net example, if the responses in the two columns under ice hockey were *identical* to those under road hockey, we would know that Type of Hockey was not a useful basis of segmentation for this market. We would then revisit the analysis and seek other, relevant bases of segmentation.

Targeting

Historically, the marketing literature (Kotler & Armstrong, 2016) has offered three ways to target markets.

1. *Undifferentiated Targeting:* The marketer ignores market segmentation and the differences it reveals between groups and targets the entire market with a single message. This is

TABLE 5.3 Questions by Segment

Income	High				Low			
Age	Y		O		Y		O	
Personality	A	B	A	B	A	B	A	B
Geography	U	R	U	R	U	R	U	R	U	R	U	R	U	R	U	R
Who?								
What?								
Where?								
Why?								
How?								
When?								

TABLE 5.4 Segmentation Table: Market for Ice Hockey Nets

Market	Ice Hockey/ Personal Use	Ice Hockey/ Institutional Use	Road Hockey/ Personal Use	Road Hockey/ Institutional Use
Who are they?	rural families and backyard rinks	arenas, municipalities, parks and rec, clubs	children and young adults at home	bars, arenas, teams, leagues, clubs
What do they want?	an enabler for game-like fun, competition, and practice	regulation-size net that conforms to rules; durability, quality, and safety	a way to have game-like fun, competition, and practice	regulation-size net that conforms to rules; durability, quality, and safety
Why do they buy it?	to keep puck in play, practice, skill development, dream, fun	to provide a regulation game to players	to keep ball in play, practice, fun, pickup games	to provide a regulation game to players
How do they buy it?	pressure from children, parents go to purchase	based on client need and owner-ship decision	pressure from children, parents go to purchase	based on client need and owner-ship decision
Where do they buy it?	large sporting-goods stores	wholesaler or larger retailer	large sporting-goods stores	wholesaler or larger retailer
When do they buy it?	fall or early winter	year-round	spring or early summer	year-round

rarely used, and even those organizations that once did so (e.g., Coca-Cola) are now opting for more complex approaches. It is our opinion that this approach is not advisable.

2. *Multisegment Targeting or Differentiated Targeting:* The marketer selects more than one of the segments identified in the segmentation process and develops distinct marketing strategies, one per selected target market, designing separate offers for each. For example, the automakers (e.g., General Motors, Ford, Honda, Tesla)

develop, promote, and offer numerous vehicles, each specifically targeted to specific markets. Similarly, the footwear manufacturers (e.g., Nike, Reebok, Adidas, Puma, Li Ning) develop, promote, and offer numerous styles of sporting footwear, each designed for specific markets.

3. *Concentrated Targeting:* Similar to multi-segment targeting, this involves focusing on only one target market. This decision may be made for resource reasons or as part of a niche strategy, and it is particularly attractive when

financial resources are limited. For example, Felt bicycles are specially designed for, and marketed to, only triathletes and cyclists.

Targeting, although vitally important to the success of any marketing plan, is the simplest step in STP. It involves assessing the work done in the segmentation to determine which market or markets will be pursued in the marketing strategy. In this regard, a marketer generally seeks to consider segments that have sustainable profitability, are measurable, and are accessible through existing marketing channels. Specifically, targeting seeks to identify those segments with the greatest potential for profit or return on investment, as well as to consider the feasibility, simplicity, and cost of reaching a segment.

The 80/20 Rule

The marketing literature on targeting often discusses the 80/20 rule. In this context, the 80/20 rule reminds us that typically 80 percent of revenue comes from 20 percent of customers: Our high-volume customers drive our business and must be considered in our targeting decisions (Crane et al., 2006, p. 234). In carrying out a detailed and sophisticated segmentation, we often reveal potential target markets that are interesting but may require significant investment to reach and whose profit potential is limited. For example, the Ottawa Senators' strategy may be to spend more time, money, and human resources on customers who have engaged in an exchange with the team by buying one or several tickets than people who have never done so. Thus, by targeting those fans, the Senators can develop a number of marketing strategies to deepen the team's relationship with them. The result may be more ticket sales (with the ultimate goal a season ticket), more merchandises sales (e.g., jerseys, mugs), and more revenue from concessions.

Using the Segmentation Grid for Targeting

The six-question grid provides the marketer with a tool to analyze the various markets to consider and the data necessary to make an informed targeting decision. Specifically, targeting involves the analysis of each segment and the selection of one or more segments that will enable the marketer to achieve their goals.

The process involves two steps: (1) assessing size, reach, profitability (or ROI), and measurability of each potential target market identified in the segmentation, and (2) selecting one or more target markets.

Step 1: Assessing Size, Reach, Profitability, and Measurability

This step involves going across the completed segmentation grid segment by segment, and asking the following questions of each segment:

Size

- Is the segment too large (i.e., difficult to differentiate from) for a marketing effort?
- Is the segment large enough to justify a marketing effort? If not, will it grow to that size in the near future?
- Is our target market too narrowly defined?

Reach

- Are we able to communicate with this segment? If not, will future technology enable this communication to happen?
- Is the segment compatible with the goals and image of our organization?

Profitability

- If we're seeking profit, can we achieve our profitability requirements from this target market?
- If we're not seeking profit, can we achieve our objectives in a cost-effective manner through this target market?
- Do we possess the resources (financial and human) necessary to pursue this segment?
- Is it possible to achieve a competitive advantage in this segment?

Measurability

- Can we measure the size of the segment?

- Can we estimate the purchasing power of the segment?
- Can we determine if we can access this segment?

There are a few things to note about these questions. First, the largest segment may be too large to pursue if the marketer cannot find a point of difference in the form of a specific feature to demonstrate how their product is superior to competing products. A smaller segment where a niche strategy is likely to work may be a better choice. For example, the new Major League Soccer franchise in Toronto targeted specific cultural groups in the city that were known to support soccer (e.g., Italian Canadians, Brazilian Canadians) in its ticket sales programs. Second, in considering reach, the marketer must be aware that new forms of communications and consumer engagement are developing all the time (e.g., online forums, blogs), which may change our answer to this question.

The responses to these questions will provide the data and direction that marketers require for selecting the target or targets they wish to pursue.

Step 2: Selecting Target Markets

Armed with the responses to the 12 questions for each identified segment from the segmentation step, the marketer is able to determine which segment or segments to select for marketing action. This involves analyzing the segments and determining which ones to pursue, based on available resources. The number of targets is specific to each target decision, which considers how attractive they are and the resources and market conditions that the marketer faces in each case.

Positioning

Marketers assume that consumers arrange competitive offerings in their minds according to factors (e.g., price, quality, luxury) that are important and relevant to them for the product. Position is the place that each product offering occupies, relative to others, in the minds of the consumers of that target market segment.

Practically speaking, positioning involves looking for that place in the minds of your target market or markets where you can fit your product or where there is currently a **hole in the market**—no direct competitive offering. The trick to effective positioning is to have carried out segmentation and targeting properly in order to identify clearly articulated target markets, and then to view your product versus competitive offerings (competition and substitutes) specifically in the minds of the consumers in each target market.

For each target market identified in the targeting stage, a separate positioning strategy is developed. For example, if three target markets are selected, then three positioning strategies are developed, one for each target market.

Positioning Story: Clean and Clear B-Ball Skills Days

The Clean and Clear B-Ball Skills Days is an excellent example of STP in action. Clean and Clear, an acne treatment product, ran a program known as B-Ball Skills Days in high schools throughout Ontario. Program staff went into the schools and ran basketball skills camps and scrimmage games with girls while the boys watched. No product was given out, but the name Clean and Clear was attached. Why was it brilliant STP? Research had revealed that a large segment of teenage girls did not participate in sport because they believed that sweating would cause skin problems (e.g., acne) and they were afraid this would limit their attractiveness to boys. Thus, in combination with playing a cool sport in front of the boys, Clean and Clear could be positioned in girls' minds as the product able to help them to counter these fears.

Positioning Strategies

Marketing theory provides a number of strategies by which a marketer can position their product in the marketplace. Table 5.5 lists these strategies.

Marketers must be careful in their positioning strategies. First, positioning against a clear market leader (e.g., Puma versus Nike,

TABLE 5.5 Strategies for Positioning

Strategy	Example
By attributes	Seek a specific characteristic (e.g., Nike and high performance) by which to position.
By price–quality association	Position by the value proposition offered to the target market (e.g., student discounts on ski passes at Mont Tremblant ski resort).
By use	Determine why the product is purchased (e.g., Cobra KING F9 Speedback golf club for long drives).
Advantage over competition	Seek a difference from competitors (e.g., Gatorade scientifically proven to enable a runner to absorb more energy than competing products) or seek to mimic a successful competitor's offering.
By benefit	Seek a difference by benefits offered to consumers (e.g., Nike Vaporfly running shoe claimed to be 4 minutes faster in the marathon than other shoes).
Find market gap	Assess the marketplace and find a niche where competition is limited or absent (e.g., PowerBar [energy bar] and endurance sport athletes).
By usage environment	Use situations or times of use as point of difference (e.g., road hockey net or goalie pads designed for hockey on the street).
By association with endorsers	Use endorser to position or reposition (e.g., Sidney Crosby and Tim Hortons).
By association with something unique	Use a unique or exotic aspect or fact to position or reposition (e.g., Drake partnership with the Toronto Raptors).
By product of choice to certain users	Select a specific product for a specific group where the product becomes their option of choice (e.g., Gatorade for athletes).
Differentiate brand	Stress your differences and avoid head-to-head competition (e.g., the Canyon Speedmax CF 8.0 as the fastest triathlon and time trial bike).
Reposition	Adapt the product to a new market (e.g., golf to senior women).
Be the leader	Set the tone—be the one that others follow (e.g., Speedo as the manufacturer of performance swimming products).
Appeal to lifestyle	Seek a fit between lifestyle and product appeal for your target segments and use it to differentiate your offering (e.g., Chariot baby strollers for active parents offer a multiuse stroller for running, bicycling, hiking, and cross-country skiing).

Powerade versus Gatorade) is not recommended due to the influence of the market leader on all target markets. Second, positioning in a crowded market is unlikely to work well because confusion will reduce or limit the ability of the message to effectively reach its target. Third, overpositioning may lead to a narrow image being communicated to an overly small and likely unprofitable market segment. Fourth, it is generally not recommended to position a product on an attribute that is not important to the target market (e.g.,

a waterproof tennis racquet). Finally, product modification that is not needed or wanted by the target is likely to be ineffective.

Examples of Positioning

The positioning of a product via sport within a specific target market is illustrated in the following four Canadian examples briefly mentioned above.

1. Dairy Farmers of Canada: The classic repositioning of chocolate milk from a dessert

or special drink for kids to a postevent recovery drink via sponsorships of triathlons and running events, including product giveaways at the end of the race (i.e., handout of a cold chocolate milk to marathon/triathlon finishers).

2. AMJ Campbell: In the early 2000s, this national firm sought to enhance their positioning as a dependable mover through its role as the official mover of Canada's Olympic Team, via its partnership with the Canadian Olympic Committee. As of 2020, the firm also sponsors the Canadian Curling Association, Special Olympics Ontario, Soccer Canada, Tennis Canada, and Rogers Hometown Hockey.

3. Nicorette: This is an example for the late 1990s and early 2000s, when venues still had smoking sections, but the positioning was very well done. Nicorette, a smoking cessation product, enhanced its positioning as the number 1 product in its category by sponsoring all the smoking sections and the "no smoking" signs in the Bell Centre, the home of the Montreal Canadiens.

4. Gatorade: The Gatorade Sport Science Institute (GSSI) engages scientists in research sport performance. In Canada, at the University of Guelph, it researches elite hockey players as well as athletes in other sports. The idea is to position Gatorade as a superior product due to the science used in its development and testing.

The Positioning Map

In continuing the process that we have developed from the 6-question segmentation grid and the 12-question targeting approach, we now move to positioning the offering in the minds of the consumers in the target market or markets

that were selected. The key tool that we will share to undertake this is known as a *positioning map*, or a **perceptual map**. It is important that we consider and carry out a positioning for only the target market or markets that we selected. Effective positioning is built on three required stages:

1. The marketer assesses a given market segment and determines where each competitive offering is currently positioned.
2. The marketer does background research to determine the important dimensions and drivers that lead to this positioning.
3. The marketer selects a position for their product to occupy in the mind of the target market segment.

As suggested by one of the authors' former professors, this process can be referred to as "cherchez le creneau" ("look for the hole"): The marketer seeks to understand what is happening in the minds of consumers in the target market and identify holes, or gaps, where they can position their product for success. For example, if all the competitors in the running-shoe market are launching high-quality shoes with big-name athlete sponsors, why not offer a low-priced shoe? If all the events in town are free and convenient, why not offer a prestige event?

Perceptual Mapping

The perceptual map, a positioning tool also known as a positioning map, displays the location of products or brands (or sometimes product classes or groups) in the minds of consumers (both current and future) in the

IN THE KNOW

Canada's Team

Another informative example of positioning is professional sport franchises in Canada and those who take on the role of Canada's Team at certain times and with certain segments of fans. The NBA's Toronto Raptors have done this very well, with their "We Are the North" campaign, particularly during their run to the 2019 NBA Championship.

target market of interest. Perceptual maps are usually displayed in two dimensions but can be constructed in three or more dimensions using special software.

One perceptual map is designed for each target market of interest. The design process involves three steps.

1. Draw the axes: The two most relevant dimensions of the target market are selected along with ranges of each dimension, based on the views of consumers in the market of interest.

2. Plot all offerings: All competing offers (substitutes as well) are positioned on the graph in one of two ways: by feel and understanding of the market or by scoring via the perceptual-mapping technique (figure 5.2). The latter is always recommended, and the more sensitive the scale used to do the scoring the better (see "In the Know" about Likert scales).

3. Determine the position of product of interest in target market of interest. Based on the market and research, determine the position of the product. With existing products, this may involve repositioning, whereby the product's current position is altered based on a changing market or environment.

Figure 5.2 is a typical perceptual map, based on the results of work done by Lance Warwick, a graduate student at the University of Ottawa, on consumer perceptions of running-shoe brands in relation to their cost (high prices to low prices) and their marketing spending (high marketing investment as compared to low marketing investment). In figure 5.2, two dimensions were selected to determine the perceived price (premium to value) and marketing spend by the brand (high or low). In reviewing figure 5.2, consider how the map would change if you substituted other attributes such as market share (regional to global), product focus (technical to casual), product diversity (general to specialized), or annual revenue (high to low). The number of attributes to pick from shows just how versatile a tool the perception map can be. Note that the perceptual map in figure 5.2 is based on the opinions of one person and is meant to be an example of a perceptual map and not a validated representation of running-shoe brands.

Common Target Markets in Canadian Sport

Some specific target markets in Canadian sport should be well known to the Canadian sport marketer.

• *Aboriginal Peoples:* Aboriginal Peoples represent a group of considerable interest in amateur sport in Canada, particularly in participation, where sport is seen by government as a way to improve the lives and health of this group. Sport Canada, the Aboriginal Sport Circle, and other organizations work in this segment. Examples of targeted activities in Canadian sports include the North American Indigenous Games, the Canadian Sport Policy, which includes specific action targeted at Aboriginal sport, and Hockey Canada youth programs to encourage Aboriginal youth to participate in hockey.

• *Canadian women and girls:* Female Canadians represent an important interest group to the government as well as to professional sport, resulting in initiatives to engage women at all levels of sport, ranging from the creation

---

IN THE KNOW

Positioning Using the Perceptual-Mapping Technique

In this technique, a sample of consumers from the target market of interest are asked to use Likert scale questions (e.g., putting answers on a 1 to 5 scale such as 1 = very similar and 5 = very different) to rank product pairs (e.g., Nike and Adidas, tennis and soccer) or product comparisons (e.g., the entertainment value of a Halifax Mooseheads hockey game), with the results used to position competing offerings in a perceptual map.

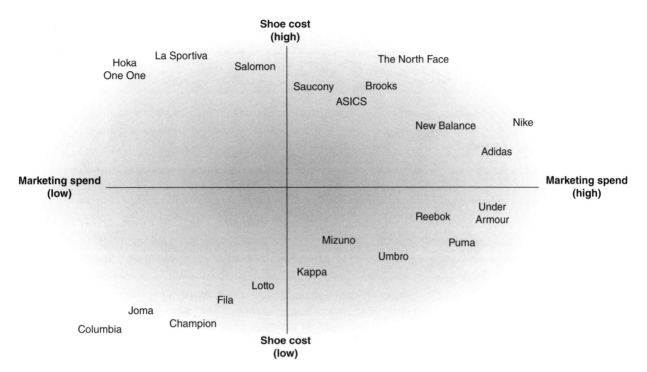

FIGURE 5.2 Perceptual map of the perceptions of running-shoe brands on price and marketing spend by the brand. Created by Lance Warwick.

of new female professional sport leagues to youth programs to get girls involved in sport. For example, Canadian Women & Sport, created in the early 1980s, has been successful in developing strategies that have led to more opportunities for girls and women to engage at different levels in the sport system (participants, athletes, administrators, etc.). In 2019, Canadian Women & Sport received $3 million in funding from the government of Canada to expand its programming and impact over a four-year period.

- *Young Canadians:* Young Canadians are a focus of government, particularly Health Canada and Sport Canada, due to increasing health issues (e.g., obesity) in youth. Thus, developing specific strategies for engaging youth into sport and physical activity is a priority for governments (national, provincial, municipal), sport clubs, corporations, and health-care professionals.

- *Official language groups:* Canada is a country of two official languages, English and French, and sport organizations, activities, events, and programs that cater to both languages are sought after and supported. For example, national sport organizations must develop marketing programs that appeal to both segments.

- *Paralympic athletes:* The emergence of the Paralympic Games has provided huge opportunities for physically challenged individuals to pursue their athletic dreams (see the case of the Special Olympics Ontario and positioning efforts by AMJ Campbell). The Canadian Paralympic Committee (CPC) is responsible for the Paralympic movement in Canada.

IN THE KNOW

STP in Action: The International Triathlon Union (ITU)/Toronto World Cup Triathlon

In 2000, one of the authors (O'Reilly) worked for the Toronto 2008 Olympic bid as event manager for the ITU Toronto World Cup Triathlon. He used STP in developing the marketing program for the event, which ended up with six specific target markets:

1. *International decision makers:* As part of the Olympic bid, the main goal of the event was to influence those voting to determine the location of the 2008 Olympic Games. A specific marketing strategy was developed to pass Toronto's message to these individuals.

2. *Spectators:* The event was held following the Molson Indy car race in Toronto on the same course. Extensive seating was still up following the event, which organizers had to fill since empty seats look bad on television. STP identified potential Toronto fans and a marketing program was developed to encourage more than 5,000 spectators to show up.

3. *Participants—Elite:* To impress the international decision makers, a top field representing many countries was needed to participate in the event. Thus, a strategy was developed that saw participation by the vast majority of the top 50 male and female athletes in the world, representing over 30 countries.

4. *Participants—Amateur:* A further source of spectators for the elite race and of goodwill for the event is the amateur triathletes doing the event. This marketing strategy was adopted to try to attract 1,000 participants that day. That objective was not achieved, and the strategy was altered for the following year.

5. *Participants—Celebrity relay:* A few celebrities (e.g., actors, politicians, business executives) were sought to garner media attention and fanfare.

6. *Sponsors:* To access a major source of funding for the event, we developed a detailed sponsorship program and implemented it with partners. We reached the target amount, with Pizza Hut as the title sponsor.

CHAPTER SUMMARY

Chapter 5 introduces STP, the bridge to marketing strategy, and outlines the important process of turning research data about consumers' internal and external environments of interest into effective and efficient marketing strategy in order to achieve organizational objectives. The three-step STP process includes, in order, segmentation, targeting, and positioning. Segmentation involves reducing the entire market of interest down to manageable groups with similar characteristics. Targeting is the selection of one or more segments that will have the greatest potential for marketing success. Positioning is the act of determining how to best present your product in the minds of consumers in one or more target markets of interest versus your competition. The chapter provides a number of tools for STP (e.g., perceptual mapping, the six-question segmentation grid), which enable marketing action that is efficient and reduces risk.

TEST YOUR KNOWLEDGE

1. Complete a six-question segmentation grid for a sport product of your choice.

2. Complete a positioning map for one of the market segments you identified in your answer to Question 1.

Chapter 5 • Segmentation, Targeting, and Positioning in Canadian Sport

3. Selecting at least three bases of segmentation, create a segmentation grid and respond to the six questions for launching a new driver into the golf market in Canada.

4. Explain the role and give an example of each of the following in developing marketing strategy: segmentation, targeting, and positioning.

5. If the targeting process reveals two target markets of interest, how many perceptual maps and marketing strategies must be developed?

6. Create a perceptual map for sport entertainment options for a couple on a Saturday night in the Greater Toronto Area.

7. List as many bases of segmentation as you can that might help segment the market of CFL fans.

8. What risk does a marketer take if they build a marketing strategy without considering or doing an STP?

KEY TERMS

B2B	measurability	sensitivity
B2C	perceptual map	segmentation, targeting,
hole in the market	positioning	and positioning (STP)
market segmentation	responsiveness	targeting

CASE STUDIES

Visit HK*Propel* for case studies organized by chapter.

CHAPTER 6

The Sport Product

LEARNING OBJECTIVES

After studying this chapter, you will be able to do the following:

- Understand what is meant by a product
- Expand the concept of a product to a sport product
- Become acquainted with the various product forms and the elements of product strategy
- Build out the range of sport products in the market, from tangible goods to ideas
- Outline some of the feature of sport products

Nothing inspires passion and emotion quite like sport. One kick of the ball or swing of the bat can energize and excite a crowd or dash the hopes of a nation. In many cases, an ingrained emotional connection exists between the consumer and the product, something most marketing professionals in other industries can only dream of achieving. However, there is much more to the **sport product** than emotion: Many characteristics challenge the sport marketing professional. Sport is not a product form that can be easily defined as a good or a service, but rather it is made up of a variety of forms representing both categories. Some argue that the core of the sport product is an athletic

event and that all other product forms support and expand on that core. It is on this basis that we discuss the sport product. This chapter begins by looking at the unique features of the core sport product: Why is this product different from all others? It then examines numerous forms of the sport product, including events, **athletes, facilities, teams, leagues, clubs, merchandise, media,** and **skilled services,** providing a general description of each form along with examples taken from Canadian sport. The chapter ends with a brief overview of the concept of the sport **brand** and sport **packaging.**

The product is the most important element of the marketing mix, so it is vitally important for sport marketing professionals to clearly understand the product in all its forms. They must appreciate the aspects of sport that make it a challenge to market but that also form the basis of its appeal. This chapter outlines and highlights these aspects to provide that understanding.

What Is the Sport Product?

Sport is a product like no other; however, to understand it, we must examine the more general definitions and elements of a product. The numerous definitions of product all contain similar elements. Central to the definition is the assertion of Pitts and Stotlar (2013) that a product should be understood as a concept, rather than a singular item. Solomon and colleagues (2018, p. 237) define a product as "a tangible good, a service, an idea, or some combination of these that, through the exchange process, satisfies consumer or business customer needs; a bundle of attributes including features, functions, benefits and uses." Another definition, that we have developed, of a sport product is any offering of any form that any market may have interest in in order to satisfy a need or want.

A product is something that satisfies a need and that exists in more than one form—a good, service, idea, person, organization, place, or activity. A product may be made up of any one or a variety of these forms. This is a particularly relevant observation in the context of the sport product, which encompasses a wide variety of these forms. To gain an even deeper understanding of a product, we can also define critical elements of these definitions—goods and services. A good is a tangible, physical entity that offers specific benefits to the consumer. For example, shoes are physical, tangible objects that offer the consumer something to cover the feet with. A service, on the other hand, represents the opposite, a nonphysical entity that is intangible but that still offers specific benefits to the consumer. For example, a piano lesson does not offer the student a physical object but rather a new skill that benefits them.

Since the tangibility of the product is the most important determinant in classifying it as a good or service, it is important to understand the meaning of tangibility. Pitts and Stotlar (2013) define a tangible product as "something that is concrete, definite, discernible, and material . . . it physically exists" and an intangible product as "something that is indefinite, indiscernible, indistinguishable, and imperceptible. It is not a physical object." All these definitions and concepts are key to understanding the product and will be discussed again in the context of the sport product.

Product Life Cycle

The product is the core of the marketing mix. It is important for marketers to not only define the product they are dealing with but also understand how it evolves over time so they can adapt it accordingly. The most widely accepted way of explaining the evolution of a product is with the product life cycle model (see figure 6.1). This consists of four stages—introduction, growth, maturity, and decline—each representing distinct challenges for the marketing professional. Therefore, marketers must recognize where their product fits in the cycle so they can respond to those challenges. In the *introduction stage*, the product first enters the market, few consumers have heard of the

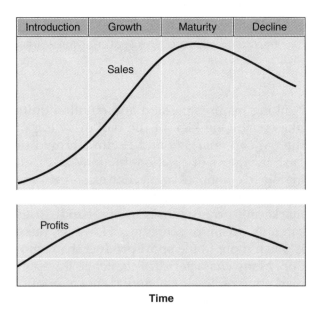

FIGURE 6.1 The product life cycle.
Based on Solomon et al. (2003).

EXECUTIVE PERSPECTIVE
The Varied and Extensive Nature of Sport Products

DARRYL BOYNTON, Former Associate Vice-President Partnerships, Canadian Tire Corporation

At first glance, you might not expect the world of retail sports products to be particularly complex—but every day, thousands of Canadians shop at our stores both in person and online to purchase popular items like hockey sticks, soccer balls, yoga mats, and running shoes, just to name a few. With over 500 Canadian Tire Retail locations and many more retail stores across various banners like Sport Chek, Atmosphere, Pro Hockey Life, and Sports Experts, considerable research is done by our teams at Canadian Tire Corporation (CTC) to continually provide a compelling assortment of sports products.

Canadian Tire Corporation is unique when it comes to sporting goods. Along with carrying some of the most well-known global sport brands, we also develop products for our own private label brands in several categories. Canadian Tire's internal brand-development teams are researching and developing new products with the help of consumer testing, to ensure our sporting goods are truly made for life in Canada. The Sherwood hockey brand is one such example; it has undergone a complete relaunch since being acquired by CTC and is once again being used in hockey dressing rooms at all levels of the game. Sherwood has a unique hockey stick assortment to meet the demands of both recreational hockey players and NHL pros. Another prime example is Helly Hansen, whose quest in making high-quality products to withstand all weather conditions has led to many different opportunities, from creating industrial work wear trusted by professionals, to having the brand worn by maritime teams in the prestigious America's Cup Sailing Championship. Helly Hansen's attention to detail, functionality, and quality have been key elements of the brand for over 140 years.

In my experience at Canadian Tire, I have learned that products need to achieve different results, based on consumer expectations. A mother purchasing her son's first pair of skates will consider variables such as cost, quality, and fit, while a professional hockey player will need them adjusted at the factory level and specially tailored to precise specifications. Historically, sporting goods have typically been sold as aspirational products, leveraging endorsements from professional athletes. For many young consumers, these aspirations influence their purchasing decisions and often foster lifelong brand affinity. Though parents generally pay for sports equipment, it's more often the kids who inform these decisions most, based on the products their peers or favourite athletes use.

We often talk about how a hockey player's journey begins and ends at Canadian Tire. Whether you're a kid picking up your first pair of skates, an adult shopping for specialized equipment, or maybe a parent passing the love of the game on to your family, Canadian Tire is here to help Canadians with all their sporting needs.

DARRYL BOYNTON is the associate vice-president, partnerships, at Canadian Tire Corporation. Prior to this, Darryl worked at Hockey Canada for more than 10 years in different capacities. He was the general manager of the Toronto component of the 2015 IIHF World Junior Championship. He received his degree in sports administration from Laurentian University before starting his career at the Canadian Hockey League as a manager of marketing.

IN THE KNOW

What the Golf Industry Knows about the Driver in Your Golf Bag as a Sport Product

Over the years, we—the authors—have studied closely many products in sport, one of which is the most talked about of golf clubs, the driver, or "one-wood." It's the club that a golfer uses when they need to maximize the distance of their shot, the one that leading professionals use to hit the ball more than 300 yards. It is the quintessential sport product. It has legendary brands (e.g., Big Bertha), it has an impact on performance (i.e., hitting the drive farther makes subsequent shots easier), and there are many options at many price points. In a previous edition of this book, Chris Walling, at the time director of marketing for Callaway Golf Canada, shared his views on the driver as a sport product, which we summarize here as key takeaways about the sport product.

1. Brand matters: The brand of the driver is stronger than price when a golfer is considering which driver to purchase.

2. Timing: The average golfer replaces their driver every 2.5 years, so brands need to product develop on similar timelines (i.e., product life cycle).

3. Professional endorsement: The use of a driver by a leading pro influences purchase decisions.

4. Consideration set: A golfer has a set of options already in mind when they go to purchase a driver. If your product is not in that "consideration set," they will not buy it.

5. Trial: Demo days, indoor driving ranges, and similar features are key to letting a buyer try before they buy.

6. Performance: Golf is a performance-based sport (i.e., no one plays without keeping score), so the driver's impact on performance (score) is very important.

7. Product availability: Simply, when they decide, the golfer needs to be able to get their driver quickly.

As you can see, the purchase of a driver is a highly involved decision for a serious golfer and a sport marketer needs to consider this deeply—and at many levels—when developing the product.

---

product, and sales are low. A product in this stage requires extensive promotion to create awareness; and if this is successful, then a slow but steady increase in sales should be expected. In the *growth stage*, the product has been recognized and accepted by most consumers. This stage is characterized by a steady, rapid increase in profits; however, it also entails the introduction of competitors and a resulting peak in profits followed by a decline. During the growth stage, marketers must appreciate the impact of the arrival of competitors on the profitability of the product (Kotler & Armstrong, 2016) and take measures to counteract such an impact. When sales have levelled off and the competition is firmly established, a product has reached the *maturity stage*. During this stage for tangible products, the majority of

purchases are made to replace worn-out products, and so the number of new consumers is relatively low (Solomon et al., 2003). While the levelling of profits symbolizes the beginning of the maturity stage, competition is the most pressing issue, and the costs of promotion and competitive pricing strategies eventually lead to further profit decline. Finally, the *decline stage* is reached when a product becomes obsolete. New technologies may mean that a significantly improved product is taking over and sales will steadily decline. During this stage, it is up to the marketer to realize when a product should no longer be produced. Table 6.1 describes sport products in various stages of the product life cycle.

What else can we learn from the product life-cycle model? First, a product can leave or

TABLE 6.1 Examples of Stages of the Product Life Cycle

Stage	Athlete	Equipment	League
Introduction	Quinton Byfield	Hybrid golf clubs	Canadian Premier League
Growth	Connor McDavid	Yoga	Major League Soccer
Maturity	Sidney Crosby	Snowboards	National Hockey League
Decline	Wayne Gretzky	Scooters	Canadian Football League

enter the marketplace in any stage. Products that are a duplicate of an original idea can skip the introduction stage and come in later in the cycle. For example, a new brand of snowboard may be introduced to the market, but it does not have to gain consumer recognition for the product, and the majority of its sales may come from replacing boards that have worn out. This means the product has joined the cycle at the maturity stage and so should be marketed in a way that reflects this. As well, different products will move through the life cycle at different speeds, product life cycles are getting shorter, and the early bird generally makes the greatest profit. Since all these factors must be considered when creating a marketing plan, marketing professionals must be aware of them all.

The Sport Product

The definition of a sport product is similar to that given earlier for general products but placed in a sport context. Pitts and Stotlar (2013) define the sport product as "any good, service, person, place, or idea with tangible or intangible attributes that satisfy consumer sport, fitness, or recreation needs or desires." Key to this definition, like the generic product definition, are the concepts of the product taking many forms and fulfilling the needs or desires of the consumer. For example, one form of the sport product is sport equipment, which fills the needs of athletes as it provides the material necessary to facilitate their participation in a sport.

Why Is Sport Special?

Despite the existence of numerous sport product forms, the core sport product is the production of an athletic event, and it is elements of this core product that give the sport

product its unique nature. Many authors have written about the unique characteristics of the sport product and what makes it different from other products or at least special (Foster et al., 2020; Mullin, 2000), which we summarize and expand on here.

1. The sport product is intangible and subjective: A sport event is intangible in that consumers are unable to physically touch the experience of attending or viewing a sport event. Instead, the benefit they receive is the value provided by the product, which is the entertainment they have experienced. Indeed, a sport event is subjective: What one person considers a positive experience, another may perceive as negative. For example, if the Toronto Blue Jays beat the New York Yankees, then, despite the fact that they attended the same game, the Blue Jays fans may be pleased with the product while the Yankees fans may be disappointed.

2. The sport product is inconsistent and unpredictable: The human element of sport makes it impossible to predict from one game to the next. This is true in both the spectator and the participant aspect of the sport product. While the Blue Jays may have beaten the Yankees one week, that is no guarantee that the next game will bring the same outcome. Similarly, a person participating in figure skating may skate the same routine at every competition but may win at some and not at others. So many factors go into the outcome and production of a sport event that it becomes unpredictable. The weather, injuries, the crowd atmosphere, or unexpected events can have a huge impact on a game. For instance, a professional team in a hotel may be woken at 3 a.m. by a fire alarm and be forced to stand outside for an hour before going to bed. That is something that cannot be predicted and could possibly

affect the outcome of the next day's game. It is this unpredictability that makes sport so exiting, frustrating, and bothersome.

3. The sport product is simultaneously produced and consumed. It is also perishable and must be presold: Both a spectator sport event and a participant event are being produced as they are being consumed. The crowd at a football game is watching the sport product as the players on the field are creating it. This leads to the sport product being classified as perishable, which means that it has a limited shelf life. Once the football game is over, the sport product can no longer be sold. Even the most talented marketer cannot sell a ticket for a game that has already taken place. Similarly, for a participant event, the experience of playing a game of golf is being consumed by the golfers as they make their way around the course. When they are finished, the product no longer exists.

4. For marketing professionals, there is a greater emphasis on product extensions than the core product: The inconsistent and unpredictable nature of the sport product cannot be controlled by the marketer. Therefore, there tends to be a focus on product extensions, which can be controlled to a great degree. The marketing professional has no say on which players will be signed or how the team may perform, and, as these things can significantly alter the core product, it does not make sense for a marketing plan to centre on them. Instead, the packaging of the event becomes even more important. The experience of attending the game can be affected by product extensions such as cheerleaders, esports, mascots, gambling, fantasy sport, and promotions.

5. Sport is generally consumed in public and so the experience is affected by group dynamics: For the most part, sport is a social product, which is consumed by a large group of people in a public location. The behaviours and activities of the other consumers can have a significant impact on an individual's experience. It is the job of the marketer to ensure that programs and plans are in place to facilitate the needs of different groups so that they have a positive experience. For example, many NHL clubs in Canada create family fan zone seating to meet the needs of families coming to the games, including low ticket prices, no alcohol in the section, and games for kids nearby.

6. The emotional attachment and personal identification associated with sport are incomparable. In many cases, committed sports fans feel as though they are part of the team and often use phrases like "*We* won the other day in Edmonton" in an effort to affiliate themselves with a win that they technically had no part in (Mason, 1999). The strong degree of emotional attachment makes sport an excellent opportunity for selling product extensions like merchandise and collectibles because, in purchasing these items, fans often feel they are supporting their team. However, there is also a negative side to such an attachment. The backlash that can result from selling a team's best player or losing an important game can have a negative impact on the sport product. For example, when Wayne Gretzky was traded from the Edmonton Oilers to the Los Angeles Kings, the grief of Canadian sports fans was so great that it prompted *Sports Illustrated* to publish an article titled "A nation in mourning" (Taylor, 1988).

7. Sport pervades all elements of life and enjoys an almost universal appeal: Across all provinces and territories, among the many cultures, and through all classes in Canada, sports fans exist. This is the same in every country all over the world and is one of the few things which all countries have in common. Soccer is often referred to as the world's game because of its universal appeal and popularity. Sport is linked to country pride, gambling, government funding, and much more. The FIFA World Cup is one of the few events that stops life in hundreds of countries all over the world to focus on the host city and the many nations competing for the title of world champions. In the upcoming 2026 FIFA World Cup, which Canada will cohost with the United States and Mexico, the event will welcome 48 teams.

8. Sport is both a consumer and industrial product: A consumer good is typically classified as the end product, which is consumed after production, while an industrial good is a product that is manufactured for use in creating another product (Mullin, 2000). In most

cases, a product is either an industrial good or a consumer good; however, different forms of the collective sport product represent both. For example, a hockey game is a consumer product as it is consumed by the fans as it is produced; however, it is also an industrial product as it fuels the production of other products such as sport media. This interaction will be discussed further in the next section.

These eight elements make the sport product unique and provide special advantages and challenge for a sport marketer. The key to marketing success is to recognize these elements and capitalize on those that offer an advantage and preempt the possible negative impact of those that offer a challenge.

Sport Product Forms

The sport product takes a variety of forms—goods and services, consumer and industrial products. The core of the sport product is an athletic event where the consumer is either a participant or a spectator. Other sport product forms are no less important, but they are dependent on the core product for their existence. The sport form model in figure 6.2 indicates how the forms interconnect. The athletic event, the core product, is part of a group of primary products. These primary products also include athletes, teams, leagues, and clubs, which all depend on the athletic event for their existence. For example, if no actual hockey games were played, the National Hockey League would have no reason for existence, the Montreal

EXPERT PERSPECTIVE
The Role of Rivalry within the Sport Product

TERRY EDDY, Assistant Professor of Sport Management, University of Windsor

The Battle of Alberta. El Clasico. The Backyard Brawl. The Game. Simply mentioning these contests evokes all sorts of memories and emotions in sport fans, and they are usually among the first that team supporters note on their calendars when the schedule for a new season is released. Rivalry games carry greater importance beyond placement in the standings, and are highlights in sport seasons that can often be long and somewhat repetitive. Given that these events take on a "life of their own," often having their own brand names, they also show us the importance of sport rivalry as a product extension and can even be considered unique sport products in themselves.

Although there are several definitions of rivalry in the academic literature, rivalry is often considered an adversarial relationship, which can be driven by past competition between the teams and/or other factors like geographic proximity and historical factors outside of sport (Havard & Dalakas, 2017). For example, the Old Firm derby (derby is a synonym for rivalry outside North America) between Celtic and Rangers football clubs in Glasgow, Scotland, is one of the oldest and fiercest rivalries in sport due to its basis in religious and political divisions in the city. Similarly, rivalries can manifest from a general dislike between residents of two cities (e.g., New York and Boston, Toronto and Montreal) or can span multiple levels of sport (e.g., rivalries between Oshawa and Peterborough, or Cape Breton and Halifax, are most apparent at the CHL level, but rivalries also exist at the youth level across multiple sports).

Rivalry is also important because it can increase the efforts of sport participants and can impact fan behaviour (Havard & Dalakas, 2017), because both athletes and fans measure themselves against their rivals (Berendt & Uhrich, 2016). In fact, past research suggests that sport fans have a fundamental need for rivalry—as people, we compare ourselves to others, both positively and negatively, so having rivals is important to our self-concept (Havard &

> continued

> **The Role of Rivalry within the Sport Product** > *continued*

Eddy, 2013). Thus, sport rivalry offers us more than just an opportunity to gain bragging rights over our friends and family—it satisfies deeper, psychological needs.

Because of all of these factors, understanding rivalry and leveraging it for marketing purposes are very important to sport organizations. Research indicates that people are more likely to attend or watch rivalry games than nonrivalry games, particularly women (Havard et al., 2016; Reams & Eddy, 2017). Further, fans are willing to pay more to attend a rivalry game (Sanford & Scott, 2016), so the organization can charge more for tickets (Tyler et al., 2017)—if you check the ticketing website of any sport organization implementing variable pricing, you will see that rivalry games usually come at a premium. Fans are also more engaged on social media than usual during traditional rivalry games (Watanabe et al., 2019). In addition to these tangible outcomes, rivalry is an important brand association for teams and a key aspect of product differentiation (Mullin et al., 2014). Rivalries facilitate links to the past and are a vital piece of a team's history and traditions; they contribute substantially to brand image and brand equity.

Sport organizations adopt a variety of strategies marketing contests with rivals, as well as how they use rivalry to market their products more generally. In recent years, major professional sport leagues (e.g., MLB, NHL) have altered their divisional structures to ensure that rival teams play each other as often as possible during each season. Some leagues, including the MLS and Quebec Major Junior Hockey League (QMJHL), have instituted "rivalry weeks," whereby all the games played in a week are between rival teams, to create greater attention to these matchups.

In addition to these structural changes, rivalry games are often labelled with their own brand's names. This practice is especially common in U.S. intercollegiate sport, where almost every major team has a named rivalry game, but there are examples from all over the world. Branding these games attempts to show that they are more important than average and offers teams new opportunities for marketing (e.g., merchandising, ticket packages). Some organizations have used the potential to name a rivalry contest to engage with fans. For example, the "Freeway Face-Off" between the Los Angeles Kings and Anaheim Ducks was named through a contest in which fans could submit possible names and submit votes for their favourite names among a group of finalists selected by the teams.

Although rivalry is clearly an important piece of the sport product, marketers must resist the temptation to try to manufacture rivalries. Rivalry needs to develop organically from the factors mentioned previously (e.g., time, notable events, close competition) to be accepted by fans (Havard & Eddy, 2013). Although organizations can work to grow rivalries in a low-key way, forcing new rivalries on fans could have a negative effect. One area where organizations could make some safer efforts to grow rivalry might be on social media—fans don't naturally engage as much during newer rivalry contests than they do with traditional rivalries (Watanabe et al., 2019), so providing extra content and opportunities for fans to engage online during these newer matchups could help to push along the development of the rivalry.

TERRY EDDY is an associate professor of Sport Management at the University of Windsor. Originally from St. John's, NL, he holds a PhD in sport administration from the University of Northern Colorado. Before moving to UWindsor in 2017, he held assistant professor positions at the University of Arkansas and St. John's University in Queens, New York. Terry's research interests lie in sport sponsorship and consumer behaviour, and he has also performed research on sport rivalry. His work has been published in over a dozen academic journals, including *Sport Management Review* and *Sport Marketing Quarterly*. He also serves on the editorial review boards for *Sport Marketing Quarterly*, *Frontiers in Sports and Active Living*, and *Case Studies in Sport Management*.

Canadiens would have no purpose, and the athletes would have nothing to do. The second group of product forms, the derivative products, include merchandise, skilled services, facilities, and media. The derivative products are an expansion of the primary products—and they are no less important, as they also support the primary products. For example, sport-specific media are an expansion of events, leagues, athletes, and teams: *The Hockey News* could not exist without the NHL, its teams, and its athletes, as it would have nothing to report on. However, in return, they offer the products exposure and a direct communication channel to their consumers, the fans. To provide a better understanding of the collective sport product, the rest of this section will discuss each product form with examples from Canadian sport.

Events

The sporting event is the core sport product form: It stimulates and drives production of all the other sport products. The athletes, leagues, teams, clubs, facilities, merchandise, skilled services, and media all exist as a result of the events. Although the first association made with the sport event product is professional sport, an event can actually represent a wide variety of competition levels, including professional games, the Olympics, the Paralympics, national championships, intercollegiate athletics, minor sport, and recreational activities. For example, an organized minor soccer game influences the production of a league; and within that league, there must be teams. It also requires the completion of a soccer pitch (facility) and the production of equipment such as balls, cleats, nets, and shin pads. On the other end of the scale, the Olympics and Paralympics stimulate the mass production of facilities, merchandise, and equipment, and they provide the media with countless hours of programming and inches of newspaper and magazine column space. Events offer consumers various benefits, including the entertainment experience, the vicarious thrill of victory or agony of defeat, and for some fans, particularly in baseball, the numbers of the game (the percentages and stats) can be exciting.

Athletes

Athletes are the participants who produce a particular sport event or competition. They train and prepare to develop and perform during an event. There are both amateur and professional athletes, and both are forms of the sport product. The benefits offered by the athlete product form

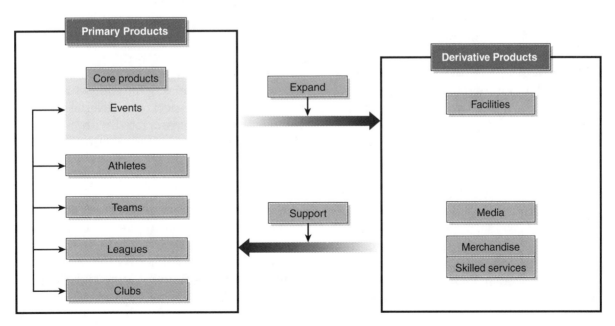

FIGURE 6.2 Sport product model.

can be twofold: Highly successful athletes not only aid the production of another product (the event), but also provide their image as a marketing tool for their team, league, or sport, as well as outside companies through endorsement deals. A prime example of this is Connor McDavid, a rising hockey superstar who has been in the limelight since he was touted by experts while a teenager. Much like superstars before him, his rise to stardom in the NHL has benefited not only his team and the fans but also the league as a whole. Sidney Crosby, now an established star in the league, was already a household name and had been on the *Tonight Show* with Jay Leno and in *GQ* magazine as the new face of the NHL before he had even played a game in the league. It was also reported that Crosby made more in endorsements than his salary as an NHL rookie in 2005 (Spencer, 2005).

Teams

Teams are a collective product comprising a group of athletes who not only work together to create the on-field performance but also represent a brand that can be sold to consumers. While specific athletes may come and go and success may be fleeting, the team product usually remains the same and is best represented by its name and logo. The Toronto Raptors went through the eras of stars Vince Carter and Tracy McGrady in the early 2000s and then an NBA championship run in 2019 with Kawhi Leonard. These three stars all came to Toronto and then left, but the entity of team product has remained and grown in value and following. Regardless of who is on the roster, the Toronto Raptors team goes out and competes each year. The team product can be shaped by many elements, including the current players, its coach, and the team's former players and coaches, along with such factors as the history of the team, ownership, and marketing. It is the marketing professional's responsibility to recognize those aspects of the team product that will be the most beneficial in selling the team and exploiting them to their fullest advantage. What works for one team may not work for another, so a detailed examination of the team product is required when putting together

a marketing strategy. For instance, while a hockey team like the Toronto Maple Leafs or Montreal Canadiens may be able to use their vast history as an aspect of their marketing, a newer sports team like the Ottawa Redblacks must focus on something else because history is not a strength of their team product.

Leagues

The league product form is very similar to that of the team product. While a team is made up of a group of athletes, the league is made up of a group of teams. The league is a service that provides the framework for sport competition. It is also a sellable brand that, like a team, can be sold as merchandise and is best represented by a logo and official name. However, the league product can offer other benefits to the consumer, such as pride and nostalgia (Mason, 1999). The Canadian Football League (CFL) is a league product that offers its consumers a number of benefits. First and foremost is a sense of "Canadian-ness." The CFL is the only major professional league made up of only Canadian teams. Fans feel a sense of pride about the Canadian nature of the league: The threat to this from possible expansion into the United States was met with resistance, as fans felt that they were losing an integral part of the league product (Nauright & White, 2002). Once again, as with the team product, it is the responsibility of the marketing professional to identify the elements of the league product that are of most value to current and potential consumers. The service of organizing the competition itself will always be an aspect of the league product, but it is the images associated with the league that can provide the best marketing potential.

Clubs

The club form product is a service that offers consumers a chance to become involved with sport as a participant rather than just a spectator and fan. All across the country are gymnastics clubs, figure skating clubs, curling clubs, golf clubs, and more. Each of these can provide the consumer with the opportunity, infrastructure, and coaching needed to participate in a sport. They also provide a social venue. Many people see socializing as a benefit of sport participation, and clubs (especially golf clubs) offer an opportunity to get together and socialize with fellow participants. Some clubs are private and only allow people who fulfill certain criteria and obligations to become members. Sometimes members may feel that the club membership offers them the opportunity to not only socialize but also make business contacts, all while perhaps getting in a great round of golf.

Facilities

The facility product form has seen many changes over the past 30 years because venues have expanded considerably in terms of sophistication, comfort, technology, architecture, design, and quality (Foster et al., 2020). Today, spectator comfort and satisfaction are a top priority, much more so than in years past. Not only has the facility product become an extension of the event product, today it also is a destination itself. Facilities now offer visitors more than just a place to sit when they attend a game—they offer a full entertainment service. The Rogers Centre in Toronto is an excellent example of a facility that offers more than just sport spectating. It is home to the Toronto Blue Jays and the Toronto Argonauts. It features a hotel with luxury suites, major restaurants, a retractable roof, one of the world's largest video boards, a fitness centre, and specially commissioned public art. It is an attraction that has the ability to attract tourists to Toronto on its own. New venues, such as the new NHL arena being built in Calgary (opening in 2021), are known to have the most impact (described as the stadium novelty effect), where increased attendance is typically observed in the first five years of the life of a new venue (Howard & Crompton, 2003).

Skilled Services

The skilled services product represents those aspects of the sport product form that involve a set of different skilled professionals who provide services that improve the performance of athletes or teams. Examples include chiropractors, team doctors, fitness trainers, sport scientists, data analysts, massage therapists, nutritionists, and athletic therapists. Recent trends toward more healthy and active lifestyles have led to an increased demand for skilled sport product services.

In addition to fitness- and health-related services for elite athletes and teams, the skilled services product form includes coaching and instructional services. For instance, tennis professionals who give lessons are providing a service to their students in order to enhance the sport performance levels of their students. This product form can also include the provision of legal services. For example, professional sport agents look after their athlete-clients' interests in negotiating with clubs, leagues, schools, and sponsors.

Finally, sport agents and sport marketing agencies provide services to athletes, coaches, and sport properties. For example, the William Morris Endeavor–International Management Group (WME-IMG), a firm that has its roots in the IMG agency created in the 1960s by the late Mark McCormack, provides a bundle of services to their clients, including Canadian tennis player Vasek Pospisil, who was one half of the 2014 Wimbledon champion doubles team (his partner was American Jack Sock). The WME-IMG agency may manage Pospisil's appearances at various events (sports and charities), sponsorship deals (National Bank), and media tours and offer financial and other services as well.

Media

Another sport product form is the sport-specific media form. Numerous all-sport television stations, radio stations, blogs, websites, newspapers, and magazines depend of the production of sport events, athletes, leagues, and teams to provide them with the information they need to produce their own sport product. The number of sport media products grew early in the 2000s and continues today. In Canada, the first sport-specific television channel was the Sports Network (TSN), which was launched in 1984. When it first aired, people questioned how TSN would fill 24 hours of each day with sports. However, despite initial doubters and a rocky start, the channel broke even in its third year and became profitable shortly thereafter.

More recently, the increasing number of specialty channels as well as direct competition from other all-sport networks (e.g., the Tennis Channel, the Golf Channel), Rogers Sportsnet, and the Score have made for a very competitive environment for TSN, which is now rivalled by Rogers Sportsnet as the leading sport network in Canada. League, club, network, and private websites offer both traditional television and web streaming, including a large amount of sport content, such as stories, stats, scores, interviews, news articles, and pundits' opinions.

Merchandise

Many items and types of items can be classified under the heading of merchandise, including sport, fitness, and recreation equipment; sport and fitness apparel; and collectibles and memorabilia. Sport, fitness, and recreation equipment as well as some of the sport and fitness apparel are then used in the production of the core sport product (a sport event), which further classifies them as a form of a sport product. For instance, a curling broom is produced in a factory and is a tangible product whose purpose is to be used in the production of a game of curling. The merchandise sport product form is also tied significantly to the idea that sport is an entity that inspires emotions and creates a deep sense of personal attachment by the fan to the sport, league, or team.

Sport Brands

The importance of branding is very evident in sport marketing. While many professional teams and sporting good products have put significant time and money into branding for many years, it is only in that past decade that most sport organizations in Canada—from individual athletes to national sport organizations, provincial sport organizations, and university athletic departments—have included branding as essential to their marketing plans. Shank and Lyberger (2015, p. 265) define branding as a "name, design, symbol, or any combination that a sports organization uses to help differentiate its products from the competition," with the aim to have a positive impact on the behaviours of the desired target markets. These positive impacts could include such objectives as an increase in attendance, more merchandise sales, or increased athlete recruiting opportunities. In most cases, an organization's brand involves a brand name, brand mark (logo), brand colours or style, and a trademark (for legal protection, to prevent competitors from copying it). The brand name is that which can be vocalized, such as the BC Lions, Callaway, or the Calgary Stampede. It is important for a brand name to conjure up a positive and memorable image in the consumers' mind. Conversely, a brand mark is the element of a brand that cannot be spoken (e.g., the flaming C of the Calgary Flames). Both should reflect the image the product is trying to sell. It is for this reason that many professional teams update their brands or have third jerseys. The third important branding concept is the trademark, which enables the sport property to license the mark for merchandise production and sales.

One of the most important elements of building a brand is creating an emotional attachment between the consumer and the product, which in turn can lead to fan loyalty and trust. Here, many sport products have an advantage since sport has the ability to create strong emotional ties between the fan and sport product forms like teams, leagues, and athletes. Both the team and its league are typically represented by a brand name and a brand mark. This means that in many cases, the positive attachment associated with the team can be transferred to the brand name or mark, which can have a positive impact on brand equity (Richelieu, 2018).

Brand Equity

Shank and Lyberger (2015) define brand equity in economic terms as "the difference in value between a branded product and its generic equivalent." The development of brand equity has the ability to provide numerous benefits for the sport product, including increasing the probability of brand choice (by consumers), consumer retention (e.g., season ticket holder renewal), profit margins, willingness to pay premium prices, marketing effectiveness, licensing opportunities, positive word of mouth, trust, social media traffic, reach, and potential for **brand extensions**. The ability of brand equity to increase licensing opportunities as well as the potential for brand extensions are two further benefits for the sport product with high brand equity.

Licensing

Licensing is a vital aspect of the sport product brand. Licensing is the process whereby the sport brand signs a contract with a manufacturer to use their brand on products, in return for a fee or a proportion of sales revenues. Licensing is seen everywhere one looks in Canada, with Montreal Canadiens or Toronto Maple Leafs logos on clothing, household items, flags, license plates, and more. While almost everything has been licensed, traditional sport products are apparel, collectibles, and sports equipment. Digitally licensed products, including video games, fantasy sports, and esports, are on the rise.

Licensing offers many benefits to both licensor and licensee. For the licensee, benefits include a positive association with a sport entity, greater brand awareness, and the ability to charge higher prices. For the licensor, it may allow reach into new markets and increase brand awareness. However, there can also be disadvantages for both parties. The licensee is taking a risk that an athlete or team might do something that would damage their brand. The licensor is running the risk of being associated with a product over which it has little control. For example, if the Canadian Football League signs a licensing agreement with a company that is going to produce footballs with the CFL brand mark on them, the league may not be able to ensure the quality of the finished product, and a poor product could negatively affect the CFL brand.

Brand Extensions

This chapter has noted a series of unique characteristics of the sport product. In particular, it makes more sense for marketers to focus on product extensions rather than the core product, because the latter is usually an athletic event that is not under the control of the marketer. The coach will decide on the team and the tactics and it is up to the players to provide the win, with the marketing professional having no say in on-field performance. While it is not always

possible for the marketer to have a say in the brand extensions either, that is more likely. A brand extension is defined as "a new product sold with the same brand name as a strong existing brand" (Solomon et al., 2018, p. 277). The key element in this definition is the use of an already established brand and the loan of a brand from one entity to another. Examples include a specialty cable pay channel owned and operated by a team (e.g., LeafsTV), mascots, cheerleaders, team publications, youth leagues, merchandise stores, and sport camps and clinics. The success of a brand extension depends on a variety of factors (see Apostolopoulou, 2002):

- The strength of the parent brand
- The perceived fit between the parent brand and the extension
- The promotional support (resources) offered by the sport organization to the extension
- The quality of the extension product
- The distribution strategy to get the extension product to the target market(s) of interest
- The management of the extension

Packaging Elements of the Sport Product

Throughout this chapter, we have discussed the idea of the sport product being made up of a collective group of product forms. This feature of the sport product makes it ideal for promotion as a package (i.e., a bundle of benefits). Since each element of the sport product is interrelated, it is easy to combine the elements to make a full entertainment, or participant, sport package. For instance, when fans go to the baseball park, they no longer expect just to sit, watch the game, and be entertained by what is happening on the field. They want entertainment at all times, especially during breaks in the game. They seek an overall experience, of which the game (or the core product) is only a part. Consequently, the package may get under way even before the game does. With a hotel on the premises, fans may arrive the night before to get an early start on their fan experience.

For those not staying in the hotel, there are still ways to start their night before the first pitch is thrown (e.g., restaurants at the venue). During the game, numerous products are being produced and consumed simultaneously. The video board shows replays, birthdays, and out-of-town highlights, and people often find they are watching the game on the big screen rather than on the field. There are also bands, cheerleaders, and mascots, which all create an atmosphere of excitement and involvement among the crowd so that they can feel engaged even during the most boring games. The concourse is filled with things to do and see: In addition to numerous concession stands and merchandise outlets, there are usually games for children, draws, and promotional offers for adults. All this leads to the creation of a total sport entertainment package or experience. In many cases, someone could go to a game and be entertained all night without ever actually watching the game.

Other elements of the sport product can also be packaged. Many gyms and training centres bring in skilled professionals to meet the needs of their clients all under one roof. For example, a gym may offer fitness training, massage therapy, nutrition counselling, athletic therapy, and sports psychology to its members, along with the standard fitness classes and exercise equipment. It may also have a juice bar and a tanning salon, just to add a little bit extra to the experience.

CHAPTER SUMMARY

This chapter discusses the well-developed marketing concept of a product as a bundle of attributes that satisfy a particular market need and then presents the first element of the sport marketing mix—the sport product. The special nature of the sport product is emphasized throughout the chapter, along with how it takes on one of the four product forms (tangible good, service, behaviour, idea). Examples include a running shoe (tangible good), coaching (service), antidoping (behaviour), and believing in sport participation as a solution to childhood obesity (idea). We introduce strategic elements of sport-product marketing, including the product life cycle, brands, licensing, and packaging, as well as the nine specific sport product forms—events, athletes, teams, leagues, clubs, facilities, skilled services, media, and merchandise.

TEST YOUR KNOWLEDGE

1. What must a marketer do before defining their sport product?
2. What is a sport product?
3. Is a sport product different from other products? Explain.
4. List the nine forms of sport products provided in the chapter and give an example of each.
5. Why is a skilled service a sport product?
6. What is the difference between merchandising and licensing?

KEY TERMS

athletes	facility	skilled services
brand	league	sport product
brand extension	media	team
club	merchandise	
event	packaging	

CASE STUDIES

Visit HK*Propel* for case studies organized by chapter.

CHAPTER 7

The Digital Sport Product

LEARNING OBJECTIVES

After studying this chapter, you will be able to do the following:

- Expand the concept of the sport product to a digital sport product
- Appreciate the digitization of products and services in the sport industry
- Become acquainted with the elements of digital product integration
- Provide direction on building and expanding sport products to be digital or hybrid
- Define the digital sport product life cycle

In chapter 6, we introduced the idea of the sport product, one of the four Ps of sport marketing. There, some of the key goods and services in the sport industry were presented, such as the core sport product (i.e., athletes, teams, leagues) and supportive product forms (i.e., merchandise and licensed apparel), leading to brands that develop equity and product extensions thereafter. But, as the sport product is comprised of a multitude of characteristics, we must not overlook the changes in the modern environment and the importance those elements may have for the strategic sport marketing process. For instance, there have been significant economic ups and downs since the 1980s that have had

an impact on sport organizations and their ability to offer sport products (Parent et al., 2018). Over that same period, much of what sport marketers learned and understood about the sport product was very much in **analog** form; sport products were viewed in much the same way as other products in the 20th century: in their physical, nonelectronically impacted form. Going to a large facility like BC Place in Vancouver did not, for the most part, include any electronic or digital aspects. A fan could physically walk up to the ticket box office, purchase that ticket with cash, have that ticket "stubbed" by a ticket taker at the appropriate facility gate, and consume the sport product

115

in person. On top of that, that fan could walk along the facility's concourse and purchase a host of affiliated sport products, such as team hats, jerseys, and foam fingers, all physical items to wear or show their support for the team. Now, two decades into the 21st century, this process has fundamentally changed. The COVID-19 pandemic only further accelerated this shift. While you will read more about technology and the effect it has had on sport organizations in chapter 16, in this chapter, you will learn more about the **digital sport product** as it relates to expanding sport-product offerings.

This chapter begins by looking at defining the digital sport product: Why are these products different from all others? It then examines several forms of digital sport products, including esports, over-the-top (OTT) services, **mobile apps**, wearables, and **extended reality** (XR), providing a general description of each form along with examples taken from Canadian sport. Given that product is the most important element of the marketing mix, it is vitally important for the modern sport marketing professional to understand the product in all its forms, including its digital form. They must appreciate the elements of sport as well as the engaging proposition that digital provides in its appeal to the modern consumer. This chapter outlines and highlights these aspects to provide that understanding.

EXECUTIVE PERSPECTIVE
NFL Canada's Digital Sport Products

DAVID THOMSON, Vice-President, Managing Director, NFL Canada

Keeping our fans at the centre of everything we do has been a hallmark of the National Football League since our inception over a hundred years ago. That focus has ensured that with each passing season, we are constantly challenging ourselves to explore, test, and bring to life innovative ways to help our fans stay close to their favourite clubs, players, and communities of fans around the world.

The rapid growth of global digitization, combined with the global footprint of the NFL, has helped accelerate our need to connect with our fans in new ways. Whether it's through our game-day broadcasts or new product innovation, meeting the needs of our evolving fan base has been critical to the long-term sustainability and financial health of the league. If you think about television, there has been an incredible amount of innovation and data technology developed by the league and our partners over the years to bring the excitement of the NFL into fans' homes each week. Recently, Next Gen Stats has started using real-time data captured on the field through RFID tags on players' uniforms, bringing to the fans new insights and analysis. For the viewer, the creation of the NFL RedZone all-in-one channel allows fans to watch scoring updates from up to eight games at a time in real time. NFL RedZone can be accessed by our fans through a variety of subscription-based and digital streaming services across all devices, which meet the needs of a constantly evolving fan base.

NFL RedZone is also a fan favourite and ideal companion for the millions of people every week that participate in NFL fantasy football leagues. Fantasy football has become an integral part way for fans to engage with and follow the NFL each season, as the owner, GM, and head coach of their own fantasy team. NFL Fantasy strongly appeals to our more avid fans, driving their passion throughout the season as they track their own performance and compete in their leagues. NFL Fantasy also has evolved digitally, as players can update and set their rosters weekly online or via the NFL Fantasy app on their mobile devices.

As fans also explore new ways to consume content and media around the world in a digital format, services such as NFL Game Pass are becoming important and provide complimentary ways for fans to follow the NFL each week. NFL Game Pass gives fans access to every single game each week, streamed live to their various digital devices. Whether through a direct NFL Game Pass subscription or through a digital service provider, NFL Game Pass is an emerging and dynamic way for fans across the world to follow the NFL.

Gaming has become another critical way of enabling our fans to immerse themselves in the NFL. Since its inception in 1989, the Electronic Arts (EA) Madden NFL Football franchise has become a global sensation, putting players truly in the game. As technology has evolved, so too has the interactivity of the EA Madden NFL Game. No longer are players limited to playing against the computer system or their friend sitting next to them; now they can go head to head with players around the world online. And we are thinking about gaming in the broadest sense, as reflected in recent collaborations with EPIC Games, the creators of the global phenomenon Fortnite. Fortnite players have been offered NFL uniform skins that can be applied to their in-game avatars. That's just another way to extend the reach and connection of the NFL with the broader gaming community. Creating new and innovative touchpoints for our fans in all these ways will help the NFL stay relevant in an ever-evolving sport landscape, across the world.

As managing director of National Football League Canada, David is accountable for the business aspects of the league in Canada. Throughout his career, David has had a passion to build some of the most iconic brands in Canada, including Clorox, Molson, Coca-Cola, and now the NFL. He continues to spearhead a number of initiatives to fuel the growth of the NFL and its fanbase in Canada. David worked at Coca-Cola for 15 years prior to joining NFL Canada and has a wide range of experience in marketing and development.

What Makes a Sport Product Digital?

By now, we know that sport is a product unlike any other or at least one with a series of special attributes, and that its properties of tangibility can represent both a challenge and opportunity (Shilbury et al., 2014). But what happens to the sport product when you throw the Internet and electronic capabilities into the mix? The answer is a new growth pathway for sport marketers to consider, as the breadth of sport products doubles to include both traditional (i.e., in-venue) and digital (e.g., web, social, digital) benefits, as well as hybrid benefits (e.g., a conference with both digital and traditional offerings) options. The COVID-19 global pandemic led to major advances in thinking concerning digital offerings, such as the Tokyo 2020 Olympic Games, which were delayed to 2021 with a drastically reduced traditional, in-person component.

Consider the example about the fan attending a live sporting event at BC Place. While the initial engagement was the fan physically purchasing a ticket from the box office, digital technology has advanced to mediate this interaction, allowing the fan to purchase the ticket at home on a computer or even conveniently with their mobile smartphone device. Along the same lines, that fan can also show the ticket's barcode on their smartphone to gain entry into the stadium. This example underscores one of the key distinguishing features of the digital sport product: using electronic, especially computerized, technology to enhance or complement consumption. The BC Place fan was going to consume the live game anyway, but digital technology facilitated the process, complementing their overall sport experience.

The role that digital sport products can play as mediators of consumption is another key feature. As Pegoraro (2013) noted, changing wants, needs, and habits of sport consumers have been met with changing digital processes and connections. Thus, as consumers have become more connected with one another, digital products have also been aligned to facilitate interactivity between fans and other sport stakeholders, such as athletes, teams, leagues, and sponsors (Naraine, 2019). The specific role of social media in sport marketing is further discussed in chapter 12, but it is important to recognize that digital sport products (such as social media) can enhance sport consumption, not just complement it. To understand this

EXECUTIVE PERSPECTIVE
Digital Products and the Canadian Olympic Committee

MARK NADOLNY, Canadian Olympic Committee, Product Manager, Digital and Data

The Digital Stadium

The Olympics is a 16-day event that takes place every two years, alternating between winter and summer editions. In an effort to extend the limited time Canada's best athletes have in the limelight, one of our major initial goals was to shift the focus to instead driving interest 365 days a year. Beginning with changing the way we referred to ourselves online from "The Canadian Olympic Team" to "Team Canada," we set out to tell our athletes' stories year-round and become a go-to source for Canadian sports content. Most pro sports teams have a physical stadium that acts as the home for their fanbase to watch their team compete and celebrate together. Given that each edition of the Olympic Games takes place in a different country and many of our fans will never attend in person, we saw an opportunity to leverage our digital channels as a virtual stadium. With a focus on creating compelling and insights-driven digital experiences, we at the Canadian Olympic Committee (COC) were able to rally fans year-round to Team Canada (Équipe Canada en français).

Reaching New Heights

Flip the calendar from 2018 to today and it's clear that we've come a long way. Some of our major highlights include:

- Increasing our annual web traffic by more than 20 times. During the PyeongChang 2018 Olympic Winter Games window, we saw over 21 million page views on our website (Olympic.ca in English and Olympique.ca in French).
- The fan-following on our primary social media channels increased exponentially and now includes a combined 2 million followers across Facebook, Twitter (in English and French), and Instagram. During PyeongChang 2018, we drove more social media interactions than any other National Olympic Committee.
- We established our digital fanclub (the Canadian Olympic Club, presented by Bell), where fans could harness their competitive nature by earning points and entering for a chance to win unique prizes. Since its creation ahead of the Sochi 2014 Olympic Winter Games, the club now features over 400,000 registered members.

Digital Products and Data

Over the years, my role on the digital team has shifted from creating content, to reporting on analytics, and to my current area of focus—leading the Digital Products and Data team. This is split into two parts:

1. Digital Products: Championing the highest standards across Olympic.ca, the Canadian Olympic Club, and all Team Canada's digital products, with a focus on quality control and user experience
2. Data and Analytics: Ensuring the greatest level of implementation for all data, analytics, and insights programs for all of Team Canada's digital properties

The Team Canada Mobile App

The next major product development in our digital evolution is a Team Canada mobile app. This new owned channel will provide our fans with a more personalized content experience, with recommended content based on selected favourite athletes and sports. Push notifications can let users know when their favourite athletes are competing and ensure that they never miss another Canadian Olympic medal moment. Geogated notifications (i.e., notifications only to those in certain countries, cities, or other geographic regions) and location-based triggers will allow fans to engage with us digitally as they move around in the real world. The app will truly bring the Team Canada experience right to our audience's fingertips in a way that mobile web simply can't. This new digital touchpoint will also provide an opportunity to expand on the value offered by joining the Canadian Olympic Club, presented by Bell. That will come in the form of improved sweepstakes, perks offered by Team Canada partners, as well as access to enhanced engagement activities such as interactive games, trivia, and augmented reality (AR) features. In addition to improving the way in which fans connect with Team Canada, the mobile app will also provide access to new data points related to audience demographics and behaviours. While maintaining a focus on ever-improving privacy, consent, and data governance practices, Team Canada will leverage enhanced tracking and measurement capabilities offered in a mobile app environment. These improved insights and audience segmentation capabilities will help us continue delivering the content that our fans want most, as well as allowing us to drive incremental value for Canadian athletes, sports, and Team Canada partners.

Reach for the Top

To stay relevant in the digital marketing world, you must always be learning, innovating, and evolving. Like our athletes, Team Canada will continue to improve our game until we rest firmly atop the digital marketing podium. Go, Canada, go!

MARK NADOLNY'S Olympic journey began a few months before the London 2012 Olympic Games, when he accepted a position at the Canadian Olympic Committee (COC). Having now been at the COC for over eight years, he was able to play a role in the organization's ambitious digital transformation. Vancouver 2010 lit a patriotic sports flame in Canadians, and following London 2012, it was clear that Canadians were no longer content with being participants; we expected to be on the podium. With the COC's online following at an all-time high, the decision was made to create a digital team, sitting within our Marketing department. Mark then moved from his initial placement within the brand team to help drive the growth of the COC's digital footprint.

---

point further, let us briefly discuss this in the context of social media. While on social media, a passive, casual sport fan may come across a post from an "influencer" or high-profile sport celebrity indicating that they will be giving away an authentic game-worn jersey on Twitter, the social media microblogging platform. The contest involves social media users finding digital clues on the influencer's website or other social feeds, thus stimulating interaction from die-hard fans and casual fans alike. This engagement piece, an entirely online endeavour, highlights the enhancement function that digital sport products, as mediators, can provide to sport marketers.

Besides complementing or enhancing the needs and desires of sport, fitness, or recreational consumers, the other distinctive feature of the digital sport product from the sport product generally is perhaps the most obvious one: the use of electronic, specifically computerized technology. The Internet, primarily, has been a driving force in allowing digital sport products to develop. Initially allowing businesses to develop online storefronts through web pages, the Internet allows fans to access schedules, events, and game times; buy merchandise; and purchase tickets. Putting aside the Internet's ability to facilitate connectivity, the advancements in modern computer technology have created standalone digital sport products. Smartphone devices like Apple's iPhone, Google's Pixel, and Samsung's Galaxy are all pedometers, heart-rate monitors, and calorie counters, on top of their telephone and text-messaging functions. However, these devices are not sport-specific or sport-focused. Consider other sport, fitness, and recreation-focused products like fish finders or wireless fitness-oriented earbuds, which exist without the need for the Internet because of computerized technologies such as global-positioning systems (GPS), Bluetooth wireless connectivity, and graphical user interfaces, which allow consumers to engage in their sport, fitness, and recreational pursuits even without Internet connectivity.

Enhancing or complementing sport, fitness, and recreation using electronics, especially computerized technology, is a key feature that distinguishes digital sport products from traditional sport products. Because of these digital features, consumers often have more choices for their sport consumption. Revisiting our BC Place example, the fan wanting to attend the game at BC Place can, more often than not, still purchase a ticket in person at the box office. Therefore, the presence of digital sport products provides more options to consumers in the market. However, over time, there is the potential for digital sport products to replace traditional, more physical sport products (and services), particularly when the former acts as a mediator or facilitator (such as the case of purchasing tickets using mobile devices).

Why Is the Digital Sport Product Special?

Because the consumer, in certain cases, has a choice between traditional and digital sport products, it is critical for sport marketers to recognize why they would opt for the latter. There are five specific qualities of the digital sport product that would cause a consumer to choose digital products over traditional analog sport products and services:

- Convenient
- Instantaneous
- Dynamic
- Interactive
- Gamified

Convenience

In the modern sport environment, convenience for the consumer is one of the most important characteristics that shapes whether or not a good or service is accepted and embraced. When analog products and services are complex (requiring significant effort or thought), difficult to locate, or require the consumer to travel long distances, the consumer might question whether they wish to consume that product—if they even know about it. For instance, an at-home workout apparatus might have significant advantages over purchasing a fitness gym's monthly membership, but the consumer may not want to spend the time and effort required to build the apparatus (and those do-it-yourself tasks can be tedious). On top of that, products might be difficult to find; some products might be local or regional, tucked out of sight for consumers living on the other side of the country. For example, a sports fan living in Nunavut might not be aware of the sport product offerings in major and small townships across the country. Likewise, the baseball fan living in Summerside, Prince Edward Island, may refrain from consuming Vancouver Canadians games given the length of travel required to attend a minor league baseball venue. Compounding these considerations is the factor of price; if a sport product is not affordable, that lessens its convenience for the consumer.

Digital sport products are much more convenient than analog sport products. While there is certainly an argument that some electronic equipment and computerized technology might be challenging to learn, there are many digital products that are **user-friendly** (i.e., they are easy to adopt and use for any user, even one not familiar with the product or the technology platform). Digital sport products are also quite easy to locate. In the current environment, digital products are widely advertised and maintain significant popularity in the market (mostly because they are new and "cool"), increasing the ease of access for potential consumers. Digital sport products also do not require significant travel. Of course, it is possible that a consumer will have to travel to a retail store to purchase certain products, but more often than not, consumers can purchase and consume their digital sport products completely in a digital environment. Imagine sitting in a living room browsing an **e-commerce** storefront like Amazon.ca and locating a **smartwatch** to track running habits (or making any purchase that occurs in a digital format). The consumer is able to purchase that smartwatch with a simple click and have the product shipped directly to their home in a day or two. In the case of that baseball fan from Summerside wanting to watch minor league baseball, instead of having to travel across the country to watch the minor league baseball game, the event can be streamed through an over-the-top (OTT) platform directly to the fan's smartphone, tablet, laptop, or television. *OTT* refers to those apps and streaming services that do not require a traditional cable or satellite subscription service and offer a variety of channels that often go unwatched. These examples highlight the convenience of the digital sport product: It's user-friendly, it's easily accessible, and it requires no intensive travel.

Instantaneous Access

The digital sport product is also known for its immediacy and speed. Consumers do not need to wait to access a website, tune in to a live-streamed sport event, or begin to play the latest NBA 2K title on their Xbox or Playstation. When the consumer wants to consume, they are not limited by time. This is not always the case with analog sport products. If a sports enthusiast wanted to go out and play a game of box lacrosse with some friends, they would need to collect their sticks and balls and their protective equipment, travel over to the arena at the designated time of the facility rental, and

then, after gearing up, go and play. While this example is about sport participation, the same applies to attending a sporting event (especially with friends or family members) or even going to a store to purchase a product. The tools and logistics required to set up an analog sport experience are time-consuming and require some additional planning and foresight. However, with digital products, consumption is immediate. If some friends are interested in passing time with a little competition, they can each log on via their readily available smartphones and access an online eight-ball pool game and start playing. No need to locate pool cues, commute to a pool hall, or rent a table. All those time-consuming activities are absent with digital sport products. Whenever the consumer wants to consume, they can.

Dynamic Selection

In addition to being instantaneous, digital sport products are also dynamic. With analog sport products, goods and service offerings are usually stagnant and do not change. When a consumer purchases a new, composite ice hockey stick from their local sporting goods store, that stick is just that: a stick. It does not change over time, especially in terms of refinement. Perhaps there might be an initial "break-in" period when the stick is flexed, and the athlete learns and gets a feel about its kick point, weight, and general usability. But fundamentally, that stick remains just a stick, and it's certainly not going to get lighter or stronger or evolve with use. In fact, that hockey stick is more likely to deteriorate over time, compelling the consumer to purchase a replacement analog sports product at some point. With the live sport event product, there may be incremental changes to gameplay and the fan experience, but more often than not, the product is fairly consistent. To keep with our ice hockey example, certainly the National Hockey League product has changed from its "dead puck" defensive trap style in the late 1990s and early 2000s to a higher goal-scoring era in the present, but fundamentally the game is the same. This is not the case with the digital sport product. Because of their inherent electronic and computerized technological

EXECUTIVE PERSPECTIVE
Media Representation of Athletes and Athletes' Presentation on Social Media

ALANNA HARMAN, Assistant Professor in the Kinesiology and Physical Education Department, Laurier University

The power of presentation and representation cannot be minimized. Recognizing the impact of who is represented and in what manner is critical to understanding the power of the media. The power of an image is best captured through our understanding of our "reptilian brain." This region of the brain helps govern our instinctual responses and also "processes visual stimuli without the use of the visual cortex. This is why we prefer images over words and experiences over explanations" (Morin, 2011, p. 134). Our instinctual preference for visual media is further supported by the exponential growth of social media platforms that allow us to share and connect through visual imagery (e.g., Instagram, SnapChat, TikTok). Traditional media outlets such as newspapers, magazines, and television were once the sole gatekeepers to what sports received coverage and what narratives were created about athletes. With the increasing adoption of social media by leagues, athletes, and consumers, many people believed social media could break the echo chamber of traditional media and could be the promised land for new stories and perspectives. But before considering the opportunities of social media it is important to understand how traditional media framed sport and athletes.

Traditional Media

When it comes to sports in the traditional media there appears to be a warm embrace, but only for a select few, namely, the major professional and college male sports; basketball, football, baseball (Cooky et al., 2015), and in Canada, presumably hockey as well. Even as women continue to participate in sport at higher rates and there are more professional leagues for female athletes, women's representation in traditional sport media appears to be lost in plain sight. With the limited coverage that female athletes receive there has been an identified shift from sexualizing athletes to a greater focus on motherhood (Cooky et al., 2015), neither of which celebrates the athletic feats of female athletes. The exclusion of women from sport media is not a new phenomenon, and even attempts to better highlight female athletes have been criticized for labelling female athletes as "other." For example, espnW, which was created to focus on the accomplishments of female athletes, in some measure reinforces the notion that women do not belong with the "real" sports and that's why they require their own channel. Why are women's sports not included in the ESPN umbrella? Adding the W suggests that women athletes are different and other than the real athletes, and therefore need their own space as they do not belong in the traditional sport sphere. While female athletes have faced a lack of representation, male athletes tend to be represented using preconstructed narratives that do not allow for individual nuance. "The most prevalent racial sport stereotype, Black brawn versus White intellect" (Deeb & Love, 2018, p. 98), has been found to be perpetuated in the media representation of athletes.

Social Media

As a result of the constrained portrayal of sports and athletes in traditional media outlets, there is optimism that social media will provide a space to break from these traditional representations, as athletes and leagues have complete control of their online self-presentation. As athletes and leagues increasingly utilize social media platforms to connect with fans, it is critical that they are careful they don't reinforce traditional stereotypes and instead strive to break the echo chamber that has dominated traditional media. As the use of social media continues to evolve from simply sharing content to becoming a broadcaster (e.g., NFL on Twitter), a critical review of how these platforms are managed is necessary. The algorithms that select which content makes it to our social media feeds are not perfect and can develop biases as a result of the criteria developed by humans to classify the data (Diakopoulos, 2014). So, while social media provides a new and exciting frontier for representation within sport, it should not be consumed without a critical eye. If social media is to truly embrace sport in all its variances, new narratives, voices, and stories need to be celebrated rather than revelling in the sensationalism of the same old sound bites.

ALANNA HARMAN is an assistant professor in the Kinesiology and Physical Education Department, Wilfrid Laurier University. Her multidisciplinary research platform is focused on answering questions that will enhance the sport environment, in particular for women and girls.

---

capabilities, the goods or event offering can radically change. Whether it is an esports title that has new maps, characters, and gameplay; a wearable with new features; or consumers now having access to different types of sport through their OTT platform, digital sport products are subjected to routine (software) updates. Because of this ever-changing nature, the consumer will remain intrigued with such enduring and seemingly long-lasting products.

Interactive

Digital sport products are also engaging and interactive for consumers. While there is an allure to the live sport product because the final result is never known, the same also applies in a digital setting. Fans consuming the sport product live through an OTT platform are also intrigued by the unknown. However, where those fans attending the live product at the venue are locked in to just that product, consumers of the digital sport product can jump back and forth between games on their OTT or even use a picture-in-picture mechanism to watch two games simultaneously. To do so, the consumer has to interact with the product. Using a remote accessory, fans can choose which sport product they are consuming digitally at any moment. Today, fans may also make this choice on their smartphone, tablets, or laptop computers, providing full mobile access. But the interactivity of the digital sport product does not end there. Other products require ongoing fan and consumer input to be consumed. A mobile sport app would require

consumers to click on different tabs and elements in order to access content, multimedia, and even games, and they may have to swipe or gesture to move from one content piece to another. Another example of the interactivity in the digital sport product is the inherent nature of social media platforms. Facebook, Instagram, Twitter, Snapchat, TikTok, and Twitch are just a few of the major names in the social space. They are all predicated on fans consuming content pieces driven by sport stakeholders such as athletes, teams, and leagues—key facets of the traditional sport product—and then interacting with those pieces by liking, sharing or retweeting, and commenting on that content. This is a very important distinction; whereas consumption of the analog sport product is very much a one-way process, digital sport products are often two-way, with an interaction between the sport entity and the consumer.

Gamified Products

The fifth defining feature of the digital sport product is that it can also be gamified. As analog sport products are not interactive in nature, they often keep fans and consumers away from the action. Fans are not directly involved in the production of the product, nor are they competing for any particular goal, prize, or notoriety. The digital sport product is different in this respect. Newer, technological sport products such as sports video games best exhibit this particular trait. Certainly, sport consumers can just play video games as a leisurely pursuit, but those titles are inherently competitive. In other words, the consumer is trying to win the game. This concept also exists in other digital sport products such as mobile apps. Often sports teams and leagues will embed "mini-games" or competitive activities to stimulate consumer engagement. For instance, the Toronto Raptors have been known to integrate mini-games sponsored by key partners into the team's mobile app. Some of those mini-games have included a 32-bit video-game character with a jetpack who flies through the air collecting coins and refuelling with jugs of milk, an engagement sponsored by the Dairy Farmers collective. This mini-game was not just for fun, either; fans with high scores could win Raptors tickets and jerseys just by playing. This idea of **gamification** is not new, but there has been a significant rise in taking regular, everyday tasks and keeping score, adding rules, and making them more competitive (Heere, 2018). By gamifying sport products, there is greater incentive for the consumer to choose those products over another. Part of the reason for that is the natural competition that encompasses sport. Consumers like sport because it tests human abilities with a standard set of rules and results in a winner. This competitive element, while not the primary driving force behind the digital sport product, is a key differentiator from the analog sport product, and it highlights why in the modern era, consumers may opt for a digitized product.

What Are the Two Types of Digital Sport Products?

There are two types of digital sport products: those that are discontinuous innovations and those that are dynamically continuous innovations (Shank & Lyberger, 2015). Discontinuous innovations are products and services that are completely new and require significant consumer learning. This category is most often associated with the digital sport product. Social media is one example of a discontinuous product because when it truly became a mainstream activity, around the late 2000s and early 2010s, it provided an opportunity for consumers to engage with sports brands in a

two-way process, something that had not been the norm before. On top of that, the consumer (and sport brands) then had to learn about the differences among social platforms because not all platforms are used for the same purpose (e.g., Facebook is for long-form content and Twitter is for short-form content). This process has taken some time, and sport organizations still struggle with balancing the needs of the consumer with the ability to constantly engage (Naraine & Parent, 2017). While that battle remains to this day, the key takeaway here is that a digital product can be so radical that it drastically changes behaviour.

However, there are also digital products that are not radically different from what currently exists in the marketplace and serve to provide incremental improvement to consumer purchase and usage habits because of the integration of technology. These products are known as dynamically continuous innovations. For instance, the smartwatch is not a radical innovation. People were wearing wristwatches as early as the 16th century, with quartz watches emerging in the mid-20th century. Even the shift from analog to digital watches, while seemingly impressive, is not radical because, at the end of the day, the function of the watch remains the same: It can tell time. However, as digital watches were increasingly accepted by the consumer, more features were added, such as a chronograph with stopwatch capabilities. But that did not stop this product from evolving. Today, the watch is now known as a smartwatch because it can be used as a calculator, camera, text messaging device, and cell phone. Even though the smartwatch hardly resembles the watches produced in the 16th century, it is an example of a dynamically continuous innovation because both iterations have the same function: They tell time. It is important that sport marketers understand this distinction as there might be an initial feeling that all digital sport products must be new, radical, and, therefore, discontinuous innovations.

Similar to the analog sport products discussed in chapter 6, digital sport products also experience a product life cycle (PLC), the important marketing concept described in detail in that chapter. Applying the PLC to the ever-increasing numbers of digital products in the sport industry is, thus, important to this chapter. To reiterate, sport products—both traditional and digital—go through an introductory stage, growth stage, maturation stage, and decline stage. However, it may be helpful for sport managers to understand some of the variations that digital sport products experience. We can refer to these as life cycle variants (LCVs). In particular, as shown in figure 7.1, there are four primary variants that impact digital sport products: slow adoption, rapid adoption, fads, and revitalized products (Shilbury et al., 2014).

Slow adoption follows the PLC but in a more subdued manner. Digital sport products that are too daunting for the marketplace are often susceptible to this type of LCV. In this variant, what occurs is acceptance and utilization of the product but over a much longer time horizon relative to other market products. Consumers are hesitant to embrace certain products, fearful of the time required to learn about the product, the ongoing technical competence required, or other factors such as price. The life cycle of products of this variant looks very similar to the natural PLC curve except for a key distinction: The curve is flatter and does not receive a large amount of market share even after some consumers understand its value.

Another variant of the digital sport product life cycle is known as rapid adoption. In direct opposition to the slow-adoption variant, products experiencing rapid adoption are embraced and utilized much quicker by consumers. In this variant, consumers who do not hesitate when new products arrive in the market are known as "first-movers." There is a significant advantage for those consumers (including sport organizations) who accept first-mover status because they use the product before other people, which allows them to become competent and even expert. There are many reasons why a digital sport product would experience such a rapid accession in the market. One of those reasons could be a high-profile and well-trusted company offering the product. Another reason could be the fact that it's a dynamic continuous innovation rather than a discontinuous product. In those situations, if the sport product is a small, incremental change but meets consumer demand, acceptance is likely to be high as soon as the product comes on the market.

A third digital sport product variant is the fad. Fads are products that experience a rapid rise and a steep decline in quick succession. To distinguish fads from rapid adoption, it is important to consider the time horizon. With rapid adoption, consumers embrace the digital sport product during its introductory stage and there is a quick ascent in its growth period, followed by a longer time period of maturation and decline. Conversely, fads not only have rapid ascent but their maturation period is almost nonexistent and their decline is equally as rapid as its growth. Fads are also linked to products that **go viral**; products that receive a lot of notoriety or attention from a celebrity consumer or social media campaign tend to experience the rapid ascent and quick decline that characterizes this LCV.

The fourth and final variant presented here is known as revitalization. In this variant of the PLC, digital sport products experience all four stages but in shorter intervals or periods and then experience them over again as time passes. This is often the case for products that consumers find an initial benefit or need for

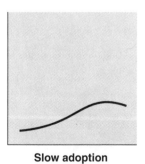 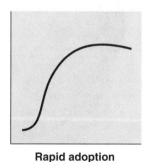 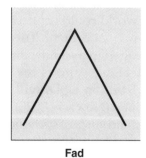 

Slow adoption   **Rapid adoption**   **Fad**   **Revitalization**

FIGURE 7.1 Digital sport-product life cycle variations.

but then lose interest in, only to return back to the product once time passes and the benefits of the product are reintroduced to the market. Nostalgia also plays an important role for this variant. Oftentimes products may be in their decline stage and remain dormant for several years and, in some cases, decades, before reentering the spotlight because consumers feel good about the product and remember the good times they had consuming it.

Understanding that there are different types of digital sport products (i.e., discontinuous and dynamically continuous) that experience the PLC differently (e.g., the four LCVs), it is important for sport marketers to get a sense of the current product offering in the market. Although there are many digital sport products in the modern era, progressive and innovative Canadian sport marketers should focus their attention on esports, OTT, mobile apps, wearables, and XR.

Esports

Esports (this is the shortened form for electronic sports) is the most representative digital sport product given that it encompasses many of the analog sport forms presented in chapter 6. Esports are organized video-game competitions, a concept that might be a confusing concept for consumers of analog sport products. However, esports are not a new phenomenon. Organized video-game competitions began as a niche activity in the 1980s and remained that way for some time (Funk et al., 2018). However, esports truly began to gain mainstream appeal in the 2010s with the rise of social media and broadband Internet access. Instead of just competing in esports matches, athletes could stream or display their match on their social feeds and fans from different parts of the world could connect to those feeds to engage with that content. This increased exposure has resulted in a significant popularity boost. In 2020, global esports revenues were more than 1.1 billion USD, with global audiences of 495 million (Newzoo, 2020). Those figures are staggering and surpass some of the analog sport products that have operations in Canada, such as Major League Soccer, the National Basketball Association, Major League Baseball, and the National Hockey League. But these massive numbers are not solely accountable to social media content and faster Internet speeds. The esports product is quite complex, and while it shares elements of the analog sport product, it has unique characteristics too. Figure 7.2 illustrates this complex environment.

Initially, the esports ecosystem begins with all forms of gaming, competitive and noncompetitive, across mobile devices, personal computers (PCs), and **consoles** (i.e., hardware devices made for video gaming, such as the PS5 and XBox). This would include those casual gamers or people who use video games to pass the time. Most esports games or "titles" exist with a computerized function so that an individual consumer can play solo. From there, play becomes a little more focused with amateur competitive gamers. Those consist of gamers who do not just want to play the game but also want to compete against friends, family, and other gamers in their city or province, across the country, or even internationally. This particular group is not small; it is very easy for consumers to jump online and compete against other consumers instead of simply playing against the device. These amateur competitions are a critical first step into the esports realm because they distinguish those who play for a purpose (i.e., to

FIGURE 7.2 The esports ecosystem.

win) versus those who simply play for fun. After competing against other amateurs, the next stage is streaming or using various esports channels to broadcast their gameplay. Thus, instead of just some amateurs competing without anyone knowing or watching, this involves competitions that are, in fact, streamed to a broader network of esports consumers. Similar to the analog sport product, viewers also tune in to this particular digital sport product because of the excitement of the unknown. Additionally, esports athletes utilize these channels to help get them noticed and scouted by gaining them more notoriety and attention. This culminates with the most focused part of the system, professional competitions, where there are professional esports athletes who train and compete for major prize purses around the world in events presented to audiences by **casters**. This process, illustrated by the concentric circles in figure 7.2, highlights how a casual video gamer can move through to become a professional esports athlete, much in the same way a youth athlete would work through an analog sport product system, get scouted, and work toward their professionalization. However, there are other key forms within this specific digital sport product that need to be further explored.

Tournaments

The esports tournament is core to this digital sport product form, akin to events for analog sport products. Tournaments encompass multiple aspects including the esports athletes themselves, teams, leagues, and publishers, as well as traditional entities such as merchandise and media (discussed in the previous chapter). There are a wide variety of esports tournaments held around the world including DreamHack, the Electronic Sports World Convention, and the World Cyber Games. These tournaments are multigenre and multititled, and they attract the top esports athletes. Table 7.1 lists some examples of the types of genres played at these tournaments. In reality, these esports tournaments function a lot like circuits series in tennis, golf, and auto racing. The events are usually held in different spots around the world, and the athletes, teams, media, and fans travel to the various locations if they wish to watch those competitions live and in person.

One of the most well-attended tournaments is the Intel Extreme Masters (IEM) events which routinely feature Canadian teams or athletes. IEM tournaments are known for their rowdy, rambunctious fans and elite competitions (Naraine & Wear, 2019). Besides the opportunity to connect in person with other esports fans, tournaments provide consumers with the ability to connect with technology providers and vendors, who often have displays at these events to demonstrate new products, services, and gaming titles, resulting in increased sales and purchase behaviours. Therefore, it can be an exhilarating feeling going to an esports tournament to watch the elite competition as well as to try and play games while attending. This is something completely different from the traditional sport product; imagine going to a baseball game and after the third inning, deciding to head to small area within the stadium and take some practice swings in a batting cage or play catch with a fellow fan. While that usually does not take place in the modern sport environment, it certainly does happen at esports tournaments.

Teams

Esports teams are also a collective product, comprising professional athletes, coaches, and trainers who work together to achieve successful performances. Esports teams build significant

TABLE 7.1   Examples of Esports Genres and Titles

Multiplayer Online Battle Arenas	First-Person Shooter	Fighting	Sport-Based
League of Legends	Counter-Strike: Global Offensive	Street Fighter	Madden NFL
Defence of the Ancients 2	Overwatch	Tekken	NBA 2K
Heroes of the Storm	Call of Duty	Super Smash Brothers	PGA Tour 2K
Smite	Halo	SoulCalibur	MLB The Show

brand value that is instantly recognizable by consumers. Some of the most well-known teams include Team Liquid, Fnatic, Cloud9, Astralis, and Ninjas in Pyjamas. Unlike traditional sports teams that play just one sport, like the Saskatchewan Roughriders only playing Canadian football, many esports teams field several squads across genres and titles. This maximizes the exposure of the team so that if a fan only likes one specific title, they will still be able to cheer for that team.

However, in Canada, many esports teams focus on one particular gaming title. For instance, the Vancouver Titans, Toronto Defiant, and Montreal Rebellion exclusively compete against other Overwatch teams. Then there's the Raptors Uprising GC (the abbreviated form of Gaming Club), the esports offshoot of the Toronto Raptors, who compete only in NBA 2K, the professional basketball simulation. Conversely, at the Canadian intercollegiate level, teams focus on multiple titles. Many universities and colleges offer esports teams as recreational or varsity clubs, spinning off their school's athletic logos with an esports theme. For instance, the Sheridan College esports team utilizes a computer-generated, stylized bear paw, a riff on the intercollegiate mascot, the Bruin. While the number of teams in the Canadian landscape is small relative to other countries, this is an area of growth, and future sport marketers need to be cognizant of these opportunities.

Leagues

While esports teams are made up of groups of athletes, leagues are made up of teams competing for championship notoriety and the prize purses and sponsorships that winning yields. Unlike tournaments, which are rotating, circuit-style events, leagues are enduring products, similar to those in traditional sport, which allow teams to compete over an extended period of time. Like their analog forms, esports leagues are also sellable brands that sell and offer merchandise using an official logo and name. Some of the major international leagues include the Overwatch League, ESL Pro League, League of Legends Pro League, and, possibly the most similar to the traditional North American sport leagues, Major League Gaming (MLG). In 2007,

MLG expanded into the Canadian market, with competitions hosted in Toronto. There is also the Ontario Esports League, whose goal is tap into the 7.6 million amateur competitive gamers in the province of Ontario. However, leagues, especially in Canada, are susceptible to expansion by new players. For instance, in the western provinces, SKL esports is the choice of competition for many athletes. Additionally, because of the many brands in the esports ecosystem—teams, game titles, and leagues—it is important for marketing professionals to identify what it is about their esports league that is a key connection point with consumers, whether it be the eliteness of the competition or camaraderie among athletes and teams.

Publishers

The fourth key stakeholder in the esports ecosystem is the publisher. This is a difficult aspect for many traditional sport marketers to understand. Whereas the analog sport product might be affected by an international or national federation that governs the rules and regulations about a sport, esports are not only subject to those same groups, but also the creators and designers of gaming titles. Indeed, the sport is the sport product, which they own. As an illustration, the Toronto Raptors might be impacted by the NBA and even FIBA, the global body governing basketball, but the game of basketball is just that—a game created by a Canadian, Dr James Naismith, in 1891. The Raptors and other Canadian basketball teams in the National Basketball League of Canada or the Canadian Elite Basketball League do not have to fear their sport product will undergo any significant changes or upgrades, like adding a four- or five-point shot, changing the size and angle of the backboard, or lengthening the court to the size of a Canadian football field. However, esports athletes and teams are subject to these experiences. Game publishers create their titles for sale to the mass marketplace, and it also so happens that competitive gamers become experts and elite at those titles. But over time, publishers can offer software updates to improve gameplay, add new features, or make a title more difficult for gamers. There is also the ability to create a completely new title. Electronic Arts (EA), one of the largest publicly traded sport video-game publishers, has an office in Burnaby, British Columbia, where employees work on the popular NHL and FIFA sports-based simulations. Each year the team at EA Burnaby helps to release a new edition of NHL and FIFA, which seek to build on the foundation built from the previous year. Another example is Ubisoft, a publisher who has a Canadian operation in Montreal. This Quebec-based publisher does not focus on sport-based titles, but instead opts for first-person shooters like Tom Clancy's Rainbow Six, adventure titles like Far Cry and Assassin's Creed, and fighting titles like For Honor.

The world of esports is a growing part of the sport industry that sport marketers need to recognize. Even during COVID-19, when most of sport was under pressure and lost revenues, esports was stable and growing, albeit slowly. Because of its local, national, and global reach, esports has the ability to be a very important platform for advertisers looking to connect with consumers. This is critical because esports consumers tend to skew younger and male, in the highly coveted 18-to-34 age group (Gough, 2020). So, for companies looking to partner with a sport entity to get in front of the younger audience who may also want their products and services, esports is a highly visible and valuable route.

Over-the-Top Networks and Channels

While esports is the digital sport product that most resembles its analog counterparts in terms of form and operation, there are other popular digital products and services that merit attention, including over-the-top (OTT) channels. Examples like CTV GO, Crave, and CBC Gem are all examples of OTT channels that stream those networks' content directly to the consumer via their smartphone, tablet, laptop, or, of course, their television. The rise of OTT in sport and other industries can be attributed, at least in part, to the significant popularity garnered by Netflix, the movie and television show streaming service.

Before sport OTT platforms became the norm, it was Netflix that began to change con-

sumer preferences. For home entertainment consumers, weekday evenings and weekends were spent visiting Blockbuster, the movie and video-game rental chain. The U.S.-based company had been successfully operating in Canada since 1990, and it did not appear that Blockbuster would be overthrown by any major competitor. In fact, Blockbuster Canada employed nearly 2,500 employees at its peak and existed for just over two decades before ceasing operations in 2011 (Berkow, 2011). So what would derail a seemingly untouchable business? The answer is, of course, Netflix and their OTT product. Instead of consumers having to go to a Blockbuster store and choose from a limited selection of movie titles, Netflix provided a large assortment of titles, easily accessible on multiple devices, and without the need to return a physical video tape or disc back to the store. Through Netflix's popularity, much of which continues to this day, as the brand has now expanded into other markets worldwide, as other businesses, including those in sport, have viewed OTT as a more direct, convenient way to connect to sport consumers.

In Canada, sport OTT platforms fall into two primary categories: traditional broadcasters and digital-focused broadcasters. Traditional Canadian sport broadcasters include TSN and Sportsnet. TSN, of which 80 percent is owned by Bell Media and 20 percent is owned by ESPN, the famed U.S. sports broadcaster, began offering its TSN Direct product free for traditional cable subscribers and for a charge for **cord-cutters** (i.e., individuals who have cancelled their cable subscriptions and instead purchased online streaming packages). As of June 2021, for a consumer without a current cable subscription, TSN Direct costs 7.99 CAD a day, 19.99 CAD a month, or 99.99 CAD for six months, providing flexibility to the consumer if they are seeking to watch just one or two days of programming. The other major sports broadcaster in our country, Sportsnet, also offers an OTT platform called Sportsnet NOW and an enhanced platform called Sportsnet NOW+. Similar to TSN Direct's offer to consumers, cord-cutters have several price options (as of June 2021) from which to choose: a monthly pass for $19.99 for Sportsnet NOW or $34.99 for Sportsnet NOW+, and a yearly pass which works out to $16.67 per month for Sportsnet NOW or $20.83 per month for Sportsnet NOW+. Sportsnet NOW+ also offers a seven-day package for $9.99. Sportsnet's pricing may be attributed to the more expansive sport coverage such as the Canadian national rights to the National Hockey League, as well as its rights to Major League Baseball games in Canada. Sportsnet offers multiple television feeds including Sportsnet Ontario, East, West, Pacific, 360, and World, while TSN maintains five channels, TSN1 through TSN5.

Beyond these two major players, there are other emerging broadcasters that can be accessed through traditional means, as well as OTT platforms such as beIN Canada, which currently owns the rights to La Liga global football (soccer) matches in Canada. Digital-focused OTT players cannot be accessed through traditional cable programs. One example of these types of OTT providers is DAZN (pronounced "Da Zone"). DAZN has been able to occupy a unique space in the OTT market, acquiring rights to stream key sports content in Canada including NFL Sunday Ticket, MLS, tennis, and global football (soccer) matches, such as European global football leagues (e.g., English Premiership). Additionally, DAZN is the official streaming service of the MLB Network. Other digital-focused broadcasters include social media giants Facebook and Twitter, as well as Amazon, the e-commerce company. Facebook has worked with the Toronto Blue Jays to stream a couple of games each season, while Twitter has agreements with Golf Canada and Tennis Canada. Amazon has utilized its Amazon Prime OTT application to stream certain Thursday night NFL games across Canada. For some of these players (e.g., DAZN), subscriptions are in the hundreds of thousands. This may not seem like a lot relative to the number of subscriptions of cable broadcasters, but each month more Canadians cancel their cable service and start streaming. For the 2018 FIFA World Cup, for instance, Canadians aged 16 to 64 flocked to the Web (18 percent), their smartphones (7 percent), and their tablets (7 percent) to stream matches using OTT services (Briggs & Verna, 2019). Therefore, sport marketers in Canada should not overlook the value of OTT as an important digital sport product. As teams and leagues seek innovative ways to connect to consumers, OTT is a viable option given the increasing number of cord-cutters in Canada.

Mobile Apps

One of the most important digital sport products in the modern era use the mobile application (mobile app for short). Mobile apps have transformed how consumers at home interact and also engage. Individuals have freedom to access software applications in different parts of their house or as they engage in other life activities such as driving, shopping, and, of course, leisurely pursuits like running, walking, biking, boating, or hiking. This is where the power of mobile apps truly shines. Certainly there are productivity mobile apps such as Microsoft Word and Adobe Reader that many sport marketing professionals utilize on a daily basis, but for consumers, the ability to have instantaneous engagement with brands or enhance their sport participation is more important.

Earlier, the example of the Toronto Raptors jetpack mini-game was presented as just one element of the team's mobile app. Fans can utilize the app to access scores, standings, highlights, and other tidbits of information, all from the convenience of their phone or tablet. Imagine a fan who is out shopping with their family and gets a sudden urge to check the schedule for the Raptors' game against one of their rivals, the Brooklyn Nets. Instead of having to rush home to use a desktop computer or try and fiddle around with their smartphone's browser, which could provide the information but at a smaller scale, which might be difficult to read and navigate, the fan can just tap the team's mobile app, which is perfectly optimized for viewing on a small screen and for the user experience. Voilà, an instantaneous connection between the team and the fan has been created. But what makes the mobile app even more important for sport marketers is what it can yield in terms of data and market research.

While sports teams and leagues do have information on their website analytics and, to a lesser extent, their social media analytics, mobile apps are an important anchor for digital sport market research. Thus, brands are able to track the number of downloads, time spent on apps, and which aspects of the app are being engaged more or less often and track the partnership activations like the dairy farmers' jetpack game for the Raptors. Fans are also able to use team mobile apps to store their tickets for games, adding convenience for the consumer instead of making them go to a box office and hang on to physical tickets that could be lost or stolen. In addition, brands often incentivize mobile app usage with loyalty programs and discounts for merchandise and food concessions at games, which enhances a consumer's usage.

Notably, mobile apps are not just limited to sports teams and leagues. Major sportswear brands like Nike and Under Armour use apps to mobilize digital communities of consumers to cheer one another on with their health and fitness goals, as well as provide opportunities for consumers to get early access to products and services. For example, Nike's SNKRS app serves as a digital catalogue for consumers to view past and upcoming shoe releases and even enter a lottery to be one of the first fans to purchase an upcoming design or colour combination that will likely sell out fast. This has been the experience of many consumers attempting to purchase limited-edition Jordan or Nike Air Max footwear, which has brought significant digital activity to the SNKRS app over the past few years. Other products, such as **fantasy sports** and sport gambling, have also found significant value in the mobile app environment. Major players like Yahoo! Fantasy Sports, DraftKings, and FanDuel have become more prominent, and much of that is largely due to their ability to have consumers engage and interact in real time via mobile apps. Whether that a fan forgot to set her fantasy team lineup for the day or found out there's been an injury to a star player and wants to put down a bet in favour of the opposition before the money line drastically changes, these types of apps reflect a shift as consumers desire their digital sport products to be more instantaneous and responsive to complex tasks. These examples are not an exhaustive list, but they demonstrate the variety and range of the current market offering; there are other important mobile apps that track steps, flights of stairs climbed, heart rate, and other biometric details and seamlessly integrate with another key digital sport product: wearables.

Wearables

Wearable technology presents another opportunity for sports brands to connect with fans. Wearables are devices that consumers wear close or near to the skin, which track, analyze, and transmit information and data. The most well-known wearables in the market are smartwatches, a dynamically continuous innovation. Smartwatches, which allow consumers to access text messages, e-mails, and phone calls, are also able to store sport event tickets, integrate mobile team and league apps, and track fitness activities. Popular smartwatch choices include the Apple Watch, Google's Fitbit, and Samsung Gear, though there are dozens of manufacturers who have created specific types of smartwatches for luxury, lifestyle, and fitness. What makes the smartwatch an important digital sport product is its integration with other consumer products like smartphones and tablets and digital-sport products like mobile apps, as well as the ability to create another ongoing touchpoint with the consumer. For example, consider a runner looking to train for an upcoming marathon. An important part of their training is making sure they are tracking their time splits per kilometre, as well as monitoring calories burned, heart rate, and elevation gains. These are all activities that can be tracked through these smartwatches and provided to the runner in real time.

While running might be the activity most associated with the smartwatch, these tools are now able to track swimming, cross-country skiing, biking, hiking, dog-walking, and yoga activities, which makes them ideal for triathlon athletes. However, in addition to tracking these information tidbits, the consumer can also share their statistics and recorded information with others in a digital community to gamify their training. Smartwatches are an important part of this digital sport community where consumers can track their personal records, as well as those of friends, family, and even competitive foes. They can share their training results with coaches and fellow runners as well. This explains why sport brands like Nike and Under Armour have developed mobile apps like the Nike+ app and MapMyRun to integrate into existing smartwatch ecosystems like the Apple Watch. In fact, both these sportswear companies have developed a digitally integrated process for consumers that begins with running shoes and smartwatches that both track data, send it to the appropriate mobile app, and maintain a constant stream of connectivity and engagement. In Canada, sport participation and physical activity advocate ParticipACTION has developed its own app, the ParticipACTION app, to support Canadians seeking to increase their participation in sport and physical activity.

Beyond smartwatches, wearables can also manifest in smart jewellery, smart clothing, and head-mounted displays. Smart jewellery is similar to smartwatches but includes things such as wristbands, anklets, and earrings. One particular company, Joule, which is based in Kitchener-Waterloo, creates earrings focused on the female consumer, tracking activity levels with a discreet wearable that is also fashionable. It is important to note that smart jewellery can also have sport-branding implications. One of the common trends in sports apparel is jewellery and accessories worn around the neck and wrist. This has been the case with the sport of baseball. Nearly a decade ago, the titanium ion jewellery company Phiten, based in California, developed a line of necklace and bracelet products using MLB licensed teams, including the Toronto Blue Jays, that claim to improve athlete healing and wellness via their proprietary technology. Given the technology that exists in other smart products like Joule, it may not be long before sport marketers benefit from the integration of tracking devices in team- and league-licensed products. Part of the reasoning behind prediction is that this is exactly what has happened with smart clothing. From suits to bikinis and sports bras and from arm sleeves to socks, there is an abundance of smart clothing on the market to service the digitally focused sport consumer (Sawh, 2018).

Major companies such as Google and Samsung have jumped on the wearables trend, prompting consumers to improve their yoga and running postures with alerts, mapping their walks with location-tracking features, and even paying for other goods through mobile payment sensors. Sports brands have also used clothing to enhance the consumer's experience, such as QR barcodes that lead to mobile apps and sites displaying supply-chain information and other exclusive content. Nike and Adidas are well known for these activities and integrate them into their professional team jerseys (e.g., NBA, MLB, MLS), and these activities will continue to spill over into new smart clothing for sport consumers. Finally, wearables can also manifest in head-mounted displays. These devices provide a display to the consumer's field of view, reducing the need to look at a smartwatch or wear other smart jewellery and smart clothing. Thus, a consumer might be running on a treadmill and want to have constant access to several biometric information without having to look down or interact with a product on their body. However, the true value of these display units is their ability to project extended reality, another important digital sport product.

Extended Reality

Extended reality (XR) is the umbrella term used to describe new, immersive technologies. While XR might seem like a foreign concept to some, it has grown to become an important consumer engagement tool, commonly used in other industries. Indeed, XR is a hundred-billion-dollar industry, which is poised to grow even higher as more businesses harness immersion to engage consumers (Marr, 2019). Therefore, the future sport marketer needs to know about this digital product and how it connects to sport.

There are three segments of XR that are most prevalent: **augmented reality** (AR), virtual reality (VR), and **mixed reality** (MR). There are several use cases of AR that many consumers are very familiar with. However, they may not be aware of the related technology applications. For instance, AR has been prominently featured in the "hawk-eye" system used for

EXECUTIVE PERSPECTIVE
ParticipACTION Launches a Digital Sport Product

ELIO ANTUNES, President and CEO, ParticipACTION

ParticipACTION is a Canadian not-for-profit legend, an organization known for its advocacy and role in promoting healthy lifestyles through physical activity and sport participation across the country. Following a successful period of activity from its launch in the 1970s until budget cuts shut it down in 2001, and now since its relaunch in 2007, ParticipACTION has a record of successful activities to get Canadians moving.

It's this longstanding history of success that brings me to the topic of this chapter. Specifically, I'd like to talk to you about our first major digital product, the ParticipACTION app. Launched in 2019, our evidence-informed app has built-in machine learning to provide a more tailored experience for its users and has content and applications that are grounded in and based on validated behaviour change theory. This grounding has help us program the app with a number of behaviour change techniques (BCTs) to help support and enact change in its users.

What is it? Quite simply, it's like any other app on your smartphone, but one that is specific to *your* health and physical activity goals. It is free to use and works on both Android and Apple (iOS) platforms. The app integrates and syncs with most of the common fitness tracker wearables and apps in the market. It offers incentivizes to reward users for improved and ongoing physical activity with weekly, monthly, and quarterly prizes based on the user's physical and app activity levels. In terms of content, the app includes articles and videos to inform and motivate a user to be more physically active. Importantly, it uses targeted custom motivational push notifications based on how users are tracking toward their weekly goal. Fortunately, based on evaluation metrics, we know these "nudges" are working as they are opened at a rate five times higher than industry averages. Badges are awarded to recognize physical activity achievements, such as two- and four-week streaks, survey completions, article consumption, completion of "Take 10" activities, app opens, and so on. Importantly, the app is designed to enable collaborative and competitive team-based challenges to drive accountability and connect family, friends, and coworkers in a fun virtual setting.

ELIO ANTUNES is the president and CEO of ParticipACTION, a national not-for-profit, charitable organization that helps Canadians sit less and move more. He is a visionary leader with expertise in marketing, creative development, government relations, partnership building, and sponsorship procurement. Elio has 30 years of experience in the physical activity sector. Prior to joining the organization, he was executive director of the Ontario Physical and Health Education Association (Ophea), where he was responsible for the steady growth and success of the organization over a 21-year period. In 1994, Elio founded Active Healthy Kids Canada, a national charitable organization focused on engaging children and youth in physical activity.

---

virtual-referee decision making in tennis, cricket, global football (soccer), badminton, and Australian-rules football (Joshi, 2019). While these on-field decisions are often lamented by fans, AR has drastically changed the outcomes of sport events and other games by reducing the human error in refereeing. Some would also say that cheating (i.e., paying off officials) may also have been reduced by this technology. AR has also been used to improve coaching and athlete training regiments by displaying virtual athletes with correct form and positioning and highlighting the real-life player who shows poor form or is out of position.

AR's impact is not just limited to the on-field sport product. Sport consumers watching sport on their television or **second screen** can be unknowingly subjected to AR features in the broadcast. The term *second screen* refers to the increasing occurrence of consumers being on more than one screen at the same time, with the television typically being the second screen (i.e., secondary focus), behind the user's phone, computer, or tablet. This specific technology can bring consumer attention to Canadian football receiver routes or open spacing in the penalty box in global football (soccer) and can even provide shot and skating speeds in hockey. Consider Connor McDavid, one of the fastest skaters in the NHL. For the average viewer, his speed can often be overshadowed by his excellent puck handling and scoring prowess. But with the capabilities of AR, broadcasters such as TSN and Sportsnet can provide a small overlay above McDavid's head with his real-time speed, emphasizing his abilities and captivating the consumer. These add-ons are not necessarily obtainable when consuming the live, analog sport product, but they can be provided to consumers through digital means during digital consumption of the sport product. Similarly, broadcasters can use AR to overlay sponsor logos and images on the playing surface, maximizing the amount of revenue they can generate through exposure through the sport product. Rogers Communications, a telecommunications giant and the owner of Sportsnet and the Toronto Blue Jays, has been using AR to maximize baseball broadcasts, overlaying sponsors near the first- and third-base coaching boxes, as well as using the "hitters' eye" in centre field. These are just a few examples of AR in sport. There are certainly more, including the ability for fans to add filters to selfies with team jerseys or to superimpose themselves into a team action shot. While AR has significant benefits for sport, VR changes the perspective for the consumer completely. Whereas AR uses the physical environment and adds digital pieces on top, VR creates an entirely new, digital world. In these VR settings, brands can create whole new environments where consumers can "play" and engage while enjoying a full 360-degree experience (Marr, 2019). For instance, a consumer could wear a head-mounted device like an Oculus Rift or HTC Vive and enter a virtual basketball arena and gesture to shoot virtual basketballs into a basket. This is also a great way for less popular sports (in Canada) like lacrosse, badminton, rugby, and archery to immerse consumers in an environment where they can try out their skills.

VR is also a great way to connect to younger audiences who appreciate imagination and creativity. With VR technology, children could play bowling on the moon, play mini-golf near dinosaurs, or go fishing on a pirate ship sailing the seas. The types of environments and activities where implementation is possible are endless with VR, and this flexibility is incredibly useful for sport marketers looking to connect and engage with consumers separate from the analog sport product. In Canada, AR and VR have grown exponentially because of their activation and consumer interest abilities: Companies currently spend more than 600 million CAD on these immersive technologies, and that number is set to be $8 billion in a few years' time (Kim et al., 2018).

Beyond AR and VR, the third type of extended reality is MR. MR involves both real-world settings, new virtual settings and objects, and the ability to alternate and mix both simultaneously. This is different than AR, which just overlays digital objects on top of physical environments, or VR, which is just an entirely simulated environment altogether. To date MR has not been extensively used in sport, but that does not mean it cannot be used in the future. One example of how MR could be used in sport is to design sports venues in a way that is more appealing to consumers. Sport executives could wear a special MR head-mounted device like a Microsoft Holo-Lens and look at their empty stadium concourse as a canvas on which they can digitally integrate seats, concessions stands, exits, stairs, and bathrooms and simulate what congestion would look like for a high-profile game in the playoffs. Thus, while MR is not widespread in its use currently, it has considerable future potential that can be harnessed to enhance the consumer experience.

CHAPTER SUMMARY

In this chapter, we discuss the emerging sport marketing concept of the digital sport product. While the digital sport product is an offshoot of one of the four Ps—the sport product—its uniqueness has been emphasized throughout this chapter. Digital sport products can be found throughout the sport industry, whether esports, OTT, mobile apps, wearables, or XR. We explain that the digital sport product, like the analog sport product, is subject to the PLC, and we specifically emphasize variants of the PLC to show how digital products can be rapidly adopted, slowly adopted, a fad, or subject to decline in interest followed by periods of revitalization once consumers find renewed value. In each element of the process, examples from the Canadian sport sector are provided to highlight how sport brands integrate new technologies to engage consumers. As sport marketing continues to be affected by new improvements in the digital space, it is important to stay on top of how these products can be harnessed to engage consumers and maximize revenue for sport organizations.

TEST YOUR KNOWLEDGE

1. What is a digital sport product?
2. What is the difference between a digital sport product and an analog sport product?
3. What devices would consumers use to access digital sport products?
4. List the four forms of life cycle variants for digital sport products provided in the chapter and give an example of each.
5. What is esports? Provide some examples of popular esports titles.
6. Who are the major OTT operators in Canada?
7. List four types of wearable products.
8. How has extended reality been used in the sport industry?

KEY TERMS

analog	e-commerce	mixed reality
augmented reality	esports	mobile apps
casters	extended reality	second screen
consoles	fantasy sports	smartwatches
cord-cutters	gamification	user-friendly
digital sport product	go viral	

CASE STUDIES

Visit HK*Propel* for case studies organized by chapter.

CHAPTER 8

Branding in Sport

LEARNING OBJECTIVES

After studying this chapter, you will be able to do the following:

- Appreciate the role of branding in sport
- Understand and apply the concept of brand equity in the sport settings
- Understand the role of brand management in sport
- Appreciate the consequences of strong brand equity

A **brand** is the most valuable intangible asset of an entity at a corporate, product, or individual level. The concept of brand has been studied widely across the marketing industry. Many marketing scholars suggest that a brand is a company's greatest asset and one that should be managed carefully. This is mainly because brands can be destroyed or damaged, just as easily as they can be built and expanded. In sport, the passion from customers is as high as in any industry on the planet, so capitalizing on this emotional attachment to a team, club, national team, sport, athlete, or league is a must for any successful sport marketing effort.

An effective **branding** strategy can foster an associative symbolism for the brand that can trigger trust and loyalty from fans and customers (Richelieu, 2004). If loyalty and trust are achieved, this, in turn, can help the sport organization generate additional revenues through the sale of a variety of goods and services (e.g., merchandising, media, sponsorship), both within and beyond the sports arena (Kunkel & Biscaia, 2020). Think of strong Canadian sport brands like Hockey Canada, the Toronto Raptors, or the Montreal Canadiens, or even global brands that have a strong presence in Canada, such as the Olympic brand, which has been identified as one of the most recognized brands in the nation (Séguin et al., 2008). The fans of these national and international sport properties live through these brands at many different levels in

137

their daily lives (e.g., wearing the jersey of their favourite player proudly, waving the Canadian flag, etc.) with unwavering loyalty. This has been seen in professional sport franchises (e.g., Edmonton Oilers, Winnipeg Jets) and Olympic sport organizations (e.g., Hockey Canada, Skate Canada, Rowing Canada).

A strong brand enables a sport organization to differentiate itself from its competitors and create close relationships with consumers (Watkins, 2014.). This is especially true in sports, where the connections between the brand and consumers usually happen in a highly charged emotional environment (Richelieu, 2004). A well-established brand is usually one that consumers are aware of and associate with trust, quality, and perceived value. Consider brands like the Olympics, Toronto Raptors, Montreal Canadiens, X-Games, and, for baby boom–generation skiers, the Crazy Canucks. Just mentioning their names invokes, in the minds of consumers, a certain image, a memory, associated attributes, and other related products and services. These values of a brand to a sport organization can outlast its equipment, its employees, and even its products. This chapter introduces the concept of a brand, clarifies branding, and discusses **brand equity** and how to manage it.

Branding and Sport

Today, a brand can be defined as the name, logo, or other outward symbol that distinguishes a product or service from others in its category. The seminal work of Aaker (1991) suggests that a brand points to the source of the product and also serves to protect the customer and the producer from competitors who attempt to provide products that appear to be identical. A brand's value comes from establishing a unique set of **brand associations** in the minds of customers that create positive **brand images**, form differentiation, build customer loyalty, and establish competitive superiority (Keller, 2003). (The latter is important, especially in light of ambush marketing, which we discuss in chapter 15.) In relation to sport

EXECUTIVE PERSPECTIVE
The Hockey Canada Brand—A Source of Revenue and Inspiration

SCOTT SMITH, President and CEO, Hockey Canada

Since the mid-1990s, Hockey Canada has adopted a brand strategy that has been very successful. In fact, our merchandising has gone from minimal levels in the early 1990s to more than $50 million in revenue (retail values) each year since the mid-2000s. Next to the NHL teams, our brand is the most valued sport property in Canada. One agency has estimated that Hockey Canada holds 15 percent of the sport-merchandising market in Canada.

How did it all begin? The mid-1990s was a time of great on-ice performance by our teams. The National Junior Men's Team won five World Championships in a row and our National Women's Team won all four Women's World Championships between 1990 and 1997. With the merger that created Hockey Canada in 1994, we decided to create a brand that would be instantly recognizable as hockey and Canada. Additionally, the senior management made the decision that all of Hockey Canada's teams would start playing in the same uniform with one look and one brand. This was a major change as up until then, all teams (e.g., men, women, sledge, junior, under-18) had played in their own distinct jerseys. After considerable discussion and deliberation, we requested proposals for a new brand design that would achieve this goal. Of the many proposals submitted, we selected three for further consideration. The suggestion determined to be best for Hockey Canada was a proposal that asked only for a small percentage of future merchandise sales. However, our negotiators, determining the brand would be a revenue-generating success, said no and offered a lump sum so that we would be free of any future takes on revenues. That turned out to be a very wise decision.

And how did it become a success? Clearly, we did not do it alone. We focused on activation and encouraging our sponsors and cosponsors to activate it with us. This means that our partners used our brand in their own communication programs, giving us great brand visibility and, in turn, maximizing the impact of the sponsorships. As our brand increased in value, so did the desire of our sponsors (and also nonsponsors) to link to our brand as well. Partners like Esso, Telus, Nike, Tim Hortons, and TSN have all leveraged their investments in Hockey Canada significantly, and their promotions of hockey in their marketing programs further build the Hockey Canada's brand. Brand building is a long-term process, and we have made a few changes along the way. For example, the humorous message in a series of television commercials of one of our partners during the 2002 Olympic Winter Games caused some negative consumer reaction toward the sponsors and our brand. In fact, after a few broadcasts of that commercial, complaints arrived from all over the country with people upset at the way the promotions were referring to the other nations. Later we decided that the presentation of our brand would always be in a positive light. This policy, I believe, has had an enormous effect on the continually increasing value of our brand and its presentation, and it is one we have now continued for nearly 20 years.

What else happened to develop our brand? First, the incredible growth in fan interest, media coverage, and youth participation in the women's game—a more than 10-fold increase since the mid-1990s—has really created a property of value with a significant following. Second, the steady and rapid growth of the World Junior Championships (for men) has really played into the growth of the brand, as this event emphasizes Canadian pride through introducing future top stars who are playing for their country prior to playing in the NHL. Third, the growth of the Women's World Championships, which we also host regularly, has showcased our best women athletes. Fourth, the inclusion of ice hockey on the program of the Olympic Games in 1998, where the top male and female players in the world were wearing our mark, was a tremendous step forward. And fifth, we have continued to expand and grow our social media channels, the women's game, and our Paralympic development.

If I had to summarize the key factors of our brand, I would say:

1. Canadian pride—a vital component of our success, a huge value to our brand, and important to the Canadian marketplace
2. Hockey success on the ice
3. Playing in a healthy, high-quality way

Today, we protect our brand with diligence. Our law firm in Calgary handles trademark protection. This entire process is known as brand protection, which basically means countering the ambush marketing that damages our brand equity. Here our efforts include a variety of activities designed to enhance the equity of our brand and to protect the interests of all our stakeholders, including working with external partners to proactively deal with the key issues of the day, such as ambush marketing and the antidoping movement.

What is next? We want to continue to our efforts to support Hockey Canada's core mandate, the game on the ice, and to follow the lead of great sport marketers like the NHL and NBA to make our brand international.

SCOTT SMITH joined Hockey Canada's head office in 1997 as the director, operations, and has been chief operating officer since 2007 and president and COO since 2017. He is responsible for the overall day-to-day operations of Hockey Canada.

brand, Gladden and Funk (2002) identified 16 different dimensions of brand associations that are classified into three main categories:

1. Product-related attributes (successful star player, head coach, management) and nonproduct-related attributes (logo design, stadium arena, product delivery, tradition)

2. Benefits (fan identification, peer group acceptance, escape, nostalgia, pride, and place)

3. Attitudes (importance, knowledge and affect)

Notwithstanding the period of the COVID-19 global pandemic, the sport industry has grown tremendously in this millennium. There are more spectators at events (onsite, television, and streaming), more media covering and specialization in sport, more jobs and internships, more sport merchandise being sold, and more sponsorship spending on sport. This has created a highly cluttered environment, which has made it extremely difficult for sport organizations to attract and maintain consumers' attention and, more importantly, loyalty. Sport organizations have to appeal to a variety of consumers, including spectators who observe sporting events (onsite or via television or streaming), participants who take part in sporting events, and sponsors who exchange money or product for the right to be associated with a sport. Sport brands exist in a dynamic ecosystem, particularly those of professional sports. In professional sport, for example, players, coaches, and managers are mobile and may change teams and teams may lose or win. Such instabilities impact fans' association with a team and imply the need for sport brands to evolve and respond to the dynamics of the ecosystem (Kunkel & Biscaia, 2020).

The need to break through the clutter has led many sport organizations to adapt business principles to manage their products. An increasingly popular business technique used by sporting bodies is branding, the process of creating a brand with an image that matches the image with which one or more target markets seek association. The purpose of branding

a product, such as an event, is to allow the organization to distinguish and differentiate itself from all others in the marketplace (Gladden & Funk, 2002). A brand can enable differentiation via product-related effects (i.e., perceived quality in consumers' minds), price-related factors (i.e., a stronger brand reduces the number of customers lost following a price increase), messaging effects (i.e., a strong brand results in better promotional effects), distribution channel factors (i.e., retailers are keen to include well-known brands on their shelves), or effects of the purchase decision process (i.e., strong brands are more likely selected when consumers scan the alterative choices available to them). For example, the Toronto Maple Leaf brand ("Leafs Nation") has a very rich history and is very well known across the country, as are the more recent (but 2019 NBA Champion) Toronto Raptors ("We the North" or "Jurassic Park" brands). Even though sport marketers have little control over the core product (i.e., the team's performance), its product extensions have been of high quality (e.g., the Scotiabank Arena, entertainment, promotions). This is reflected in the price of tickets, which, for the Maple Leafs, has traditionally been higher than for other NHL teams. Few tickets are available game in and game out. In addition, television ratings, Web traffic, social media following, merchandising sales, and sponsorship dollars have skyrocketed. These are all signs of a very strong brand.

Consumers know a brand first by its brand name, which can be one or more words (Winnipeg Blue Bombers), a logo or trademark (the Nike swoosh), or a sound representative of the brand name (the rally song or motto of a sport team, e.g., the "Let's Go Raptors" chant), since the brand can be communicated physically and emotionally. Often accompanying the brand name is a slogan, such as Nike's "Just Do It" or the NHL's "Hockey, the fastest game on earth." In selecting brand names, marketers must consider a number of important aspects or risks affecting the long-term viability of the brand and the equity it could generate. Brand name selection must recognize both the semantics and the phonetics of the name itself and how easy the name is to read, say, and memorize. A name that is difficult to pronounce may affect brand development. Further, cultural and linguistic differences must be accounted for, especially in a country like Canada, where a majority of the population of Quebec speaks French and there are large pockets of French-speaking Canadians in Ontario and the Maritime provinces, in particular New Brunswick, Canada's only officially bilingual province. Yes, a company interested in creating a brand must consider the language and cultural differences. Similarly, the marketer must be aware of differences when engaged in international business, where the brand name must function in different countries. A name with a negative meaning in another country can hinder the brand's performance there. Well-planned and selected brand names and slogans help build consumer brand awareness, increase the brand's perceived quality, create the associations consumers make with the brand, and support consumer loyalty. Further, when a brand is known to have a high level of awareness (such as the Raptors), it is often perceived as a quality product (including extensions and entertainment) with strong associations, a high level of loyalty (sold-out games, merchandise sales, ratings), and have high brand equity (Keller, 2003).

Building Brand Equity

Brand equity is the value of a brand that a consumer places on that brand (Watkins, 2014). Brand equity is built via a four-stage process (awareness, perceived quality, association, and loyalty) that will be described in detail in this chapter. The assets and liabilities linked to any brand differ from context to context and from brand to brand. As sport marketers strive to build equity in their brands, they need to benchmark their successes by measuring brand equity at different times. For example, measures before and after a marketing campaign, a new product launch, or a specified period of time (e.g., quarter, year) will reveal—controlling for external influences—the changes in brand equity.

An important concept for building brand equity is brand identity, which comprises all the unique or special associations that a brand possesses and that brand managers seek to create, maintain, or—in the case of a negative association—move away from. For instance, the Canadian Olympic Committee has marketed hard in recent years with its "Be Olympic" campaign launched around the 2018 Winter Olympic Games. This campaign is part

IN THE KNOW

The Value of a Running Shoe Brand

How much would you pay for this shoe? Let us assume that you are given $250.00 CND and told to buy any basketball shoe of your choice from the following selections. Before you pick one, you will be asked to say how much you would pay for each.

1. How much would you pay for a shoe with no logo on it? There is no brand. Give any price.
2. Now, you know that the same shoe is a Converse. How much would you pay for it?
3. This is the same shoe but the brand is now changed to Mizuno. How much would you pay for it?
4. This is the same shoe but now it is Adidas. Do you pay a different price, and if so, why? How much would you pay for this shoe now?
5. This is the same shoe, but now it is a Nike Air Jordan shoe. How much would you pay for this shoe? Would you pay more or less?

Brand is what people think about an offering. It is a mental image of an offering (e.g., one of the shoes in the previous example). Brand is the perception or impression that people have of an offering. If you offered different prices for each of the shoes, the difference in prices would be the brand equity for you as a consumer. That is what that brand means to you as a consumer—the brand equity.

of their goal to be a relevant brand year-round in Canada, not just during the two weeks of the Summer and Winter Olympic Games, which are each held once every four years and have an identity that is clearly tied to the athletes, their success, and Canada. Brand identity associations represent what a brand stands for and imply a promise to customers from the organization. The brand identity can help a brand express its benefits to its customers.

Brand-related activity and concepts have increased in importance in sport over time, especially in relation to professional team sports (e.g., Montreal Canadiens, Toronto Raptors) and major Olympic and Paralympic sport (e.g., Hockey Canada, Canadian Paralympic Committee). As a result, a number of academics have studied brand concepts in sport. Brand is one of the most valuable assets a sport entity possesses (Kunkel & Biscaia, 2020). Teams such as Manchester United (global football, or soccer), the Toronto Maple Leafs (hockey), or the Dallas Cowboys (football) trigger a memory, an image, a sense of belonging, certain attributes, and similar other connections among their fans. In this regard, Underwood and colleagues (2001) noted that sport teams build their brand partly through their history, rituals, fan experiences, and the stadium, where the oldest brands (e.g., the Toronto Maple Leafs) establish a rich relationship with fans. Watkins (2014) also reported that group experience, venue, and ritual have a significant impact on brand equity.

Step 1 of Building Equity: Brand Awareness

Building the first component of brand equity, brand awareness—the likelihood with which a brand name will be recalled or recognized—is introducing your potential markets to you and your products. For a local triathlon club

EXECUTIVE PERSPECTIVE
The NBA Brand in Canada—Growing Equity

LEAH MacNAB, Managing Director, National Basketball Association (NBA) Canada

The NBA brand is synonymous with competitive, fun, fast-paced action, as well as global stars and our collective support of social justice. With a fan-first approach offering compelling live-game viewing experiences, the foundation of our brand is built upon core values, including respect, teamwork and innovation.

The History

The NBA's first game was played in Toronto between the New York Knickerbockers and the Toronto Huskies at Maple Leaf Gardens in 1946. Despite the league's Canadian roots, the NBA didn't see a rise in national popularity until 1995 as the Toronto Raptors and the Vancouver Grizzlies were added as expansion teams. Team identities took shape, fans familiarized themselves with this new league, and one player in particular left an indelible impact—Vince Carter. His electrifying play, amazing dunks, and commitment to the community put Toronto on the basketball map. At the time, only a handful of Canadians made it to the NBA, but a few—including Steve Nash—became household names. Fast-forward to the beginning of the 2019-2020 season; 20 Canadians were on opening night rosters for NBA teams, and several of them cite Vince Carter as the inspiration for their dreams to play in the NBA.

The relocation of the Vancouver Grizzlies created an opportunity to work more closely with Maple Leaf Sports & Entertainment (MLSE), to position the Toronto Raptors as "Canada's team." Together, we broadcast all 82 regular season Raptors games nationally, and our partners TSN and Sportsnet air all NBA All-Star, Playoffs, and Finals games. This commitment to broadcasting basketball has no doubt impacted the huge increase in NBA fans from 1995 to present.

League Objectives

Our ultimate objective is to grow the number of NBA fans in the country while finding new ways to engage our core and casual fans. We produce new content for broadcast, NBA App, NBA.com, NBA Canada social media channels, and email on a daily basis. Every fan touchpoint is measured and analysed with the goal of better understanding our fan base and informing how we evolve content going forward.

In addition to content, we host NBA preseason games in markets outside of Toronto called NBA Canada Series presented by Bell. This enables us to bring fans into a live NBA atmosphere for an authentic game experience with friends and family. Through our marketing partners, we create unique fan activations including the NBA Playoff Bracket Challenge presented by Tangerine and sweepstakes offers on boxes of Post Cereals, increasing our brand's exposure to new audiences.

Finally, to sustain our growth, we look to youth as our next generation of fans. The Jr. NBA Youth Basketball program introduces the fundamentals of basketball to children across the country thanks to coaches and training provided by Canada Basketball. We believe basketball teaches important life and leadership lessons as well as provides a sense of belonging for youth. These instructions are delivered in age- and stage-appropriate play-based settings.

The future of the NBA in Canada has never been brighter. Canadian talent will continue to shine on a global stage, and we are confident this will inspire even more youth to engage with the game.

As managing director of NBA Canada, Leah MacNab is responsible for the development and growth of the league's business in Canada, including television and digital media, marketing and retail partnerships, licensing, special events, and basketball development. MacNab assumed the role in August 2019 following a record-setting year for NBA viewership, marketing partnerships, and merchandise sales in Canada.

In 2015, MacNab was promoted to NBA Canada's senior director of global marketing partnerships, leading new business, strategy, and relationship management for the league's marketing partners in Canada. She has played a significant role in the league's biggest events in the country—including NBA Canada Series presented by Bell—and created the annual NBA Canada Partner Summit, which began in 2018 and brings together the league's Canadian partners, executives, and industry thought-leaders. In 2018, MacNab received the Canadian Sports Business "5 to Watch" Award, recognizing her as one of the top sports executives in Canada under 40 years old.

MacNab sits on the Sponsorship Marketing Council Canada's Steering Committee for Education. She is passionate about critical and creative thinking, marketing, women's empowerment, and food. A graduate of the University of Toronto, MacNab also has a postgraduate marketing certificate from Ryerson University.

---

such as the Canadian Cross Training Club in Caledon, Ontario, brand awareness can refer to the familiarity of the residents of Caledon and surrounding areas with its name and logo. The club may be competing for attention against other triathlon clubs and clubs from other sports. Therefore, a high level of awareness can help it get noticed. The marketer of the club should pay close attention to the quality of services and programs it offers since quality is closely related to awareness. Consumers often assume that a familiar brand is probably reliable and of reasonable quality. For the Canadian Cross Training Club, quality can be measured in many ways, such as certification level of coaches in the club, number of athletes competing for the club, performance results at competition, quality and number of educational programs, social benefits of being a member, or quality and number of events organized. Awareness is important when measuring brand equity for a number of reasons (Ross, 2006). In particular,

- it increases the likelihood that a brand will be part of a consumer's consideration set,
- it can impact the purchase decision, and
- it influences the strength of brand associations.

Previous research indicates that the Olympic symbol, the five interlocking rings, is the most recognized symbol in the world. For instance, a study done by the International Olympic Committee (2006) in 11 countries found that the Olympic Games have over 94 percent recognition, ahead of the brand symbols of such multinational corporations as Shell, McDonald's, and Mercedes and such other well-known organization as the Red Cross and United Nations. Olympic brand work by Séguin and colleagues (2008) outlined a model for brand equity maximization for the Olympic Games based on the high levels of awareness globally.

By attaining a high level of awareness, a company can benefit from having something with which other associations can be attached. For example, the Montreal Canadiens hockey club has a long-standing reputation of success and a fan base that reaches far beyond Montreal; and this attracts the interest of corporate sponsors (e.g., Bell, Molson) that seek a similar reputation. Brand awareness creates liking or familiarity with the brand and signals the substance and commitment of the firm over a long period of time. This sends a message to consumers that the brand is worth considering (Christodoulides & de Chernatony, 2010).

Step 2 of Building Equity: Perceived Quality

The second component of brand equity, perceived quality is "the customer's perception of the overall quality or superiority of a product or service with respect to its intended purpose, relative to alternatives" (Aaker, 1991, p. x). Once a sufficient level of awareness is established (see

Step 1), the sport marketer focuses on building the quality of their brand, as consumers perceive it: The higher the perceived quality of one's brand, the more likely consumers are to build strong associations with it and become loyal customers. Perceived quality is measured by recall, a market research technique that also enables a marketer to discover if potential consumers remember the product and its associations. Note that perceived quality is a perception by customers, an intangible, overall feeling about a brand. Since perceived quality is linked to purchase decisions, it can make all elements of the marketing program more effective. Perceived quality can be increased by factors such as on-field performance, star athletes, positive stories, improved diversity, quality spectator experiences, and much more. To illustrate further, consumer perceptions of high quality can benefit a brand in many ways, including

- validating why a consumer should buy that product,
- articulating how the product differs from its competitors and substitutes,
- justifying a premium price,
- encouraging retailers to offer and promote the product, and
- supporting the building of brand extensions.

Step 3 of Building Equity: Brand Association and Brand Image

A brand association is any image that a consumer retains (in their memory banks) about a given brand (e.g., Michael Jordan and Nike). These associations can be categorized as experiential (what it feels like to use the product) and symbolic (benefits that satisfy underlying needs for social approval and personal expression) (Ross et al., 2006). For example, a local curling club can link a number of associations to its brand. Consumers may associate the club with fun, togetherness, friendship, community, competition, health, and more. The marketer who knows what consumers associate with the club can develop outreach programs, sales promotions, and communication strategies to reinforce those associations between the club and consumers.

Brand association is closely related to brand image. An association and an image both represent perceptions that may or may not reflect reality. Positioning is closely related to association and image concepts except that it implies a term of reference, the reference point (usually the competition). A well-positioned brand has a competitively attractive position supported by strong associations. A brand position does reflect how people perceive a brand; however, positioning can reflect how a firm is trying to be perceived. The underlying value of a brand name often is its set of associations—its meaning to people. In the case of sport, brand associations refer to the intangible attributes of a brand, the experiential and symbolic attributes offered by an athletic team, sport event, or league. It is critical that sport organizations/events begin to understand the attributes associated with their sports or events. Ultimately, some combination of tangible and intangible attributes creates a brand identity. In this regard, Richelieu and Pons (2009) noted that the brand associations that a sport entity's stakeholders (e.g., consumers, sponsors, media) make toward the entity are important in establishing brand equity. Clear and positive brand associations help consumers retrieve and retain information about the brand and lead to consumers differentiating and positioning that brand from its competitors.

Step 4 of Building Equity: Brand Loyalty

The brand loyalty of the customer base is often at the core of a brand's equity. Thus, if customers pay little attention to brand features, price, and convenience and to the brand name, it is unlikely that they would equate much equity in that brand. If, on the other hand, they continue to purchase the brand, even in the face of competitors with superior features, price, and convenience, substantial value exists in the brand and possibly its symbol and slogan. Brand loyalty is a widely accepted measure of the attachment a customer has to a brand. Many major brands track the loyalty of their customers regularly. Previous brand research has identified a number of ways that marketers can build the loyalty to their brand, including

- ensuring that the brand promise (i.e., what customers expect from the brand) lives up to expectations,
- being innovative (i.e., show customers that the brand is on the cutting edge),
- implementing marketing activities that are focused on loyalty into their programs, and
- having the marketing resources necessary to support loyalty programs.

Bauer and colleagues (2008) refer to sport brand loyalty as fan loyalty. According to the authors, repeat attendance is the most evident indicator of a person's behavioural attachment to a team and, thereby, fan loyalty. However, it does not tell the whole story about a fan loyalty, nor does the concept of psychological relatedness (i.e., the need to feel connected with others, or a sense of belonging). Hence, they argue that the concept of fan loyalty is better captured by including both behaviour and attitude criteria. Fans' attitudinal dimension is represented by the psychological commitment of a fan to a team, which in turn is defined as the emotional or psychological attachment to a brand.

Loyal customers are great assets to a brand. They are familiar with the brand, they have developed associations with it, and they know what to expect from it. For some firms, loyal customers provide opportunities to leverage as brand ambassadors or word of mouth to reach other potential customers. The ability to accomplish these outcomes stems from increased awareness and by reassuring potential customers that the brand is of high quality. For example, the Vancouver Canucks may be able to leverage their relationship with bloggers focused on the club to increase web traffic, social media chatter, and following on the club's social media platforms. Finally, having loyal customers provides a firm with time to respond to competitive threats or in times of crisis as the loyal customers are known stay with the firm's products longer than would disloyal customers (Bauer et al., 2008).

The Branding Process

In striving to achieve a unique brand that gives their organization an advantage over the competition, sport marketers follow a process to develop that brand. In his class work on brand equity, Aaker (1991) built a brand equity model to encourage brand loyalty based on the previously discussed steps of brand associations, building to perceived quality, and leading to brand awareness. Later, in regard to the equity of the team sport brand, Gladden and colleagues (1998) added the following requirements:

- A successful team and head coach
- An established organization with tradition and a brand
- A home market with sufficient media coverage

In sport, a number of outcomes of a branding process exist, including media exposure, merchandise sales, donations, sponsorship, game atmosphere, season ticket sales, single game-day ticket sales, suite sales, website traffic, and social media activity.

As we described in chapter 6, the inconsistent nature of the sport product makes it difficult for the sport marketer to plan around on-field success. Therefore, customer satisfaction must be emphasized as the main reinforcement tool for repeat purchasing. Since the sport product provides largely intangible benefits, determining the requirements for generating customer satisfaction is more difficult than in other areas of marketing where the outcomes are certain. This enhances the importance of loyal customers (fans) who are less affected by poor on-the-field performance and provides the assurance of a predictable level of ticket sales following a losing season. In the case of sport properties that attract the attention of ambush marketers, such as the Olympic Games, a strong brand can put the sport organization in a better position to protect its own brand and the brand of its sponsors (Séguin et al., 2008).

In putting a branding process in place, sport marketers need to develop the brand and understand their target markets. The secret to success in branding is creating a brand with an image that perfectly matches the image that the target markets seek association with. Figure 8.1

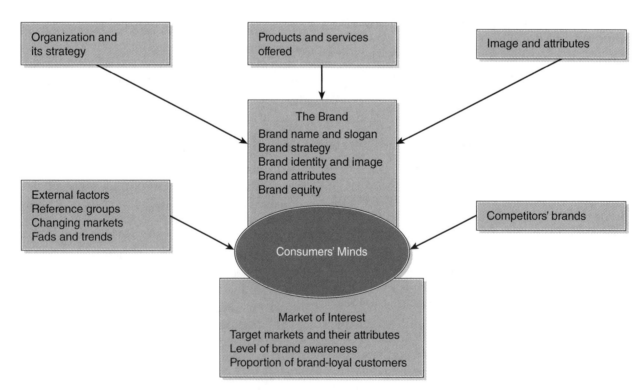

FIGURE 8.1 The branding process.

outlines the branding process and emphasizes how it takes place in the minds of consumers.

The importance of brands and their management has led to the common practice of the brand audit, which refers to an extensive review of an organization's brand, its attributes, its equity, its association, and its levels of awareness with important markets. This involves assessing each element of figure 8.1 to examine how all aspects of the organization relate to its brand. The objective is to identify any elements that do not support the brand and alter them so that they do. A good marketing manager always plans their marketing-related activities to align with their brand.

Real-Life Brand Management

Throughout this chapter, we have outlined many of the key aspects of branding theory and provided a diagram of the branding process, which clearly demonstrates how and where it works. But what does this mean and how does one use it?

Whether a marketer is working in a multinational organization or running their own local company, the noted branding concepts will enhance their success. As the identity by which their business will be known to consumers and other stakeholders, the brand is essential to its long-term survival. An organization benefits from managing its brand and not letting it develop on its own. It is the job of the marketer to do this and to strategize and implement all aspects of the brand, aligning all its attributes for maximum effectiveness and ensuring that all actions made by the organization do not compromise the brand.

EXECUTIVE PERSPECTIVE
Implementing a Brand Strategy: Tactics and Applications

VIJAY SETLUR, Sport Marketing Instructor, Schulich School of Business, York University

Branding Is Everything

I have heard this axiom often, but it really holds true in both business and life.

As an undergrad sport marketing instructor for more than 10 years, I cover an array of interesting topics in my class. One of them is **brand management**, for which I devote a session, along with the associated topics of athlete marketing and licensing and merchandising.

At the start of the session, I like to demonstrate the power of branding by drawing on my favourite analogy of three white tee-shirts in a retail store. Consumers would view the tee-shirts to be functionally similar in size, quality, colour, and type, but once a Nike, Adidas, and Puma mark are affixed to them their perception of the tee-shirts is drastically changed.

When asking students which one they would purchase, most typically say Nike since the various associations linked to the brand contribute to stronger purchase consideration than for the other brands, particularly in North America. That is the power of branding.

While differentiation is a key outcome of effective branding, it alone is insufficient to ensure optimal revenue generation and future business success, especially in the current hyper-competitive attention economy. Relevance is critical, and essential.

Amid the competing interests for our time, mindshare, and discretionary income, many companies realize the importance of maintaining the relevancy of their brand to as many consumers as possible. Relevance means something matters, and the more a brand is relevant, the better it can withstand competition.

> *continued*

> **Implementing a Brand Strategy: Tactics and Applications** > *continued*
>
> One strategic approach many sport properties are increasingly drawing on to implement brand strategy and achieve relevance in the marketplace is leveraging popular culture. Popular culture consists of various elements that impact the lives of consumers in some way. They include music, film and TV, fashion and beauty, food, comics, video gaming, and celebrity, as shown in figure 8.2.
>
> These elements represent platforms for brand building via storytelling, and thus new content, at a time when content is the top priority and distribution a close second. Media, both traditional and digital, plays a key role in amplifying content and heightening fan engagement.
>
> Equally important is the interconnectivity of the elements—each is connected to every other element—creating the potential for beneficial synergies. Your ability as marketers to effectively decipher these relationships and maximize them to a brand's advantage correlates with the potential to build brand equity and achieve strong business results.
>
> The NBA has long served as a leader in this area and a best-in-class example. In danger of ceasing operations in the early 1980s, the league embraced Black culture and its ties to hip-hop music, celebrity, video gaming, and most recently, fashion to become a thriving multibillion-dollar business viewed by many to be at the forefront of popular culture.
>
> The following is an overview of some of the key elements along with notable industry examples.
>
> - *TV and Film:* As key platforms for brand storytelling, TV and film are important for properties aiming to expand their brand internationally. Along with promotional marketing initiatives (e.g., Carolina Panthers and *Black Panther*) and cross-promotional partnerships (e.g., MLB and *Game of Thrones*), developing content for documentaries, films, and animated series has been a core focus. NASCAR has integrated stock car racing

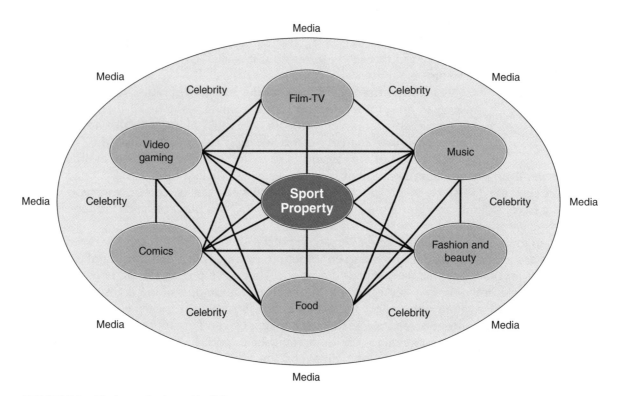

FIGURE 8.2 Platforms for brand building.

and its drivers in TV shows, cartoons, movies, awards events, and digital programs by pitching programming concepts, creating short-form content, and collaborating with partners such as the children's network Nickelodeon.

- *Music:* Properties have drawn on music extensively, creating ancillary programming (MLS Summer Beat), building partnerships (Apple Music and Bayern München), establishing a new and complementary line of business (Professional Bull Riders' record label), and developing merchandising programs (Minnesota Twins and Prince), all intended to cultivate an all-encompassing entertainment experience for fans. The NHL has made music the crux of a larger content strategy to grow the league and sport of hockey by creating Spotify playlists for use in league content and staging outdoor concerts ahead of marquee games featuring headline artists.

- *Fashion and Beauty:* Fashion has extended well beyond licensed apparel as properties have developed fashion programming (the NBA All-Star Game Fashion Show), created partnerships (MLB and Gucci), and rolled out fashion-conscious apparel lines (NFL's women's line).

  Paris Saint-Germain of France's Ligue 1 capitalized on its location in one of the world's fashion centres to collaborate with Jordan Brand, develop a merchandise line with the rock band the Rolling Stones, partner with various product manufacturers, and be featured in Paris Fashion Week, resulting in its successful positioning as a global lifestyle brand.

- *Video Gaming:* EA Sports's *Madden* has become a pop culture phenomenon, propelling consumer interest in the NFL. Likewise, the global popularity of EA Sports' *FIFA* title has built consumer affinity for soccer, helping raise the sport's popularity in North America. As esports continues its ascent, driven by the rise in video gaming, many properties are aiming to use eSports to build their brand among younger consumers by signing players (Manchester City), buying teams (Philadelphia 76ers), and staging competitions (NBA 2K League).

- *Food:* Driven by the explosion of foodie culture, properties are incorporating food programming into events (Taste of the NFL), organizing culinary-specific events (MLB Food Fest), and creating new hospitality concepts (LaLiga TwentyNine's), resulting in an elevated fan experience.

As these examples demonstrate, leveraging popular culture enables sport properties to reach new target consumer markets, enhance the gameday experience, grow fan engagement and . . . attain relevance. The combined effect of these results is stronger brand equity and, ultimately, greater revenue generation.

VIJAY SETLUR has been teaching sport marketing and tourism marketing at Schulich School of Business–York University since 2009 and working with Concacaf since 2018. Aside from teaching, Vijay plans career-centric sport industry events at Schulich, including Canada's only annual university-based Sports, Media and Entertainment Career Fair, which he founded in 2015. In addition to his academic work, Vijay has worked professionally in the industry for sport properties, as well as a product company and a marketing agency.

CHAPTER SUMMARY

Sport marketers pay attention to the role of brands in building successful sport organizations/teams. The goal of brand building is to create brand equity: a high level of awareness, perceived quality, strong brand association, and loyalty for your product. This can be achieved through long-term investment. To develop brand equity, a brand must be consistent and coherent over time. The outcome of brand equity can benefit a sport organization with a high level of support from the community, increase in sponsorship dollars, higher attendance at events, strong media following, strong television ratings, or additional revenue from merchandise programs.

TEST YOUR KNOWLEDGE

1. Define brand.
2. What constitutes a strong brand?
3. Why is brand management important to a sport organization? A sport team?
4. What are the four key elements of brand equity?
5. What are the consequences of brand equity for a sport team?

KEY TERMS

brand	brand equity	branding
brand association	brand image	brand management

CASE STUDIES

Visit HK*Propel* for case studies organized by chapter.

CHAPTER 9

Pricing in Sport Marketing

LEARNING OBJECTIVES

After studying this chapter, you will be able to do the following:

- Understand the importance of price for a product and identify price-setting strategies
- Understand the importance of value in setting a price
- Identify the steps in setting the price for a product
- Recognize key issues that can affect pricing in sports

Following the trade of a star player on their team, a fan may ask rhetorically, "You traded my favourite player, so why should I buy a ticket?" Although such a question may seem mundane at first, it points to price. Yes, pricing is actually fascinating, affected by many factors and a very powerful strategic tool of business. Some even call price a marketer's best friend. It is the one strategic element that can be changed immediately (or within a few minutes) to move product (i.e., encourage immediate sales). The economic concept of **supply** and **demand** explains how this works: If a team is struggling to attract fans, its management can lower the price of tickets immediately to increase attendance. Generally speaking, the price a consumer is willing to pay for a particular offering is tightly linked to the supply available. For instance, if the demand for a Montreal Canadiens playoff ticket includes 200,000 people willing to pay the list price (i.e., demand) but a supply of only 20,000 tickets is available, the price can and will go up. Although profitability is a challenge, the immediate effect of the action is clear: product will sell. Not one of the other four Ps is able to achieve this kind of immediate return.

This chapter looks at the different aspects of pricing in sports marketing. It provides the basic theory and concepts of pricing and applies them in the sport context. It shows how the issue of pricing is not simple but rather calls

151

on concepts from marketing, economics, management accounting, and business strategy.

Price: What Is It?

Price takes many forms. Some people pay tuition to attend school or rent to have a place to live. Others pay a fare to ride a bus or a toll to drive across a bridge. Anyone with an overdue credit card bill pays interest. Firms pay lawyers a retainer to have them at the ready, salaries to their managers, commissions to their salespeople, and wages to their staff. Each form of price differs in its application and is affected by different factors. But pricing is strategy, as the following example illustrates. Following continued financial problems, a local high-school basketball team recently repriced its tickets to improve attendance at their games. All tickets used to cost $5 but now there is a more elaborate pricing scheme in place: Adults pay $9, students pay $4 in advance or $7 at the door, seniors pay $5, and groups of eight or more pay $3 per student or senior and $5 per adult. Will this make a difference? The answer is yes. The team has taken a marketing approach to pricing and sought to understand the needs of each target group. The adults are typically parents of the players. What parent is not going to come to their child's game even if it costs a few dollars more? Students are fickle and often change their plans at the last minute, so the upfront pricing scheme is appropriate. Seniors (either grandparents of the players or interested local boosters) are a growing market for the team but one that is price sensitive. Group pricing also makes sense as it encourages groups of students to find a few more friends to come to lower their price or may bring the entire family of a player to a game.

Defining Price

Merriam-Webster's Dictionary (n.d.) defines price as the amount of money or goods for which a thing is bought or sold. It is determined by not only what a firm chooses to charge for the item but also what a consumer is willing to pay for it. The actual price is based on several factors. Consumers are introduced to price early in life, which establishes references in their minds of how various products should be priced. This price reference point permits or limits consumption patterns and can affect social standing. For some people, price can even become part of a sport or hobby, as shopping for the best price becomes an important activity for them.

Price is one of the four main components of the marketing mix—the four Ps. However, understanding how a price is determined is not easy. To explain, this chapter examines several important pricing factors including value, the pricing window, ethics of pricing, and **break-even points**. Nagle and Müller (2018) note that there is wide agreement in industry that pricing plays a different role in marketing than product, promotion, or place (the other three Ps) and note that pricing, therefore, has a different purpose than the other elements and that a pricing strategy should be constructed to capture the value created by the other three Ps.

The Pricing Window

Many marketers use the idea of the pricing window when setting price. At the bottom of the window is the lowest price possible (that the marketer can set), which is determined by the total **costs** or the minimum return demanded by investors. At the top of the window is the maximum price possible, which would be defined (theoretically) as the price that could be charged where one unit of the product would still be sold. Within these boundaries is the window in which pricing can be set.

Price and the Four Ps

To build a strategy, marketers use the four Ps to target their product to a certain segment of the population by properly combining these elements. For price, a marketer must consider and establish what the target group is able and willing to pay to receive the product. Thus, to determine the price, the marketer must consider all the decisions that precede offering the product, such as the costs of manufacturing, the customer's first reaction to the price, the perceived value of the product, any additional costs involved in the purchase by the customer, and finally the **discounts** and **allowances** offered by the seller. The total impact of these factors allows the marketer to determine a price that will meet both the customers' needs and the company's need to cover its expenses and—ideally—make a profit.

Price provides firms with different strategy options to present their product to consumers. For instance, the particular pricing strategy and actual price for their products will be determined by whether they want to introduce a new product, maintain market share, or become the market leader. There are a number of accepted pricing strategies that marketers use regularly, as listed here.

- *Cost-oriented price setting* (cost-plus pricing) involves calculating the estimated costs (variable and fixed) and adding a markup suitable for the firm to achieve a profit. Example: It costs Canadian Tire $35.50 (fixed plus **variable costs**) per Sidney Crosby hockey stick to get each stick on the rack ready for sale. To obtain a 10 percent margin, the sticks are retailed for $39.05 (cost plus 10 percent).

- *Experience curve price setting* is a variation of the cost-oriented price setting that involves adding future average costs to the calculation. It assumes that future costs will decrease due to efficiency and volume. Example: ABC Inc., a manufacturer of tennis balls, has forecasted that its future cost to manufacture each ball will go from 11.5 cents today to 4.5 cents in five years' time. Therefore, it has established a price of 9 cents per ball to attract business today, enable price stability for the medium term, and generate profits in the short term.

- *Target-return price setting* is another variation of cost-oriented pricing, in which the markup is a specific percentage return or dollar amount. Example: Canadian Tire has reconsidered its cost-plus–10 percent strategy and has set a (strategic) target-return price of $39.99 per stick, which results in approximately a 13 percent margin.

- *Leader and bait price setting* (loss leader pricing) involves retailers setting their price for a particular item very low to attract consumers into the store, where they will be encouraged to purchase additional products at regular prices.

Example: A new driving range opens its doors in St. John's, Newfoundland. To encourage people to try the range, it offers the first bucket of balls free of charge, with additional buckets costing $2.50 each.

- *Psychological price setting* involves setting the price of items at specific points that appeal to specific consumers to encourage higher-volume purchases. Example: A Junior C Hockey team in northern British Columbia offers tickets at various price points to appeal to certain markets: adults, $19; students, $12; seniors, $10; children under 5, free; children ages 6 to 12, $5, and ages 12-17, $10; and groups of eight or more, $9 each.

- *Odd-even price setting* involves retailers using a particular number to end their prices to give the impression of lower prices. Example: Wal-Mart often prices items at $18.99 or $19.97 rather than $19.00 or $20.00.

- *Price lining* sets the price of all products at a series of specific prices. Example: Nike prices products in its line of running shoes from about $50 to about $250, based on various factors.

- *Demand-backward price setting* establishes the final price of the product and working backwards to determine the amount available for markup and cost for a particular item. Example: NB Inc., a start-up sport marketing consultancy in Saskatoon, has established a business offering full marketing plans for sport events priced at $5,000. The organization works backwards from there to determine expense line items.

- *Prestige price setting* involves retailers setting a higher-than-average price to give the impression of superior quality and class. It is interesting that if the price of the product goes below an acceptable point, often demand from consumers will decrease. Example: During the 2019 Stanley Cup playoffs, the Toronto Maple Leafs increased their ticket prices significantly over the regular season to reflect the prestige of the games. A second example: Red Bull, the well-known energy drink, is typically priced 50 percent higher than its competitors and often sold in small quantities, signalling a prestige product.

- *Full-line price setting* is used when many different models of one type of product must be priced to indicate the added values and features of each item. Example: Calloway offers a line of golf balls with an escalating price based on their quality, features, flight, and durability.

• *Complementary product price setting* involves adjusting the price of items that are used together since future sales of a complementary item will increase profits. Example: Ink-jet printers are inexpensive; replacement ink cartridges are not. Thus, a consumer may be enticed to purchase the inexpensive printer (often the manufacturer takes a loss) while later paying a premium for ink cartridges whereby the manufacturer recoups its losses and accumulates profit. Sport examples of this approach are rare.

• *Product-bundling price setting* involves selling a group of items or services for one price that is lower than the sum of the individual prices. Example: The Montreal Canadiens offer fans flex-packs of tickets for multiple games at a discount from the regular prices of tickets purchased individually.

EXPERT PERSPECTIVE

Price/Cost of Sport Participation

MIKE ALCORN, Researcher, International Institute for Sport Business and Leadership

While there have been numerous studies over the years examining the various factors that influence sport participation, few studies have focused on understanding the many contributors to the monetary cost that an individual must incur in order to participate. In Canada, it is widely accepted that almost all amateur sport involves a pay-to-play model, meaning that in many cases the participant is required to spend an increased amount of money to participate at a higher level. As a former collegiate athlete, and more recently as a coach, this pay-to-play model became abundantly clear over my time in sport, and similar to many of my peers at the time, the dollars I would need to spend to further my development as both an athlete and a coach encroached the territory of becoming a barrier to my participation. This lived experience, in addition to conversations with participants of numerous other sports, is what led to my research on understanding what factors contribute to the overall cost of participating in amateur sport in Canada.

Understanding Price versus Cost

Anyone who has ever taken part in amateur sport would be aware that in order to participate, they are required to pay a fee to their sport club, team, or organization. While this registration fee is often viewed as the most significant expense required to participate (Coalter, 2004), there are numerous additional costs that are often overlooked when making the decision to partake in sport. This is in essence the difference between "price" and "cost." An easy analogy to think of this difference would be the money you would need to pay to attend a sports event. The fee that everyone would be familiar with would be the price of the ticket (registration fee); however, there would be numerous additional costs associated with attending the event, such as gas money to drive to the event, the hotdog and drink you buy from vendors before the event, or the hotel you stay at after the event. When considered all together, attending the sport event comes at a much larger price tag than the ticket price, and it is the same when participating in amateur sport. In addition to the registration fee, individuals are often required to pay costs associated with equipment, travel, and medical and nutrition costs in order to get the full sport-participation experience.

Significant Drivers of Sport Cost

In order to identify and understand the many factors that contribute to the financial cost of participating in sport, I engaged participants of many of Canada's sport organizations, ranging from recreational members to upper management of national sport organizations (NSOs). From these conversations and interviews, coupled with diving into the literature on the cost of sport, I put together a framework of the financial cost of participating in sport, breaking down the numerous financial components into primary and secondary drivers of cost. Primary drivers of the financial cost incurred by the participant—those mentioned consistently and emphatically across sports—included registration fees, equipment, travel, and facility costs. In general, registration fees often include costs associated with equipment and facilities (and occasionally travel) incurred by the sport club, which are then passed along to the participant in order to cover the cost of providing the sport service or program (Young et al., 2010). Secondary drivers of cost included factors such as staff, human resources, and medical, and nutrition costs. The inclusion of these financial costs were mentioned less often than the primary drivers but were identified as having the potential to be significant costs under certain circumstances. For example, in many cases it is unlikely that an athlete would require sport-related medical care, but in the event of a severe injury the financial costs of the injury have the potential to be significant. Additionally, not every sport participant has regular access to sport-specific staff (e.g., sports psychologists or private coaches), but for those who do, the costs associated with these professionals are not small. It is also important to note that regardless of the cost driver, there is variability in the costs based on both the level of participation (e.g., recreational or leisure as compared to national team competition) and the availability of the sport (i.e., number of individuals participating in a given sport). The pay-to-play model found in most amateur sports leads to increased costs at higher levels of competition, whereas at the grassroots level, greater participation numbers generally result in reduced costs to the participant because the cost is spread across more individuals.

Subsidization of Costs

While the costs of participating in sport have the potential to be significant, there are numerous initiatives and funding opportunities available to individuals to reduce the overall cost. For example, and as has been widely documented, multiple sports organizations cover many of the costs of their national team athletes, coaches, and other staff, ranging from providing top-quality equipment and a food per diem, to covering travel and accommodation costs associated with competitions and training events. Perhaps less widely recognized by many sport participants is that sport organizations also act to reduce the cost passed on to the participant by providing sport clubs with aid when it comes to policy development and staff training, thus reducing the costs incurred by the sport club itself. Finally, there are numerous sport funding and sponsorship opportunities available to all sport participants at various participation levels, with the magnitude and availability of these funds often dependent on the sport.

Bringing It All Together

Overall, there are numerous costs associated with amateur sport participation. When marketing sport, it is important to consider the numerous drivers of cost, both to the sport organization or club as well as those directed at the participant because it is essential that these costs be communicated to the participant in order to avoid negative experiences for them.

As a graduate student at the University of Guelph and a researcher at the International Institute for Sport Business and Leadership, Mike has a diverse background. Following an undergraduate degree in the biological sciences, Mike completed his MSc in integrative biology, specializing in the neuroendocrine response of Carassius fish to hypoxic stress. Following his MSc programme, Mike switched streams to an MA in management, specializing in the financial cost of participating in amateur sport. Over his time at the University of Guelph, Mike made the transition from athlete to coach with the varsity rowing program. Once transitioned to "the other side of the megaphone," Mike took on roles in recruitment, fundraising, and alumni relations.

Price and Value

The price decision for any particular product always has a "value" element. A marketer must consider how value is created, particularly through the promotion of the intangible benefits that the product offers and how the product is priced as a driver of value. This process of creating value can best be described when a firm's marketing mix and the costs associated with the product effectively meet consumers' needs and wants (benefits/price). Whether the need or want is met will depend on a given customer's perception of the quality of the product based on its brand image, availability (or lack thereof), durability, and performance, as well as how much it cost them to meet that need or want. In other words, if a firm can effectively determine the needs and wants of consumers in a particular segment and then create a marketing strategy that communicates the benefits of their product to meet those needs at the appropriate price, consumers will recognize the added value as they consider which product to purchase. An increase in the quality of the product, in turn, allows firms to charge consumers higher prices. This illustrates the formulaic dimensions of value, whereby the relationship between quality and price determines how consumers assess value. Thus, value is defined here as:

$$value = perceived\ quality\ /\ perceived\ price$$

This equation reflects the fact that a marketer can increase value by either (i) improving the perception of quality of the offering (product, promotion, or place) or (ii) decreasing the price charged.

The amount customers are able and willing to spend on a product will largely be influenced by what quality of offering they will receive for their money and what they expect at that price. If you have exceeded their expectations, you have succeeded in giving additional value from your product. Value will typically be different in each consumer segment for the product, as their perceptions of quality will differ. For example, a radically decorated piece of sports equipment at a premium price may add value for the segment of the market that prefers items that reflect their individuality and prestige. However, the same item may be considered garish and overpriced by an individual looking for a less-expensive standard item.

Ethics and Pricing

An interesting issue in pricing concerns companies' ethics. In Canada, consumers are protected by the Competition Bureau of Canada, which enforces the Competition Act (2020), a federal law designed to enhance competition and protect Canadians from anticompetitive and predatory practices related to pricing of products and product availability and choice. In this regard, there are a few unethical pricing practices that organizations have been known to use. In most cases they are not illegal but are certainly viewed as unethical. A few of these are noted here:

- *Price fixing* occurs when competitors in a geographical area collude to set market prices for a product above the average price point, whereby high margins are achieved to achieve higher profits. Example: A group of race directors in a major city agrees to all charge the same, elevated price for their running events.

- *Price discrimination* occurs when manufacturers charge different prices to different consumer segments for reasons not associated with differences in cost. There are many forms of price discrimination. Example: Charging a lower unit cost price for a box of three golf balls (price $11.49) when buying a high quantity (the price drops to $9.99 when more than five boxes are purchased) is a way of targeting buyers who need a few balls (often a last-minute or only time golfing that year) at a higher price versus regular golfers, who will be attracted by the higher-volume/lower-price offering.

- *Predatory pricing* occurs when a firm in an industry prices its product much lower than the regular market price to reduce competition. This forces competing companies to abandon the market and discourages new competitors from entering. The firm then raises its prices to regain lost profits. Example: Wal-Mart prices racquets at a very low level to gain a competitive advantage over sport retailers. Once other retailers stop offering the product, Wal-Mart can then increase its price.

Setting Price

One of the most challenging yet most important elements of pricing is determining the actual price to charge (or set) for a given product offering. It is a decision not without risk. If you overprice, it can lead to economic problems, even failure, while if you underprice, you may sell well but you are missing out on profit or even incurring losses. Understanding supply and demand for your product is necessary to inform the setting of price.

Estimating Demand

One of the first steps marketers take in pricing is to estimate the consumer demand. The information required to determine consumer demand can often be acquired from such sources as the company's historical data (e.g., how many units the company sold of a similar product last year) or it may require intensive market research (e.g., to calculate how many units of the new product can be sold in this particular market at this particular price). The better the forecast, the better the decisions the marketer can make.

Figure 9.1 shows the inverse relationship between price and quantity sold, which is a well-known principle of economics. Thus, as the price of an item increases, fewer consumers are willing to purchase the item, and demand drops—and as the price of the item drops, more consumers are now willing to buy, and demand increases. Consumer demand can be influenced by many factors, including the price of the product, competitive offerings, current economic situation of the consumer, consumer lifestyle, consumer trends, and the availability of substitute products.

Identifying Restrictions

There are two caveats to note before using the price-demand curve in determining price. First, the **elasticity** of demand of a given product must be considered: With products having a

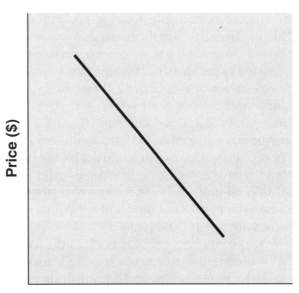

FIGURE 9.1 Price-demand curve.

more elastic demand, changes in price have a greater impact on quantity sold. Second, the ends of the curve are neither reliable nor valid for forecasting: It is difficult and unreliable to forecast demand at very low or very high prices.

Estimating Cost, Volume, and Profit

After determining demand, the marketer must estimate the costs that will be incurred, volume to produce, and profits to be made. To produce a product or service, a company incurs costs, which can be estimated by the management and production staff. These include costs for the components of the item and for equipment and tools for production, and wages for the employees to build the item. The firm, however, must not stop there but rather must identify every cost that is associated with the product. Considering two distinct categories of costs (variable costs and fixed costs) is a useful method to organize and analyze expenditures.

A variable cost is the firm's added cost to build just one more item. For example, the individual parts that make up the item are variable costs: If you make six items, you incur the cost for the parts of those six items. Shipping costs and the cost of labour to manufacture may also be considered variable costs depending on the product. For example, Quebec-based Racing Rowing Shells makes the boats that rowers use (known as shells), where variable costs would be stated as per shell (i.e., per unit), such as additional labour or wages of $750 per shell (unit), shipping $295 per shell (unit), and parts and materials of $1,250 per shell (unit). Note that this example is fictional and is used to illustrate the concept only. This example illustrates the point that variable costs are costs incurred with each additional unit sold versus those costs that are incurred regardless of the number of units sold, which are called fixed costs.

Fixed costs are costs for such items as the heat, electricity, and taxes for the building; wages for management and administrative personnel (these wages are incurred regardless of number of items made); and promotional and marketing costs. These costs are usually identified by a fixed amount over a unit of time and are incurred regardless of the number of units sold. For example, a firm making racing rowing shells will incur a series of administrative costs, facility (i.e., factory) costs, and overhead (i.e., administrative staff and full-time salaries) that must be paid regardless of shells (units) sold. Examples would include full-time wages for an office manager of $90,000 per year, utilities for the factory of $4,500/month, and office supplies of $125/month.

Once the variable and fixed costs are identified, a marketer can focus on performing an analysis of costs, volumes, and profit. Often called a cost-volume-profit analysis (CVP), the objective is to determine a price to first cover costs and then to generate profits. The most useful and best known of such analyses is the break-even analysis.

Break-Even Analysis

The break-even analysis is a calculation that focuses on determining the minimum quantity of products that must be sold to break even, so that the expected total revenue is actually zero once all the costs have been paid. The break-even point becomes an indispensable tool that management can use to make production decisions. You can also use the analysis to assess potential profits at certain price points.

To determine the break-even point, we must first determine the contribution margin (marginal income) from each unit. The contribution margin is the amount of money that the sale of a single item (i.e., the sale of one product) will contribute to covering the organization's total fixed-cost expenses. This is calculated by first subtracting the variable costs from the selling price:

$$\text{contribution margin} = \text{selling price} - \text{variable costs}$$

Second, we divide the total fixed costs incurred by the firm by the contribution margin to determine the number of units required to reach the break-even point:

$$\text{number of units to break even} = \text{fixed costs} / \text{contribution margin}$$

The result of this equation will be a total number of units. If the answer includes a fraction, you round up to the next single unit (e.g., if the result is a need to sell 125.6 tennis racquets to break even, the result is 126).

Controlling Costs

In today's global markets, competition is fierce. Canadian firms are looking to increase their market share or even maintain their current position. In seeking to do so, these firms learn quickly that failure to control costs decreases their competitiveness since firms operating in regions of the world with lower production costs and fewer regulations often are able to gain a critical competitive advantage over other firms. Therefore, to stay competitive, firms must continuously scrutinize every aspect of operation and production to reduce operating costs and stay competitive.

Many Canadian firms have been creative in competing against lower production costs in other countries by gaining competitive advantages in other areas. Ottawa-based Shopify, for example, became one of the world's leading ecommerce platforms by providing its customers with not only a service but also a place where they could be more profitable. In essence, they reduce the fixed costs (and thus increase the contribution margin) of its business clients, thereby enabling them to price

IN THE KNOW

Break-Even Analysis Example: Baseball Gloves from O&S Manufacturing

This example will help clarify the break-even analysis process. O&S Manufacturing in Montreal has designed a premium baseball glove. Based on last year's sales and secondary research on the market, the firm believes it can easily sell 2,500 gloves at a retail price of $150 per glove. In reviewing the documents provided, we also know the following:

- Variable cost: $98.50 per glove (includes leather, padding, and thread; labour to cut the leather, stuff the glove, and sew it together)
- Fixed cost: $150,000 (sales and marketing costs, new sewing machines, cutting tools, and wages for salesperson, manager, and secretary)

We solve the first equation as follows:

$$contribution\ margin = selling\ price - variable\ costs$$

$$\$150.00 - \$98.50 = \$51.50$$

Thus, the sale of each glove contributes $51.50 to the fixed costs (and then profits) of the firm. To calculate the unit sales the firm needs to break even and pay for all their fixed costs, we solve:

$$number\ of\ units\ required\ to\ break\ even = fixed\ costs\ /\ contribution\ margin$$

$$\$150,000\ /\ \$51.50 = 2912.6,\ or\ 2,913\ baseball\ gloves$$

Therefore, at the retail price of $150, the firm must sell 2,913 baseball gloves to pay all the fixed costs incurred and break even. For each glove sold beyond 2,913, the contribution margin will go entirely to profits. This calculation is easily repeated to gather data on the number of gloves required to break even at different retail prices. For example, if we maintain variable and fixed costs, the firm would have to sell the following to break even:

- 1,961 gloves at $175 (the contribution margin of each glove is now $76.50)
- 5,661 gloves at $125 (the contribution margin of each glove is now $26.50)

---

products more competitively and increase sales (which in turn helps Spotify, who earn more as its clients sell more).

We consider again the O&S Manufacturing case. At the retail price of $150 per baseball glove, we calculated that the firm would have to sell 2,913 gloves to break even. However, following some market changes, the estimated consumer demand is now only 2,500 gloves for next year, and the failure to sell the 2,913 baseball gloves will cause the firm to incur a loss. Therefore, the firm must scrutinize every facet of its operation and production to find additional ways to cut costs. One response for O&S manufacturing would be to potentially decrease its variable costs for the glove by:

- switching to new suppliers of raw material offering lower costs,
- outsourcing selected activities that can be done by others for less, or
- using manufacturing process innovations to increase efficiency and reduce labour costs (which may increase the company's fixed costs from the purchase of new technology and equipment but may reduce labour time per glove sufficiently to bring about a savings via decreased variable costs).

O&S Manufacturing may also be able to find ways to decrease the company's fixed costs by negotiating better rates for telephone services or outsourcing such clerical tasks as bookkeeping and payroll. Taking the example of O&S Manufacturing further, we can better demonstrate the variable–fixed cost relationship. For example, let's say that due to recent changes at O&S Manufacturing, the firm now has the following cost structure:

- Variable costs: $79.75/glove (includes leather, padding, and thread and labour to cut the leather, stuff, and sew it together)
- Fixed costs: $140,000 (sales and marketing costs, new sewing machines, cutting tools, and wages for salesperson, manager, and secretary)

Now, we can solve:

$$selling\ price - variable\ costs = contribution\ margin$$

$$\$150.00 - \$79.75 = \$70.25$$

This item now contributes $70.25 to the fixed costs (then profit, beyond the break-even point) of the firm. To determine the break-even point and cover all the fixed costs, we calculate:

$$fixed\ costs\ /\ contribution\ margin = number\ of\ units\ required\ to\ break\ even$$

$$\$140,000\ /\ \$70.25 = 1992.9,\ or\ 1{,}993\ baseball\ gloves$$

Thus, at the retail price of $150, the firm must sell 1,993 baseball gloves to pay all the fixed costs that are incurred. The company still anticipates selling 2,500 gloves, with an additional contribution from 507 gloves worth a total of $35,616.75, all as profit. This example emphasizes the point that profits are not encountered until a firm has met its break-even point and has paid off its fixed costs. Any additional sales over the break-even point will begin to accumulate profit for the firm; conversely, sales below the break-even point will result in a loss.

Key Pricing Issues

Now that you have an understanding of pricing and a set of tools to set price and determine the ideal price point for a given product, we will share a number of additional issues that are important in pricing. Pricing is affected by many uncontrollable things, including competition, market changes, and access to materials and facilities.

Discounts and Allowances

Discounts and allowances are both *decisions* that involve adjusting the existing price of an item. In marketing, the seller gives discounts to the consumers to shift some of the marketing function from the retailer to the consumer. Examples of discounts from the marketing literature include the following:

- *Quantity discounts* are given to consumers who purchase large quantities; however, in doing so, the customer must agree to inventory the product (which takes space), as they are buying more quantity than they need. For example, the big-box sporting goods retailer Sport Chek may do this with products such as running shoes, exercise clothes, and golf balls.

- *Seasonal discounts* are given when consumers choose to purchase an item off-season, such as a discount offered on a downhill ski, boots, and poles package in March. The consumer once again chooses to inventory the item as they likely will not use the ski package until the following winter.

- *Payment term discounts* are often observed when a business sells to another business. In these cases, the discounts are offered in order to encourage early payment. For example, a company may offer a 2 percent in 10 or net 30, meaning the buyer can deduct 2 percent from the total of their invoice if it is paid within 10 days and otherwise the net amount (not discounted) of the invoice is due within 30 days. This shifts the economic burden to the buyer more quickly in order to improve the seller's cash flow. For example, the wholesaler that supplies Warrior with the materials for its hockey sticks offers the firm a 1.5 percent discount if it pays within 30 days of receiving the invoice. With such a discount offered, it is likely that they will pay within the 30 days.

- *Trade and functional discounts* are passed down to retailers to compensate them for additional services they must perform. For example, sport drink manufacturer Gatorade could provide a 10 percent discount to a chain

EXPERT PERSPECTIVE
Pricing and Talent: Teams Garner Talent by Four Methods

PETER TINGLING, Associate Dean, Undergraduate Program, and Associate Professor, Management Information Systems, Beedie School of Business, Simon Fraser University

Starting with the best ingredients is good advice for cooks and manufacturers, but what if your main resource were people? More importantly, what if the primary acquisition method was designed to equalize performance by allocating early, presumably better, choices to organizations with the worst performance?

Welcome to the strange world of entry drafts where the most popular professional sport leagues (football, basketball, baseball, and hockey) operate in cartels. Rivalries are encouraged but the overall objective is competitive parity and dynastic reduction by distributing athletes to aid the weak and disadvantage the strong.

Free agency is the simplest and fastest way to improve. In a market environment, teams choose athletes using identifiable performance records or characteristics; a process that favours affluent teams and those that manage their salary caps.

Trading, exchanging assets such as players, cash, and draft picks, is heavily dependent on the skill and reputation of management but is a special method of assembly because it is not inherently zero-sum. Swapping redundant or unneeded assets enables teams to simultaneously improve, although research has shown this occurs less often than expected and teams avoid trading with or improving direct competitors.

Developing players, coaching, and culture, for example, or using junior or affiliate teams or combining complementary skills can create synergy but is the most difficult process. Leadership, the role of the general manager, coach, and captains, is demonstrably important and, once instantiated, creates a positive feedback loop. A process where athletes become their best is a magnet that attracts talent at a discount and is hardest to imitate.

Drafting is the most heavily regulated systematic allocation of talent. It not only rebalances performance by granting high-potential athletes to low-performance teams but also diminishes the advantage of affluence or the effects of those who have made ineffective or suboptimal decisions. In practice, however, drafting is more luck than skill and more art than science. Research has shown teams to be notoriously poor at selection, and there is ample evidence that beyond the first few choices, no teams have been able to repeatedly select well. The essence of drafting seems to be the hope that decision makers avoid bad luck in the first few choices and hope for good luck in later ones and that luck often masquerades as skill. Despite a wealth of research into good decision-making processes, drafting remains characterized by a variety of biases and poor process, and no team or general managers have demonstrated ongoing ability. In the NHL, for example, although the league has implemented improvements—scouting services and lottery elements to reduce the incentive to lose and gain the possible franchise-making first choice (Crosby or Lemieux)—every year great players are overlooked (Salming, Joseph, and Oates) and others are drafted late (Hasek, Gilmour, and Datsyuk).

Despite much attention, bigger budgets, and the beginning adoption of "moneyball" style approaches to player selection, the draft remains a gamble that is no better than guessing.

PETER M. TINGLING is the associate dean for undergraduate programs at the Beedie School of Business at Simon Fraser University. He holds a PhD from Western University, and his research focuses on decision making. Widely recognized as an expert in drafting, he has consulted to a wide variety of business, government, and high-performance sports organizations.

of grocery stores in return for product placement in an ideal shelf location near the entrance to the store or at the end of an aisle.

- *Chain discounts* are passed down by the manufacturer to the different members of the distribution network, such as wholesalers and retailers. For example, a logging company, lumberyard, canoe maker, wholesaler of outdoor equipment, and chain of retailers might form an alliance and share discounts. Another example would be a chemical lab, a fibreglass manufacturer, and a manufacturer of tennis racquets sharing a chain discount.

- *Sale price discounts* are temporary savings featured by the retailer to consumers to meet certain marketing strategies. For example, Speedo could offer women's swimsuits for 50 percent off to reduce stock before launching new designs for the next season.

In marketing, an allowance is given (typically) to a retailer for having accomplished something in terms of sales. The following are a few of the allowances that are common in marketing practice.

- *Advertising allowances* are granted to retailers based on a percentage of total sales; this allowance normally takes the form of the manufacturer providing a rebate or dollars to the retailer to promote their products. Example: The North Face, a manufacturer of mountain climbing wear sold at Canadian retailer Mountain Equipment Co-op (MEC), offers an allowance to MEC to enhance their promotions of North Face jackets and hiking boots once a certain number have been sold in a given time frame.

- *Stocking allowances* are typically seen in supermarkets where manufacturers pay a fee to promote their new products on the supermarket shelves. Example: Nike enters into a deal with retailer Sport Check that includes an allowance paid if their shoes are displayed prominently instore and online to attract buyer attention.

- *Spiffs or push money allowances* are targeted to retail salespeople to encourage them to push a particular product. Often called "kickbacks," these allowances are illegal in some places and are not always considered

EXECUTIVE PERSPECTIVE
Earned Revenue in a Pandemic Environment

MATT AFINEC, President and COO, Hamilton Tiger-Cats Football Club, 2021 Grey Cup Festival, and Forge FC Hamilton Soccer Club

The Context

When the COVID-19 pandemic hit in March 2020, clubs operating in the Canadian Football League (CFL) and Canadian Premier League (CPL) had sold and collected approximately 85 percent of the upcoming season's season seat revenues but had yet to play any games to earn that investment from their most loyal fans (CPL season commences in April and CFL season in June). Season seat revenue accounts for approximately 75 percent of total ticket revenue for the average club in both leagues.

The Challenge

With the pandemic's health regulations making games with fans in attendance an impossibility for 2020, clubs in both leagues had to work to avoid issuing mass refunds to season seat holders for the 2020 season. It should be noted that fans, especially season seat holders, were positive and proactive about their will to support their team during these unprecedented times and their impacts on the team's operations. Clearly an opportunity existed for teams to minimize the negative impacts of mass refunds, but that opportunity was dependent on creating a compelling value proposition, at the right price.

The Opportunity and the Solutions

All season seat holders were provided the value of their 2020 season seat account in credit that could be applied against several options, including a refund.

The first and most common outcome was to take the account credit balance and pay for their 2021 season seat renewal. Some clubs went one step further to add value and show appreciation by offering an incentive to reward this action (merchandise or food and beverage gift cards are primary examples). While rolling account credits toward 2021 renewal is a much-preferred outcome to a refund, it creates a future liability for the team in the context of future cash flows used to operate the business. If people weren't paying for their tickets incrementally in 2021, or at least some portion of them, the cash flow impact would be significant to ongoing operations.

The second option was classified internally as earned revenue programs. Specifically, creating a product or service(s) that the season seat holder could chose to purchase with their account credit. In so doing the team would earn the revenue in 2020 and not have that balance remain as a future liability. In most cases the products created to earn 2020 revenue did not equal the value of the account credit owed, which proved to be advantageous for both the fan and the team. The fan could use the balance to roll forward into their 2021 renewal paying less than the traditional price, and the team earns some part of the revenue immediately, secures the coveted season seat renewal for 2021 and has the positive cash flow of the incremental dollars equal to the delta amount of the earned revenue and 2021 renewal value.

The specific products or service created to earn 2020 revenue by the CPL and the CFL differed. In the CPL, a league-wide supporters group was created to augment the strong club-level supporters group that already existed. This product, dubbed The Collective (see https://canpl .ca/thecollective), sold for $149 per person and featured a series of benefits highlighted by members receiving their club's 2020 official on-field kit (a $120 retail value). The pricing decisions around this product were heavily influenced by the target-return approach to pricing.

In the CFL, the approach was to seize the unique connection fans have with the teams and players by creating a product that connected them through the CFL's most visible and significant brand attribute, the Grey Cup. No mechanism existed to hold the iconic Grey Cup trophy or serve as its base when it's not being hoisted by the winning club. Combining the fans' passion for the CFL with the opportunity to create an official base resulted in the Grey Cup Fan Base. For the first time ever in professional sports, a base to support the championship trophy would be created and feature the names of the fans who supported the initiative by allocating a portion of their 2020 season seat credit. Given the aspirational nature of the value proposition, and the target audience being the most passionate of CFL fans, the $349/person price for the Grey Cup Fan base most closely resembled that of psychological price setting strategy (see www.greycupfanbase.ca).

MATT AFINEC serves as the president and COO, business operations, for the Hamilton Tiger-Cats (CFL), Forge FC Hamilton (CPL soccer), and the 2021 Grey Cup. He's entering his 11th year with the Bob Young Group of Companies (owners of both franchises) and was appointed president and COO in June 2018. He oversees all business affairs for both clubs and the 2021 Grey Cup and serves as a representative for both clubs on the board of governors or executive council in both the CFL and CPL. He also oversees the club's nonsoccer (global football) commercial event business for the clubs' home venue, Tim Hortons Field (concerts, live events, etc.). A graduate of McGill University, Afinec entered the professional sports industry in 2005 with the CFL's Toronto Argonauts. He held various positions including director of corporate partnerships for Toronto's 2007 Grey Cup Organizing Committee and vice president of corporate partnerships for the Argonauts.

IN THE KNOW

The Fan Cost Index

The fan cost index (FCI) is a data report prepared by Team Marketing Report that shares the prices of items for a consumer attending games in the major sport leagues in North America, including the NHL, MLB, NBA, and MLS. Many Canadian teams are included. The costs for a consumer attending a game are calculated based on a formulate that includes the following:

- Four average-price tickets
- Four small soft drinks
- Two small beers
- Four hot dogs
- Two game programs
- Parking
- Two adult-size caps.

For the 2018-2019 NHL season, the Team Market Report (2020) calculated the median FCI for the league, including the seven Canadian teams, to be 424.62 USD, a considerable increase over the previous year (2017-2018) of 388.71 USD. This is strong evidence of the importance of cost over price as shown in figure 9.2, which provides the average ticket prices for the NHL clubs in the 2018-2019 year, with the median value being less than 80.00 USD, about one-fifth of the total cost.

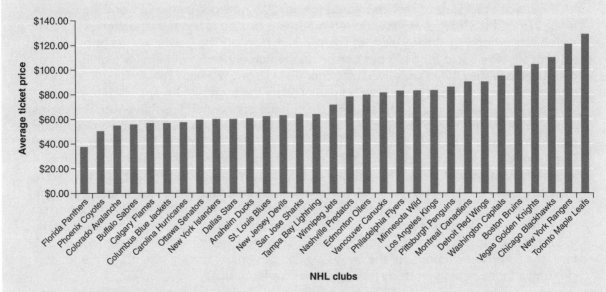

FIGURE 9.2 TEAM marketing report (2020), average ticket prices for NHL clubs in 2018-2019

Data from Team Marketing Report, *Fan Cost Index* (2020). http://www.teammarketing.com/.

The FCI is an example of a tool that looks at costs versus price (see figure 9.2), showing how significant the difference is. There are other tools (or you can develop your own) to look at cost, but the key is that you consider cost in your marketing efforts and value calculations. It also allows for longitudinal comparisons. For example, the FCI for the Toronto Maple Leafs has gone from 271 USD in 2006-2007 to 617 USD in 2018-2019, almost tripling in 12 years. Similarly, one can compare market to market, such as the NHL teams in Canada's two largest cities in 2018-2019, where FCI was 617 USD for Toronto versus 470 USD for Montreal.

ethical. Example: a salesperson for a major golf retailer receives bonuses when specific sales targets are reached.

• *Trade-in allowances* are often used in the automotive industry, where a consumer can receive a cash value for their older vehicle that must be applied to the new purchase. Example: The Play-It-Again Sports chain buys and resells used ski or hockey equipment.

One of the marketing advantages of discounts and allowances is that they allow retailers, wholesalers, and manufacturers to adjust (lower) the price of an item on a temporary basis without changing the posted regular retail price. Thus, it enables them to achieve specific marketing goals on a short-term basis without compromising the brand image or the positioning of the product in the marketplace.

Price versus Cost

Cost is the broader construct of price that includes all costs incurred by a consumer. For example, the price of a new driver for a young golfer might be $349, but the cost is that price plus all other costs incurred (e.g., gas to drive to the store, taxes, upgraded handle, cover to protect the driver, pack of balls purchased with it). Thus, although the price may be $349, the cost is closer to $500.

Sport consumers are faced with many different elements of the true cost of a purchase—above and beyond the ticket price—when attending or participating in an event. This becomes apparent when we consider that the cost includes a number of things beyond the ticket price:

• Online processing fees to purchase ticket
• Transportation
• Parking
• Food
• Beverages
• Memorabilia

A sport marketer must be aware of these costs and must price their product properly relative to the total cost of attendance, as an informed consumer will typically view the exchange based on cost, not price. They will assess the overall value of the purchase, based on cost not price. This type of thinking led the Team Marketing Report (n.d.) agency to develop the **fan cost index** in 1998.

CHAPTER SUMMARY

Pricing and the tools to set price represent knowledge that the sport marketer needs to understand because they directly affect sales revenue and profits. Specific to the sport industry, a number of important tools were shared for determining price, including break-even analysis. Price is used to capture the value of all other elements of a product. For example, consider the price of a ticket to a Calgary Flames game: While the price may be considered high, it represents the highest quality of hockey in the area, delivered in a first-class sport entertainment facility, with upscale promotions before and during the games. In addition, the games are sold out every year, making the demand for the product high.

TEST YOUR KNOWLEDGE

1. What two issues affect price?
2. Name two ways to estimate demand.
3. How do you calculate the break-even point for a product?
4. What effect will reducing variable costs have for a manufacturer? What about reducing fixed costs?
5. Name two types of pricing discounts and two types of pricing allowances.

6. What is the difference between price and cost?

7. State what each item stands for in this equation:

$$\text{Profit} = (P \times Q) - [FC + (VC \times Q)]$$

8. Fill in the blanks in the following definition.

When demand is elastic, a _____ percentage price change results in a _____ percentage demand change.

9. Marie has started her own business making custom wetsuits for triathletes. The total cost of materials and her time is $4,500 per wetsuit. Last year she had expenses of rent at $12,000 annually, equipment at $60,000 (total), and monthly utilities at $200. Assuming that fixed costs remain the same, how many designer wetsuits does she have to sell at $7,500 each to break even for the year?

KEY TERMS

allowance
break-even point
costs

demand
discount
elasticity

fan cost index
supply
variable cost

CASE STUDIES

Visit HK*Propel* for case studies organized by chapter.

CHAPTER 10

Sport Promotion

LEARNING OBJECTIVES

After studying this chapter, you will be able to do the following:

- Understand the tools available in the promotion mix
- Appreciate the link between promotional mix and communications mix
- Put together a promotion plan for a sport organization
- Recognize the importance of using each of the elements of the promotion mix collaboratively and strategically

Sport promotion is one of the most dynamic and exciting areas of sport marketing. You will certainly work in **promotions** at some time during your sport career, possibly on an event like your local 10-kilometre fundraiser run (also known as a "fun-run") for cancer awareness and research. Let's dig into that example a bit.

A few months before the race, you create a plan to attract participants, volunteers, and businesses that will support your event. You create a website that communicates information about the event: the affiliated cause, when and where the event will occur, prizes to be won and drawn, and marquee sponsors already lending their support. You share the website via social media and email. You seek to distribute

this content to raise awareness of your event and garner public support. The spokesperson for the event, a well-known person in the community such as a former professional sport star or a local politician, conducts media interviews and meets with key business contacts to help drive sponsorship sales and registrations. The event is promoted by your local grocery store, the official food and beverages supplier of the event, and sporting goods retailer Running Room, another official event sponsor, through a number of activities leading up to the race. The grand prize for the participant who raises the most money for cancer research, donated by a local business leader, is a $500 Amazon gift card. During the race, a number of local businesses set up tents on-site to sell merchandise, offer interactive displays about their products and services, and so on. The organizations also had a presence on the event website and local channels. Each and every one of these many activities are promotional activities. They serve a multitude of purposes, from raising awareness for your product to enhancing participants' experience at the event. This chapter examines the various forms of promotions, known as the promotional mix, and the execution of a promotion.

Promotion

Promotion plays a key role in the marketing mix. Once decisions have been made about product, price, and place, the marketer must plan the most effective way to communicate critical information about them to the various publics. The recent proliferation of media outlets—including new technologies (chapter 16) and ever-advancing social media (chapter 12)—provides the marketer with effective and efficient means to reach very specific targets with very little waste. Preparing and executing a promotion requires support from a number of employees within a sport organization or an enterprise marketing through sport. A successful promotion is one that makes the consumer aware of the product or service, generates interest in it, creates desire, and ultimately leads to action, typically a purchase. This four-stage promotion model is known as AIDA, the acronym for awareness, interest, desire, and action. Using AIDA, the ultimate

---

EXECUTIVE PERSPECTIVE
The Gameday Promotional Mix

CAMERON KUSCH, President, Guelph Nighthawks Basketball Club

Since the launch of the Canadian Elite Basketball League and the Guelph Nighthawks professional basketball club in 2019, the team's core strategy has been to deliver a gameday experience focused on an immersive entertainment that resonates with basketball fans, casual sport fans, and nonsport fans alike. In Guelph, Ontario, a city of 135,000 people, hockey has a rich history in the fabric of the community and has always been the go-to option for those looking to spend time and money on local sport entertainment. When the Nighthawks launched in Guelph, it was done with a clear focus to deliver an exciting night out for all members of the community, not just our local basketball fans. The goal for the organization was an "entertainment-first" model that would resonate with a wider spectrum of the community, and those attending the games would actively promote their positive experience with their network via word-of-mouth, in turn, leading to greater ticket sales and long-term success for the club.

Basketball naturally lends itself to a rich history built on an entertainment-first, game day experience model. One can thank David Stern, former commissioner of the National Basketball Association, for his vision in shifting the sport to an entertainment-focused model that opened the door to a far larger cross-section of the North American population. Live music, dance teams, mascots, tee-shirt guns, spotlights, fireworks, and lasers are now synonymous with professional basketball, and the Nighthawks have adopted these activations as part of our model.

One of the most important parts of the entertainment-first model is easing frustration for the consumer. Before a Nighthawks game even begins, many consumers are subject to the challenges of transportation, especially locating car parking close to the arena. To alleviate this concern, our organization has provided complementary public transportation to ticket holders and offered reserve parking for premium ticket holders who choose to drive. Once downtown, the consumer gets to experience the array of partnerships the organization has with local restaurants and breweries, allowing groups to congregate together, grab some food and drink prior to the game, and cultivate their allegiance to the team through this feeling of belonging and community. This is a critical element to the Nighthawks marketing strategy; the brand, colours, and excitement shared by fans intuitively promote our product to anyone else they interact with before, during, and following the game.

Once inside the arena, the Sleeman Centre, fans get fully immersed in the entertainment-first, game day experience. Live DJs are playing music, buskers entertain, fans can shoot hoops, and inactive players are often holding autograph signing sessions. These immersive experiences enhance the sounds, smells, and feelings of being at a Nighthawks game and build upon our goal of extended promotion via word-of-mouth in the community.

However, one of the drawbacks of this model is the potential discontent from passionate sport fans. As many of these activities are ongoing, including playing live music during game-play, there is a bit of a learning curve for the traditional fan to embrace these experiences alongside live sport. This is a tricky balance that our organization has had to navigate but, given our organization's goal of building the casual and nonsport fanbase in our region, it is important to remain authentic and implement the actions that align with this goal, which includes the entertainment-first experiences.

Additionally, as with all professional sport teams, sponsored content and activations are a key revenue driver for the club. The Nighthawks sponsorship mandate is to ensure every team partnership augments the fan experience, enhancing our entertainment-first focus. Instead of scrolling corporate logos on digital displays and ribbon boards and running commercials on the centre-hung video board, team sponsors are integrated as part of the immersive consumer experience. An example of this is McDonald's Restaurants, which worked with the Nighthawks to bring the McDonald's "Hawks Nest Family Zone" to life. The zone is a court level space, accessible for all ticket holders, filled with various activities such as face painting and confectionary food fare. This sponsorship has allowed McDonald's to secure naming rights to the space, while the restaurants' investment in the club assists in offsetting the cost of creating the augmented family experience at the games. Similarly, other partnerships with the club have improved the fan experience through team-branded items that are thrown into the crowd, branded on-court contests during TV timeouts, and the opportunity for a randomly selected fan to win a new vehicle by hitting a half-court shot. All of these activations maintain our entertainment-first dynamic.

As the Nighthawks aim to develop and nurture new fans in the Guelph region, player interactions are also becoming a more intricate part in the development process of the team's fandom and community-based focus. Inactive players are available pregame and at halftime to sign autographs and chat with ticket holders. Moreover, following the final whistle of the last home game of the season, ten lucky fans are selected to come onto the court to receive a jersey off the players back, which is subsequently signed by that player and kept by the fan as what will hopefully become a lifelong keepsake. And following each home game, a Nighthawks gameday concludes with the Post Game Player Party at an establishment in downtown Guelph. Nighthawks players and fans are encouraged to socialize and interact, while the Nighthawks DJ spins music late into the evening.

These examples highlight the entertainment-first model, which is at the core of the Nighthawks' operations. By showcasing an immersive, entertaining product for consumers, we are able to ensure the Guelph Nighthawks are synonymous with positive feelings and outcomes. While there are other ways to market our product, providing an entertainment-first model fits our club and has made the product more accessible to a wider cross-section of the community looking to spend their time and money on local sport entertainment.

CAMERON KUSCH has spent the last 20 years immersed in the Canadian sport industry, most recently as the president of the Guelph Nighthawks. Cameron has been directly involved with some of the most influential and internationally recognizable sporting events in Canada, including the 2015 FIFA Women's World Cup, HSBC World Rugby Canada Sevens, the PGA and LPGA Tour, and the Canadian Football League's Grey Cup.

goal for marketers is to get consumers to try the product or service and build loyalty for that product or service over the long term. Notably, it is very important to recognize that promotion does not work in isolation; it is an integral part of the overall marketing plan and must be consistent with the organization's objectives.

Promotional Mix

A number of promotional tools are available to marketers, which, as a group, are commonly referred to as the promotional mix. Since the open market is extremely competitive, sport marketers must be creative to make their promotions break through the clutter and attract people's attention concerning their product or service. A promotional idea does not have to be an entirely new one. In fact, it can be borrowed from many sources and changed to suit individual needs. For example, golf's "skins game" concept has been modified to suit the sports of curling and bowling. These events focus on entertainment, and the rules of the sport can be altered for the specific promotional event. The number of variations evolving from these starting points is limited only by one's imagination and creativity.

The traditional promotional mix consists of the following six activities:

- **advertising**
- **publicity**
- **personal selling**
- sales promotions
- **public relations**
- sponsorship

Advertising

Despite a fragmented and cluttered environment, advertising remains an important marketing tool for marketers. Essentially, advertising is used to create brand awareness and brand loyalty (Shank & Lyberger, 2015). Since advertising is paid for by the focal organization (i.e., the organization that is seeking consumer attention), the sport marketer controls the message to be communicated to consumers as well as creative aspects, choice of media, and timing. In other words, they shape and control the content of the advertisement. The available advertising budget will dictate the quality of the production and the choice of media. For example, a local sport club with a limited budget can be successful in creating an in-house video promoting its various summer clinics to its local, focused audience on a community television station or its own YouTube channel. Since television stations run a limited number

---

IN THE KNOW

Mix Up Your Promotional Mix

This chapter outlines the promotional mix and all its elements, with later chapters focused on some of the specific elements, such as **sponsorship**, in great detail. However, and this is very important as you learn about the marketing mix, the smart sport marketer uses each and every tactic and strategy available to them in their promotional mix in a collaborative and strategic way. A few examples include:

- Activating a sponsorship with a well-timed advertising campaign
- Launching a publicity campaign concurrent to a mass market sales promotion
- Ensuring that your public relations agency is aware of your sponsorship, advertising, and sales-promotion efforts

Coordinating the tactics within your promotional mix is of such importance and with the ability to lead to positive outcomes that it is its own subfield of marketing, which is known as Integrated Marketing Communications (IMC).

of public service announcements (PSA), the club may be able to get its announcement to air free of charge. On the other hand, major corporations like Nike are well known for creating powerful global advertising campaigns that evoke strong emotional connections with consumers, often using high-profile athletes to generate those responses. For example, Nike works with tennis superstar Serena Williams via a multiyear, multimillion-dollar agreement to build advertising campaigns around certain products that Williams endorses (e.g., tennis apparel) and general inspirational categories that she supports (e.g., women's sport). Moreover, if Nike wants to buy advertising time on television, they have the resources to purchase high-impact slots, such as the approximately 5 million USD cost for a 30-second commercial to air during the NFL Super Bowl.

Shank and Lyberger (2015) suggested a five-step approach to developing an advertising campaign (also known as an ad campaign). Decisions have to be made at each step about:

1. developing clear objectives for the campaign,
2. the amount of money available,
3. messaging and creative content,
4. the media strategy (e.g., television, print, social), and
5. evaluation and measurement of the campaign.

An ad campaign should support and reinforce a brand's positioning and overall corporate strategy. The media choices, or the vehicles which will help broadcast or deliver the ad campaign, include print (e.g., magazines, newspaper, direct mail) or electronic (e.g., television, web, social, blogs) media, as well as posters, billboards, event signage, brochures, balloons, and even athlete bibs or uniforms. These examples demonstrate the variety and range of media available for promotional activity. Some can be physical, while others may be digital. Some media might be contained within or very near to the event, while others might be in a different city, region, or even province altogether. The decision to choose certain media over others largely depends on the target

markets of interest and the available budget. For instance, printing costs for brochures or balloons may be relatively inexpensive compared to advertising on television or through the World Wide Web. However, certain media, although cheaper, may not be as effective in reaching certain audiences, such as a national Canadian audience. A billboard on the side of the highway may be perceived to be effective given its large size and the amount of passersby in their cars each day, but drivers may be too concerned with operating their vehicle to pay attention to billboard signage or may not see the ad due to their high rate of speed, or the campaign may simply not be relevant to them. Conversely, campaigns that select web advertising, which is a more expensive ad medium, can engage in search engine optimization to specifically target groups and demographics seeking certain web content, thereby concentrating efforts on likely interested consumers. A key distinction between advertising and any other element of the promotional mix such as publicity is that advertising is wholly paid for by the marketers who, consequently, maintain control over what is said, as well as where, when, and to whom.

Publicity

Publicity is an important component of the promotional mix for sport marketers. Contrary to advertising, marketers do not pay (directly) for publicity. The opportunities to get one's brand into the mass media are numerous, whether at the local, regional, provincial, national, or international levels. Every day, hundreds of reports on sporting events, athletes, and other types of sport information are presented by numerous media outlets nationwide (e.g., television, newspaper, radio, web, social, blogs). While a majority of airtime in traditional mass media outlets such as television and radio is devoted to professional sports, the opportunity to get the story out through these platforms depends in part on the media relations effort. Effective media relations usually takes months (and sometimes years) to implement and may include news releases, PSAs, demonstrations of product or service, press conferences, media days, interviews, partnerships with bloggers, and photograph sessions. These activities do require costs for the focal sport organization, which is why publicity bears indirect costs. An important component of any media-relations strategy is the relationship that a marketer, coach, athlete, or spokesperson develops with the content producer (e.g., journalists, bloggers). Since publicity is what a third party decides to say about the organization, this has the ability to add credibility to the focal organization more generally. Therefore, getting one's story out through the media can provide excellent public-relations benefits to an organization. In addition, good, consistent mass-media coverage is closely tied to sponsorship opportunities since one of the key benefits sought by companies involved in sponsorship arrangements can be mass-media coverage given that sponsors seek to maximize the visibility of their brands to their target markets. While it is true that an organization has less control over the timing and content of publicity than advertising, it remains an interesting, essential, and often effective platform within the promotional mix.

Personal Selling

A key characteristic of personal selling, another marketing communications tool used by sport organizations, is its approach—which is targeted and personal, rather than broad and impersonal. Personal sales can take numerous forms. A varsity basketball player visits local schools to share personal experiences; a swimming coach lobbies community groups for the construction of a new pool; a volunteer calls potential donors for a local soccer tournament; a 10-year-old lacrosse player goes door-to-door selling chocolate bars to subsidize the travel cost to play at the upcoming provincial championships. A key element of personal sales is the dialogue created between the organization offering a product or service and the targeted publics. That dialogue is designed to be intimate, connecting to a particular attribute or element that is valued by the targeted consumer group. For example, the marketing director of a university's athletic program may meet with representatives of a student association, such as a sport management council, to sell a block of group tickets to a marquee football game (e.g., alumni homecoming). While the director meeting with students is personal on its own, appealing to the group's school spirit and camaraderie demonstrates the targeted nature of personal sales.

Selling a sponsorship is also a form of personal selling. For example, the director of corporate partnerships of Alpine Canada may tailor a sponsorship program to meet the needs and objectives of a specific organization (e.g., Audi motor vehicles). Prior to making a formal presentation, Alpine Canada invites key senior executives of marketing at Audi Canada to a World Cup event (hospitality), which happens to be at a beautiful resort in Whistler, BC. The environment, hospitality, and special events may strengthen relationships and, in the end, create a favourable atmosphere when the pitch is finally made.

Since personal selling is about creating human contacts, a key to its success is developing long-term personal relationships. In fact, personal selling is a great example of relationship marketing—creating, maintaining, and enhancing strong, value-laden relationships with customers and other stakeholders—which is critical to sport marketers.

Sales Promotion

The aim of **sales promotion** is to stimulate immediate demand for a product or service. It can also create consumer goodwill and/or reinforce the relationship between consumers and a brand. Sales promotions can take the form of price-oriented or non-price-oriented tactics (Mullin et al., 2014). For example, a ski resort that offers two-for-one tickets on Tuesday nights uses a price-oriented strategy, while a sales promotion that gives a free team calendar to the first 10,000 spectators to arrive for a baseball game uses a non-price-oriented strategy. In both the price-oriented and non-price-oriented promotions, sport marketers must decide if their activities should be associated with weaknesses (e.g., weekdays are slow sales days, games against low-performing ranking teams are less appealing for ticket purchasers) or strengths (e.g., matchups against teams performing well or with marquee athletes are attractive to ticket buyers). Specifically with regard to the latter, it is important for sport marketers to remember that strong attributes may not always result in positive outcomes. Just because the Ottawa Senators have an upcoming home game against the Edmonton Oilers, a team with superstar forward Connor McDavid, does not necessarily equate to higher ticket sales and attendance figures. Although McDavid is an important selling feature, consumers may not want to attend the game because of Ottawa's lack of talent or because the team is unable to contend in the playoffs. In this respect, marketers may employ price-oriented or non-price-oriented tactics (or even both) to drive consumers to the game. Whatever strategy is used, it is important that loyal customers do not feel alienated by the promotion. In this regard, a sport marketer looking at discounting tickets for half the traditional cost needs to carefully assess the potential impact of short-term revenue versus long-term alienation of season ticket holders who are loyal to the team and do not reap the rewards of certain discount schemes. A good rule of thumb is that the season ticket holder always pays the lowest price (even in the situation of a sales promotion).

Sales promotions take a multitude of forms, including **premiums**, contests and **sweepstakes**, sampling, **point-of-purchase** displays, and coupons (Shank & Lyberger, 2015). The decision on which form to choose depends on the objectives of the sport organization.

Premiums

Premiums include giveaways that are tied with a brand's product as part of the sales promotion. For example, spectators purchasing a VIP ticket (which are sold at a higher price point than regular tickets) to the Rogers Cup tennis tournament in Toronto are given a care package that includes a bottle of La Roche-Posay sunscreen. This premium enables the consumer to feel valued through their purchase of the higher-priced ticket. Concurrently, premiums allow sport marketers to distinguish between ticket price tiers and categories, thus reaching a wider array of audience segments. This type of promotional activity is particularly popular among sponsors as it gets their products into the hands of a targeted audience. In the example of the Rogers Cup, La Roche–Posay was able to get a specific clientele of tennis spectators to use their product for their skin-care needs, thus building loyalty among the desired consumer segment and attributing their product with a premium price point as well.

Contests and Sweepstakes

This form of a promotion offers consumers the chance of winning a prize. Sweepstakes are games of chance (e.g., lottery) where the purchase of a product is not required to play, while a contest is skill based (e.g., selecting the top three finishers in a horse race). For example, the Toronto Blue Jays worked with one of their premier partners, TD Bank, to establish the TD Grand Slam Contest. Fans of the team fill out an online entry form for the chance to win tickets for four to attend the Blue Jays' home opener that season. Additionally, the fan selected as the grand prize winner also receives round-trip economy airfare for all four people, hotel room stays, Blue Jays merchandise, spending money, team store gift cards, and an opportunity to meet a star Blue Jays player (e.g., Vladimir Guerrero Jr. or Bo Bichette).

To successfully promote the organization, premiums or prizes offered in a contest or sweepstakes must have key consumer appeal, be new, or be tantalizingly unavailable to the average person (e.g., an all-expenses paid trip, a luxury vehicle). Cash, trips, and cars are often powerful hooks proven to attract consumers to enter a contest.

Sampling

A company introducing a new product can get participants or spectators to try it by offering samples. For example, a company specializing in organic ice cream products may use its sponsorship of a beach volleyball tournament to distribute samples of its product to athletes or spectators on-site. Or the company may decide to install a tent and have a representative providing product information on the health benefits and differentiation of their organic product versus their competitors. In the case of a service, the sampling is in the form of an opportunity to test it out (e.g., massage after a triathlon given by a local massage therapy clinic).

Point-of-Purchase

The point-of-purchase (POP) display is a popular form of promotion in retail environments. For example, General Mills uses Olympic-themed POP displays featuring Team Canada athletes at several Sobeys grocers (also a Team Canada partner) for its Cheerios cereal brand. On occasions, the POP promotion may be supported by the presence of well-known athletes and a contest or sweepstakes. In general, the objectives of POP programs are to:

- enhance the sport's connection and image with the consumer,
- generate consumer awareness, interest, and involvement,
- provide sales support over a longer than normal period,
- maximize in-store display, feature price, and consumer visibility, and
- provide further incentive for the retailer to feature focal products over competitors.

Public Relations

Public relations is everyone's business, from the top to the bottom of any sport organization. Every athlete, coach, volunteer, and administrator must be conscious of the public-relations aspect of major decisions that an organization makes and at every point of contact with the public and all its stakeholders. Since sport organizations connect with the public in many ways, the essence of public relations is to plan for and manage all connections. Public Relations is an essential aspect of brand management, and it is no coincidence that for most professional sport teams, community relations is an important aspect of their public-relations strategy. For example, when the president of the Saskatchewan Roughriders is invited to speak at the Regina Rotary Club, plays at a golf tournament, addresses the media during a major game or trade, or speaks at a business school or any other public or private function, they are taking on a public-relations effort.

The president is representing the Roughriders brand every time they interact with the public. Similarly, when players have speaking engagement in schools, visit a children's hospital, or take part in a charity event, they are engaged in public-relations activities. However, executives and athletes are not the only personnel within a sport organization that are subject to public relations. Any staff member of the organization, whether it's in sport operations, finance, human resources, or sport marketing, can affect how the public relates to the brand because of the staff member's association. Therefore, if a sport marketer is out in the community wearing a team-affiliated polo and donning their work identification badge and lanyard, their actions can positively or negatively impact how the public views that team. Because of this, it is critical to maintain a positive attitude toward public relations. Therefore, public relations is an essential component of what is known as an integrative sport management (ISM) system.

Progressive organizations have a communications plan as part of their business strategy. Such a plan should identify publics of interest, the messages to be sent, and the communication vehicles to be used. If a concern arises, the integration of an image communication program into the corporate strategy can often lead to less criticism by special interest groups. For example, the National Hockey League (NHL) has been very proactive with respect to the LGBTQ+ community, celebrating the league as an inclusive space for athletes, fans, and other stakeholders from that particular community. In situations where an athlete or coach voices noninclusive perspectives about LGBTQ+ rights and lifestyles, it is critical for the league to have a proactive corporate strategy of promoting inclusivity. To be specific, sport marketers must identify sources and channels through which the organization's image is conveyed, making sure relevant concerns are addressed. In the modern era, this is especially important on digital and social media channels such as websites, apps, and engaging platforms like Facebook and Instagram. In the NHL example, it would be important to proactively communicate on these various channels that the

IN THE KNOW

Public Relations and an Integrative Sport Management System

Managers working for sport organizations make decisions all the time. What may be considered a minor decision at the time may have future consequences that lead to a public relations fiasco. Naturally, it is best to have the time to thoroughly think through a decision, take the correct action, and report on that action, but in reality, this does not always happen. The integrative sport management (ISM) system considers how sport marketing works with the other departments of an organization (e.g., operations, finance, human resources) to provide a broader understanding of issues and the roles that everyone should play in public relations. For example, coaches do not just coach; they are salespeople to athletes, organizational members, sponsors, governments, and the public. Therefore, media training is essential to enable coaches to shape a positive public image of the organization. When a coach or other representative of an organization stays silent when given the opportunity to speak to the media, they are basically inviting the media to shape the public image of the organization—a risky choice.

league is an inclusive space and is welcoming of LGBTQ+ through its "You Can Play" and "Pride" events. Communicating to its publics in this particular, positive way can reduce the likelihood of public outcry and harmful public relations for the league.

Since public relations programs have a direct impact on organizational image, staff with good communication skills tend to be successful within a sport organization and elevate to positions of importance. The involvement of sponsors, media, and governments in sports has encouraged sport organizations to develop public relations policies. These policies would typically outline interactions and interview requests from the mass media, social media interactions and behaviours, sharing documents and information with stakeholders, attending conferences or representing the brand at public events, speculating or commenting on current events, and key things to avoid. What is important to remember here is that these policies are not just for key sport stakeholders like athletes and coaches but rather extend to other figures within the sport organization, including staff, volunteers, and other applicable administrators. Especially in the case of volunteers who may not be associated with the sport organization on an ongoing basis, it is important to remember their impact to the public at large as the latter develops

beliefs and assumptions about the brand as a whole. Thus, a sport organization's public perception should be assessed continually, both internally with members and externally with various publics, including government, suppliers, sponsors, and media. It is a valuable activity to survey people or corporations that have no present dealings with the sport organization because a poor impression may affect external business relations. For instance, if, from surveying an unaffiliated and unattached party, it is learned that there is a misunderstanding about a policy or directive, the organization should reword the policy to ensure that the wording, characterization, and delivery of the policy are made clear because this approach to the public can reduce negative publicity in the future. This can, in turn, be assessed with future evaluations.

Sponsorship

Sponsorship is a promotional practice that has moved from its roots as a tool for corporate donations to a highly developed course of action in which both the sponsor, or investor, and the sponsee, or property, benefit in a marketing partnership (Cornwell, 2020). Its rapid adoption into practice by organizations is reflected by the growth of sponsorship spending (rights fees plus activation) in Canada, which rose from an estimated 1.6 billion CAD in 2006 to just over 3.0 billion CAD in 2018 (CSLS, 2019). Globally, sponsorship spending was projected to be more than 71 billion USD in 2020 (Statista, 2019). The momentum of sponsorship in Canada is not an anomaly; over the course of the past two editions of this textbook, sponsorship has continued to grow in importance, and the global and Canadian spending in this promotional mix category have followed suit. Accordingly, two chapters (13 and 14) of the present edition are entirely dedicated to sport sponsorship in the Canadian context.

In the published marketing literature, the role of sponsorship in the marketing promotional mix ranges from no inclusion at all—from a marketing as communications perspective—to full-scale recognition that it is an integral part of the mix, alongside advertising, publicity, personal selling, and sales promotion. The full-scale recognition view emphasizes the importance of sponsorship from a perspective of marketing as revenue generation. In this regard, Tripodi (2001) recognized several decades ago that sponsorship in sport was an incredibly powerful tool for sport marketers and should not be discarded from the promotional mix. Given the consistent rise of sponsorship spending, Tripodi has not been proven wrong. However, one of the key challenges that remains for sponsorship (and researchers on the topic) is to provide evidence that it is more effective than advertising or sales promotions. On one hand, advertising seeks to exploit consumer emotion by connecting the brand directly to the consumer; it connects to a feeling, belief, or attitude and drives awareness and, hopefully, additional purchase behaviour. On the other hand, sponsorship strives to connect with the emotions and feelings inherent between two brands, organizations, or properties. The association between the two parties, known as the sponsor (brand) and property (sponsee), differentiates sponsorship from advertising. Because of this distinction, sponsorship should be integrated with the other elements of the promotional mix (publicity, advertising, sales promotion, and personal sales). A synergetic effect will not only maximize effectiveness but will also contribute to building equity in the focal brand. For more detailed information on sport sponsorship, refer to chapter 13 and chapter 14.

Executional Elements of Promotions

The implementation of the promotional mix, particularly when using an integrated approach with all the different tactics, requires particular attention to the execution. This section provides directions on the elements of an execution to increase the potential for success.

Preliminary Planning

When deciding whether to use a promotion, a sport marketer must have sound knowledge of the total business operation so that the promotion complements the organization's overall strategy and brands. Promotions that are inauthentic to the organization's brands may potentially have an adverse effect (i.e., a negative impact). It is also important for the sport marketer to be intimate with the specific details of the product or service they are seeking to promote; just because there is a good promotional idea does not necessarily mean it works for their brand. For instance, consider the bobblehead doll promotion, often considered as the most engaging, embraced promotional giveaway in sport. Bobbleheads, more often than not, are considered a good promotional tool to entice consumers to purchase the sport product. But what if there was a Parkinson's disease awareness night at the Ballpark? Would a bobblehead be a good promotional item or detract from the awareness of the night due to the poor taste in giveaway? What if a team created a bobblehead doll of a former player who had made insensitive remarks about race and ethnicity during Black History Month? These examples show that while a sport marketer could have a good promotional idea in mind, that might not always be the most prudent choice given the circumstances. Finally, sport marketers need to have a strong understanding of the audience and consumer demographic they are trying to reach with the promotion. For example, a 1960s nostalgia day promotion may not necessarily be suitable if the target audience consists of Millennials and Generation Zs.

Timing

Although it is a crucial element of the preparation process, if timing is not well planned by a promoter, a mistake can result that can harm an otherwise good promotional idea. For example, many organizations force a promotion during the wrong time of year for a segment of their target market. A mass-market promotion during the month of Ramadan, the holy month observed in Islam when Muslims around the world fast, if the potential audience is 40 percent Muslim and therefore unable to participate and engage, is not a well-timed plan with strategic foresight. Sport marketers should consider not just major holidays and religious events, but also days and times of the week and how those connect to the event, product release, or service offering. For example, the COVID-19 global pandemic led to the cancellation of many promotions, as they were no longer appropriate or relevant during such a time. Researching competing, additional, or unexpected events scheduled in the same location for the same proposed date and time is thus an important task for any sport marketer. This research must be coupled with sufficient lead time to book space, activities, and entertainment for the promotion. Even during the traditional off-season period for sports (e.g., the winter months for baseball), arrangements and bookings could have occurred over a year ago from another business or organization within or outside the sport industry. Chambers of commerce and local business associations can be useful resources to find information on upcoming events; having this information while planning a promotion can prevent a potentially embarrassing or ineffective campaign and allow consumers to engage with and experience multiple promotions across industry sectors.

Ideas

Once sport marketers take preliminary steps and consider the timing of the promotion,

brainstorming (sometimes call "ideation") can be a useful technique to generate creative input from as many sources as possible. In an initial group discussion, negative thoughts and opinions should not be welcomed; rather, each idea should be presented and discussed until there is consensus from the promotions team or unit that it is an unacceptable choice. The most promising ideas should then be assessed against the organization's objectives. It is also useful to secure opinions from sources located outside the inner trust of the marketing team. For example, one enterprising promoter could discuss ideas with "gig economy" workers who often drive the public to sporting events (e.g., Uber) or deliver food to their homes during major sporting events. Another would be to target promotions and efforts to support frontline health-care workers during the COVID-19 pandemic. Once ideas have been assessed inside and outside the organization, it is also critical to develop mock situations that seek to address the idea's potential pitfalls or shortcomings. In other words, it is important to play "devil's advocate" and address what might go wrong with this promotional idea. Thorough preparation results in greater promotional success.

Follow-up

The follow-up stage ensures that all the elements of a promotion fit together. First, the chosen idea must be checked against both promotional and budget requirements. Then, the promotion must have the proper lead time, not only for the staff or members, but also for the commercial and community sectors. Everyone must execute their assignments within the specified period of time. A good promoter also attempts to secure the necessary equipment or personalities at minimal cost. A successful promoter must be aware of people and resources in the community and then negotiate contracts and deals accordingly. For example, if an upscale hotel suite is required for a visiting celebrity personality, offering the hotel prominent publicity in exchange for getting the suite at no cost is a logical strategy to limit costs (this is sometimes called an in-kind or contra sponsorship). Another example of follow-up is the coordination of advertising to support the promotion. A newspaper could begin a digital subscription drive by offering a season ticket as the prize for a lucky, random new subscriber. In exchange for the season ticket, the newspaper would provide free advertisements for the promotion day. When considering these follow-up tasks, organizing an itemized list of what has to be done, by whom and when, as well as what could go wrong and how the situation could be rectified, can be extremely beneficial. For example, to prevent a disaster if special microphones are required for the promotion, have those present learn how to check power source and microphone trouble spots. Arrange for a standby backup unit and technician in case of emergency. Maintaining a "run-sheet" or organized list of tasks, persons, and potential issues reduces the potential for a misstep or unknowns that can derail a promotional activity.

Activating the Promotion

Personnel must check their individual lists to ensure all elements are operative. Every promotional element must be rechecked on the day of the event. In addition, a group meeting should be held to delineate staff responsibilities so that an error in assignment can be corrected before the event begins. No promotion is too small for this kind of commitment to detail. For digital or virtual promotions, it remains an important task to check and recheck systems, databases, and other technological infrastructure. For example, a digital promotional activity should be broken down into key time segments pre-, during, and post-activity. The names and responsibilities of each person should be laid out on an internal plan page and each person should be ready to execute in their position. For certain social media promotions, one staff member might be allocated to curate and post content while another might be allocated to search through comments and analyze the metrics as they develop. However, even less-complex digital tasks can be challenging. For instance, an element as simple as an online ballot-entry form causing an error to the user can be frustrating and adversely affect the

flow and viral nature of the online promotion. Remember, the promotion reflects the state of professionalism within the organization.

Preparation cannot guarantee a trouble-free promotional activity, but it can provide contingency plans that turn problems into positive outcomes. For example, if the facility heating system fails, perhaps the concessionaire can be convinced to provide free coffee, tea, or hot chocolate during the event. While this idea might seem far-fetched, the strategy of providing free food items is mutually beneficial for the sport brand and food provider because the free item may actually result in increased purchases and, ultimately, revenue. For instance, an ongoing promotion with the NBA's Toronto Raptors results in fans obtaining a medium-sized order of fries from food outlet McDonald's if the club scores at least 12 three-pointers in any playoff game. While McDonald's gave out over 2 million orders of fries during the Raptors' championship season in 2019 (Tsekouras, 2019), the food supplier also generated significant purchase sales as a result: McDonald's customers do not typically just eat fries; they also purchase drinks, meals, and other complementary food items. Thus, working with food providers to problem solve and react to a situation or proactively create a promotional circumstance like the Raptors did with McDonald's is a strategy an enterprising promoter should discuss prior to the event. A mutually beneficial arrangement is characterized by sound planning. It is critical to remember that whatever is offered during the promotion must be delivered, even if a situation results in additional cost to the promoter. To do otherwise, regardless of the reason, alienates the public and affects the success of future promotions.

As a final promotional assessment, the sport marketer should carefully consider hidden promotional costs; this is especially important for a volunteer association. For instance, if advertising costs are $1,000 and the expected net profit is $3,000, the promotion may be worth the effort. However, generating the net profit will entail the time, energy, and talent of many volunteers to develop promotional kits and posters, make community contacts, and distribute printed material. Personnel will also be required to contact the media before and after the event and, of course, work at the event. This effort could represent 150 person-hours depending on the scale of the event. Minor salaries calculated at only $3.00/hour (as a modest stipend) decreases the actual net profit to $1,550. This may still be an acceptable profit to an organization, but at what cost? Since the volunteers gave 150 hours to make the promotion a reality, it may be unrealistic to expect similar service more frequently than once each season. Overloading volunteers can be a risky venture, which can affect the availability of human resources within that organization. Using different volunteers for each promotion entails additional person-hours involved in training or explaining tasks on each occasion. Moreover, changing the personnel dealing with individual community contacts prevents the establishment of a long-term cooperative relationship throughout the season. In professional sport contexts, salaries are much higher than the $3.00/hour calculation used here, but this is where the use of interns is critical. Internships are valuable work placement experiences for sport marketing students across Canada and serve as a useful labour force for the sport organization. With growing minimum wages across the country as well as increased benefits and incentives packages, delivering a promotion with paid, in-house staff could be an extremely costly venture. This is where the industry has sought to take advantage of the valuable human resource represented by interns. However, interns supply their talents with the expectation that there may be a full-time position available in the organization in the near future. Therefore, if a firm is unable to provide interns with full-time work in the future, this may result in a negative image and impact the organization's ability to attract future interns and deliver promotions at a later time. Another common strategy to minimize costs is to outsource promotions to third-party companies that specialize in promotional activity. Those firms often require a monthly or yearly cost, but they take care of the hiring, training, and development of human resources so that the focal organization can maintain a more strategic, higher-order focus.

EXECUTIVE PERSPECTIVE
Promoting the Canada Games

ERIN MATHANY, Vice-President, Marketing and Partnerships, Canada Games Council

Held once every two years, alternating between winter and summer, the Canada Games represent the highest level of national competition for up-and-coming Canadian athletes. Recognized as our country's largest multisport event, the Canada Games see teams from each province and territory compete against each other for medals—much like the Olympic Games.

Since their inception in 1967 as part of Canada's centennial celebration, the Canada Games have served as a nation-building event contributing to the country's sport development system and produce lasting impacts through community pride, national unity, and the infrastructure legacies they leave behind.

The Games feature events for athletes with physical and intellectual disabilities as well as able-bodied athletes and are designed to bring the next generation of Canadian leaders from across the country together in a celebration of sport, art, culture and community. Over the last 50 years, the Games have been held in every province at least once, with 22 communities across Canada hosting the Games, each welcoming athletes from over 700 communities nationwide.

> continued

> **Promoting the Canada Games** > *continued*

In total, nearly 100,000 athletes have participated in this multisport competition, while hundreds of thousands have engaged in tryouts and qualifying events. When you add that to the more than 100,000 coaches, officials, and volunteers who have been directly involved in the planning and staging of the Games, you get an idea of the enormous reach they have had throughout their proud history.

The Games play a prominent role in developing Canada's next generation of national, international, and Olympic champions. More notable alumni who have counted the Canada Games as one of their first multisport experiences include Sidney Crosby, Eugenie Bouchard, Steve Nash, Hayley Wickenheiser, Cindy Klassen, Chris Pronger, Clara Hughes, Andre De Grasse, Adam van Koeverden, Desiree Scott, Bo Hedges, and Stephanie Dixon.

Many Canada Games alumni like the ones listed here go on to compete at the Olympic and Paralympic Games. Recently, Canada Games alumni contributed to 14 of the 22 medals that Canada won at the Rio 2016 Summer Olympics, and they also contributed to 12 of the 29 medals Canada earned at the PyeongChang 2018 Winter Olympics.

The governing body that oversees the Canada Games as they move from one host community to the next is the Canada Games Council (CGC). The CGC provides the continuity, leadership, and support to host societies in key games areas such as sport technical, transportation, organizational planning, protocol events, ceremonies, marketing, community relations, and sponsorship. In addition, the CGC also manages the effective long-term partnerships with national sport organizations, multisport organizations, national partners, government stakeholders, and provincial and territorial teams.

The Canada Games are promoted in a wide variety of ways both locally and nationally. Most recently, during the Red Deer 2019 Canada Winter Games, approximately 80 hours of live competition and ceremonies were broadcast on TSN and RDS in both official languages nationwide. In total, over 475,000 people tuned in to TSN and RDS to watch the 2019 Canada Games, while the same number of viewers watched the Games webcast—consuming over 9.9 million minutes of coverage online.

Between various Games and during the event itself, the CGC works to develop the Canada Games brand, promote the Games nationally, engage fans through social channels, establish long-term national sponsorships, and ensure that host societies have the tools they need to promote their unique Games.

In host communities, a wide variety of marketing strategies are undertaken by the host society in an effort to: (1) boost awareness of the Canada Games, (2) recruit the thousands of volunteers necessary to run the event, and (3) raise additional funds through sponsorship engagement as well as ticket and merchandise sales.

Given that many consumers and potential sponsors in a host community have not been widely exposed to the Canada Games before, the host society will activate a variety of programs to ensure that the Games are promoted at an unprecedented level within their host community, region, and province or territory. This approach often features a mascot program, an education program, and milestone or community events, including a torch relay.

Recognizing that a mascot is an essential community ambassador for each Games and a playful way to engage and inspire a young audience, the official mascot of any Canada Games plays an important role in promoting its key messages. The mascot program also works harmoniously with the host society's education program that features touch points and activities with local schools and their students in the years leading up to the Games— serving as another mechanism to build up knowledge, engagement, and excitement for the Canada Games.

To further promote and celebrate this unique competition, the host society will organize community and milestone events in the run up to the Games, which include groundbreaking ceremonies, a torch relay, and countdown celebrations that typically feature Two-Years-Out and One-Year-Out celebrations. These types of events will not only engage the public with a memorable experience but also further develop awareness and buzz for the Games. In addition, they produce important opportunities to highlight and showcase funding partners, sponsors, and participating municipalities of the event.

Host Societies also pursue local and regional sponsors and work collaboratively with the CGC to recruit prominent Canadian brands to sign on as national partners in order to elevate the Canada Games brand. Sponsorship packages developed for these partners often seek to recognize the different contributions and needs of each sponsor in the hope of maximizing revenue and allowing sponsors to personalize their activations, thereby increasing the overall awareness of those activations and the Games.

The host society will adopt robust earned media and social media strategies to gain a broader audience, while developing recognition and sentiment for its brand. In order to support this, the host society produces dynamic and high-quality content online to optimize its reach, drive engagement on social media platforms, and build lasting relationships with its audiences. Part of the host's aim also strives to drive visitors to their website with the goal of investing them further into the Games by prompting them to sign up for a newsletter or register for an event.

The latter is a particularly important tactic in the recruitment of over 4,500 volunteers (including over 300 pre-Games planning volunteers) required to service and support all operational areas of the Games. Given that the Canada Games are fundamentally a volunteer-driven event, a critical component of any successful Games involves the recruitment of these volunteers from the host community. In order to meet this requirement, the host society will also invest in digital, radio, and out-of-home (OOH) advertising, while also targeting community events and groups to find the volunteers needed to run the Games.

Two areas that impact both revenue generation and stakeholder experience are merchandise and ticketing. A host society's merchandising plan, built in collaboration with their merchandise supplier and the CGC, will focus on creating a merchandise lineup of hard and soft goods that are sold both online and at specific events and venues during the Games. The Canada Games family of stakeholders (sponsors, athletes, provincial and territorial teams, etc.) are typically encouraged to participate in a Games-wear campaign that takes place prior to the event to build up excitement for the Games and its merchandise lineup.

A host society's ticketing plan will aim to not only generate revenue but also maximize spectator attendance. Similar to merchandise, the host society will work with their selected ticketing agency to develop a program that outlines the variety of tickets, packages, or passes available for sale to the general public. The host society will also work to determine which sports and venues are ticketed and the allotment of seats that need to be reserved for VIPs, media, same-sport participants, and the general public. Tickets are predominantly sold online through either the host society or ticketing agency website, while box-office purchases are also made possible during the Games.

ERIN MATHANY is vice-president, marketing and partnerships, at the Canada Games Council. She is responsible for leading the innovative growth of the Canada Games brand, highlighting the stories of the athletes, coaches, volunteers, and communities that bring the Games to life while engaging corporate partners in the Canada Games movement. Erin was previously with the Canadian Olympic Committee as the director of commercial affairs and business development. Erin holds a bachelor's degree in sport management from Brock University and an MBA from Wilfred Laurier University.

CHAPTER SUMMARY

This chapter provided an overview of the importance of promotion within the marketing mix. The promotional mix comprises six components: advertising, publicity, personal selling, sales promotion, public relations, and sponsorship. The promotional mix is used to communicate information about the product or service and is interchangeable with the communications mix. The chapter also includes some advice on how to plan and execute a promotional strategy, including outlining the executional elements to implement to maximize the potential success of a promotional strategy. The chapter further outlines the importance of an integrated (i.e., all-components) approach to promotions for sport marketers.

TEST YOUR KNOWLEDGE

1. Explain the relationship between promotion and each of the other Ps of the marketing mix and give an example.
2. What makes a promotion successful?
3. Describe an experience when you have seen all elements of the promotional mix in action.
4. Visit a sport retailer in your local area (or a sport retailer's website) and describe how it uses sales promotion. What tactics do you believe to be most effective in reaching consumers, and why?
5. Visit a sport organization's website and describe how it uses the site as a promotional vehicle. Assess whether it uses the site effectively.
6. When do sports marketers use personal selling? What are some key elements of personal selling?
7. Describe the elements of the promotional mix and give an example of each.

KEY TERMS

advertising	promotion	sponsorship
personal selling	publicity	sweepstakes
point-of-purchase	public relations	
premium	sales promotion	

CASE STUDIES

Visit HK*Propel* for case studies organized by chapter.

CHAPTER 11

Media and Distribution in Sport

LEARNING OBJECTIVES

After studying this chapter, you will be able to do the following:

- Understand the sport media business in Canada
- Identify the three models of delivering sport content to consumers
- Understand the importance of building positive media relations
- Identify the different ways of generating media coverage
- Describe the value of media training
- Understand the distribution process in relation to the media, facilities, and retailing

Suppose that you have been hired as a sport marketing coordinator by a company that organizes a series of running events in your hometown. The company's flagship event is an annual half-marathon that is staged every year in October. During the first week of your hire, the race director asked you to share some of the topic areas about the management of sport media that you covered during your degree program. What would be your response to the race director? This chapter discusses the main points that a student of sport marketing should

know about the management of sport media. The management of sport media requires an understanding of both the sport media business ecosystem and the management of content production within your organization. The chapter also includes details related to preparing press releases, creating social media content, developing script for a 30-second promo video, and leveraging television coverage.

The chapter mainly consists of two different but interrelated parts, namely, the sport media business (external) and the management of **media**

relations (internal). The third part discusses the related topic of **distribution** in sport. The first part starts with a brief discussion of the history of the sport media business in Canada and with a presentation of an overview of media rights revenue. Then the chapter discusses the three commonly employed models of sport-content delivery, followed by a discussion of the key players in the Canadian sport media business. As important as understanding the ecosystem of the sport media business may be, it is also essential for sport marketers to look inward and recognize the key undertakings in managing media relations, which is the purpose of the second part of the chapter. Specifically, the second part discusses the importance of building positive media relations, the significance of servicing the media, the different ways of generating media coverage, and the value of media training.

A Brief History of the Sport Media Business

Sport has always attracted the interest of audiences above and beyond those attending live games at the stadium. For a number of reasons, people may be unable to make it to a stadium and watch live games. Not enough time, cost of tickets, or living far away from a game venue could be some of the reasons. Those people who could not make it to a stadium have always relied on the media channels to follow game updates. The media channels can be newspaper, radio, magazines, TV, and, in today's world, streaming services, podcasts, blogs, or social media platforms. For example, if we look at the 2016 Rio Games and the 2012 London Olympic Games, while not more than 100,000 people attended the Game's opening ceremonies live at Olympic venues, a reported one-seventh of the world population viewed the ceremonies live on the media. The Tokyo 2020 Olympic Games, held in 2021, took place during the COVID-19 pandemic, and no spectators were allowed to attend the events. Therefore, the media channels played a significant role in bringing the Games to audiences worldwide. There is little doubt that media channels (especially television) have greatly influenced the advancement of the sport industry as we know it today.

Looking back, however, the sport media industry had a humble beginning. If we start with the first radio transmission of the National Hockey League games in Canada, the 1931 season games were broadcasted by radio stations in Ontario and Quebec initially, and later different radio stations from different parts of the country started covering the games (Canadian Communications Foundation [CCF], 2014). By then, most radio stations in Canada were run by private capital such as radio equipment manufacturers and newspaper companies, without much intervention by the state (Cavanagh, 1992). According to CCF (2014), General Motors (GM) of Canada was sponsor of the 1931 season games, and due to repeated requests the company it was receiving from dealers in the different part of the country, the number of radio station covering the games increased significantly between 1931 and 1934. The radio stations were covering the games only after the second period was under way, so the media coverage of the games does not deter stadium attendance or risk ticket sales to the games.

For the 1934-1935 games, the pioneer of Saturday night hockey, GM, was replaced by Imperial Esso Oil, which continued its sponsorship until 1976 (Cavanagh, 1992). The MacLaren Advertising Agency, the agency handling the media management of the games at the time, selected radio stations that carry the radio coverages and set up a network to connect them (CCF, 2014), which is shown in figure 11.1. As the figure shows, the local radio stations have been networked together with the help of telephone to evolve into radio broadcast. In radio broadcast, the same event will be covered and distributed to different radio stations, so that an event can reach a wider audience at the same time through a network of different radio stations. The Imperial Esso Hockey Broadcast, in due course, became Hockey Night in Canada, and the program was later carried over to TV when the games began to be televised in the 1950s (CCF, 2014). Following the national coverage of the hockey games and Canadians' love for the sport, businesses became interested in associating themselves with the games as advertisers or sponsors. The national advertising or sponsorship opportunity,

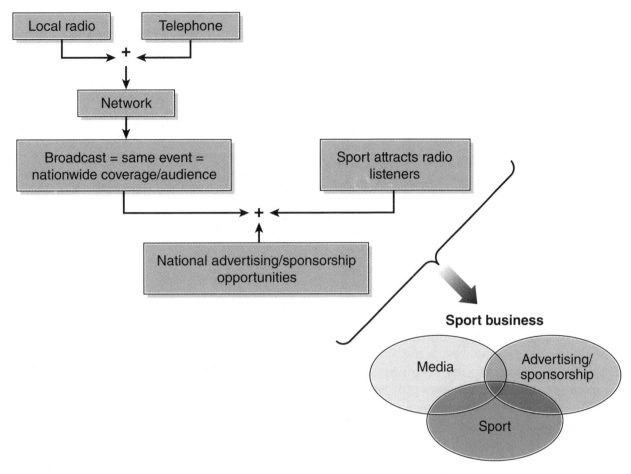

FIGURE 11.1 Evolution of the media business.

as shown in figure 11.1, leads to the symbiotic relationship that we know today among the sport, the media, and businesses.

In terms of televised sport event, the first televised sporting event in Canada was Hockey Night in Canada on CBC, which started with the 1952-1953 season (CCF, n.d.). In fact, the first trial televised sport program was the Memorial Cup hockey game, which was broadcast from Maple Leaf Gardens in April 1952 (CCF, n.d.). The trial was closed to the CBC's top management, the then sponsor Imperial Oil, and the MacLarens advertising agency. Three years before the first broadcast, the then NHL president Clarence Campbell was voicing his concern against a televised hockey game. The president was concerned that the TV would take away fans from the stadium and ticket sales would decline. However, as shown in table 11.1, it turned out that the president was wrong, and television became a new revenue source. The

TABLE 11.1 Hockey Night Canada: Early Days Radio Rights Fee (in CAD)

Year	Rights Fee
1952-1953 Season	$100 per game
1954-1957 Season	$150,000 per three seasons
Early 1960s	$9,000,000 per six seasons or $21,000 per game

Data from Canadian Communications Foundation (2020b).

media rights fees (i.e., the total revenue from all media sources) have grown from the first-rights fee of 100 CAD per game (1952-1953 season) to 21,000 CAD per game in a period of seven years (early 1960s seasons). Hockey Night in Canada was produced by the CBC until 2013, when the rights to broadcast NHL games were acquired by Rogers Communication through the 2025-2026 season.

Overview of Media Rights Revenue

The sport media business in Canada has had a humble beginning during which both radio and TV were initially considered a threat to ticket sales and stadium attendance. Today, media rights fees are the major sources of income for a few major sporting entities. A good example is the International Olympic Committee (IOC) for its Games. The IOC generates a significant amount of revenue from media rights fees, which is shared with the National Olympic Committees, including the Canadian Olympic Committee.

As table 11.2 shows, the IOC generates 47 percent of the Olympic Games revenue from media rights fees, followed by sponsorship, and then ticketing and licensed merchandise. This shows the significance of the symbiotic relationship among the media, the sport, and the business world. For the 2016 Rio Games, for example, the IOC received approximately 2.9 billion USD in media rights fees, and for the 2018 PyeongChang Games, the IOC received approximately 1.4 billion USD (International Olympic Committee, 2020).

To further highlight the sizable growth of media rights fees over the past six decades, it is interesting to look at how much the IOC generated from media rights fee for the 1960 Rome Olympics and then for the 2016 Rio Olympics. As shown in table 11.3, the IOC broadcast rights fee grew from 1.2 million USD in the 1960 Rome Olympics to about 2.9 billion USD in the 2016 Rio Olympics. This is a significant growth in media revenue in just over the period of 56 years. Two Olympic Games, in particular, saw the biggest jump in media rights fees;

namely, fees for the 2000 Sydney Olympics grew by 434 million USD and the London Olympics Games by 830 million USD. These dollar figures show the importance of media not only in terms of satisfying the need of those who could not make it to the stadium but also as a major source of revenue for the Olympic Games, which makes the subject matter one of the key topic areas in sport marketing.

The substantial growth in media rights fees, however, is not representative of what is happening in all types of sports. Similar to the IOC, a significant portion of National Football League (NFL) revenue comes from media rights. By definition, the media rights fee is the fee that a broadcasting company (e.g., CBC) pays to a property owner (e.g., the IOC) to have the official right to produce, distribute, and transmit content related to an agreed property. For example, CBC was the broadcaster of the 2014, 2016, and 2018 Olympic Games. The CBC pays the IOC to have the right to broadcast the Summer and Winter Olympic Games in Canada on its different outlets. The outlets could include CBC Television, radio networks, digital properties, and so forth. Another example is Rogers Communications' 2013 deal with the NHL to be the league's exclusive Canadian national broadcaster for 12 years for a fee of CND $5.2 billion (Settimi, 2013). In addition to TV, Rogers' deal included the mobile rights, Internet streaming, and terrestrial and satellite radio rights.

One may, therefore, wonder how the media companies generate revenue to recoup their expenses and then make profit. Media companies use different methods to make up their expenses and make profit. In a typical sport-media business, the broadcaster produces the telecast, distributes it, and generates revenue by selling advertisements aired in between the broadcasts and by distributing the content to other TV network stations. The main revenue sources for the sport media companies are advertising sales, subscription fees, and regular cable fees. While major sport properties (e.g., the Olympics, NHL) and established media companies (e.g., CBC, SportsNet) have the typical rights arrangements of content production and distribution, this specific type of rights arrangement (i.e., the network both produces

TABLE 11.2 Olympic Revenue 2016

Revenue Source	Percentage of Contribution to Total Revenue
Broadcast	47%
Sponsorship	45%
Ticketing	5%
Licensing	3%
Total	100%

Based on IOC (2019).

TABLE 11.3 Broadcast Revenue History: Summer Olympic Games

Olympic Games	Broadcast Revenue (in USD millions)	Growth from the Preceding Games
Rome 1960	1.2	
Tokyo 1964	1.6	0.4
Mexico City 1968	9.8	8.2
Munich 1972	18	8.2
Montreal 1976	35	17
Moscow 1980	88	53
Los Angeles 1984	287	199
Seoul 1988	403	116
Barcelona 1992	636	233
Atlanta 1996	898	262
Sydney 2000	1,332	434
Athens 2004	1,494	162
Beijing 2008	1,739	245
London 2012	2,569	830
Rio 2016	2,868	299

Based on IOC (2019).

and distributes the content) is one of the three common types used in the business of sport broadcasting. The second type of arrangement is rights only agreement, where production expenses are covered by sport properties and the media company will be responsible for the distribution of the content and the revenue is shared. The third type of rights arrangement is commonly used by small local and regional events (e.g., a regional 5K run) that cannot find broadcasters interested in their property's content. These types of properties usually produce the content themselves and buy airtime from the media companies to broadcast the content. These property holders cover their expenses by selling advertising and seeking sponsorship. This type of arrangement is commonly referred to as a time-buy rights arrangement (Masteralexis et al., 2011).

In the case of a time buy, the amateur sport organizations generally hire a producer to broadcast their events on a private sport cable network such as TSN. By paying for the production, the sport organization usually has more control over the content and creative of the broadcast. For example, you may want to consider an interview with a key sponsor representative, place the signage in the right television spots, and develop a special vignette. Sport organizations are also often given advertising inventory to share with a broadcaster (e.g., 30-second spots, opening and closing billboards, or in-program graphics). The value of such advertising should be acquired ahead of time. Finally, understanding event broadcasting is critical when negotiating a fee with potential production companies. Consider the following requirements:

- Number and types of cameras required to provide a quality broadcast
- Number of technicians needed to produce the broadcast
- Commentators
- Lights and equipment
- Production crew and truck

These three types of rights arrangements include different clauses in their media rights agreement. In the most common media rights agreements, media companies enter in agreement with sport properties covering key clauses such as the amount of rights fees, the length of the agreement, broadcast distribution territory, copyright ownership, number of commercials to be aired, and sponsorship exclusivity. These clauses impact media companies' potential in raising funds to recoup their expenses and then make profit. For example, while TVA has the French-language broadcasting rights for NHL games, SportsNet covers a larger geographic area and reaches a wider audience in the country. The larger the broadcast territory is, the higher advertising and sponsorship opportunity, and, by extension, the bigger the revenue. On this note, the next section discusses the three typical content delivery models employed by sport media companies.

Models of Delivering Sport Content

In delivering sport content to consumers, there are four value-adding steps that are historically employed in the media businesses (Foster et al., 2020). These include

1. the sport rights holders (e.g., NHL, CFL, IOC),
2. the production of content (e.g., SportsNets studio producing NHL games for broadcast and distribution),
3. the distribution of content (e.g., cable companies as Rogers, digital Over-The-Top services as Sportsnet NOW, subscription as TSN Direct), and
4. the consumer of content (e.g., sport viewers using TV, radio, laptop, smartphone, or tablet).

According to Foster and colleagues (2020), these four steps are managed under one of the three common distribution models:

• *Model 1: Direct to consumer model.* A model through which a sport property holder delivers content via Internet directly to the consumers. These are often called OTT (over-the-top) networks. In other words, for the consumer to get access to live game content, they have to commit to a pay-per-view agreement. A good example of this model, according to Foster and colleagues (2020), was World Wrestling Entertainment's

WWE Network, which is a **subscription-based video-on-demand (SVOD) service**. Subscribers pay a monthly subscription fee to access content. The property holder can also generate income from advertisers and sponsors.

• *Model 2: Partner with broadcasting channel.* This model is the oldest and most commonly used method in various regions of the world such as UK with BBC, Australia with ABC, and Canada with CBC. These three providers receive government funding and are state owned, and consumers often access the sporting content free of fee. In fact, they also enter into an agreement with sport-property owners to produce a program and recoup their fees through selling airtime for advertisers and charging redistribution fees from other broadcast companies.

• *Model 3: Via a double set of partnerships.* This third model is the dominant form of content distribution today, although it is under pressure as consumers move from cable packages to Model 1. This model can be better understood through the illustration shown in figure 11.2. The NHL entered in an agreement with SportsNet in 2013 as the league's exclusive Canadian national broadcaster for a 12-year period. SportsNet's parent company, Rogers, is a telecommunications (telecom) firm that offers TV cable, streaming, and OTT packages to consumers. Therefore, if Rogers offers a cable package of sport programs for 50 CAD for consumers, for example, the provider may channel 10 CAD of the fee to SportsNet. SportsNet recovers the fee it made to the NHL from the subscription fee plus selling airtime for advertisers and charging redistribution fees.

Key Players in the Sport Media Business in Canada

The sport-media business in Canada is dominated by two of Canada's largest providers of cable television service, namely, Rogers Communication and Bell Canada. These two telecom companies own the majority of the sport broadcasting rights in Canada. As shown in table 11.4, seven media companies take the significant market share of the Canadian sport broadcasting rights among the six major league

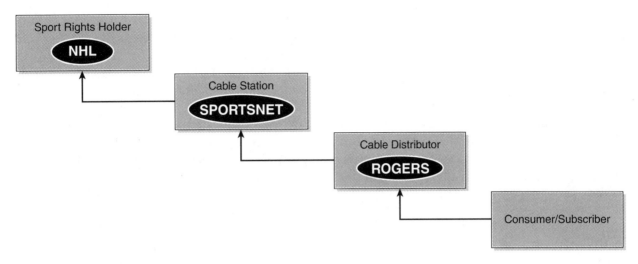

FIGURE 11.2   Distribution model 3: A double set of partnerships.

TABLE 11.4   Key Players in Sport Media in Canada

Major League Sports	National Rights	Parent Company
National Hockey League (NHL)	SportsNet	Rogers Communications
	TVA Sports	Groupe TVA (sister channel of SportsNet)
Major League Baseball (MLB)	SportsNet	Rogers Communications
National Basketball Association (NBA)	TSN	Bell Canada
	SportsNet NBA TV	Rogers Communications
	Canada	Maple Leaf Sports and Entertainment (MLSE)
Major League Soccer (MLS)	TSN	Bell Canada
	DAZN	DAZN Group–Access Industries
	TVA Sports	Groupe TVA (sister channel of SportsNet)
Canadian Football League (CFL)	TSN	Bell Canada
	RDS	Bell Media and ESPN
National Football League (NFL)	CTV	Bell Canada
	TSN	Bell Canada
	RDS	Bell Media and ESPN
	DAZN	

sports. These are CTV, RDS, TSN, SportsNet, TVA Sports, NBA TV Canada, and DAZN.

Please note that table 11.4 only shows the contract as of the 2020 seasons, only lists the six major league sports, and does not include international markets. In basketball, for example, the international market includes the Canadian national men's basketball team and FIBA tournaments, for which DAZN has the broadcast right in Canada. Also, TSN and NBA TV have the Canadian TV rights for the NBA's subsidiary leagues such as the NBA Summer League and NBA G League.

Media-Relations Management

Effective media relations depends on relationships between the sport organization and media representatives that are built over time. Media relations refers to the relationship between the sport organizations and the media, with the goal of improving both the volume and quality of media coverage that the sport organization receives. Media outlets provide sport organizations with the opportunity to reach large numbers of consumers at minimal cost. Hence, understanding the inner workings of media is an important aspect of a sport marketing strategy.

There are three main categories of media: media, print, and electronic. Print media include newspapers, magazines, and special publications; electronic media are all forms of radio and television broadcasting; and digital media are based on the Internet and include websites, social networking sites, blogs, content communities, and discussion sites. The later are discussed in more detail in chapter 12.

Why Is Media Relations Important?

With the increased attention devoted to sport, the media can be a great source of promotion for a sport organization. However, if used poorly, media relations can damage the sport. Often marketers and managers in sport organizations find themselves in the eye of a media storm, either as the central figure or as the spokesperson for an athlete, their sport, the organization, or a government. Therefore, all sport-organization personnel must be prepared to weather the storm. In a crisis, interaction—rather than reaction—with the media holds the greatest potential for defusing a problem and creating a positive interpretation of a situation. Proactive beats reactive every time. One must attempt to create positive attention for their sport organization and, in the process, gain respect from the media.

Building long-term relationships with the media can be a great asset to your sport organization. As a sport marketer, it is your role to service the media by providing information that is timely, professional, and accessible, both in good times and bad. Having good relations with the media is an integral part of any sport marketing strategy. A newspaper, a news media website, bloggers, and others may provide such information on your events as the price, product (information on individuals or teams participating), and place (where to get tickets, where the event is taking place), and it can

promote the event (interesting stories, things to watch for)—all at no or little cost to your sport organization.

In terms of the tactical activities undertaken by the sport marketer under the media-relations function, it is essential to understand the people in the media system and media relations. First, one must appreciate the influence that sport journalists have on the public. Sport journalists attain recognition and power because they provide breaking new and behind-the-scenes stories that the public craves. Since sport journalists have the power to shape the image and reputation of athletes, teams, leagues, coaches, and owners, a number of amateur sport organizations train athletes, coaches, and key staff in media relations. For example, most Canadian professional sport clubs have media relations departments (or agencies who work on their behalf) whose job is to connect with the media, create opportunities for athletes and coaches to get media, provide media-relations training for athletes and coaches, and support the activities of the clubs' marketing departments.

Ways to Get Media Coverage

The media can be a great source of content distribution to sport organizations. There are a number of ways that a sport organization can get media coverage of its events, athletes, or coaches. Key factors are the development of relationships and the quality of the servicing. To service the media, a sport marketer can use methods such as news releases, **press conferences**, and interviews. For the effectiveness of these methods, a sport marketer needs to develop relationships with journalists that are based on trust and understanding. These methods are briefly discussed in the following section.

News Releases

News releases are among the most common forms of communications between sport marketers and the media and are used by all levels of sports from major league sports to the little league soccer team competing in a city tournament. Ideally, the press release is written in a style that conforms to the needs of the media. It should include not only basic information but also quotes, pictures, or both and video clips when available. With fierce competition to get space in the media, one needs to provide a news release that will be newsworthy, timely, and interesting to the media audience. It is important to know that every sport event represents three major news opportunities, during which the press is legitimately interested in timely information: pre-event, event, postevent.

O'Reilly and Séguin (2013) listed eight basic elements that need to be included in a press release. Six of those basic elements are most relevant today and are discussed here.

1. Use official letterhead with information on the sport organization. If you use an electronic format, send the press release as an attachment to an email. It is essential to have the name, email address, and phone number of a person to be reached if a journalist needs clarification or additional information.

2. Mark the release with the words "immediate release," indicating that media can use the press release as soon as they wish, depending on their own schedule.

3. Write a meaningful headline to catch the attention of the media sport editor. The first paragraph, or the lead, should be two to three lines below the headline. The lead should include the Five Ws: who, what, when, where, and why.

4. In the body, write the facts to support the lead. The general rule is to use the inverted pyramid: The lead is the most important paragraph, and each succeeding paragraph contains less important information.

5. Use short sentences and short paragraphs because they are easier to read.

6. Put a page number at the top and bottom of the release. Indicate the end of release with "30" or "end" centred on the last line. Last, make sure that your press release is sent out on time.

Press Conference

The sport marketer must assess the value of a press conference, which is an organized event—in person or online—prior to a game or an event, where managers, coaches, athletes, and other celebrities are engaged to bring attention to an upcoming content. They are typically held a few days prior to the competition, and if enough attention can be garnered, they can be very successful. Media representatives are busy people and do not like to be called in for something of little or no value to them. In addition, especially in big cities, the competition for getting the media's attention is fierce. Too often sport organizations believe they have something newsworthy when in fact that is not the case. Can a press release be issued instead? This is usually where previous relationships with the media can pay dividends. Prior to sending an invitation it may be wise to check with a few prominent media representatives to find out their availability for the event. If you decide to go ahead with a press conference, send out invitations with information for an RSVP on it. Make sure that everything is ready on the site, including staff and volunteers, equipment including **media kits**, parking spaces, podium and microphone if needed, key personalities confirmed (athletes, coaches, administrators), master of ceremonies confirmed, refreshments, and lighting. Bring a media list to confirm which media attended. Usually, a press conference will be held in the late morning (11:00 a.m.) or mid-afternoon to get the maximum electronic coverage—news broadcast at noon, repeat coverage in evening, and late-night news. Once again, it is essential that the reasons for the press conference be newsworthy.

Whether at a press conference, in a media room, or delivered directly to the media, a press kit should be provided to the journalists. This kit should, at least, include the following:

- Biographies of personalities
- Schedule of events
- Previous statistics (e.g., results, records)
- Interview request form
- Accreditations
- Fact sheet on sport
- Technical information
- History of the sport
- Names of sponsors
- Action shot photos
- Video clips on memory sticks
- A folder

Interviews

The media are most interested in what the audiences would like to hear. In this regard, the most sought-after content for the media is interviewing high-profile sport personalities. Therefore, whether you work for a local hockey club or for a college wrestling team, you need to try to use one of your own high-profile personalities (a player or director) or one of the big names in your sport to attend your event and arrange a program for the media to interview that high-profile personality. Securing the attendance of a high-profile personality has never been easy, but it can be very rewarding. In doing so, the interviewee can speak about a given story on your behalf and get the word out much faster, wider, and better than you would possibly do it yourself. Also, that high-profile personality's attendance in itself could play a major role in enhancing your image and increasing your trustworthiness among journalists.

Media Training

The media training of athletes, coaches, administrators, and volunteer boards is essential for a successful media-relations strategy. The athletes and coaches in particular are most likely to be sought after for interviews. Some may be asked to face the media on a frequent basis (e.g., professional hockey players and coaches). Others may only get the opportunity to be on television once every four years during the Olympic Games. Either way, athletes and coaches are sports' best ambassadors, and good preparation can contribute to building awareness and interest for a sport organization.

While a sport organization may wish to get as many athletes as possible in the media under normal circumstances, there are times when only one spokesperson should be speaking on behalf of an organization (e.g., doping infractions, harassment cases, conversations about selection criteria for teams). Selecting a single spokesperson has merit as long as other personnel within the organization are informed of the facts. Reporters will seek multiple opinions for a story, and you must not leave a news coverage opportunity to chance. The possibility for misrepresentation is decreased if the reporter is unable to uncover conflicting opinions. This is critical especially in time of crisis. Preparation is essential when dealing with the media.

A briefing session (or press conference) in time of crisis is a useful tool because a planned response reduces the chance of harm for an organization. The briefing session allows personnel to obtain correct information on many topics. Key messages should be developed and distributed to the individuals who may be speaking to the media. Preparing answers to questions that are most likely to be asked by the media is also an effective way to get ready for a media interview. The key messages and the question-and-answer (Q&A) documents must not be disseminated to a few individuals on a "need to know basis" but rather to all personnel when contact with the media is possible. Remember that opinion makers are not limited to media personnel.

Completely briefed personnel increase the chance for positive reporting in general. The idea is to eliminate the uninformed response and replace it with facts delivered in a positive manner. This type of planned media strategy will position the sport organization as a leader in the eyes of many opinion makers, especially in the media themselves.

Alongside media training, the issue of crisis management is an important one. A good media-relations strategy usually includes a crisis-management plan. A crisis is a turning point for better or for worse, and the way a sport organization deals with a crisis can be a deciding moment. Crises are usually brought on by an issue or event that has potential for widespread, long-lasting impact. Crises require the attention of senior executives.

Distribution of Tangible Sport Products and Events

This section focuses on getting attention for a tangible sport product or event. Let's assume that you have a good sport product, a nice price, great media, and impressive promotions: How do you deliver the product? The final strategic marketing element is distribution, connecting with customers. Distribution, the "place" in the four Ps, involves the management of channels, or the chain of organizations that a product flows through from its origin to the end-user. Distribution is the process of moving a product from the producer to the consumer through one or many channels of distribution. If we consider a tangible good (e.g., snowboard, tennis shoes, basketball), this process of moving the good to a consumer is important in many ways, not just geographic (i.e., from location of manufacture to location of purchase) but also relating to time. In other words, it is not enough to provide a potential buyer with a store to buy a specific brand of snowboard, but the board must be available when they want it—just in time to hit the slopes. It is also important for the buyer to gain possession of the product in the form that they want—proper design, colours, style, and so on. Simply, the buyer gets "the" snowboard they want, where they want, and when they want.

The same distribution concepts apply to sporting events. For example, the fans for curling's most prestigious event, the Brier, may prefer to have games played during the week in the evenings in a facility that offers top-notch amenities (concessions, jumbotron, parking, public transportation) and broadcast on a major network (CBC). They may also want easy ticket access (Internet) and have a choice when buying tournament passes and selecting seat locations. As demonstrated in the previous examples, the marketing function of enabling consumers to access products conveniently and when they want is considered one of the most important strategic tactics that sport marketers implement. This can range from making sure local tennis players can get your rackets or that the televised product of your team is available to fans nationally or even globally. In accomplishing such goals, *distribution* refers to getting the product to the end-users and *channels* to the route the product takes to get to them, with each organization along the way known as a channel member. The form of the channels, or delivery systems, depends on the nature of the sport product being distributed. For example, telecasting a National Hockey League game is very different from selling hockey sticks.

In terms of the function that **distribution channels** provide to organizations, consider the efficiencies in the interactions between producers and consumers that they provide. Specifically, it is important to note that some large sporting goods stores sell as many as 5,000 different items. If the manufacturer of each of those items needed to have a way of accessing the consumer directly, the number of outlets required would be unmanageable. However, the department store—as a channel member—allows for the producer of each of those 5,000 products to access many customers in a very efficient way. In the past few years, the Internet played a significant role in making sport products accessible to consumers. Whether consumers desire a ticket to a sport event (e.g., buying from Ticketmaster) or a new pair of

IN THE KNOW

TSN and Sportsnet Offer a Portfolio of Channels

As the offerings of sport products expanded in the past decade, both the major networks in Canada gradually and extensively expanded their slots (channels) on cable packages and via streaming. For example, on the Virgin TV streaming platform (similar to cable) as of October 1, 2020, the following channels were available.

- TSN: Channels from 393 to 404 (13 total), including TSN1, TSN2, TSN3, TSN4, TSN5, and 8 TSN bonus channels.
- Sportsnet: Channels 405 to 409 (5 total), including Sportsnet Ontario, Sportsnet East, Sportsnet Pacific, Sportsnet West, and Sportsnet One.

Sometimes the network carries the same content on all its offerings (e.g., a high-profile NHL game), while other times it broadcasts different programming on all the slots (or channels).

running shoes (e.g., buying from NIKE website), the sporting goods are easily accessible online.

Channel Management and Sport Products

Sport marketers can manage distribution channels, or the set of companies and individuals who participate in getting the product from the producer to the consumer, in a variety of ways. First, there are direct and indirect channels. In a direct channel, the end-user deals directly with the manufacturer or producer of the sport product. For example, a national team cyclist works directly with a bicycle manufacturer to have a custom bike made for racing and training. In an indirect channel, at least one channel intermediary exists between the producer and the end-user, and often there are more. These channel intermediaries, which are often called middlemen or middlepersons, can be wholesalers, who purchase the product and resell it to another channel intermediary, or retailers, who sell the product to end-users. Examples in sport include the person scalping tickets to a professional sport event and a large wholesaler who buys hockey cards and resells them to a local wholesaler. Intermediaries provide the following functions:

- Taking ownership (and therefore risk) of the product
- Managing the physical storage of the product (risks associated with stocking the product)

- Gathering, sorting, and delivering the product
- Providing information about the product
- Facilitating purchase including financing of the product.

Each of the channel members—wholesalers, retailers, dealers, distributors, brokers, franchises, and agents—is influenced by key factors that affect the distribution in most industries.

Key Influencers on the Distribution Process

Not all channels have the same number of channel members. For example, the Toronto Blue Jays do not sell their game tickets to each customer in the same way. They may sell directly on the Internet or through a sales agent such as Ticketmaster, a sponsor (grocery chains), or at the gate. Shorter channels, those with fewer levels, exist when there are fewer consumers (e.g., business consumers) and higher service needs, the product is complex or perishable, and the producer has the resources and ability to reach the consumers directly and requires a high degree of control over the process. Longer channels are required when the consumers are highly dispersed, products are standardized and inexpensive, the producer does not have expertise in distribution, or the need for control is low.

CHAPTER SUMMARY

Given the tremendous coverage of sport by the media, a sport marketer's solid understanding of the sport media business ecosystem (external) and the management of media relations (internal) are key objectives of this chapter. In terms of understanding the sport media ecosystem, the first part of the chapter covered the brief history of the sport media business in Canada, the overview of media rights revenue, different models of sport content delivery, and the key players in Canadian sport media business. It showed how essential it is for sport marketers to understand the ecosystem of the sport media business and its different implications. Then, looking inward and focusing on the media-relations management, the second part of the chapter covered different topics related to the management of media and journalists, such as the importance of building positive media relations, the significance of servicing the media, ways of generating media coverage, and the value of media training. The last and final part presented the concept of distribution in sport marketing in relation to the media, facilities, and retailing.

TEST YOUR KNOWLEDGE

1. Identify the three models of delivering sport content to consumers and briefly describe each.
2. Who are the key players in sport media business in Canada?
3. Describe the significance of servicing the media and relate that to the value of media training.
4. If you were tasked with getting media coverage for a local 10 km run, what would you do? Outline all the steps.
5. Define media relations, and briefly discuss its significance in sport marketing
6. Discuss how the concept of distribution is applied to sport marketing situations.

KEY TERMS

distribution
distribution channel
media kit

media relations
media rights fee
press conference

subscription-based
video-on-demand
(SVOD) service

CASE STUDIES

Visit HK*Propel* for case studies organized by chapter.

CHAPTER 12

Social Media and Distribution in Sport

LEARNING

After studying this chapter, you will be able to do the following:

- Recognize the distinguishing features of social media
- Identify the different types of social media platforms
- Understand the different types of social media users
- Recognize social media use in branding, endorsement, sponsorship, and ambush marketing
- Identify the 10 practical steps in managing social media platforms
- Understand the measurement of return on social media investment

Take a moment to consider the following questions: What is social media? How do you define it? What is included (or not included) in social media? What is unique about it? For how long has social media been around? What kinds of social media users are there? How do sport marketers use social media? How is managing a personal social media account different from running an organization's account?

How can one justify a return on social media investment? This chapter addresses these questions and offers insight into the use of social media in an organizational setting. Social media allows users to reach a wide audience at a time, place, and frequency that is convenient for the audience. Similarly, organizations across all industries are increasingly creating content and running social media platforms

197

as a means of connecting with their stakeholders. In this regard, sport is an industry that uses social media as a medium to carry out different marketing endeavours, such as news updates, sales, advertising, public relations, sponsorship, branding, ambush marketing, and relationship marketing. This chapter discusses the use of social media as a tool to implement these different marketing efforts.

While running a personal social media account can be fun, managing an organization's social media offers a totally different experience. Successful management of an organization's account demands skill, creativity, dedication, ethics, and personality. The goal of this chapter is to explain how that's done.

Social Media and Its Distinguishing Features

Social media platforms include Facebook, Twitter, LinkedIn, YouTube, TikTok, Snapchat, and Instagram. However, social media as a whole extends beyond just these popular sites. The term **social media** is defined as online resources open to the public (e.g., blogs, social networks, content communities, and discussion sites) that people use primarily to share content (e.g., text, photo, audio files, and video) and engage in conversation on Internet applications (e.g., Facebook, Twitter, YouTube). According to this definition, there are four core concepts of social media: online open resources, content sharing, engagement in conversation, and Internet applications. The most unique feature of social media among these four concepts is engagement in conversation. For an online open resource that allows people to share content on Internet applications to be considered a social media platform, it should primarily allow users to exchange content and engage in dialogue. For example, Wikipedia is an online open resource that allows people to share content on Internet applications; however, it does not have a feature that allows users to exchange content and engage in conversation and is not considered a social media platform. Therefore, **social media platforms** are sites that carry content generated through users' participation

and collaboration. In generating content, users read or view content online, learn, voice their view, circulate their interests, and share their experiences. The process, as Constantinides and Fountain (2008) noted, creates an opportunity for connectedness, openness, network, and community.

Some people also assume that social media started with the launch of Facebook. However, the historic record shows that the first recognized social network site, Six Degrees, dates back to 1997. In fact, most of the popular social media sites started to emerge around 2003-2006 (e.g., LinkedIn, YouTube, Facebook, Twitter). Some social media sites have experienced a short life span; at some point they were popular but they failed to maintain their popularity. For example, Vine was a popular short-form-video hosting service on which users could share six- or seven-second-long looping video clips. The site was launched in 2013 and had 200 million users in 2015. Three years after its launch, the service was discontinued, and the full Vine archive was no longer available as of 2019. Some of the popular sites, such as Instagram, Snapchat, and TikTok, did not even exist in 2010. While some social media sites experience a short life span, a number of different social media sites are also available for use in addition to the most popular ones. Some examples include Triller, Vero, Yubo, Gab, Likee, Thriller, Parler, and Pod.

Serving as online resources that people use primarily to create and share content and to engage in conversation, these sites share some common features that distinguish them from other online communication mediums. Some of these updated and extended features were originally discussed by Hennig-Thurau and colleagues (2010) and Abeza and O'Reilly (2018) and are listed here:

- *User-generated content:* Users produce the content (e.g., text, photos, videos) as opposed to the original Web, in which one-way messages were largely supplied by publishers.

- *No "gate keeper":* Users can create and post content without permission, which has made real-time information exchange an inherent characteristic of today's society.

- *Content availability:* Users' social media activities are visible to others and can be seen immediately after being produced and also long afterward.
- *Community driven:* Users can create, listen, learn, contribute, and circulate interests, experiences, and comments that provide opportunities for connectedness, openness, participation, conversation, and community.
- *Omnipresence:* Social media has overcome time barriers and erased borders. Users can reach other users almost anywhere at any time.
- *Multipurpose:* Social media platforms can be used for a range of purposes, including a simple birthday wish, political debate, event promotion, and livestream shopping.
- *Dynamism:* Social media is continuing to reinvent itself. Platforms are constantly evolving in terms of features and tools. They are also evolving rapidly in their nature, scope, and extent of use across the globe.

Social Media Platforms

While the **distinguishing features** inform us of the unique characteristics that separate social media from other forms of communication mediums, and, at the same time, contributed to social media's expansive reach and popularity, it is also important to clarify the widely held assumption about what is included in social media (and what is not included). When someone mentions social media, many people think of social networking sites such as Facebook and Twitter. But social media also includes online resources that people use to share content and engage in conversation, such as blogs and discussion sites. Based on the work of Constantinides and Fountain (2008) and Abeza and O'Reilly (2018), social media platforms can be classified into four major categories: social networks, content communities, blogs, and discussion sites. Each platform is briefly discussed next.

- Social network: A platform that allows users to initiate communication with other users who share their interests by posting information, comments, messages, and images and creating a community for participation. Common communication points with which to initiate conversations on social networks include status updates in Facebook and tweets on Twitter. Some examples include Hockey Canada's Facebook (@HockeyCanada), Toronto Raptors' Facebook (@TorontoRaptors), TSN Hockey's Twitter (@TSNHockey), and *The Hockey News*'s Twitter (@TheHockeyNews).
- Content communities: Content communities are platforms that are predominately dependent on videos, photos, and audio files from the users themselves. Like social networking sites, users can engage in discussions with other content community members regarding video or photo content posted on a site. Some examples include Toronto Star Sports's Instagram (@thetorontostar), The Calgary Stampede's YouTube Channel, Sportsnet's Snapchat (@sportsnetcanada), and Toronto FC's TikTok (@#torontofc).
- Blogs: Blogs are online journals or personal websites that are usually managed by an individual. Entry times are stamped on each posting and displayed in reverse chronological order. Readers can post a response to a specific entry, allowing the author of the initial content to read these responses and react to readers' comments, thus creating a virtual dialogue. Regular readers of blogs can develop relationships with one another through their own frequent comments. Since the development of social networks, blogs have become traditionally fan-driven and -created, including pages for the Toronto Maple Leafs (www.mapleleafshotstove.com) and the Toronto Sports Media (https://torontosportsmedia.com/).
- Discussion sites: Discussion sites are platforms (e.g., forums, community sites) on which users with similar interests share ideas on different topics, activities, and concerns. On discussion sites such as forums and message boards, messages are often approved by a moderator before they are made available to the public. Once they are approved, users

engage in conversations in the form of posted messages. Examples include the Calgary Flames forum (http://fans.flames.nhl.com /community/) and the Vancouver Canucks, Canucks Talk forum (https://forum.canucks .com/forum/24-canucks-talk/).

Social Media Users

Social media users are producers, contributors, distributors, and content consumers. Users' intentions for joining social media platforms can differ, and the most common motivations include social interaction, information seeking, a way to pass time, entertainment, relaxation, communication utility, and convenience utility (Whiting & Williams, 2013). In sport, Abeza and colleagues (2019) identified seven different reasons social media users in sport join and use social media platforms:

1. Knowledge, whereby social media provides sport consumers with the opportunity to create, listen, converse, and learn about their favourite sport,

2. Voicing, whereby social media gives sport consumers the opportunity to express, endorse, entertain, or provide alternative views,

3. Bonding, whereby social media fosters an environment for consumers to influence each other's views, attitudes, and knowledge and bond together around their favourite sport,

4. Access to information, whereby social media provides sport consumers access to live updates, breaking news, and insider information,

5. Resource convenience, whereby social media reduces (if not removes) the corresponding costs involved in communicating with their favourite sport and fellow consumers (e.g., speed and volume of reach),

6. Economic benefits, whereby social media platforms enable sport organizations to promote special offers, discounted tickets, and so forth, and

7. Input for management, whereby social media enables consumers to contact and interact with the team management directly. Traditionally it has been difficult to make and maintain contact with consumers offline or interact on an ongoing basis.

While these reasons explain why users sign up on a social media site, it is important for sport marketers to know that not all their social media followers are the same. Users' levels of participation range from less frequent users to **social media influencers** (SMIs). For example, while some of Calgary Flames fans visit the team's Facebook page multiple times a day, other fans log on much less frequently. Also, a Calgary Flames fan may use platforms such as Facebook (@NHLFlames) and Instagram (@ nhlflames) often but never visit the other social media sites of the team, such as those on Periscope (@NHLFlames), Snapchat (@nhl-flames), and TikTok (@nhl-flames). Similarly, a Calgary Flames fan might be active on one platform but not on another. For example, a Flames fan might be simultaneously a new user to TikTok who started studying the platform and familiarizing themself with the culture before making contributions, a socialized user on Snapchat who has just started posting but is not fully engaged or committed to the site, a bystander on Facebook who is comfortable with the site but has a private profile and uses the site to stay current within the online community, or a committed user on Instagram who invests time and resources in making frequent posts and comments about the team.

Some social media users and ordinary fans of the past have managed to become influencers in the social media sphere; these users are commonly referred to as social media influencers or opinion leaders. Social media influencers are those who have a large number of followers, who post content that addresses the needs and interests of their followers, and who are considered by their followers to be advocates, representatives, sources, and guides. These influencers share fresh and rich information with the community and their information is often considered to be compelling and reliable by their followers. In particular, they are perceived as relatable, accessible, and intimate, features that by extension give these opinion leaders the authority to potentially sway opinions in a positive or a negative way. Their opinion as a third party is often considered to be more "real" and authentic. In this regard, some hockey teams offer behind-the-scenes stories and exclusive content directly to these influencers to maintain a healthy relationship with them. Three common features characterize SMIs: what one knows (level of expertise), whom one knows (network size), and who one is (traits and values) (Uzunoğlu & Kip, 2014).

Dimensions of Social Media Use in Sport Marketing

Social media has been used for a variety of purposes in the sport industry. It is used by local community sport organizations, youth sports, professional sports, college sports, international sports, and Olympic sport. It is also used by athletes, fans, and the media. It involves legal issues (e.g., college athletes' use of social media), social issues (e.g., social media and homophobia, misogyny), governance (e.g., athletes' social media use guidelines from the International Olympic Committee and Hockey Canada), marketing (e.g., use of social media for endorsement), and communication (e.g., use of social media in crisis management). Social media touches almost every aspect of the sport industry. In sport marketing, as shown in figure 12.1, sport organizations use the different social media platforms (e.g., Facebook, Twitter, YouTube) to communicate content (e.g., text, photo, infographic, videos) with their audiences by engaging in multiple ways and dialogues. In the communication process, organizations use social media as a medium to implement marketing objectives such as branding, endorsement, sponsorship, sales, ambush marketing, and relationship marketing. By considering the dynamic interrelationship between sport and social media and recognizing that social media can be used for a number of different sport marketing purposes, this section illustrates the use of social media in sport marketing by discussing four of the six selected topic areas as noted in figure 12.1. Commentary on the other two areas is also included. The four discussed in detail are branding, endorsement, sponsorship, and ambush marketing, with relationship marketing and sales addressed in less detail.

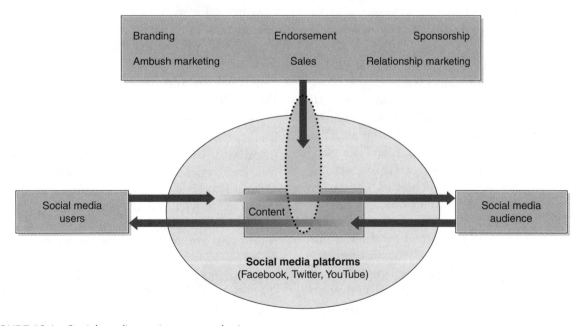

FIGURE 12.1 Social media use in sport marketing.

Brand and Social Media

Sport organizations have been creating, developing, maintaining, and advancing their use of social media as a sport marketing tool since the early 2000s. Sport entities from a local rowing club connected to the Toronto Raptors are using social media to communicate directly with their consumers without a third-party intervention (e.g., radio, TV), which was a rare opportunity before the early 2000s. Social media has particularly become a key branding tool for a number of users such as sport teams (e.g., Ottawa Redblacks), athletes (e.g., Jonathan Toews), and sport organizations (e.g., Athletics Canada). One example that shows the quickly evolving and intertwined nature of social media and branding today involves the parallel nature of a team's brand value with the size of its social media following. The Toronto Raptors, for instance, is the most valuable sport franchise in Canada, worth an estimated US$1.8 billion (Rubin, 2019). At the same time, the team is the most followed sport team in the country, with 2.6 million followers on Facebook (@TorontoRaptors) and 2.2 million followers on Twitter (@Raptors). It is clear that the most valuable sport team in the country is a leader on both popular social media platforms, which emphasizes the importance of social media in brand management.

Another example that shows the interconnected nature of social media and branding is the openness of sport teams to adopt newer social media platforms. As of October 2020, for example, the Edmonton Oilers had an official TikTok account (@edmontonoilers) with 102,900 likes, and the Canadiens Montréal's (@canadiensmtl) official account had 126,600 likes. After the league adopted the platforms in November 2019, the NHL director of social media, Sean Dennison, underscored the importance of TikTok, stating that it "has carved out a niche that's separate from all the other social platforms," Dennison said. "Not only in terms of the types of content that's produced and consumed for TikTok but also the audience. So, we see it as an opportunity to start engaging with a much younger and diverse audience" (Moran, 2019). Whether an organization has adopted new platforms (e.g., TikTok) or continues to use the existing popular ones (e.g., Facebook. Twitter), each social media platform includes an organization's name, logo, graphic designs, symbols, and hashtags (e.g., #GoHabsGo of Montreal Canadiens). These are elements of a brand, a product, or service that has unique components (e.g., name, symbol, or design) making it distinguishable from its competitors. An eventual goal of brand management is increased brand equity. A brand equity is assets and liabilities linked to a brand name that add to or subtract from that product's value (Aaker, 1991).

A brand, therefore, enjoys high level of brand equity when the following components of brand management are prominent: brand awareness, brand associations, perceived brand quality, and brand loyalty. These components are discussed in chapter 8. To briefly describe them in relation to social media, we can use the Toronto Raptors as an example:

- Brand awareness: Brand awareness could be, for example, the Raptors social media profile, its logo, its colours, its motto, or content communicated on the organization's Twitter, Facebook, and Instagram sites to help users learn more about the team's performance, high-profile players, merchandises, services/goods, and the organization.

- Brand associations: Brand association is based on the unique attributes of the brand that are communicated on social media to consumers. In other words, it's what comes to a person's mind when they think of the Raptors, which can be the 2019 playoffs, winners, the city of Toronto, Kyle Lowrey, Jurassic Park, We the North, Scotiabank Arena, and so on.

- Perceived brand quality: Perceived brand quality can be based on the large following and popularity of the Raptors, which is the most followed sport entity in Canada both on Twitter and Facebook. Also, the Raptors are always perceived as a team with success in the playoffs. Those types of perceived qualities can be communicated and enhanced by the team through social media by actively interacting with fans and humanizing their team with the use of humour, wittiness, and clever comments when both interacting with fans and sharing information (Abeza et al., 2017a). Interacting with the fans, showing appreciation of their support, and responding to their requests all add to the perceived brand quality.

• Brand loyalty: Brand loyalty could be displayed on social media in different ways, such as a frequently changing a profile picture with the Raptors logo or a picture of a favourite player. On the team side, social media can be used to enhance and maintain team loyalty by creating a LinkedIn Group and Facebook Group for avid fans, including season-ticket holders. The team can also produce graphics and short video clips that can facilitate the display of loyalty on social media.

Brand equity is the sum total of the efforts put into these four components of brand equity. Hence, it is important to create a brand with an image that matches the impression that the target markets seeks association with. Note that social media platforms can also be used to release a new brand (e.g., a new 5k run in town, by introducing its name and logo) or to refresh a brand (e.g., Calgary Flames announced their "full retro" in October 2020, returning to the team's roots by promoting throwback jerseys to primary status beginning in the 2020 season).

Endorsement and Social Media

Before the expansion of social media in early 2000s, sport personalities used to rely on a third-party medium (e.g., broadcast media) to reach out and communicate with their fans and the public. However, the emergence of social media platforms has changed that tradition by allowing athletes to communicate directly with their deeply engaged followers, on their own personal social media account, to do so in their preferred content format, and, most importantly, to be able to create, develop, mould, and stage their own brand (Abeza et al., 2017b). With the expansion of social media in size, reach, and scope, celebrity athletes have also started lending their names to endorse causes, products, and services on their social media sites. Today, a number of celebrity athletes, such as Sidney Crosby (e.g., with Tim Hortons), Kyle Lowry (e.g., with AXE), and Wayne Gretzky (e.g., with Canadian

Tire) are using their celebrity status (e.g., names and image) to endorse products and services in advertising in an exchange for financial reward. A celebrity endorser is an individual "who enjoys public recognition and who uses this recognition on behalf of a consumer good by appearing with it in an advertisement" (McCracken, 1989, p. 310).

Athletes' endorsements of products and services are a common phenomenon on social media today. They use their agents (and professional assistants) to manage their social media sites by producing well-designed graphic designs and video. Cristiano Ronaldo's Facebook, Twitter, and Instagram accounts are good examples for this. In using their social media platforms for endorsement purposes, celebrity athletes such as Lowry and Gretzky are transferring their celebrity status (e.g., names and image) to the brand they are endorsing. Their celebrity status includes the athletes' reputation, likeability, believability, attractiveness, and trustworthiness. The endorsement of brands on athletes' personal social media sites is much more effective than the traditional mediums such as TV advertisements. This is mainly because social media provides an opportunity for athletes to interact directly and engage in real-time dialogue with their fans. The celebrity athlete's image, combined with the "emotional attachment that fans usually form with them[,] can create a greater influence on potential consumers' attitudes about the brand partners. Such influences can be higher on those followers who admire and identify themselves with the particular athlete" (Abeza et al., 2017b, p. 351).

Abeza et al. (2017b) studied the world's highest-paid athletes' use of their own social media channel for the purpose of endorsement and identified the different roles and modes that celebrity athletes displayed in their endorsement of brands on social media. In their endorsement of brands on social media, the highest-paid athletes played five different roles: expert, ambassador, personifier, spokesperson, or observer. A brief description of each role along with corresponding examples follows.

• As an expert, an athlete's account can be found endorsing a product for which the athlete has an authoritative knowledge (e.g.,

Andre De Grasse, a Canadian sprinter, sending a tweet that endorses Puma's running shoe).

- As an ambassador, an athlete is presented as an accredited representative of a product about which the athlete may not have an authoritative knowledge and with which there is a clearly demonstrated material connection (e.g., Jamal Murray, a Canadian professional basketball player, posting on Instagram about Western Union, the money transfer company with which he partners).

- As a personifier, an athlete endorses a product that is presented as an embodiment of the athlete's own personal motto or professional qualities, which are typically embedded in the brand's campaign message (e.g., American professional basketball player Kevin Durant's "Dream Fearlessly" with American Family Insurance: "@AmFam I want to inspire kids to lead healthier lives #DreamFearlessly").

- As a spokesperson, an athlete acts as an informal representative or advocate of a cause or product with which the athlete has no official association (e.g., Donovan Bailey, a Canadian sprinter and former Olympian, tweeting about racial inequality and voicing his concern).

- As an observer, an athlete makes a simple positive public comment about a product but does not communicate any recommendation to try or use it (e.g., Eugenie Bouchard, a Canadian tennis player, posting on Instagram a picture of her purchasing food at a grocery store with the mention of the store's name).

With regard to the modes assumed by celebrity athletes in their endorsement on social media, four endorsement modes have been identified. These modes are explicit ("I endorse this product"), implicit ("I use this product"), imperative ("You should use this product"), and copresentational (simply appearing with the product). Examples of each of these modes follow.

- Explicit mode: In an explicit mode, a social media post communicates an athlete's endorsement of a product on Twitter (e.g., Georges St-Pierre, a Canadian former professional mixed martial artist, tweeting about Belairdirect (an insurance company): "Happy to start working with @belairdirect and take part in their #insurance. Take a look their website and I endorse it. #dontcallitacomeback #actorslife").

- Implicit mode: In an implicit mode, a social media post informs social media followers that the athletes themselves are consumers of the endorsed product (e.g., Maria Sharapova, a Russian retired professional tennis player, about Avon: "My secret to natural beauty is out thanks to @AvonInsider! Learn more: a link to Avon's website").

- Imperative mode: In an imperative mode, a social media post encourages fans to try and use the endorsed product (e.g., Christine Sinclair, a Canadian soccer player, tweeting about A&W burger "Buy a burger, beat MS (Multiple sclerosis)! $2 from every @AWCanada Teen Burger®. Support Canadians affected by MS. I'm participating for my mom and all Canadians, who live with MS.").

- Copresentational mode: In a copresentational mode, the athlete is presented with the product in pictures or videos, or the brand or organization's name is simply mentioned in the tweet (e.g., Bianca Vanessa Andreescu, a Canadian professional tennis player, tweeting a picture of herself taken standing next to a car she drives).

Sponsorship and Social Media

While it will be discussed more in chapter 14, it is worth mentioning here that sponsorship is a three-way relationship between the sponsors, the sponsored party, and consumers. Moreover, sport takes the lion's share of the total sponsorship spending in North America (70 percent) (IEG, 2020), mainly because it is an ideal avenue that allows sponsors to be placed in an emotional connection with consumers. In other words, consumers will be drawn to a sponsor that supports the property that they cheer for and of which they are fan. Particularly, consumers perceive that corporate messages are less obtrusive and have a goodwill effect when delivered through a sport property that is sponsored by a company. In the emotional connection that fans form with a sport property, a sponsor effort can be best facilitated by social media. Social media is a participatory and collaborative medium, and sponsors will have a chance to communicate directly with fans by humanizing their brand and hearing back from them.

The global reach and magnitude of social media along with its unique features make it a useful medium for sponsors to communicate with consumers. The unique features include speed, easy access, real-time functioning, connectivity, and provision of a public forum. Particularly, by using social media, sponsors will have the opportunity to have frequent interactions with consumers, set the tone of communication, use and capitalize on brand personalities, and humanize their brands. As discussed further in chapter 14, when a sponsor enters in an agreement with a sponsored party, the fee that they pay for a property is only to have an official right of association. For example, when Scotia Bank sponsors the Toronto Waterfront Marathon and the Calgary Marathon, the fee that the bank pays to the two marathons is only to have the right to an official association and to publicly announce that the bank is supporting the events. But in order to promote their sponsorship to the wider public, the bank needs to invest more money in things such as billboards, TV commercials, flyers, posters, and, most importantly, using social media. This type of initiatives is referred to as sponsorship activation. Simply put, activation is additional investment beyond the rights fee or different communication efforts implemented to support one's sponsorship.

There is industry-wide agreement that sponsorship is much more than simple logo placements, and sponsors need to invest in activation to realize the full potential of their sponsorship investment. In early days of social media, Abeza et al. (2014) found Olympic sponsors using social media to achieve and activate three sponsorship objectives: promotion (of services, products, and the company's image), customer appreciation, and athlete encouragement. As official partners of the Games, the Olympic sponsors were using Twitter for the purpose of congratulating, cheering, and spreading the words of athletes' victory, which in turn allows them to establish an emotional connection with the sponsorship audience. Even though the Olympic sponsors used their social media platforms for these limited purposes, a sponsor's objectives may include creating awareness, educating consumers, making consumers like the company's products and services, generating sales, and actual sales. For all these sponsorship objectives, social media is an ideal medium. On the property holders' side (e.g., Rogers Cup, the Canadian Open), social media can be used to service sponsors. Using social media sport properties provides sponsors an added platform to publicize their association through appreciation of their support, promoting their services and products, and sponsors gestures' (Abeza et al., 2017a).

Ambush Marketing and Social Media

The practice of nonsponsoring companies attempting to associate themselves with an event without having an official or direct commercial connection is referred to as *ambush marketing* (Chadwick & Burton, 2011). During major events, it is common to observe nonsponsoring companies developing creative strategies to take advantage of the attention, good will, and other benefits associated with mega events such as the Olympic Games. While the topic of ambush marketing will be discussed in more detail in chapter 15, we will be looking at the practice of ambush marketing via social media in this section. You may find companies attempting to associate themselves with major events that they have not paid for and doing so for a range of different reasons. For some, that is unethical, but for others, the practice is creative marketing approach. Regardless of the argument, companies engage in ambushing practice mainly to benefit from the reputation of a sponsored property's wider media coverage and large audience. The other factors that lead companies to become involved in ambushing include sponsorship fees being too expensive, exclusivity (e.g., Coca Cola chosen as an exclusive sponsor in the soft-drink product category, which leaves Pepsi with no option), and length of sponsorship agreement (e.g., most Olympic sponsors sign up for four to five Games, and four Olympic Games means 20 years).

Understandably, ambush marketing may create anger and frustration among official sponsors, and the practice can threaten the sponsorship industry (e.g., sponsorship renewals). To address the issue, sport-governing bodies have introduced different protection strategies. The three most common counter-ambush strategies include (per O'Reilly et al., 2015) legislation (law to punish parties found involved in ambushing practice), communication (increasing public awareness about event properties, including trademarks), and surveillance (identifying intellectual property infringement). In the face of these strategies, staging an ambush-free event is still difficult (Abeza, et al., 2020). In particular, social media opened up a new avenue for ambushers to implement their creative marketing strategies. The features of social media such as its ability to break border restrictions and the flow of information make the practice difficult to control by national boundaries or institutional gatekeepers (Abeza, 2020).

Recently, ambushing has been prevalent on social media platforms among the figurehead rivals of the sponsors of major sporting events. Following this, the global sporting events such as those of FIFA (the governing body of global soccer) and the International Olympic Committee (IOC) introduced a social media antiambushing regulation. For example, while the IOC encourages athletes to use social media during the Games to share their experiences with families and friends, for advertising purposes, the IOC has used Rule 40 to limit athletes from associating themselves with nonofficial Olympic sponsors immediately before, during, and after the Games (Abeza, 2020). The IOC specifically has issued social media guidelines that include tweets and various other Internet postings in 2014, 2016, 2018, and 2020. Within the context of these guidelines and protection strategies, Abeza et al. (2020) found direct industry competitors of the Olympic sponsors continuing to use social media for ambushing purpose. There are four types of **ambush marketing strategies** employed on social media:

- *Associative ambushing:* Associative ambushing is the use of imagery or terminology to create a suggestion that an organization has links to

the event. For example, Michelin employed associative ambushing during the PyeongChang Games by tweeting "The UK snow has got us in the mood, so we've taken a look at the top 10 snowboarding videos on the Internet!—https:// sole-power.com/skiing-snowboarding-spring/ ::: " with a picture of a skier taking a break from training on a field covered with snow and having his skates by his side. Bear in mind here that the timing of the tweet matters, and this specific content was posted during the Olympic Games.

- *Values ambushing:* Values ambushing is the use of an event or property's central value or theme to imply an association. The direct industry competitors of the Olympic sponsors were found using the themes centred on the Olympics to gain the attention of their social media followers. An example is Pirelli, where the company employed value ambushing by communicating a tweet with pictures that revolve around the Winter Olympics' central value of racing on a snowy downhill slope: "When you are late for a meeting, but you have a @Lamborghin#WinterChampion."

- *Coattail ambushing:* Coattail ambushing is attempting to directly associate with a property using a legitimate link, such as participating athletes. The direct industry competitors of the Olympic sponsors were found to be directly associated with the Games by using a legitimate link, such as participating athletes. An example is Subway's use of Twitter during the Rio Games, when the company retweeted the NBC Olympics Twitter account with Aly Raisman's USA gymnastics performance. In the retweet, Subway used the caption "NBC fresh focus presented by @subway." It should be noted that NBC had a legitimate partnership with the Olympics as an official broadcaster; however, instead of directly seeking a sponsorship with the Olympics, Subway engaged its brand with NBC to "piggyback" off its legitimate link to the event.

- *Property infringement:* Property infringement involves the intentional unauthorized use of protected intellectual property, such as a logo, a name, and words. Examples of this fourth strategy include, for example, Subway offering "congratulations" to participating teams or athletes with the mention of Olympic names and words and Ford communicating a congratulatory message using a protected Olympic term.

Social media and sport marketing have a dynamic relationship, as demonstrated in the four topics discussed here. These dynamics will be more intertwined and heightened in the coming years, which highlights the important place and value of social media in sport marketing.

Practical Guide: Managing Social Media Platforms

Sport organizations at all levels—local, regional, provincial, national, and international—use social media for several different purposes. Social media is accessible and simple to use. However, managing a social media platform for personal use is different from managing for an organization, which requires strategic planning. Whether an organization has been active on different social media platforms for years or is just getting started, it must take basic practical steps when managing social media sites. The key to overseeing a successful social media platform is to develop a plan and design a strategy that fits the organization's intended purpose. Sport organizations should adhere to the following 10 practical steps to create, build, and professionally manage a social media platform successfully:

1. Collect information
2. Establish objectives
3. Set goals
4. Identify your target audience
5. Choose platforms
6. Strategize your content
7. Create a content calendar
8. Monitor your performance and evaluate your accomplishments
9. Prepare a report
10. Communicate your report

Step 1: Collect Information

Every organization is unique and every social media channel is different. Because organizations offer different products and services within the market, they all have unique audiences and thereby provide different types of content on social media. Therefore, within your organization, you must first study your environment and industry. Research what others in your area of business are doing. For example, when a rowing club in St. Catharines, Ontario, plans to create and run a new social media platform, the club must collect information by researching its competitors to determine what similar rowing clubs and other sport organizations in the city, the province, and the country are doing on social media. This involves identifying the most commonly used social media platforms in your industry, detecting the content type that you observe appealing most to the consumers of your sector of business, uncovering the nature of the users' interaction on a given platform, and so on. To identify organizations in your area of business, you can simply run a Facebook or Google search. You can also use specialized services. For example, you can use BuzzSumo to identify what content performs best on your competitors' social media channels or the most trending content within your industry. In like manner, to monitor specific social media accounts and hashtags, you can use Hootsuite.

Once you finish performing an assessment or scan of your environment, the next step is to look inward. Understand your organization's mission and its strategic short- and long-term plans. Consult with your top management team to strategize your social media use in accordance with your organization's strategic goals. You can start by reviewing the written strategic plans available in your organization. Your internal assessment should include potential interested audiences, such as board members, employees, volunteers, fans, participants, the general public, governing bodies, media, sponsors, partners, and suppliers.

Step 2: Establish Objectives

Define the reasons for creating, building, and running a social media platform. Organizations use social media for advertising, sales, direct marketing, public relations, promotion, news update, customer service, internal communication, or corporate communication. You can focus on a combination of these purposes. You may also come up with some specific objectives, such as to increase brand awareness (e.g., increase followers and page likes), increase community engagement (e.g., replies, comments, shares, likes, favourites, clicks, follows, mentions), and increase website traffic. Regardless of the scope of your objectives, you must have a defined list of objectives for which you can measure the success after a specific time period (e.g., a month, three months, six months, a year).

Identifying the short- and long-term objectives and your top managements input in step 1 can help you specify your objectives for the use of a social media platform. For example, the 5k Foam Fest Fun Run in Vancouver might choose Facebook to provide video-recorded training guides to runners, announce a high-profile personality attendance at the event, call for registration, promote giveaways, and sell entry tickets. The event may set an objective, for example, to increase its followers' numbers from 317,000 to 500,000 in two years. Therefore, the organization should set objectives that guide its social-media management strategy as well as its day-to-day activity.

Step 3: Set Goals

Running a social media platform without specific goals is like walking in the dark. The objectives outlined in step 2 can help you narrow your focus but they may still not be specific enough to help you achieve your intended goals. In order to achieve your objectives, each objective should be supported by a list of goals that are specific, measurable, achievable, realistic, and time bounded (commonly referred to as the SMART goal outline). An example of a SMART goal can be, for example, bringing 600 Facebook fans who have not attended the home games of an NHL team to the stadium during the first six months of the season. This goal satisfies the SMART requirements; it is specific, measurable, achievable, realistic, and time bounded. Having this defined goal can be part of your organization's overall goal of increasing stadium attendance as identified in step 2. Also, having such specific goals can help you design effective goal-centred strategies. For this goal, for example, you can develop a strategy to reach out to Facebook fans who have not attended home games by developing and posting messages that encourage attendance, which in itself requires specific tactics. In short, objectives drive goals, goals lead to specific goal-centred strategies, and specific goal-centred strategies help generate tactics.

Step 4: Identify Your Target Audience

In order to be successful in any business, you must first identify who your customers are. As discussed in chapter 4, sport marketers must develop a clear understanding of who an organization's consumers are. One way to identify your consumers is to apply segmentation, targeting, and positioning tactics. Your target market should be reachable so that you can communicate with customers who are responsive to your marketing communication efforts. If you have a younger audience, Instagram posts might be more effective in reaching them than tweets on Twitter. Similarly, if you run a sport-media business, Twitter might be a more appropriate platform than Instagram or Facebook.

Step 5: Choose Platforms

Your organization's social media presence should focus on platforms that allow you to reach your target audience, attain your goals, and achieve your objectives (as outlined in steps 2 through 4). Each platform has different users and formats. It is advisable not to create an account on a specific type of social media platform (e.g., Twitter) if it does not help you reach your target audience or will not be run well. Your management of a social media platform reflects the image of your organization. For example, Red Deer Tennis Club in Alberta must decide which platforms it should use. Addressing the following questions can help this organization identify the suitable platforms for the organization: Why should my organization use this platform? Who will be reached on this platform? Do we have the resources to run it? What types of post works best on this platform? How are my organization's posts unique on this social media site?

Step 6: Strategize Your Content

In the social media world, content is king. Content can include text or written content, audio files, video, photo, graphic designs, and GIFs. Your social media content and its presentation reflect your brand. Sharing objective-based quality content across your social media platforms is key to engaging your audience and attracting new followers. Beyond using quality videos, photos, and graphic designs, you should figure out the type of content that resonates with your audience and how often to post on each of your platforms. Posting high-quality content could also involve identifying the best and most purposeful hashtags to use and creating good visuals.

For instance, Abeza and colleagues (2017b) identified Cristiano Ronaldo's Twitter account as an exemplary site in terms of social media use. According to the authors, Ronaldo's account exhibited quality in the clarity and message tone, the manner in which the communicated messages were framed, the frequency of use, the combination of tweet types and types of content employed, and the clear and consistent narrative/images created about the athlete on Twitter outside his sport practice. The athlete used a **balanced combination** of social media content of text, mentions, hashtags, and web-links to video clips and pictures. Another exemplary sport entity is the Chicago Blackhawks. According to Abeza and colleagues (2017a), the Chicago Blackhawks employed **appealing social media content**, in which the team actively interacted with fans and humanized the team with the use of humour, wittiness, and clever topical comments when both interacting with fans and sharing information. The team interacted with fans in a variety of contexts, such as engaging in casual exchange, answering customers' questions, rewarding fans, appreciating fans' support, conversing about the team's slogan, and responding to fans' request for content.

Step 7: Create a Content Calendar

Whether you want to have a professionally managed social media platform or you want to avoid a last-minute struggle to find shareable content, having a social media–content calendar that was developed in advance is essential to success. You can create a yearlong calendar including major events that have already been planned. Most important, however, is to create a month's worth of content and a schedule for its release. This is not to say that you will not post any breaking-news updates, but you need to be prepared for situations in which you may not have access to the news or the freedom to post at the timing of a specific goal you want to achieve. For example, if you are organizing a running event in your area in the month of August, you can schedule a social media post (a prize, a contest, or at least a nicely done graphic design) of Terry Fox in advance, to be posted on August 3 (Terry Fox Day). After you have developed a content calendar, make sure to update it weekly or monthly. The schedule can be built using a spreadsheet in Excel or Google Sheets. Your schedule can have the following headings: (a) content title, (b) content format (e.g., text plus photo, infographic, graphic design, video, GIF), (c) keywords (e.g., mentions @, hashtags,), (d) calls to action (e.g., like or follow us, learn more, share now, comment now, visit a website), (e) social media platform type (e.g., Facebook, Twitter, Instagram, Snapchat, LinkedIn, TikTok), (f) description (e.g., specific actions and task, responsible person), and (g) remarks (e.g., for comments on the scheduled content).

Step 8: Monitor Your Performance and Evaluate Your Accomplishments

Evaluation and monitoring are critical steps in the assessment of plans, undertakings, and outcomes and to help provide learning for future informed action. Therefore, you must assess how well your plan matches the objectives. Year-end accomplishments are the sum total

IN THE KNOW

Some Tips to Manage Social Media Content

The following recommendations, though not an exhaustive list, can help guide sport marketers in managing their social media content:

- *Be consistent:* Some platforms (e.g., Twitter) involve urgent and frequent, multiple posts, whereas others (e.g., Facebook) can benefit from relatively less frequent postings. Therefore, you need to take into account the varying nature of different platforms, maintain your pace, and stay consistent. Industry practice, for example, recommends 1 or 2 posts per day on Facebook and Twitter and 8 to 16 stories on Instagram.

- *Use trending stories:* Stay alert to trending stories in your business. Pay attention to popular trends emerging on social media and communicate them with your audiences to keep your platform interesting, fresh, timely, and relevant.

- *Optimize your social profiles:* To connect with your existing and new customers, fill in as much information as possible on your profile page. An example could be the SportsNet Facebook page (@sportsnet), which includes the company's motto, a description of the company, its website, top fans, privacy policy, links to Soundcloud, and links to its different social media pages on Tumblr, Instagram, Snapchat, Twitter, and YouTube.

- *Use automated-scheduled social media posts:* Social media platforms, for example Facebook, have automated process that allows you to deposit and **schedule content** on the sites well in advance and release it at a predetermined time on your page. This option helps you target your given content to coincide with a major event. For example, a small, local hockey club in Fredericton, New Brunswick, can create, deposit, and schedule a post on its Facebook site that can be released during the week of NHL playoffs. The option can also help social media personnel manage their time by allowing them to create meaningful content at their convenience. For more on this, see step 7.

- *Consider paid content:* With improved targeting options and a budget limit, you have the option to maximize your social media content reach and engagement. If you want to reach a new target demography and a wider audience than your followers, you can combine organic and **paid content**. Paid content services are available to businesses; for example, Facebook-boosted posts represent a paid service that enables your message to reach a wider audience beyond your followers and thereby to reach potential new followers.

- *Join community groups:* Community groups such as LinkedIn Groups and Facebook Groups help you expand your reach and connect you with like-minded people. Among other benefits, joining a community group helps organizations gain useful audience insights and stay up to date about the state of their specific business sectors.

- *Don'ts of social media:* Do not leave your followers' messages unanswered; do not let your platform to be quiet for a long period of time, and at the same time, do not overwhelm your followers with too much content. Do not post too many promotional messages, and do not forget the social aspect of social media.

of the outcome of your periodic performances. Therefore, monitoring your progress can help inform you whether you need to build on your success or adjust your social media plan and its management. For example, after setting a goal of bringing 600 NHL fans from Facebook to the stadium in the first six months of the regular season, you can evaluate your progress at the end of the first six months. For a detail discussion on this step 8, please see the next section on return on investment from social media in sport.

Step 9: Prepare a Report

Like any other department in most organizations does, you must prepare a report for the organization's top management. Your report can be a quarterly, biannual, or year-end report and can be structured in different ways. To secure the required resources from the top management in terms of a video editor, a photographer, a graphic designer, or equipment including software programs and analytic tools, you must clearly present the accomplishment of your objectives that you set at the beginning. Your report not only demonstrates your commitment but also helps you justify the organization's investment in terms of time, money, hiring, office supplies, and other, similar resources. Also, in preparing your report, be sure you know your audience. For example, the report you present to the head of your organization might be more condensed than the detailed report that you prepare for your immediate manager. In your report, highlight your accomplishments in relation to the objectives that were established. If you fail to accomplish any goals, prepare to justify this with concrete evidence. If your objective is cyclical, propose adaptive strategies to avoid the shortfall from happening again.

Step 10: Communicate Your Report

Celebrate your accomplishment and propose adaptive strategies for the areas on which you need to improve. If you have accomplished much more than expected or achieved something unique (e.g., interviewing a high-profile personality), you should share those accomplishments internally with employees of your organization. Success is meant to be celebrated, and it inspires others.

EXECUTIVE PERSPECTIVE
Social Media and Major League Professional Sport

JOHN DELANEY, Manager, Social Media, True North Sports + Entertainment—Winnipeg Jets

The skillset required to manage social media platforms professionally in sports continues to grow as the varying platforms advance. To succeed in social media, I see three primary pillars in which social media managers need to be proficient in: marketing, communications, and content creation. So much of marketing relies on digital efforts, and as a social media manager, you are often responsible for developing campaign strategies, executing organic postings, and booking paid ads to generate awareness and drive revenue for the company. Social media is often the principal point of communication between teams and fans, and with that fact comes a lot of responsibility. Social media managers need to know how to navigate through the treacherous waters of corporate communications and be aware that posting something that may be interpreted negatively by some people can have major ramifications. Finally, as social media has become reliant on content, skills to create and edit content have become more important than ever. This includes copywriting, photography, and videography, plus all the editing that comes with it. A feed has become a noisy place and strong content is crucial if you wish to stand out.

> continued

Social Media and Major League Professional Sport *> continued*

The social media world is advancing at a rapid pace. Tie that in with the precipitous nature of the sports industry and you end up having to adjust your social strategies nearly every other month. Just 10 years ago, social media was simply a checkbox of things to do for any sports public relations professional—just send a tweet to recap a game and post a photo gallery for fans on Facebook. The five years that followed required a content foundation to be built by teams, and those who did so efficiently still reap the benefits as those foundations flourish into full-on departments. Today you see leagues and teams with social media departments comprising community managers, strategists, content creators, and more.

The biggest challenge that I face regularly in social media is managing demand and prioritization in our strategies. In social media, there is no limit to what one brand can do. There is always more content that can be created, graphics that can be enhanced, stories that can be published, but never enough resources to meet the demand any strategist desires. As the social headcount grows, more opportunities open up, and almost simultaneously, social media platforms expand their offerings, creating new ways (and demands) to engage fans. (The "stories" boom seen on Instagram, Facebook, Messenger, LinkedIn, and Skype is a good example of this and the introduction of live streaming across all social platforms is another.) Prioritization remains difficult too; with all of the opportunities available, knowing which strategies are musts and which are just wants can be a challenge.

The importance of social media has never been more prevalent than today. Social media has become the primary tool for communicating with fans and consumers alike. It is a tool that not only keeps audiences up to date on happenings with their favourite teams but also generates fans, pushes marketing support, and most importantly, drives revenue. Advertisements in social streams and sponsored content pieces have begun to generate significant revenue for sport organizations as more fans follow along through social media.

The varying social platforms all offer strengths of their own, for example:

- Facebook Groups has been a way to connect with some of the most dedicated fans on social media. We have been able to build a sense of community within the platform for Jets fans while passively learning more about our audience.

- Twitter's Amplify program has been a new source of revenue for us. With our largest follower base being on the platform, Twitter's introduction of a way for publishers to monetize at scale through video content has made a significant bump in the income generated by social media.

- I am looking forward to exploring Instagram's Shopping features more as our e-commerce business grows. The direct relationship between Instagram and Shopify makes some of the social media marketing initiatives seamless.

- Along with every home game that we put live on YouTube (among other platforms). before and after each game we post a pre- and post-game show. YouTube's live streaming platform is nearly flawless, and the ability to archive, download, and post shows in-platform is excellent.

- With some of our major present and past players being Finnish, Finland is our number one country on Snapchat. This stat is unique to this platform for us, and as a result, we use the platform to engage with that Nordic audience.

- As TikTok introduced a brand-new way to think about social media content, we have had some fun creating unique pieces specifically for our audience there. The For You page has shown off the viral potential the platform offers, with one of our videos taking off, getting tens of millions of plays, and generating over 100,000 followers from one short video alone.

My name is John Delaney, and I am the manager of social media at True North Sports and Entertainment. I am responsible for managing the social media channels for the National Hockey League's Winnipeg Jets but also oversee our other social media channels for our other brands, including the American Hockey League's Manitoba Moose, our arena Bell MTS Place, and many others.

Return on Investment from Social Media in Sport

The adoption and utilization of technological advancements have always faced the scrutiny of top management in organizations. Understandably, top management would like to see concrete results from their decision, and new technologies involve uncertainties (both risks and rewards). In fact, social media is not a new media anymore; however, there is still pressure on the social media team in organizations to justify their investment in terms of time, money, office resources, and other similar resources. Therefore, management support is critical to exploit the full potential of social media in sport marketing. In particular, when employees see the top management acting reluctant, employees in other departments of an organization will follow suit, hampering social media's full potential. Hence, the pressure increases on social media managers to demonstrate accountability for their investments. In this regard, the measurement of return on social media investment becomes essential to show value from investment and to defend spending on social media.

The measurement of a return on social media investment is not an easy task, mainly because social media encompasses an element of emotion and engagement. However, there are some methods that can help us produce insights to help justify investments. This section will discuss those approaches. Yet again, one should take note of the **measurement fact** that there is no magic metric to process and identify all the gains and losses in the measurement of return on social media investment. None of the methods are capable by themselves to give the full picture of return on all your investment on social media. Instead, the methods help us gain insights about the level of accomplishment of preestablished and specific marketing objectives. As such, setting benchmarks will be essential, where objectives of using social media are identified and measurements are done against those established and defined objectives. In this regard, a number of analytical methods exist that provide information to help make some level of informed investment or decisions. This will be discussed next, preceded by a discussion on the simple and direct measure of return on social media investment against a SMART objective. A return on investment means that the organization receives value for investing time, money, or other resources. Simply put, cost of investment minus financial gain resulting in a positive return would be considered a gain.

EXPERT PERSPECTIVE
Social Media and Your Career

OLAN SCOTT, Assistant Professor of Sport Management, Brock University

It is increasingly important for sport-management students undertaking a sport marketing course to have a grasp on the importance of social media for sport organizations that seek to engage with and market to their following. Sport fans are active users of social media, so it is vital for sport marketers to understand that social media is an important element of the marketing and communications mix. Since the advent of the Internet and the proliferation of social media, consumers can communicate with their favourite businesses, athletes, celebrities, and other Internet users in ways that were not possible before the 2000s. The rise of social media platforms provides consumers with new opportunities to communicate. Further, contemporary media has never been more personalized, individualized, and pleasurable to use. Moreover, social media users both simultaneously produce and consume media content, which suggests that consumers are actively engaged. Students in sport marketing should learn about social media because it is becoming increasingly important for their career start

> *continued*

Social Media and Your Career > *continued*

and early progress. Many of my current and former students have started their careers using social media in a variety of roles at sport organizations, so keeping abreast of evolutions in the use of these platforms may provide current students with a leg up at the start of their career.

When students connect with each other on social media, there are many opportunities to share course-related materials and real-world examples with others to cocreate course content and stay abreast of relevant stories quickly rather than having to search for news by oneself. Social media also allows students to take offline discussions from the classroom to social media platforms, which enables communication to continue beyond the classroom setting. Thus, the quantity of discussions about course materials can be enhanced, use media, and increase the engagement with course materials that was not possible prior to the advent and proliferation of social media platforms. The use of social media in a classroom environment enables instructors to create a course that promotes cooperation and collaboration among the instructors and students and aids in the long-term information retention of course materials. Therefore, the use of social media by both students and instructors is encouraged.

My advice for current sport management students and their social media profiles is to ensure that all content is sufficiently moderated and reflects positively on each individual. For those with public profiles, ensure that the content you share is interesting and reflects your values and interests. Recruiters will scour the Internet to learn more about each applicant, so having a good public profile on relevant social media platforms can help you stand out and show your ability to engage with others on social media. However, your profiles can also be a deterrent to gaining meaningful employment, so maintaining a positive profile on social media is important to allow future sport managers to build their personal brands in the most positive way.

OLAN SCOTT is an assistant professor in sport management at Brock University. His research is predominately in sport communication, with the bulk of his work in sport media seeking to understand how sport events are communicated to viewers on television or readers in newspaper or online. Another of his areas of research is understanding fan engagement on social media and the types of content published by sport organizations that generates the most engagement from their followers. He is heavily involved in industry-focused research, including social media marketing, fan development, strategic planning, and brand-awareness market research.

Measurement Based on Platform-Generated Metrics

The return on investment (ROI) for social media can be assessed against established objectives. For example, what is the objective that a marketer is trying to accomplish with the investment? The investment can be employee salary and office resources or an investment in posts. If one is interested in assessing the effectiveness of investment (in terms of payment made for an ad boost or boosted post), one way to evaluate would be the number of likes, reaches, engagements, messages received, and shares. In this regard, Facebook provides data (for business Facebook accounts) to inform the level of reach and engagement of a post. Facebook (n.d.) lists

some of the metrics it uses to help businesses assess their investments on boosted posts. Some of the common metrics by post type are presented in table 12.1. It is worth noting here that other social media platforms also provide analytical assessment of posts. These include Twitter Analytics, Instagram Insights, and YouTube Analytics.

The effectiveness of an ROI depends on what one attempts to achieve, and the metrics in table 12.1 can help you assess the awareness and reach of your product (e.g., likes) and the level of understanding (e.g., messages received, conversation, and comments). Platform-generated analytical data can also inform you as to who saw your social media posts by location, language, and demographics. These types

TABLE 12.1 Metrics for Boosted Posts

Post Type	Metric	Description
Post with an image or text	Post engagement	The total number of actions that people take involving your ads.
Video post	ThruPlays	The number of times your video was played to completion or for at least 15 seconds.
Post with a call-to-action button (i.e., like/follow us, learn more, share now, comment now, visit website)	Link clicks	The number of clicks on links within the ad that led to destinations or experiences, on or off Facebook. For ads promoting Instagram profile views, link clicks include clicks on the ad header or comments that led to the advertiser's profile.
	Messaging conversations	If your page has the send message button, you should look at the messaging conversations started metric.
Event post with tickets	Link clicks	The number of clicks on links within the ad that led to destinations or experiences, on or off Facebook. For ads promoting Instagram profile views, link clicks include clicks on the ad header or comments that led to the advertiser's profile.
Event post without tickets	Event responses	The number of people who responded interested or going to your Facebook event, attributed to your ads.

of data are informative in segmenting your target market for a number of different marketing initiatives. However, one should understand that translating Facebook likes to liking a product or service is wrong and misleading. For example, a post by a small local 5K run might be liked by a number of people, but it does not necessarily mean that those people who liked the post are going to pay the entry fee and register for the event or to donate money for charity. Therefore, in thinking on measuring an ROI in social media, one should first define the objectives.

The existing metrics do not reflect the sum total of benefits that one may gain from social media investment, and one cannot rely on a single measure to get the whole picture of a multifaceted benefit that an organization may get from social media. To illustrate this point, figure 12.2 outlines our model of measuring return on investment on social media, which uses a hierarchy of effects approach that builds from awareness to purchase in six steps. The purpose of the model (figure 12.2) is to outline the progression of learning and decision-making that consumers go through as a result of advertising. It also informs how advertising influences a consumer's decision to purchase a product or service. Based on the hierarchy of effects model, one may want a social media platform and the content posted on that platform to have one or more of the following objectives included in the hierarchy of effects model (per Kotler & Keller, 2006): awareness, knowledge, liking, preference, conviction, and purchase, with the ideal outcome being the final phase, purchase (the ultimate goal of any business).

As you see in figure 12.2, the hierarchy of effects model is extended to social media, where the first two stages are cognitive stages in which a company attempts to create awareness and provide knowledge and understanding of its offerings on social media. In other words, that is the stage where social media followers acquire their knowledge and understanding of an organization or its offerings. Once, the first two stages are met, the next stage is affective stage, which includes liking, preference, and conviction. This is the stage where sport organizations attempt to influence the feelings and emotions of their followers (e.g., Q&A with a player, birthday wish by a team to fans, Facebook live meet-and-greet with a player). The last stage is behavioural, which is about purchase. It is a stage where social media followers act or buy an offering, for

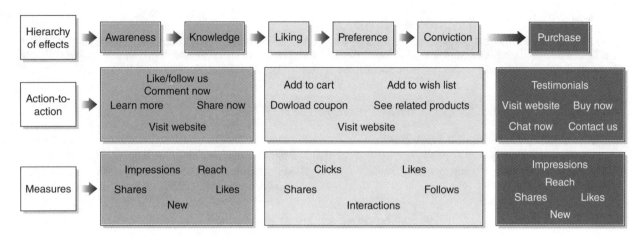

FIGURE 12.2 Model of measuring return on investment on social media.

example, social media followers responding to a post such as "Buy a ticket and get 30 percent off the next game" or registering for a 5k run using a Facebook events page.

Guided by figure 12.2, for example, a sport organization may set the objective of creating awareness and then educating its customers. For instance, a new local 5K run in the city of Halifax, Nova Scotia, it may announce that there is a 5K run taking place at a given time and location in the city, reveal the entry fee and the location of the race, and announce any high-profile personality attending the event on its social media. In doing that, the race organizers can select one of the following buttons available on Facebook such as like/follow us, comment now, learn more, share now, and visit website. These actions help you create awareness as well as educate your potential audience about your event. Once you establish your objective, you can use the analytics offered by the different social media platforms to assess your effectiveness in terms of measures such as impressions, reach, shares, likes, and new followers.

Similarly, in order to attract potential runners to your new event and for them to like what you are offering (liking), to get them to prefer your event over other running events in the city (preference), and then, to lead them to have an intention to register for your event (conviction), you can post messages such as an offer of free training for four weeks in the days running up to the race day. You can also provide them with a video-recorded training program, offer advice on the best running shoe, and boost your post about the event's flat racecourse. When these messages are posted, they need to be accompanied by actions or buttons available at the platforms (e.g., Facebook) such as add to cart, add to wish list, download coupon, see related products, and visit website. You can assess the effectiveness of these actions using measures such as clicks, likes, shares, follows, and interactions.

Finally, to convert all the efforts you put into the first few stages and turn them into purchase, you need to post contents accompanied with actions or button such as testimonials, visit website, buy now, chat now, contact us, and claim your reward or discount. Sales can be measured in terms of the number of people who purchased your offerings. For the 5K run example, if the organizers sell tickets on Facebook, they will be able to find the number of people registered on Facebook event. If the organizer uses specialized registration websites such as Eventbrite, the registration websites themselves have analytics that inform how the registered participants accessed the registration link, which can tell you if people made the purchase on Eventbrite using the link posted on Facebook. Even if these methods do not reflect the sum total of benefits that you received from your social media investment, the metrics provide you with some insight to justify investments to the top management in your organization. Finally, figure 12.2 includes a set of measures as a reminder to always track your efforts with benchmarks and data to see what is working and what is not.

CHAPTER SUMMARY

This chapter highlighted the place and value of social media in sport marketing. The chapter opens with the basic concepts of social media, followed by a discussion of the different dimensions of social media in sport marketing and the measurement issues associated with social media investment. The first part specifically provided an overview of social media, including its definition, the distinguishing features and various types of users of social media, and the different platforms of social media. The chapter clarified the widely held assumption that social media started with Facebook and explained that it has been in existence since the late 1990s with the launch of Six Degrees. It also clarified that social media is much broader than social networking sites such as Facebook and Twitter. Social media includes discussion sites, blogs, and content communities in addition to social networking sites. In addition, the chapter brought to our attention that all social media users are not alike and discussed the different types of social media users.

With the understanding of the foundational concepts of social media, the chapter covered the use of social media as a sport marketing tool for purposes such as branding, endorsement, sponsorship, and ambush marketing. These selected dimensions of social media used in sport marketing demonstrated that managing an organization's social media account is different from running a personal account. It demands skill, creativity, dedication, ethics, and personality. To help guide the management of a professionally managed social media platform, the chapter identified and discussed 10 different practical steps and detailed the undertakings in each step. In its final part, building on the practical guidelines, the chapter articulated and introduced the different approaches that can be employed in the measurement of return on social media investment.

TEST YOUR KNOWLEDGE

1. Define social media and briefly describe each of the four concepts included in the definition.
2. Identify the distinguishing features of social media and discuss each one briefly.
3. What are the major social media platforms?
4. What are the different types of social media users? Identify and briefly describe each.
5. Identify and list the 10 practical steps in managing social media platforms.
6. What are the five stages of the hierarchy of effects model that facilitate the measurement of return on social media investment? List metrics that can be used to measure each stage.

KEY TERMS

ambush marketing	distinguishing features	social media
appealing social media content	measurement fact	social media influencers
balanced combination	paid content	social media platforms

CASE STUDIES

Visit HK*Propel* for case studies organized by chapter.

PART III

IMPORTANT STRATEGIC ELEMENTS OF SPORT MARKETING IN CANADA

CHAPTER 13

Sport Sponsorship

LEARNING OBJECTIVES

After studying this chapter, you will be able to do the following:

- Appreciate the history of sponsorship and its use in sports today
- Understand the place of sponsorship in the promotional mix
- Know the differences between sponsorship and advertising
- Integrate a sponsorship strategy within a sport organization
- Understand the corporate objectives associated with sport sponsorship

In the early days of marketing and sport marketing and up until the 1970s, **sponsorship** was no different than philanthropy. It was conducted as an individual interest of corporate managers rather than a sensible evaluation of the benefits of sponsorship (Foster et al., 2020). In the 1980s and early 1990s sponsorship started to be viewed primarily as an alternative to advertising and as a way of obtaining media exposure (Crompton, 2004). Today, according to International Event Group (IEG) (2018), sponsorship has exceeded both media advertising and promotions in terms of year-to-year growth in expenditure. But what is sponsorship?

Although it is somewhat dated, the most widely accepted definition of sponsorship is from Meenaghan (1991, p. 36), who defined the concept as "an investment, in cash or in kind, in an activity, in return for access to the exploitable commercial potential associated with that activity." In this definition of sponsorship, we find four main concepts that remain today as the most important aspects of sponsorship.

1. Sponsorship is an *investment* in a property, and it is not a gift or a donation. For example, each of the Olympic Games sponsors pay a sponsorship rights fee of an estimated 100 million USD. Each sponsor is spending this sum of money with an expectation that their investment will allow them to achieve targeted objectives.

2. Sponsorship investment is not always in the form of cash; it can also be in kind, in other words, by offering services or products as a sponsor. For example, Air Canada may sponsor a soccer team by giving free airline tickets, a hotel may sponsor a sport conference by providing free hotel rooms, Adidas may provide complimentary sport wear for a major event's volunteers, and so on.
3. Sponsorship is an investment in different sport activities such as sport teams (e.g., Toronto FC and Bank of Montreal), players (Axe and Toronto Raptors' Kyle Lowry), venues (e.g., Scotiabank Saddledome and Calgary Flames), and a few other, similar properties.
4. Sponsors expect a return on their investment (ROI).

Sport sponsorship is big business. How big a business? According to the Canadian Sponsorship Landscape Study (CSLS), total corporate spending on sponsorship in Canada exceeded 3 billion CAD for the first time in 2018 (Canadian Sponsorship Landscape Study [CSLC], 2019). For the same year, global sponsorship spending was expected to reach 66 billion USD (IEG, 2018). The CSLS has reported major sponsorship growth in Canada since 2006, and sponsorship spending more than doubled from the first year CSLS started measuring spending in the country. There have been a few major milestones as well, including the Vancouver 2010 Winter Olympic Games, which generated 703 million CAD in sponsorship revenue (COC, 2014), and the landmark 800 million CAD Scotiabank Arena deal, which gave Scotiabank the naming rights to the home arena of the Toronto Maple Leafs and Toronto Raptors for 20 years (CBC, 2017). These major deals are accompanied by a number of deals of various sizes across Canada each year, bringing revenue to national sport organizations (NSOs) such as Hockey Canada, Speed Skating Canada, and Alpine Canada; professional sport leagues (e.g., Canadian Football League, National Lacrosse League); and events of all sizes, from 5k runs to esports tournaments. This chapter details sport sponsorship, a **promotional mix** tactic that was introduced in previous chapters. Notably, the chapter emphasizes the importance of sponsorship in generating resources for sport organizations that have the ability to offer value back to a potential sponsor.

EXECUTIVE PERSPECTIVE
Sport Sponsorship as a Key Strategy for Visa Marketing in Canada

BRENDA WOODS, Vice-President of Marketing, Visa Canada

Visa is a global payments technology company, connecting consumers, businesses, banks, and governments in more than 200 countries and territories worldwide. The Visa brand is one of our most valuable assets and stands for trust, convenience, and security. Our marketing programs are one of the drivers that have made Visa the leading payment brand worldwide. Sponsorship is an important component of our marketing strategy, in Canada and around the world.

In Canada, we activate our global sponsorships of the Olympic Games, FIFA, and NFL, as well as our Canadian sponsorship of the Toronto International Film Festival. We view sponsorships as a powerful way to connect our brand to sponsorship properties that have complementary brand attributes and provide a connection to events that consumers are passionate about.

Let me give you a few examples of some of our sponsorship programs that I've been involved with during my time with Visa.

Text used with permission from VISA. In addition, the VISA trademarks are being used with permission. The VISA trademarks are registered trademarks of Visa International Service Association. Permission to use does not constitute endorsement of any products or services. Any other use is expressly prohibited.

Olympic and Paralympic Games

One of our longest sponsorship partnerships has been with the Olympic and Paralympic Games. Since 1986, Visa's commitment to the Olympic Movement, National Olympic Committees, and individual athletes has been an important factor in ensuring the continuance and success of the Olympic Games and Paralympic Games. As a proud Worldwide Sponsor of the Olympic Games, Visa will be the exclusive payment technology partner and the only card accepted at the Olympic Games through 2032. This global sponsorship gives Visa the rights to activate in every country around the world where Visa operates.

The Olympics platform is used to drive key outcomes:

- Strengthen the Visa brand through the association with the Olympic brand, which remains strong and differentiated and has been a proven platform to drive Visa brand preference.
- Provide a platform for Visa's over 900 bank clients around the world to use to drive acquisition, activation, usage, and loyalty for Visa products.
- Showcase new product innovation—the two-year cycle of Summer and Winter Olympic Games gives Visa a platform to debut new innovations on a global stage.

Visa communicates its sponsorship of the Olympic Games by running Olympic-themed advertisements in the television broadcast of the Games, through promotions such as "Win a Trip to the Olympic Games when you use Visa" and through the sponsorship of Olympic athletes in our Team Visa program.

Toronto International Film Festival

A truly Canadian property, the Toronto International Film Festival (TIFF), is a sponsorship we have been part of for 24 years and one that I have been involved in building our activations around. The celebrity attendance and global profile of the TIFF, as well as its location in the heart of Canada's biggest market and financial hub, provide many activation opportunities and a positive return on investment for us. Our focus has always been on delivering an elevated experience for clients and cardholder, through an exclusive branded theatre experience at the Visa Screening Room at the Princess of Wales Theatre, advance tickets for Visa cardholders, and a special entrance line and lounge for Visa Infinite cardholders. In 2020, the Film Festival had to pivot its program to show screenings at outdoor venues and online. Visa took on this challenge to still provide a unique experience despite the largely virtual setting. We created a unique drive-in experience at the Visa Skyline Drive-In on Toronto's waterfront that hosted film lovers in their cars during 10 nights of TIFF premieres. Three screenings were held exclusively for cardholders, clients, and small businesses.

FIFA

Finally, I'd like to comment on another of our popular sponsorships, FIFA. Visa is one of just five global FIFA Partners, and we have exclusive rights in the financial services product category for all FIFA World Cup activities around the world. We first began our sponsorship at the 2010 FIFA World Cup South Africa. Our FIFA partnership provides Visa with the opportunity worldwide to use the FIFA World Cup and more than 40 other FIFA competitions in our marketing programs. Our rights to the FIFA World Cup events also allow our financial institution clients and merchant partners to activate in their programs which provide a powerful opportunity for the sponsorship to drive business, achieve maximum exposure, and improve brand lift, global reach, and local relevance.

These celebrated FIFA competitions create economic benefits for host nations and provide Visa with an opportunity to build business for its financial institution clients and merchant partners. Working together, Visa and FIFA create exclusive and unique programs at FIFA tournaments that drive incremental value to Visa account holders and clients.

> *continued*

> **Sport Sponsorship as a Key Strategy for Visa Marketing in Canada**   > *continued*
>
> Visa is carried by millions of football fans across the globe, and by creating integrated cardholder promotions, access to tickets and experiences that capitalize on fan passion for the game, Visa is able to enhance the FIFA World Cup experience for fans.

> BRENDA WOODS is the vice-president of marketing for Visa in Canada and is responsible for leading all aspects of Visa marketing to support the achievement of business and brand objectives. Brenda has more than 30 years of marketing and brand management experience. Brenda is also past chair of the Sponsorship Marketing Council of Canada and previously worked at Kraft General Foods.

Market Trends in Canadian Sponsorship

The Canadian Sponsorship Landscape Study provides a number of important trends over the period 2006 to 2018 that show how sponsorship is growing and thriving in Canada, despite some challenges. First, as noted in figure 13.1, sponsorship represents about one in four of the total marketing communication dollars spent by Canadian sponsoring brands (CSLS, 2019).

As noted in figure 13.1, in 2018, 23.3 percent of marketing communications budgets were invested in sponsorship in Canada. The highest percentage of spending was in 2011. After going down in 2012, the percentage of spending increased for three years, until 2015. It started decreasing in 2015 and then started to increase again in 2017. In the period 2012 to 2018, on average 23.96 percent of the marketing communications budgets of Canadian sponsoring brands has been spent on sponsorship.

The Canadian Sponsorship Landscape Study (CSLS) measures a number of aspects of sponsorship in Canada and has done so since 2006. It is significant that CSLS (2019) reported an ongoing increase (in fact, a 5.06 percent cumulative annual growth rate) from 2006 to 2018 of sponsor spending in Canada, comprised of both their investments in rights fees (i.e., costs to partner

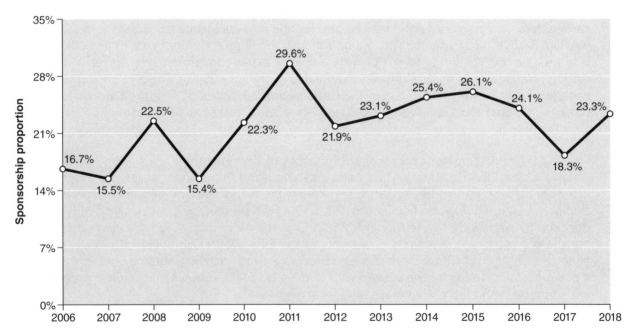

FIGURE 13.1 Percentage of marketing communications budgets spent on sponsorship in Canada from 2006 to 2018.

Reprinted by permission from N. O'Reilly, *Sponsorship Landscape Study* (2019). 13th Annual Canadian Sponsorship Landscape Study. www.sponsorshiplandscape.ca

with a given property) and activation investment (i.e., what they spend to promote their sponsorship) by the brands. Figure 13.2 reports on these results.

As reported in figure 13.2, the overall spending (the top line) has gone from 1.59 billion CAD in 2006 to 3.02 billion in 2018, a growth of just over 5 percent year-over-year. Of that growth, the amount spent on rights fees (the middle line) has gone from 1.11 billion to 1.80 billion, while that activation spend (the bottom line) has gone from 0.48 billion to 1.22 billion. Rights fees refer to the amounts paid by sponsors to acquire the rights to sponsor a given property, while activation refers to the additional spend to support that investment and the sponsorship's success overall.

Sponsorship and Activation

Activation will be discussed in much detail in the following chapter; however, it is important to provide some initial description here. It is often described using the *activation ratio* (O'Reilly & Lafrance Horning, 2013), which is what the brand spends in addition to the rights fee purchase. For example, if a brand pays a property 10 million CAD to be an official sponsor of that property and then spends an additional 4.5 million to activate it, the ratio of activation to the rights fee spend is 0.45. The rights fee only covers the ability to associate with the partner, but to promote the association, the brand needs to invest more (e.g., tv and radio commercials, a newspaper advertisement, billboards, flyers, social media advertising, and other activations tactics), which is the activation spend.

There are three major stakeholder groups in sponsorship:

- Sponsors are the parties that seek association with a particular sport property in order to further their own marketing objectives (e.g., Canadian Imperial Bank of Commerce [CIBC]).

- A property (sometimes called a sponsee) is a sponsored party, a property owner, or a rights holder (e.g., Hockey Canada).

- Agencies are companies that work on behalf of a sponsor or property (e.g., Wasserman, the T1 Agency, Elevant, Lumency). They conduct research, undertake valuations and evaluations, develop sponsorship agreements, sell sponsorship, and often negotiate on

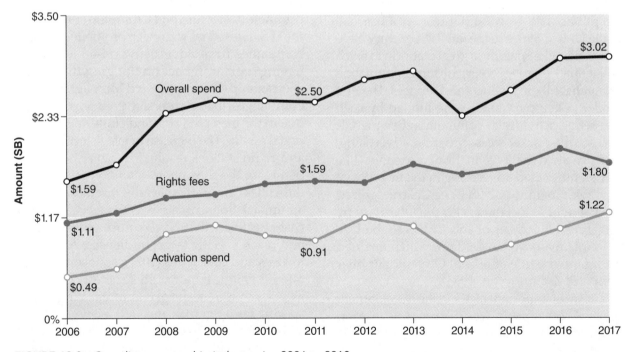

FIGURE 13.2 Canadian sponsorship industry size 2006 to 2018.
Reprinted by permission from N. O'Reilly, *Sponsorship Landscape Study* (2019). 13th Annual Canadian Sponsorship Landscape Study. www.sponsorshiplandscape.ca

behalf of their clients. Agencies work for sponsorships of all sizes and in all industries and range from very large organizations to those with only a single professional.

History of Sponsorship

The sponsorship of sports organizations is not a new phenomenon. In fact, it can be traced back to the ancient Olympic Games (dating back 3,000 years), when wealthy patrons helped athletes in their training and supplied them with equipment, including chariots and horses (McMahon, 1996). In return for their contributions to the Olympic Games, these wealthy Greek men gained not only goodwill and enhanced civic standing in the community and the state but also a variety of privileges including the rights to special seats.

The origins of sponsorship as we know it today may be more recent, dating to the 19th century. Brooks (1994) notes that transportation industry companies in the United States were the first businesses to be associated with sponsorship. As early as 1852, the New England railroad transported rowing teams from Yale and Harvard to a competition and used various promotional strategies to communicate their involvement to the public. The growing popularity of baseball in the United States in the late 19th century gave companies like Spalding a great platform to reach and influence a burgeoning consumer population to purchase their products and services. The first modern Olympic Games were funded by such marketing activities as commemorative medals and stamps, ticket sales, program advertising, and private donations. In 1896, companies like Kodak purchased advertising in the first official Olympic program. In 1928, Coca-Cola recognized the value of association with the Olympics by donating 1,000 cases of soft drinks to the U.S. Olympic team in Amsterdam, which enabled it to claim the title of official Olympic supplier (Howard & Crompton, 1995).

The most important factor in the development of sport sponsorship was the progress in communications technology in the 1950s and 1960s, which set the stage for future radical changes in the world of sport. Technical progress and growing prosperity accelerated the spread of television, which became the driver of the growth of sport and the marketing of sport. Specifically in the 1955 to 1960 time frame, the sale of television sets was so rapid that it was described as "contagious commercialism" (Schantz, 1995). At the time, the symbiosis between television and sport influenced the development of one another. One result was the acceleration of the commercialization and professionalization of sport. This led to the commodification of sport, the rise of professional sport, fan interest, the celebrity status of athletes, increased revenues, intense media coverage, and an overall growth in the popularity of sport around the world (Schantz, 1995).

Commercial sponsorship has mainly been a phenomenon since the late 1950s (Sandler & Shani, 1993). Until the early 1970s, corporate sponsorship of sporting events, clubs, and athletes was done first and foremost for philanthropic reasons (Sleight, 1989). In this way, corporate decisions to sponsor sports were not necessarily made as a business decision but as ones that could generate public goodwill. This corporate attitude greatly shifted in the 1980s, as companies started devoting substantial resources to sponsorship.

Technological changes, especially in television and web streaming, have had the most profound effect on making sport an attractive commercial commodity. Howard and Crompton (1995) credit the U.S. Television Act, which prohibited tobacco companies from advertising on television, as having a great impact on the growth of sport sponsorship. Otker (1988) and Meenaghan (1991) both suggest that sponsorship grew in popularity due to the increased cost and cluttering of traditional media. The increase in television channels and radio stations resulted in advertisers competing for the consumers' attention and made it difficult for any particular advertisement to make an impact. Sponsorship was therefore seen as a cost-effective way to break through the **clutter** and reach specific target audiences. According to Dees and colleagues (2021), sponsorship also offers a unique opportunity for lifestyle marketing, which is a means of communicating with a specific target market through leisure and lifestyle activities. This evolution has resulted in the symbiotic relationship between sport properties, media, and sponsors that is commonly referred to as the sponsorship triangle.

In the case of the Olympic Games, which Canada hosted in 1976 (Montreal), 1988 (Calgary), and 2010 (Vancouver), the IOC's decision to open the door to commercialization in the early 1980s played a key role in the growth of sponsorship with the 1984 Olympic Games. The great success of the 1984 Los Angeles Games and subsequently the IOC's Olympic marketing program may have contributed to legitimizing the commercialization of sport by the sport governing bodies. Irwin and Sutton (1994) believe that the Games served as the catalyst for the phenomenal growth in American sport sponsorship. Prior to the 1984 Games, financing had primarily come from government funding, lotteries, and donations. According to Meenaghan (1998), interest in associating with desirable positioning values through clean, exclusive, and cost-efficient access has always been the key driver in the development of sponsorship as a medium of promotion. However, the clutter resulting from multilevel deals negotiated by such properties as the Olympics and the effects of ambush marketing may inevitably wreck the purity of the transfer of values between event and sponsor.

Sponsorship and Its Roots in Philanthropy

In the early days of sponsorship research, Shanklin and Kuzma (1992) suggested that sponsorship's foundation is philanthropic giving. However, the lines between pure philanthropy and sponsorship blurred in the years that followed, and today they are viewed as distinct strategic elements (Foster et al., 2020).

According to Arthur and colleagues (1997), the confusion between sponsorship and philanthropy in the early days of the concept made it difficult for researchers to agree on a precise definition of sponsorship as the field developed. In turn, this lack of a precise definition confused consumers and businesses alike concerning the delineation of sponsorship, charitable donation, and patronage (Arthur et al., 1997), since brands differ in their expectations of the return coming from each. Indeed, pure philanthropic donations, in which the individual or corporation donates funds for

altruistic benefit and charity and in which an individual or corporation makes a donation and publicizes the fact, are very different from sponsorship primarily because the commercial orientation core to sponsorship is absent in these other elements

Today, the common view is that financial support of a philanthropic nature should not be part of sponsorship since a firm making a donation does not (or should not) expect any direct benefits in return. It may be possible to place various forms of corporate giving along a continuum defined by the extent to which giving is linked to corporate marketing objectives. On one end would be pure philanthropy, with no direct link to marketing objectives; on the other end would be sponsorship marketing, with explicit ties to sales of the sponsoring companies; and in the middle would sit public–private partnerships (a mix of philanthropic and marketing objectives by the private-sector partner) (O'Reilly & Brunette, 2013).

Relationship of Sponsorship to Marketing

The rapid growth of sport sponsorship has led to the misuse of the term *sponsorship*. While sponsorship is part of the promotional mix, it cannot be used, for example, to describe marketing. Although sponsorship is now considered a legitimate element of a company's communications mix, it is important to understand its place within the broader concept of the marketing mix, as well as within the promotional mix. The process of marketing begins with the identification of the needs and wants of consumers: A consumer-oriented organization tries to understand consumers' requirements and satisfy them in ways that are beneficial to both consumers and the organization. This is usually achieved through the marketing mix (the four Ps)—product, price, promotion, and place—which were discussed in previous chapters. A transaction occurs when equitable terms of exchange are agreed upon by the two parties; this is a common element of the American Marketing Association (AMA) definition of marketing introduced in chapter 1. In the realm of sports, consumers have demonstrated an intense want for sport, which has translated into demand, since these wants were backed up with purchasing power.

Sport promotion plays a significant role in the marketing mix. While the term promotion is often used synonymously with *advertising* (Shank & Lyberger, 2014), it is much more than that, since it involves all forms of communication to the consumers. This is why contemporary marketing theorists often refer to the promotional mix as the *communications mix*. The role of the communications mix is to inform and persuade consumers and thus influence their purchase decisions. For a growing number of organizations, sport has become an effective and efficient way to communicate to current and potential target markets. An increasingly popular method used by corporations to market their brands through sport has been sponsorship.

Since corporations typically use sponsorship to achieve a number of different objectives, for example, sales, employee satisfaction, brand equity, relationships, and market share (O'Reilly & Madill, 2009), many sport properties offer a variety of strategies and tactics to seek to help their partners achieve these objectives. This approach consists of carefully integrating and coordinating the promotional mix elements to deliver a unified message and take full advantage of the synergy between all the elements of the promotional mix. For example, an integrated marketing communications program for Canada's Olympic women's hockey team may include the rights to athlete images, corporate hospitality, media advertising, sponsor recognition programs, social media posts, and sales promotions. A sponsor may choose to leverage its investment by using a variety of communications tools: Leveraging, or the activation of rights, refers to incurring additional costs to support a sponsorship program by many or all of the other elements of the communications mix (O'Reilly & Lafrance Horning, 2013). For example, Pepsi's sponsorship of the Canadian Football League (CFL) may only provide the company with the right to associate with CFL and its eight teams. Thus, Pepsi will be required to spend additional money to activate its rights through such promotional mix elements as advertising, social media, and sales promotions. Tactical examples could include advertisements placed during TSN's broadcast and stream of CFL Friday night games, getting players from each of the eight teams to come to Pepsi offices for signing sessions, building a joint web platform, providing content for CFL social media platforms, creating in-store promotions, offering a hospitality experience to key customers and suppliers at the Grey Cup, or most likely a combination of all of these (and additional) tools. Sponsors who activate heavily can spend up to seven times the original investment in leveraging (O'Reilly & Lafrance Horning, 2013).

Legitimizing sponsorship as an important element of the communications mix has contributed to making sports big business. Worldwide expenditure on sponsorship has grown from about 500 million USD in 1982 (Shanklin & Kuzma, 1992) to an estimated 66 billion in 2018 (IEG, 2018). In Canada, the total spend has gone from 1.5 billion CAD in 2006 to just over 3 billion in 2018 (CSLS, 2019). These figures support the argument that sponsorship is an integral part of the marketing communications mix alongside advertising, public relations, sales promotions, and personal selling, in that its basic function lies in achieving communications objectives. It should be noted here that even though these elements of the promotional mix are different, it does not mean they work in isolation. In fact, ideally, they work in an integrated fashion. All these forms of communications and messages are carefully linked together as an integral part of an effective marketing plan.

Relationship between Sponsorship and Advertising

Since moving on from its roots in corporate philanthropy, sponsorship today fits nicely within the promotional mix. However, there is a lack of consensus among contemporary marketing scholars as to *how* it fits. While some marketers consider sponsorship as part of advertising, others position it as different from advertising and as a promotional strategy unique in its application and benefits (Foster et al., 2020). In fact, as suggested in the Pepsi-CFL example earlier in this chapter, sponsorship fits quite naturally alongside advertising, public relations, sales promotion, and personal selling as an element of the marketing communications mix because its basic function lies in achieving communications objectives.

According to Meenaghan (2001), a comparison between sponsorship and advertising in terms of goodwill, intent to persuade, and emotional relationship reveals some distinct features. Regarding the goodwill factor, corporate sponsorship as a generic form of marketing communications is seen as involving a benefit to society. Sponsorship is also seen as offering benefits to a property with which consumers (i.e., fans) have relationships, which has led to sponsorship to be considered as "advertising plus" (Meenaghan, 2005, p. 245). Advertising, by contrast, is seen as directly addressing a corporate agenda. Similarly, in terms of the intent to persuade, advertising is a direct, verbal, and visual method of communication capable of product demonstration and information provision. On the other hand, sponsorship—if done in a sophisticated manner—is an indirect, relatively subtle mode of communication that operates through the sponsored property to address sponsors' objectives. For this reason, Meenaghan (2001) suggests that sponsorship involves a disguised intent-to-persuade feature and posits that sponsorship is a three-way emotional relationship between sponsor, property, and (potential) consumer.

An additional important difference between sponsorship and advertising lies in how each works to persuade customers. Advertising exploits the construct of emotion and sponsorship seeks to connect with the emotion inherent in sport or the arts or the charity (depending on the property of interest) (Meenaghan, 2001). Sponsorship is fundamentally different from advertising because it persuades consumers indirectly via the association that exists and the fact that consumers are influenced by the sponsor, the association, and the property, not just the sponsor (as is the case in advertising). If a firm is seen to support a property (e.g.,

team, charity, venue, event, athlete), the sponsor's expectation is that the consumer, who is interested to some extent in the property, will view the sponsor positively provided there is a good fit between the image of the sponsor, the property, and the association. Sponsorship is further differentiated from advertising because it offers an interaction with consumers, where advertising only talks to them. This, in theory, allows sponsorship to create a bond with consumers via the values they both share by association with the property of interest (O'Reilly & Madill, 2012). For example, Coca-Cola's long-time sponsorship of the Olympic Games and the Canadian Olympic Committee allows for the transfer of attributes from the image of the Olympic Games (e.g., global, high-performance, amazing stories) to the images of Coca-Cola's products via the promotion of the association between the two in Canada. Hence, sponsorship is widely believed to be different from advertising (Foster et al., 2020).

Another scholar who articulated this difference was Bloxam (1998), whose three key points of difference between sponsorship and advertising are noted and illustrated in table 13.1. As the table outlines, what differentiates sponsorship from advertising is the association between the two parties (sponsor and property), which enhances the relationship beyond a basic cash purchase of promotional value (advertising). Sponsorship is a form of promotion, but it differs from advertising in that the medium and created messaging are not as tightly controlled by the sponsor as they would be by an advertiser (Javalgi et al., 1994).

A brief analysis of the objectives sought by advertising and by sponsorship reveals the similarities and differences between the two promotional tools. Like advertising, sponsorship may sometimes be employed to enhance public awareness of a sponsor or to improve or change a previously established image, and, similar to advertising, sponsorship may seek to increase sales or increase media exposure (O'Reilly & Madill, 2009). However, a sponsorship can achieve more diverse objectives than an advertisement, including increased awareness, change in the image of a brand, or an enhanced ability to improve business relationships with

TABLE 13.1 Sponsorship's Distinction from Advertising

Distinction	Meaning	Example
Sponsors are viewed as part of the program.	Due to the association effect, consumers perceive a sponsor as more involved with the property than an advertiser who lacks the association.	The Subaru Ironman Canada event in Penticton, BC (sponsor) versus a Subaru TV commercial (advertising) playing during a Toronto Blue Jays MLB game on Rogers Sportsnet.
Advertising and sponsorship function differently.	The process by which the communication takes place differs: In sponsorship, the message is coded, delivered, and decoded in collaboration with the property; in advertising, the process occurs independently.	Leading up to and during the Olympic Games, the IOC and its TOP sponsors work together on developing promotions, while Ford purchasing an advertisement in the *Globe and Mail* develops the promotion on its own.
Sponsorship is widely believed to benefit a wider audience.	Consumers often believe that supporting a sponsor has greater benefit than supporting an advertiser, as they perceive that the property also will benefit. This is particularly important in the sponsorship of causes (e.g., amateur sport, charity).	The CIBC Run for the Cure is a great example where CIBC is viewed by many as supporting finding a cure for breast cancer via their support for this event.

Based on Bloxam (1998).

customers. Cornwell and colleagues (2001) point out two additional objectives that differentiate sponsorship from advertising: achieving corporate hospitality and advancing the personal agendas and interests of senior executives, both of which are enabled by the ability to leverage a sponsorship, which more readily allows for associated events and activities.

Corporate Objectives and Sponsorship

Since companies today look for a **return on investment (ROI)** from their sponsorship, they must allocate their sponsorship dollars—both what they spend as rights fees and what they invest in activating those rights—wisely. In this context, sponsorship is now considered to be an important element of the promotional mix. Researchers have identified more than 150 outcomes that sponsors seek to achieve with sponsorship (O'Reilly & Madill, 2009), which still fit with the three main groupings of objectives associated with sponsorship sport

that Sandler and Shani (1993) identified many years before:

1. Broad corporate objectives (image based)
2. Marketing objectives (brand promotion, sales increase)
3. Media objectives (cost effectiveness, reaching target markets)

One advantage of sponsorship is that it can achieve a number of objectives simultaneously and independently, as noted by O'Reilly & Madill (2012), who reported that the most often cited specific objectives for corporate involvement in sport sponsorship are as follows:

- Increasing public awareness of the company, brand, or both
- Altering or reinforcing public perception, or image, of the company, brand, or both
- Identifying the company with particular market segments
- Generating media benefits
- Achieving sales objectives

- Creating a competitive advantage through exclusivity
- Gaining opportunities in terms of hospitality and entertainment

Each objective provides sponsors with an ROI that might be in monetary form but could also be in media exposure (number of **impressions**), the ability to exclude competitors, and so on.

Awareness as a Sponsorship Objective

Awareness is widely accepted by practitioners and academics alike as an objective which sponsorship can help achieve. Indeed, exposure to an association between a brand and property has the ability to lead to positive affect toward it and the transfer of images from the property to the event, which can lead to the consumer having improved understanding of the sponsor and its products (Faganel & Bratina, 2013). Awareness of the sponsorship and, ideally, a positive feeling about it can provide numerous benefits to the brand image and corporate image. For example, consumers may pay greater attention to subsequent commercial communications and may be more likely to include the sponsor's products in their consideration sets. If a local grocery store is actively involved in supporting the activities of local children in boys' and girls' ice hockey year in and year out, their parents may become more aware of future communications by the store. Meenaghan (1998) suggests that awareness is created at events where sponsors intrude on the consciousness of event audiences, which implies that awareness is closely linked to image objectives since a sponsor's image may be enhanced by the association of the sponsor with the event, thus transferring values from the event to the sponsor.

The importance of increasing a consumer's level of awareness is significant in light of ambush marketing, whereby a competitor of a sponsor seeks to take some of the benefit achieved by association with a given property. Meenaghan (1996) coined the term **ambush marketing** to describe "a practice whereby another company, often a competitor, intrudes upon public attention surrounding the event, thereby deflecting attention to themselves and away from the sponsor." A number of additional studies on ambush marketing (e.g., Séguin & O'Reilly, 2008; Burton et al., 2018) demonstrate that consumers with relatively low levels of awareness of sponsors are easier to fool (by ambushers) than those who are aware and identify with the sponsorship due to having both knowledge of the event and an emotional link to the activity or event or to the sponsor. As a result, event organizers use an integrated approach to sponsorship communications, which may include strategic use of signage, rights in naming events or stadiums, jumbotron advertising, in-stadium promotions, or sales promotion. These methods are a way to highly targeted segments.

Note that recall and recognition of sponsors is key to achieving many other objectives such as image and sales. If consumers do not remember (i.e., are not aware of) the Tim Hortons affiliation with the week-long Brier (Canadian Men's Curling Championship), there will be little if any impact on the company's image, sales, or market share, thus resulting in a low ROI.

Image as a Sponsorship Objective

Brands have long attempted to enhance their corporate image by creating awareness of their "good deeds" in the hope of ultimately increasing sales and profitability. Even when they refrain from explicitly promoting their altruistic efforts, they expect to generate goodwill, enhance their image, and ultimately increase sales. Many want to be good corporate citizens as well and do their part in making society a better place. The opportunity to capitalize on image association and transfer makes sponsorship very attractive to businesses as a communications tool.

This possible impact of sport sponsorship on corporate image has been the focus of many researchers, who agree that a majority of companies involved in sponsoring are attempting to meet an image objective, normally involving associating some of the images of the chosen property partner with the sponsor's corporate or product images. By definition, image is the sum of beliefs, ideas, and impressions a person has of a business or its products (Gwinner et al., 2009). Image benefits are most frequently sought by companies that are striving to create interest and a favourable attitude toward their products by "borrowing" the image of a sport to enhance the product's image with its target audience. Gwinner and colleagues (2009) suggest that the image of a sporting property is a social representation and propose that the property, as a social object or phenomenon, embodies a stock of image capital. In turn, a sponsor can leverage this image capital, via activation, to transfer images (Faganel & Bratina, 2013; Foster et al., 2020). In turn, by transferring the positive image of the sport property, a sponsor can distinguish itself from its competitors, thereby achieving a competitive advantage.

The choice of a sport property with particular attributes can help a company achieve the transfer of a desired image that will reinforce or change consumers' perceptions of the company and its products. There are numerous examples of brands that improve their image via the sponsorship of a sport property. For example, Kia Motors, in 2020, is a sponsor of the Canadian Hockey League (CHL) and its four key properties (Ontario Hockey League (OHL), Quebec Major Junior Hockey League (QMJHL), Western Hockey League (WHL) and the Memorial Cup. In sponsoring the CHL, a long-standing and national-local property (there are more than 50 Canadian clubs in nine provinces) with strong "Canadian," "grassroots," and "future NHL players" images, all of which are valuable associations for Kia, a Korean car manufacturer seeking to build its connections to Canada and its communities.

Additional aspects of a sport property that can impact the ability of a sponsor to generate awareness are event type (e.g., World Championship or local), event characteristics (e.g., professional, traditions, look and feel, and venue), and individual factors (e.g., consumer perceptions of the property) (Faganel & Bratina, 2013; Gwinner et al., 2009). Sponsorship potential will be at its maximum when there is an association between the target group of the sponsor and the target group of the property, between the desired image of the company and the image assets of the sport property, or between the product characteristics being promoted and the credibility of the sport property helping to promote the product (O'Reilly & Madill, 2009).

The degree of similarity between the event and the sponsor (often called "fit") is a key factor in the image transfer process. A sponsor's product can have either functional or image-related similarity with the event (Faganel & Bratina, 2013; Gwinner et al., 2009; Gwinner, 1997). Functional similarity means a sponsoring product is actually used by participants during the event (e.g., Speedo sponsoring Swimming Canada). Image-related similarity means the image of the

IN THE KNOW

COVID-19 and Sponsorship in Canada

In 2020-2021, sport sponsorship in Canada (and around the world) was impacted at a significant level by the global pandemic of COVID-19, which impacted almost every part of the world leading to tens of millions of cases and hundreds of thousands of deaths. At the level of sport, it led to the cancellation or postponement of major events including the Olympic Games and the Euro, professional sport league seasons, and the cancellation of almost all local and grassroots sport competitions. Many people in sport lost their jobs or were laid off.

The pandemic was devasting to the field of sport, and to sponsorship as well. The SponsorshipX COVID-19 global studies (SponsorshipX, 2020), of which most of the sample was from North America, found that sponsors expected to invest about 50 percent less than planned in rights fees in 2020 and close to 70 percent less in activation spend. Results from properties (on expected sponsorship revenues and activation spend by their partners) and agencies (on expected billings and activation spend by their clients) were similar.

event is related to the image of the brand (e.g., the Kia sponsorship of the CHL). Thus, companies should consider not only the potential customers the sponsor will reach but also the image of the event, as both are achievable through well-activated sponsorships.

Reaching the Target Market

Corporations searching for an optimal event or team to sponsor need to find a link between their product and the property. While Speedo has a direct link to aquatic sports and Nike has one to basketball, the link between pizza and the Edmonton Eskimos football team may not be as obvious. Sponsorships where there is a direct link are termed **endemic** (i.e., the sponsor's products are directly used in the sport property), while without a direct link they are **nonendemic**, meaning the sponsor has no functional relationship with the sport but is using the images associated with the sport and the property to market their own products. Tim Horton's ongoing sponsorship of curling properties in Canada is a very good example of a nonendemic sponsorship. Tim Hortons may not have a direct link to curling, but its sponsorship of Canadian curling events reinforces its presence at events important to its target market. In other words, prior to selecting a property, corporations should have a clear understanding of their target market. On the flip side, the sport marketer should also have a good understanding of its consumer base. Companies evaluate their potential consumers and produce a product that best adheres to the needs and wants of their own particular target market. A company using target market strategies is considering entering segments of the market where it can offer superior value and gain an advantage over competitors.

With the proliferation of media outlets (e.g., television, print, streaming, web, social media, radio) and new areas (e.g., esports, sport gambling, fantasy sports) that can be activated, sponsorship can provide brands with the ability to break through the clutter and reach the specific target markets they seek. Sponsorship is known to be effective in such a complex market, and, as marketing and advertising have become increasingly cluttered, sport organizations can use sponsorship to navigate the clutter and reach their target markets. For instance, Kruger Products Canada has sponsored the Canadian Women's Curling with their Scotties' facial tissue, Cashmere bathroom tissue, Purex bathroom tissue, and SpongeTowels as title sponsor of Scotties' Tournament of Hearts. The Scotties Tournament of Hearts sponsorship illustrates that certain events can help companies reach specific segments, such as heavy users, shareholders, and investors, or specific groups that have been demographically, psychographically, or geographically segmented.

One way by which a company can use sponsorship to reach its target consumers is by targeting their lifestyles. Lifestyle marketing is "a strategy for seizing the concept of a market according to its most meaningful recurring patterns of attitudes and activities, and then tailoring products and their promotional strategies to fit these patterns" (Hanen, 2000, p. 261). The rationale behind a brand embarking on this kind of sponsorship is that certain types of leisure activities (e.g., CrossFit, triathlon, mountain biking, adventure racing, mountaineering, trail running) appeal to individuals who share similar lifestyles, values, and behaviours. Hence, the consumers in these target groups may be more receptive to a message from a brand that shares those values. In other words, lifestyle sponsorship creates opportunities to reach consumers who partake in similar activities and possess similar interests and opinions. These sponsorships often involve sporting events, which are environments where sponsorships activation can occur directly with these markets. For example, Dairy Farmers of Canada (DFC) have sponsored many triathlons and runs over the years to provide an opportunity to market to this segment with chocolate milk, as a postrace recovery beverage (including product sampling).

Media Benefits

Media exposure or coverage has been identified as a key benefit sought from sponsorship as well as being a key objective of many sponsorship programs. Early studies found that media objectives were the first priority for sponsors (Abratt et al., 1987) and that potential media coverage that a property can provide is a key aspect for most sponsors (Howard & Crompton, 1995). Major sporting events often achieve significant media coverage, which can provide sponsorship with a cost-effective means of reaching specific target markets. Media benefits can also include achieving publicity (e.g., blog coverage, newspaper coverage) related to the promotional efforts surrounding the sponsored property.

A sponsor can achieve media-related objectives in many ways. Shank and Lyberger (2014) identified alternative forms of advertising, from conventional stadium signage to the most creative media. For example, an advertising message may be an actual advertisement during a specific event. During the 2004 Grey Cup, Pfizer developed an advertising campaign that used a number of complementary media to promote one of its products. The in-stadium spectators were exposed to a specially designed vignettes aired on the jumbotron, while a 30-second commercial was aired during the broadcast of the event. The spectators and viewers were also exposed to in-stadium signage throughout the game. Sponsor signage is often prominent in photographs that are included in web, newspaper, and social media content, providing impressions for the sponsor with consumers.

Impressions are the number of viewers (television or streaming), followers (social media platforms), readers (all print forms), and listeners (radio) exposed to the message. In the social media platforms, followers also have the ability to share the messaging further, with the ability to amplify the reach (and impressions) of the sponsorship. It is important that not all impressions are considered equal and, as such, the source of impressions is of interest to a sponsor. For example, coverage and a photograph in a leading national newspaper (e.g., the *Globe and Mail*, the *National Post*) is much more powerful in terms of impressions than one in a local newspaper because of the subscription base, the perceived value, the online reach, and the national distribution of the publication. The same applies for television and streaming exposure by a national broadcaster, such as CBC, TSN, or Rogers Sportsnet. Clearly, a strong media program is an important aspect of any sponsorship program.

Unfortunately for some sponsors, there are times when they are promised media benefits from a sponsorship (e.g., recognition, percentage of reach in target market, sales), but for some reason (e.g., insufficient activation, competitor activity, ambush marketing), those benefits fail to materialize.

Sales

Perhaps the most important sought-after outcome of sponsorship for brands is achieving bottom-line sales results. Indeed, many of the other objectives (image transfer, awareness, brand, relationship building, etc.) are all directly or indirectly related to encouraging the buyer to purchase. After all, it is unreasonable to believe that organizations would spend tens of millions of dollars to lend their names to stadiums or to major events if they did not feel comfortable about the ROI. The Canadian Sponsorship Landscape Study finds, year after year, that sales are one of the key objectives of Canadian sponsors (CSLS, 2019).

Sponsorship provides brands with opportunities to drive sales via activities such as providing product sampling and developing point-of-sale merchandising. Sales objectives can also relate to product use as a benefit of a sponsorship or licensing agreement in the form of **exclusivity**. Exclusivity (or the protected use of the sponsored product as the only one in its category) is often included in the sponsorship agreements and contracts with a property (CSLS, 2019), whether an event, a venue, or even an entire university campus, which may require the exclusive use of a product at all events, functions, or facilities. For example, Coca-Cola's strategy is to sign sponsorship or licensing agreements that ensure product exclusivity (i.e., no Pepsi-related products or communications) and utilization: The ethics of such deals on university campuses has created a lively debate in many postsecondary institutions. As noted by Brenda Woods in the Executive Perspective earlier in this chapter, Visa uses sponsorship to drive business for itself and its partners. The brand, which globally has sponsored the Olympics since 1986, required exclusivity as Visa is the only credit card accepted to buy Olympic tickets and merchandise on-site at any Olympic Games.

Exclusivity

Exclusivity is a core element that most sponsors seek in their partnerships with sport properties. It is described as providing the sponsor with a clean (i.e., competitor free) platform from which to promote their products and/or services. This is known as exclusivity, or blocking the competition, and it is a key requirement for most sport sponsorships. In the case of Olympic Games sponsorship, top sponsors pay tens of millions of dollars for the rights fees. In return, these corporations are guaranteed exclusivity in their product category, exclusive rights to use the five-ring logo worldwide marketing campaigns, and many other benefits. Canadian sponsors (CSLS, 2019) continue to report that exclusivity is one of the most important elements they want to see in a sponsorship package.

Exclusivity provides an opportunity for the sales-driven use of the sponsorship agreement while prohibiting competitors from using the event, venue, product, or activity to transmit a message to the audience. It also prevents the property from allowing competitors to access any of their assets. This limitation can improve the ability of the marketing messages or activation programs to increase sales, and, in turn, may enhance the profitability of both the sponsor and the competitor. Exclusivity allows the marketer to position brands or products as supporting an event or the efforts of a particular team, while implying that a competitor's product does not, thereby encouraging consumer support where it counts.

The Canadian Sponsorship Landscape Study (CSLS, 2019) has outlined the importance of exclusivity for sponsors. As shown in figure 13.3, CSLS reported on the most valuable benefits that sponsors identify in Canada. According to the study, exclusivity ranked at the highest (on a scale of 1 to 5) for the years 2016, 2017, and 2018. Thus, as figure 13.3 supports, a brand may choose to sponsor an event only if it offers exclusivity to prevent the competition from accessing it. Ideally, for the sponsor, exclusivity also limits the ability of their competitors to copy their activation strategies, among other benefits.

Hospitality

Hospitality and entertainment play a critical role in the packaging of sponsorship programs. They enable the sponsor to construct certain benefits and opportunities that are often unique and

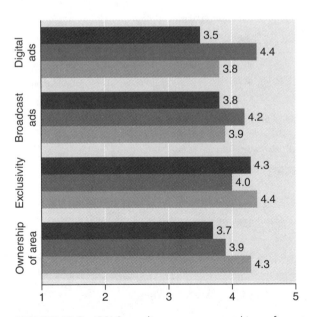
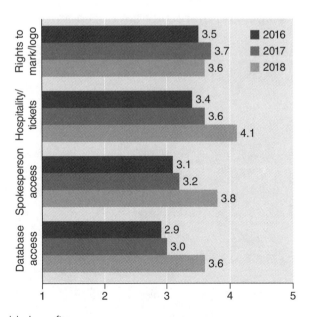

FIGURE 13.3 CSLS results on sponsor ranking of most valuable benefits.
Reprinted by permission from N. O'Reilly, *Sponsorship Landscape Study* (2019). 13th Annual Canadian Sponsorship Landscape Study. www.sponsorshiplandscape.ca

unavailable in the marketplace. Such opportunities may include winning trips to prestigious events such as the Stanley Cup finals or curling's Brier, both including special treatment through on-site hospitality and special events. Often, the hospitality programs are targeted at top clients, attractive prospects, and key suppliers. Hospitality opportunities have become an integral part of sponsorship agreements for professional and Olympic sport organizations, which may package hard-to-obtain tickets in prime locations along with tents, catering, and other amenities provided by brand ambassadors. Luxury boxes in the venues of professional sport teams are another example of hospitality-based programs, as corporate suite holders use the suite benefits to reward their own personnel, clients, or potential clients. Often, the use of suites is reviewed each year to assess if they led to increased sales or ROI from the hospitality efforts.

Results from the Canadian Sponsorship Landscape Study (CSLS, 2019) on how brands have spent their activation dollars in sponsorship since 2010 show a varied and ever-changing result as to where activation dollars go each year. In essence, it appears that Canadian brands have different and customized approaches to how they activate their sponsorships, with certain trends also evident (e.g., social media at its highest in 2013 and 2014 and dropping since then). Hosting and hospitality have been an important part of Canadian sponsors' activation mix since 2010, with their importance increasing in 2018 over the years prior. Public relations (PR) is normally not a major area of spend, although in 2012 and 2013 it increased. Branded content (or the creation of a brand's own activation platform) has been on the rise in recent years, with more than 15 percent of all activation spending in Canada on branded content in 2016, 2017, and 2018. Product sampling and advertising are the two other areas of activation spend, with advertising being the highest in both 2016 and 2018. See figure 13.4 for the graphical results.

In the context of the Olympic and Paralympic Games, sponsors and broadcasters use their hospitality resources to maintain or increase revenues, influence potential customers, reward existing customers, and even reward key employees. One of the major benefits of the Olympic and Paralympic partnership is the right to entertain these guests and customers in an exclusive manner. This includes access to premium hotel rooms, tickets, transportation, and accreditation, which creates an exceptional VIP experience. Many sponsors view hospitality as an effective strategy to strengthen relationships with distributors, brokers, consultants, and employees, sometimes as a part of a larger relationship marketing strategy. Often, these programs involve access to athletes or coaches in a hosting setting.

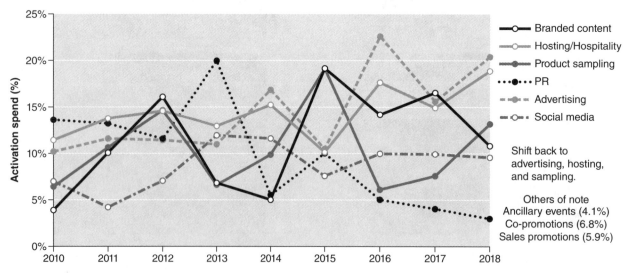

FIGURE 13.4 Activation investments by tactical area in Canada, 2010 to 2018.
Reprinted by permission from N. O'Reilly, *Sponsorship Landscape Study* (2019). 13th Annual Canadian Sponsorship Landscape Study. www.sponsorshiplandscape.ca

EXECUTIVE PERSPECTIVE
Sport Sponsorship: A Researcher's View

DON MAYO, Global Managing Partner, IMI International

The Beginning: Flashback to 1985

I was 20 years old and just finishing my second year of business school at Sir Wilfrid Laurier University in Waterloo when I was offered an internship job at Petro-Canada in an entity called Research One. It was March 1985, and I started a month later and was immediately thrown into a project focused on a thing called "Sponsorship," which I knew nothing about. Little did I know that I had the good fortune to be immersed in one of the best examples of sponsorship impact ever in our country, watching and working on the insights behind the 1988 Olympic Torch Relay. The story? Petro-Canada had secured the rights to the Olympic Torch for the 1988 Calgary Winter Olympics. At the same time, Shell Oil had secured the rights to the 1988 Olympic Games. Two major petroleum companies both had rights to the biggest event in Canadian History. Petro-Canada's rights included the Torch Relay, which precedes the Olympic Games, while Shell Oil's rights included the Games and were all-encompassing except for the torch.

The internal question was how does Petro-Canada win the hearts and minds of Canadians? Shell certainly had the upper hand, as western Canadians had a large disdain for a government-owned oil company that was Petro-Canada, and Petro-Canada only had the rights to the Torch Relay. To make a long story a little shorter, Petro-Canada won the hearts and minds of Canadians, thereby changing perceptions of the government-owned oil company through their use of the Olympic Torch Relay and exceptional activation efforts, including the following:

1. *Community Activation:* 10 million applications to run in the Torch Relay were submitted from a country of 30 million people. A random sweepstakes from towns across Canada led to 7,000 runners participating in an 11,000-kilometre cross-country journey.
2. *Inclusion:* A group of 300 torchbearers was added by special selection, composed of persons with disabilities, First Nations representatives, athletes, and officials.
3. *Retail Activation:* Offering commemorative Olympic Torch glasses in sets of six or eight for $1 per glass at every retail location, eventually sold 60 million glasses.
4. *Cause:* A portion of the sale of each glass funded future Olympians, raising about $6 million.
5. *Mass Employee Engagement:* Petro-Canada utilized employees to help organize, plan, and execute the Olympic Torch Relay, which enabled them to drive pride across the company and their thousands of retail outlets across Canada.
6. *Continuity:* Petro-Canada continued their Olympic involvement for decades following 1988.

Concurrent and competing with Petro-Canada, Shell activated their rights with a significant campaign of on-air broadcasts, collectible pins at retail, and extensive signage. In March 1988—after the Olympics had ended—Research One asked 1,000 Canadians one powerful, unaided question: "Please name as many as you can of the brands, products, or services that supported the 1988 Winter Olympic Games." Petro-Canada achieved the #1 rank with over 27 percent respondents mentioning them spontaneously, far exceeding the unaided awareness of every other sponsor. This is a case study in executional excellence: a first-year partner, with rights to only the Torch Relay, dominated every other Olympic

> *continued*

> **Sport Sponsorship: A Researcher's View** *> continued*

Sponsor by activating in communities and in their retail locations, building emotions and pride while integrating the cause and retail sales. Even though this happened more than 30 years ago, it is difficult to name another sponsorship as impactful.

Current Levels of Engagement in Properties in COVID-19

Let's fast-forward to 2021 now. I define property engagement as engagement through broadcast, digital platforms, social, celebrity, merchandise, fantasy, and day-to-day discussion. For all types of properties—sport, entertainment, community or lifestyle, cause—engagement remains very high and consistent over time. Table 13.2 shows a consistent strength and engagement in properties—sport and others—that cannot be hindered even by a global pandemic.

TABLE 13.2 IMI Research on Engagement of Properties

Property Engagement	Sport	Entertainment	Community/Lifestyle	Cause
Feb 2020—Prepandemic	83%	78%	87%	93%
Feb 2021—Postpandemic	83%	79%	86%	91%

Property Engagement (Source: sponsorpulseimi.com.)
Note: IMI International's SponsorPulse evaluates over 1,200 properties—global and local—across 18 countries representing 4.4 billion people and is conducted monthly.

The interesting thing when you evaluate people's engagement in sport, entertainment, cause, and community events is that the vast majority of people engage with many properties of all shapes and sizes, not just one. In fact, the average person who is 13 years of age or older engages with an average of 43 different properties per year.

Put another way, people are not NFL only fans in the United States or NHL only fans in Canada—rather, the average person who is engaged is sport engages with 19 different sports. Thus, it is critical for brands, properties, and media outlets to realize and embrace the fact that people are not a fan of one property but rather a fan of the theme. This results in a far greater competition for capturing the consumer's mind and heart. It is not about blanketing athletes, clubs, events, and facilities with logos. Rather, for success it is critical to: (i) engage the consumer with value and entertainment, (ii) elevate the experience for the end-consumer making it better because your brand or product is involved, and (iii) create memories that people can talk about and share socially and on social media. In turn, this will provide a true win–win–win situation, where the consumer is happier, the property earns their rights fees, and the sponsor enhances the consumer experience, thus driving a measurable return on investment (ROI) that makes CFOs and CMOs want more.

COVID-19's Impact on Sponsorship

In the past four decades (and likely much longer than that), we have never experienced or planned for such a devasting situation for the world, ourselves, our families and friends, or our businesses. Few areas have undergone a more negative impact than live events. Who could have planned for a world that had almost no (or very limited) live experiences for 12 months and most likely close to 2 years? Fortunately, we have some research that will help you consider a few contextual realities considering consumer attitudes and perceptions.

Over the past 12 months, IMI completed over 1.5 million consumer interviews across 40 countries, measuring and assessing perceptions from a representative sample accounting for over 5 billion people. The goal of this research is to assess and quantify the impact of the pandemic on people's willingness to return to life. The results showcase a few harsh realities about 2021. First, IMI International's Global Recovery Study (released February 2021) reports that the world's population believed (and hoped) that Covid-19 would be behind us in 2021. Second, unmatched personal and financial health concerns existed globally, with 7 in 10 people currently concerned about "their personal health" and more than 5 in 10 people currently concerned about "their personal financial health."

And yet, people's *future* intention to attend *live* has never been higher. This is fact-based, quantitative research showing future intention to attend and engage in community events. Live events, sports, concerts, charity events, return to restaurants, and travel have also never been higher, with results showing an "increased intention" of from 25 to 60 percent.

So, what about sponsorship? Well, whether it is 1988 or 2022, if you add value and give people options on how they can engage with your property or brand—live or virtually—you will be very successful. Effective and efficient sponsorship can deliver a very positive ROI for a brand. This can be measured and quantified easily and cost-effectively, and it is as effective and oftentimes more effective than other marketing options. We at IMI International measure the ROI of over 90 different marketing tactics globally, with results supporting this fact. Effective sponsorship creates memories for people by advancing their passions in what they already love. The experience is long-lasting and makes a big impact on their attitudes, emotions, and behaviours for months—and sometimes years—after the actual experience.

Starting out in sponsorship research in 1985, Don Mayo has been immersed in insights to help clients make profitable decision for the past three decades. During this time, he has completed work for thousands of brands, properties, and agencies across over 45 countries. This work includes investments and sponsorships of all shapes and sizes—from the largest events in the world to small regional or community events. Don is currently based in Toronto, where he leads IMI International's North American and European efforts from the head office. Don can also be found speaking on the optimization of sponsorship ROI at conferences and webinars and on podcasts and social channels.

Sponsorship and Olympic and Paralympic Sport Properties

In Olympic and Paralympic sport in Canada, success on and off the field does not come easy, and for many, they are highly connected since these sport organizations rely on the reach of the Games and (possible) success at those Games to generate the attention and interest that many sponsors desire. Quite simply, winning medals is important to Canadians, the media, and—in turn—sponsors. Success at the Games requires Canadian teams and individual athletes to compete at the highest level against international competition from all countries of the world, many of whom have access to considerably more resources. In an effort to achieve these results, Canadian NSOs build detailed and holistic high-performance plans to put their athletes in contention to reach the podium. Although there are a few exceptions (e.g., hockey, golf, tennis), for the majority of Canadian NSOs, the Olympic

and Paralympic Games are the pinnacle of their sport. Thus, full attention is put toward these plans, including staff, facilities, assessment camps, coaching, technology, sports sciences, competition needs, and athlete support, which requires significant financial resources. Government funding, funding resulting from revenue sharing from the IOC, and donations and support from multisport organizations (MSOs), such as Canadian National Sport Centres, Own the Podium, the Canadian Olympic Committee, and the Canadian Paralympic Committee are all important sources, but support from the corporate section in the form of sponsorship is vital to expanding these programs.

An important element of any high-performance financial plan for a Canadian NSO is a successful sponsorship program. For the NSOs that are successful in generating sponsorship, this can mean millions of dollars of discretionary resources. Of course, the ability to generate these sponsorships requires the NSO to offer a partner an opportunity to provide value back to (potential) sponsors. This can take the form of logos on the athletes' competition uniform, access to athletes and their images to include in the sponsor's promotions, ability to implement hosting programs, digital assets around the NSO's website and social media platforms, chances to sample their products, ability to have athletes use their equipment, and much more.

An NSO seeking to build a strong sponsorship program needs to focus on providing assets to sponsors that enable them to achieve their objectives, including a positive return on the investment they would make. Conducting research to understand sponsors, offerings, and consumers is an important task, as is implementing sponsorship-focused resources and efforts across the NSO. The support of the NSO leadership, including its board of directors, is significant.

CHAPTER SUMMARY

Sponsorship has experienced phenomenal growth since the 1980s. From its modest roots as a form of philanthropic giving, sponsorship is now a 3 billion CAD industry in Canada and a 66 billion USD industry worldwide. Progress in communications technology has had a great impact on sponsorship by being the catalyst that moved sports into the "entertainment" industry. Another factor that led corporations to sponsorship was the cost combined with the cluttering of the traditional media. Many corporations were looking for new avenues to communicate with consumers, and sports appeared to be an effective and efficient way to reach them. Finally, as corporations poured more money into sports, the decision to sponsor sports became a business decision with an expected return on investment. Today, sponsorship is recognized as a legitimate part of a corporation's promotions mix alongside advertising, sales promotion, personal selling, and publicity, and—as a result—sponsorship programs are developed to meet a variety of corporate objectives, in particular sales, increasing awareness, changing or enhancing corporate image, creating experiential opportunities, and reaching specific market segments.

TEST YOUR KNOWLEDGE

1. What is sport sponsorship?
2. What is a sponsor? A property? An agency?
3. What are the key differences between sponsorship and philanthropy?
4. Why do corporations invest large sums of money in sponsorship? Explain.
5. Explain the place of sponsorship within the promotional mix.
6. Explain how sponsorship is not advertising.
7. What is activation? Give three examples.
8. Give an example of a company that uses sponsorship effectively and explain why you think that is the case.

KEY TERMS

ambush marketing
clutter
endemic
exclusivity

impressions
nonendemic
promotional
mix

return on investment
(ROI)
sponsorship

CASE STUDIES

Visit HK*Propel* for case studies organized by chapter.

CHAPTER 14

Building Successful Sport Sponsorships

LEARNING OBJECTIVES

After studying this chapter, you will be able to do the following:

- Appreciate the resources an organization must commit to implement a successful sponsorship program
- Understand the place of sponsorship in the marketing/communications mix
- Understand conceptually the complexities involved in activating a sponsorship
- Understand the key success factors to sponsorship in Canada
- Identify best sponsorship practices

Chapter 13 introduced in detail sport sponsorship, setting up this chapter, which focuses specifically on the "how" of developing or building out sport sponsorship programs for success. Whether a **sponsor**, a sport **property**, or an agency, the content is applicable to you and will aid in building successful programs. It is important that, regardless of the sponsorship, this must involve **activation**. Support of this notion comes from industry experts. Notably, when we were writing the second edition of this book, the marketing director at the International Olympic

Committee at the time told us, "I suggest that investing into a sport property without any kind of 'activating' poses a threat to sponsorship."

Finding and developing successful partnerships with corporate sponsors is, and will continue to be, a challenge for professional and amateur sport organizations of all sizes. A **sponsorship deal** is an agreement entered into between the sponsoring party and the party that is being sponsored in the form of cash or payment in kind. The decision to sponsor a sport property (e.g., athlete, sport organization,

241

national team, event, or festival) by a company is usually made following an **evaluation** of the property's value and the ability that a **sponsorship** of that property will provide to reach corporate objectives. Some companies have sophisticated evaluation criteria, while others may just look to gain some goodwill by supporting a local event. Whatever the reasons for sponsoring a property, once an agreement is reached, the property and the sponsor will most likely work together to maximize the benefits from the relationship. This will involve some kind of activating from the sponsor. Activation refers to additional investment beyond the rights fee or different communication efforts implemented to support one's sponsorship. For example, when Scotiabank sponsors the Edmonton Oilers, it pays the NHL hockey club a rights fee. The rights fee is only for the right of official association. But Scotiabank also invests in a number of activities to make that sponsorship work and get it communicated widely, such as the Scotiabank Skater program that runs to promote the partnership. The purpose of this chapter is to take you through the process a sponsor, such as Scotiabank, goes through to gain a positive experience with sport sponsorship. A four-step approach to sponsorship will be presented along with a list of key success factors and best practices in Canadian sport sponsorship.

EXECUTIVE PERSPECTIVE
Sponsorship Sales

GAVIN ROTH, Founder and Managing Partner, Gavin Roth + Associates Revenue Consultants Inc.

"You can't control the outcome, so control the process."

That's my favourite sales quote. I like it because it's my own (cue the eye roll). Shockingly, there've been no bumper stickers sold yet. I also like the quote because it applies. In sponsorship sales—in life, really—so much is outside of our control. We can't know when a prospect will have to suddenly shut down operations due to a cyber-attack. You are so close to wrapping up a deal and all of a sudden you get an email from the head of marketing informing you she's leaving for another job. A pandemic hits and budgets get frozen. You get the picture.

I've had the pleasure of training sponsorship sellers from MLSE, NBA Canada, COC, TIFF, Princess Margaret Cancer Foundation, and more. I advise them to focus on themselves; to control what they can—to develop a sales process that will put them in the best possible position to win business, all things being equal. So let's talk process. Don't worry, this won't be as dry as that sounds. In fact, I think of it more as a *gameplan*, and I bet it'll be useful to you down the road.

I break sponsorship sales into three key segments—the *approach*, the *proposal*, and the *feedback*. How you navigate and manage each of these three phases will determine your chances of a successful outcome. For football fans out there, it's akin to offence, defence, and special teams. To win the Grey Cup, Super Bowl, or Vanier Cup, you need to be strong at all three phases.

The Approach

This stage is all about *preparation*—learning as much as you can about your target. What's happening in their category? How is their company doing? Is there any news? Who are the decision makers? What are they like? Is there someone in your network that can facilitate a warm introduction?

Once you land that intro meeting, phone call, or video chat, prepare for how to approach the meeting. Remember, first impressions are lasting. Ensure you know who will be attending the meeting from their end so that you can match up and bring subject matter experts from your team (marketing, digital, leadership) if warranted. Embrace team selling. You may be the point guard or quarterback, but you will succeed by engaging your teammates.

That first meeting should be more about asking questions, listening, learning, qualifying—and establishing next steps. Your goal isn't to close the deal in that first meeting (although that would be nice, wouldn't it?). Your goal is to develop trust, demonstrate credibility, and secure a second meeting where you can share a custom proposal.

Here are the types of questions I like to ask at the first meeting:

- What are your marketing objectives?
- What are your business challenges?
- Who is your target consumer?
- Is there a regionality or seasonality to your business?
- Are there any best practices?
- If we built a proposal that addresses your needs, do you have room in your budget for it?
- If we mutually agree to continue our discussions, when should I reconnect with you?

If you can't help them do things like drive sales or trials, grow awareness, reward their stakeholders and customers, or amplify their corporate social responsibility platform, then chances are pretty strong that you won't end up closing a deal with them. The only way to get there is to learn about their business and their objectives, needs, and challenges and then work internally with your colleagues to come up with a solution.

It's important to note though that a solution won't always be there. In that case, you need to respectfully advise the prospect and move on to another. Time is your most precious commodity, so make sure you are investing it with prospects that will yield you and your organization the maximum return.

The Proposal

The proposal stage is all about demonstrating that you have a solution that addresses your prospect's needs. You ideally want to find a time to meet in person (or over video) to present a proposal. That allows you the chance to address questions and objections in real time.

In terms of content, I recommend the following fundamental sections:

- Their objectives—a brief summary to demonstrate you heard them.
- Your solution—an overview of the benefits you are offering, presented with sufficient detail to show what they will be receiving, yet presented in a way that is easy to read and digest.
- Terms—length of deal and fee; ensuring the fee you are proposing is defendable. In other words, be prepared for the "how did you come up with that?" question. Maintaining credibility throughout the sales process is key. It takes a long time to establish trust—and only a second to lose it.
- Next steps—leave the room at the end of the meeting to get their alignment on next steps. The key step is to decide when you will reconnect to get their feedback. I also like to ask them about their internal review and decision-making process. This will give you insight into how you want to manage the follow-up process.

The Feedback

The prospect has reviewed the proposal. They have socialized it internally. Questions arise. Objections are relayed to you. How you deal with those questions and objections will often determine if you move forward or they walk away. This stage is all about *qualifying*.

Before answering their questions, ensure you understand them. It's human nature to hear a question and jump to answer. But human beings are imperfect. Sometimes the question

> *continued*

Sponsorship Sales > continued

they pose is framed incorrectly by the buyer or absorbed incorrectly by the seller. So a simple "let me make sure I have this right" never hurts. By qualifying the question, you give them a chance to clarify. Qualifying leads to clarity.

The same thing applies to objections. Before you jump into feedback, ensure you understand the nature and context of the objection. Often the problem the client relays to you isn't really the problem. For example, they may say the fee is too high. Sometimes that means they don't have budget for it. Alternatively, they may be saying they don't feel there's enough value relative to the fee you are asking. So before simply adjusting one variable (price), ensure it's not really about the benefits you've included. You may be able to adjust the assets or benefits while maintaining the fee.

So let's recap. The key to sales success is developing a gameplan—a system or process to find, qualify, and move prospects through the sales funnel. The three key phases to focus on are the approach, the proposal, and the feedback. To establish and maintain credibility and trust, you must apply focus and thought to each encounter with your prospect. Can you dictate that the prospect ends up buying from you? No. There are too many variables outside of your control. But if you stick to your plan and invest your time wisely, you will give yourself the best chance at success. Happy selling!

GAVIN ROTH is one of Canada's top sponsorship strategists and partnership architects. He has over 25 years of experience and success in sponsorship sales and marketing, sports marketing, integrated media sales, and sales training and coaching. Currently the managing partner at Gavin Roth + Associates Revenue Consultants, a sponsorship agency Gavin founded to help properties grow sponsorship revenue through sales strategy, business development, and sales training. He also hosts the Influencers of Sponsorship Marketing podcast. Prior to running his own agency, Gavin was chief commercial officer at Golf Canada, where he was responsible for revenue and marketing for all Golf Canada properties, including the RBC Canadian Open and CP Women's Open. He was formerly vice-president of multiplatform sales at Rogers Media and vice-president, sales, at Canada's Olympic Media Consortium (the official media rights holder for the 2010 and 2012 Olympics), where Gavin led a team that developed and negotiated some of the largest integrated media partnerships in Canadian media history. Gavin has also held senior sales and marketing roles with the Canadian Football League and WWE Canada and spent six years on the agency side with two multinational advertising agencies.

Sponsorship Stakeholders

The sponsor (e.g., Coke, Pepsi, Nike, Adidas, RBC, General Motors, Scotiabank) is the investor who provides resources and in return seeks promotional value and fulfillment of other objectives from the association. The property (e.g., Alpine Canada, Kelsey Serwa and Brittany Phelan, Canada's Men's National Junior Hockey Team, a fundraising dinner, the Atom AA hockey team) is receiver of resources from the sponsor and often seeks to achieve its own objectives from the association. Affiliated entities or agencies are companies that work on behalf of a sponsor or properties to facilitate sponsorship negotiations. They are intermediaries that support the sponsor–property relationship, such as a benefiting charity, a sponsorship sales agent, a cosponsor, an event manager, or a facility provider.

Sponsorship is attractive to these stakeholders for several reasons. First, most organizations can no longer promote themselves through traditional promotional techniques alone as they are faced with the challenge of a cluttered marketplace and an ever-expanding digital world. In 2019, the Canadian Sponsorship Landscape Study (CSLS) reported that about 23 percent of marketing communications budgets by sponsoring Canadian brands are allocated to sponsorship, supporting sponsorship's value as an efficient way by which to differentiate a brand from its competition. Second, evidence of the attractiveness of sponsorship relative to other promotional tools is supported by activation, which the CSLS (2019) assessed at 68 cents for every dollar spent on sponsorship rights fees. *Activation* refers to strategies that the sponsor (and sometimes the property) funds and implements to increase the effectiveness of the sponsorship, such as serving as the title sponsor of a televised event developing commercials and paying for their broadcast leading up to, during, and following the event; producing billboards; placing newspaper ads; printing the sponsored property's logo on the company's promotional materials, and so on.

In today's highly competitive marketing climate, Olympic and Paralympic sport properties (often called amateur sport) are seeking alternative strategies to financially support their athletes, programs, and events. On the international stage, international sport federations (IF) such as FINA (aquatic sports), IIHF (hockey), and IAAF (athletics) look for sponsorship as a noninstitutional source of funding in the form of cash contributions and in-kind product. At the national level, national Olympic committees (NOCs), national Paralympic committees (NPCs), national sport organizations (NSO), and multisport organizations (MSOs) seek sponsorship opportunities. At the provincial or territorial, municipal, and individual levels, the pursuit of sponsorship is carried out by a number of stakeholders including provincial or territorial sport organizations (PSOs), municipalities, facilities, coaches, athletes, clubs, teams, sport centres, and others.

Research has shown that sponsoring Canadian brands use their sponsorship to achieve multiple different objectives, with more than 100 different ones identified (O'Reilly & Madill, 2009). Examples of these objectives include increased sales, involvement with the local community, increase in awareness, enhanced company image, changed public perception, trade relations, enhanced employee relations and motivation, competition blocking, employee retention, increased sales, increased market share, reaching target market, and business development (O'Reilly & Madill, 2009).

Sponsorship success is known to rely on three fundamental aspects of a sponsorship management:

- Effective activation: In the case of activation by the sponsor, this is assessed using the activation ratio (i.e., the measure of the amount of spend on activation versus the rights fee investment), which must be greater than zero and with some recommending ratios of at least 2:1 or 3:1 depending on the nature of the specific sponsorship (O'Reilly & Lafrance Horning, 2013). In other words, for a 1-dollar sponsorship, an activation worth of 2 to 3 dollar is recommended.

- Attentive **servicing** by the property: Servicing, or the fulfilment of all the contractual elements promised to the sponsor by the property, is an area where Canadian properties have not delivered to sponsors' expectations (CSLS, 2019) and one that is important to any successful sponsorship. Here, servicing refers to providing the assets agreed to in the contract (e.g., website content, signage, social media posts, access to celebrities or athletes, rights to marks or logos, etc.).

- Evaluation of the sponsorship: evaluating the impacts of a sponsorship and its leveraging activities on achieving corporate objectives is another important aspect of a sponsorship program. While research and practical tools for **sponsorship evaluation** have improved in recent years, there is no widely accepted valuation method, thereby suggesting that each sponsorship should follow its own process based on the objects sought by the sponsor. Particularly, focusing on return on objectives (ROO) evaluation, which involves measuring sponsorship against clearly defined or established objectives that can be agreed upon prior to the commencement of the evaluation program. For this, sponsorship objectives are recommended to be SMART (Specific, Measurable, Achievable, Results oriented, and Time bounded) to provide the best possible understanding of what the evaluation must be designed to measure.

Sponsorship in Canada: A Model for Sport Sponsorship Success

Brands in Canada sponsor sport properties in all four facets of Canadian sport—professional (Ottawa Senators), Olympic (Canadian Cycling

Association), university or college (U Sports women's championships), and grassroots (little league baseball). Within each facet, sponsorable events are omnipresent at the local, regional, provincial, national, and international levels. However, the strategic use of sponsorship varies greatly within the Canadian sport industry. While most professional sport organizations (e.g., Toronto Blue Jays, Edmonton Oilers) and "big" NSOs (e.g., Alpine Canada, Hockey Canada) rely on professional marketing or sponsorship staff or on sport marketing agencies to develop sponsorship programs, it is common for smaller sport organizations (i.e., many NSOs, PSOs, and clubs in Canada) to have their office staffs or volunteers direct the sponsorship function.

A four-step approach for properties to developing successful sponsorship partnerships is presented below. The four-step approach to successful sponsorship includes the following steps:

- Step 1: *Presponsorship practices.* Developing product(s), creating digital assets, building organizational capacity, building long-term relationships, and planning.
- Step 2: *Negotiation stage.* Finding the right fit, terms of contract, and commitment to activation.
- Step 3: *Sponsorship life.* Organizational support, joint planning, implementing activation tools (activation), putting in place a service plan, and developing an evaluation framework.
- Step 4: *Sponsorship termination.* Collaborative succession planning, gradual decrease of involvement, and termination.

Figure 14.1 summarizes these steps, which are explained in detail in the pages that follow.

Step 1: Presponsorship Practices

The first step, presponsorship practices, involves establishing the prerequisites for future success—developing the sport organization's properties (both traditional and digital), along with associated hospitality events, to a point where they can provide value to a potential sponsor. While a number of the smaller sport organizations in Canada believe that they have nothing of value to attract the corporate sector, it is worth mentioning that the ones that are successful "invest" resources (e.g., human resources expertise, web content, advertising, digital content, PR expertise, etc.) in their properties to increase marketability. Later in this chapter, we will learn about a Canadian Paralympic program that was designed, in part, as a presponsorship effort.

An important part of the presponsorship phase involves developing relationships with potential sponsors from each **sponsorship category** that may be a fit with your offering. A property should understand that sponsorship is a three-way relationship, which is about placing a sponsor in an emotional relationship between a consumer (for example, a sport participant) and a sponsored activity (for example, a 5K run). Therefore, a property should put an effort to identify the possible avenues available with its property that a sponsor can use to form emotional connection with participants of the property's event or, simply, consumers of the property. A property should undertake market research to identify categories and potential partners within each category. Then, seek to build those connections and share its potential value to them as a partner. A second important aspect of the presponsorship phase is to achieve buy-in from the larger organization (i.e., the board of directors of an NSO, senior management of a professional club) that sponsorship is important to the organization and that resources will be invested in sponsorship. A sponsorship plan and budget should be developed, and an assessment of capacity undertaken. Properties need to assess if they have (i) the expertise, (ii) the understanding of their fans/members (demographics, psychographics), (iii) the assets that a sponsor would be interested in (events, digital platforms, social media following, television ratings, etc.), and (iv) products that a sponsor can activate.

An assessment of capacity is a necessary part of the presponsorship phase for a sport property. This involves assessing the level of expertise, commitment, and resources (human and financial) needed to build a sport sponsorship program and offering that to a brand that might be inter-

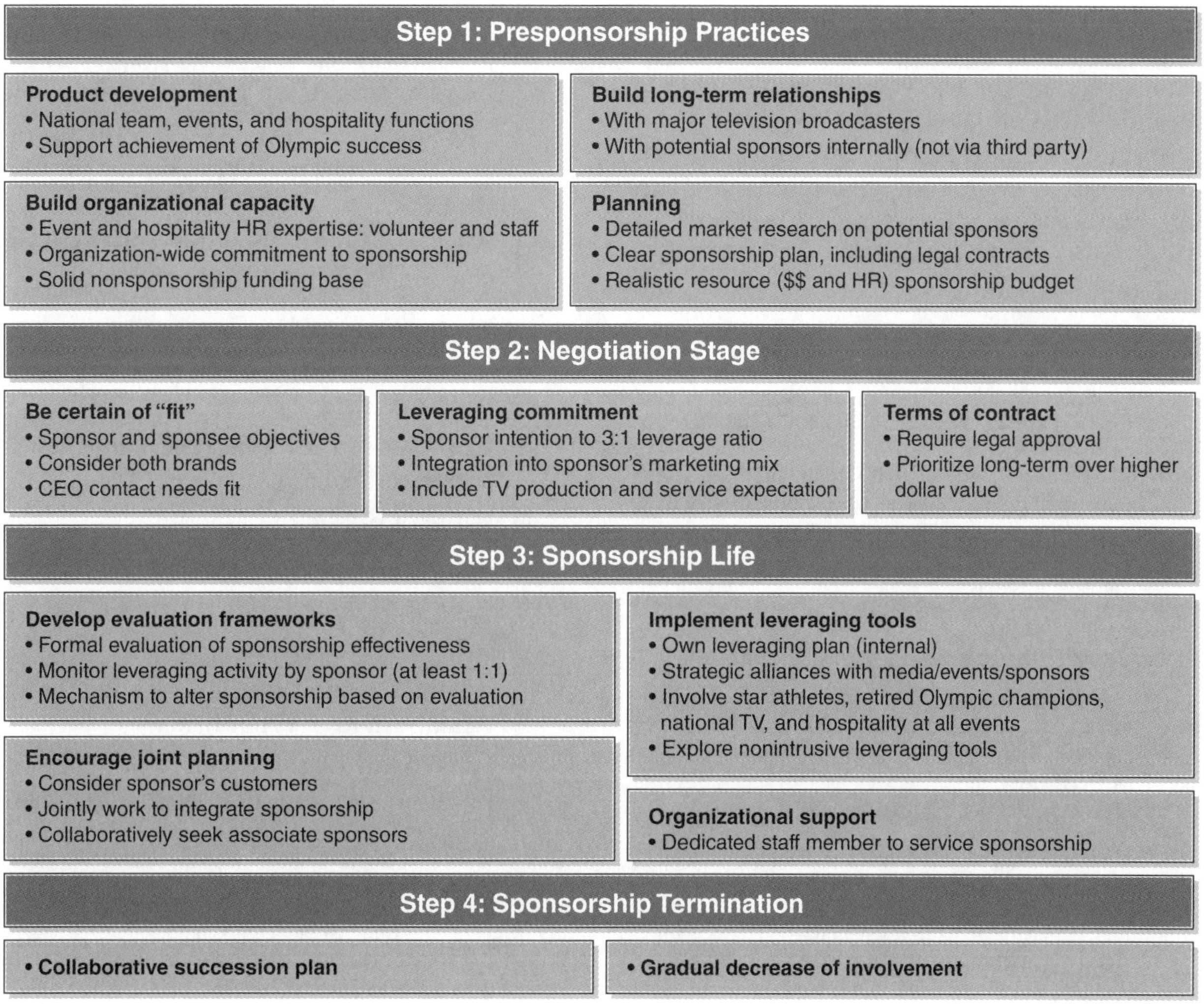

Step 1: Presponsorship Practices

Product development
- National team, events, and hospitality functions
- Support achievement of Olympic success

Build long-term relationships
- With major television broadcasters
- With potential sponsors internally (not via third party)

Build organizational capacity
- Event and hospitality HR expertise: volunteer and staff
- Organization-wide commitment to sponsorship
- Solid nonsponsorship funding base

Planning
- Detailed market research on potential sponsors
- Clear sponsorship plan, including legal contracts
- Realistic resource ($$ and HR) sponsorship budget

Step 2: Negotiation Stage

Be certain of "fit"
- Sponsor and sponsee objectives
- Consider both brands
- CEO contact needs fit

Leveraging commitment
- Sponsor intention to 3:1 leverage ratio
- Integration into sponsor's marketing mix
- Include TV production and service expectation

Terms of contract
- Require legal approval
- Prioritize long-term over higher dollar value

Step 3: Sponsorship Life

Develop evaluation frameworks
- Formal evaluation of sponsorship effectiveness
- Monitor leveraging activity by sponsor (at least 1:1)
- Mechanism to alter sponsorship based on evaluation

Implement leveraging tools
- Own leveraging plan (internal)
- Strategic alliances with media/events/sponsors
- Involve star athletes, retired Olympic champions, national TV, and hospitality at all events
- Explore nonintrusive leveraging tools

Encourage joint planning
- Consider sponsor's customers
- Jointly work to integrate sponsorship
- Collaboratively seek associate sponsors

Organizational support
- Dedicated staff member to service sponsorship

Step 4: Sponsorship Termination

- **Collaborative succession plan**

- **Gradual decrease of involvement**

FIGURE 14.1 A model for sponsorship success.

ested in your property. Most professional sport organizations (e.g., Saskatchewan Roughriders, Toronto FC), major sporting events (Montreal Formula One Grand Prix, the Brier, Scott Tournament of Hearts), and large NSOs (e.g., Hockey Canada, Soccer Canada) are fully committed to sponsorship and rely on professional marketing staff or sport marketing agencies to develop, sell, and implement their sponsorship programs. Smaller sport organizations, however, may have limited staff compliments, volunteers, and only rare agency involvement in their sponsorship function. Thus, building organizational capacity is essential for large and small properties alike.

On the brand and sponsor side, many Canadian companies have considerable experience and have developed sophisticated sport-sponsorship programs (e.g., Scotiabank, Bell, RBC, Telus, Esso, etc.). However, many companies of all sizes do not engage much (or at all) in sponsorship. Hence, a company that is supportive of sponsorship is essential for the success of the program, as the required time, energy, and money are significant. Ideally, they integrate the sponsorship into their overall marketing communication plans and invest in activation to enhance the sponsorship outcomes. In establishing a sponsorship program and before entering into any agreement with a sport property, a brand needs to (i) articulate its objectives as to why it is investing in sponsorship, (ii) build a list of potential properties to invest in who could help achieve the objectives, and (iii) assess the risk of each potential partner in not achieving those objectives. A sponsorship plan for a brand typically includes the identification of potential properties to sponsor that will help achieve the sought objectives. Examples include an individual athlete (Sidney Crosby), a team (national triathlon team), an event (national synchronized swimming championships), an organization (Canadian Olympic Committee), a program (learn to skate), a league (NHL), or a club (Ottawa sailing club).

Sponsor-Side Research in the Presponsorship Phase

Market research, as outlined in chapter 3, is a fundamental component of sport marketing. At the presponsorship phase, a sponsor (or their agency) typically researches some of the following:

Information on participants or members

- Description of the property (mission, values, strategic objectives, etc.)
- Programs offered (grassroots, national team, events, coaching, etc.)
- Number of participants (athletes, coaches, officials, volunteers)
- Demographic information on participants (age, gender, education, income, etc.)
- Other

Information on spectators or viewers

- Number of spectators at events
- Number of spectators on television and via streaming
- Number of followers on social media
- Profile of spectators (demographic information, reasons for attending, etc.)
- Information or profile of TV/streaming audience (ratings, demographic profile, etc.)
- Attitudes and behaviours (research on consumer attitudes and behaviours)

Information on media coverage

- Interest of media in the property (athletes, events, etc.)
- Coverage by the media (television, newspaper, radio, etc.)
- Value of publicity in media

Information on competitors

- Who are the competitors (i.e., whom else could I sponsor)?
- What other sponsors do they have? From what industry? What firms?
- What kind of attendance information ratings and ratings data do they achieve?

Restrictions from sport organizations, leagues, or governments

- Restrictions in terms of sponsorship (e.g., no tobacco sponsors, no alcoholic beverages sponsors, etc.)
- Policies about finder's fee and other deductions on rights fee (e.g., sales commission to sponsorship selling/agency, revenue sharing, etc.).

IN THE KNOW

Sport Properties Changing the Rules Can Enhance Sponsorship

There are a number of cases of sport organizations changing the rules of their game that led to improved sponsorship outcomes, as these steps made the sport offering more attractive to spectators in person or via media. The classic example is basketball and the NBA adding, first, the 24-second clock, and second, the 3-point line. Two examples from Olympic sport are the dropping of compulsory figures in figure skating and changing the cycling portion of a triathlon to be draft legal (i.e., riding in groups or packs). The NHL famously lost its 2004-2005 season to labour negotiations, one of the outcomes being rule changes to make the game faster and higher scoring. Often, these were done to make the sport television friendly. While sometimes risky, the ultimate goal of investing in a property is to increase marketability.

- Restrictions in terms of conflicting sponsors (e.g., a national team athlete cannot have a sponsor conflicting with NSO sponsor; if the NHL has a league-wide sponsor in the same category, a club-level sponsor will have restrictions in what they can activate)

What Can Be Sponsored?

On both the sponsor side (what can we sponsor or activate?) and the property side (what can we offer to a sponsor?), there are a number of categories of assets to be considered, including:

- *Programs:* An offering by the sport organization that is participation based. Examples include coaching education programs, official clinics, learn-to-skate, alumni appreciation event by a university, elite athlete development programs.
- *National Teams:* Canadian NSOs manage their national teams who pursue Olympic and Paralympic qualification/performance and compete at world championships. Examples include the Canadian Alpine Ski Team, the National Sledge Hockey Team, and Under-18 Women's National Soccer Team.
- *Owned Events:* Events that the sport property owns and operates. Examples include National Championships, World Cups, All-Star Games, Junior National Championships, Provincial Championships, made-for-TV events (e.g., curling, figure skating), fundraising events (e.g., golf tournaments, auctions), invitational events, esports tournaments, and so on.
- *Ancillary Event Activities:* Other activities around an event that could be sponsored. Examples include promotional events, press conferences, media announcements, and hospitality.
- *Digital Assets:* Online assets that can be sponsored or used in activation efforts. Examples include the property website, property social media channels, blogs, YouTube or Twitch channels, and new platforms (web, social) designed just for the sponsorship.

- *Merchandising:* apparel, swag (i.e., giveaways), and educational videos are examples of merchandise products that could be sponsored and activated.

What Levels of Sponsorship Are Possible?

Although there is much debate over how to classify sponsors of a given property and determine a price for that classification, there are some accepted industry practices to be aware of, even though many different approaches are used. For instance, some properties only offer one level of sponsorship, whereby each sponsor sits at the same "level" and is the only sponsor in that category (e.g., Pepsi from the soft drink industry). Others organize sponsorship into two levels, such as sponsor and supplier, and still others have more elaborate structures, such as gold, silver, and bronze or Tier 1 through Tier 4, with each tier different in terms of price and the assets included. Within these varying structures, however, there are some commonly agreed-on levels.

- *Title sponsor:* This is the highest level of sponsor for a property whose name is well used and can provide high value to a sponsor whose name is part of the property. Examples are usually venues (e.g., Scotiabank Centre, Labatt Centre) or events (e.g., Rogers Cup, RBC Sports Day in Canada). These tend to be high-priced sponsorships with many assets provided.
- *Major sponsor:* This could be the single sponsor level, gold, or tier 1, or another designation, but what is common is that it is an important sponsorship and the brand is recognized as a major contributor to the property through its financial commitment and supporting activity and typically offers a high level of assets and activation opportunities.
- *Cosponsor:* A relatively new area of focus, whereby two or more sponsors of a given sport property work together to enhance the value they received, thereby benefiting the property as well.
- *Presenting sponsor:* This is not as integrated as a title sponsorship, but a presenting

sponsor has name recognition in the overall event (typically) as supporting or presenting (e.g., ParaTough Cup presented by Petro-Canada).
- *Supplier:* A brand that supplies product (usually at no cost) as part of a value-in-kind (VIK) or contrasponsorship deal with the property. In return, awareness of its contribution (e.g., official ski supplier of the Canadian Nordic Ski Team) and the use of the products of the supplier by the athletes are provided.

EXECUTIVE PERSPECTIVE
Petro-Canada and Canadian Paralympic Committee: A Great Partnership

FRANÇOIS ROBERT, Executive Director, Partnerships, Canadian Paralympic Committee

As part of my role as executive director of partnerships with the CPC, I'm tasked with building, managing, servicing, and seeking to renew our partnerships. We are fortunate, as an organization, to have built many great partnerships over the years. With each of our partnerships, we seek to find programs that deliver strong value for the Paralympic system and also to support the partner's needs.

Let me tell you about one of our partnerships, a very good one. This partnership is an example of one that supports three key stakeholders—athletes, coaches, and families. That partner, which has been more than a 20-year partnership, is Petro-Canada. Whether it's helping athletes reach their full potential with Petro-Canada's Fuelling Athlete and Coaching Excellence (FACE) Program or bringing them closer to their families with the Canadian Athlete Family Program, Petro-Canada believes in its motto, "Living by the Leaf," and that this means supporting those who wear it.

FACE Program

Many athletes dream of representing Canada at the Paralympic Games. However, this goal requires years of hard work and dedication, often before an athlete qualifies for government funding. Petro-Canada's FACE Program helps support athletes at this crucial stage in their journey by awarding eight Paralympic FACE grants of $10,000 every year, to be shared between promising para-athletes and their coaches. Petro-Canada has increased the visibility of this program in the past years by supporting the Paralympic Games broadcast for the past three Games (Sochi 2014, Rio 2016, and Pyeongchang 2018) and are scheduled to continue their commitment for the Tokyo Paralympic Games.

Family and Friends Program

Petro-Canada believes one of the best ways to support Canadian Paralympic athletes is to help their biggest supporters—their families—be there to see them compete on the biggest global stage. The Canadian Athlete Family Program helps to make this a reality by ensuring their families have the opportunity to watch their Paralympians compete live on the world stage. Here are a few details of the program:

- All family members receive two free tickets per event to see their kids compete at the Paralympic Games.
- CPC and Petro-Canada host a Family and Friends Reception during the Paralympic Games. This allows family members to interact with other parents and spend some time with their kids during the Paralympics.

- This program is important to the CPC as it provides us an opportunity to support the family members during the Paralympic Games and means that they are well taken of while travelling. This alleviates one of the largest distractions for the athletes, which allows them to focus on their Games performance.

Paralympic Games Coaches Reception

Paralympic coaches are one of the most critical stakeholders in an athlete's success. In addition to the support of coaches through the FACE program, Petro-Canada supports the Paralympic Coaches Reception, where the CPC and Petro-Canada formally recognize all Team Canada's coaches at the Games. It has become a tradition that we host a private reception for all coaches before the start of the Games to provide Petro-Canada the opportunity to thank our coaches and be recognized for the continuous support they provide on an annual basis.

Why Is This Partnership Successful?

In summary, the Petro-Canada CPC partnership has been built over the years and has been successful for a few reasons:

1. It provides Petro-Canada with owned properties that can be activated without clutter from other CPC partners.
2. It is integrated within their corporate marketing program, "Living by the Leaf."
3. It allows joint activations with their other sport property partnerships (Canadian Olympic Committee and Coaches Association of Canada).
4. The funds received from this partnership have a direct positive impact on CPC's strategic priorities.
5. It provides Petro-Canada with a storyline that resonates with Canadians.
6. Research shows that Canadians have a stronger emotional connection to Petro-Canada because of the Paralympic partnership.

FRANÇOIS ROBERT leads the corporate partnership team at the Canadian Paralympic Committee, which includes both servicing and strengthening relationships with current partners, and the recruitment of new sponsors and business. He joined the organization in January 2011. Under his purview, CPC's corporate partnership program has greatly grown and diversified, bringing more partners into the Paralympic fold and enhancing their involvement within our community to be truly engaged. Prior to joining the CPC, he was a senior corporate account manager with Senators Sport and Entertainment and has many years of marketing and management experience as the sales manager of Labatt Breweries Ontario. He holds an EMBA from the University of Ottawa's Telfer School of Management.

Pricing a Sponsorship

Determining the price of a sponsorship, also known as **sponsorship valuation**, is a challenging undertaking and one that requires research and analysis. Typically, the property has a price in mind, and the sponsor an amount that they want to spend, and it is determined in the negotiation stage. Often both sides have a valuation done internally (or by an agency on their behalf) in the presponsorship stage, prior to any negotiations. A key determinant of price is what is included in the sponsorship package (e.g., access to athletes, tickets, hospitality, signage, media time, inclusions in digital/social, etc.). Another method for determining the price of a sponsorship is by knowing what the competitors are offering. This may be difficult to obtain; however, information may be available via agencies or from public sources as trade publications and/or conferences. In Canada, the *Canadian Sponsorship Landscape Study*, the Sponsorship

Marketing Council of Canada, *The Sponsorship Report*, and *Marketing* magazine are all good sources of information.

For small new properties (e.g., a new 5K run in town), property holders will be recommended to assess the market and put a value to the different sponsorship categories. For this, a property needs to first assess its financial need by starting from the basic revenue versus expense scenario. Once financial needs have been assessed, a number of other factors should be taken into consideration in pricing the different sponsorship categories and, thereby, the total sponsorship value of the property. The factors may include the local economy, local companies' interest in your property, the appeal of your property, the history of your property, a high-profile person's involvement in your property, and so on. Figure 14.2 outlines the media reach a property can offer a potential sponsor. Here, a property needs to make sure the sponsorship ask is not overstated and the property is not undervalued, both of which can have negative consequences. While overstating primarily turns off a potential sponsor, even if a sponsor agrees to pay an overstated fee, that sponsor may not continue its sponsorship because the property will have failed to deliver what it promised. New properties, over a course of period of time (e.g., for annual events), can move their valuation to a demand versus supply scenario (i.e., the interest potential sponsors show to your property). This becomes important when a property builds its brand.

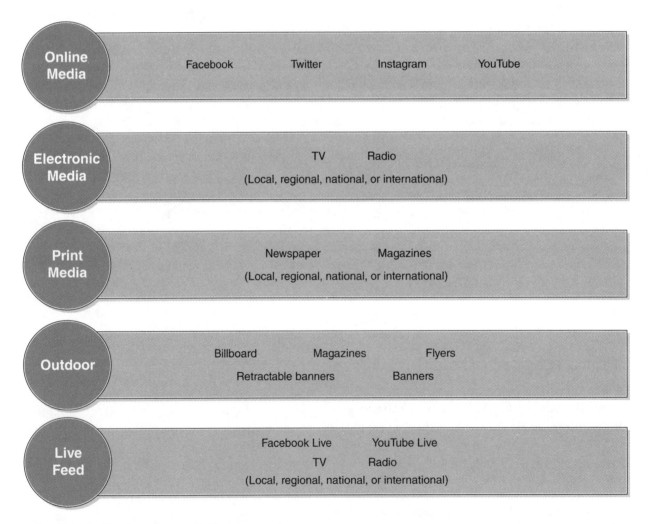

FIGURE 14.2 Media outlets available to properties.

Finding a Sponsor

This is tedious work, but it is a key to sponsorship success. One way to identify potential sponsors will be to identify and investigate companies in different industry sectors such as banking, insurance, soft drinks, energy drinks, sport-goods producing, automotive, electronic supplies, hotels, restaurants, airlines, water bottle–manufacturing companies, and so on. Small properties can also list similar events in their region and study the type of organizations that are sponsoring those similar properties. Identifying the sponsors of those properties would help you craft a proposal to a similar company in a given product category or to that same company. Deep research on all potential sponsors will enable the property to tailor a sponsorship offering to each potential sponsor's needs. An annual report is an excellent source of information, as it includes the brand's mission, vision, strategic objectives, financial situation, and marketing plans. The brand's website and social channels are sources of information on its products, marketing orientation, brand, and distribution processes. Other sources include business magazines, blogs, trade journals/web portals, newspapers, Statistics Canada (http://www.statscan.ca), and conferences. The purpose of gathering this information is to understand potential sponsors' needs. There is little value in pursuing a sponsorship without understanding the potential sponsor, its business, and its industry. Practically, your background research should include a potential sponsor's

- mission, values, corporate philosophy, history, culture,
- financial situation,
- products or services,
- marketing approaches and activities,
- promotion/communications mix (advertising, personal sales, sales promotions, use of social media),
- current and historical sponsorship (who do they sponsor, who have they sponsored),
- customers—who they are and how they are reached,

- place of distribution/supply chain,
- any partners in cross-promotions or cosponsorships,
- selling process—how their products or services get to customers,
- annual donations/philanthropy,
- annual marketing communications and advertising budgets, and
- the person responsible for making sponsorship decisions.

In addition to doing the research and building a case for how sponsorship of a property can help the brand reach its objectives, a key factor in getting to a negotiation stage with a sponsor is building meaningful and long-term relationships with more than one person in the potential sponsor's organization. This can be accomplished by keeping regular contact; engaging in hospitality opportunities, webinars, and conferences; and sharing information about how the property can help the sponsor achieve its objectives. While relationships help make an existing sponsorship stronger, they are also invaluable for acquiring sponsorship. It is well known that a key driver of sponsorship deals is the presence of existing relationships between individuals within the partnering organizations.

Step 2: Negotiation Stage

Once the presponsorship practices (antecedents) are in place, a sport property will be in a better position to seek corporate sponsors. If the property is able to enter into discussions and **pitch** a brand, we are now in the second step of the process: negotiation. This is the phase that involves developing with and attempting to sign a sponsorship agreement. In most cases in sponsorship, three main areas need to be addressed before any agreement can be signed (or even considered) by the brand. First, there must be a fit between the sponsor and the property in terms of the objectives they seek and the brands they offer. Second, prior to signing any agreement, the property should ensure that the sponsor has both the resources and motivation to activate the sponsorship with an investment beyond the rights fee. In most cases, a suggested activation spend of twice the rights fee would make sense. Remember from chapter 13 that activation spend is the investment in addition to the rights fee, so if the rights fee was $100,000, then double that on activation would be an additional $200,000 invested to activate the sponsorship. Ideally, the deal would also include the sponsor integrating the sponsorship into the company's overall marketing mix. This could include things like a new social media content or digital presence for the sponsorship, sharing in TV production costs, or enabling cosponsorship with some of the property's other sponsors. Finally, during the negotiations, unless the property has multiple brands interested in that category, they should prioritize a long-term contract over seeking higher sponsorship dollars.

Fit

The fit between the potential partners will be an important consideration in the negotiation stage. Whether it is through image, associations, or objectives, the fit must be clear to both parties. Consider the example of Purolator and its sponsorship of Team Gushue, the curling rink of Brad Gushue and his Newfoundland-based rink, one of the most successful curling teams in Canada, where both image (high-performance, accurate) and corporate objectives (good corporate citizen, nationwide) are illustrated through the sponsorship. Team Gushue is engaged in Purolator's "Tackle Hunger" campaign in Newfoundland, and the fact that they are some of Newfoundland's celebrities helps stress that Purolator can ship as well to Newfoundland as anywhere else.

Commitment to Activate

The initial sponsorship investment only buys the rights to an association. Thus, there is a further need to exploit the sponsorship by investing additional resources in activation, including advertising, sales promotion, point-of-purchase promotions, packaging, and merchandising. These activations should be designed to help the sponsor achieve its goals, whether they are about sales, market share, purchase intention, brand awareness, or brand image. By activating appropriately, a

corporation can position itself better and help out its sport partner in an increasingly cluttered sponsorship environment.

Terms of the Sponsorship Contract

Although obtaining legal advice is highly advised, it is important for the sport marketer to understand a sponsorship contract. These contracts have the intention to protect both parties throughout the duration of the sponsorship. A number of important elements should be in the contract:

1. Price and any allowances or additional fees
2. Time sponsorship fee should be paid
3. Level of the sponsor (e.g., title, supplier)
4. Category of the sponsor (e.g., beverages versus soft drinks)
5. Exclusivity (i.e., does the sponsor have exclusivity for the category of the sponsorship)
6. Event signage (how many, where, who pays)
7. Digital assets (web, social, other, where, how much)
8. Advertising credits (where—on stationery, event name, program cover/ad)
9. Merchandising rights (Can the sponsor sell tee-shirts, mugs, or other souvenirs? Can the sponsor manufacture its own souvenirs or buy from the promoter at cost? Who gets the profit?)
10. Ownership of television, web, or digital rights (who owns and controls, rights of refusal for advertising spots, opening and closing billboards, rights to use footage of event)
11. Public relations and personal appearances (athletes as spokespersons, mention of sponsor's name in media interviews, ticket availability, hospitality)
12. Future options (right of renewal)
13. Trademarks (ownership and usage of special logo, sponsor quality control, promoter's quality control)

14. Liabilities (to observers, participants, site; infringement of trademarks; event cancellation)

Step 3: Sponsorship Life

Assuming a successful negotiation, the sponsorship will come to life. The property receives revenue and the sponsor will have its marketing tactic ready to launch. Of course, this is not the time to celebrate, relax, and lose focus. It is at this step that effort and action coordinate so that the benefits of the sponsorship can be maximized by both sponsor and property. The property must appoint a dedicated person to service the sponsorship and develop the relationship with the sponsor. The property must collaborate with the sponsors to support the activations they want to engage in. For example, the presence of high-profile athletes (both active and retired) at hospitality functions or in digital activations is effective. In addition, the presence of television, streaming, and social media are important for many sponsors. Internal marketing plans through which the brand and the property leverage the sponsorship within its organization also need to be launched independently. This could include an opportunity for employees to attend the event or sharing merchandise promoting the sponsorship or an associated charity to campaign to fundraise around the sponsorship. Strategic alliances with media, additional sponsors, and events should be developed by the property with the support of the sponsor.

An evaluation plan to measure the effectiveness of the sponsorship must also be implemented, including setting benchmarks based on the sponsor's objectives, and putting in place methods to measure the impact of the sponsorship (and activations) on those objectives before, during, and after sponsorship. The results of the evaluation will allow for improvements to be made to the sponsorship if it is to be renewed in the future. Throughout the entire evaluation process, ideally the two organizations work together.

An important element in Stage 3 is the human resources allocated to the sponsorship. These can be internal or via an agency working on behalf of either the sponsor or the property. On the property side, at a minimum, a dedicated staff member or volunteer should be responsible for servicing the sponsorship. However, all members of the organization (staff and volunteer) need to understand the sponsorship to support the efforts of the sponsor in activating it. Many sport organizations have special sessions with athletes and coaches to educate them on the value of sponsorship. The participation of athletes and coaches can be of high value to many sponsors. The objective in servicing is to ensure that a high-quality program is created for the sponsor.

At the tactical level, servicing a sponsorship includes keeping regular communications on activities of the property (e.g., press releases, telephone calls, emails, texts, sharing of digital and social posts, visiting in person), making sure that all materials needed from the sponsor for a specific event are in place (e.g., signage, digital content, sample material, ad in programs, etc.), inviting the sponsor to special events (e.g., press conferences, webinars, blogs, visits with athletes, shows, competitions), knowing the sponsor's objectives so that one can create innovative promotions, keeping track of all the things a property does for a sponsor (log), working with media to ensure your sponsor gets publicity, ensuring the sponsor's logo specs are respected in all collateral materials (e.g., digital, social, posters, signs, advertisers), and providing added-value benefits to sponsor without asking for more money—because people enjoy getting a deal. Servicing is essential in sponsorship, but Canadian properties have not historically done a good job at servicing their sponsors, with results showing that sponsors are not pleased with the services provided since 2006 (Canadian Sponsorship Landscape Study, 2019). Thus, properties need to overdeliver because too often, a sport organization signs a sponsorship deal with a company, promises a number of benefits, and then fails to deliver on its promises. This will not only damage a property's reputation but also hurt others in the industry. The key in servicing is to keep your sponsor happy. Take every opportunity to make your contact a "star" in their own organization. Providing added value is also looked on favourably by sponsors.

For sponsors, it is essential that they also support the sponsorship, either directly or via an agency (or a combination of the two). The property should know who is responsible for managing the sponsorship from the sponsor's side, as well as other people in the sponsoring organization.

Developing an Evaluation Framework

Evaluation along with activation and servicing are the three key tactical elements of a sponsorship. Evaluating a sponsorship program may be one of the greatest challenges facing the sponsorship industry. Although processes and approaches exist, there is no easy method like we find in advertising due to the many, and often hard to measure, objectives that sponsors seek with sponsorship programs. Thus, the measurement of any sponsorship program is a difficult task, requiring research to identify the objectives and expertise to determine ways to measure them. Often, sponsorship evaluations are custom projects, specific to the sponsorship they are seeking to evaluate. According to the marketing representative of a major Canadian sponsor, as reported in Séguin et al. (2005), "It takes time, and repeated exposures, for a communications plan to register upon one's target audiences (both internal and external) and for them to fully understand all that the sponsoring company is trying to accomplish" (p. 79). Thus, as a takeaway on evaluation, there are published models available to support your evaluation, but as a base, the goal is to measure a sponsorship's ability to help a sponsor achieve its objectives, so you must identify what those are, set a benchmark to where they are at presponsorship, measure during the sponsorship, and determine a return for the sponsor based on those results. When identifying the objectives, it is important to establish clear and measurable objectives. Examples include sales, awareness levels, attitude changes, media coverage, advertising space, image transfer (images associate with property transferred to sponsor), **tracking** employee satisfaction, trials achieved, merchandise sold, numbers reached through sampling, impressions, sponsor recall, and so on. In any major sponsorship with large investment, sales or market share are almost always one of the primary objectives pursued. Common in

sponsorship is that some of these objectives will be tangible (easier to measure) and others will be intangible (difficult to measure).

- *Tangible benefits:* These are the quantifiable assets in a sponsorship package. They may include activities that take place in or around an event: signage, public service announcements, web banner, social media post, collateral materials produced by the property or sponsor (e.g., posters, flyers), website content, sampling or coupons, blog posts, and hospitality. The sport marketer must be able to track the number of fans, spectators, or participants that can be reached through these activities. Some that can be measured in sheer numbers include visit to a sponsorship mini-site, newsletters signup, downloads, coupon redemptions, employment participation. Some that one can measure in dollar value may include on-site sale, new product order, new customer acquisition

- *Intangible benefits:* These are the qualitative assets that a property delivers, such as borrowed imagery, image transfer, brand equity, and audience loyalty. These are much more difficult to measure than the tangible benefits, although there do exist ways to estimate these concepts. Some additional examples may include brand image, showcasing community responsibility, hospitality, and employees' morale.

In evaluation, a presponsorship benchmark will be needed for each objective of interest to the sponsor. This could include presponsorship sales figures or market share relative to the competition, or results of a customer survey or employee satisfaction study presponsorship. You must have a benchmark if you want to assess any changes due to the sponsorship and measure a return for the sponsor. In addition, if a company is involved in a number of promotions at the same time, and so are their competitors, it may be difficult to determine if an increase in sales is the result of the sponsorship rather than other promotions. This is called **attribution**, and it must be kept in mind when building out the evaluation plan. For example, if one is measuring whether Tim Hortons's sponsorship of the Women's World Ice Hockey Championships is influencing coffee brand choice of Canadians, the researcher must also consider the other marketing efforts that Hortons is doing as well as the programs offered by its competitors.

As a final note on evaluation, the ever-important objective of sales for sponsors can be assessed in a few different ways that impact sales in the short or long term or at different points in the supply chain. For example, a sponsorship could (i) generate more inbound calls or emails, (ii) produce an increased number of leads, (iii) increase loyalty levels in heavy users or most attractive market segments, (iv) boost web or retail traffic, or (v) increase the number of outlets (web and retail) selling the sponsor's products. Methods to look at these outcomes could be tracking sales in the two- to three-month period surrounding the sponsorship compared to the same period in previous years, tracking sales in the immediate area where the sponsorship took place versus national sales, and looking at sales tied directly to the sponsorship (e.g., online purchase with a special discount code).

Media Impacts of Sponsorship

Questions such as "What is the value of a Twitter post highlighting the sponsor's brand?" and "What is the value of a 30-second ad on television?" need to be answered. Fortunately, today, many tools are available to sponsors, properties, and agencies, or they can be purchased (in most cases) at a reasonable cost to measure many of these items. One example is GumGum Sport. Twitter and Facebook both have analytics tools built in and there are applications available to do further analysis. A media-monitoring system should be used to keep track of media coverage, on web, digital, blogs, newspaper, radio,

---

IN THE KNOW

Athletes in Sponsorship

A derivative of sponsorship is called athlete endorsement, whereby a brand sponsors an athlete directly so that the athlete is perceived to be endorsing their products, brands, or services. The rationale is that an athlete (or any celebrity) supporting a product, brand, or service validates that offering provided their image stays positive and performance on the field stays strong. There are many examples of an athlete's image being tarnished and in turn hurting their sponsors. Another element in sponsorship is a property including athletes or access to athletes within a sponsorship of an event, organization, venue, or team. In these discussions, the sponsor and property follow the process described here:

- Determine which athletes would fit with the brand.
- Contact the athletes or agents that were identified.
- Sign a contract with the athletes (including payment terms sent to the athlete directly).
- If a contract is signed, get information on each athlete (bio, stories) and get any necessary rights to pictures, videos, and other content.
- Determine how to include the athlete in the activation of the sponsorship.
- Produce the activation content.
- Develop promotional materials or communications to support the program (point-of-purchase plan, signage, photos, advertising, sales support material).
- Plan the athletes' appearances.
- Implement the program.

television, magazine, and blog coverage. The monitoring system should also be able to measure the success of media and public relations efforts (e.g., press conferences, press releases, web releases, and social media posts). One way to monitor media coverage is by the time when the sponsor's brand and images were visible to the reviewer. For example, a one-hour broadcast of a diving event on CBC may provide Speedo with 15 minutes of clear identification. Another method is by counting the number of signage impression a sponsor gets during the coverage (the number of times the signage appears in camera view).

Clearly, going through the life of a sponsorship (Step 3) requires proper planning, timing, and execution by a number of stakeholders. It is a complex process. Here are a few steps to follow during Step 3.

1. *Review the details of the contract and ensure that all parties (sponsor, property, and—if relevant—agencies and cosponsors) are clear on their roles and responsibilities:* status of sponsor, event signage, merchandising, and so on.

2. *Set clear sponsorship objectives (from the point of view of the sponsor):* sales, image, hospitality, market share, and so on.

3. *Develop activation strategies and tactics:* athletes or teams at the point-of-purchase (**POP**), incentive programs for trade, consumer contests, property brand in collateral materials, cross-promotions with other sponsors, and so on. See In the Know for some examples of activation tactics. In the case of POP, packaging

IN THE KNOW

Examples of Activation Tactics

Clearly, activation is a key activity toward maximizing the impact of any sponsorship and with respect to just ensuring success from sponsorship. There is almost an endless list of tactics that can be used in activation, with a sample list provided here.

- Sponsor name used as official team name
- Official property poster
- Website title and weblink
- Owned property (create a traditional or digital property)
- Sponsor or property signage at the track
- Front cover of event program
- Content in related publications (e.g., newsletter)
- Sponsor logo on equipment or the team uniform
- Mailing lists (effective use of)
- On-site product sampling
- Use trademarks, logos, and slogans of property (or athletes) in advertising, packaging, and promotions
- Leverage prestige of property
- Provide category exclusivity
- Include cross-promotional benefits from sponsor
- Networking opportunities
- Block ambush marketing
- Public relations announcement

or sales promotions at retail or digital imagery online can incite a purchase.

4. *Develop a sponsorship or activation plan:* timelines, tasks, resources, and deadlines.

5. *Evaluate:* benchmarks, methods, data, analysis, and media analysis.

Step 4: Sponsorship Termination

The final step of the sponsorship process is termination, when the agreement comes to an end. This can be due to nonrenewal, the end of a contract, or if the sponsored property was not continuing (e.g., the 2015 FIFA Women's World Cup). If the previous stages of the sponsorship process were well executed, then termination is normally rewarding as discussions about renewal and what to change (price, assets, activations, etc.) will be in progress. In cases where the sponsorship opportunity is continuing, the property should find out well in advance of the termination date whether the sponsor wishes to renew the deal. If they do, then the renewal process can proceed. but if not, a succession plan to find a new sponsor for that category needs to be developed. In some cases, the outgoing sponsor may help.

In an ideal situation, a sponsorship is terminated slowly over a number of years, with both parties feeling satisfied and a new sponsor taking over to help the sport property continue its operations.

Best Practices in Canadian Sport Sponsorship

Our experiences have led to the following list of suggested best practices in sponsorship.

- Building relationships: This is identified as a *must*, a key success factor for most sponsorship programs. Emphasis should be on building meaningful and long-term relationships with more than one individual within the sponsoring organization. This can be accomplished through keeping regular contact, hospitality at events, and servicing all aspects of the sponsorship. A number of sport properties report that they devote much effort to that one key contact within corporate sponsor's organization—the "champion" for the sponsorship.

- Professionalism: Corporate sponsors have high expectations that sport property will deal with them in a professional and business-like fashion. This goes for the entire sponsorship management process, from acquisition to servicing to evaluation. Follow-up appreciation letters or emails, progress reports, invitations to events or webinars are all important. If involved with

---

IN THE KNOW

The Vancouver 2010 Olympics Were Landmark in Canadian Sponsorship History

In Canada, the hosting of the 2010 Olympic Winter Games prompted Canadian companies to spend an unprecedented amount for the rights to be associated with the Vancouver Olympic and Paralympic Games. Bell Canada reported that its sponsorship of the Games amounted to an overall commitment of 200 million CAD, of which $90 million was in cash. Petro-Canada, RBC, General Motors, Hudson Bay Company, and RONA each committed more than $65 million to the Games. These were unprecedented numbers at the time, but as reflected in the Canadian Sponsorship Landscape Study (2019), they have led to nearly a decade of growth and expansion to where Canadian sponsors spent an estimated $3 billion on sponsorship rights fees and **activation** in the 2018 calendar year. Of course, there is little doubt that the 2010 Games in Canada were the biggest event the country has hosted to date (from a sponsorship perspective). However, there is also little doubt that those Games, at least in part, ushered in a new era of sponsorship in Canada.

events, attention to details involving the look of the event and its execution are all important factors that create a professional impression for sponsors.

• Community involvement: Many corporations look for opportunities to leverage involvement sponsorship deals with the consumers. Sometimes this is referred to as grassroots marketing.

• Quality of product or success: Having a successful team, athlete, club, or event helps attract interest from fans and the media.

• Innovation and creativity: A number of previous studies have shown the importance of being creative—suggesting new promotional ideas and new ways to activate a sponsorship.

• Sponsorship evaluation: Property owners must evaluate all aspects of the sponsorship, both tangible and intangibles assets. The Canadian Sponsorship Landscape Study (2019) tells us that this is the most concerning challenge in the industry for sponsors.

• Deliver more than expected: Provide sponsors with added value—people want to get a deal.

• Television, digital, social, or media support: It is essential for successful sponsorship programs that sponsors and properties should spend time forging solid relationships with media in all forms and build their own platforms where they can.

• Define priorities: Clearly identify segments of the target market you wish to reach, review your marketing mix, and identify the role you want your sponsorship to fill.

• Set clear and measurable objectives.

• Understand your consumers: Understand what is important to them, identify their interests and motivations, and make the sponsorship relevant to them.

• Measure success: Analyze the property and its effect on your company.

• Activation: Activate and support activation by your partners.

• Servicing: Service and deliver on the contract, all elements.

• Leverage volunteers: Harness them to drive your ROI.

• Train front-line staff: Hire and train your staff in all relevant business aspects and select staff that fit your brand.

• Ensure and coordinate brand consistency across all promotions and activations.

In addition to this list, table 14.1 provides a summary list of six general best practices in sponsorship that complement the key success factors just listed.

TABLE 14.1 Best Practices from Author Experience

Fit	Ensure a good fit between the partners, whether through image, associations, or objectives.
Exclusivity	Know that most companies demand exclusivity in their product category.
Leveraging	Understand that companies seek sport organizations who offer and create leveraging opportunities for their sponsorship.
Relationship building	Build good relationships and networks with sponsors. Consider offering sponsors the opportunity to network with each other.
Market expansion	Understand that many companies use sponsorship to break into new markets and create brand awareness.
Community/Cause	Consider that many organizations want to be seen as good corporate citizens that support the community. They often see sport sponsorships as a way to give back to the community.
Employee motivation/education	Know that many companies see sport sponsorships as an opportunity to get their employees involved and motivated toward the company's goals.
Know both parties' objectives	Understand what both parties are trying to gain through the sponsorship agreement to make it easier to reach those objectives.

CHAPTER SUMMARY

This chapter provides practical instructions for building a successful sponsorship. The four-step approach—presponsorship practices, negotiation, sponsorship life, and sponsorship termination—gives the necessary building blocks for successful sponsorship programs. The commitment of the sport organization to sponsorship is a key component of a successful program. In the life of the sponsorship, activation, servicing, and evaluation are vital and were highlighted. While short-term success may be gained from some sponsorship programs, the emphasis should be long term, which must be understood by the decision makers (board of directors, senior leadership). Resources (time, staff, financial) will have to be invested throughout the sponsorship process. The sport organization should develop a strong relationship with its partners. Sponsors should be encouraged to activate their sponsorship by integrating some or all aspects of the sponsorship within their communications mix. Best practices in sport sponsorship include fit, exclusivity, digital, social, relationship building, market expansion, community, employee motivation, and understanding objectives.

TEST YOUR KNOWLEDGE

1. What is activation? Explain with an example.
2. Explain the presponsorship practices. Why are they critical in the sport-sponsorship process?
3. What are five of the many objectives usually sought by sponsors?
4. You have been asked to research a potential sponsor for your sport. Where do you start? What information will you look for?
5. How can you create your own property that might interest a sponsor?
6. Explain how the four-step approach presented in this chapter could help your local soccer organization to get sponsorship.

KEY TERMS

activation
attribution
pitch
POP
property

servicing
sponsor
sponsorship
sponsorship category
sponsorship deal

sponsorship evaluation
sponsorship valuation
tracking
sponsorship valuation

CASE STUDIES

Visit HK*Propel* for case studies organized by chapter.

CHAPTER 15

Ambush Marketing

LEARNING OBJECTIVES

After studying this chapter, you will be able to do the following:

- Understand the objectives of ambush marketing
- Identify the different ambush marketing strategies
- Identify the different ambush marketing protection strategies
- Recognize the concerns associated with ambush marketing
- Recognize the ethical debates around ambush marketing
- Understand the role of brand management in controlling ambush marketing

Take a moment to consider the following scenario: Assume that you own a local coffee shop, and your coffee shop sponsors a high school soccer team in your neighbourhood. There is another coffee shop in the area that competes with your business. The high school soccer team that you sponsor hosts home games every other weekend. During those home games, as an official sponsor of the team, you display your coffee shop's banner around the high school soccer field and you distribute flyers and discount coupons to people attending the event. You also air a weekend radio commercial wishing your sponsored soccer team good luck. During those

home games, the competing coffee shop, which does not have an official association with the soccer team, also puts a radio commercial on the air sending good luck wishes to that same soccer team. They also hire a number of brand ambassadors (i.e., people who attend the game), who attend the games carrying signs advertising the competitor's coffee shop that they display every time the home team scores.

Think about this for a moment. If you are the sponsoring coffee shop (i.e., the one who makes a financial contribution to the high school in return for the right to be their official sponsor), would you be happy with what the

263

competing coffee shop is doing at the venue and on radio? Why or why not? The actions of the competing coffee shop are referred to as **ambush marketing**, and the same practice can happen at sporting events at the local, regional, provincial, national, and global levels. In cases where the sponsorship investments made are in the millions of dollars, it quickly becomes evident that event organizers and sponsors are not amused by what some may consider a business game. This chapter discusses this practice of ambush marketing by presenting the objectives of ambush marketers, outlining the factors that stimulate ambushers, providing examples of ambush marketing strategies, sharing some of the concerns associated with ambush marketing, and describing the different protection strategies that property holders can use.

The Business Impact of Ambush Marketing

Many properties rely on revenues generated from the sale of marketing rights (e.g., ticket sales, broadcast media rights, pay-per-view sales, sponsorship, naming rights, licensing, merchandising, etc.) to subsist. Companies (or brands) pay fees, in cash or goods and services, to governing bodies or event organizers in exchange for the right to use an event or a property's intellectual assets such as logos, terminology, images, or video footage. These revenue sources allow sport properties to finance the staging of events, pay appearance fees or prize money, contribute to the development of athletes, and build infrastructure to help sport grow and to prepare the next generation of high-performance athletes.

Some companies conduct marketing campaigns around a given event or property without paying rights fees. This not only misleads consumers into believing that they are a sponsor of the event but also ambushes the rights of companies (i.e., the official sponsors) that have paid fees that entitle them to an association with the event. Companies that imply a false association with or make unauthorized use of a sports organization's intellectual property pose a serious threat to the industry, or at least to the revenue sources of the sport properties. Some refer to them as cheaters, pirates, or parasites—they are companies conducting ambush marketing, a practice that can have severe business repercussions on properties.

Ambush marketing can have financial consequences for a property, beyond the obvious costs incurred in the case of legal action by a sponsor. Commonly, properties enter into contractual promises to their sponsors to prevent and fight ambush marketing, and these contracts need to be upheld. For example, in the Olympic Movement, the International Olympic Committee (IOC) is at the forefront of the fight against ambush-marketing practice. The IOC generates billions of dollars to distribute to (i) organizers of the Olympic Games, (ii) the more than 200 national Olympic committees (NOCs), such as the Canadian Olympic Committee, and (iii) international federations (governing bodies for a given sport at the international level). To protect this revenue base and the value it provides to its sponsors, the IOC develops extensive ambush prevention and education initiatives and, when required to do so and where it can, it takes measures against ambushers.

What Does Ambush Marketing Look Like?

Ambush activities can take many forms. During mega-events such as the Olympic Games or the FIFA World Cup, organizers face a challenging situation where the direct industry competitors of their official sponsors attempt to associate themselves with their properties in an effort to reduce the benefits that the official sponsors accrue. Direct industry competitors are companies that market similar products, at a similar price point, and to the same customers as Olympic sponsors. Well-known competitor sets include Visa vs. MasterCard, Heineken vs. Guinness, Coca-Cola vs. PepsiCo, and Nike vs. Adidas. During the major events, it is common to see direct industry competitors of the sponsoring companies employing creative strategies to take advantage of the media exposure, attention, goodwill, and other benefits associated with mega-events such as the Olympic Games. Often, direct industry competitors of sponsoring companies engage in ambush-marketing practices to take advantage of the reputation of a sponsored property's wider media coverage and large audience, or to diminish the communication effectiveness of a competitor's official association with an event. Along the same lines, the factors that stimulate companies to engage in ambush-marketing practices include sponsorship fees being too expensive, exclusivity (e.g., Visa is an exclusive sponsor of IOC for the payment solutions product category, which leaves MasterCard with no option), and length of sponsorship agreement (e.g., Visa may sign up for four to five Games, and four Olympic Games means a total time period of 20 years).

Historically, for example, a number of ambushing practices have been observed during major events. As far back as the 1984 Los Angeles Olympics, Kodak was observed successfully ambushing the official Olympic sponsor (and their fierce competitor at the time) Fuji. During the 1996 Olympics, Linford Christie wore Puma-branded contact lenses at a press conference while the official sponsor at the time was Reebok, and the tactic drew much media attention, reflecting the sophistication of ambushing practice. Around the time of the 2000 Sydney Olympic Games, a leading Australian airline—which was not a Sydney 2000 Games sponsor—used one of Australia's most recognizable athletes in its advertising campaigns. Through this athlete's participation in the Olympics, the company was able to gain an association, thereby undermining the investment made by Ansett, the official airline sponsor of the Games. In the lead-up to the 2004 Athens Olympic Games, a potato chip company—which was not an Olympic sponsor—conducted a television campaign that mocked the delayed construction of the Olympic stadium. By imitating the sound of the starting pistol for a race and using actors as athletes and construction workers in the stadium, the company connected with viewers through sight and sound. All the more challenging was the fact that this company openly used a visual disclaimer at the end of its commercial, which stated, "Obviously, this company is not a sponsor."

Similarly, around the 2008 Beijing Olympics, while Adidas was the official sponsor of the Olympics, one of the greatest Olympians of all time, track sprinter Usain Bolt, broke a world record and posed next to the time clock (showing his world record) while carrying a Puma shoe, which created confusion as to which sporting goods–manufacturing company was the sponsor of the Games. During the 2012 Olympics, Nike communicated several messages on social media using Olympians who took part in the Games. During the 2016 Rio Games, Under Armour installed branded outdoor exercise areas in Rio for the duration of the Games and communicated a well-crafted "Rule Yourself" video featuring Michael Phelps on different social media platforms.

Ambush Marketing: An Alternative to Traditional Sponsorship Strategies?

As discussed in chapters 13 and 14, the continued growth in sponsorship expenditures in Canada suggests that sponsorship continues to be an effective marketing tactic. Both global sport properties (e.g., Olympic Games) and national properties (e.g., Hockey Canada) have optimized their revenues by offering exclusive sponsorship opportunities. In turn, they have become commodities that are sought after by potential sponsors. Given the desirability of these sport properties, in conjunction with the increase in rights fees necessary to become officially associated with them, there has been a practice in companies wishing to reap the benefits of sponsorship but without paying the fee. Such activities are considered ambush marketing. The pioneers of ambush marketing research, Dennis Sandler and David Shani, define ambush marketing as "a planned effort (campaign) by an organization to associate itself indirectly with an event in order to gain at least some of the recognition and benefits that are associated with being an official sponsor" (Sandler & Shani, 1989, p. 10). This definition suggests that ambush marketing is similar to sponsorship since strategies are put in place to gain specific benefits associated with a specific sponsored property.

The subject of ambush marketing first garnered major media attention following the 1984 Los Angeles Olympic Games, when Kodak successfully ambushed official Olympic sponsor Fuji. Since then, ambush marketing has grown both in the number of occurrences and in the number of sport properties that have been subject to it. Even though it has recently become less intensive than what had been observed in the 1990 to 2010 period, the use of ambush marketing by some companies is still a common practice in the sport world. Today, it is considered to be a strategic alternative to formal association through the purchase of legitimate sponsorship rights. However, many people believe that ambush marketing can be detrimental to sport because it diminishes the value of sport properties and increases an already cluttered sporting environment.

While some consider ambush marketing to be a legitimate competitive response, others believe that ambush marketing is ethically questionable. Still others believe that such claims are made in a way that justify one's position as either the ambusher or the ambushed. Some argue that sponsored properties are not different from any other commercial effort, and one should expect a nonsponsor to try to associate itself with the sponsored property of its key competitors. Based on this perspective, marketers that are successful at creating effective ambush-marketing campaigns may appear to be "intelligent" marketers, since they are able to neutralize the competitive advantage by confusing the consumer as to the legitimate sponsor of an event. They consider such behaviour to be legitimate competitive marketing. The adage, "May the best marketer win!" applies to this viewpoint.

For others (often including property holders), ambush marketing is a form of cheating since no authority to associate with the event has been provided. The notion of an exchange between a sponsor and an event organizer is violated through the use of ambush marketing, since "a third party is seeking to benefit from an exchange without making a proportional contribution to that exchange" (McCarville & Copeland, 1994, p. 109). As a result, the sport entity is threatened by ambush marketing since it diminishes the corporation's dependence on the sport group. The existence of ambush marketing suggests that the sponsor may be able to enjoy comparable benefits without contributing to the sport group (McCarville & Copeland, 1994). Regardless of one's opinion on the matter, it is the responsibility of the property to develop programs that will both enhance and protect the sponsors.

Research on Ambush Marketing

Previous literature in ambush marketing can be broadly categorized into five research streams:

1. Defining, and describing the practice, aims, and objectives of ambush marketing
2. Consumer perception of ambush marketing
3. Ethical issues surrounding ambush marketing
4. Legal issues related to ambush marketing
5. Ambush marketing–prevention strategies

A few studies exist on the topic of ambushing strategies (e.g., Burton & Chadwick, 2018; Chadwick & Burton, 2011) and the use of social media as an ambush-marketing medium (e.g., Abeza et al., 2020; Grady, 2017). Consumer studies on ambush marketing report mixed results. Some found varying level of consumer confusion, while others reported that consumers do not empathize with sponsors and do not feel concerned with issues such as ambush marketing. The emphasis on maximizing revenue rather than creating value to sponsors may have contributed to an increasingly cluttered environment, resulting in a confused marketplace. In turn, there has been increased emphasis on managing sponsorship programs as part of an integrated brand-management system. Regarding research related to the ethical issues in ambush marketing, some have argued that the practice of ambush marketing may be ethically questionable, while others believe that there is nothing wrong with such behaviour.

While research on ambush marketing in Canada has been sparse, two notable early consumer-based studies were carried out in four countries (including Canada) around the 2000 and 2004 Olympic Games. The findings showed that Canadians felt that ambush marketing was unethical, unfair, and inappropriate, suggesting that nonsponsors should not lead consumers to believe that they are sponsors of the Olympic Games since it was not fair for companies to associate themselves with the Olympics without being an Olympic sponsor (Séguin et al., 2005). It is interesting to note that in both the 2000 and 2004 studies, Canadians were most disposed to view the practice of ambush marketing as unethical than people from other countries. In fact, across each of the statements related to ambush marketing, Canadians were more opposed to ambushing than the American, German, or French respondents (Séguin et al., 2005). Such findings reveal significant differences between countries in attitudes toward ambushing. This is of particular interest for the Olympic Games since this may require specific strategies country by country. In this regard, it is likely that Canadians would be more responsive to communications strategies that would position ambush marketing as an unethical practice.

Whether ambush marketing is ethical, legal, or simply smart business practice has been the topic of the studies undertaken by a handful of researchers. While some argue that ambush marketing is ethically problematic, others believe that the practice is a creative and legitimate competitive response. In fact, the choice of definition often depends on the position that one holds as either the ambusher or the ambushed (Ellis et al., 2011). It is important to note that the official sponsor who has purchased the rights normally views any such activities by a competitor as an intention to ambush, although they often acknowledge that it is part of the competitive marketing landscape (Abeza et al., 2020). When reflecting on ambush marketing, former IOC vice-president of marketing Richard Pound explained: "Our attitude is that the practice wasn't wrong just because money wasn't paid to be a sponsor, but because someone has appropriated something that did not belong to them" (Ettore, 1993, p. 55).

Strategies of Ambush Marketing

Event organizers and sponsors understand that ambush-marketing efforts are essentially promotional tactics. Examples of ambush-marketing strategies include increasing advertisements at the time of an event with no specific reference to it; booking TV, web, social media, and radio advertising slots during the time of an event that are sponsored by a competing company; sponsoring entities other than the event itself (e.g., athletes, national teams, national sport federations, etc.); purchasing advertising spaces in close proximity to an event such as billboards; creating connection through key visual and word elements that make event-related references; and launching a social media program at the same time as the event (without specific mention). In summarizing these strategy efforts of ambushers, Chadwick and Burton (2011) identified three broad types of ambush-marketing strategies: (a) a nonsponsoring agency using suggested references to an event, which they refer to as indirect ambushing, (b) a nonsponsoring agency gaining the benefits of association without clear intention of ambushing, which they refer to as incidental ambushing, and (c) a nonsponsoring agency using protected intellectual property, which they refer to as direct ambushing.

These authors (Chadwick & Burton, 2011) further divided ambush strategy groupings into 11 specific ambush marketing practice types: indirect (distractive, values, insurgent, sponsor self, associative, and parallel property); incidental (unintentional and saturation), and direct (property infringement, predatory, and coattail). According to Abeza and colleagues (2020), 6 out of the 11 identified typologies are adaptable to social media (a relatively recent avenue used by ambushers), while the remaining 5 strategies are those that are applicable in an offline setting or geographically near an event's venue. The offline strategies include insurgent ambushing (e.g., the use of aggressively promoted, one-off, street-style promotions at an event), predatory ambushing (e.g., distributing branded giveaways around an event venue), distractive ambushing (e.g., displaying products around the event venue), sponsor self-ambushing (e.g., a sponsor promoting itself above and beyond what has been agreed to in the sponsorship contract), and parallel property ambushing (e.g., the creation of, or sponsorship of, a rival event or property to be run in parallel to the main ambush target).

As Chadwick and Burton (2011) discussed and Abeza and colleagues (2020) further developed, the strategies that are specifically applicable to social media are the following:

- **Coattail ambushing:** An ambusher attempts to directly associate itself with a property using a legitimate link, such as participating athletes.

- **Property infringement:** An ambusher intentionally using protected intellectual property, such as a logo, a name, and words, without authorization.

- **Associative ambushing:** An ambusher uses imagery or terminology to create a suggestion that an organization has links to the event, leading to consumers believing that the organization is involved with (or supports) the event when it does not.

- **Values ambushing:** An ambusher uses an event or property's central value or theme to imply an association.

- **Unintentional ambushing:** Consumers inadvertently identify a nonsponsoring company as an official sponsor based on a previous association with an event.

- **Saturation ambushing:** An ambusher increases the volume of advertising at the time of an event with no reference or association to the event.

It is not uncommon that all these ambush techniques are used in part or all together to maximize the desired effect. For the most part, the context in which the online applicable strategies are used is legal. However, from an event organizer (e.g., Olympic Games) point of view, ambush activities may result in complaints from official sponsors, suggesting that these tactics reduce the value of their investments. If sponsors truly believe that the value is diminished, there is the potential risk of event organizers losing revenue and, in the end, of damaging the event's brand. Some of the strategies and corresponding examples are presented next.

Using Media during the Time of a Competing Company's Sponsored Events

A number of sport properties include media extensions such as online (e.g., YouTube) and commercials on traditional television or streaming broadcasts. At times, a company may have the opportunity to purchase advertising during the broadcast of an event without being a sponsor of that event or to use YouTube advertisements. By purchasing media airtime during such events, an ambusher may not be doing anything illegal yet may create the impression that it is a sponsor of that event. For example, Nike used YouTube to release creatively developed short videos associating itself with athletes and the name of the host city during the Olympic Games. During the 2016 Rio Olympic Games, Nike released its "Unlimited" campaign about everyday athletes that was promoted on YouTube, and during the 2012 London Olympic Games, Nike released its "Find Your Greatness" campaign showcasing "everyday" athletes finding their greatness in towns around the world called London (Abeza et al., 2020).

During the 1996 Olympic Games, the official broadcaster for Canada, CBC, sold advertising packages to a number of companies that became "sponsors" of the broadcast and received recognition in the opening segment of the broadcast (e.g., "The 1996 Summer Olympics Games broadcast is brought to you by Compaq"), when in fact, the official worldwide sponsor of the 1996 Olympic Games was IBM. While the onsite spectators are unaffected by such advertising, it created confusion among a large and global television audience. Clearly there are important differences between the official sponsor of an event and the official sponsor of a broadcast of that same event. The official sponsor provides resources directly to the event organizers and, in effect, buys a license to spend more money to activate this investment, while the media sponsor buys airtime during the broadcast of the Games and employs ambush marketing.

The practice of sponsoring a broadcast by a direct competitor of an official sponsor has declined in frequency over the course of time, partly due to public awareness, social media, and antiambush legislation in host countries. Regardless of this trend, it is important for a property to employ a **sponsor recognition program**. Sponsor recognition programs are promotional activities developed by a property to increase consumer awareness of its official sponsors and to help the sponsor differentiate between themselves and their competition (ambushers). A similar tactic may be to purchase **advertising inventory** during or around the broadcast of an event. Advertising inventories are opportunities available for purchase during or around the broadcast of an event, such as 30-second commercial spots, in-program graphics, or opening and closing segments of a broadcast. While some properties may arrange with broadcasters to offer official sponsors first right of refusal to the advertising inventory (e.g., Olympic sponsors and CBC), it remains a popular tactic among competitors, especially if they use sport images in their commercials. Thus, the buying of television advertising inventory by a competitor of an official sponsor should be considered an ambush marketing tactic since it has the ability to confuse consumers as to who really is the official sponsor of the event.

Sponsoring Subcategories and Aggressively Activating This Investment

The proliferation of sponsorship categories may create many opportunities for corporations that do not wish to pay the rights fees required for official sponsorship. In major mega multisport events (such as the Olympic Games), there are many events, hundreds of teams, and thousands of athletes participating, providing many opportunities for exploiting a subcategory sponsorship. While the practice has been declining over time, aggressive ambush campaigns related to subcategory status have the potential for great effectiveness at a significantly lower cost. In particular, by sponsoring individual athletes, teams, or national sport federations, ambush-

ers can gain the type of associations they seek without paying the cost of a full-event sponsorship. For example, Nike used athletes such as Mo Farah, a well-known British distance runner and Olympian, and communicated its message and association itself with the athlete during the Games. Nike showed its relationship with the celebrity athlete both online and offline in a country where the athlete's achievement was celebrated at the highest sporting stage in the world (the Olympic Games) and at an Olympics hosted by the athlete's country, Great Britain. On social media, Nike used pictures, GIFs, and emojis to promote its association with Mo Farah. Offline, Nike used an outdoor advertising campaign to celebrate Farah's double Olympic gold medal–winning performance.

Engaging in Advertising and Similar Events That Coincide with the Sponsored Event

Corporations may resort to large-scale promotional campaigns directly at or in close geographic proximity to the venue of the event. In fact, during the bid process, Olympic Games host countries are expected to demonstrate that they can deliver a "clean city" during the entire month of the Olympic Games. However, some companies are still observed to be adopting this ambush strategy, whereby they find a way to acquire outdoor advertising space, including billboards, bus advertising, and subway ads, for the one-month period around (and including) the Games. Through the use of imagery on these displays, billboards, and banners, companies try to get consumers' attention in the surrounding of the event itself. For example, during the Rio Olympic Games, the association between Under Armour (UA) and Michael Phelps was in full display during the 2016 Games. Protection policies against ambush restricted UA from any use of official associations, including imagery and key phrases like "Olympics" or the "Rings." UA used its own marketing phrases along with associated signifiers to connect Phelps with its brand. The opportunistic use of Phelps, his rivalry with South African swimmer Chad Le Clos, and his victory in the 200-meter butterfly had UA posting on Twitter about the athlete with its own "Rule Yourself" campaign, the American flag, and emojis signifying applause and celebration. The creative outlook worked for them, as they did not break any IOC regulations while capitalizing on the success of Phelps, one of the greatest Olympians of all time.

Sponsors and ambushers (brands) are also observed choosing to use a heightened social media presence to promote other properties in their sponsorship portfolios. For example, during the PyeongChang Games, Visa was the official sponsor, yet American Express frequently tweeted out the NBA All-Star Game promotion: "Don't miss the hardwood come alive. Reserve your spot in an immersive Amex Experience open to all fans at NBA All-Star 2018," which was an ambush tactic. Additionally, American Express also focused on the ATP World Tour New York Open with, "Calling all Amex Card Member tennis fans! You can get discounted tickets to the @NewYorkOpen @NYCBLive now thru February 18, 2018." Similarly, Kia was tweeting out a number of messages during the Games about other sports it sponsors, such as the Australian Open "#Kia is a proud partner of the #AusOpen for another 5 years. Read more about how we are set to become the longest-running major sponsor of the tennis tournament on #KiaBUZZ!" Kia also tweeted a 1 minute and 23 second Olympic-related video with this text: "Ready to break your limits? Stay undefeated with our invincible #Kia SUVs."

Using Thematic Advertising and Implied Association

Some properties have developed such well-known brands that association with the event and brand is possible without the use of logos or trademarks. This is accomplished by creating thematic advertising that may imply an association with the sponsored property. By most accounts, hockey arguably is the primary cultural sport for Canada, and values linked to being Canadian are often linked with the sport of ice hockey. For instance, just prior to the 2018 PyeongChang Winter Olympics, Budweiser Canada launched a digital campaign celebrat-

ing hockey with its brand. The promotions included Wayne Gretzky and limited-edition gold-coloured Budweiser merchandise, with Budweiser clearly seeking symbolic reference while making no direct association with the Games themselves. The credibility of Gretzky (one of Canada's most famous people) and the social media reach of Budweiser amplified the effort while hinting at the support for Canada winning the gold at the Games. The timing of the campaign created a platform of inciting confusion (in consumers' minds) by hinting at potential association with hockey, Canada, and the Olympic Games themselves. As Abeza and colleagues (2020) noted, Pirelli's use of imagery or terminology to create a suggestion that an organization has links to the Games is another example of an ambush-marketing strategy: during the 2018 Winter Games, Pirelli tweeted "Winter Champion" along with different winter sport–related pictures, more than 10 times over a period of 17 days.

Historically, the use of imagery or terminology to create a suggestion that an organization has links to the property has been a commonly adopted ambush-marketing strategy. For example, Hockey Canada has been very successful in building a powerful brand and in making associations between its own brand—Team Canada—and the Canadian Olympic hockey team. In fact, since the 1998 Olympic Games, the jerseys worn by the Canadian Olympic hockey team have been branded with Hockey Canada's logo. Over this time frame, sales of Hockey Canada merchandise have skyrocketed, especially following the gold-medal performances of the men's and women's hockey teams at the 2002 Salt Lake City Olympic Winter Games and later at the 2010 Vancouver Olympic Winter Games. A number of Hockey Canada's sponsors have been successful in leveraging its brand by integrating it into their own promotional activities.

For instance, the Hockey Canada "theme" can be observed at the thousands of Esso gas stations across the country. A few months prior to the 2006 Winter Olympic Games, Esso used a creative and effective thematic promotion titled "Cheers for Canada in Torino, Italy." This promotion was executed at the pumps of all

Esso stations across Canada. While Esso was careful to not use the word "Olympics" or any Olympic symbols, the fact that Torino was the host city for the Games implied the connection to the Winter Olympics. This promotional campaign played to Canadians' passion and strong emotional connection to hockey and indirectly to the Olympic Winter Games. Today, the COC and Hockey Canada work together to create a Games specific logo that players wear at the Games. Both organizations share royalties on the sale of merchandise. This example illustrates the complex situation when numerous promotional opportunities are linked to a specific event. The many levels of official sponsorship available with the Olympic Games adds to this complexity, since a company can be a global sponsor, a national Olympic sponsor, a domestic sponsor of the Games, a sponsor of a national sport federation, a sponsor of an athlete, or a sponsor of a team.

Other Ambush-Marketing Strategies

The practice of ambush marketing has relatively subsided since the early 2010s, even though the staging of an event (by a property and its agencies) without ambush remains challenging. Clearly, the three groupings of protection strategies (i.e., legislation, communication, and surveillance) have played a significant role in minimizing the practice. However, the nature of ambush marketing has evolved over last few years, which changed from evading the rules and creating obvious direct associations with events to less overt and creative strategies (Abeza et al., 2020). It is important to note that the new strategies include strategies that are low-risk from a legal or sanction perspective (Abeza et al., 2020). In particular, social media has emerged as a platform of choice for ambush marketers, enabling them to implement clever and sophisticated ambush efforts without breaking the rules.

Since the 2012 London Olympic Games, many cases of creative and prominent ambush-marketing initiatives have appeared on social media (Abeza et al., 2020), which has led the IOC to take action and release subsequent social media guidelines that redefined Rule 40 of the IOC charter. Originally, bylaw #3 of Rule 40 stated that, "Except as permitted by the IOC Executive Board, no competitor, coach, trainer or official who participates in the Olympic Games may allow his person, name, picture or sports performances to be used for advertising purposes during the Olympic Games" (International Olympic Committee, 2015, p. 79). However, since the first Blogging Guidelines were released in 2008, successive revised guidelines have been released for the 2014, 2016, 2018, and 2021 Olympic Games. The guidelines released prior to the Tokyo Olympics state that "Competitors, team officials and other team personnel who participate in the Olympic Games may allow their person, name, picture or sports performances to be used for advertising purposes during the Olympic Games in accordance with the principles determined by the IOC Executive Board" (International Olympic Committee, 2020, p. 76). This is a noticeable shift, which is indicative of the changing marketing landscape.

While the impact of Rule 40 cannot be fully attributed to the changes observed over the past few years, Abeza and colleagues (2020) reported that the two common ambush-marketing strategies (coattail and property infringement) employed during the 2014 Games, and to some extent during the 2016 Games, were not observed during the 2018 Games. These are strategies whereby ambushers attempt to directly associate themselves with a property using a legitimate link such as participating athletes or engage in an unauthorized use of protected intellectual property such as a logo, a name, and or words.

Counter-ambushing Strategies

How do you prevent unauthorized companies from associating with or implying an association with one of the world's most widely recognized brands? Abeza and colleagues (2020) noted that there are three common counter-ambushing strategies: legislation (laws to punish parties found involved in ambushing practice), communication (increasing public awareness about event properties, including trademarks), and surveillance (identifying intellectual property infringement).

Prevention is the key. To effectively combat ambush marketing, sport properties need a well-stocked toolbox. Extensive trademark and copyright registration as well as other legal instruments are essential for developing a legally robust intellectual property inventory for the modern-day property. However, legal tools are often insufficient when dealing with ambush marketing. Today's sophisticated marketers craft creative campaigns that steer clear of registered trademarks yet manage to create a connection with consumers. As such, laws often need to be supplemented or, in many cases, created to specifically address ambush marketing. This gives law-enforcement bodies the legislative grounds to act should the need arise. Legislation is an effective strategy but must be complemented by communication campaigns and operational plans designed to ensure compliance and enforcement of rules and laws. In this regard, FIFA and IOC ask host country governments to enact special legislation prohibiting ambushing and protecting the goodwill associated with their events. This has occurred in countries such as Australia (2000 Sydney Games), Greece (2004 Athens Games), China (2008 Beijing Games), Canada (2010 Vancouver Games), South Africa (2010 World Cup), and the United Kingdom (2012 London Games).

Legislation can be a very effective strategy when complemented with communication. If done properly, the combination can increase awareness of those companies that are legitimately supporting and financing the property of interest, where this angle can be used in a communication campaign. For instance, the advertising campaigns commonly paid for by the property that are designed to recognize and often thank its sponsors can enhance consumers' awareness levels of the "real supporters" of the event or property. In recent Olympic Games, the organizing committees have developed integrated communication campaigns to recognize their sponsors and condemn ambush marketers. In major markets, certain NOCs have undertaken similar strategies. For example, in the lead-up to the Athens and Torino Olympic Games, the IOC took unprecedented steps to create a significant, multinational advertising campaign.

Surveillance is the third strategy. Surveillance ranges from assigning a dedicated law-enforcement agency to undertake ambush policing (i) around the host city to hiring, to (ii) tracking people or organizations posting or sharing content of unauthorized association of a brand with

IN THE KNOW

Ambush Marketing Today

Ambush marketers are becoming increasingly sophisticated, often indirectly leveraging investments made by official sponsors. In most cases, ambushers will not use any registered trademarks or copyrighted materials. Their ability to operate in a grey zone makes enforcement more challenging since legal recourse is not always an effective means to resolution. The consequences of ambushing practices are significant. Understanding the stakes and the means to counter an ambush will better serve you, your organization, and your sponsors. In this regard, social media has opened a new avenue for ambushers by expanded the territory to execute creative marketing initiatives. It offers ambushers the ability to take part in breaking border restrictions and time barriers, particularly as the messages communicated over social media can hardly be stopped either by national boundaries or institutional gatekeepers (Abeza et al., 2020). The practice noticed on social media, in fact, led the International Olympic Committee (IOC) to release subsequent social media guidelines through revisions to Rule 40 of the Olympic Charter.

an event. For example, during the South Africa 2010 FIFA World Cup, 36 women who dressed in Dutch orange minidresses attended a match promoting the Dutch beer company Bavaria and stole the match's media spotlight while the official beer sponsor was Budweiser. During the match, the women were detained by police over claims that they were advertising for an unofficial beer company, Bavaria.

Ambush Marketing and Clutter

Sponsorship has been argued to be a lower-cost way to break through the clutter in the modern marketplace and reach specific targets. An inherent problem linked to ambush marketing is its contribution to a cluttered environment (which can undermine sponsorship overall). However, other factors contribute to the clutter. For example, newer sports and events (skateboarding, ski cross) and repackaged existing sports (beach volleyball, TopGolf) now offer entertaining products that may be attractive to sponsors looking for access to a specific audience. The Canadian sport industry has thousands of sport properties available in its five segments—grassroots sports, sporting events, university and college sports, professional sports, and Olympic sports. These segments can be broken down further. For example, in Olympic sport, sponsorship opportunities exist with Olympic Games, local organizing committees, NSOs, national teams, individual athletes, coaching programs, multisport organizations, national training centres, and so on. Each opportunity may attract numerous sponsors and different levels of contribution, activation, and value. This increasingly clutters the environment and, if not controlled, can add to confusion in the marketplace and a lessening of the effectiveness of sponsorship. In fact, consumers may not differentiate an Olympic sponsorship from a national sponsorship of an Olympic sport. Thus, rights holders should be concerned with clutter both on its own and as a result of ambush marketing. On its own, clutter leads to a general fragmentation of the market and difficulty in diffusing messages. Clutter is further increased with each case

of ambush marketing. In both cases, clutter can diminish the value of a specific sport property or of sport in general.

Figure 15.1 details how ambush marketing in a cluttered marketplace is related to key stakeholder groups, which demonstrates that ambush marketing and clutter are closely linked issues. The figure also identifies brand management strategies for each partner of the Olympic property—IOC, NOC, OCOG, and sponsors—to protect the brand against potential ambush-marketing attacks. This figure was the result of extensive consumer research and expert opinions in Olympic sport marketing. These are some key elements of a brand management system.

1. Managing and protecting the Olympic brand is vital for the future of Olympic marketing programs.

2. A strategic marketing communications program is necessary to develop brand consistency at all levels.

3. Integrated public-relations plans play an important role in the Olympic marketing communications program. A team of "brand masters" made up of representatives of IOC, NOC, OCOG, and sponsors should develop the plan, which would then be integrated within each NOC and OCOG.

4. Activation of rights by sponsors: the Olympic brand should be integrated into sponsors' marketing and communications programs. Sponsors must claim their space within the Olympic landscape.

5. IOC, NOCs, OCOG, and sponsors must work closely with each other. All must truly comprehend the Olympic brand and work toward integrated marketing communications. This approach can contribute to making the brand more coherent, which is an area that was identified as weak in this research.

6. NOCs must be educated in brand-marketing management. NOCs lack competency and expertise in marketing, which has caused a lack of coherence and uniformity in Olympic brand worldwide.

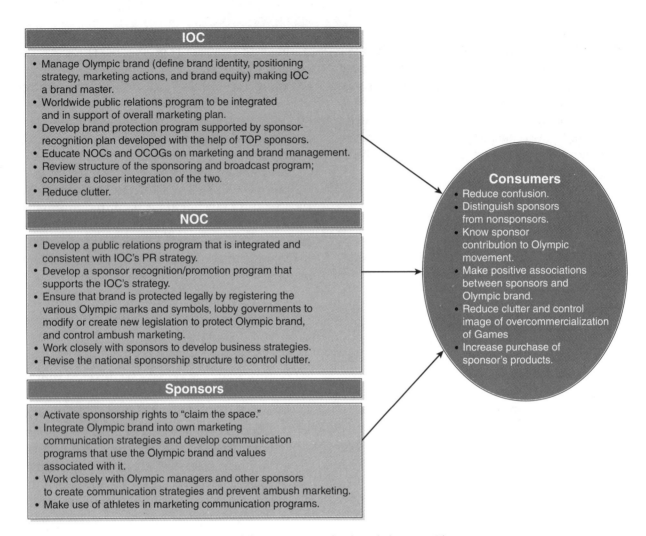

FIGURE 15.1 A brand management model to manage ambush and clutter in Olympic sport.
Reprinted by permission from B. Séguin and N.J. O'Reilly, "The Olympic Brand, Ambush Marketing and Clutter," *International Journal of Sport Management and Marketing* 4, no. 1 (2008): 62–84.

CHAPTER SUMMARY

Although the prospects for sport properties and sponsorship remain encouraging, the increased cost of sponsorship combined with a highly cluttered sponsorship environment raise concerns about its effectiveness in helping brands achieve their business objectives. Thus, the emergence of ambush marketing can be a threat to sponsorship. If sport properties do not effectively respond to ambush marketing, the benefits and ultimately the value to sponsors may be diminished. While some have questioned the ethics of ambush marketing, sport organizations should reconsider the way in which they conduct business and adopt sound marketing strategies that protect exclusivity and combat ambush. The use of a brand-management system is shown to be useful in managing ambush marketing. In particular, with the expansion of social media and the convenience of the platforms for the execution of ambush strategies, property holders need to design proactive measures to manage the practice of ambush marketing.

TEST YOUR KNOWLEDGE

1. Why is ambush marketing considered a problem by both sponsees and sponsors?
2. What is clutter? Why is clutter an issue in sponsorship?

3. Do you consider ambush marketing an ethical or a business issue? Explain your position. Ethical debates around ambush marketing have attracted different views from different groups.

4. If you were in a position to employ an ambush-marketing strategy, would you do it? Why or why not?

5. Have you noticed any ambush-marketing activities? If so, what are they? Bring some examples of advertising or promotional materials you consider ambush marketing and present them to your classmates.

KEY TERMS

advertising inventory

ambush marketing

associative ambushing

coattail ambushing

property infringement

saturation ambushing

sponsor recognition program

unintentional ambushing

values ambushing

CASE STUDIES

Visit HK*Propel* for case studies organized by chapter.

CHAPTER 16

Technology in Sport Marketing

LEARNING OBJECTIVES

After studying this chapter, you will be able to do the following:

- Understand the importance of technology in the contemporary sport environment
- Acquire a basic understanding of enterprise resource planning or ERP
- Understand the types of technologies that can affect the sport marketing cycle
- Understand current technological trends and advancements in sport
- Forecast future technological trends and advancements that will impact sport

It might seem like the world of zeros and ones should be solely for those studying computer science or engineering, but technological advancements over the past decade have reached multiple aspects of the sport business enterprise. Moreover, the COVID-19 pandemic has only enhanced this trend. Whether it is a ticket sales team reaching out to season-ticket holders via email, a graphic designer creating a poster promotion using Adobe Illustrator **software,** or anything similar in between, there is no question that technology has become an important part of sport marketing. In chapter 7, we first looked at this concept by highlighting different types of

digital products, namely, mobile apps, wearables, and fantasy sport, as well as social media. But the importance of technology in sport marketing goes far beyond the ability to create new digital product offerings for consumers. For example, technology has enabled the collection and storage of vast amounts of data, which, in turn, can be analyzed to drive new insights and inform the strategic marketing plans of sport organizations. Teams, leagues, and agencies invest significant capital to build these **databases** along with the required infrastructure and human resources to analyze this data to connect different technological touchpoints to one another, all in the quest to gain more information toward competitive advantages over other teams, leagues, and agencies. As such, **information technology** (IT) and **information systems** (IS) have become key components of sport marketing, informing all the major topic areas from market research to marketing strategy.

Today, information gathering is not just an insular, back-of-house activity. Senior managers of sport organizations are increasingly emphasizing technology in their practice, realizing that to manage technology is to manage the business and make it competitive. Take, for instance, the COVID-19 global health pandemic that impacted multiple sectors, including sport, at a very significant level, in 2020. While the operations of many sport organizations were decimated by the pandemic, sport managers at the professional and amateur sport levels still needed to direct their staff and meet the needs of their members and stakeholders. Without prior investment in technology, these managers would not have been able to invest in work-from-home (WFH) scenarios and reposition their organizations to advance new marketing strategies or campaigns postpandemic. But managing technology is quite different from managing other aspects within sport.

Technology includes both the tangible (e.g., computer laptops, desktops, peripherals, routers, tablets, cellular phones) and intangible (e.g., Wi-Fi connectivity, operating software [OS] systems, "office suite" software), and it requires an intricate balance of people and processes. Some sport marketers are better versed in technology than others, with certain groups often possessing higher comfort levels than others, such as millennials (born in the early 1980s to mid-1990s) versus boomers (born in the late 1940s to mid-1960s). In general, millennials are able to respond to and appreciate the dramatic shifts in technology (e.g., dial-up vs. broadband Internet) more than the boomer generation, with those in Generation X (born in the mid-1960s to early 1980s) falling somewhere in between. For the new entrants into sport marketing, such as those in the Generation Z (those born in the late 1990s and early 2000s) or even Generation Alpha (those born in 2010 onward) cohorts, the use of technology is, in many cases, a natural, native

activity. Clearly, the differing views and (general) abilities to deal with technology across cohorts for both sport marketers and their customers (fans) can be problematic for the operation of the sport organization due to the differing levels of knowledge by cohort. This emphasizes the need for all sport marketers to appreciate and understand IT and IS and how these developments might affect the marketing cycle.

Information Technology and Information Systems

Specific to business environments, information systems comprise five elements: **hardware**, software, data, communications, and people. Only two of these elements are inherently technical—hardware and software, or information technology. The remaining three can be affected by IT, enabled through IT, or partially consist of IT, depending on the specific situation. In this section, we discuss each of these elements.

Hardware

Whether you work for a large sport organization or in a grassroots recreation club, you will be tasked with using IT, the hardware and software that enable your organization to interact and perform a variety of digital tasks (e.g., marketing, communications, human resources, data management, etc.). In the previous edition of this text, references to hardware included personal digital assistants (PDA), computers (as a general category), and servers, the latter acting as a conduit for resource sharing and activity distribution across multiple computers in an organization. However, these tangible examples of hardware show how far the sport industry and society in general have advanced. Instead of PDA with limited capabilities, sport business professionals now have mobile devices with expanded capabilities to access, view, and modify spreadsheets, documents, and emails, as well as perform simple tasks such as text message communication and phone calls. In the modern IT landscape, hardware is not just tangible assets located within the brick-and-mortar side of a sport organization; rather, hardware is fluid and can exist inside and outside the physical headquarters. This need was accentuated during the COVID-19 pandemic, when the majority of operations of sport organizations in Canada went remote.

This concept is best depicted using a "small, medium, large, and extra-large coffee cup" typology. Small hardware devices are those that are pocket sized such as smartphone devices. They exist for rapid, instantaneous connectivity and allow users who are on the go or in transit to maintain a constant link to the rest of the organization and other stakeholders. Medium-level hardware devices such as iPads and tablets still afford the user increased mobility, especially away from the physical location of the organization, but also has increased capabilities, given its larger screen and computing power. Typically, modern iPads and tablets are built with a computer architecture to perform more complex tasks such as creating and modifying graphic illustrations and presentation decks, and in some cases serving as the point-of-sale system hub for mobile retailers. Larger portable hardware, namely, laptop computers, provide the functionality of the traditional desktop computer but allow users to take the processing capability with them. While they are not as portable and often run on battery power, their computational capabilities expand the horizons for sport marketers as they create videos, spreadsheets, and reports and send emails. Small, medium, and large hardware devices are critical for the modern sport marketer. It is very common for a sport marketer to capture media content on a medium-sized device, utilize the computation power of a larger, laptop device to package the content, and maintain constant communication with colleagues using small devices to text-message the completion of the project.

This leaves the extra-large hardware devices. These are the larger, stationary desktop computers that are hard-wired into the organization's network infrastructure and have significant computational capabilities, especially with regard to pulling information from databases such as customer-relationship management (CRM) systems. Often, for sport marketers working in analytics, this hardware is a supercomputer that can quickly and efficiently house and manage **data warehouses**, sometimes with millions of data points. The reason for this "coffee cup" typology is that it ultimately explains the capacity of hardware for the sport marketer. Smaller cups are easy to manoeuvre and be mobile with, but they do not pack the same amount of "caffeine," or computational power, as a large or extra-large cup. However, given the increased WFH and mobile environments in which sport marketers operate, more peripheral devices are being created to augment small and medium-sized devices to expand their capabilities, such as keyboard attachments, styli for sketching and notetaking, and wireless mouse pointers.

Software

IT also consists of important software programs that run on hardware. There are two critical elements of software: operating systems (OSs) and software applications. OSs serve as the functional interface that allows a user to use hardware, whether small, medium, large, or extra-large. In the modern landscape, there are three OSs of primary importance for sport marketers: Apple's iOS, Microsoft's Windows, and Google's Android OS. Apple's proprietary OS runs exclusively on Apple hardware such as the iPhone (small), iPad (medium), MacBook Pro (large), and iMac (extra-large). Although it is not available on other hardware brands, its market share is considerable. Over 70 percent of Canadian sports fans gravitate toward Apple's OS (Naraine et al., 2019). Part of the reason for its consumer popularity is the ease and accessibility for both younger and older consumers and the seamless integration of the OS across its suite of hardware in the Apple ecosystem. By contrast, Microsoft's Windows OS is more widespread and focused on larger hardware devices (e.g., laptops). Windows has been the traditional powerhouse platform for businesses as Microsoft's popular "Office" suite of software applications (e.g., Word, PowerPoint, Excel) was predominantly used on Windows-based machines. However, this has since changed and many of Microsoft's software applications are now available on Apple and Google OSs. Windows is still a key OS for many businesses, especially in sport, due in part to the fact that there are software applications by third parties that operate only in this system. For instance, the popular business analytics and intelligence platform, SAS, which is used by Maple Leaf Sports and Entertainment (MLSE) and the Canadian Olympic Committee (COC), primarily operates on Windows OS (there are ways to operate SAS on Apple hardware, but it is very complex as compared to use with Windows-based machines). Finally, a newer entrant into the OS landscape, Google's Android OS, has primarily focused on small and medium hardware devices. In Canada, Android OS accounts for roughly 25 percent of sports fans (Naraine et al., 2019). More recently, Google has offered a variant OS for larger devices that is also contained in their ecosystem, known as Chromebooks. It is important to consider these OSs as sport organizations build out their IT infrastructure. A few important questions to ask include:

1. What types of software applications (e.g., word processing, creative design) are required?
2. How much capital (i.e., financial resources) can be invested in this area?
3. What is the technological competence of staff (e.g., skills, training)?

Once questions have been answered, the organization may begin to purchase the required hardware (of any or all sizes) for its staff, including sport marketers, to use for work purposes. For instance, if the marketing department of the Winnipeg Jets of the NHL decides to take a very analytical approach to the marketing of its suites, they would need to determine what software they require, what supercomputers are needed, and if they have (or need to hire) the appropriately trained staff.

After determining its hardware needs and identifying the applicable OS, sport organizations need to consider what software applications they require to perform essential business tasks. Microsoft's Office suite of applications is a mainstay of business, and its pervasiveness is the sport industry is also quite prevalent (although competing products, including a suite of applications by Apple, are available). Microsoft also offers additional software applications to supplement its business product offering. Specifically, prospective and current sport marketers should familiarize themselves with Microsoft OneNote, SharePoint, and Teams. Microsoft OneNote is very useful for taking notes during meetings, sketching drawings or quick charts, and consolidating memos and notes from other colleagues. Microsoft SharePoint then allows the organization to create a central repository to consolidate important files, documents, and presentations and share them across the firm. Finally, Microsoft Teams is a business communication platform that equips the business with video conferencing and real-time messaging. With sport businesses increasing their WFH capacity, these software applications are becoming increasingly important. As noted, there are competing and complementary applications outside the Microsoft ecosystem that are central to the sport marketing operation. Programs like Adobe Acrobat and Photoshop are critical for their ability to create and sign documents and produce stunning visual content to distribute across the organization's social and web channels. Table 16.1 provides a (nonexhaustive) list of other applications that are often considered or utilized in the sport industry.

Another software solution often found in sport organizations, predominantly the larger ones or ones that are part of larger conglomerates, is known as the **enterprise resource planning system**, or ERP system. This common business software package consists of many linkable application modules purchased from a single vendor and meant to draw from a single repository of data. The goal of ERP systems is to integrate the functions of an organization, from finance to logistics, under one unified system architecture such that the organization's processes become streamlined and more efficient—a task that is often easier said than done. One of the more popular ERP systems in the sport industry is *Sports One* by SAP. SAP, like many modern software companies, developed its solution as software-as-a-service (SaaS), which enables users throughout a sport organization to access the software on any device, small, medium, large, or extra-large and from any location (via secure Internet connection). The development of SaaS coincides with the rise of

TABLE 16.1 Selected List of Useful Software Programs for Sport Marketers

Software Program	Developer	Type	Other Alternative Products
Zoom	Zoom	Videoconferencing	Google Meet, Skype, LifeSize, Cisco WebEx
Slack	Slack	Collaborative Communication	Microsoft Teams, Google Hangouts, Discord, Chanty
Dropbox	Dropbox	Cloud Storage	Microsoft OneDrive, Google Drive, Box, Apple iCloud
Premiere	Adobe	Video Editing	Final Cut Pro, Vegas Pro, DaVinci Resolve, Blackbird
Docs	Google	Word Processing	Microsoft Word, Dropbox Paper, Zoho Workplace, LibreOffice
Sheets	Zoho	Spreadsheets	Microsoft Excel, Google Sheet, Apple Numbers, Spread32
Project	Microsoft	Project Management	GanttPro, Zoho Sprints, Wrike, Teamwork
Tableau	Salesforce	Data Visualization	Google Charts, Microsoft Power BI, Sisense, Domo

the **cloud**, a system of on-demand access where users can store, manage, and run applications. There is a growing trend of SaaS in business, including the Microsoft Office suite of products, which now includes a new service, Microsoft Office 365, while Google has developed a competing suite of SaaS products known as the G-Suite. The benefit of software being stored in the cloud and not requiring physical storage space located on large and extra-large hardware devices is that it significantly increases work productivity for sport organizations because employees travel for meetings but might still be required to access or publish information and data in real time. This is especially important for ERP systems. Employees who are able to travel locally, provincially, nationally, or even internationally are no longer constrained and can use their small and medium-sized hardware to access the organization's ERP system and synchronously collaborate on supply-chain issues, human resource management, and sales. For example, you could be pitching to a potential new corporate sponsor in another province and be able to pull up a key file or data repository to answer a question mid-meeting.

In the case of SAP's Sports One, these traditionally ERP elements are combined with sport-focused elements such as athlete training, fitness, health, scouting, and front-office management, allowing athletes, coaches, scouts, and administrators to develop insights and manage the organization's resources accordingly. Another popular ERP system in sport is Workday. Unlike SAP's Sports One platform, Workday focuses on core business elements, namely, payroll, recruitment, time tracking, and e-learning and training. Sport organizations at the grassroots, amateur, collegiate or university, and professional levels have migrated to ERP systems in response to increasing WFH demands, but in the 21st century, these decisions are still difficult. Sport organizations may resist change, especially technological change, because of the high financial cost required.

Technological change in sport organizations also requires a fundamental cultural shift: as organizations and their people are accustomed to their routine operations, adopting a new technological system (such as ERP) requires a "champion" within the organization to lead the cause and influence others about the technology's benefits (Hoeber & Hoeber, 2012). Thus, while adopting an ERP system that seems logical to younger, aspiring sport marketers and the vice-president of marketing, the reality faced in integrating these systems into the business is difficult when one considers the financial, time, and human resource cost, as well as the need to manage the change within the organization. In most cases, both technical *and* change management consultants are hired for ERP adoption. Typically, a detailed cost-benefit analysis is recommended before undertaking such an installation. To perform a cost-benefit analysis, managers typically utilize a spreadsheet application like Microsoft Excel and create columns of the elements that draw a cost from the organization and those that offer a benefit, providing a dollar figure or ranking to each item or idea.

Data, Communication, and People

Beyond the IT components, IS encompasses data, communication, and people. One of the certainties about technology in sport is that it will continue to expand its capabilities and evolve (Slack & Miah, 2021). For example, shortly after the turn of the century, the "big thing" in sport was the development of high-definition television (HDTV) for sport broadcasts. MLSE, Canada's largest professional sport conglomerate, was the topic of research about whether HDTV was worth investing in or whether sport organizations should wait for the market to fully adopt the technology (O'Reilly & Rahinel, 2006). Today, not only have we adopted and further expanded HDTV toward 4K, ultra-high-definition (with 8K on the horizon), but conversations have advanced to things like artificial intelligence and blockchain in sport (Naraine, 2019a; Naraine & Wanless, 2020). If that is the case, how does technological advancement help those in sport? The answer surely depends on whom you ask, but for sport marketers, the answer is about being able to collect, manage, and access data.

Data is information and arguably one of the most important assets an organization can possess in the analytics age. It is critical for sport marketers and other staff within sport organizations to have access to information to develop new paths and strategies. To maintain a repository of information, sport organizations use a database in their operation. One of the simplest forms of a database is using a Micro-soft Excel spreadsheet to store data about such things as students and employees, along with the transactions and relationships that unify them. Each entity is represented by a table with a series of records, stored as rows in each table, which identifies specific instances of that entity. Across each column are the attributes that each entity might possess. For example, we could have an entity named "NHL player" that stores data about all the players in the NHL. Each row would represent a different player, while the columns could include such attributes as "years-in-league," "team," or "position." This database might be used in its raw form for NHL employees to keep track of each player or as a table on the NHL website where fans can look up information about their favourite player. However, organizations with multiple sheets or complex records might consider streamlining their data repository with a more comprehensive database. For example, MLSE uses Salesforce, one of the leading SaaS databases for customer-relationship management. By using Salesforce, the organization can easily identify and distinguish between customers based on location, sex, income, number of family members, email accounts, ticket and concession purchases, and other facets to provide detailed reports back to the marketing team to help refine their plans and targeted efforts. Once that information is contained in the database, it has to be accessible, since communication plays a large part in the use of an IS. Technologically, we can accomplish this by using a *network* that connects hardware (in its various sizes) to other hardware. Earlier, there was mention of cloud storage SaaS providers such as Dropbox and Microsoft OneDrive. For sport organizations that have leaner operations and do not have the resources to purchase and adopt an application like Salesforce, these cloud storage solutions are preferred given that they simply require Internet connectivity.

Traditionally, sport organizations have relied on connectivity through fibre optic cabling (or simply fibre) to connect their IT infrastructure. Today, fibre remains the preferred method for physical connectivity given its ability to take on greater **bandwidth**. However, with the increased use and deployment of large, medium, and small-sized hardware, sport organizations can no longer solely rely on fibre to conduct their business activities. In the current landscape, there is also a focus on wireless connectivity to supplement fibre within sport organizations and to support staff working remotely (a trend that was enhanced during the COVID-19 pandemic). Thus, it is very important for sport organizations to have holistic network schemes that allow all sizes of hardware to communicate through both wired and wireless means. In some cases, leaner sport organizations may not invest into their own physical network infrastructure and instead will wholly rely on wireless telecommunications providers. For instance, a sport organization may simply purchase a consumer wireless access plan through a major telecommunications company such as Rogers, Bell, or Telus and communicate via Wi-Fi. Ten years ago, this concept would not have been fathomable, given the limitations of Wi-Fi and cellular data services and capacity. Today, Wi-Fi and 4G wireless speeds are much faster, and 5G networks have the ability to allow all stakeholders, including lean sport organizations, to communicate without interruption or concern (Naraine et al., 2020).

Although in IT circles the idea of object-to-object communication is endearing, we often think of technological communication as connecting *people*. People work with software, make decisions based on data, and communicate over a network. People are the component that brings value to the information system in an organizational context and therefore must be managed as its most crucial asset. Therefore, it is critical for sport marketers to recognize that embracing technology solutions is not just about the technical components and their ability to perform the desired tasks, but whether the people within the organization will be able to harness those components and use the technology to its full extent.

Earlier we alluded to the challenges of adopting ERP systems, but this holds true not just for ERP, but for any technological investment. Users must first buy into the idea of using the given technology and then be taught how to use it. Without support in both areas, any technology will fail. In this regard, two trends set to continue in the foreseeable future are important to be aware of. First, Generation Z is entering the workforce (with Generation Alpha close behind), bringing with them a natural affinity for technology—which is both a boon and bane for organizations, as the inherent assumption that staff are competent with and knowledgeable about technology may be offset by the threats felt by older workers, leading to tension, disputes, and change-of-management issues. It is important to note that you should not assume that just because an employee is a millennial or a Gen Z, they are technically competent. Second, and as a partial response to the previous point, life-long technological learning is becoming more prominent in organizations, especially for more complex technological solutions (e.g., data visualization, ERP management). Some employees are learning as a way of coping with the increasing demand on users to be more technologically proficient while others see technology as a way to make their jobs easier. In either case, supporting this personal growth with adequate resources is a healthy investment for organizations.

Information Systems in the Marketing Cycle

With our basic understanding of the IS, we can look more closely at how it fits into the specific context of the (sport) marketing cycle. Previous chapters covered the three general zones in the marketing cycle—the information mainland (situational analysis), the bridge (STP), and the strategy mainland (the Four Ps). Technology enables and supports activities in each zone. This section breaks down technology's role in each and shows how both understanding and managing these technological components are critical in sport marketing. Figure 16.1 describes the process of marketing-strategy development from a technology perspective.

Situational Analysis

Technology applications perform the role of host, gatherer, and compiler in the situational analysis phase. Secondary data that spans television

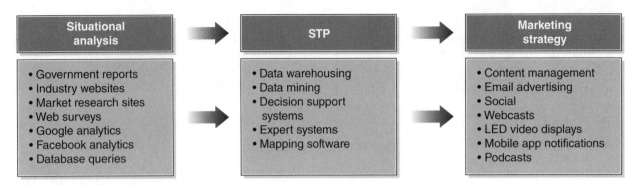

FIGURE 16.1 Technology-based marketing-strategy development.

ratings, performance metrics, and other insights are available online. A high-quality and often overlooked source of secondary information can be found through government sources. For example, Statistics Canada provides key statistics regarding demographics and trends from surveys administered to the public, including the census (done every 10 years) and regular surveys of small portions of the Canadian population. Additionally, the Government of Canada's Ministry of Innovation, Science and Economic Development (formerly known as Industry Canada) is a robust source, providing market size, labour characteristics, and performance data for various sectors. Beyond official government sources, it is also worthwhile to explore more concentrated and focused reports offered by market research websites. Such websites are wide and varied, and prices for reports (both custom and standard) have dropped in many cases due to increased competition in the market research space, although high-end or customized research remains an expensive investment. Canadian firms such as IMI, Charlton Research, and Ipsos, as well as global providers like Statista and NewZoo, can save time and energy but can be very costly for sport organizations. One of the historic trends within situational analyses via technology is to outsource the operation to these well-established securities and consulting firms with the expertise and capacity to pull data and reports.

A series of less formal and inexpensive routes toward acquiring secondary data exists. These include news sites offered by major media or web portals. Google News, for example, compiles its news using algorithms to determine what is most prominent and pressing among a large and representative sample of news websites. Google News is flexible and can be personalized to your interests and needs. Another way to acquire news updates is to use rich site summary (RSS) feeding. RSS is an aggregator of websites and information into an easily digestible format for consumption. This not only allows you to personalize your news, but also to have it delivered to your email inbox, akin to a newspaper delivery. Specially designed aggregator software automatically accesses RSS feeds you have subscribed to and retrieves them. These feeds contain snippets of information and sometimes small pictures. More in-depth information is usually available at the click of your mouse. Overall, RSS feeds are an efficient and personalized way to stay on top of news sites with irregular updating cycles.

Technology also supports the gathering of primary data. The simplest way to do this is to ask website visitors to complete a short questionnaire (with services like Qualtrics and SurveyMonkey). Responses can be collected automatically by a back-end database and stored in the organization's cloud storage solution for future analysis. A more unobtrusive method to obtaining primary data on the Internet is to track customer movement through your website or social channels. Using Google Analytics to look at how users are searching for your brand, click-through rates for online advertisements, and tracking path of pages visited are incredibly useful digital footprints for analysis. Similarly, deriving insights from social channels like Facebook (including Instagram) and Twitter are important given that some of the younger demographic segments are much more inclined to visit social pages than traditional websites.

Ultimately, when a sport marketer is seeking to glean insights from the marketplace, seeking out the engagement behaviours and demographics of consumers in the digital environment can be extremely useful.

Segmentation, Targeting, and Positioning (STP)

In the STP process, as described in chapter 5, considerable focus is placed on technology's ability to analyze data and aid in decision making. Segmentation requires that we establish both mutually exclusive and homogeneous groups of people. This process implies that data about a given population is available to the marketer and can be analyzed. Two database technologies are especially helpful in the segmentation analysis—data warehousing and **data mining**. A data warehouse is a large repository of historical data that allows an organization to analyze trends in financing, market performance, or consumer taste over a specified time and on a broader scale than a regular medium-format database, as is typically used by organizations and individuals, such as a reference database of baseball statistics. Historically, many data warehouses did not update in real time and instead were done on a weekly schedule. Today, data warehouses are equipped to handle the volume and velocity of data and provide immediate updates. KORE software, one of the leading sport business solutions, offers this real-time data warehouse capability, breaking down siloed data and storing it in one easily accessible repository.

Data mining involves uncovering previously unknown trends in the data warehouse. Often this is fully or semiautomatic and relies on complex algorithms or statistical methods. The role of data mining in segmentation is to uncover relevant bases of segmentation for the sport marketer, as chunks of data about consumers are often lost in the depths of a data warehouse. For example, a data mining project could reveal that fathers with male children under 10 years old are more likely to attend Major League Baseball (MLB) games. Teams in the MLB can therefore include age and gender of child as two relevant bases of segmentation and subsequently choose to target this segment. However, segmentation is not relegated simply to physical engagement activities like attendance. Online fans and consumers can be segmented based on their behaviours and demographic attributes. For instance, social followers of MLB's Toronto Blue Jays can be segmented into 20 groups, including mothers, postsecondary students, business enthusiasts, and video gamers (Naraine, 2019b). Therefore, data mining should be considered for both physical and digital consumers. As a cautionary note, data mining comes with ethical concerns. For example, consumers often overlook the fact that their digital behaviours are tracked and recorded, so there is an ethical dilemma for sport marketers as to whether to use that data or if that would violate the privacy of the consumer. Therefore, sport marketers should familiarize themselves with any applicable customer privacy laws before proceeding with this method of analysis.

Choosing the method of identifying and selecting target markets is often complex and cumbersome without adequate support from technology. Technology offers several tools to sport marketers to aid specifically with this decision making. The most common of these is the *decision support system*, which uses mathematical models to represent complex decisions. The systems often use data warehouses, summary data from transaction databases (or data mining), and user input as the data component to arrive at decisions. They can help marketers answer questions related to the size, profitability, and measurability of a segment. *Expert systems* provide yet another supplement to the targeting process. As the name implies, their purpose is to deal with problems the way an expert would. Expertise can be stored in these systems in three ways:

- *Case-based reasoning:* A repository of past cases is kept on reference for access by the ES engine. This reasoning is particularly useful for complex situations with many variables and nuances.
- *Neural networks:* The system "learns" as it goes along by noting which factors have determined success and failure in previous situations.

- *Decision tree structures:* Decisions are made by running data through a series of simple if–then programming structures formulated collaboratively with experts. SAS offers an SaaS product known as Viya to sports business professionals, which is particular adept at performing neural network and decision trees.

Finally, competitive positioning involves developing perceptual maps to visualize the insights gleaned through the segmentation and targeting processes. Furthermore, it allows sport marketers to visualize their brand versus competing brands in the same sector. Visualizing data can be done through a variety of means. Marketers may use SaaS they already subscribe to, such as SAS Viya, or opt for alternative software programs. Microsoft's Visio software is a popular choice within the sport industry given its association with the Office suite of products. However, MindManager presents sport marketers with the ability to create charts, flows, and mind maps as well.

Marketing Strategy

Technology performs the role of distributor and enabler in marketing strategy. While marketers who understand consumers' propensity to use and purchase technology capture only incremental customers today, they almost certainly stand to capture large and fruitful segments of consumers tomorrow. From a consumer perspective, we take advantage of these impacts almost carelessly: We buy online, use various-sized hardware products and SaaS software ourselves, and share our recommendations about popular technology with friends, family, and colleagues. This section will cover the ways in which product, price, place, and promotion have been altered by the technological frontier and its impact on sport from both marketing and consumer perspectives.

The dynamics of promotion and pricing have changed considerably as a result of technological advancements (e.g., social media). Marketers now include digital advertising as part of their integrated communications mix. The most common and wide-reaching tool that marketers use in this capacity is web-based marketing.

Organizations routinely look to advertise their brands, products, and services through services like Google Ads, the advertising program that showcases advertisements on Google's search engine system, as well as partnering websites that host Google Ads for a price. While Google is not the only player in this space—Amazon, Facebook, and Microsoft have also robust online advertising networks—they are seen as the most visible and wide-reaching platform for online advertising given the breadth and pervasiveness of the Google search engine. Whereas online ad promotions of the past would be relegated to simply a banner promotion on the brand's own webpage, today sport marketers are able to specifically target users who search for certain keywords directly on the search engine site or indirectly on a partner website in the future. One of the reasons why this form of online advertising has become more prevalent is the decreased costs associated with online advertising, notably, the price-per-click (PPC) scheme. Traditionally, brands would have to pay other content producers for space on their webpage for an advertising banner. However, with PPC, brands bid for certain key words shown to targeted groups and are only charged if a user clicks on the ad (Choi & Sayedi, 2019). This has led online advertising spending to approach 10 billion CAD per annum (Briggs, 2019). While the total costs of online advertising will vary by firm, sport marketers should expect to spend just under 1.50 CAD per user click given the current climate. While that figure might seem like a lot (approximately the cost of a cup of coffee), consider how much advertising would cost for other, nondigital means such as billboards and newspaper ads and the effectiveness of those means versus the digital medium.

In the modern business and academic environment, sport marketers may also enhance their digital-marketing strategy by using social media advertising. The Digital Media Zone, Future of Sport Lab, and Next Big Idea in Sport innovations described by Cheri Bradish in her perspective are good examples from academia.

In addition to targeting potential customers through search engines and general web browsing, brands are able to target specific groups through their social media usage. Popular social

EXPERT PERSPECTIVE
Sport Innovation in Action

CHERI BRADISH, Ryerson University

Ryerson University in Toronto, Ontario, has been at the forefront of supporting student entrepreneurship and innovation, in 2010 establishing the Digital Media Zone (DMZ), ranked as Canada's leading business incubator, to broadly support and grow tech startups and entrepreneurs. Through a variety of integrations, the DMZ supports bold ideas and solutions for a variety of business problems via digital technologies.

In turn, one industry that Ryerson has well supported in this innovation space is sport and sport business, in 2015 launching the Next Big Idea In Sport (NBIS) Competition, an incubator program between Ryerson University and Rogers Communication, with the mission to identify and address emerging technologies and opportunities in sport, targeting early sport startups via innovative technologies generating creative solutions for the sports industry, as specific to the Canadian market. A number of stakeholders were engaged in this project, including students, sport entrepreneurs—both from the Canadian sport system and the professional sport community—as well as corporate and media partners, leading to the curation and development of Canada's sport innovation ecosystem: a network of like-minded people and partners interested and engaged in "thinking big" about solving unique and emerging problems for the sport industry.

What is particularly important to note about this initial program, as it relates to the global sport innovation and technology landscape, is that Ryerson in fact had become the earliest mover in the sport incubator and accelerator space, being the first external-facing institutional program launched in North America. Subsequently, other industry leaders in this space followed with similar announcements, with the Dodgers Accelerator (Los Angeles) becoming the first MLB team to announce a sport tech program focusing on sports, technology, and entertainment (April 2015), followed by the Stadia Accelerator. The Stadia was announced (June 2015) as a spinoff from St. Louis University's Sports Innovation Hub, to serve as a business venture development accelerator for sport-related startups, providing equity investment, intensive mentoring, and connections to sport business executives. Finally, from the first cluster of sport business incubators in North America, the NBA-related Sixers Innovation Lab (Philadelphia) was created (April 2016) to focus on sport and consumer products, in partnership with the Wharton School of the University of Pennsylvania.

With these announcements, an overwhelming interest and business case for understanding and embracing new sport technology and innovation could be seen emerging from leading sport-business professionals, properties, and partners, and Ryerson continued to be engaged in the sport innovation space, announcing in fall 2018, in partnership with Maple Leaf Sports and Entertainment, the establishment of the Future of Sport Lab (FSL).

The work of the FSL is all aligned to drive new and meaningful, innovative thinking and products to support the "future of sport" via some of the following areas: providing entrepreneurs and startups with access to leading sport franchises, elite athletes, and top sport business leaders; providing entrepreneurs and startups with opportunities to access Canada's top academic faculty and student resources for applied research, needs assessments, insight challenges, and research forums; and facilitating the delivery of complementary sport-business programming at Ryerson.

There are many lessons to be learned from the work of FSL for the sport-business industry and emerging professionals, including the following:

- A solid understanding and integration of sport innovation and technology (including related disciplines, such as analytics) will be a pivotal factor in the future of sport.

> *continued*

Sport Innovation in Action > *continued*

- Experience with multidisciplinary teams, including engineers, sport scientists, and computer science professionals will be part of our reality. Innovative problem-solving (including design thinking) will be crucial in new sport business modelling and related strategy development.

The skills of the sport entrepreneur are often honed early in one's career (especially as an athlete), and these need to be cultivated and translated to business careers, integrated sport-industry partnerships, and related challenges and is key to ensuring relevant sport business education standards. Finally, a broad and open commitment from the leadership of the sport-business community for relevant and rigorous sport business education must be matched by corresponding curriculum that is new and innovative.

CHERI BRADISH is an industry leader and pioneer in sport business education, with areas of expertise in sport business, sport marketing, and female sport leadership. She currently is the founder and managing director of the Future of Sport Lab (FSL), a sport innovation lab and sport tech incubator supported by Maple Leaf Sports and Entertainment (MLSE). She is also the Ted Rogers Director of Sport Business at the School of Management at Ryerson (TRSM), which she joined in 2013 as the Loretta Rogers Research Chair in Sport Marketing, after coming from Brock University, where she spent 16 years at the founding professor of their department of sport management. Bradish has considerable consulting and industry experience with a number of leading sport organizations, including the Canadian Olympic Committee (COC)–Vancouver Olympic Organizing Committee (VANOC), Nike Canada, and the Vancouver Grizzlies (NBA). She is a proud alumna of Florida State University and the University of Guelph—where she was a member of the Gryphons varsity volleyball team (Ryerson Communications, 2020).

---

platforms like Facebook, Instagram, Twitter, and Snapchat, also known by the acronym FITS, experience hundreds of millions of monthly active users (Naraine & Karg, 2019), a seemingly ripe environment for brands to promote their brands. Except, unlike Google ads, which are predicated on search terms, sport marketers promote their own content as "sponsored," interspersing it with other user-generated content (UGC). So, while a user might be hoping to view the Instagram stories of their close friends or family members, every so often a "sponsored" story may appear promoting a new product,

services, or discounted sale price. What makes these social advertisements effective is that they are often decided by *algorithms* that consider multiple factors such as recent UGC, recent content viewed, and demographics (e.g., location, age, gender, sexuality, interests). This is one of the major reasons why a user might experience a social advertisement about purchasing new swimming apparel after posting a recent photo about going to the beach; social advertising can be very effective, especially for those lesser-known brands trying to efficiently counter larger brands with significant market share.

IN THE KNOW

Email Advertising

Email advertising is another way sport marketers use technology to promote their products. In this approach, email addresses of the target market are gathered and included in a mailing list. The mailing list is sent advertisements—new product updates, special one-time promotions, or notifications of in-store events. This has led to much controversy due to annoyed consumers, as some organizations have simply chosen to purchase email addresses from other organizations, resulting in large batches of unwanted junk email, or spam, in consumers' email inboxes. Organizations engaging in these practices run the risk of generating negative consumer perceptions.

In terms of pricing, brands enjoy the increased freedom of selling their products and services online, and typically price them equal to or lower than their physical, brick-and-mortar operations. With respect to things such as sporting goods and event ticket sales, consumers are likely to experience similar prices as simply selling online does not necessarily have an impact on consumer demand and supply (it simply creates a new and facilitated avenue to sell the product). However, because the digital frontier allows sports brands to expand their market reach, different types of products can be priced at marginal costs. Consider the shift toward over-the-top (OTT) sports content. OTT allows brands to circumvent the traditional television broadcasting scheme in favour of a direct-to-consumer product. These OTT products exist online and can be accessed by the consumer using any size of the hardware products mentioned previously (e.g., cell phones, tablets). While subscribing to traditional Canadian sports media channels like TSN and Sportsnet would probably force the consumer into purchasing a cable package, which can often cost upwards of 100 CAD per month, both TSN and Sportsnet offer OTT products for all their content and channels priced at about 20 CAD per month each. Sports leagues offer OTT platforms, too. For example, MLB has an OTT in the form of its MLB.tv offering, which costs much less than similar television-based options provided by regional cable companies. The savings of transporting the sport product via the digital frontier have been passed on to the consumer.

Place, on a smaller scale, has also been significantly affected by technology change. Certainly, the sport product is no longer limited to physical brick-and-mortar stores, stadiums, and arenas. Being able to offer OTT and other digital products means the "place" element of the promotional mix is not in any one location; rather, it is everywhere and anywhere consumers wish to consume. The results of the COVID-19 pandemic, during which many sports were offered digitally only and without fans in-venue, emphasized this point. Consider, for instance, the QR barcodes that evolved from radio frequency identification (RFID) tags. Whereas consumers would previously use the RFID tags, which are no larger than a grain of salt, to track and verify their official memorabilia purchases, QR barcodes also allow consumers to experience additional services and consume more information about their purchase. Using small hardware devices like smartphones, consumers can scan the QR barcode on an item (or even simply a promotion on a poster or social media site or even on a television broadcast) to unlock additional information about the item's supply chain and upcoming sales events. This feature allows sport marketers to amplify their products and services through this exclusive, nonintrusive technology; when consumers scan QR barcodes, sport marketers are able to gather records on where in the world the scans are coming in, from what software OS they originate, and other information that can be used to further the STP process. What is important to remember about QR barcodes is that, as opposed to RFID tags, which can only be realized postpurchase, QR barcodes can be available anywhere the sport marketer believes the consumer will be present. For instance, Nike has recently begun to integrate QR barcodes into professional sports jerseys (e.g., NBA). When the consumer scans the barcode with their smartphone, they can view additional information about the jersey and even see highlight packages of the individual athlete whose name is on that specific jersey. Thus, QR barcodes in sport highlight how technology has shifted the sport place to everywhere and anywhere individuals consume.

Technology can also be directly or indirectly involved with the sport product. With the increased consumption of small-sized hardware and the applicable software applications and programs for the hardware, technology is involved in the whole product and thus is directly involved. In indirect cases, technology can be used to enhance or complement a core product, as is the case with live sport (which was largely nonexistent in Canada during the COVID-19 global health pandemic). Whether attending a hockey, baseball, basketball, or football game, technology was used enhance the live product for spectators. Consider the large video displays (e.g., videotrons), scoreboards, and ribbon signage activating partnerships; there are intricate technological details of consuming the live sport product that are often overlooked by the average sport consumer. In today's sport marketing environment, there are also added technological enhancements, such as providing Wi-Fi to consumers so that they can engage with teams, players, and other brands while spectating (Naraine et al., 2020). However, the indirect effect can also be felt with the technological enhancements to sport equipment. Today, golfers can hit a golf ball further than they ever did before, and this is due in part to advances in both golf club and golf ball technology. Steel iron shafts would have been commonplace for Canadian legends like Moe Norman and Lori Kane, but today's golfers are swinging carbon fibre graphite shafts that are lighter and stronger, allowing for quicker, more responsive swings. In hockey, sticks that were once made of maple or ash wood have largely been replaced with composite graphite shafts, which are much lighter for the athletes to wield on the ice; and "comp" hockey sticks in the modern day weigh in at roughly half of a comparably sized wood stick and have increased flexibility and kick points relative to their predecessors, resulting in quicker and harder shots on goal. These technological developments have resulted in a more exciting (e.g., more goals in hockey) live sport experience, thereby indirectly affecting the sport product.

Technology has affected sport much more than simply in the equipment used to play. Consider more recent developments such as the "Hawk-Eye" in Tennis, which allows athletes to challenge linespersons or umpire calls with enhanced video zooming, or the Virtual Assistant Referee in global football, which can detect whether the ball crossed the goal line in those often-chaotic moments of a match. These technological advancements have also increased the quality (and outcomes) of the sport product consumed by fans.

Perhaps the most wide-reaching impact of technology in sport has been in the distribution of products. With digital capabilities to offer a website and various social media (i.e., the FITS), Canadian sport organizations, whether small and lean or large and robust, have the ability to reach fans locally, provincially, nationally, and internationally in both official languages and many other languages beyond English and French. Over a decade ago, one of the more promising technological pushes was the concept of webcasting. For those smaller or lesser-known sports brands that did not have the opportunity to be televised and reach mass audiences, webcasting was seen as a way to circumvent that broadcast paradigm and maximize key sport events like world championships or Olympic qualifiers. For instance, prior to increased mass-media acceptance, the Paralympic Games utilized webcasts to air the competitions at the 2006 Winter Paralympic Games in Torino, Italy. Today, webcasting is still used, but not in the same way. Observing the benefits of broadcasting more sport events to concentrated audiences, major media properties like CBC Sports, TSN, and Sportsnet have used webcasts to air niche, second-tier sports such as lacrosse, strongman competitions, triathlons, and athletics and track and field competitions with a scaled-down presentation package. However, these webcasts may still require consumers to subscribe to the broadcaster's OTT service, which can be a deterrent for some consumers. In response, sport organizations with limited capacities, such as Soccer Canada, the National Sport Organization responsible for soccer in Canada, have opted for social live streaming services (SLSS). This new form of television broadcast circumvention allows organizations to live-stream events (of all levels), interviews with athletes, and other behind-the-scenes content to their fans and stakeholders via social media platforms. All four of the FITS platforms offer a form of SLSS, allowing organizations at various levels to distribute their product to those who wish to consume, irrespective of place.

Combining this with other aspects of globalization and the relative specialization of nations in their media consumption interests, there is also an increasing focus on issues of supply-chain management (e.g., the various stages required to produce a physical sport good like running shoes) related to the sourcing of inputs from foreign nations. Some broad challenges for supply-chain managers include products taking longer to arrive, complex power dynamics (especially in nations with authoritarian regimes), and intercultural communications. ERP and other logistical systems contribute to coordination, but only so much can be done on the technological front. Therefore, good supply-chain management ultimately requires good technology management as much as good technology.

CHAPTER SUMMARY

This chapter introduces the concept of technology to sport marketing. It provides sport marketers with a perspective on technology and knowledge of the modern tools of IT that are applied to all business environments. The chapter outlines and describes key IT components, including the various types of hardware and critical software applications that have an impact on or have the potential to affect all steps of the sport marketing process. In particular, there are structural, fundamental technology pieces for the sport organization, such as CRM and ERP, and also useful digital enhancements to assist with the STP process. Finally, the chapter provides an overview of how technology impacts the Four Ps.

TEST YOUR KNOWLEDGE

1. Define technology.
2. What are the four types of hardware? What size hardware do you think is most important to conduct business in today's environment?
3. What software applications are critical for the modern sport marketer?
4. If you were a marketing director for Swimming Canada, on what social platforms would you recommend the organization maintain a presence?
5. What is SLSS? Do you see a future for it in sport marketing?
6. Define and describe each of these sport technology-based acronyms:
   a. OS
   b. ERP
   c. SaaS
   d. PPC
   e. UGC
   f. OTT
7. Select any two of the media technologies listed in question 6 and forecast their future impact on a sport of your choice.

KEY TERMS

bandwidth
cloud
database
data mining

data warehouse
enterprise resource planning system
hardware
information system

information technology
software

CASE STUDIES

Visit HK*Propel* for case studies organized by chapter.

CHAPTER 17

Social Marketing in Sport

LEARNING OBJECTIVES

After studying this chapter, you will be able to do the following:

- Understand what social marketing is and its potential in the sport context
- Know when to use social marketing
- Adapt commercial marketing concepts to social marketing
- Understand the complications arising from this adaptation

Many do not realize it, but marketing can also be about **behaviour** change, and behaviour change is an important part of the sport business. Indeed, the impact of sport on society is tremendous: It contributes to economic vitality; it fosters activity and exercise in the population; and it boosts municipal, regional, and national morale. Just like any other industry, however, sport is not without flaw. Behaviour change, whether trivial or major, is sometimes a necessary objective of key stakeholders, including athletes, potential athletes, coaches, administrators, media, funding agencies, and regulatory boards. This is where marketing is most useful. Marketing *owns* the business of behaviour influence. Thus, in these situations where the

"purchase" of new *behaviours* is required, we can use *social marketing*. It is important to note that social marketing is not social media marketing; it predates social media and is simply about using marketing practices and principles to use marketing when the product is a given behaviour. Examples of behavioural change where social marketing has been used effectively are practising safe sex, avoiding drinking and driving, quitting smoking, and curbing alcoholism.

As a marketer, one touches on many different fields (e.g., microeconomics, psychology, etc.), which allows us to coordinate, strategize, and approach the field of behaviour management with a holistic and integrated perspective. Finding situations where social marketing can be applied, assessing the context of the "product" and organization, understanding the various segments of "consumers," choosing a target segment, and executing a behaviour-management strategy are all marketing processes. In doing this, we just have to take the relatively small step from one field of exchange to another.

EXECUTIVE PERSPECTIVE
Gender Equity in Sport: Building a Better System for Everyone

ALLISON SANDMEYER-GRAVES, CEO, Canadian Women & Sport

Since 1981, Canadian Women & Sport (formerly CAAWS) has been recognized as a leader and expert on gender equity and sport in Canada. Our mission is to create an equitable and inclusive Canadian sport and physical activity system that empowers girls and women as active participants and leaders—for the benefit of all involved. In other words, we strive to build better sport through gender equity.

We believe that by supporting women and girls to be active and valued contributors and participants in sport, we can achieve equity for women and girls in society. We advocate to change the sport system, which requires us to look at the culture of sport and the ways that systemic **barriers** like sexism, racism, and transphobia (among others), are discouraging women and girls from staying involved or actively pushing them out. This requires us to focus on changing attitudes and mindsets, as well as behaviour.

Why Do We Advocate for Gender Equity?

Sport can be a powerful catalyst for social change. We saw striking examples in the summer of 2020 as athletes like Naomi Osaka and players in the WNBA and other leagues called for action to address anti-Black racism. Our role as an organization is to help sport leaders and decision makers understand what they can do to maximize the potential of sport in support of equity for diverse women and girls.

Our research shows that while there are enormous physical health, mental health, and leadership development benefits to sport participation, the participation rates of women and girls in Canada are too low to realize these positive outcomes (Canadian Women & Sport, 2020). We know from decades of research that inclusive organizations are better organizations, with stronger understanding of diverse target audiences, more efficient decision making, and more creative thinking. Currently, women are not well represented in sport leadership roles at the coaching, board, or management levels (Canadian Women & Sport, 2020). This needs to change.

Our Approach to Social Change

Everything we do is based on our Theory of Change—a framework that identifies three essential focus areas that will shift the sport sector toward equity. These focus areas are (1) retaining girls in sport, (2) increasing the number of women leaders in sport, and (3) influencing the decision makers and culture setters who impact sport environments (government, media, and corporations).

Our efforts in these three areas are focused on three behaviour change strategies: building knowledge, changing attitudes, and developing competence. We do this because we know that there are many deep-rooted negative beliefs and stereotypes about women in sport, and we cannot assume that our target audience sees gender equity as a priority in their work. Many individuals who want to learn are often unsure of where to start or if they have the right information to make good decisions. Once these decision makers understand the benefits of gender equity, believe in its importance, and have the right tools to move forward, their work to include girls and women will be meaningful and sustainable.

How We Collaborate and Build Partnerships

Our partnerships with the organizations we support are the most important part of our business. We cannot achieve systemic change alone. We collaborate with sport organizations, governments, and leaders to help them understand how they can leverage gender equity to achieve their strategic priorities, from the bench to the boardroom and beyond. We know that our stakeholders have a lot to consider when it comes to the complexities of managing a modern sport organization—and with the impact of COVID-19 on top of already limited resources, many sport organizations are struggling just to keep doors open.

Before a potential partner becomes interested in the solutions we offer, we need them to buy in to our cause and understand their stake in it. Our approach to building knowledge and changing attitudes has always been to meet sport organizations where they are on their own gender equity journey. We communicate to them how using their resources to address the needs of women and girls can help grow their membership (and their bottom-line with it); provide development opportunities for their staff, volunteers, and coaches; and position them to be more attractive to funders. Instead of focusing on "selling" our ideas, we need to convince others to "buy into" them. Real buy-in happens when stakeholders cocreate the change process, inviting discussion, debate, and allowing everyone to feel invested in the outcome.

Advocacy for inclusion has traditionally been associated with charity and philanthropy. But those approaches alone are often insufficient to motivate organizations to make big structural changes or to create widespread adoption. Effective advocacy requires an understanding of the different ways you can articulate the value of your cause to your key stakeholders. It starts with listening to them carefully to understand their goals and needs and identifying how acting on this cause can help them achieve their goals.

Canadian Women & Sport is dedicated to creating an equitable and inclusive Canadian sport and physical activity system that empowers girls and women—as active participants and leaders—within and through sport. With a focus on systemic change, we partner with sport organizations, governments, and leaders to challenge the status quo and build better sport through gender equity. We are champions of women and girls in every arena, from the field of play to the boardroom.

ALLISON SANDMEYER-GRAVES is an experienced nonprofit leader with a passion for social innovation that challenges the status quo. As CEO of Canadian Women & Sport, Allison is committed to achieving gender equity in society through the power of sport. She joined the organization in 2016 as the only full-time staff member and has grown the organization to a staff of 10 employees who are all dedicated to its mission and vision.

What Is Social Marketing?

Social marketing is a relatively new subfield of marketing that was born in 1969 (Kotler & Levy, 1969) as part of a thrust to broaden the field of marketing. Many definitions have been offered since then; however, there is still no consensus on what social marketing is. Some writers have taken a narrow approach, arguing that social marketing is present only where a clear mutual exchange of value has taken place; others have taken a wider approach,

arguing that social marketing is any sort of application of commercial marketing principles for behaviour change. In fact, the question, "What is social marketing?" is often the topic of discussion in keynote speeches and panels at social-marketing conferences. For the purposes of this chapter, we will adopt the seminal definition of Alan Andreasen (2002), a leading scholar in the field who conceptualized social marketing as "the adaptation of commercial marketing technologies to programs designed to influence the voluntary behaviour of target audiences to improve their personal welfare and that of the society of which they are a part" (p. 5). Thus, social marketing involves all the following components:

1. *An adaptation of commercial marketing technologies:* The three 3 Cs (company, competition, and consumer), 4 Ps (marketing strategy), and STP (segmenting, targeting, and positioning) as the bridge between the two concept islands (i.e., commercial marketing and a behavior) are all transferred into the new context of behaviour management. We use this analogy of two islands and a bridge as a guiding schema for this chapter.

2. *Influencing voluntary behaviour of target audiences:* The goal is not to coerce or force target audiences to act in a way that is in line with your goals. As you might know from casual experience with your parents or supervisors at work, negative effects often arise when this approach is used.

3. *Improving the personal welfare of target audiences and that of the society of which they are a part:* The impetus of a social marketing program is usually to foster behaviours that sustain or improve the social welfare of the target audience or society at large—social marketing is benevolent.

In adopting this definition, we note that competing definitions of the field are neither right nor wrong, but simply that this definition is better suited to this book. Using this definition, we can to explore a wide range of situations where social marketing has been or might be used and an array of tools and tactics to use. However, before we can embark on the adaptation of commercial marketing principles for social-marketing programs, we must first address the issue of when to apply social marketing.

When Is Social Marketing Appropriate?

In a landmark social-marketing article published in the *Journal of Marketing*, Michael Rothschild (1999) compared three tools for social change: education, social marketing, and law. Education refers to the change agent's messages that attempt to convince the target audience to change or behave in a specific way but don't offer rewards or punishments in return. Education is the least persuasive of the three tools and will work on its own only when the target audience can perceive that its self-interests will be served. For example, an educational message might read: "Engage in physical activity; it's good for you." According to Rothschild (1999), law is "the use of coercion to achieve behaviour in a non-voluntary manner . . . or to threaten with punishment for noncompliance or inappropriate behaviour" (p. 27).

Law is the most persuasive tool and will work even when the target audiences does not perceive that its self-interests will be served. For example, a change agent's message might read: "Those who do not exercise regularly will not receive health-care benefits." In the middle ground between these two approaches is social marketing, which was defined earlier. In this context, Rothschild adds that social marketing involves the reinforcement of incentives and consequences to shift the balance of costs and benefits so that voluntary exchange is encouraged. For example, a social-marketing message might read, "Tell us your address, and we'll drive you to the gym." Here, the additional costs that one would incur from driving to the gym (cost of gas, physiological effort, and psychological effort) are taken away by the social marketer's offer to take on this responsibility. And so, the question persists: In what situations should one use education, social marketing, or law?

Table 17.1 shows that this largely depends on three characteristics of the target audience: *motivation*, *opportunity*, and *ability* (MOA) (Rothschild, 1999). The table also shows the difference between the eight different segments in terms of a target audience's reality in terms of change. Target audiences are motivated when they believe their self-interests will be served by engaging in the behaviour. In using our first example, the target audience might see the benefits of increasing their engagement in physical activity—getting healthier, living a better life, reducing stress. These people are motivated. Conversely, someone may be very content just sitting on the couch watching television and playing video games and might not see the benefits: In other words, this person has no motivation. Target audiences have the opportunity to

Chapter 17 • Social Marketing in Sport

TABLE 17.1 Applications of Education, Marketing, and Law

Motivation	Yes		No	
Opportunity	Yes	No	Yes	No
Ability	#1	#2	#3	#4
Yes	prone to behave	unable to behave	resistant to behave	resistant to behave
	education	marketing	law	marketing, law
	#5	#6	#7	#8
No	unable to behave	unable to behave	resistant to behave	resistant to behave
	education, marketing	education, marketing	education, marketing, law	education, marketing, law

Adapted by permission from M. Rothschild, "Carrots, Sicks, and Promises: A Conceptual Framework for the Management of Public Health and Social Issue Behaviors," *Journal of Marketing* 63, no. 4 (1999): 24–37.

behave when a known environmental mechanism is at hand. For example, consider children in underprivileged families. They may not have access to recreational programs and so may be more likely to engage in deviant behaviours (e.g., gangs, drugs). These children are said to have a deficient level of positive opportunity. Finally, ability includes the basic skills of the target audience to counter peer pressure, break a habit, and comprehend rational appeals. This also includes the self-confidence of the target audience to make the behavioural change. For example, a coach may be too easy on his players and may not have the "heart" to tell them that they are performing below expectations, even if it is in the team's best interests. This coach lacks the ability (or at least the willpower) to behave in a way to best achieve the team's goals. Depending on the mix of motivation, opportunity, and ability in the target audience, different combinations of education, marketing, and law are suggested. As shown, social marketing's potential as a tool of social change is vindicated by its recommendation in six of the eight possible situations.

Some social marketing scholars have taken the approach of comparing and contrasting Rothschild's work with other frameworks or approaches to behaviour change. However, we feel that this comparison is unfair: The aims of such competing frameworks are divergent because they were developed for a variety of purposes. Whereas Rothschild looked at places where social marketing is appropriate, many other scholars merely describe the best ways to go about social marketing once it has been chosen as a tool for social change. Thus, many (if not all) of the frameworks contribute to the field of social marketing.

Some issues have been raised over the Rothschild MOA framework and its applicability. One issue is the difficulty in evaluating motivation, opportunity, and ability as binary constructs. For example, in looking at college athletes who binge drink, one can discern that motivation to change one's behaviour may differ widely among the target audience. Some students may see the health benefits in halting their excessive drinking, while others may not, considering binge drinking a part of the university experience. Even assuming that the other two dimensions—opportunity and ability—are equal across the target audience, what the change agent decides on as the motivation will determine which tools are chosen. This decision is further confounded by the difficulty and expense of research in social marketing. One can take the approach of using more tools than necessary, but this has a tremendous impact on resources—money, time, and people—which are often scarce in social marketing environments.

This brings us to our second criticism of the model. Often, deciding on social marketing requires significant coordination and buy-in from several different agencies, from internal administration to the media department. This entails the commitment of many resources, some of which the change agent may not have. Thus, although an MOA analysis might confirm that social marketing is appropriate in a situation, careful planning and budgeting are still needed to ensure the resources to execute a social-marketing strategy. In other cases, sufficient resources may be available but the societal costs of the behaviour might not warrant such expenditure. In these situations, change agents must question why they are interested in such behaviour change and the nature, recipient, and volume of potential benefits. In answering such questions, change agents will be able to move toward developing a behaviour-management program they know can work.

Understanding Social Marketing and the Company and Consumer

Chapters 3 and 4 discussed sport marketing research and the sport consumer. As with any other subset of marketing, social marketing is highly consumer focused, and tapping into the needs and wants of each consumer is paramount when formulating any marketing strategy. In doing this, the company and its ability to meet those needs and wants must also be assessed.

Analyzing the company in a social marketing context is similar to that activity in commercial contexts. The main difference is that the findings are often less pleasant. Organizations engaging in social marketing are often in the nonprofit sector and rely largely, or at least in part, on volunteer employees. Even those organizations that are in for-profit industries often only have limited and dispersed resources (if any) devoted to behaviour management. For those organizations without dedicated resources, the first step involves moving the problem up in the organizational or governmental agenda, so that people start to care about behaviour management (and the behaviour change of interest) in the first place. Thus, if you do not head up your organization or if behaviour management is not a normal activity for your department, someone else—an individual, group, or organization— will have to, first, believe in your cause, and second, support your cause with the resources you need. Good candidates for this may include parties whose interest in curbing behaviours are perhaps less altruistic than yours. For example, the highly successful 10,000 steps (daily) initia-

tive in Australia, which as of September 28, 2020, had more than 476,000 members who logged over 243 billion steps (http://10000steps.org .au), was founded in 2001 by a collaboration of Queensland Health, CQ University, the University of Queensland, Queensland University of Technology, Sports Medicine Australia, and the National Heart Foundation.

Another hurdle that social marketers encounter on the path to behaviour change is resistance from individuals, groups, and organizations from other intellectual disciplines who dislike taking a "business approach" to efforts considered to have considerable societal benefit. Since overcoming this resistance will not be easy, we recommend that sport marketers arm themselves with the data and knowledge required as an important step in the right direction. How you frame the social problem, your persuasiveness versus that of your opponents, and other miscellaneous company- and political-centred factors will determine how you fare.

Regardless of the characteristics of your target audience, every target audience member goes about the process of change in a stepwise fashion. Andreasen (2006) calls these four steps the *stages of change*:

1. *Precontemplation:* Target audience members have decided against or are unaware of the social marketer's desired behaviour. In either case, they are not thinking about behaviour change.

2. *Contemplation:* Members of the target audience are weighing the benefits and costs of changing their behaviour. Self-efficacy is an important influencer at this time.

3. *Preparation and action:* Some target audience members are ready to act and do so. Others, however, hesitate to change and need the final push. Andreasen suggests that a potential motivator toward action may be offering some sort of trial behaviour.

4. *Maintenance:* Social marketers often seek to encourage repetition of the behaviour, similar to a habit. For example, it is really no good if an athlete changes their unsportsmanlike behaviour or conduct the first time they are reprimanded. This change has to be turned into a long-standing record of emotional control and self-discipline. The difficulty of achieving this

goal often depends on the type of behaviour, how behaviour change was accomplished, and how constant the change was.

In social marketing, the goal should not be to move members of the target audience from the precontemplation to the contemplation stage, as some behaviours are low involvement, but rather directly to the preparation and action phases. These differences between consumers at each of the four stages of change will be addressed in the "Product" section of the chapter.

Segmentation, Targeting, and Positioning for Social Marketers

The process of segmentation, targeting, and positioning (STP) has implications for resource allocation and competitive strategy in social marketing, which are important in light of generally low budgets (in these situation) and often intense competition in the market (i.e., competing behaviours). Therefore, not employing segmentation in planning could lead to a mass misallocation of resources, which could ultimately go unnoticed in the light of positive (though suboptimal) program results.

Segmentation and Targeting

Segmentation in social marketing requires thinking outside the box and undertaking analysis deeper than what was presented in chapters 4 and 5. Although traditional bases of segmentation might provide information on which segments are larger or growing fast, usually these provide little insight about which segments are most susceptible to social-marketing programs or how prevalent the behaviour is in each segment. The important concepts in segmentation in social marketing are (i) that behaviour is the product, and (ii) that the most influential bases of segmentation are lifestyle and psychographic related. Specific to sport-related behaviours (e.g., doping, sport participation, sportsperson-like conduct, etc.), these bases are very relevant.

Targeting in social marketing targeting usually involves choosing between two strategies—differentiated targeting and concentrated targeting. As with commercial marketing, undifferentiated targeting is not recommended, especially in light of resource constraints. In differentiated targeting, two scenarios are possible. First, if the target can select from a number of alternative behaviours, you may wish to concentrate on different offerings for different segments. For example, in considering an effort by the Canadian Centre for Ethics in Sport (CCES) to reduce doping in Canadian development-level athletes, there are different behaviours, including regular ongoing doping (e.g., steroids, human growth hormone), onetime doping (e.g., painkillers, erythropoietin [EPO]), and not doping. There is also the consideration of those athletes who do not dope and encouraging them to maintain that behaviour (not change). Each of these behaviour options differs by segment of athletes as well, such as type of sport (weightlifting versus curling) and training environment (independent versus club). Thus, the sport social marketer must consider both behaviour maintenance and behaviour change in any social-marketing strategy.

Positioning

In a similar fashion to segmentation and targeting, positioning depends on the social marketer's objective (e.g., to entice the target audience to leave behind a behaviour or to engage in a new one). If it is to change behaviour, then positioning is relatively easy. The only rational appeal a social marketer must make is that the costs of the existing behaviour must clearly outweigh the benefits and that other, alternative behaviours are much better. In commercial marketing, this is referred to as *demarketing*. The quantity and nature of these alternative behaviours need to be closely researched and evaluated to understand the target audience's options to try and eventually adopt one (or more) of them. If the objective is for target audience members to engage in a new behaviour (e.g., a league commissioner would like athletes to be more active in their local communities), this will have to be positioned in consumers' minds in opposition to the alternative behaviours, which presumably are not the objective of the social marketer.

EXPERT PERSPECTIVE
Social Marking and the Paralympics

DAVID LEGG, Professor, Mount Royal University

Let me start by saying that a key outcome that the social marketer seeks in positioning is to communicate clearly to the target audience that engaging in the suggested behaviour is more congruent with their desired self-image and long-term benefits than the competing alternative behaviours. An example of this is the Paralympic movement's approach to changing attitudes toward persons with disabilities through sport and the hosting of Paralympic Games. The social marketing–based efforts of the International Paralympic Committee to build a more inclusive world through Para-sport by challenging assumptions about ability, inclusiveness, and belonging are relevant to this chapter.

Some might question if persons with disabilities can be "elite" or "high-performance" athletes or whether persons with disabilities can be physically active, participate in physical education, or go hiking. The direct and indirect social marketing by the Paralympic movement was aimed at influencing these beliefs.

What the Paralympic movement hoped to influence was the understanding and valuing that participation is not "nice possibility"—it is "a right." The United Nations Convention on the Rights of Persons with a Disability (Article 30.5—The Right to Sport for All Persons with Disabilities), states that "the sport, recreation and play domain, far from being trivial, is essential for fully realizing the human rights promise" (Hubbard, 2004, p. 256).

It is interesting that this premise was the origin of the Para-sport system, with Ludwig Guttmann pioneering the idea of using sport to help rehabilitate injured World War II veterans. His premise was that through sport society and perhaps the service, people themselves would believe that they were capable contributors and worthy of accommodations to enable integration and inclusion. Years later, Robert Jackson, seen as one of the founding fathers of the Paralympic movement in Canada, argued "that if someone saw a person with a spinal cord injury bench press 400 pounds, then surely they could understand that the same person could also work a 40-hour week and be a contributing member of society" (Canada's Sports Hall of Fame, n.d.).

Through the showcasing of athletes and para-sports, the International Paralympic Committee (IPC) and its national associations hoped to reinforce the benefits of being inclusive and demonstrate that the consequences of doing so outweighed the costs. This was also directed to multiple audiences including business, government, and society at large. Each had differing motivations, abilities, and opportunities, so at times the social marketing campaigns had be nuanced. For instance, for corporations, perhaps a "Handicapitalism" approach was best, suggesting that making a restaurant accessible would increase the number of patrons, not just based on the number of people with disabilities themselves, but multiplied by their friends and families. For society it was increasing awareness of the abilities for persons with disability while avoiding patronizing and paternalistic presentations of people that disabilities that have been coined by some as "inspiration porn."

While these social media campaigns have been employed since the end of World War II, much still needs to be done. Society still does not easily associate disability with beauty, and rarely have persons with disabilities been portrayed in the media as "normal" let alone "attractive." James Bond movies are notorious for using persons with disfigurement (or disabilities) as the evil characters and never as the charming, gorgeous hero. A more recent reported example is TikTok, which suggested that moderators suppress uploads from users with flaws such as abnormal body shape, dwarfism, eye disorders, or other "low-quality" traits that would keep uploads out of the "algorithmic fire hose" (Biddle et al., 2020). *Vogue Magazine* got flack, and rightly so, for photoshopping able-bodied persons to appear as if they had amputations to help promote fashion for persons with disability.

A final example was a commercial that was produced during my presidency of the Canadian Paralympic Committee in 2013. Guinness Beer launched an advertisement including a person with a disability playing wheelchair basketball with five able-bodied friends (who used sport wheelchairs). At the end of the commercial the five able-bodied friends stand up and walk out of the gym and all six go the local pub for a beer. The tag line was, "Dedication, Loyalty, Friendship: The choices we make reveal the true nature of our character." When I first saw it online, I loved it, but it didn't take long for me to question and challenge a number of assumptions. Was the voiceover speaking about the person with the disability or his able-bodied friends? The online reviews were mixed, with advertising agencies bestowing awards and disability advocates expressing concerns about the promotion of condescending stereotypes. The advertisement may have been an effort to promote inclusion and bring sport for persons with disability into the common discourse, but it may also have perpetuated negative stereotypes.

DAVID LEGG is a professor and past chair in the department of health and physical education at Mount Royal University with a specialization in adapted physical activity. He is the president of the International Federation of Adapted Physical Activity, the past president of the Canadian Paralympic Committee, and a former member of the International Sports Science Committee for the International Paralympic Committee.

Social-Marketing Strategy

At this point, you can see that marketing can be applied to the product class of "behaviours," just like it can to tangible goods and services. This leads to the next section of this chapter, which is specific to creating the four Ps of marketing strategy in the social-marketing realm.

Product

In commercial marketing, products evolve with the ever-changing needs and wants of the market, and thus, many ultimately fail: Indeed, sometimes, the market does not want what you have to sell. The same is true for social marketing. No matter how many resources are dedicated to convincing a target audience that they should undertake one behaviour or cease another, sometimes people just resist, fail to see the value in that decision, or believe the benefits of the alternative behaviours outweigh the sought-after one. The difficulty in this situation, clearly, is that behaviours are behaviours: You cannot make a behaviour out of better material or put more gadgets on it. It is not a tangible good. All you, as the social marketer, can control is how

the behaviour is *framed*: Is the behaviour called "unsportsperson-like conduct," "trash talking," or "motivating your teammates"? Which of these is more politically correct? Which of these is more likely for people to notice? Which of these is more likely to help you in your social-marketing crusade? Which stakeholders would be inspired by which behaviour? Recognizing that the way by which you define your social-marketing product may be your only leverage point is vitally important to your product strategy.

Price

In social marketing, price is a simpler construct than in commercial marketing. Chapters 6 and 7 explained that a product, including a digital product, can be initially priced in several ways—low to penetrate the market and capture market share or high to skim off the segment of users who are willing to initially pay more for a product. Social marketing *always* takes the former approach. The objective is to frame or design replacement behaviours and products while keeping target audience costs as low as possible. In fact, this "let's make a deal" mentality is largely at the heart of social marketing. For example, if a government's objective is to encourage youth to participate in sport, offering free "learn to play" programs in low-income neighbourhoods may be a viable product offering. Because it is free, the target audience should be more motivated to participate: Costs have been more than offset (for most) by the benefits (e.g., having fun, getting outside, spending time with friends, being active, learning a sport). With audiences that are more resistant, this product might be augmented with other cost-reduction strategies, such as providing transportation, security guards, equipment, babysitting (if the target audience includes parents), or free league membership.

Promotion

The same promotional tools of commercial marketing are available to social marketers. You can choose from advertising, publicity, sponsorship, public relations, sales promotions, and personal selling, although some contextual differences do exist. Table 17.2 summarizes the potential advantages and disadvantages of each tool in the social-marketing context.

Depending on the target audience, a social marketer also has to choose the kind of appeal to make—rational or emotional. In rational appeals, the social marketer lays out objective costs and benefits for the audience to show that leaving behind old behaviours for new is a logical decision: Everybody wants to believe they act rationally. In an emotional appeal, the social marketer appeals to the emotions of the targets, whose behaviour they are seeking to maintain or change.

Place

Place is a relatively minor strategic element in social marketing, although it still requires attention. In seeking behaviour change in sport environments, the distribution of "change" may work through other individuals such as coaches, referees, technical experts, parents, and teammates. In these cases, each member of the chain must also be convinced of the value of the behaviour.

TABLE 17.2 Promotional Mix Assessment

Promotional Tool	Advantages	Disadvantages
Advertising	Wide reach Control the message	Costly Longer development process May not be as credible
Publicity	Wide reach Credible perception of third party	Costly Loss of control of message
Sponsorship	Focused ability to reach targets Differentiation from other behaviours Resource generation	Sponsor may take attention away from cause
Public relations	Not as costly Unbiased third party may signal credibility Ability to leverage brand equity of third party	No control on message Must have human resources with contacts Long-term process
Sales promotions	Wide reach Immediate effects Target gets to try desired behaviour Engage third party (corporate) into promotion	Incur extra costs of communicating sales promotion
Personal selling	Can reach socially "detached" audience members Message can be tailored for specific member Ideal for high-involvement decisions Power of speech	Very expensive Limited reach Variance of sales agent skills Time consuming

IN THE KNOW

Learning from the World Anti-Doping Agency and Social Marketing to Overcome Barriers

Sport faces an enormous threat from doping. In recognition of this threat, the International Olympic Committee (IOC), in collaboration with numerous sport organizations and governments worldwide, founded (in 1999) and continues to support the World Anti-Doping Agency (WADA) and its mission to eradicate doping from sport. WADA was formed with a structure based on equal representation of the Olympic Movement and public authorities, with a funding model of 50 percent provided by the Olympic Movement and 50 percent by various governments around the world. WADA's World Anti-Doping Code defines the rules and policies that it follows.

Target Market: High-Performance Sport

Sport, as an industry, is not homogeneous, and this is particularly important from the perspective of the **antidoping movement** (O'Reilly & Madill, 2007). The segment of sport that is most likely to be affected by doping is the high-performance stream of sport. High-performance sports are those in which performance is the principal goal (Olympic Games, professional sport) rather than development or participation.

This stream is not limited to elite international athletes: It includes any athlete who is on-track to high performance, beginning at quite young ages in some sports. In practical terms, the stream includes varsity athletes, national-level athletes, development-level athletes, and participation-level athletes in high-performance training environments with the objective of achieving performance success (junior national athletes). WADA's programs must target not only the athlete but also their entourage—coach, trainer, family, doctor, massage therapist, and so on.

CHAPTER SUMMARY

Social marketing is a field of study in marketing that has received sporadic attention over the years. However, its effectiveness in encouraging behaviour change in health-related issues (e.g., safe sex, drinking and driving, smoking, alcoholism) is widely accepted and supported empirically. Some marketing theorists and practitioners believe strongly that, as a product form, a behaviour should receive as much attention as a tangible good, service, or idea. This chapter applies the situational analysis, sport marketing mix, and STP concepts to social marketing and uses Rothschild's MOA (motivation, opportunity, ability) framework to describe behaviour change. The chapter closes with the case of WADA and its work in antidoping behaviour in sport, where social marketing strategies and tactics could be applied to support its overall mission.

TEST YOUR KNOWLEDGE

1. Define social marketing.
2. Provide at least three examples of a social-marketing product in sport.
3. Distinguish between education and social marketing.
4. If you were the CEO of the World Anti-Doping Agency, would you invest in social marketing expertise? Support your decision.
5. Provide an example for each of the eight boxes in Rothschild's MOA framework.

6. Explain why the law and legal sanctions are often ineffective in achieving the following social-change objectives: (a) doping, (b) drinking and driving, and (c) safe sex.

KEY TERMS

ability

antidoping movement

barriers

behaviour

motivation

opportunity

social marketing

CASE STUDIES

Visit HK*Propel* for case studies organized by chapter.

CHAPTER 18

Sport Marketing Strategy Implementation and Evaluation

LEARNING OBJECTIVES

After studying this chapter, you will be able to do the following:

- Recognize the significance of marketing strategy implementation in sport
- Describe the three most commonly used budgeting methods
- Identify organizational design elements essential for successful marketing strategy implementation
- Identify project management tools used to schedule tasks in implementation process
- Recognize the importance of marketing strategy evaluation in sport
- Understand the different approaches used in marketing strategy evaluation

This chapter presents the final, and most important, step in the strategic-marketing process—putting your research, creativity, and strategy into action and assessing your success. Initially, this may sound like an exciting step and one that most sport organizations would be willing to embark on immediately. However, this is often not the case. Many strategies, white papers, and planning documents collect dust on the shelf, with no money or work allocated to make them a reality. Taking strategy to action involves three general steps, which are the three key components of this chapter: developing the strategy into resourced action (allocating resources to the

305

proposed strategy), implementing the strategy (e.g., who, when, how, resources), and evaluating the effectiveness of that strategy to determine future action. This chapter reviews each step and presents possible tactics. Developing the marketing strategy is covered throughout the rest of the book, whereas this chapter focuses on **implementation** and **evaluation**.

Marketing Strategy Implementation in Sport

Implementation is a stage when actions are taken and plans are executed in a manner that accomplishes stated objectives. As we discussed thus far in this book, sport marketing strategies are first based on the three Cs of marketing: consumers, company, and competitors. Some marketers seek to prioritize the environment, so they take a green marketing approach and add a fourth C, called climate. Once a sport marketer gathers sufficient internal information (the three Cs), they start to develop strategies about the four Ps of marketing—product, price, promotion, and place—and their mix. In the implementation stage, those marketing strategies are executed and turned into action. Whether termed implementation, operational excellence, activation, or marketing action, the act of putting a developed strategy in place is important to any business, including sport. At its roots, implementation involves the allocation of resources to a developed strategy. The resources may include human resources (e.g., a staff member), financial resources (e.g., an allocated budget), information resources (e.g., developing an online presence and a chain of communication), and physical resources (e.g., office supplies and equipment).

Of all these resources, human resources (e.g., a leader, or a project team) is key to implementing a marketing strategy, while the other three are also vital. Human resources involves a coordinated action across the entire organization to implement a marketing strategy both efficiently and effectively. For this, recruiting and involving team members who are skilled in and knowledgeable about the project area will become crucial. For example, if television

is a key element of the marketing plan for the Canadian Diving Championships finals of the women's 3-metre springboard competition, expertise in television production is required. Similarly, the activation of an in-stadium tee-shirt giveaway at a Toronto Blue Jays home game requires many trained, part-time staff who are energetic, safe, and good with children.

Financial resources or budget realities are also important in implementing marketing strategy. Financial resources facilitate and, at the same time, constrain the execution of any marketing strategy. For example, the budget can affect the human resources involved as a function of salary, incentives, or bonuses. A poor forecast of the required resources during the development stage of a strategy will often lead to a failed implementation. In an attempt to overcome this challenge, sport marketers use several budgeting techniques. Stevens and colleagues (2006) discussed the three most commonly used budgeting methods:

- A percentage of revenue approach— forecasting potential sales and then using actual sales to determine a budget based on a preset number (say 10 percent).

- Task- or objective-based—allocating a budget to each objective of the sponsorship based on its importance and priority.

- An "all-you-can-afford" approach, or maximum allocation—aggressively supporting the implementation with as many financial resources as possible.

Clearly, no one budgeting method is preferable over the others. The budget for implementation should ideally be based on an assessment of the amount required to achieve the objectives of the marketing activity.

Successful Marketing Strategy Implementation

Since an excellent and well-planned marketing strategy is worthless if not implemented properly, it is important for sport marketers to follow tested guidelines in implementing their marketing strategies. In particular, to facilitate the marketing strategy implementation process, a sport marketer will be expected to ensure that a number of organizational design elements are in place. According to Shank and Lyberger (2014), there are seven organizational design elements that make possible the implementation process of a marketing strategy:

- Communication: To begin, an organization must effectively communicate the plan and its rationale to all the members of the marketing team who will execute it. The communication of a marketing strategy and its schedule both internally (within an organization) and externally (with stakeholders) will be important. In particular, the leadership team sets the tone for communication within as well as outside the organization.

- Staffing and skills: Human resources is essential for the success of a marketing strategy. In particular, having a sufficient number of staff who are skilled and have the expertise in the area of the developed strategy are vital for effective execution.

- Coordination: This involves determining the best structure for the organization to achieve the developed marketing strategy. For example, for the best execution of a sponsorship agreement, a public relations department in an organization needs to work hand-in-hand with the sponsorship team.

- Reward: It is important to include a reward system in the execution of a marketing strategy to recognize those who successfully perform their implementation duties. The reward scheme should be available to all in the team and needs to be a performance-based incentive.

- Information: Gathering data at the right time and for a specific purpose and reason and disseminating it to the people who need the information is essential for the successful implementation of a marketing strategy.

- Creativity: Shank and Lyberger (2014) noted that in order to enhance employee creativity in an organization, a creative process consisting of four steps should be used: knowledge accumulation, idea generation, evaluation, and implementation.

- Budgeting: Financial resources are essential for the successful implementation of any marketing strategy and must be allocated to areas of priorities in the implementation process.

Crane (2006) identified a few considerations that were not fully covered in the work of Shank and Lyberger (2014):

- Develop a project calendar that outlines clearly these three items for each specific action:
  1. Task to be accomplished.
  2. Name of the persons responsible for completing the task.
  3. Dates by which by the task must be completed.

- Develop systems to avoid "paralysis by analysis" so that analysis is sufficient but not excessive. This will ensure that resources are balanced between strategy development and strategy implementation and that decisions are made promptly.

- Include a communications plan to encourage open dialogue about issues or problems that may arise in implementation. A suggested course of action to marketers includes the following actions:

  - Develop an open system of problem identification, where
    - problems are identified and communicated quickly,
    - individuals feel comfortable and safe in raising these issues,
    - anonymity is offered, and
    - solutions are developed efficiently and ethically.

  - Provide and communicate about the resources available to help with problems or issues, including mentors, coaches, and resource people.

  - Foster the development of an environment of problem solving rather than one that seeks to attribute blame.

EXECUTIVE PERSPECTIVE
Resourcing Strategy Implementation

PAUL AUSMAN, Manager, Event Services, Ottawa Sports and Entertainment Group

If you were to follow the social media account of either of our teams (the Ottawa RedBlacks and the Ottawa 67s) at any given time during a season, you might think that each post, email, and interaction with our followers and subscribers is made up on the spot and the marketing team is simply "going with the flow" of the given game or the season overall. Although that is true in a few cases because some things that happen spontaneously are prime opportunities to enhance the brand, the large majority of the entire marketing strategy is planned before the season even begins, sometimes even just weeks after the previous season ended.

For each of our teams, we get a committee of staff involved in the marketing strategy who work in different departments who bring their own ideas and perspectives. For example, the Front of House staff (i.e., ushers and ticket hosts) speak to the fans and hear what they want to see, so they bring that back to this committee to be acknowledged. The merchandise staff can bring sales reports and brainstorm about what pieces of apparel sell the best and what could use a push via marketing for the next season, including theme game jerseys. The ticket sales department can tell us which games sold the best and what seat packages could be part of the next season's strategy. Every department has a say and is made part of the planning process.

After throwing all our ideas against the wall, we prioritize them and the marketing strategy begins to take shape. Each department representative is then assigned a task and deadline, and other departments can discuss how they could help each other to achieve a task or how they could compliment it in their own area. For example, for the Ottawa 67s hockey season, we were in the theme game–planning portion of our strategy and my department was assigned the task of figuring out how we could decorate the entrances, concourses, and other public areas for Halloween and Christmas. As the concessions department is part of the concourse area too, the staff shared some ideas on how they could help decorate their line-ups and service counters, which helped us in our planning. Another example is when the partnerships department had a Teddy Bear Toss game, which is part of a fundraiser for charity where guests can either bring their own teddy bear or purchase one, and when the home team scores their first goal, they throw the bear on the ice. All bears and proceeds from purchased bears go to charity. As my department has the most staff on game days, I volunteered to assign some of them to collect the bears from the ice in order not to delay the game. Although it might not seem like a significant contribution to the overall event, it was a big logistical nightmare.

All this is to show that a marketing plan doesn't have to be the sole responsibility of the marketing team. For our organization, it is a collective effort from the first meeting all the way through the season. We attend biweekly meetings to check up on the status of certain action items to ensure that nothing is falling through the cracks, and we help each other out where we can. And in the end, our marketing efforts have been extremely successful in terms of our ticket sales and have also garnered attention on television networks like TSN (Bell Media) and Sportsnet (Rogers Telecommunications).

PAUL AUSMAN is a graduate of the University of Toronto and the University of Ottawa. Currently, he is manager, event services, at Ottawa Sports and Entertainment Group, where he is responsible for event planning and execution for the RedBlacks, 67s, Fury, concerts, and major events. He is responsible for guest services, customer service, in-venue operations, and postevent reporting and evaluation.

Tools for Activity Scheduling

Activity scheduling is a method most organizations use to effectively organize tasks, set timelines, and allocate resources. The wide array of tools available in the marketing literature include Gantt charts, project calendars, operational plans, the **program evaluation review technique** (PERT), and the **critical path method** (CPM). A PERT is a project management tool that provides a graphical representation of a project's timeline. CPM is a project management tool used for scheduling a set of project activities, including tasks along with deliverable dates. The last two methods use critical path analysis to define the order of tasks in the most efficient way to support implementation. Although we present only two methods here, we encourage you to learn more about the others. The project calendar tool is easy to use and adaptable for many implementation situations. PERT is an example of a critical path method that is more sophisticated and therefore suitable for larger and more complex marketing situations.

A project calendar can be created with any calendar software on a desktop computer, laptop, or smartphone. It can also be developed with a hard-copy calendar or spreadsheet. Whatever the recording mechanism, the content of the calendar involves four things: identification of all tasks required to implement the marketing strategy, timing and order of these tasks, estimation of the time required to complete each task, and identification of which tasks can be performed simultaneously and which cannot. PERT involves multiple stages. Anderson et al. (2018) outlined a nine-step approach:

1. Develop a list of activities that make up the project.
2. Determine the immediate predecessors for each activity in the project.
3. Estimate the completion time for each activity.
4. Draw a project network depicting the activities and immediate predecessors listed in steps 1 and 2.
5. Use the project network and the activity time estimates to determine the earliest start and earliest finish time for each activ-

ity by making a forward pass through the network. The earliest finish time for the last activity in the project identifies the total time required to finish the project.
6. Use the project-completion time identified in step 5 as the latest finish time for the last activity and make a backward pass through the network to identify the latest start and latest finish for each activity.
7. Use the difference between the latest start time and the earliest start time for each activity and determine the slack for each activity.
8. Find the activities with zero slack: These are the critical activities.
9. Use the information from steps 5 and 6 to develop the activity schedule for the project.

Marketing-Strategy Evaluation in Sport

Once the implementation of a marketing strategy has begun, the evaluation of that implementation should already be well under way. Although the importance of evaluation is well known to researchers and practitioners in marketing, it is also considered one of the most challenging tasks to accomplish. Evaluation, sometimes referred to as **control** or monitoring, is a critical assessment of plans, undertakings, and outcomes to provide a basis for future informed action. Simply put, the evaluation strategy in marketing assesses how well a plan is corresponding to the objectives and then provides recommendations for adjusting the plan to achieve the intended results (Shank & Lyberger, 2014).

The benefits of a properly planned and implemented evaluation are clear. The results will show what factors are contributing to the success or failure of the overall marketing strategy and provide direction for future marketing activities. To successfully evaluate a marketing strategy, the marketer must assess all factors that influence the reaction of targets, including customers, employees, potential customers, and partners: Did sales or intent to purchase increase? How

EXPERT PERSPECTIVE
Strategic Marketing Alliances

DANA LEE ELLIS, Associate Professor, School of Sports Administration Management, Laurentian University

The sport industry is made up of a series of disparate organizations and institutions, but despite their differences they can, and often do, come together to form strategic partnerships of all kinds. While the structure, purpose, and duration of these partnerships can vary a great deal, when it comes to understanding marketing strategy, one of the most important types of relationships is the strategic alliance. Strategic alliances are defined by the coming together of one or more organizations to meet collective and individual strategic objectives, for the purpose of developing sustained competitive advantage.

Strategic alliances are evident everywhere you look in the sport industry. For example, you may see arrangements between sport organizations and the tourism sector that bring together nongovernmental organizations and sport organizations to facilitate sport for development, and close to my heart, alliances created between multiple cities seeking to act as joint hosts for a sporting event like the Olympic Games. Alliances are generally sought to enhance efficiency, stability, or legitimacy within the partnering organizations by combining their skills and resources; they may form for a variety of reasons or be more focused. When entering into a sport marketing alliance there are any number of objectives the partners may wish to meet, which could include:

- Facilitating: product and marketing innovation, image transfer, and knowledge transfer,
- Providing access to new distribution channels, geographic markets, and market segments, and
- Enhancing messaging credibility, competitor differentiation, and brand equity.

With these objectives in mind, let's look at a few of my favourite examples of sport marketing strategic alliances.

Coca-Cola and Olympic Games

While not all sponsorships may fit the criteria of a strategic alliance, those with long-term staying power and meaningful integration between partners certainly do. One of the best examples of such an alliance is the partnership between Coca-Cola and the Olympic Games. Coca-Cola is the longest serving partner of the Olympics, having been a sponsor since 1928. One of the key benefits of the alliance is mutually beneficial positive image transfer. The Olympic Games benefit from the professional prestige of partnering with one of the world's most powerful companies and Coca-Cola benefits from the positive attributes associated with the Olympic brand. Coca-Cola also played an integral role in developing and promoting TOP, the IOC's multibillion-dollar global sponsorship program. The Olympics have undoubtably thrived financially because of the marketing innovation and knowledge supplied by Coca-Cola in this regard.

Bell and OverActive Media (OAM)

Esports has changed the sport industry landscape in recent years, bringing with it new markets and innovation. Seeking access to new markets (both geographic and target markets), Bell Media entered into a strategic alliance with OAM, the global leader in esports entertainment, in 2019. With 15 teams in seven countries, and three franchised leagues, OAM offers Bell unparalleled access to a growing global market while also providing access to the hard-to-reach 18 to 34 demographic. As a minority partner and founding sponsor, Bell also collaborates with OAM on marketing innovation related to event production, content integration, and experiential activations, among other benefits.

Adidas and Parley for the Oceans

To address consumers' increasing environmental awareness, many sport organizations are looking to integrate environmental considerations into their marketing strategy. However, justified consumer skepticism about the true nature of such efforts can limit their effectiveness. One way to overcome this skepticism is by forming an alliance with a respected environmental organization. Adidas and Parley for the Oceans provide a good example of this. They came together in 2015 with a stated goal of reducing ocean pollution, specifically plastics. Since then, they have collaborated on numerous projects, the most significant of which is the fact that Adidas has produced more than 30 million pairs of shoes, like the UltraBOOST DNA Parley sneaker, using plastic collected from the oceans by Parley. The partnership provides Parley with funds and awareness to help fulfill its mission, while offering Adidas much-needed credibility for their marketing messaging concerning the environment.

Like all marketing strategies, the evaluation of strategic alliances should be comprehensive and ongoing. However, strategic alliances should be evaluated both cooperatively between partners and individually. The reasoning and methods for evaluating a strategic alliance are no different from those for any other strategy. Nevertheless, some specific metrics for measuring success should be considered in addition to determining whether the alliance met its strategic objectives. These metrics mostly relate to the quality of the relationship between alliance partners and can include trust, support, compatibility, flexibility, conflict resolution mechanisms, and the ability to meet expectations.

DANA ELLIS is an associate professor in sports administration at Laurentian University in Sudbury, Ontario. Her main research interests include sport sponsorship and branding, ambush marketing, mega-event management, and organization theory. She has published on related topics in journals such as the *Journal of Sport Management, Sport Management Review,* and *European Sport Management Quarterly* and has contributed to books including the Sage Handbook of Sport Management and the *Routledge Handbook of Sport Management.*

did employees respond to an internal marketing program? Did the organization meet customer expectations? How did it respond to customer complaints? How did it analyze customer feedback? How did it manage relationships with its customers?

Several studies have identified different methods for evaluating marketing activities. From surveys of customer or employee satisfaction to the analysis of sales figures and opinions of experts, these are applicable to a broad range of marketing objectives that may need to be evaluated. Recently, with the help of big data, sport marketers have made observations using sentiment analysis, social media analytics, social network analytics, look-alike modelling, and similar methods. Marketing activities that sport marketers may wish to evaluate include purchase intention, employee satisfaction, product

trials, repeat purchase, donations encouraged, inquiries generated, and public perception. Sometimes developing a measurement metric is difficult. Measuring implementations against objectives that have been set out from the outset of implementing a marketing strategy is an applicable approach for various marketing initiatives.

In evaluating the effectiveness of sponsorship investment, for example, one can assess sponsorship against clearly defined and established objectives that are agreed upon prior to the implementation of sponsorship and the commencement of the evaluation program. If the objectives are SMART—specific, measurable, achievable, results-oriented, and time-bounded—then they give clear direction as to what the evaluation must be designed to measure (Abeza et al., 2020). As Abeza and colleagues noted, companies may seek different outcomes from their sponsorships (e.g., awareness, image, employee morale, product trial, product sales), and different types of measures and designs will be required for each individual objective, along with quantifiable data.

EXECUTIVE PERSPECTIVE

The Business of Asset Development as a Nonprofit Governing Body for Sport

JOHNNY MISLEY, CEO, Ontario Soccer, and Board of Directors, League1 Ontario

Founded in 1901, Ontario Soccer is comprised of more than 600 clubs and private academies servicing over 24,000 teams with 380,000 registered players, 70,000 coaches and managers, and 10,000 match officials, as well as countless volunteers, parents, and supporters, comprising a direct multicultural community of over 1 million Ontarians. Ontario Soccer is one of the country's oldest and largest sports organizations in Canada. Ontario Soccer also operates the Ontario Player Development League (OPDL): the province's premier, standards-based youth development high-performance program and proudly supports Canada Soccer's National Teams, the Canadian Premier League, and Toronto FC of Major League Soccer.

In 2014, at the same time as launching the OPDL, Ontario Soccer introduced League1 Ontario, which was recognized by Canada Soccer and FIFA as a Division 3 senior, semiprofessional or pro-am league. Over a five-year period, League1 Ontario licensed 30 soccer clubs and academies (17 men's division and 13 women's division teams). Also during this time, the league developed and transitioned 190 players (175 men and 15 women) into professional leagues around the world, including the first overall pick in the 2015 MLS draft, Cyle Larin (Brampton) from Sigma Academy of Mississauga.

Ontario Soccer, while dependant on up to 80 percent of its revenue generation from its membership, operates in the modern times as a business and invests resources in securing alternative revenues through a number of creative partnerships.

Approach Your League as a Marketable Asset through Nontraditional Means

In 2012, Ontario Soccer, led by its Technical Advisory Committee and with support of the board of directors, went all in with the implementation of its Long-Term Player Development (LTPD) plan. In 2014, both the OPDL and League1 Ontario were launched to provide a high-performance, standards-based league pathway for aspiring youth and senior ages male and female players who wish to prepare and launch themselves to higher levels of the game. Over a six-year period, the programs (leagues) evolved through marketing of their subbrands of Ontario Soccer, which benefitted off and on the pitch.

While some corporate partnerships were established that identified with this level of soccer in Ontario, it was the higher levels of the game, which in turn invested back into the future of the game, that have proven successful for both leagues. Toronto FC of MLS became invested partners in the OPDL and, through a long-term marketing-rights deal, now has a talent-identification pipeline to their TFC Academy program. In the case of League1 Ontario, rather than a marketing-rights partnership, it became a full sales acquisition of the league in 2019 when it was purchased by Canada Soccer Business, the Canadian Premier League's parent company and marketing agency. With the launch of the CPL in Canada in 2019, what better way to not only launch the country's professional division 1 league than to also announce League1 Ontario as its official development league?

Know Your Organizational Mandate and Programming Asset Priorities

It takes considerable resources to operate a provincial high-performance, standards-based program and league in any sport. With 80 percent of Ontario Soccer's registered players under the age of 18, over time it became apparent that sustainability of both programs and leagues for the long term would require knowledge of their mandate as an organization and the priorities that go with it.

Ontario Soccer's core programming is centred on the development of youth age players and the supporting grassroots structure below it. Therefore, in order to focus on the key resources to further develop the OPDL, it was decided that League1 Ontario needed to be managed and operated by an outside organization. This was a difficult decision for the organization, but it was necessary for the good of both leagues. The key was finding a suitable partner that would allow the linkage between the OPDL and League1 Ontario or its player development pathway would remain intact.

Timing Is Everything

The CPL, Canada's domestic professional soccer league made for Canadians by Canadians, arrived on the scene and launched in 2019 with seven franchises across Canada. The league filled a huge void within the pathway for men's soccer talent in Canada. A future women's professional league is also a part of a long-term vision for soccer in Canada.

For Ontario Soccer, the fit was perfect. Rather than working with a traditional third-party service provider to operate the league, it was decided to sell the league to Canada Soccer Business, which owns and operates the CPL, and uses the transaction to garner both cash and value-in-kind (VIK) assets to reinvest back into Ontario Soccer's programming. Furthermore, League1 Ontario was structured as a new associate member organization of Ontario Soccer. This membership structure maintains the link of channelling graduating players from the OPDL directly into League1 Ontario, all while under the governance of Ontario Soccer. The deal was conceived, approved, and announced in December 2018.

It Is All about Partnerships with a Vision, Not Just Selling an Asset

The most difficult deal to accomplish was the valuation on selling a four-year-old league that is made up of predominantly male and female amateur players and built under a business model of license holder clubs and academies rather than franchisees. In the end, the valuation of sale was agreed to by both parties motivated, congruent with a vision of CSB's professional soccer model in Canada and supported by Ontario's strength and ability to produce high-quality national team and professional soccer players through its high-performance, standards-based programs.

JOHNNY MISLEY has served as Ontario Soccer's chief executive officer since 2015 and is leading the modernization of the organization, including the implementation of innovative business practices to support the emerging demand of its membership at all levels while expanding opportunities for players, coaches, and referees at the higher levels of the game. He holds a bachelor of physical education degree (coaching sciences) and a master's degree (sports management) from the University of British Columbia. He spent 27 years of his professional career in hockey, working at the national level, and has been a part of national team management of 14 gold medal championships, including five Olympic Gold Medals (2002, 2006, and 2010 Olympics). He is passionate about everything from the playground to the podium and about the power of sport.

IN THE KNOW

Implementation Plans Need to Be Designed to Use

Although we, the authors, are professors, we also have many years of experience between us working in sport, sitting on boards, consulting, and working at major events. One thing we have learned and that we cannot stress enough is a very simple tidbit of advice but one that we would say is among the most important in the entire book: It is essential to create your strategy and implementation plans in such a way that they get used. There are many very good and well-researched strategies and implementation plans that sit on the shelf or on a hard drive or in the cloud that are never used. For us, the best indicator of a great strategy is one that gets adopted and implemented, and the best implementation plans are ones that get tested and revised.

How do you make that happen? Here are few things we have learned.

1. Keep your strategy in an easy-to-use format—one page if you can do it.
2. Make sure all your strategy goals and implementation steps (i) have timelines and (ii) are measurable.
3. Put key staff (and the most appropriate staff) in charge of each element of the implementation plan.
4. Revise your plans, as a group and with buy-in from all key staff, often (monthly if possible).

CHAPTER SUMMARY

The process of implementing and then evaluating a marketing strategy is vital to a sport organization. These processes, which are based on the principles of performance and feedback, are actions that must not be neglected by marketers; however, they often are. This chapter provided content, direction, and tools for implementing and evaluating marketing action. It should be clear that no marketing action is implemented without a detailed plan, which includes tasks, human resources, financial resources, time, and evaluation (the last task occurs at all stages. The chapter specifically (a) identified the three most commonly used budgeting methods (percentage of revenue, objective based, and "all-you-can-afford"), (b) the seven organizational design elements essential for successful marketing strategy implementation (communication, staffing and skills, coordination, rewards, information, creativity, and budgeting), and (c) two project management tools used to schedule tasks in the implementation process, the program evaluation review technique (PERT) and the critical path method (CPM). The chapter concluded by briefly discussing the different approaches employed for evaluating marketing activity, including evaluation against clearly established objectives.

TEST YOUR KNOWLEDGE

1. Define marketing strategy implementation.
2. Briefly discuss the significance of marketing strategy implementation in sport.
3. Identify the three most commonly used budgeting methods.
4. List the seven organizational design elements essential for successful marketing strategy implementation.
5. What two critical path analysis methods are used for activity scheduling?
6. Define marketing strategy evaluation.

KEY TERMS

control
critical path method

evaluation
implementation

program evaluation review technique

CASE STUDIES

Visit HK*Propel* for case studies organized by chapter.

CHAPTER 19

Olympic Marketing

LEARNING OBJECTIVES

After studying this chapter, you will be able to do the following:

- Appreciate the history of Olympic marketing
- Understand the place of television in the Olympic movement
- Know the significance of the Olympic Program (TOP) for the Olympic movement
- Understand the role of branding in the Olympic movement
- Learn about the structure of the Olympic movement in Canada
- Appreciate the benefits and risk of hosting the Olympic Games

The Olympic Games have become a global icon of sport. They are best described as a mega-event. Held every two years—alternating between the Olympic Games and the Olympic Winter Games—this multisport spectacle draws thousands of the world's best athletes, millions of attending fans and tourists, and billions of television viewers worldwide. It has evolved into a big business. This chapter provides a historical perspective on the development of the Olympics, including the role of marketing (television, digital, and sponsorship), key events that have had an impact on the **Olympic movement**, which includes all the organizations, associations, and events associated with or linked to the Olympic Games, the impact of the 2010 Olympic Winter Games in Vancouver, and the future of the Olympic movement in Canada.

EXECUTIVE PERSPECTIVE

A High-Performance Approach to Preparing Canada for the Olympic Games

ANDREW BAKER, Vice-President, International Relations and Public Affairs, Canadian Olympic Committee

There is much talk, and debate, when it comes to the hosting of Olympic Games. This is no surprise: As the world's biggest sporting event, it has a significant impact on the host city, region, and country.

In Canada, we have hosted three editions of the Games: one Olympic Summer Games (Montreal 1976) and two Olympic Winter Games (Calgary 1988, Vancouver 2010). Vancouver 2010 included the first Paralympic Games to be hosted in Canada. In addition, Canada has hosted three editions of the Pan Am Games and the Commonwealth Games four times. For a country of our size, we have rich and meaningful hosting tradition.

As described throughout this chapter, the Olympic Games are a complex undertaking, the operations of which could fill a textbook on their own. Thousands of stakeholders play a role in bringing the event to life, planning for everything from venue construction to transportation and to providing meals and accommodation for thousands of athletes, coaches, staff, and volunteers. Every Olympic Host City creates a local organizing committee (LOC) that is charged with delivering the Games and generating significant revenues to cover organizational costs.

In addition, the more than 200 national Olympic committees around the world work to best prepare their teams for successful competition. In Canada, this process starts more than five years before the Games and involves hundreds of trips to the host city to prepare Team Canada for all elements of the Games. We work to ensure the best possible performance environment for our team by building strong relationships with the LOC and other local groups that can help us deliver our operations with a high-performance focus. In addition to our operations in the athletes' village and work with the LOC, we secure hundreds of hotel rooms for additional staff, host a Canada Olympic Hospitality house, secure vehicles and drivers, and source storage and warehouse space, among hundreds of other logistical elements. Olympic operations are no small feat for anyone involved.

So why host an Olympic Games? The easy answer is *impact* and *legacy*. Hosting Games has the ability to leave a lasting positive impact on a host city and its residents. Each legacy is different and focused on different outcomes, but the strongest hosts will "begin with the end in mind," to use a term coined by Stephen Covey.

In Montreal, where cost overruns of the Olympic Stadium from the 1976 Games dominate the legacy discussion, many positive impacts and legacies remain untold. The Montreal Games drove an improved structure of the Quebec sport system, increased support for high-performance athletes and coaches, and left a meaningful venue legacy in use to this day, nearly a half-century later. In fact, I personally spent a significant amount of my nights and weekends as a teenager running track at Centre Claude Robillard, a 1976 Games venue that has become a high-performance hub in the city.

In Calgary, the 1988 Games legacies are significant, positive, and wide-ranging. The 1988 Games venues support the training of hundreds of Olympic and Paralympic athletes and continue to host international competitions in numerous sports. Legacy funds from 1988 Games surpluses still support sport development, coaching, and venue operations in Calgary and across the country. The Canadian Olympic Committee benefits from a legacy fund that has grown to over 150 million CAD.

The 2010 Games in Vancouver brought the country together like very few things in our history. Canada's success on the field of play continues to be an important legacy of those Games. A reorganization of high-performance sport-funding systems and additional investment were the driver of a record-setting performance in 2010 and the Games that have followed. Vancouver 2010 left a significant number of well-used legacies—sport and otherwise—that have added immense value to communities in and around Vancouver. In some cases, infrastructure priorities were accelerated, such as the "Canada Line" transit from Vancouver Airport, the sea-to-sky highway that connects Vancouver to Whistler, and the Vancouver convention centre. In many cases, Olympic and Paralympic venues continue to serve the community in which they stand (e.g., Richmond Oval, Hillcrest Community Centre, Whistler Olympic Park).

In recent years, the International Olympic Committee (IOC) has sought to make hosting the Games more efficient through its Agenda 2020, an approach that seeks to lower the cost and complexity of hosting and ensure that the Games leave a lasting positive legacy for host cities. Canada is well positioned to capitalize on these changes as it considers the future of hosting of another Games. The only question is "Where next?"

ANDREW BAKER joined the Canadian Olympic Committee (COC) in 2005 and has participated in six Olympic Games, four Pan American Games, and three Youth Olympic Games. Named as director, Games, in 2013, Andrew oversaw the planning and delivery for Canada's largest ever multisport Games delegation at the Toronto 2015 Pan Am Games and Canada's most successful Winter Olympic Games team, at PyeongChang 2018. Following the PyeongChang Games, Andrew joined the COC's senior leadership team as the executive director, Games and international relations, and in October 2019, he became vice-president, international relations and public affairs. In this role, he is responsible for leading the COC's efforts to bring the Olympic Games back to Canada. Andrew is a graduate of the sports administration program at Laurentian University and the Queens University and Cornell University Executive MBA Americas program. In 2015, he was recognized as one of the "5 to Watch" in Canadian Sport Business.

History of Olympic Sponsorship: 1896 to 1976

Baron Pierre de Coubertin's dream of reviving the Olympic Games was to establish a broadly based social movement that, through the medium of sport, would celebrate physical culture and art, promote international understanding, and inspire people to reach higher and farther while growing stronger in mind and body. He was convinced that the Olympic ideal would help promote universal values such as mutual understanding, friendship, and tolerance, which, in turn, would contribute to build a better and more peaceful world (Muller, 1986).

Since the revival of the Olympic Games in 1896, the commercialization of the Olympic movement has led to many strong and heated debates. Yet this was not a new phenomenon. The ancient Olympic Games, held in the honour of the god Zeus, could not have been celebrated without the financial support from various Greek states and wealthy Greek men. As far back as 525 BCE, commemorative medals were sold to finance the Games (McMahon, 1996). This suggests that even in those days, the organizers of the Games were concerned about how they could stage the event.

Like the Greeks of ancient times, de Coubertin was concerned about the cost of hosting the Olympic Games and the source of financing. It should be no surprise that marketing would play a vital financial and supporting role in the Olympic movement from the beginning. The 1896 Athens Games was funded by stamps, ticket sales, commemorative medals, program advertisements, and private donations (McMahon, 1996). The donation by Greek philanthropist George Averoff of 390,000 USD—a very large sum in 1896—combined with the issuance by the Greek government of the first series of commemorative stamps of the Olympic Games to provide the funds necessary for their success (Landry & Yerlès, 1996). The

IN THE KNOW

Vancouver 2010: A Look Back at a Well-Marketed Olympics

The following points illustrate the smart marketing that happened around the Games.

- The Canadian Olympic Committee (COC) and Canadian Paralympic Committee (CPC) signed an agreed to transfer all commercial sponsorship and licensing rights to its marks from 2004 through 2012 to the Vancouver Organizing Committee for the Olympic and Paralympic Winter Games (VANOC), leading to a joint marketing program and a revenue-sharing agreement.

- For the first time in the history of the Olympics in Canada, the Games were not broadcast by CBC. A coalition of networks led by Bell Globemedia outbid CBC to broadcast both the Vancouver 2010 Games for $90 million and the London 2012 Games for $63 million. Note that this is the first time that payment for the Olympic Winter Games has exceeded that for the Olympics in Canada, demonstrating the value of hosting in Canada. CTV's subsidiaries for 2010 included TSN, the French-language RDS, and the Outdoor Life Network. Rogers's holdings, as of 2010, included Sportsnet and the Omni and 43 radio stations. In Quebec, TQS was the main carrier, with RDS helping out in coverage. This decision was reflective of the IOC's strategy to change from having one broadcast partner per country to a diversification of partners, or multiple broadcasters (e.g., CBC, TSN, TQS, RDS), thus maximizing the hours broadcast on television. By having a national carrier like CTV, it also accomplished its policy (at the time) of ensuring that the Olympic Games were available free of charge to the largest audience possible. If consumers want more, they can turn to (and purchase) the specialty channels.

- The opening and closing ceremonies of the Vancouver Games are the second and third most watched television programs in Canadian history, drawing 14 and 13 million Canadian viewers, respectively.

- Vancouver's sponsorship program is arguably the most successful sponsorship program in Canadian history. In focussing on quality over quantity, and given that TOP sponsors already had a number of categories spoken for, VANOC limited the number of domestic sponsorships to 57 partners using a three-tier system: Tier I consisted of 6 national partners, Tier II was 15 supporters, and Tier III was 36 suppliers. In total 688 million USD in revenue was generated for domestic sponsorship (IOC, 2020). The program was managed with many resources, and the Tier I partners included some extensive activations, including (i) the Bell Athletes Connect Program, (ii) RONA's "Growing with Our Athletes," (iii) RBC's "Olympians Program," and (iv) Petro-Canada's "FACE—Fueling Athlete and Coaching Excellence."

- VANOC build a successful licensing program, which granted companies the right to use VANOC and COC marks on goods for retail sale. In total, VANOC sold 48 licensees for a total of 51 million USD in revenue (IOC, 2020).

- Vancouver 2010 was one of the first Games to embrace a digital offering of its content, reaching 130 million digital views globally, in addition to 1.8 billion via television and 2,700 hours of content (IOC, 2020).

- Ticketing was a focus of VANOC, leading to 97 percent of the 1.5 million available tickets being sold for 250 million USD in revenue (IOC, 2020).

- Almost four years before the Games, VANOC hired a number of individuals who were dedicated to brand protection (against ambush marketing—see chapter 15). Such a commitment was a first for any Olympic Games. In addition, VANOC has created a comprehensive education program to provide its stakeholders with information about the meaning and importance of protecting the brand. Further, antiambush legislation aimed at increasing its effectiveness in protecting the Olympic brand from grey ambush, Bill C-47, the Olympic and Paralympic Marks Act, was put forward by VANOC and supported by the federal government.

official Olympic program of the 1896 Games had advertisers (including Kodak, who later become a TOP sponsor). The Games of 1900, 1904, and 1908 were closely connected with international trade. The 1900 Olympic Games in Paris were conducted within the program of the International Universal Exposition in Paris, whose central objective was the promotion of industry and trade. Its financing was assured mainly by the French state through global subsidies granted by the Ministry of Commerce and Industry (Landry & Yerlès, 1996). The 1904 Olympic Games in St. Louis were held adjacent to the St. Louis World's Fair. The 1908 London Olympic Games were linked with the Anglo-French exhibition, which covered all capital costs of the Games, which were reported to be £60,000, or 75 percent of their total costs (Landry & Yerlès, 1996).

Financing the Olympic Games continued to be a challenge through the years and is still an issue today. The responsibility to finance Games has always been left up to each organizing committee. The 1912 Stockholm Games were a milestone because they marked the beginning of true marketing in the Olympic movement and were reported to be a financial success, with direct contributions from the states and the city of Stockholm accounting for only 2.5 percent of the total revenues, while sponsorship contributed twice as much to the revenues of the Organizing Committee for the Olympic Games (OCOG), and a Swedish lottery accounted for 51 percent of the revenues.

De Coubertin was troubled by the escalating financial considerations of hosting the Games and the potential cost that commercialization could have on the Olympic ideals (Landry & Yerlès, 1996). He was also concerned about the excessive usage of the title "Olympic Games" in many countries. This led the IOC to protect the title and establish guidelines about its use in 1913 (Martyn, 1996).

In the years that followed, **commercialism** grew. Commercialism is widely described as a profit-motivated approach to business. It was reported that the official program for the 1920 Antwerp Olympic Games had so many advertisements that was difficult to find content related to the Games themselves (McMahon,

1996). Four years later, at the 1924 Paris Olympics, venue advertising (i.e., signage) was permitted for the first (and only) time.

In the 1928 Amsterdam Games, revenues from ticket sales, **rights fees**, and various contracts were able to cover over 60 percent of the total costs of the Games. In addition, the first forms of merchandising were observed (Preuss, 2000), leading to the first instances of logo registration, trademarks, and copyrights to protect those marks.

During the 1932 Los Angeles Games, the relationship between businesses and the Olympics continued to expand and is widely reported to be responsible for the Games' success. Following the 1932 Games in the second largest city in the United States, the Olympics became a platform for businesspeople, hotels, and travel agencies to use to boost tourism in the area (Trumpp, 1998). Several advertising agencies were contracted by the organizing committee for the right to use Olympic symbols and emblems for a variety of advertising campaigns. Despite the efforts in 1928, however, the word "Olympics" and "Olympiad" continued to be used by other entities without permission.

The first live coverage of an Olympic Games for people watching at home was provided by the British broadcaster BBC at the London Olympic Games in 1948. Only 80,000 homes in Britain could receive the signal, and the BBC paid about $4,000 for the television rights (Landry & Yerlès, 1996). Two Games later, in Melbourne in 1956, television network executives reportedly refused to pay for the rights to telecast what they perceived as news footage on a tape-delayed basis (Wenn, 1994). This resulted in a virtual **blackout**. After Melbourne 1956, the IOC added to its charter a new rule, Rule 49, governing publicity, which provided strict controls on bona fide news coverage of the Games, stipulating that live television rights to the Games were to be sold by the OCOG as approved by the IOC. Many view this as the first step toward the concept of "exclusivity," a driver of future revenue for the Game.

Starting in the 1950s, the Olympics were attracting a very large number of television viewers, leading to increasing rights fees paid by network, which in turn charged advertisers ever-increasing fees to promote them during telecasts of the Olympic Games. This trend represented a key turning point as television shifted its coverage of the Olympics from news to entertainment. By the 1960 Squaw Valley Olympic Winter Games and Rome Olympic Summer Games, the principle was established that the Games were entertainment and therefore could be sold.

As technology involved with the quality and diffusion of televised content increased, television emerged as the driver of international growth for the Olympic Games and the global communication of the Olympic ideal, as well as revenue for the OCOG and the IOC. The television rights to the 1960 Rome Games were sold for 2.88 million USD and the Games were shown live in 18 countries throughout Europe. Now, for the first time in the history of the Olympics, people anywhere could watch the Games live from afar. The 1964 Tokyo Games were transmitted around the world "live," which created new dynamics, and entertainment became an integral part of the now "global" Olympics, which was watched by millions.

Later in the 1960s, television network ABC decided to make sport a focus of its programming, including acquiring the television rights to the Olympic Games in the United States, which resulted in improved quality of programming, increased audiences, rights fees, and advertising, and increasing sport content on television. The value of these Olympic rights was demonstrated in 1968, when ABC secured 20 million USD in advertising revenue from corporations such as Coca-Cola, Ford, Texaco, Pan American Airlines, and Goodyear, having paid only 4.5 million USD for those rights (Wenn, 1995). This led to a trend of increased television coverage of sport, increasing demand for that coverage, and resulting growth in rights fees and advertising revenues. In 1967, the IOC created a finance commission to improve its business and negotiate its television deals; and in 1972, television rights replaced ticket sales as a principal source of income (Wenn, 1995).

Despite the increasing revenues, the IOC president at the time, Avery Brundage, was con-cerned about the loss of autonomy due to the increased influence exerted by economic (e.g., television, advertisers) and political interests. His strong opposition to the commercialization and the professionalization of the Olympic Games led to a struggle between people who defended the traditional Olympic ideology and others adapting to the reality of marketing and sponsorship in the Olympic world itself. Brundage's efforts to achieve two divergent aims—the pursuit of commercial television revenue for the IOC and its affiliated organizations and the preservation of the IOC's image—made for some interesting debates during the 1960s, since money was a dominant topic of discussion in the Olympic movement. The troubled Brundage questioned the commitment of the International Federations (IF) and National Olympic Committees (NOC) to amateur sport and to the Olympic ideals. To him, they seemed more interested in pursuing a sizable share of Olympic television money. The IFs, in Brundage's mind, had adopted a "disgraceful" profit-making stance with respect to television revenue generated at both the Olympic Games and the World Championship (Wenn, 1994, 1995). Brundage was also displeased with the lax enforcement of the rules of amateurism by a number of IFs in such sports as soccer (world football), figure skating, skiing, and basketball. However, television contributed to making athletes in those sports into huge celebrities, and it became important for athletes and for some sports to resist benefitting from their successes and popularity (Preuss, 2000).

The 1972 Munich Games reported a deficit of 667 million USD, while Montreal 1976 had a reported loss of 1.2 billion USD (Preuss, 2000), not positive figures for the IOC and cities interested in bidding for future Games.

Under Lord Killanin's presidency, the IOC had put in place some changes that paved the way for future commercialization of the Olympic Games. In 1973, the IOC decided to grant permission to the Montreal Organizing Committee to use the Olympic emblems for publicity or commercial purposes. The OCOG for Montreal launched a marketing program with what, at the time, was an innovative three-tier sponsorship program:

Chapter 19 • Olympic Marketing

IN THE KNOW

Financial Stakes of Hosting Olympic Games—1976 Montreal Olympic Games

Montreal won the rights to host the 1976 Olympic Games over Los Angeles and Moscow by promising very modest Games with a price tag of 125 million USD. It was the first time Canada would host an Olympic Games. In 1973, Mayor Jean Drapeau famously stated: "The Games could no more have a deficit than a man could have a baby" (Ludwig, 1976), which proved to be very wrong. The expenditure directly related to hosting the organization of the Olympic Games amounted to about 1.6 billion USD—$1.2 billion for the Olympic Park and Olympic Village and $380 million for the OCOG operating costs and related expenses (Landry & Yerlès, 1996). The official report of the 1976 Montreal Games established the overall deficit of the OCOG at $981 million as of April 1977. The fact that the cost of the Olympic facilities increased more than 10-fold between the forecast in 1969 and the reality in August 1976, with a gap equivalent to $1.2 billion, received much press coverage and did little to enhance the Olympic movement (Landry & Yerlès, 1996). When including the interest paid on the debt over the years and the additional $537 million required to complete the facilities after the Games, the Olympic debt totalled an estimated 1.6 billion USD (Todd, 2016). According to reports, the debt was finally paid off by municipal and provincial tax dollars in 2006.

Regrettably, the financial situation tarnished the otherwise well-organized and successful 1976 Olympics Games in Montreal and their positive effects on the development of amateur sport in Canada through the onset of government funding for sport. The Games also led to considerable publicity and television coverage for the Games in Canada.

- Official Sponsor: 150,000 USD or more
- Official Supporter: 51,000-149,000 USD
- Official Promoter: up to 50,000 USD

A total of 628 companies with branches in 47 countries signed sponsorship agreements with the Montreal Games and 42 companies were recognized as "official sponsors" (Landry & Yerlès, 1996). About 20 million USD ($7 million in cash and $13 million in-kind) was raised through the sponsorship program. Had the organizers recognized the potential of marketing sooner than 18 months prior to the Games, it is believed that this figure could have been much higher (Stauble, 1994).

IOC's Sponsorship Expansion: 1976 to the Present

Following the financial losses incurred at the 1972 and 1976 Games and the 65-country boycott of the 1980 Moscow Games, for many years

public opinion seemed to be consistent worldwide: Hosting the Olympics was not worth the financial risk. This was clearly demonstrated when only Los Angeles bid for the rights to host the 1984 Olympic Games, with the organizers promising that they would be financed by the private sector and that no subsidies or loans would be obtained from the local, state, or federal public administrations.

Another important precursor to commercialization implemented by the IOC was the introduction of the new eligibility Rule 26 in 1974, which made each IF responsible for determining who would be eligible to participate in the Olympic Games. This decision opened the door to the advanced professionalization of the Olympic Games since this led to the IFs structuring eligibility requirements to gradually allow athletes to compete while receiving money from sponsors, governments, and universities. In 1987, the IOC decided that professional tennis players would be eligible to compete in the 1988 Olympic Games, and in 1992, professional basketball players debuted at the Games, highlighted by the "dream team," including Michael Jordan.

The 1984 Los Angeles Games were a tipping point for **Olympic marketing**, even though it had been part of the modern Games since 1896. However, after Montreal and leading into Moscow 1980, Los Angeles was the only city making a formal bid to host the 1984 Games, promising that their Games would be financed totally by the private sector. Under the guidance of Peter Ueberroth, sound business principles were applied to the organization of the Games, which was a major shift for the Olympic Games (McMahon, 1996). Indeed, for the first time in their history, the Olympic Games were totally organized, administered, and financed by private enterprise.

Following 1984, television and corporate sponsorship became the two pillars on which the Olympic Games were funded. The potential value for commercial sponsorship was validated. The Los Angeles Olympic Organizing Committee (LAOOC) (Los Angeles, 1985) sold the Games on the premise that companies were willing to pay to be involved with the Olympic Games for such benefits as "an improved public image, increased product name recognition, improved employee morale, and the exclusion of competitors from similarly associating themselves with the Games" The LAOOC developed a three-tier program for corporations to become sponsors, suppliers, or licensees. In most cases, the sponsors were large multinational firms that paid at least 4 million USD to the LAOOC in cash, goods, and services (Los Angeles, 1985), and the suppliers were companies that provided a combination of products, services, and cash needed by the LAOOC in staging the Games. Finally, the licensees were companies authorized by the LAOOC to manufacture and sell souvenir products featuring all LAOOC symbols: On average, the licensees paid 10 percent royalty fees to the LAOOC (Los Angeles, 1985). An important element of the sponsorship program for the 1984 Games was that it was based on a new concept of offering corporations exclusivity within a limited number of product categories (e.g., beverages, credit cards). In return, corporations were given certain rights to use Games symbols in their advertising and marketing. As early as 1979, the LAOOC signed sponsorship agreements with Coca-Cola and Anheuser-Busch worth more than $20 million (Los Angeles, 1985). These early signings served as a benchmark for other negotiations and indicated that a privately financed Olympic Games was possible. This resulted in fewer sponsors than in previous Games, but they paid more money to be associated with the Games. LAOOC signed 35 companies as sponsors, 64 as suppliers, and 65 as licensees—164 in all. LAOOC took in $157 million in sponsorship, almost 10 times that generated by Montreal in 1976. Television revenue also reached new heights with revenue of $236 million compared to $35 million in Montreal. The final result was an unprecedented $222.7 million in profit (Landry & Yerlès, 1996). Los Angeles clearly demonstrated that with sound business practices, the Olympic Games could make a profit.

Shortly after becoming IOC president in 1980, Juan Antonio Samaranch expressed serious concerns about 95 percent of the IOC revenues coming from selling television rights for the Olympic Games, with 83 percent of this deriving from American networks. As a result, the IOC established the New Sources of Finance Commission in 1982 to identify potential areas of opportunity for the generation of revenues (Landry & Yerlès, 1996). In 1985, the IOC, with the help of International Sports, Culture and Leisure (ISL), created its first worldwide sponsorship program, the Olympic Partner (TOP) Program, to establish a more diversified revenue base for the Olympic movement and Games. The first TOP sponsor was Visa, which remains a TOP sponsor to this day. In 1989, the commission led by Canadian IOC member Richard Pound reported that TOP had achieved its objective of diversifying the IOC's revenues and reducing dependence on television. Following the resounding success of the **TOP Program**, the percentage of television revenues had gone down to about 50 percent of total revenue.

Throughout the balance of the 1980s, and into the 1990s, Olympic sponsorship quickly evolved into one of the world's most sophisticated and successful sport marketing programs, an achievement it has maintained during the first two decades of the new millennium. Recognizing the increased importance of marketing, the IOC gradually played a significantly greater role in coordinating all aspects of marketing the Olympic Games and the financial health of the Olympic movement. In 1989, the IOC executive board decided to create its own marketing department, primarily to generate income for the Olympic movement on a stable, long-term basis in accordance with the general policy of the IOC (Preuss, 2000).

For more than 30 years, Olympic marketing has generated significant and increasing revenues from sponsorship (as well as broadcasting, which will be discussed later in the chapter). Ticket sales have also become an important source of revenue for OCOGs. For example, Vancouver 2010 sold approximately 200 million USD in tickets for its two-week event. In the period from 1985 to 2016, sponsorship generated an increasing amount of revenue for each quadrennial, eclipsing 1 billion USD for the first time for the 2013-2016 quadrennial. Table 19.1 shows the rise in Olympic sponsor-

ship revenue since 1985, and table 19.2 shows OCOG sponsorship and ticketing revenues over the 1993-to-2016 time frame.

At the level of the OCOG, marketing revenues have also grown significantly following the 1984 Los Angeles Games, and most notably in recent years. Table 19.2 outlines this growth over the past six Olympic quadrennials on sponsorship and ticketing. Licensing is flat. Due to the delayed Tokyo 2020 Games, this information was still not public at the time of printing.

Olympic Broadcasting

In addition to sponsorship, broadcasting has been a significant and quickly growing source of revenue for the IOC. Interestingly, this has emerged despite former President Avery Brundage saying at the 1956 Winter Olympic Games: "Dear Friends, we in the IOC have done well without TV for 60 years and we will do so certainly for the next 60 years, too" (IOC, 1999). Despite these efforts to stay "amateur," broadcasting emerged

TABLE 19.1 Olympic Sponsorship Revenue by Quadrennial, 1985-2016

Olympiad	Games	Partners	No. participating NOCs	Revenue (in USD millions)
1985-1988	Calgary/Seoul	9	159	96
1989-1992	Albertville / Barcelona	12	169	172
1993-1996	Lillehammer / Atlanta	10	197	279
1997-2000	Nagano / Sydney	11	199	579
2001-2004	Salt Lake City / Athens	11	202	663
2005-2008	Turin / Beijing	12	205	866
2009-2012	Vancouver / London	11	205	950
2013-2016	Sochi / Rio	12	205	1003
2017-2021	PyeongChang / Tokyo	14	Not available	Not available

Reprinted by permission from International Olympic Committee, *Olympic Marketing Fact File 2020 Edition*, 15. ttps://stillmed.olympic.org/media /Document%20Library/OlympicOrg/Documents/IOC-Marketing-and-Broadcasting-General-Files/Olympic-Marketing-Fact-File.pdf

TABLE 19.2 OCOG Revenues (in USD millions): 1993 to 2016

Source	1993-1996	1997-2000	2001-2004	2005-2008	2009-2012	2013-2016
OCOG Domestic Partnership	534	655	796	1,555	1,838	2,037
OCOG Ticketing	451	625	411	274	1,238	527
OCOG Licensing	115	66	87	185	170	74
Total	1,100	1,346	1,294	2,014	3,246	2,638

Reprinted by permission from International Olympic Committee, *Olympic Marketing Fact File 2020 Edition*, 9. https://stillmed.olympic.org/media /Document%20Library/OlympicOrg/Documents/IOC-Marketing-and-Broadcasting-General-Files/Olympic-Marketing-Fact-File.pdf as the most important driver of future revenue growth for the IOC. The "marriage" between television and the Olympic movement was inevitable. Starting in the 1950s, sport became a significant advertising vehicle for television and has continued to grow and expand and internationalize ever since. Television is given credit for attracting new fans to sport and help sport grow and athletes to become celebrities. Sport and television have enjoyed a symbiotic relationship. Schantz (1995) noted that "the spiraling effect of media exposure, popularization and commercialization had been set in motion: the popularity of sport increased, and, with it, financial interest in sport as a commodity; this in turn intensified its media exposure which ultimately helped to promote sport itself" (p. 51). This resulted in an acceleration of the commercialization of sport. Despite strong resistance from some of its members, the IOC finally embraced commercialism and went quickly from a practically bankrupt organization to a multibillion-dollar business.

The first significant revenue from broadcasting rights was obtained in 1960, when American broadcaster CBS paid 660,000 USD to broadcast the Rome Olympics in the United States. Broadcast rights revenue continued to increase with each Olympics in the 1960s and 1970s. Then, beginning in 1984, these revenues started increasing dramatically. From 1980 to 2016, broadcast revenue for the Olympic Games has grown more than 30-fold, from $88 million for Moscow 1980 to $2.868 billion for Rio 2016 (IOC, 2020). The growth of Olympic Winter Games broadcast revenue has been even more impressive, increasing more than 65-fold, from $21 million for the 1980 Lake Placid Games to $1.436 billion for the 2018 PyeongChang Games (IOC, 2020).

In addition to the growth in revenue, television has been recognized as the medium that has globalized the Olympic Games. The IOC's policy on television coverage has aimed to maximize the global coverage of the Games, both in number of countries and in overall global reach: "The world experiences the Olympics through television and the IOC wants to guarantee that if there is a television available, every family, every child can watch—not that he/she has to pay. It should be everyone's right to watch the Olympic Games free of charge" (Payne, 1998, p. 108).

This strategy has been very successful for the Olympic movement. The number of countries or territories broadcasting the Olympics nearly doubled from 111 during the 1980 Moscow Games to more than 220 jurisdictions for each of the Games since 2000 (IOC, 2020). For Rio 2016, the IOC (2020) estimates that more than half of the world's population watched some part of the Games.

By maximizing the television audience, the IOC has provided advertisers with a unique platform that reaches huge audiences. In turn, advertisers (including sponsors) have been willing to pay a premium to acquire exclusive advertising inventory during Olympic broadcasts. Ultimately, this has ensured that the IOC has maximized revenues from its number 1 source of revenue—the broadcasters.

As the broadcasting rights revenue rose rapidly in the 1980s, the role of the IOC in negotiating those rights changed from one of partnership with the OCOGs to one of sole negotiator. Since the 1992 Barcelona Games, the IOC has assumed full control on the negotiation of television rights, as indicated in the Olympic charter, Rule 11, which give the IOC exclusive rights. As the owner of all broadcasting rights to the Games, the IOC negotiates the broadcast agreements directly with each broadcaster. It negotiates the rights on a territorial basis, selecting broadcasters that provide the widest and best possible coverage. With control over the negotiation, the IOC embarked on a new long-term broadcast strategy that led to many lucrative long-term deals with networks in many countries. In Canada, CBC–Radio Canada signed a five Games deal in 2015 to broadcast all Game through to 2024. In the United States, NBC renewed in 2014, signing an extension to have Olympic broadcast rights in the United States until the 2032 Games.

The size and length of these contracts are evidence of the ability of the Olympic Games to generate revenues (e.g., advertising, cable fees, rights sharing) for the networks. Furthermore, the Olympic Games remains one of the few properties where advertisers can reach large global audiences, leading to a premium. Broadcasters are in business to make profits, and it appears that the Olympics contribute to reaching that objective in many ways. For example, for the 2000 Sydney Games, NBC paid the IOC 705 million USD for the broadcasting rights and spent an additional $125 million in production costs; it reported sales of more than $900 million in advertising (including many spots purchased by TOP sponsors) and expected a profit in the tens of millions of dollars from the Games (Associated Press, 1995).

Figure 19.1 captures the overall formula that the IOC followed to maximize revenues. This is an interpretation of both the sponsorship and broadcast revenues, and the history of IOC marketing as presented in this chapter.

By all accounts, this strategy has been very successful, with the revenues from broadcast more than tripling from the 1993-1996 quadrennial to the 2013-2016 quadrennial, reaching 4.157 USD for that period. This is shown in table 19.3.

The marketing success of the IOC has been shared with the sport community. In 2020, the IOC reported distributing 90 percent of total Olympic marketing revenues to the OCOGs, IFs, NOCs, and such other sport organizations as the International Paralympic Committee and the World Anti-Doping Agency. They note that this is the equivalent of 3.4 million USD per day (IOC, 2020). Table 19.4 provides the amounts the IOC has shared with National Olympic Committees (NOC) over previous quadrennials.

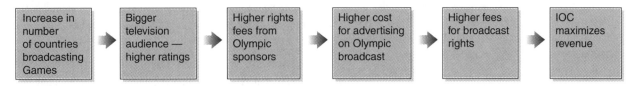

FIGURE 19.1   IOC formula to maximize revenue.
Reprinted by permission from B. Séguin, *Représentations d'Acteurs Sociaux sur les Relations Entre le Marketing et les Jeux Olympiques* [Representations of Social Actors on the Relationship Between Marketing and the Olympic Games] (2003). Unpublished doctoral dissertation (Université Marc Bloch [Strasbourg II]).

TABLE 19.3   Olympic Broadcast Revenue by Quadrennial (in USD millions), 1985-2016

Source	1993-1996	1997-2000	2001-2004	2005-2008	2009-2012	2013-2016
Broadcast	1,251	1,845	2,232	2,570	3,850	4,157

Reprinted by permission from International Olympic Committee, *Olympic Marketing Fact File 2020 Edition*, 8. https://stillmed.olympic.org/media/Document%20Library/OlympicOrg/Documents/IOC-Marketing-and-Broadcasting-General-Files/Olympic-Marketing-Fact-File.pdf

TABLE 19.4   IOC Contributions to support NOCs and IFs (Distribution in USD millions)

	NOCs	IFs
OLYMPIC GAMES		
Athens 2004	234	257
Beijing 2008	301	297
London 2012	520	520
Rio 2016	540	540
OLYMPIC WINTER GAMES		
Salt Lake City 2002	87	92
Turin 2006	136	128
Vancouver 2010	215	209
Sochi 2014	199	199
PyeongChang 2018	215	215

Reprinted by permission from International Olympic Committee, *Olympic Marketing Fact File 2020 Edition*, 10, 11. https://stillmed.olympic.org/media/Document%20Library/OlympicOrg/Documents/IOC-Marketing-and-Broadcasting-General-Files/Olympic-Marketing-Fact-File.pdf

The Olympic Partner (TOP) Sponsorship Program

Sponsorship (along with broadcasting) has been one of the key drivers of the marketing growth of the Olympic Games. The change has been extraordinary. The 1980 Moscow Olympic Games had 381 sponsors who paid an average of 10,000 USD each (Stotlar, 1993). The 2020 Tokyo Olympic Games (delayed to 2021 due to the COVID-19 global pandemic), in addition to the IOC's 14 TOP sponsors (and an estimated $1 billion+ in rights fees), had 67 domestic sponsors signed for $3 billion in rights fees as of January 2020 (SportBusiness, 2020).

Starting with the 1984 Los Angeles Olympic Games, The Olympic Partner (TOP) Program was the IOC's response to the difficulties experienced by OCOGs and sponsors with their international marketing activities in connection with the Olympic Games. At that time, Canadian IOC member Richard Pound (1986), who was also the chair of the IOC's New Sources of Finance Commission, argued that it was virtually impossible for OCOGs and sponsors to engage in efficient marketing activities. Prior to the TOP Program, the Olympic charter stipulated that no sponsor could use the OCOG marks without permission of the local NOC. Sponsors were forced to negotiate with the NOC of each country to use the emblems of the OCOG, making the sponsorship much less attractive as a marketing proposition.

The response was a program involving a limited number of sponsors, each with category exclusivity and global rights (i.e., rights to the entire Olympic movement). The IOC learned that global brands were seeking a platform to reach global audiences and that they were willing to pay more for an international sponsorship that was simple and delivered exclusively on a worldwide basis (Pound, 1986). The IOC responded to the needs of the sponsors by creating TOP and allowing multinational corporations to promote their associations with the Olympics on an exclusive basis worldwide. Exclusivity became a rule that future sports-marketing programs would have to respect to be successful.

The creation of TOP was a challenge for the IOC, which had to convince 167 NOCs to give up certain marketing rights to launch the worldwide program. This proved to be particularly difficult for the USOC and a few other NOCs that had developed successful marketing programs. Following long and complex negotiations, especially with the USOC, 159 NOCs (92 percent) agreed to participate in the program (Landry & Yerlès, 1996). As part of the agreement with NOCs, the IOC reserved 44 product categories (e.g., beverages, credit cards) for TOP sponsors, many of which remain in place today. The program was launched in 1985 as TOP I. In total, nine multinational companies became worldwide sponsors and provided the Olympic movement with 96 million USD. The nine iterations of TOP since its formation in 1985 were presented in table 19.1, which shows just over $1 billion in the 2013-2016 quadrennial from nine sponsors. Due to the delayed 2020 Tokyo Games, revenues from the 2017-2020 quadrennial are not yet publicly available. Clearly, the TOP Program has been a great success and is one of the largest revenue sources of the modern Olympic Games.

The TOP Program of the IOC was designed to meet the following objectives (IOC, 1998), a mandate that has not changed:

- Ensure the independent financial stability of the Games and the Olympic movement.
- Create a long-term structure that ensures continuing and substantial support.
- Guarantee equitable revenue distribution throughout the Olympic movement.
- Prohibit uncontrolled commercialism of the Games.

As official partners, TOP sponsors were to receive the following benefits (IOC, 1998):

- Exclusive rights and opportunities within their designated product category.
- Worldwide rights to develop marketing programs with members of the Olympic family.
- Rights to use Olympic imagery, designation of products, hospitality opportuni-

ties at Olympic Games, direct advertising, and promotional opportunities, including first rights to Olympics broadcast advertising.

- On-site concessions or franchises, product sale and showcase opportunities, ambush-marketing protection, and a broad Olympic sponsor recognition program.

TOP has helped bring financial stability to the Olympic movement. IOC (1998) also considers the TOP Program an asset in the following ways:

- Generate long-term, independent sources of revenue for the OCOGs, NOCs, and the IOC.
- Offer TOP partners a simple and unique solution for acquiring the Olympic marketing rights and the execution of a global Olympic marketing strategy.
- Provide TOP partners with a broad marketing platform from which to communicate worldwide the powerful messages about their support of the Olympic movement.
- Harness the marketing power of the partners to communicate Olympic ideals to people worldwide.
- Provide integrity to Olympic marketing and the Olympic brand through a greater authority over the use of Olympic marks and imagery.

In return for their financial commitment to the Olympic Games, sponsors seek to achieve a multitude of objectives including audience awareness and image enhancement. The sponsorship role permits marketing communicators to talk more directly to particular market segments in a manner that may be more efficient and less costly than traditional media advertising. The return on investment may take the form of improved profit figures, image, or reputation, elevated employee morale, perceived status elevation in the public perception, and more. These benefits come from an association with the imagery of the Games as the most important event in the world, the recognition of the Olympic symbol as the best known "symbol" in the world, and the qualities of Olympism (Pound, 1996).

The Olympic Brand

The foundation of Olympic marketing has been established on a set of Olympic ideals promoted as its core values. Over the years, these ideals have been "packaged" and "communicated" to a mass audience via extensive worldwide television coverage. The Olympic symbols (e.g., rings, torch relay, lighting of the flame, athletes' oath, Olympic truce) are well recognized and accepted by people of diverse cultural backgrounds all over the world. In fact, these symbols have contributed to making the Games a celebration of values and aspirations that have resulted in universal appeal and power. This has made the Olympic brand an attractive proposition for a multitude of corporations (e.g., broadcasters, firms in various industries) that hope the Olympic brand values transfer to their own brands. These ideals and values have positioned and differentiated the Olympic system from other major sport systems. As a result, sponsoring the Olympic brand can enable association to a competitively attractive position supported by strong associations and the ability for the sponsor to differentiate its brand and generate positive business outcomes. Scandals such as doping, corruption, and fixing of events all have damaging effects on the Olympic brand.

With the amount invested by partners in the Olympic brand (counted in billions of dollars since 1984), it is no surprise that they want and need a strong Olympic brand. It is the IOC's responsibility to keep the Games a viable and strong sponsorship investment choice. The brand research infuses sponsors with much-needed brand information and provides NOCs and OCOGs with supportive evidence to use in selling to national and domestic sponsors. Broadcasters also get information on the appeal and power of the Olympic image, which is critical to their programming and their goal of maximizing television ratings. This, in turn, maximizes revenue from advertisers. Thus, a well-defined brand provides partners, broadcasters, and OCOGs with the foundation for building their

Games-time image and Olympic-associated activities.

The consumer-defined attributes from an IOC internal brand study (2001) are summarized as "a peaceful and festive forum for cultural exchange and fair play" and "ideals of equality, tradition, honor, and excellence." These brand equities possess multiple dimensions, which increases the breadth and the depth of their value. For example, the friendship dimension includes friendship between athletes, between cultures, and between nations. Likewise, the peaceful dimension includes peaceful events, peaceful spectators, and peaceful hosts. Although it is nearly 20 years old, current reports (IOC, 2020) suggest that the Olympic brand is similar today. These attributes of the Olympic brand have the ability to provide Olympic partners with a powerful marketing advantage and the ability to appeal across multiple markets and diverse demographic segments around the world.

But what makes the Games different from other properties? What is the true point of differentiation in branding terms? Most importantly, this is a truly global event that unites people from around the world. With over 200 NOCs, thousands of athletes taking part in the Games, and billions of people watching on television, the Olympics are truly a global event uniting the entire world. The Games are the pinnacle of sporting achievement—a celebration of sports, cultures, and humanity. The values and ideals associated with the Olympic brand also make it unique.

Over the years, crises have plagued the Olympic movement and led to growing concerns on the part of commercial partners and the public. It is important that a failure to live up to the brand's promise could lead to serious problems for the Olympic brand. Examples include doping, the cost of the Games, terrorism, ambush marketing, unfair bidding processes, operational failure, and so on.

Brand values such as harmony, global peace, excellence, and friendship are frequently mentioned as a point of differentiation for Olympic brand. The Olympic ideals have well-defined meanings and values that consumers can relate to, thus providing a platform that is unavailable in other properties. The protection, enhance-ment, and communication of the Olympic brand are all identified as key factors to the continued success of the Olympic marketing program (Séguin et al., 2008).

Olympic Marketing in Canada

Canada's contribution to the Olympic movement is significant. Despite the financial difficulties of the 1976 Montreal Games, Canada's reputation in hosting capabilities is widely recognized internationally. Since the Montreal Games, Canada has hosted numerous multisport events—the Olympic Winter Games (1988, 2010), FIFA Women's World Cup (2015), Commonwealth Games (1994), Pan American Games (1999, 2015), and the ParaPan American Games (2015), FISU (world student) Games (1983), IAAF World Championships (2001), and FINA World Aquatics Championships (2005), as well as world championships and world cups in gymnastics, athletics, figure skating, hockey, speed skating, alpine skiing, triathlon, FIFA U-20, and many other sports.

Canada has hosted three Olympic Games: the 2010 Vancouver Olympic and Paralympic Winter Games, Olympic Winter Games in 1988 (Calgary), and Summer Olympic Games in 1976 (Montreal). Canada has also bid to host the Games unsuccessfully on other occasions, including 10 failed bids for the Winter Games by Banff (1972), Calgary (1964, 1968, 2026), Montreal (1932, 1936, 1944, 1956), Quebec City (2002), and Whistler (1976), and 5 failed bids for the Summer Games by Toronto (1996, 2008) and Montreal (1944, 1956, 1972).

Of all the NOCs, the Canadian Olympic Committee (COC) has one of the most sophisticated marketing programs, consisting of sponsorship, licensing, fundraising events, communications, and public relations. As of 2020, the COC had a robust platform of sponsors, including four Premier National Partners (RBC, Bell, Canadian Tire, and HBC), six National Partners (Cadillac Fairview, Deloitte, PetroCanada, SAS, Teck, Toyota), nine Official Supporters, four Official Suppliers, and three Media Partners.

EXECUTIVE PERSPECTIVE
The Sport Legacy of Major Events in Canada

DEBBIE LOW, CEO, Canadian Sport Institute Ontario

As the major high-performance sport legacy from the Toronto 2015 Pan/Parapan American Games, the Canadian Sport Centre Ontario was designated as a "sport institute" in 2014. Setting our vision on becoming a world-leading sport institute required over a decade of dedication, planning, and fortitude. Finally, our dream was realized when the Canadian Sport Institute Ontario (CSIO) opened its doors as a world-class sport institute in September 2014. Housed at the Toronto Pan Am Sports Centre (TPASC), the largest legacy facility of the TO 2015 Pan/Parapan Am Games, the sport institute occupies 23,500 square feet of sport performance space dedicated to Canada's Olympic and Paralympic athletes and coaches.

The Canadian Olympic and Paralympic Sport Institute (COPSI) Network) is a network of four sport institutes and three sport centres located across the country. The COPSI Network plays a pivotal role in enabling Canada to be a world leader in high-performance sport. Own the Podium, the Canadian Olympic Committee, Canadian Paralympic Committee, Coaches Association of Canada, Sport Canada, and the respective provincial government are key partners and funders of the COPSI Network.

Sport Canada and Own the Podium are responsible for designating sport institute status in Canada. Criteria include:

- sport-specific training facilities as well as generic high-performance strength and conditioning facilities,
- sport science and sport medicine services provided on-site as part of the daily training environment,
- a critical mass of nationally carded athletes using the facilities as the primary location for their daily training environment (a critical mass is defined as 100 athletes or more), and
- a critical number of nationally recognized training groups using the facilities as the primary location for their daily training environment (a critical number is defined as five or more).

CSIO shares the 312,000 square foot facility at TPASC with training spaces that includes 2 × 10 lane—50-metre pools; a separate dive tank with 3-metre, 5-metre, 7.5-metre, and 10-metre platforms and a dryland training area; a field house featuring four courts with FIBA hardwood sprung floors; a judo training centre; a 200-metre indoor track; multipurpose studios; a climbing wall; and a weight room open to University of Toronto students and the public.

There are over 60 full-time sport scientists, sport medicine practitioners, and sport administrators working at CSIO. Our purpose is to elevate people and performances. In addition to our national role, CSIO plays a significant leadership role in Ontario's high-performance sport system. In partnership with the Government of Ontario, CSIO works further down the performance pathway assisting provincial sport organizations in the development of the province's best athletes and coaches.

CSIO also operates a satellite training facility at the Mattamy National Cycling Centre in Milton. This site includes a strength and conditioning centre, a sport therapy suite, and a sport lab featuring state-of-the-art equipment for testing and training high-performance athletes. In addition, CSIO practitioners work in the daily training environment of other national training centres in the province including at the Athletics Canada's East Hub located at York University and Rowing Canada's Next Gen Centre in London. It is our goal to create future satellite centres in partnership with local municipalities and universities.

> continued

The Sport Legacy of Major Events in Canada   > *continued*

President and chief executive officer of the Canadian Sport Institute Ontario (CSIO) since November 2005, Debbie Low has re-established Ontario as a leader in high-performance sport. She led the creation of Ontario's first and only facility-based sport institute as a legacy of the Toronto 2015 Pan/Para Pan American Games. Previous roles include executive director of Parasport Ontario and director of sport for Toronto's 2008 Olympic bid. In addition, Debbie spent 10 years with the Ontario Government in the Ministry of Heritage, Sport, Tourism and Culture Industries working in the Multi-Sport Games unit. Debbie was Canada's chef de mission for the 2008 Beijing Paralympic Games and assistant chef de mission for the 2004 Athens Paralympic Games. Debbie was also involved in nine sets of Canada Games as part of Team Ontario including chef de mission in 1997 and 1999. Debbie holds a bachelor of physical and health education from the University of Toronto and a diploma in sport management from Durham College.

Olympic Broadcasting in Canada

Since the IOC negotiates broadcasting rights, the COC has little control over the choice of broadcaster. The CBC–Radio Canada has been the Olympic broadcaster for most of the Games, including from 1956 to 2008 and again from 2014 to 2024. In 2005, the IOC awarded the broadcasting rights to the 2010 and 2012 Olympic Games to an alliance of CTV and Rogers Communications, which bid 153 million USD, an increase of 110 percent over the $73 million the CBC paid for the Canadian broadcasting rights for the 2006 and 2008 Games (CBC Sports, 2005).

The total hours devoted by the broadcaster to Olympic coverage depends on a number of factors, the most important being the location of the Games. Hours and ratings are affected by the time zone (e.g., North America versus Asia) in which the Games take place. For example, the 1998 Olympic Winter Games in Nagano seriously challenged the CBC. The 10- to 12-hour time difference meant that none of the finals took place in television prime time. Despite the time zone differences (middle of the night in Canada), CBC decided to carry a number of events (e.g., ice hockey) live. Of note, the 1998 Games were also the first time the NHL stars, including Wayne Gretzky, were able to play in the Olympics, driving up television ratings in Canada. An incredible 6 of the 10 highest watched television programs in Canadian history are from the men's team competing at the Olympic Games between 2002 and 2014, include

the most watched program in Canadian history, the 2010 Olympic Gold Medal game in Vancouver, when a peak audience of nearly 17 million Canadians tuned in. Of note is the fact that the Olympic women's ice hockey matches have also drawn very large audiences since 1998, with the 2010 gold medal match being the 12th most watched program in Canadian history, reaching 7.5 million viewers in Canada.

On average, Canadians are big consumers of the Olympic Games: Their appetite is reflected in the number of hours devoted by CBC (and the consortium in 2010 and 2012) to Olympic coverage. During any Games since 2006, Canadian viewers are offered hundreds—and more recently, thousands—of hours of coverage on various networks and channels and can watch most of the competitions during the two weeks of any Games. Canadian ratings for Games programming are high. Canadians are huge followers of hockey, curling, swimming, athletics, rowing, and really any sport where a Canadian has a chance to capture a medal. Canadians also watch the opening and closing ceremonies in very high numbers.

Own the Podium

Recognizing the importance of success at the Games to the Olympic movement in Canada, including marketing outcomes, the Own the Podium (OTP) high-performance technical program was put in place by the government of Canada, working with the Canadian sport community, leading up to the Vancouver Games, and has been maintained ever since. OTP aims to make Canada a leading nation in terms of total medals won at the Olympic and Paralympic Games. OTP originally started with a focus on the Winter Games of 2010 but expanded its focus following its impressive success at the Winter Olympics. Notably, Canada won 5 medals at the 1988 Calgary Winter Games (2 silver, 3 bronze), which was the most medals won at any Winter Games since they started in 1924 (with the exception of 7 at Lake Placid in 1932). Since 1988, however, results at the Winter Games have continued to improved, jumping considerably following the implementation of OTP, with Canada winning 24 medals in 2006, 26 in 2010, 25 in 2014, and 29 in 2018. At the Vancouver Games, Canada won 26 medals, the highest of any country, accomplishing OTP's goal of being first in medals at those Games. In 2014 and 2018, Canada finished third in total medals.

EXECUTIVE PERSPECTIVE
The Olympic and Paralympic Movements in Canada

DAVID BEDFORD, CEO, Athletics Canada

Over the course of my 40+-year career in sport, I have been fortunate to have held positions—professional and volunteer—related to Canada's participation in numerous major Games including the Olympic Games, Commonwealth Games, and World Aquatics Championships. The highlight of my Games career was being chef de mission for Canada at the 2004 Athens Olympic Games and later holding the position of executive director, marketing and communications, for the Canadian Olympic Committee. Today I lead one of the largest NSOs in Canada, Athletics Canada, where the Olympic and Paralympic Games are our primary focus from a high-performance perspective.

Canada has provided the Olympic and Paralympic movements with many rich, tumultuous moments since the modern Olympic Games were started in 1894 by Baron Pierre de Coubertin. In fact, it is safe to say that, based on its small size among the world's countries (the 39th most populous country in the world (Worldometer, 2021), Canada has had a disproportionate impact on the Olympic and Paralympic Movement's. Some of these moments have been triumphant; others are iconic images of sport gone awry. One thing is sure, however—the Olympic and Paralympic Games would never have been the same without Canada, and Canada would not be the same country without the Games. In regard to my current sport (track and field), we are the source of many of these iconic events, which I will describe in further detail.

Canada has been host to three Olympic Games: The 1976 Montreal Summer Games, the 1988 Calgary Winter Games, and the 2010 Vancouver Winter Games round out the triumvirate. As of 2021, only three countries have had more Olympic Games on their soil, the United States with six, France with five, and Japan with four. Germany and Italy also have three, like Canada. Canada also hosted the Paralympic Games in Vancouver in 2010.

When Montreal hosted the 1976 Olympic Games, the Olympic movement was desperately short on cash and exceptionally long on excesses. The Montreal Games suffered many of the afflictions that were common to the Olympic movement during that era, including the building of extravagant facilities meant to eclipse those of any preceding Games. Political intrigue reared its head as well, as Montreal 1976 was the first Games to suffer a boycott (many African nations boycotted in protest over apartheid in South Africa). And yet, when the Montreal Olympic Games were all over, they not only proved to be a shining success on the field of play, including our best performance of those Games in Greg Joy's silver medal in the high jump, but also provided a legacy for Olympic sport in Canada that survives to this day. Many of the venues built for the Montreal Games are still in use (e.g., Olympic Pool, Claude Robillard Centre) as high-performance training grounds for today's generation of Olympic and Paralympic hopefuls.

> continued

The Olympic and Paralympic Movements in Canada   > *continued*

After the boycott of the 1980 Moscow Olympic Games (many nations, including Canada and the United States, boycotted in protest of the Soviet Union's occupation of Afghanistan) and the rampant commercial success of the 1984 Los Angeles Olympic Games, the International Olympic Committee (IOC) realized that they had to put the Olympic movement on much more sound financial footings. President Juan Antonio Samaranch listened closely to the commercial partners of the Olympic movement. Knowing that the future of the Olympic Games rested on financial stability, he created the New Sources of Finance Commission. Samaranch asked Canadian IOC member Richard Pound to lead the charge to find new sources of financing for the Olympic movement. Pound helped create, and launch, the TOP sponsorship program, which is still the cornerstone of IOC revenue. And perhaps we should also talk about Bob Steadward's role in building the Paralympic movement.

The year 1988 illustrated the best, and worst, of Olympism to Canadians. In February 1988, the Olympic torch was lit in McMahon Stadium, signifying the start of the magical Calgary Olympic Winter Games. The Calgary Games were the first to reap the benefits of the TOP sponsorship program, and what a benefit it was to Canadian sport. The Canadian Olympic Committee's (COC) share of profits from the Calgary Olympic Games, and its investment returns, are still fuelling the COC. Just as important, a share of those same profits has been keeping Canada Olympic Park and many of the 1988 Olympic venues producing Olympic champions ever since. Unfortunately, 1988 also saw Ben Johnson stripped of his 100-metre gold medal for doping (Seoul, Korea). The national embarrassment Canada felt has also led to good, however, as the world sat up and took heed of the call to fight doping in sport, with Canada at the forefront of that movement. The IOC created the World Anti-Doping Association (WADA), installed Dick Pound as the leader of this important fight, and named Montreal as its headquarters.

Controversy was never far from the Canadians after Ben Johnson's downfall in Seoul. In 1992, Sylvie Frechette was denied a 1992 Barcelona Olympic Games gold medal in synchronized swimming by a judging mistake, only to be awarded her gold medal a number of years later. At the Nagano 1998 Olympic Winter Games, Ross Rebagliati won the gold medal in Snowboard Giant Slalom but, testing positive for marijuana, had his medal removed. Upon appeal, Rebagliati's medal was reinstated as marijuana was not on the IOC list of performance-enhancing substances. In 2002, figure skaters Jamie Sale and David Pelletier were victims of a judging scandal that saw them placed second in the pairs competition. Fortunately, the scandal was uncovered, and Sale and Pelletier were rightfully awarded the gold medal they had earned. Also at the 2002 Salt Lake City Games, Beckie Scott became the first Canadian cross-country skier to win a medal, a bronze. After the gold and silver medal competitors tested positive for doping infractions and a long fight by Beckie and the COC, the IOC awarded Scott with the gold medal she had rightfully won.

The year 2010 was a major celebration for the nation because hosting the Vancouver Winter Games was a success operationally and performance wise, as Canada—supported by the highly acclaimed Own the Podium (OTP) program—saw its medal count go to unprecedented levels.

Triumphs for the ages, however, have far outstripped the controversies: Barbara Ann Scott's figure skating gold in 1948 (St. Moritz); Nancy Greene winning gold and silver in skiing in 1968 (Grenoble); Gaetan Boucher's four Olympic medals (a silver in 1980 at Lake Placid and two gold and a bronze in 1984 in Sarajevo); Mark Tewksbury's race of a lifetime to swimming gold in 1992 (Barcelona); Marnie McBean and Kathleen Heddle taking gold in rowing pairs in 1992 and 1996 (Atlanta); Donovan Bailey becoming the world's fastest man in the 100-metre in 1996 (Atlanta); Marc Gagnon winning five Olympic medals in short-track speed skating over three Winter Games in 1994 (Lillehammer), 1998 (Nagano), and 2002 (Salt Lake City); Cindy Klassen being named the "Queen of the 2006 Torino Games" by IOC president Jacques Rogge for her five medals; and more recently, starting with the 2010 Games in Vancouver, increased medal hauls for Canada at the Winter Games, including 26 medals at those home Games, followed by 25 in 2014 at the Sochi Games and 29 at the 2018 PyeongChang Games, making it the third highest of any country (behind only Norway and Germany).

As you can see, Canada's history in the Olympic and Paralympic Movement is chock-full of suspense and political intrigue, disappointment, and excitement. Canada has contributed to the greatest show on earth as a wonderful host, as an exciting competitor, and even as a tremendous builder of the Olympic and Paralympic Movement's. Although Calgary's attempt to host the 2026 Games was not successful, I expect we'll host the world again and, even if we don't, our athletes will undoubtedly add many more stirring chapters to the story that unfolds of Canada and the Olympic and Paralympic movement.

As chief executive officer of Athletics Canada, David Bedford brings over 40 years of sports-business expertise to his role. A graduate of both Laurentian University (sports administration) and Concordia University (marketing), David began his career in sports business with the National Hockey League in Montreal in 1980.

Highlights of David's career include being vice-president, Olympic marketing worldwide, for IMG; executive director, marketing and communications for the Canadian Olympic Committee (including through the 2010 Vancouver Olympic Winter Games); senior vice-president, business operations, for the Toronto Argonauts Football Club; and executive director, Team Canada for the Gold Coast 2018 Commonwealth Games. David was also vice-president, marketing and sponsorship, for the iconic 100th Grey Cup in Toronto in 2012.

A long-time volunteer on the Canadian sport landscape, David currently sits on the board of directors of Commonwealth Sport Canada. Previously, David was president of Water Polo Canada and sat on the COC board of directors as well as its Team Selection and Games Management Committees. During his time as a volunteer with the COC, David was an influential leader in building the summer-sport caucus and was a key member of the group tasked to deliver the Road to Excellence study on summer sport (sister study to the Own the Podium winter research). David's time with the COC reached its apex when he was selected chef de mission for the 2004 Athens Olympic Games.

David was awarded the Queen's Diamond Jubilee Medal in 2012 for his contributions to the Canadian sport system. David also was recognized by Laurentian University as of 1 of 50 distinguished graduates of the first 50 years since Laurentian's inception and was inducted into Nelson High School's (Burlington, Ontario) Wall of Fame.

CHAPTER SUMMARY

From modest beginnings in 1896, the Olympic Games has grown to be the biggest and most important sport gathering in the world. Since the Vancouver 2010 Games, the Olympic presences in Canada, led by the COC, has also grown considerably. Given the billions that are generated in Olympic marketing revenue today, it is hard to imagine that less than 50 years ago the Olympic movement was on the verge of bankruptcy. While the commercialization of the Olympics is the result of a long process, the emergence of television and sponsorship have both played a significant role in making the Olympics the global icon it is today. Television, and now streaming, provides the Olympic Games with a global platform that attracts billions of viewers worldwide. With the help of a Canadian lawyer, Richard Pound, the IOC was able to develop an exclusive sponsorship program (TOP) that has interested multinational corporations in investing hundreds of millions of dollars in the Olympics. These corporations have been instrumental in developing and communicating the Olympic brand. Canada has played a significant role in developing the Olympic movement by hosting three Games, including the wildly successful Vancouver 2010 Games, launching the OTP program, and building the Olympic brand in Canada.

TEST YOUR KNOWLEDGE

1. Why is Olympic marketing important?
2. Why are Canadian corporations more willing to invest hundreds of millions of dollars in VANOC than in other promotional activities?
3. Are the Olympics worth what sponsors pay for them?
4. If you were a marketing manager of an Olympic sponsor, how would you maximize the benefits of the sponsorship?
5. Do you agree with the commercialization of the Olympics? Why or why not?
6. Test the Olympic brand by asking five people to name three things they associate with the Olympic Games. Record their answers and bring them to class for discussion.

KEY TERMS

blackout

commercialism

Olympic marketing

Olympic movement

rights fee

TOP Program

CASE STUDIES

Visit HK*Propel* for case studies organized by chapter.

CHAPTER 20

Marketing Plan Example

LEARNING OBJECTIVES

After studying this chapter, you will be able to do the following:

- Provide an example of a marketing plan
- Capture the content of the book in an application-based chapter
- Understand how to build a marketing plan for any sport product
- Appreciate the benefits of articulating a marketing plan formally

As the culmination of the previous 19 chapters of the book, this final chapter shares an example—a detailed rendition—of a marketing plan for a sport product. It is meant to capture all that you have learned so far and provide a template that you can use to build and develop future marketing plans. Although the book is very sport focused, the templated can certainly be used for nonsport products.

The Desert Dry Rack: A Product by Desert Sports Limited

This chapter gives an example of a marketing plan developed from the teachings in this book.

The plan, including product concept and supporting research, was created, developed, and articulated by Laurentian University sports administration students Jeff Barsevich, Alex Campbell, Tim Horton, Allison King, and Brandon Mazerall between September 2006 and April 2007 and updated in 2012 and in 2020.

Executive Summary

Desert Sports Limited (DSL) has developed a product that will help hockey players dry and deodorize their equipment. This product addresses the lack of quality and durability offered by current products in the industry in an attempt to fill consumer wants and needs. The Desert Dry Rack ("Rack") is expected to

EXECUTIVE PERSPECTIVE
Strategy Needs to be Flexible and Adaptable

DAN MacKENZIE, President, Canadian Hockey League

Anyone in a leadership or management position in a sport organization in Canada has to be ready for things to happen in our environment that we do not expect or that we could not have seen coming. It is no different in the case of an established league, like the Canadian Hockey League, and is something that I experienced very recently. Let me tell you the story.

On the evening of March 11, 2020, as the Canadian Hockey League's (CHL) Executive Council, comprised of the commissioners of the three regional leagues that make up the CHL (i.e., the Ontario Hockey League, the Western Hockey League and the Quebec Major Junior Hockey League) and I (the CHL president), were having dinner at an off-site location for a strategy planning meeting. That night, Utah Jazz centre Rudy Gobert became the first professional athlete to test positive for the COVID-19 virus, and suddenly our plans changed—and changed fast.

The objective of our off-site meeting had been to discuss the long-term future of the CHL and finalize the marketing plan of the organization going forward. Instead, the discussion over the next two days shifted to the immediate-term and the halting of the CHL season in order to ensure the safety and well-being of all involved, including our players, coaches, officials, volunteers, administrators, and—of course—our fans. It eventually led to the cancellation of the Memorial Cup, our championship tournament, for the first time in 102 years. Yes, it had been more than century since a year went by without us awarding the Memorial Cup.

Looking back, even as the pandemic continues more than six months later, I can say that the COVID-19 pandemic has taught us how interconnected the world is and that the sports industry doesn't operate in a bubble (no pun intended, given the name of the solution applied by the NHL and NBA to save their 2020 playoff seasons and award their respective league championships). Leagues, teams, broadcasters, sponsors, and licensees can have ambitious and well-constructed marketing plans, yet outside forces can change them in an instant—in an instant, and for many months, if not years, to come. The key—and I stress this to you strongly—is to be able to adapt to change and develop a path forward that aligns with your individual organization's reality.

DAN MacKENZIE began the role as the Canadian Hockey League's first full-time president in September 2019, a role in which he is responsible for growing the game along with enhancing the player and fan experience across the CHL's three member leagues, the Ontario Hockey League, Western Hockey League, and Quebec Major Junior Hockey League. Dan came to the CHL after a 20-year career at the National Basketball Association (NBA). As managing director of NBA Canada, he was responsible for the development and growth of the league's business in Canada through the platforms of television and digital media, marketing and retail partnerships, licensing, special events, and basketball development. Under his leadership, both the popularity and business of the NBA reached all-time highs, and he was instrumental in the execution of NBA All-Star 2016 in Toronto, the first time the NBA's premier showcase event was held outside of the United States. Dan sits on the Licensing Industry Merchandisers' Association (LIMA) Canada board of advisors, was the former chair of the Sponsorship Marketing Council of Canada (SMCC) and was the recipient of the George Brown College Alumni Achievement Award. He holds a master's degree in sports management from the University of Ohio, a bachelor of commerce degree from McMaster University, and a bachelor of education degree from Brock University and is a graduate of George Brown College Sport and Event Marketing Program, where he received the Alumni Achievement Award.

be successful because it is designed to satisfy consumers. Market research has uncovered a market niche that DSL feels it can capture if it can implement a smart marketing plan. Based on their research, DSL has chosen to market to male and female hockey parents aged 30 to 55. DSL feels that this market will have a high intention to purchase because not only do parents in this segment still play hockey themselves, their children play in some of the age groups with the highest registration numbers. DSL's product will allow them to preserve their child's equipment (and potentially their own gear) for a longer period of time.

DSL is entering the market and launching this new product into an industry at a time where there is no competitor standing out as an industry leader. By creating a quality product and brand name, DSL hopes to develop customers who are loyal to the brand and the Rack, which will eliminate competitors and substitutes from our consumers' choice set now and into the future. With the help of personal financial investments in the business and an initial bank loan, the founders of DSL will be able to supply over 110 retailers across Canada with about 60 units per year at a selling price of $75 per unit via a distribution centre that DSL will establish. In their projections, DSL estimates a net income level of $27,631 after the first year of operations.

Market Research

The first step in developing our marketing plan was collecting primary and secondary data. This information was to form the basis from which DSL would make their marketing plan decisions. The first type of information collected were data from secondary sources such as Statistics Canada. Primary data were then collected through the use of questionnaires. The two processes of data, method, and results are discussed in the following section.

Secondary Data Acquisition

Objectives

The main objective of DSL's secondary data acquisition was determining where to market

the Rack product. Given the high proportion of Canadians who play hockey (youth and adult), the province with the highest number in such categories as population, income levels, and hockey registration numbers would be the province to target initially. The second objective was then to find the best city in the province to introduce and launch the product.

Sources

The sources of information used for analysis were the 2016 Census from Statistics Canada, CBC Sports data, Hockey Canada statistics, retailer locations, and principal city populations. Statistics Canada documents provided demographic data, including population per province, urban and rural populations, median income levels, age, and sex per province. CBC Sports provided a 2013 minor hockey player breakdown per province, as well as trends in hockey registration in selected provinces. Hockey Canada publishes key information on all registered hockey players per province, with the most recent numbers—from 2018—informing the analysis. Last, a principal-city population breakdown (from Statistics Canada) was used to identify Ontario's largest cities.

Discussion of the Data

The first piece of data reviewed was from the 2016 Canadian census. From this, it was learned that Ontario has about 38 percent of the Canadian population. DSL then looked at age and sex data for Canada and its provinces. Hockey Canada reports indicate that there are many more children/youth playing hockey than adults in Canada; however, due to the fact that parents make most of the purchase decisions for children/youth players, the consumer groups targeted will be parents and young adults. Therefore, the potential market is any parent aged 30 to 55, with a secondary market being any individual (without children who play hockey) aged 19 and up, because these individuals are likely to buy their own equipment. Finally, DSL looked at Canadian census information on median family incomes per province in Canada. When analyzing the data of families with two earners, it was observed that, in addition to being the most populous province, Ontario has among the highest median family incomes in the country.

Next, the analysis considered the number of hockey players per province and found that of the 637,000 hockey players registered with Hockey Canada, nearly 40 percent were in Ontario. It was also noted that at least 75 percent of hockey players in selected provinces were children. This further supported the selection of parents as the primary market and justified focusing direct marketing activities toward hockey parents. The results of the analysis suggested that there are potentially 6,500 new customers every year, as new youth start to play.

DSL researchers next looked at sports store locations in Canada and determined that the best opportunity for the launch of the Rack was via a partnership with SportChek, owned by Canadian Tire, which—as of October 2020—had 195 Canadian locations, 83 of which were in Ontario. Ontario also has the highest population of the provinces, the highest median family income, and the greatest number of hockey players.

The next step was to consider cities in Ontario as potential areas to begin to market the Rack product. Three candidates were identified: Toronto, Ottawa, and Sudbury. The final piece of data collected was on the Canadian sports market, which experienced a 17 percent increase in growth from 2016 to 2017, amounting to $9.5 billion in expenditures. According to the sourced research, the key driver of this growth is the apparel category, which has grown by 21 percent and accounted for $6.6 billion. Research also indicated that the millennial consumer was expected to drive the growth of the sports market.

Limitations

Many limitations were encountered due to lack of information on the number of people who play hockey in certain cities in Canada, the demographic details of minor hockey players, store locations of some major sporting-goods retailers, and expenditures for residents of various cities. Another limitation that was encountered, which unfortunately applies to most of the data, is that the most recent Canadian census was in 2016, nearly 4 years before we began our study.

Primary Data Acquisition

Background

DSL used two methods to gather primary research. First, two different surveys were administered to gather primary research for DSL—one directed at current hockey players and the other at parents of current hockey players, regardless of whether they themselves played. The objectives of this survey were to provide a better understanding of consumer buying behaviours and identify both favoured and disliked product features of the Rack. Finally, the goal was to collect data to help to identify the target markets.

Objectives

The objectives of the consumer survey were to determine the potential target markets and the usefulness of the product and to identify popular retailers. By looking for trends in different target markets, a determination of the most important purchasing factors was undertaken. Objectives for the retail research included determining industry markup standards, identifying competition and competition success, and determining the methods of distribution to retailers.

Methodology

Hockey Player and Parent of Hockey Player Questionnaires

The hockey player questionnaire was distributed based on a simple random sampling technique. Participants included spectators of hockey games, hockey players, and parents. Surveys were handed out at hockey arenas in Sudbury and at Laurentian University's residence league practices. DSL had predetermined that a sample size of 40 would be suitable to gain sufficient knowledge of potential consumers.

In the Greater Sudbury region, researchers targeted three stores to gain information for market research: SportChek, Skater's Edge, and Play It Again Sports. They asked all the interviewees (experienced sales associates) the same general questions, with follow-up questions to certain answers and individual questions specific to each store. Topics included who generally bought their equipment, whether they carried a product similar to ours, whether they felt people would buy our product, and what kind of markups they charged on hockey equipment.

Conclusions from the Hockey Player Questionnaire

Based on the results, it can be concluded that older players' equipment lasts longer because they are no longer growing and generally use their equipment less frequently. The reasons older players buy new equipment are mainly mould or wear and tear. Unlike younger players, many older players do not own an equipment rack, which has led to quicker equipment decay.

Adults were found to be less price sensitive about equipment racks as long as quality matched their dollar spent. Younger players were more sensitive to price and space for the Rack. Based on the surveys, quality and efficiency were the most important aspects of the Rack for all age groups, while price and portability were less important. This will support the effort in ensuring good quality and efficiency while we develop and market the Rack.

Conclusions from the Parent of Hockey Player Questionnaire

Conclusions from the parent survey were similar to those from the player survey. Parents of older children have kids who play more frequently, which increases the need for equipment care. As well as frequency of use, children tend to outgrow their equipment within one to three years, while parents were able to keep their equipment for five years or more.

When ranking the attributes of the Rack, in all different segments, quality was ranked first and portability was ranked last. This once again supports developing a good-quality product with a higher price ceiling.

The most visited hockey equipment retailer in Greater Sudbury based on the primary data collected and analyzed is Skater's Edge.

Conclusion of Retail Store Interviews

All interviewed retailers believed that this product has the possibility of selling in the market. The only difficulty they mentioned is creating a demand for the product. Currently, only casual sales are made; and there is no noticeable high demand for this type of product (i.e., very few could remember any customer asking for such a product). Results found that price markups on this type of item tend to vary from store to store and that larger franchise stores have a much higher markup compared to the smaller individualized stores.

Situation Analysis

The situation analysis phase of the marketing plan involves a number of steps to better understand the reality—or the "situation"—that the marketer is in and must plan from.

Consumer Market Analysis

Through experience, local retailers reported that they have noticed that the main sports and athletic equipment buyers are older men, mainly fathers purchasing for their children and themselves. However, younger fathers, younger males (without children who play), and females (as mothers and as players) are also avid equipment buyers.

Our data revealed that some consumers claimed to already own an equipment rack because they built their own. The homemade equipment rack was reported to be the most common competitor. Most individuals asked expressed some motivation to purchase an equipment rack to help dry their equipment efficiently (i.e., a need or a want was evident). However, the results showed that people were skeptical about purchasing an equipment rack from a retailer due to the lack of quality of store-bought equipment trees, noting that customers perceive existing equipment racks to be of poor quality and value.

Based on the Sudbury summary statistics provided to DSL by the regional business centre, 0.7 percent of the expenditure per year for people living in the city goes to sports and athletic equipment.

However, to build a solid marketing plan, the researchers also examined larger cities and regions in Ontario. Toronto's population has by nearly 17 percent from 2010 to 2020, and this trend was expected to continue with the continued expansion of cities within the Greater Toronto Area (GTA), including Mississauga, Pickering, and Brampton. Generally, citizens in the GTA earn more per year than other Canadians, which provides them with more disposable income to spend on "want"-type products, such as the Rack, compared to someone in a smaller city like Sudbury. Citizens of Ottawa actually earn more per year than citizens of Toronto, but the population of Ottawa is smaller than Toronto. Thus, Ottawa, is also a very attractive market for DSL. With the growing trend of people to living in urban areas, it is reasonable to assume that all three populations will increase over time.

For young hockey players under 18 years of age, research found that most hockey equipment lasts an average of one to three years, mainly due to players growing out of their equipment or due to wear and tear from constant use. Older players tend to have their equipment last longer since they do not play as often and will not grow out of their equipment. The only thing that spoils their equipment is wear and tear, mould, or rust.

Skater's Edge was reported to be the most popular Sudbury-based retailer in our survey questionnaire. The second most popular retailer for hockey equipment and accessories was SportChek. Though people may visit these retailers, the results also revealed that some consumers already owned an equipment rack that they built. Most individuals expressed that they were motivated to purchase an equipment rack to help dry their hockey equipment efficiently, noting this was something that was a bother to them. However, many respondents were skeptical about purchasing their equipment racks from retailers due to their poorly perceived quality and value. This can be viewed as an opportunity: If DSL is able to market a quality product, it may entice individuals to purchase our product from retailers rather than making their own equipment rack at home.

A final note from the research is about the potential consumer of the Rack, specific to the hockey player. The point is that hockey players generally like to play with dry equipment. Putting on wet gear is not a positive experience. The Rack will not only help hockey players get dry equipment, it will also allow them to have equipment that does not smell of sweat (another well-known issue with hockey gear). Since the Rack offers a deodorizer, hockey players will have dry, nice-smelling equipment, which will allow them to preserve it for a longer period of time and store it in a more appealing and less bothersome way.

SWOT Analysis and Key Success Factors

The following provides a summary of the analysis of strengths and weaknesses of the Rack as well as the opportunities and threats that exist in the market.

Strengths: There are many unique aspects to the Rack. Nothing directly similar is currently available on the hockey accessories market. The product is an easy-to-assemble, efficient, and durable equipment rack with an Arm & Hammer deodorizer included for customer ease (a major selling point). This product has proven to be of better quality than competing racks. The Rack is an efficient solution for drying and deodorizing hockey equipment.

Weaknesses: The Rack requires the purchase and use of very durable and high-quality materials, which makes costs higher than our competitors' and, in turn, leads to a higher selling price. Another potential weakness for this product is that it will have high advertising costs to create awareness, given that DSL is a new organization and the Rack is a new brand.

Opportunities: Some opportunities include the rapidly growing sports market, and in particular, the growth of female hockey. The ongoing move to online ordering and free delivery of products (e.g., Amazon Prime) is also a potential opportunity, as potential consumers can order from home when the smell of recently worn hockey gear is strong and bothering them (i.e., ability to purchase when this feeling is high).

Another option to sell online would be to combine it as part of a bundle with other hockey gear.

Threats: A major threat is that a competitor will enter the market, find much cheaper materials, and begin to charge less for a similar product. If the competitor is a larger organization with more resources, this could force a price war that could drive DSL out of business.

Competition Analysis

The competition analysis looks at both competitors and substitutes for the products offered by the sport marketer.

Direct Competition

The findings from the primary market research reveal that fewer than half the individuals surveyed own an equipment rack. This is partially due to the lack of effective market penetration and the inferior quality of existing products. The market for hockey equipment accessories in the sporting goods industry does not have a dominant player, leading to a wide-open market potential.

With respect to direct competition, these product offerings do not show a distinct competitive advantage. Most equipment trees currently on the market are similar in style and construction, without any qualities that would separate an industry leader from the rest of the pack. Among the retailers that were visited, only two different models of hockey equipment racks were observed in stores, with prices ranging from $45 to $65. The first of these models was constructed out of wood and the second of metal (the more expensive of the two). Via observation, researchers were unable to identify the producer of the racks because there was no brand name on the packaging. This led to the assumption that retailers may produce and sell their own customized equipment racks. For example, the Forzani Group sells its equipment rack under its own name, Sport Mart. The representative from SportChek, however, had equipment racks in stock but not on display. This means the customer must make a special request to see the product and the company gains no visual

advertising. The sales representative did not know the name of the manufacturer of the equipment rack. Based on the market research results, those consumers who do currently own an equipment rack are unhappy with its overall design, commenting on a lack of stability and durability. Figure 20.1 shows a general design of the metal equipment rack; the wood design we observed is very similar.

A review of online options found a few different brand and styles in the $30 to $90 range. These include a hanger rack, metal trees, and wooden trees. No product has the quality of the Rack. A former competitor—Sticklocker—that was on the market from 2002 to 2010 (but no longer) was a very small and lightweight product that uses a player's hockey stick as its main mast and attachable aluminum brackets that clamp to the player's stick as equipment holders. However, the product did not have a spot for skates, pants, or shoulder pads, so these pieces of equipment would still need to be laid out to dry. The stability of the product is also in question since the base is very narrow and flimsy. It appears that this product failed.

Substitutes

There are numerous substitutes for equipment racks. Equipment owners have been known to simply spread their equipment out on the floor, which eliminates any need for the Rack. Homemade equipment racks are also frequently used; however, like some manufactured racks, they lack stability and durability. The most extreme substitute for equipment owners is frequently replacing equipment before it begins to deteriorate. An innovative hockey bag called the Shock Doctor appeared on the market around 2010 and is still available today. It is a heavy-duty hockey bag that can accommodate a fan to air dry the equipment in the bag. It includes a filtration system to get rid of smells in the bag. The fan is sold separately from the bag, which itself sells for $129.95. There is no information on the price of the power-dry blower. The cost of the bag is higher than the equipment trees, and most quality "regular" hockey bags sell for less than half the price.

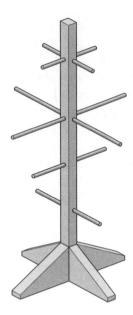

FIGURE 20.1 Patented hockey rack.

Future Competition

In the future, we predict the entry of a lot of similar products with slight variations. Due to the innovativeness of our product, there are bound to be some copycats. To keep up with the market's more innovative products, the Rack will remain adaptable to the market and continuous research will be performed to further enhance it, adding new versions and additional attributes. For instance, a Rack specific to female players or a family with more than one player (and set of gear) are possible future developments.

A primary concern for DSL lies with competitors who will create similar products but will find improvements in fan power and potentially lower-costing materials. Our material costs are nearly 70 percent of the proposed price. If a competitor is able to decrease this margin to 50 percent, they will either make a higher profit or will lower their prices and take a larger market share. Competitors may also add new features such as portability and lightweight materials, all of which would lead to higher quality products. There may also be a market expansion in children's and goalie racks, or even market development into different sports such as football or lacrosse.

Product Offering

The design of the Desert Dry Rack is unique. Both the operation and structure set it apart from any competitive product. The core structure is a dome-shaped plastic base and central pole of ABS tubing that extends upward from the base to about 5.5 feet tall. Extending off the central pole are limbs made of ABS tubing, each designed for a separate piece of hockey equipment to hang on. These limbs have tiny holes to allow air to escape from the inside of the tubing to the equipment. In the base is a fan 8 inches in diameter, mounted inside to blow air into the central pole for distribution to each of the limbs. The size of the fan allows the air to funnel into the central pole and create enough pressure to successfully flow to each part of the equipment. Also mounted near the base of the central pole will be a deodorizer that will be distributed through the rack to the equipment as part of the air flow. A diagram of the product can be seen in figure 20.2.

Innovation

DSL feels that the product is an innovative addition to the equipment rack industry for a few reasons. First, it is constructed of different materials. The current products on the market have a wood base and wood branches or are built of low-quality metal. However, customers have been complaining of the quality and stability of these wood products, and some have even decided to make their own equipment racks. With the Rack's innovative tubing, the fan, and the fact that the Rack eliminates hockey equipment odours, customers should be pleased to find a quality product on the market and consider purchasing it. No other product on the market is built with ABS tubing, which allows airflow to each piece of equipment and can take the weight of hockey equipment for repeated uses. Second, customers will be impressed with the fan, which will allow their equipment to dry faster in between uses. Third, the product is the first of its kind to include an item that will help remove the sweat smell in hockey equipment. DSL's strategic alliance with Arm & Hammer will help both com-

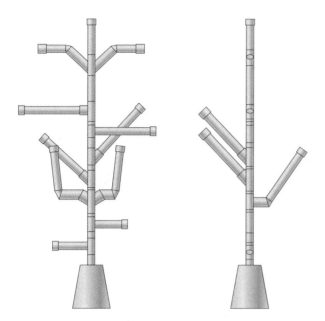

FIGURE 20.2 Product concept diagram.

panies: DSL because of the brand association and Arm & Hammer because consumers will have to go purchase another Arm & Hammer product once the initial product runs out.

Marketing Strategy

Mission

DSL has the company name Desert Sports Limited, which was selected to help the customer associate the product with the dryness of the desert. The DSL mission is to produce high-quality sporting goods for the sporting-goods consumer. By producing a high-quality product, the company aims to sell its products to consumers who are dissatisfied with the quality of other products on the market. Using our competitive advantage of a higher-quality offering, DSL looks to gain large market share quickly in these markets.

Segmentation, Targeting, Positioning

Segmentation

The segmentation begins by dividing consumers into two categories: hockey players and non–hockey players. The mass market (in Canada) generally includes many hockey affiliates. By segmenting hockey players versus non–hockey players, DSL is able to separate possible consumers from those who would have no interest or need for the Rack. Next, hockey parents are segmented from non–hockey parents. Parents can be both hockey players and have children who play hockey. Nonparents are primarily singles or couples who play hockey but do not have children who play hockey. From this, we separate them into gender, simplified here as male and female (but noting that a more diverse set of options would be important in any real life segmentation), which will apply to both mothers and fathers of children as well as male and female hockey players. Finally, using age as a base, the market is segmented into five identified age groups: 0 to 18 years old, 19 to 25, 26 to 40, 41 to 60, and 61 and over.

The 0 to 18 age group represents children who would be unable to purchase their own hockey equipment. Also, people in this age group generally do not have children, but in the rare case they do, the child will not be old enough to play until the parent is no longer in this segment. The 19 to 25 age group represents people attending the university and not married or in a common-law relationship. This group is young and has not started to work full time, so they do not have much income. The 26 to 40 age group includes people starting to settle down by getting married and having children as well as people who have been married for some time and have preteen children. This age group is also generally involved in playing hockey if they participate in adult hockey leagues after work. Part of the segment—those 35 to 39—is one of the largest population segments in Ontario. The 41 to 60 age group typically represents parents of older children who are getting ready to start high school or move on to university. These children generally participate in hockey more often due to playing in representative (aka travel) leagues within their community. Also, many of these parents are generally players of adult hockey leagues. The 61 and over age group represents grandparents or parents of adults who are just starting to get married and have children. People in this age group generally do not play adult hockey anymore. Our complete segmentation charts can be seen in tables 20.1a, 20.1b, and 20.1c.

Targeting

The target market pursued as priority #1 is the segment of male and female parents aged 26 to 40. This target market has compatible goals with DSL. The male and female segment of parents aged 26 to 40 noted in the market research survey that they wanted a quality product, stating the main reason they are not currently in the market for equipment racks was due to their poor quality. This clearly aligns with the organizational goal of producing a quality product, therefore creating compatible goals with the chosen target market. The second criterion is that the market opportunity must match company resources. DSL is currently very confident that it will be able to supply the target market with all the product and resources needed to be successful. The third criterion is that the target market must have an opportunity to generate enough sales to earn a profit. The male and female segment of parents aged 26 to 40 is an affluent segment of the Ontario population very focused on their children and investing in their children.

This positions DSL with the potential to earn a profit. In the market research, the majority of the males and females surveyed in this specific segment stated they are actively playing hockey, meaning they are potential consumers for an equipment rack. Moreover, the children's age group in this segment has some of the highest minor hockey registration numbers in the country. For instance, the tyke age groups have the most hockey players in Canada, accounting for 20 percent of the total registration numbers. As tykes are 5 to 6 years of age, they would fit perfectly into the chosen target market providing that the parents have their first child near the age of 26 or older, placing them at 31 years of age or older when registering their children. As hockey is considered to be the most expensive sport to get a child involved in, a product such as the Rack that can help preserve equipment as long as possible would be a very persuasive offer.

The final criterion for selection of the target market is based on the fact that it must allow for a competitive advantage. DSL believes it can establish a competitive advantage by targeting the male and female segment of parents aged 26 to 40 because this specific segment is frustrated with the quality of current equipment racks

TABLE 20.1a Segmentation Chart: Males and Females Who Play Hockey but Do Not Have Children Playing Hockey

Age Group	0 to 18	19 to 25	26 to 40	41 to 60
Who	youth, children, teenagers	young adults	middle-aged adults	older adults
What	something to refresh and dry equipment	something to refresh and dry equipment	something to refresh and dry equipment	something to refresh and dry equipment
When	seasonal: late summer to early fall	seasonal: late summer to early fall	seasonal: late summer to early fall	seasonal: late summer to early fall
Where	department stores	department stores and specialty sporting goods stores	department stores and specialty sporting goods stores	department stores and specialty sporting goods stores
Why	dry and preserve equipment, remove odour	dry and preserve equipment, remove odour	dry and & preserve equipment, remove odour	dry and preserve equipment, remove odour
How	parents or guardians supply equipment	purchase at department, sporting goods stores	purchase at department, sporting goods stores	purchase at department, sporting goods stores

TABLE 20.1b Segmentation Chart: Males and Females Who Play Hockey and Have Children Playing Hockey

Age Group	19-25	26-40	41-60
Who	mothers & fathers who play & have very young children just starting to play	mothers & fathers who play & have young children, teenagers who play	mothers & fathers who play & have teenagers, young adults who play
What	something to refresh & dry equipment	something to refresh & dry equipment	something to refresh & dry equipment
When	seasonal: late summer to early fall	seasonal: late summer to early fall	seasonal: late summer to early fall
Where	department stores & specialty sporting goods stores	department stores & specialty sporting goods stores	department stores & specialty sporting goods stores
Why	dry & preserve equipment, remove odour	dry & preserve equipment, remove odour	dry & preserve equipment/ remove odour
How	purchase at department/ sporting goods stores	purchase at department/ sporting goods stores	purchase at department/ sporting goods stores

TABLE 20.1c Segmentation Chart: Males Who Play Hockey but Are Not Parents of Children Who Play Hockey

Age Group	0-18	19-25	26-40	41-60
Who	n/a	mothers and fathers with very young children just starting to play	mothers and fathers with young children or teenagers who play	mothers and fathers with teenagers or young adults who play
What	n/a	something to refresh and dry equipment	something to refresh and dry equipment	something to refresh and dry equipment
When	n/a	seasonal: late summer to early fall	seasonal: late summer to early fall	seasonal: late summer to early fall
Where	n/a	department stores and specialty sporting goods stores	department stores and specialty sporting goods stores	department stores and specialty sporting goods stores
Why	n/a	dry and preserve equipment, remove odour	dry and preserve equipment, remove odour	dry and preserve equipment, remove odour
How	n/a	purchase at department, sporting goods stores	purchase at department, sporting goods stores	purchase at department, sporting goods stores

on the market. Since quality is an important component of the Rack, this has the potential to provide for a competitive advantage over the competition. If consumers purchase the Rack because it is superior to competitors' products, it is because it is both longer lasting and will save consumers money in the future. Another competitive advantage of DSL's marketing approach is that it targets the parents of children as soon as they begin to play hockey. If the Rack can successfully gain consumer loyalty early on in a children's hockey career, the potential for future sales is higher.

Positioning

With the many types of competition in the market, both direct and indirect, positioning the product in the minds of the target market correctly will be key to success. The market research undertaken informs the positioning. Once again, questionnaire results showed that the target market was primarily concerned with the quality of the product. They also believed that some of the direct competitors' products were very unstable and poorly constructed. This information led DSL to take two positioning strategies and combine parts of both. The firm adopted the "set apart" strategy to focus on the innovation and differences of the Rack product from the market's current products (specifically the fan and ABS piping product attributes) but also incorporates the "against competition" approach. These two strategies combined will show that the Rack product can be superior to the competition based on superior innovative quality.

A product position map was created to illustrate how the Rack would compare to the competition. The results of how this process are presented in figure 20.3, which illustrates how the consumer will perceive the product in terms of price and quality compared to the competitors in the industry. The placement of the Rack on the perceptual map is high in both price and quality. There is not much competition in this market of high-quality products with the exception of one substitute, the Shock Doctor hockey bag, which is much more expensive. This bag tries to incorporate a fan like the Rack does, but it is not sold with a fan and, therefore, has a combined cost of about double the Rack's proposed retail price. The other competitors have all adopted low-cost strategies that have resulted in low-quality products.

Marketing Strategy and the Four Ps

Product Strategy

The Desert Dry Rack will be a new tangible shopping good on the market. While there are similar products already on the market, the Rack has obvious differences in terms of quality and efficiency. Because there are similar products, this product will be entering this market segment in the market growth stage. This will help early sales as customers will gain awareness of the new product while investigating more established yet less effective products that are used to dry hockey equipment and prevent odour. Customers have adopted the idea of an

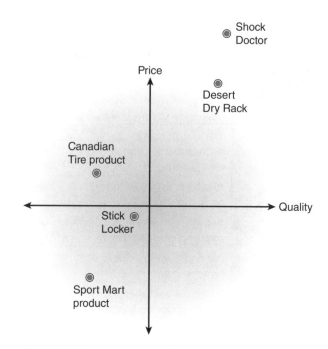

FIGURE 20.3 Positioning chart.

equipment rack but have been displeased with the quality, which has led to a deterioration of the potential market size and a large number using homemade solutions. With an emphasis on quality and efficiency, DSL feels that the Rack will be able to capitalize on part of the early adopters as well as the early majority consumers. Table 20.2 summarizes the four Ps of the marketing plan.

DSL is a business-to-consumer (B2C) company; however, it plans to use an intermediary retailer to sell the product to the consumers. Therefore, a large part of its integrated marketing plan is devoted to business-to-business (B2B) selling.

Since the market is already established and aware of similar products, DSL will attempt a product-modification strategy by altering a current product to meet the needs of customers, as well as adding new features and packaging. Through this strategy, the hope is to entice new customers to try the product as well as grab part of the existing market share.

Price Strategy

The market is based primarily on monopolistic competition, in which there is strong competition over price and product differentiation.

TABLE 20.2   Key Elements of Marketing Plan

Price	Place	Promotional emphasis	Purchase behaviour
Premium pricing to offset the costs of technology development	More selective outlets (e.g., SportChek) and online offering (e.g., Amazon, retailers' websites)	Differentiation from competitors based on quality and enhanced features	Infrequently purchased product; comparison shopping used; consumers spend time making the decision

From the market research, DSL has concluded that the potential target market is not very price sensitive and is willing to spend extra dollars to ensure high quality and purchase a product that will last.

The pricing window for the Rack has a very high floor price due mainly to the high material costs of nearly $55 per unit. After fixed costs and advertising are added on, the floor price nears $63 per unit. The ceiling price per unit was projected to be near $100 per unit sold, but research indicated that this price point could reduce the number of units sold. Therefore, the target selling price to retailers is about $75 per unit. Considering a significant margin and their costs, a manufacturer's suggested list price (MSLP) of $99 is recommended to retailers. This will provide sufficient contribution per unit but still be low enough to appeal to consumers. The $99 price point is a good example of perceptual pricing as well.

The value of the Rack product relies heavily on the perception of quality by the consumer. Marketing efforts will emphasize the improved quality of our product in comparison to competition, which will substantiate the chosen price point. However, there are constraints on the pricing because of the fact that the market is one of monopolistic competition.

In the early years of production, cost and volume analyses will not be based entirely on margins. The focus will be on break-even volume, first, and secondly on cost reduction. Unfortunately, high production costs in the early stages due to the labour needed to produce the product will be a challenge.

The pricing strategy is best described as premium pricing. Competitive pricing is not justifiable since the Rack is an innovative product with additional features beyond competitors'

products. Moreover, since the proposed return per unit is relatively low, DSL needs to recuperate costs based on the initial investment. By charging a reservation price on market entry—meaning the highest price a consumer is willing to pay based on perceived quality—DSL is aiming to associate higher price with higher quality.

In the short-term plan, a higher price is helpful in testing the market for price sensitivity as well as developing customers' perceptions of high quality and efficiency. In the long run, economies of scale will grow and production prices will drop, potentially leading to a more competition-oriented pricing strategy.

Promotion Strategy

The promotion "P" involves developing the promotional mix for the Rack as well as considering the development of the content for those various channels and tactics. In following from the advised integrated approach to promotions, a series of concurrent strategy steps are provided here.

Digital content: To create awareness of the Rack and build a following of interested customers, both a website and a series of social media platforms will be built and launched. A logo, slogans, and style will be developed.

Print material: To further create awareness of the new product in arena and retail settings, print material will be created by developing standard templates for advertisement style, logo, and slogans that will make it easier for product recognition. The main focus of the print material will be weekly Ontario Minor Hockey Association (OMHA) magazine advertisements (traditional and digital), which reach over 100,000 hockey player households across Ontario. Ads will be placed to advertise our product to Ontario residents involved in hockey, which will notify the customer they can purchase the product at their nearest SportChek. The budget and timing for these materials is found in table 20.3.

Publicity: Newspaper articles, web posts, blogger comments, and possible news coverage will provide DSL with further awareness among the public. To facilitate news coverage, various press releases will be sent to relevant media. As well, in any way possible, networking will be done with journalists, especially through existing connections in sports, to convince them to publish articles on the product.

Sponsorship in-kind: A strategic alliance will be formed with Arm & Hammer to create a sponsorship in-kind partnership, where DSL will be supplied with Arm & Hammer's new Fridge Fresh product as part of the product bundle. The Fridge Fresh will be attached to the Rack with a suction as a deodorizer for the hockey equipment. Arm & Hammer products are in nearly 60 percent of households across the United States and will help DSL expand its reach to more potential consumers. The only criterion that Arm & Hammer considers when looking to create a business relationship is that the product must be ranked either number 1 or 2 in its market. By establishing a relationship between DSL and Arm & Hammer, Arm & Hammer will receive improved reach into the sports market. Also, once the initial Arm & Hammer product has been used by the consumer, the consumer will need to go to the store to buy a new Arm & Hammer product if they want their equipment to continue to be deodorized. This benefits Arm & Hammer by driving their sales up if the product is effective in achieving continued use.

Promotional material: Each sales location (e.g., at SportChek) will have a sample display of the product, where consumers can examine and test to see how the product works. The plan is that with a sample of the product, consumers will be able to observe first-hand the quality the product offers, which will help raise their perceived value of the Rack.

Personal selling: Since key success factors for the Rack include the partnerships with SportChek, Arm & Hammer, and suppliers, the majority of the personal selling will be devoted to keeping strong and healthy distribution channels. Push strategies will be adopted to sell products to retailers, since DSL does not yet have enough financial or market pull to justify a pull strategy, which will be a longer-term consideration.

Summary of promotional mix: DSL has put in place the goal to have about 20 percent of the (potential) market share after the first five years of operation. Following the launch in Ontario, the plan is to move to a national offering quickly. Thus, by year five, achieving this goal would equate to about 100,000 consumers across Canada. Since the product is very seasonal with peak sales likely occurring during the August through December period, the majority of our advertisements will be

TABLE 20.3 Advertising Cost Breakdown

	Duration in Months	Cost per Month	Total Expense	Type of Advertisement
Magazine ads*	5	$1,467	$7,335	Total cost for eight ads and an article in two different magazines
Hockey tournament	1		$5,000	January
One-time cost	1		$16,500	Promo displays
Strictly Visual	1		$3,000	Design of all promotional materials, logo, etc.
Website	12	$20	$240	Basic website design for an information page
Total			$32,075	

Note: Costs listed are estimates.
*Estimate includes digital and traditional ads.

posted during near the beginning of the ice hockey season.

Place Strategy

Our main retailer will be SportChek/Sports Experts, which gives us nationwide reach of about 260 stores, as well as an extensive online offering. In the early stages of our development, as noted, the focus of marketing efforts will be on Ontario, with more than 90 store locations to sell our product. The majority of these are located in densely populated areas such as the GTA and Ottawa.

The two intermediaries within this group are the SportChek distribution centre and SportChek/Sports Experts retail stores themselves, as well as the SportChek website. However, DSL will also seek to establish a strategic channel alliance to ship the Rack through the SportChek/Sports Experts distribution centre to the retailers themselves.

Each part of the Rack product has a separate supply channel, ranging from the ABS tubing to the all-purpose glue, rack base, fan, and box. These suppliers are relatively close to the DSL production warehouse, the majority being based in GTA. This will reduce the stress of maintaining long-term business relations and allowing for better communications and shipping efficiency and accuracy.

Financials

Break-Even Analysis

The material costs are about $55 per unit. After fixed costs and advertising are added, our floor price nears $63 per unit. The selling price to retailers is $75 per unit. Using these figures, our break-even sales point at the most likely sales estimate of 4,638 units (figure 20.4).

Sales Forecasts

To fully analyze sales potential for the Rack, three detailed sales estimates follow.

Pessimistic sales estimate: This estimate included each of 110 stores selling 30 units, for a total of 3,300 units. This would produce sales of $242,550, with cost of goods sold totalling $175,347 for a gross margin of $67,203. The result would be a negative net income of $3,654. This amount decreases in the second year showing a promising net income for the third year.

Most likely sales estimate: This estimate included each of 110 stores selling 60 units, for a total of 6,600 units. This would produce sales of $485,100, with cost of goods sold totalling $350,695 for a gross margin of $134,405. The result would be a net income of about $27,000. In the second year, there would be a net income of about $34,000.

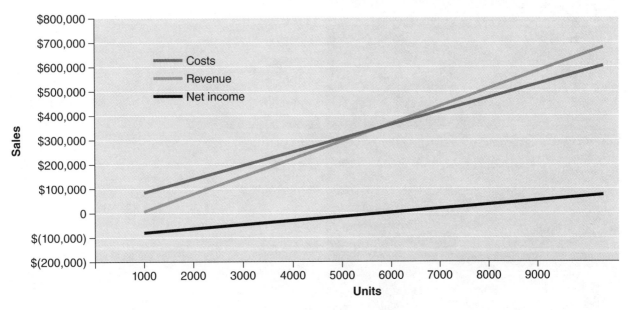

FIGURE 20.4 Break-even analysis.

Optimistic sales estimate: This estimate included each of 110 stores selling 90 units, for a total of 9,900 units. This would produce sales of $727,650, with cost of goods sold totalling $526,042 for a gross margin of $201,608. The result would be a net income of about $58,000. In the second year, there would be a net income of about $68,000.

Expenses

A warehouse lease cost was arranged via an online broker for a warehouse in Mississauga. Insurance costs were estimated by reviewing similar costs of local retailers and taking into consideration that retailers carry more inventory than manufacturing businesses typically do. Utility costs were estimated in the same way. Because of the central location to all of our suppliers and our distributor, estimated freight costs were 3 percent of the merchandise cost. Office supplies were estimated at $125 due to the small office space and reduced distributor paperwork. Selling expenses would include all travel and meeting costs. An estimated accounting cost of $5,000 per year is included, along with estimated legal fees of $10,000 for the first year on the basis of all start-up fees. Miscellaneous costs are estimated as a percentage of sales, allowing for unforeseen costs related to increases in sales. A breakdown of expenses can be seen in the projected income statement in table 20.4.

Implementation and Control

Following the product development stage (figure 20.5), DSL will ship the product to be sold through SportChek stores. Once the product is in the store, DSL will meet with the salespeople at SportChek stores to obtain customer feedback, to develop techniques for best selling the product going forward, and to learn of any challenges that exist. Additionally, depending on the information these salespeople provide

TABLE 20.4 Projected Budgeted Income Statement, Year Ending April 30, 2021

Sales	$242,550.00	
Cost of goods sold	$175,347.48	
Gross margin		$67,202.52
OPERATING EXPENSES		
Rent	$13,800.00	
Insurance	$3,600.00	
Utilities	$6,000.00	
Freight	$5,395.43	
Office supplies	$1,500.00	
Selling expenses	$1,680.00	
Accounting expenses	$5,004.00	
Legal fees	$9,996.00	
Miscellaneous	$7,276.50	
Advertising	$15,575.00	
Total expenses		$69,826.93
Income from operations	($2,624.41)	
Interest	($3,465.00)	
Income before taxes	($6,089.41)	
Taxes (40%)	$2,435.76	
Net income	($3,653.65)	

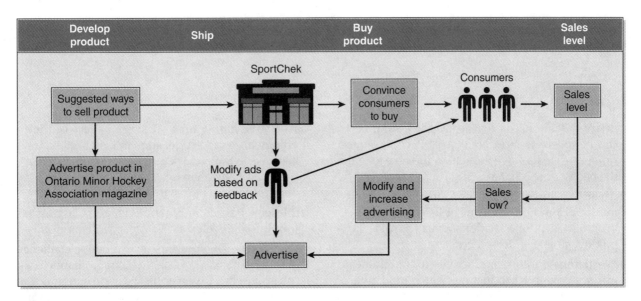

FIGURE 20.5 Implementation and control.

and the levels of sales of the product, modifications or increases to budget, promotions, and pricing may be undertaken.

A second strategy would be to switch to a different distributor. Many large department stores, such as Wal-Mart, have sporting goods sections and, as the Sudbury market research showed, there are a number of specialty stores out there.

Contingency Plan

If the outlined marketing strategy has not succeeded and the efforts at control and revision of marketing are insufficient to propel DSL to success, some changes in the marketing plan will be required. For example, if in-store sales are low, one alternative is altering the target market. Currently, the plan is to target the male and female hockey parent aged 26 to 40, but the higher-income 41- to 60-year-old hockey parent could provide a viable substitute or additional target market. Like the 26- to 40-year-olds, this market would primarily be purchasing for their children; however, there are several critical differences in the demographics of the children that could contribute to success. For instance, since these children tend to be older and have been playing longer, parents may be more likely to invest larger amounts in preserving their sporting equipment. They may even purchase more than one unit of the Rack. Additionally, since these children are reaching maturity, they will no longer replace equipment as regularly, increasing the necessity and desirability of taking better care of it. In the market research interviews with local retailers, many respondents noted that it is generally older males who come in to buy hockey equipment for their children.

CHAPTER SUMMARY

As the final chapter in the book, Chapter 20 provides an example of a sport marketing plan that was built, and has been updated over time, based specifically on the content from Chapters 1 to 19. The intention was to both provide a template for future marketing planning and also to outline how the content flows and how sport marketing is actionable.

GLOSSARY

ability—Basic skills of the target audience to counter peer pressure, break a habit, comprehend rational appeals, have the self-confidence to make the behavioural change.

activation—Integrating a sponsorship into its promotional mix, in the form of advertising, sales promotions, public relations, personal sales, hospitality, athlete endorsement, and so on.

advertising—Promotional activity to communicate information on a product or create brand awareness and brand loyalty by using paid announcement in various media.

advertising inventory—Opportunities available for purchase during or around the broadcast of an event, such as 30-second commercial spots, in-program graphics, and opening and closing segments of a broadcast.

allowance—A reduction in price given by a manufacturer to a retailer due to hitting sales targets, a form of an incentive.

amateur sport—Sport in which athletes are not remunerated.

ambush marketing—A practice whereby another company, often a competitor, intrudes upon public attention surrounding the event, thereby deflecting attention to itself and away from the sponsor. An accepted definition is, "a planned effort (campaign) by an organization to associate itself indirectly with an event in order to gain at least some of the recognition and benefits that are associated with being an official sponsor" (Sandler & Shani, 1989, p. 10).

analog—Systems and processes that are physical and do not feature or encompass computer technology.

antidoping movement—The movement, led by the World Anti-Doping Agency in partnership with governments and sport organizations worldwide, to eradicate doping (or cheating through the use of banned substances) from sport.

appealing social media content—Appealing social media content refers to the management of a social media that actively interacts with users and humanizes the organization with the use of humor, wittiness, and clever topical comments when both interacting with users and sharing information.

associative ambushing—Using imagery or terminology to create a suggestion that an organization has links to the event, leading consumers to believe that the organization is involved with (or supports) the event when in fact that's not the case.

athletes—Participants who engage in organized training to develop skills in particular sports.

attribution—The sponsorship evaluation challenge of attributing a consumer behaviour change back to a sponsorship, versus the other promotions that the sponsor and its competitors are implementing at the same time.

augmented reality—A virtual environment where information and objects are digitally overlaid or super imposed on real-world settings.

B2B—Business-to-business, or industrial, marketing, where organizations market to other organizations, which may in turn market to consumers.

B2C—Business-to-consumer marketing, where a product is marketed directly to the consumer, in contrast to business-to-business (B2B) marketing.

balanced combination—Balanced combination refers to the construction of a social media content that include written text, mentions, hashtags, and weblinks to video clips and pictures. Cristiano Ronaldo's Twitter account is a good example.

bandwidth—The rate at which information can be passed over a cable.

barriers—Structural or political elements that limit the influence and adoption of social marketing.

behaviour—The actions of human beings.

blackout—A broadcasting restriction imposed by broadcasters, professional sports teams, their leagues, and/or other sport federations (e.g., IOC).

brand—The name, logo, and other outward symbols that distinguish a product or service from others in its category.

brand association—Anything linked in memory to a brand; an intangible set of associations that can be categorized into experiential and symbolic.

brand equity—Brand awareness, perceived quality, brand associations, and brand loyalty.

brand extension—The use of an already established brand and the loan of a brand from one entity to another.

brand image—The impression a brand conveys to consumers.

branding—Creating a brand with an image that perfectly matches the image that the target markets seek association with.

brand management—Strategic implementation of all aspects of the brand, which involves aligning all the brand's attributes for maximum effectiveness and ensuring that no organization action compromises the brand.

break-even point—Point where expected total revenue is zero once all the costs are paid.

casters—Similar to play-by-play announcers in sports media, these are individuals who comment on esports gameplay by broadcasting a third-party view of the virtual gameplay arena to others.

census—Secondary research information collected by Statistics Canada.

cloud—Remote servers designed to store and manage data, run applications, and deliver content to users on demand through the Internet without physically storing and accessing files or data from a large or extra-large hardware device.

club—A service that offers consumers a chance to get involved with sport as a participant and that provides a social venue.

clutter—Advertising or sponsoring messages vying to get the attention of fans, spectators, and potential consumers, which may cause confusion in the marketplace.

coattail ambushing—An ambusher attempt to directly associate itself with a property using a legitimate link, such as participating athletes.

commercialism—Corporate interests that penetrate the Olympics (e.g., sponsorship, broadcasting, licensing) for commercial purposes.

company—The organization or entity that is offering the products or services to consumers.

competition—Another organization or product competing with you for customers.

consoles—Computerized hardware devices that are primarily designed for the consumption of video games, and that which require display monitors and controller peripherals to play.

consumer—A person who purchases a product or service.

consumption—The act of searching, identifying, purchasing, and using a product or service.

control—Feedback loop to test the effectiveness of marketing programs.

cord-cutters—A person who cancels their cable television subscription in favour of an Internet or wireless OTT product or no alternative altogether.

costs—Expenditures to produce a product or service and then take it to market.

critical path method—A project management tool that is used for scheduling a set of project activities including tasks along with deliverable dates.

database—A data management system.

data mining—Involves uncovering previously unknown trends via the analysis of existing data.

data saturation—The point when a researcher doing interviews ceases to observe new findings or inputs from any additional interviewee, thereby suggesting that the research is complete.

data warehouse—A large repository of historical data that allows an organization to analyze trends in financing, market performance, or consumer taste over a specified time, and on a broader scale than the medium-format database typically used by organizations and individuals, such as a reference database of baseball statistics.

demand—The need for a given product in a specific market.

descriptive research—Research used to determine the answer to a specific problem, such as, "What are the values of social media in sport marketing?"

digital sport product—Any goods or services which harness electronic and especially computerized technology to enhance or complement consumer sport, fitness, or recreation needs or desires.

discount—A set of reductions in price that a seller offers to a consumer to encourage early payment, the purchase of larger volumes of product, or supporting a long-term relationship.

distinguishing features—Features that make social media unique and different from other communication mediums. The features include user-generated content, no "gate keeper," content availability, community driven, omnipresence, multi-purpose, and dynamism.

distribution—The process of moving a product or service from the producer to the consumer through one or many channels of distribution.

distribution channel—The set of companies and individuals that participate in getting the product from the producer to the consumer; includes wholesalers, retailers, dealers, distributors, brokers, franchises, and agents.

dualistic typology—An approach used to classify sport fans into two categories—fans who identify themselves with a team, and those who only consume sport for entertainment purposes.

e-commerce—Buying or selling goods and services using the Internet, especially the World Wide Web.

elasticity—The change in demand for a product following a change in price—an elastic market is very sensitive to changes in price, while an inelastic market is not.

endemic—Sponsorship whereby the sponsor's products are directly linked to the sport of the property, such as a swimwear manufacturer sponsoring a national swim team.

enterprise resource planning system—Linkable application modules purchased from a single vendor and meant to draw from a single repository of data.

esports—Also called electronic sport, this is as an organized video game competition in which individuals or teams compete (in leagues or tournaments) for money or prizes and that is open to spectators (in person or online).

evaluation—A critical assessment of plans, undertakings, and outcomes, thereby providing information for future action.

event—The core sport product form which stimulates and drives production of all other sport products.

exchange—A transaction in which both parties receive value that they perceive to be greater than what the exchange costs them.

exclusivity—An opportunity for sales-driven use of the sponsorship agreement that prohibits competitors from using the event, venue, product, or activity to transmit a message to the audience.

explanatory research—Research used to determine cause and effect of relationships between known variables, such as, "Why do managers see social media as a valuable marketing tool?"

exploratory research—Research used initially to determine the real problem or issue, such as What value do sport managers place on social media in sport marketing?

extended reality—The umbrella term to describe new, immersive technologies.

facility—An extension of the event product and a destination itself, often offering visitors not only a place to sit when they attend a game but also a full entertainment service.

fan cost index—Team Marketing Report study of total costs to attend professional sport games.

fantasy sport—Fantasy sport is a type of online prediction game that allows users to build an imaginary sport team composed of real-life sports players (e.g., in hockey) and play against other users for a chosen amount of time, whether a single day (commonly referred to as daily fantasy) or the entire season.

form—The tangible properties of a product.

gamification—Adding elements of competition such as point scoring or a standard set of rules to an activity typically to encourage engagement with a product or service.

go viral—Becoming popular in a short period of time by the spread of information from person to person through digital means such as social media and the World Wide Web.

grassroots sport—Sport that is based in local communities and participation by the general public, and which may or may not be designated as an Olympic discipline.

hardware—Technical information technology objects like smartphones, tablets, and laptops that you can physically touch.

hole in the market—A niche or a particular segment whose needs or wants have not been adequately met.

implementation—A stage where actions are taken, and plans are executed in a manner that accomplishes the plan's stated objectives.

impressions—The number of viewers (television or streaming), followers (social media platforms), readers (all print forms), and listeners (radio) exposed to a given marketing message.

information system—Any electronic device or apparatus that manages, stores, and shares data to drive new insights about the operation.

information technology—The hardware and software that supports communication.

league—A group of teams; a service that provides the framework for sport competition; a sellable brand that can be sold as merchandise, is best represented by a logo and official name, and offers other benefits to the consumer, such as pride and nostalgia.

marketing—An exchange between two parties that provides a win–win benefit to both.

marketing mix—Comprises the strategic elements—product, price, promotion, and place.

market segmentation—The process of dividing a population of potential customers into homogeneous market segments.

measurability—The ability of a marketer to measure the attitudes, behaviours, and demographics of a market segment when designing its marketing actions.

measurement fact—It refers to the fact that there is no a magic metrics that processes and tells all the gains and losses in the measurement of return on social media investment. Instead, there are methods that help us gain insights about the level of accomplishment of preestablished objectives.

media—A sport product form that depends on the production of sport events, athletes, leagues, and teams to provide the information they need to produce their own sport product.

media kit—A media folder that includes a schedule of events, personalities' bios, statistics, an interview request form, accreditations, a fact sheet, technical information, a history of the sport, a sponsor list, a video clip on a memory stick, and action shots; it is given out to journalists at a press conference or media room or delivered directly to the media.

media relations—The relationships between the sport organization and the media, focusing on improving the media coverage the sport organization receives.

media rights fee—the fee that a broadcasting company (e.g., CBC) pays to a property owner (e.g., the IOC) to have the official right to produce, distribute and transmit content related to an agreed-on property.

merchandise—A tangible good that is manufactured, distributed, and marketed within the sport industry.

mixed reality—Involves both real-world settings, new virtual settings and objects, and the ability to alternate and mix both simultaneously.

mobile apps—Computer programs or software that are specifically designed and optimized for smartphones, tablets, and smartwatches to stimulate ongoing consumption.

motivation—The desire to change behaviour after being convinced that the change will lead to self-benefit.

multidimensional typology—An approach used to classify sport fans into multidimensional typologies. These typologies are proposed based on the different ways in which consumers display their level of devotion, which has an impact on game attendance, broadcast viewing, and the purchase of team merchandise.

nonendemic—Sponsorship in which the sponsor's products are unrelated to the sport property of interest, such as an auto manufacturer sponsoring a yachting race.

Olympic marketing—Revenue-generating programs, including sponsorship, broadcasting, ticket sales, and licensing.

Olympic movement—An umbrella term that includes all entities involved with the Olympic Games (e.g., athletes, coaches, administrators, fans, owners).

Olympic sport—A high-performance athletic competition in which athletes compete for personal, rather than direct economic, gain. Indirect economic gain (e.g., sponsorship, government funding) is possible in some cases.

opportunity—Known environmental mechanism at hand allowing target audiences to behave.

packaging—How the product is presented to the potential customer; it refers to everything from the design of the cardboard box or plastic container for a tangible good (e.g., golf balls) to the pageantry and ambiance around a live event.

paid content—Paid content is a service available with social media platforms that enables your message to reach a wider audience beyond your followers and thereby to reach potential new followers.

participant—People who consume sport by taking part in or playing a sporting activity.

participation—Getting involved with sports at all levels and in all forms; sport consumers' primary method of engagement.

perceptual map—A graphic representation of positioning in the minds of consumers in the target market.

personal selling—A form of promotion in which individuals representing a company provide information on the product or service to potential buyer through direct dialogue.

pitch—The opportunity for a sport property (or its agent) to present to a potential sponsor (brand) about the sponsorship that they could provide.

place—The ability to purchase or receive the product at a convenient and accessible location; ensuring distribution is set up to get the product to consumers.

point-of-purchase—Retail promotion that enhances sport's image connection with the consumer by featuring a sport, a team, or an athlete.

POP—Point-of-purchase displays include merchandising of all sorts—kiosks, cardboard cut-outs, signage—targeted at consumers at the location of the purchase decision.

positioning—Developing a marketing strategy that positions the product in the minds of consumers in relation to the competition.

possession—The ability for the consumer to take ownership of the product that was purchased.

premium—A giveaway that is tied with a sponsor's product as part of the sales promotion.

price—A cost that leads to perceived value.

product—A tangible good, service, idea, or behaviour.

professional sport—Leagues and athletes that represent private enterprise or compete in exchange for economic gain.

promotion—Communicating information to the consumers to influence them to buy a product or service.

property—An entity that can provide value to a potential sponsor; the organization being sponsored.

positioning—The use of perceptual mapping to position your offering versus that of the competition.

press conference—an invited media-covered news conference at which journalists ask questions about a newly publicized press release.

primary research—Accumulating data created specifically for the purpose of the research.

program evaluation review technique—A project management tool that provides a graphical representation of a project's timeline.

promotional mix—Tools used to communicate information about a product—its function, characteristics, price, place, and so on—to inform and persuade consumers and thus influence their purchase decisions.

property infringement—Ambushing practice that involves the intentional unauthorized use of protected intellectual property, such as a logo, a name, or words.

publicity—An important component of promotion through media outlets for which sport marketers do not directly pay.

public relations—Communicating a sport organization's activities to a group of identified and evaluated external publics through various media, ensuring positive support and awareness of the focal organization.

relationship—A long-term set of multiple exchanges between marketer and consumer.

responsiveness—How a market segment responds to marketing action.

return on investment (ROI)—Return on investment, which is usually measured in monetary or media forms.

rights fee—Amount charged for the rights to exclusively broadcast a given sport property/sponsee.

sales promotion—A marketing promotion designed to stimulate immediate demand for a product or service, generate consumer goodwill, and/or reinforce the relationship between consumers and a company.

sampling—Examining a smaller, randomly chosen selection (the sample) of group members to obtain information about a large group.

saturation ambushing—Increasing advertisements at the time of an event with no reference to or association with the event.

scheduling content—Scheduling content is an automated service available with social media platforms where a content can be created well in advance, deposited, and scheduled to be released at a predetermined time.

secondary research—Research on data already collected for other uses.

second screen—The term used to describe sport consumers using their smartphone or tablet to interact with the sport product while simultaneously watching sport on their television or computer screen.

segmentation—Dividing up the market into distinct homogeneous groups.

segmentation, targeting, and positioning (STP)—The process, or "bridge," between market research and marketing strategy, comprising the sequential steps of segmentation, targeting, and positioning.

sensitivity—How easily a group of consumers will alter their purchase patterns due to a price change, which is reflected in the number of categories used to assess a give base of segmentation.

servicing—The fulfilment of all the contractual elements promised to the sponsor by the property. This includes providing the assets agreed to in the contact, such offers as website content, signage, social media posts, access to celebrities or athletes, rights to marks or logos, and so on.

skilled services—Those aspects of the sport product form that involve a skilled professional providing a sport-related service to consumers that influences the level of sport or fitness performance.

smartwatches—A mobile device, normally worn on the wrist, with a touchscreen display, mimicking a smartphone's ability to access common mobile applications.

social marketing—Adaptation of commercial marketing technologies to programs designed to influence the voluntary behaviour of target audiences to improve their personal welfare and that of the society of which they are a part.

social media—An online resources open to the public (e.g., blogs, social networks, content communities, and discussion sites) that people use primarily to share content (e.g., text, photo, audio files, and video) and engage in conversation on Internet applications (e.g., Facebook, Twitter, YouTube).

social media influencers—These are social media users who have a large number of followers, who post content that address the needs and interests of their followers, and who are considered by their followers as advocates, representatives, sources, and guides.

social media platforms—These refer to the four different categories of social media: social networks (e.g., Facebook, Twitter), content communities (e.g., Instagram, YouTube), blogs (e.g., Maple Leafs Hot Stove), and discussion sites (e.g., Reddit, Quora).

software—Programs and applications that run on hardware devices.

spectator—People who observe the performance of a game by attending live sporting events at a stadium or following the game through the media.

spectatorship—Commonly associated with professional sport, opportunities in communities all over the country for people to get out and support local teams.

sponsor—Organization that provides the financial support or services to a property in return for marketing value.

sponsor recognition programs—Promotional activities developed by a sponsored party to increase consumer awareness of who the official sponsors are and help consumers differentiate between official and nonofficial sponsors.

sponsorship—A promotional approach in which an organization or individual offers resources (e.g., financial) or services to support a sport organization's event, program, or product offering. An accepted definition is "an investment, in cash or in kind, in an activity, in return for access to the exploitable commercial potential associated with that activity" (Meenaghan, 1991, p. 36).

sponsorship category—The industry or subindustry area of interest for which a sponsor will sell a sponsorship, often in an exclusive way (i.e., only one sponsor per category). Examples are financial services, energy drinks, fast food restaurant, beer, and so on.

sponsorship evaluation—The process of assessing the effectiveness of a sponsorship in achieving the goals that each stakeholder set out to achieve with it.

sponsorship valuation—The method undertaken to determine a value or range of potential value for a given sponsorship. This can be one by estimating the value of the assets, comparing the sponsorship to similar ones where the price paid is known or assessing past performance of sponsorship on the objectives of the brand.

sport events—Opportunities for numerous social, economic, and cultural benefits including facility legacies, job creation, and volunteer development.

sport fan—An ardent devotee of sport, who is enthusiastic about a particular sport and is motivated to engage in behaviour related to that sport.

sport product—Any good, service, person, place, or idea with tangible or intangible attributes that satisfy consumer sport, fitness, or recreation needs or desires.

subscription-based video-on-demand (SVOD) service—An Internet-based service model in which a client pays a subscription fee to gain access to a library of content.

substitute—As a form of competition, this refers to any entertainment activity that could replace going to the game.

supply—Availability of a product to satisfy a given demand.

sweepstakes—Form of promotion that offers consumers the chance of winning a prize.

targeting—The step in STP following segmentation, when the marketer prioritizes which segment or segments of one or more target markets to pursue with their marketing efforts.

team—A collective product comprising a group of athletes who work together to create the on-field performance and represent a brand that can be sold to consumers.

tiered typology—An approach used to classify sport fans into tiered typologies. It takes into account the different levels or intensities of sport fans' attachment to a team—top-tier (vested or highly committed), middle-tier (expressive and focused), and bottom-tier (social and camaraderie) consumers.

time—The ability for the consumer to access a product at the point in time when its needed or wanted.

TOP Program—The Olympic Partner Program consists of agreements with companies that are based on a quadrennial structure and therefore require at least four years' commitment; TOP partner companies are multinational organizations that provide direct support, sponsor services, or expertise for staging the Games.

tracking—Involves quantitative surveys targeted at audience and implemented through on-site intercepts, telephone surveys, surveys of employees, and customers. Topics can include knowledge of sponsorship, sponsor recall, attitudes toward sponsors, and behavioural changes resulting from a sponsorship.

unintentional ambushing—Ambushing caused by the inadvertent consumer identification of a non-sponsoring company as an official sponsor, often based on a previous association with the event based on a former official sponsorship.

user-friendly—Any electronic or computerized technology which presents an interface to consumers that is easy to use and not difficult to understand.

utility—Value provided from satisfying a need or want.

values ambushing—Using an event or property's central value or theme to imply an association.

variable cost—Added cost to build just one more item.

virtual reality—An interactive computer-generated simulation of a sport participation or spectator experience via a 3D image or environment.

REFERENCES

Chapter 1

American Marketing Association. (2017). Definition of marketing. www.ama.org/the-definition-of-marketing-what-is-marketing/

Bartels, R. (1976). *The history of marketing thought* (2nd ed.). Grid.

Dewan, T., Jensen, K., Farrell, C., & O'Reilly. N. (2005). *Marketing: What is it good for?* Copley.

Foster, G., O'Reilly, N., & Davila, A. (2020). *Sports business management: Decision-making around the globe* (2nd ed.). Routledge.

Fullerton, S., & Merz, G.R. (2008). The four domains of sports marketing: A conceptual framework. *Sport Marketing Quarterly, 17*(2), 90-108.

Gray, D., & McEvoy, C. (2005). Sport marketing strategies and tactics. In B. Parkhouse (Ed.), *The management of sport: Its foundation and application.* McGraw-Hill.

O'Reilly, N., Foster, G., Murray, R., & Shimizu, C. (2015). Merchandise sales rank in professional sport: Purchase drivers and implications for national hockey league clubs. *Sport, Business,* Management: *An International Journal, 5*(4), 307-324.

Shank, M., & Lyberger, M. (2014). *Sports marketing: A strategic perspective* (4th ed.). Pearson-Prentice-Hall.

Washington, M., & Edwards, J.R. (2016). Exploring the role of private hockey schools and academies within Canada hockey industry. *Canadian Journal of Administrative Science, 33*(1), 7-20.

Chapter 2

Athletes CAN. (2006). History of Canadian sport and accomplishments of Athletes CAN. https://athletescan.com/sites/default/files/images/history-of-canadian-sport-accomplishments-of-athletescan.pdf

Brudnicki, A. (2019, October 16). Blue Jays to wrap spring training in Montreal. MLB. www.mlb.com/news/blue-jays-2020-spring-training-montreal-olympic-stadium-vs-yankees

Brunt, S. (2011, May 19). Atlanta Thrashers moving to Winnipeg. *The Globe and Mail.* Retrieved from web.archive.org/web/20110520015341/http://www.theglobeandmail.com/sports/hockey/atlanta-thrashers-moving-to-winnipeg/article2029179/

Canadian Olympic Committee. (2020a). About us. https://olympic.ca/canadian-olympic-committee/

Canadian Olympic Committee. (2020b). Role of the Canadian Olympic Committee. Retrieved from https://olympic.ca/canadian-olympic-committee/role-of-the-canadian-olympic-committee/

Canadian Olympic Committee. (2020c). 2018 Annual Report: Operations. Retrieved from https://annualreports.olympic.ca/operations/

Central Intelligence Agency. (2019). The World Factbook: North America: Canada. Retrieved from www.cia.gov/library/publications/the-world-factbook/geos/ca.html

Chin, F. (2017, October 6). Arena funding debate: A play that always unfolds over several acts. CBC News. www.cbc.ca/news/canada/calgary/calgaryelection-2017-arena-funding-debate-explainer-eyeopener-extra-podcast-1.4342529

Doherty, A. (2005). A profile of community sport volunteers. Parks and Recreation Ontario.

Donnelly, P., & Kidd, B. (2003). Realizing the expectations: Youth, character, and community in Canadian sport. In Centre for Sport Policy Studies (Ed.), *The sport we want: Essays on current issues in community sport in Canada* (pp. 25-44). Canadian Centre for Ethics in Sport.

Fitness and Amateur Sport Act. (1961, c. F-25). Retrieved from https://laws-lois.justice.gc.ca/eng/acts/f-25/20021231/P1TT3xt3.html

Hockey Canada. (2017). Annual Report: July 2016-June 2017. https://cdn.hockeycanada.ca/hockey-canada/Corporate/About/Downloads/2016-17-annual-report-e.pdf

Lucas, K. (2019, October 2). Athletic scholarships in Canada versus the United States. *Medium.* https://medium.com/streamline-athletes/athletic-scholarships-in-the-united-states-versus-canada-5a5531a4e13f

Macintosh, D., & Whitson, D. (1994). *The game planners.* McGill-Queen's University Press.

Ozanian, M. (2019, December 11). NHL's Most valuable teams 2019: Though buried in standings, New York Rangers remain on top. *Forbes.* Retrieved from www.forbes.com/sites/mikeozanian/2019/12/11/the-nhls-most-valuable-teams-2019-new-york-rangers-on-top-at-165-billion/#2417b8907163

Ralph, D. (2019, August 30). CFL commissioner Ambrosie feels league close to resolving Alouettes ownership. *CBC Sports.* www.cbc.ca/sports/football/cfl/cfl-mid-season-1.5266595

Rush, C. (2019, October 2). Toronto Blue Jays finish season ranked near bottom in attendance. *Forbes.* www.forbes.com/sites/curtisrush/2019/10/02/toronto-blue-jays-finish-season-ranked-near-bottom-in-attendance/#125705132a4d

Sam, M.P. (2011). Building legitimacy at Sport Canada: Pitfalls of public value creation? *International Review of Administrative Sciences, 77*, 757-778.

Semotiuk, D. (1994). Restructuring Canada's national sport system: The legacy of the Dubin Inquiry. In R.C. Wilcox (Ed.), *Sport in the global village* (pp. 365-375). Fitness Information Technology.

Settimi, C. (2020, February 12). The NBA's best fans: How the Raptors turned hockey-mad Canada into hoopsville. *Forbes.* www.forbes.com/sites/christinasettimi/2020/02/12/the-nbas-best-fans-how-the-raptors-turned-hockey-mad-canada-into-hoopsville/#1d793ffd2d1c

Simpson, M. (2021). NHL helmet sponsors for 2020-2021. https://www.thesponsorshipspace.com/post/nhl-helmet-sponsors-for-2020-21

Sport Canada. (2020a). Hosting program. Government of Canada. Retrieved from www.canada.ca/en/canadian-heritage/services/funding/hosting-program.html

Sport Canada. (2020b). Role of Sport Canada. Government of Canada. Retrieved from www.canada.ca/en/canadian-heritage/services/role-sport-canada.html

Sport Canada. (2020c). Sport funding and accountability framework. *Government of Canada.* Retrieved from www.canada.ca/en/canadian-heritage/services/funding/sport-support/accountability-framework.html#a4

Sport Information Resource Centre. (2019). Canadian sport policies. Retrieved from https://sirc.ca/canadian-sport-policies

Statista. (2020a). Canada: Population density from 2008 to 2018. Retrieved from www.statista.com/statistics/271206/population-density-in-canada/

Statista. (2020b). Major league soccer teams ranked by average per game attendance in 2019. Retrieved from www.statista.com/statistics/509326/mls-average-attendance-by-team-north-america/

Statista. (2020c). Netherlands: Population density from 2008 to 2018. Retrieved from www.statista.com/statistics/276723/population-density-in-the-netherlands/

Statista. (2020d). Number of immigrants in Canada from 2000 to 2019 (in 1,000s). Retrieved from www.statista.com/statistics/443063/number-of-immigrants-in-canada/

Statista. (2020e). Population density in the United States from 2008 to 2018. Retrieved from www.statista.com/statistics/269965/population-density-in-the-united-states/

Statista. (2020f). Real gross domestic product (GDP) of Canada from 2000 to 2019 (in billion Canadian dollars). Retrieved from www.statista.com/statistics/650869/real-gdp-canada/

Statistics Canada. (2019a). Annual demographic estimates: Canada, provinces and territories, 2019. Retrieved from www150.statcan.gc.ca/n1/pub/91-215-x/91-215-x2019001-eng.htm

Statistics Canada. (2019b). Language highlight tables, 2016 census. Retrieved from www12.statcan.gc.ca/census-recensement/2016/dp-pd/hlt-fst/lang/Table.cfm?Lang=E&T=21&Geo=00&SP=1&view=2&age=1

Statistics Canada. (2019c). Population estimates, July 1st, by age and sex. Retrieved from https://doi.org/10.25318/1710000501-eng

Statistics Canada. (2019d). Population estimates, July 1, by census metropolitan area and census agglomeration, 2016 boundaries. Retrieved from https://doi.org/10.25318/1710013501-eng

Statistics Canada. (2019e). Population estimates, quarterly. Retrieved from https://doi.org/10.25318/1710000901-eng

Statistics Canada. (2019f). Sports for fun and fitness. Retrieved from www150.statcan.gc.ca/n1/daily-quotidien/190521/dq190521c-eng.htm

Strong, G. (2017, April 8). COC announces $37-million investment over next four years. *The Globe and Mail.* www.theglobeandmail.com/sports/olympics/coc-announces-37-million-investment-over-next-four-years/article32561139/

Taks, M., Seguin, B., Naraine, M.L., Thompson, A., Parent, M.M., & Hoye, R. (2020). Brand governance practices in Canadian national sport organizations: An exploratory study. *European Sport Management Quarterly, 20*, 10-29.

Thibault, L., & Babiak, K. (2005). Organizational changes in Canada's sport system: Toward an athlete-centred approach. *European Sport Management Quarterly, 5*, 105-132.

Thibault, L., & Harvey, J. (Eds.). (2013). *Sport policy in Canada.* University of Ottawa Press.

Tremblay, P. (2014, June 18). Canada–United States. Publication No. 2014-46. Library of Parliament.

U SPORTS. (2018). U SPORTS update: Strategic planning. https://usports.ca/uploads/hq/AGM/2018/Presentations/Strategic_Planning_-_2018_AGM.pdf

Wagner, D. (2021). NHL approves advertising patches on jerseys: What would be the worst ad for the Canucks? https://www.vancouverisawesome.com/canucks-hockey/nhl-approves-advertising-patches-on-jerseys-what-would-be-the-worst-ad-for-the-canucks-4230652

Wann, D.L., & Branscombe, N. R. (1990). Die-hard and fair-weather fans: Effects of identification on BIRGing and CORFing tendencies. *Journal of Sport and Social Issues, 14*, 103-117.

Chapter 3

Aaker, D.A., Kumar, V., & Day, G.S. (2008). *Marketing research.* John Wiley & Sons.

Abeza, G., O'Reilly, N., & Séguin, B. (2019). The sequential-funnel-based focus group design: Adapting the focus group for research in sport management. *Journal of Global Sport Management*, 1-28. https://doi.org/10.1080/24704067.2018.1550621

Abeza, G., O'Reilly, N., Séguin, B., & Nzindukiyimana, O. (2017). Social media as a relationship marketing tool in professional sport: A netnographical exploration. *International Journal of Sport Communication, 10*(3), 325-358.

Arora, R., & Mahankale, N.R. (2012). *Marketing research.* PHI Learning.

Babin, B.J., & Zikmund, W.G. (2015). *Essentials of marketing research.* Nelson Education.

Creswell, J.W., & Creswell, J.D. (2017). *Research design: Qualitative, quantitative, and mixed methods approaches.* Sage.

Faulkner, S.L., & Trotter, S.P. (2017). Data saturation. *The international encyclopedia of communication research methods,* 1-2.

Foster, G., O'Reilly N., & Davila, A. (2020). *Sports business management: Decision-making around the globe* (2nd ed.). Routledge.

Ipsos Reid. (2020). About us. Retrieved from www.ipsos.com/en-ca/about-us

Kozinets, R.V. (1998). On netnography: Initial reflections on consumer research investigations of cyberculture. In J.W. Alba & J.W. Hutchinson (Eds.), *Advances in consumer research* (pp. 366-371). Association for Consumer Research.

Kozinets, R.V. (2002). The field behind the screen: Using netnography for marketing research in online communities. *Journal of Marketing Research, 39*(1), 61-72.

Kozinets, R.V. (2006). Click to connect: Netnography and tribal advertising. *Journal of Advertising Research, 46*(3), 279-288.

Mullin, B., Hardy, S., & Sutton, W. (2000). *Sport marketing* (2nd ed.). Human Kinetics.

Richardson, B. (2011). Football fan loyalty and the fan conversion experience. Norwich Business School Seminar Series, University of East Anglia: Invited Seminars

Slack, T., & Parent, M. (2006). *Understanding sport organizations: The application of organizational theory* (2nd ed.). Human Kinetics.

Wong, K.B., Shapiro, S.J., Perreault, W.D., & McCarthy. E.J. (2005). *Basic marketing: A global managerial approach* (11th ed.). McGraw-Hill Ryerson.

Chapter 4

Abeza, G., O'Reilly, N., Kashuck, K., Law, J., & Speck, A. (2018). College sport and declining stadium attendance: Designing adaptive strategies. *Case Studies in Sport Management, 7*(1), 4-10.

Abeza, G., O'Reilly, N., & Seguin, B. (2019). The sequential-funnel-based focus group design: adapting the focus group for research in sport management. *Journal of Global Sport Management,* 1-28. https://www.tandfonline.com/doi/full/10.1080/24704067.2018.1550621.

Anderson, D. (1979). Sport spectatorship: Appropriation of an identity or appraisal of self. *Review of Sport and Leisure, 4*(2), 115-127.

Csikszentmihalyi, M. (1997). *Finding flow.* Basic Books.

Downward, P., Lera-Lopez, F., & Rasciute, S. (2014). The correlates of sports participation in Europe. *European Journal of Sport Science, 14*(6), 592-602.

Eakins, J. (2018). An analysis of the determinants of sports participation and time spent in different sporting contexts. *Managing Sport and Leisure, 23*(3), 157-173.

Fantasy Sports and Gaming Association. (2020). Industry demographics. Retrieved from https://thefsga.org/industry-demographics/

Finch, D.J., O'Reilly, N., Abeza, G., Clark, B., & Legg, D. (2019). *Implications and impacts of esports on business and society: Emerging research and opportunities.* IGI Global.

Foster, G., O'Reilly, N., & Dávila, A. (2020). *Sports business management: Decision making around the globe.* (2nd ed.). Routledge.

Funk, D., & James, J. (2001). The psychological continuum model: A conceptual framework for understanding an individual's psychological connection to sport. *Sport Management Review, 4*(2), 119-150.

Hunt, K.A., Bristol, T., & Bashaw, R. (1999). A conceptual approach to classifying sports fans. *Journal of Services Marketing, 13*(6), 439-452.

Lee, S., Seo, W.J., & Green, B.C. (2013). Understanding why people play fantasy sport: Development of the Fantasy Sport Motivation Inventory (FanSMI). *European Sport Management Quarterly, 13*(2), 166-199.

Madrigal, R. (2006). Measuring the multidimensional nature of sporting even performance consumption. *Journal of Leisure Research, 38,* 267-276.

Merriam-Webster. (2020). *Merriam-Webster's collegiate dictionary* (11th ed.). Thomas Press India.

Pooley, J. C. (1978). *The sport fan: A social-psychology of misbehaviour.* Canadian Association for Health, Physical Education and Recreation.

Potwarka, L.R., Drewery, D., Snelgrove, R., Havitz, M., & Mair, H. (2017). Modeling a demonstration effect: The case of spectators' experiences at 2015 Pan Am Games' track cycling competitions. *Leisure Sciences, 40*(6), 578-600.

Rein, I., Kotler, P., & Shields, B. (2006). *The elusive fan: Reinventing sports in a crowded marketplace.* McGraw-Hill.

Shank, M.D., & Lyberger, M.R. (2014). *Sports marketing: A strategic perspective.* Routledge.

Stewart, B., Smith, A.C., & Nicholson, M. (2003). Sport consumer typologies: A critical review. *Sport Marketing Quarterly, 12*(4), 206-216.

Tacon, R., & Vainker, S. (2017). Fantasy sport: A systematic review and new research directions. *European Sport Management Quarterly, 17*(5), 558-589.

Wann, D.L. (1995). Preliminary validation of the sport fan motivation scale. *Journal of Sport and Social Issues, 19*(4), 377-396.

Chapter 5

Coffee, P. (2014, June 26). Study: Advertisers don't understand women. *AdWeek*. Retrieved from www.adweek.com/agencyspy/study-advertisers-dont-understand-women/68869/

Crane, F.G., Kerin, R.A., Hartley, S.W., Berkowitz, E.N., & Rudelius, W. (2006). *Marketing* (6th cdn. ed.). McGraw-Hill Ryerson.

Kotler, P., & Armstrong, G. (2016). *Marketing: An introduction* (16th ed.). Prentice-Hall.

Nielsen Sport. (2015). Women and sport. https://www.nielsen.com/wp-content/uploads/sites/3/2019/04/the-rise-of-womens-sports.pdf

Chapter 6

Apostolopoulou, A. (2002). Brand extensions by US professional sport teams: Motivations and keys to success. *Sport Marketing Quarterly, 11*(4): 205-214.

Berendt, J., & Uhrich, S. (2016). Enemies with benefits: The dual role of rivalry in shaping sport fans' identity. *European Sport Management Quarterly, 16*(5), 613-634.

Foster, G., O'Reilly, N., & Dávila, A. (2020). *Sports business management: Decision making around the globe.* (2nd ed.). Routledge.

Havard, C.T., & Dalakas, V. (2017). Understanding the marketing implications of sport rivalry: What we know and where we are headed. *Sport Marketing Quarterly, 26*(4), 199-203.

Havard, C.T., & Eddy, T. (2013). Qualitative assessment of rivalry and conference realignment in intercollegiate athletics. *Journal of Issues in Intercollegiate Athletics, 6,* 216-235.

Havard, C.T., Eddy, T.W., & Ryan, T.D. (2016). Examining the impact of team identification and gender on rival perceptions and consumption intentions of intercollegiate athletics fans. *Journal of Applied Sport Management, 8*(2), 33-49. https://doi.org/10.18666/jasm-2016-v8-i2-6444

Howard, D.R., & Crompton, J.L. (2003). An empirical review of the stadium novelty effect. *Sport Marketing Quarterly, 12*(2): 111-116.

Kotler, P., & Armstrong, G. (2016). *Marketing: An introduction* (16th ed.). Prentice-Hall.

Mason, D. (1999). What is the sport product and who buys it? The marketing of professional sport leagues. *European Journal of Marketing, 33*(3-4): 402-418.

Mullin, B. (2000). Characteristics of sport marketing. In H. Appenzeller. & G. Lewis (Eds.), *Successful sport management* (2nd ed., pp. 127-149). Carolina Academic Press.

Mullin, B.J., Hardy, S., & Sutton, W. (2014). *Sport marketing* (4th ed.). Human Kinetics.

Nauright, J., & White, P. (2002). Mediated nostalgia, community and nation: The CFL in crisis and the demise of the Ottawa Rough Riders 1986-1996. *Sport History Review, 33,* 121-137.

Pitts, B.G., & Stotlar, D.K. (2013). *Fundamentals of sports marketing* (4th ed.). Fitness Information Technology.

Reams, L., & Eddy, T. (2017). The impact of rivalry antecedents on mediated demand for an individual sport. *Sport Marketing Quarterly, 26*(4), 247-260.

Richelieu, A. (2018). A sport-oriented place branding strategy for cities, regions and countries. *Sport, Business & Management: An International Journal, 8*(4), 354-374.

Sanford, K., & Scott, F. (2016). Assessing the intensity of sports rivalries using data from secondary market transactions. *Journal of Sport Economics, 17*(2), 159-174.

Shank, M., & Lyberger, M. (2015). *Sports marketing: A strategic perspective* (5th ed.). Routledge.

Solomon, M.R., Marshall, G.W., & Stuart, E.W. (2018). *Marketing: Real people, real decisions* (9th ed.). Prentice Hall.

Spencer, D. (2005, September 16). The selling of Sid: Crosby already helping boost league in the US. Calgary *Herald*, E1.

Taylor, J. (1988, August 22). A nation in mourning. *Sports Illustrated*, 94.

Tyler, B.D., Morehead, C.A., Cobbs, J., & DeSchriver, T. (2017). What is rivalry? Old and new approaches to specifying rivalry in demand estimations of spectator sports. *Sport Marketing Quarterly, 26*(4), 204-222.

Watanabe, N., Pegoraro, A., Yan, G., & Shapiro, S. (2019). Does rivalry matter? An analysis of sport consumer interest on social media. *International Journal of Sports Marketing and Sponsorship, 20*(4), 646-665.

Chapter 7

Berkow, J. (2011, May 6). Blockbuster Canada goes bust. *Vancouver Sun*. https://web.archive.org/web/20110509063838/http://www.vancouversun.com/business/Blockbuster+Canada+goes+bust/4737781/story.html

Briggs, P., & Verna, P. (2019, January 24). Sports OTT landscape in Canada. *eMarketer*. www.emarketer.com/content/sports-video-in-canada

Cooky, C., Messner, M., & Musto, M. (2015). "It's dude time!": A quarter century of excluding women's sports in televised news and highlight shows. *Communication & Sport, 3*(3), 261-287. https://doi.org/10.1177/2167479515588761

Deeb, A., & Love, A. (2018). Media representations of multiracial athletes. *Journal of Sport and Social Issues, 42*(2), 95-114. https://doi.org/10.1177/0193723517749598

Diakopoulos, N. (2014). Algorithmic accountability. J*Digital Journalism, 3*(3), 398-415. https://doi.org/10.1080/21670811.2014.976411

Funk, D.C., Pizzo, A.D., & Baker, B.J. (2018). eSport management: Embracing eSport education and research opportunities. *Sport Management Review, 21,* 7-13.

Gough, C. (2020, June 3). Public interest in electronic sports in the U.S. as of 2020, by age. *Statista*. www.statista.com/statistics/1108276/esports-interest-age/

Heere, B. (2018). Embracing the sportification of society: Defining e-sports through a polymorphic view on sport. *Sport Management Review, 21*, 21-24.

Joshi, N. (2019, October 26) Revolutionizing sports with augmented reality. *Forbes*. www.forbes.com/sites/cognitiveworld/2019/10/26/revolutionizing-sports-with-augmented-reality/#2c72c3ea1416

Kim, A., Dolliver, M., & Perrin, N. (2018). Canada trends in 2019: Three emerging areas for digital marketers. *eMarketer*. www.emarketer.com/content/canada-trends-in-2019#page-report

Marr, B. (2019, August 12). What is extended reality technology? A simple explanation for anyone. *Forbes*. https://www.forbes.com/sites/bernardmarr/2019/08/12/what-is-extended-reality-technology-a-simple-explanation-for-anyone/?sh=63c68b1f7249

Morin, C. (2011). Neuromarketing: The new science of consumer behaviour. *Society, 48,* 131-135. https://doi.org/10.1007/s12115-010-9408-1

Naraine, M.L. (2019). Follower segments within and across the social media networks of major professional sport organizations. *Sport Marketing Quarterly, 28*, 222-233.

Naraine, M.L., & Parent, M.M. (2017). This is how we do it: A qualitative approach to national sport organizations' social-media implementation. *International Journal of Sport Communication, 10*, 196-217.

Naraine, M.L., & Wear, H. (2019). The Esports consumer experience. In R. Rodgers (Ed.), *Understanding esports: An introduction to the global phenomenon* (pp. 85-94). Lexington Books.

Newzoo. (2020). 2020 Global esports market report. *Newzoo*. https://platform.newzoo.com/reports/d767f5a8-876c-4d13-80be-70acb6f35b59

Parent, M. M., Naraine, M. L., & Hoye, R. (2018). A new era for governance structures and processes in Canadian national sport organizations. *Journal of Sport Management, 32*, 555-566.

Pegoraro, A. (2013). Sport fandom in the digital world. In P.M. Pedersen (Ed.), *Routledge handbook of sport communication* (pp. 248-258). Routledge.

Sawh, M. (2018, April 16). The best smart clothing: From biometric shirts to contactless payment jackets. *Wareable*. www.wareable.com/smart-clothing/best-smart-clothing.

Shank, M.D., & Lyberger, M.R. (2015). *Sports marketing: A strategic perspective* (5th ed.). Routledge.

Shilbury, D., Westerbeek, H., Quick, S., Funk, D., & Karg, A. (2014). *Strategic sport marketing* (4th ed.). Allen & Unwin.

Chapter 8

Aaker, D.A. (1991). *Managing brand equity: Capitalizing on the value of a brand name.* Free Press.

Bauer, H.H., Stokburger-Sauer, N.E., & Exler, S. (2008). Brand image and fan loyalty in professional team sport:

A refined model and empirical assessment. *Journal of Sport Management, 22*(2), 205-226.

Christodoulides, G., & de Chernatony, L. (2010). Consumer-based brand equity conceptualization and measurement: A literature review. *International Journal of Research in Marketing, 52*, 43-66.

Gladden, J.M., & Funk, D.C. (2002). Developing an understanding of brand associations in team sport: Empirical evidence from consumers of professional sport. *Journal of Sport Management, 16*(1), 54-81.

Gladden, J.M., Milne, G.R., & Sutton, W.A. (1998). A conceptual framework for evaluating brand equity in Division 1 college athletics. *Journal of Sport Management, 12*(1), 1-19.

International Olympic Committee. (2006). *2006 global brand and consumer research: The power of the Olympic brand.* IOC Television and Marketing Services.

Keller, K.L. (2003). Brand synthesis: The multidimensionality of brand knowledge. *Journal of Consumer Research, 29*(4), 595-600.

Kunkel, T., & Biscaia, R. (2020). Sport brands: Brand relationships and consumer behavior. *Sport Marketing Quarterly, 29*(1), 3-17.

Richelieu, A. (2004). A new brand world for sports teams. In Brenda G. Pitts (Ed.), *Sharing best practices in sport marketing: The Sport Marketing Association's inaugural book of papers* (pp. 3-20). Sport Marketing Association.

Richelieu, A., & Pons, F. (2009). If brand equity matters, where is the brand strategy? A look at Canadian hockey teams in the NHL. *International Journal of Sport Management and Marketing, 5*, 162-182.

Ross, S.D. (2006). A conceptual framework for understanding spectator-based brand equity. *Journal of Sport Management, 20*(1), 22-38.

Ross, S.D., James, J.D., & Vargas, P. (2006). Development of a scale to measure team brand associations in professional sport. *Journal of Sport Management, 20*(2), 260-279.

Séguin, B., Richelieu, A., & O'Reilly, N. (2008). Leveraging the Olympic brand through the reconciliation of corporate and consumers' brand perceptions. *International Journal of Sport Management and Marketing, 4*(1-2). https://doi.org/10.1504/IJSMM.2008.015958

Underwood, R., Bond, E., & Baer, R. (2001). Building service brands via social identity: Lessons from the sports marketplace. *Journal of Marketing Theory and Practice, 9*(1), 1-13.

Watkins, B. (2014). An integrated approach to sports branding: Examining the influence of social media on brand outcomes. *International Journal of Integrated Marketing Communications, 6*(2), 20-30.

Chapter 9

Coalter, F. (2004). Reference pricing: Changing perceptions of entrance charges for sport and recreation. *Managing Leisure: An International Journal, 9*(3), 73-86.

Competition Act. (2020, July 1). Government of Canada. https://laws.justice.gc.ca/eng/acts/C-34/page-1.html#h-87830

Nagle, T., & Müller, G. (2018). *The strategy and tactics of pricing: A guide to growing for profitably*. Routledge.

Price. (n.d.). *Merriam-Webster.com*. Retrieved September 21, 2020, from https://www.merriam-webster.com/dictionary/price

Team Marketing Report. (n.d.). Fan Cost Index. Retrieved August 5, 2020, from www.teammarketing.com

Young D.R., Jung, T., Aranson, R. (2010). Mission-market tensions and nonprofit pricing. *American Review of Public Administration, 40*, 153-169.

Chapter 10

Cornwell, T.B. (2020). *Sponsorship in marketing: Effective partnerships in sports, arts and events* (2nd ed.). Routledge.

CSLS. (2019). Canadian sponsorship landscape study (13th ed.). Retrieved from https://www.sponsorshiplandscape.com/downloads/

Mullin, B.J., Hardy, S., & Sutton, W.M. (2014). *Sport marketing* (4th ed.). Human Kinetics.

Shank, M.D., & Lyberger, M. R. (2015). *Sports marketing: A strategic perspective* (5th ed.). Routledge.

Statista. (2019, August 19). Global advertising spending from 2014 to 2022 (in billions U.S. dollars). *Statista*. www.statista.com/statistics/273288/advertising-spending-worldwide/

Tripodi, J.A. (2001). Sponsorship—a confirmed weapon in the promotional armoury. *International Journal of Sports Marketing & Sponsorship, 3*, 82-103.

Tsekouras, P. (2019, October 22). McDonald's Canada's Toronto Raptors French fry promotion is back, with a catch. *CTV News*. https://toronto.ctvnews.ca/mcdonald-s-canada-s-toronto-raptors-french-fry-promotion-is-back-with-a-catch-1.4650512

Chapter 11

Canadian Communications Foundation. (2014, March). Hockey Night in Canada in radio. www.broadcasting-history.ca/in-depth/hockey-night-canada-radio

Canadian Communications Foundation. (n.d.). All Hockey Night in Canada—the television years. Retrieved from www.broadcasting-history.ca/in-depth/hockey-night-canada-television-years

Cavanagh, R.P. (1992). The development of Canadian Sports Broadcasting 1920-78. *Canadian Journal of Communication, 17*(3). https://doi.org/10.22230/cjc.1992v17n3a677

Foster, G., O'Reilly, N., & Dávila, A. (2020). *Sports business management: Decision making around the globe*. (2nd ed.). Routledge.

International Olympic Committee. (2020). Olympic marketing fact file 2020 edition. https://stillmed.olympic.org/media/Document%20Library/OlympicOrg/Documents/IOC-Marketing-and-Broadcasting-General-Files/Olympic-Marketing-Fact-File.pdf

Masteralexis, L., Barr, C., & Hums, M. (Eds.). (2011). *Principles and practice of sport management*. Jones & Bartlett Publishers.

O'Reilly, N., & Séguin, B. (2013). *Sport marketing: A Canadian perspective*. Nelson Education.

Settimi, C. (2013, November 26). The NHL's new broadcast deal with Rogers Communications signals Canadian team expansion. www.forbes.com/sites/christinasettimi/2013/11/26/the-nhls-new-broadcast-deal-with-rogers-communication-signals-canadian-team-expansion/?sh=4956360574e8

Chapter 12

Aaker, D.A. (1991) *Managing brand equity: Capitalizing on the value of a brand name*. Free Press.

Abeza, G. (2020). The evolving #Rule40 of the Olympic Charter: Balancing the interest of sponsors vs athletes. In D. Chatziefstathiou, B. Garcia, & B. Séguin (Eds.), *International handbook of Olympic and Paralympic Games* (pp. 139-148). Routledge.

Abeza, G. Braunstein-Minkove, J., Séguin, B., O'Reilly, N., Kim, A., & Abdourazakou, Y. (2020). Ambush marketing via social media: The case of the three most recent Olympic Games. *International Journal of Sport Communication*. Advance online publication. https://doi.org/10.1123/ijsc.2020-0266.

Abeza, G., & O'Reilly, N. (2018). Social, digital, and mobile media in sport marketing. In E. Schwarz & J. Hunter (Eds.), *Advanced theory and practice in sport marketing* (3rd ed., pp. 242-266). Routledge.

Abeza, G., O'Reilly, N., & Séguin, B. (2019). The sequential-funnel-based focus group design: adapting the focus group for research in sport management. *Journal of Global Sport Management*, 1-28. https://www.tandfonline.com/doi/full/10.1080/24704067.2018.1550621

Abeza, G., O'Reilly, N., Seguin, B., & Nzindukiyimana, O. (2017a). Social media as a relationship marketing tool in professional sport: A netnographical exploration. *International Journal of Sport Communication, 10*(3), 325-358.

Abeza, G., O'Reilly, N., Séguin, B., & Nzindukiyimana, O. (2017b). *The world's highest-paid athletes, product endorsement, and Twitter. Sport, Business & Management,7*(3), 332-355.

Abeza, G., Pegoraro, A., Naraine, M.L., Séguin, B., & O'Reilly, N. (2014). Activating a global sport sponsorship with social media: An analysis of TOP sponsors, Twitter, and the 2014 Olympic Games. *International Journal of Sport Management and Marketing, 15*(3-4), 184-213.

Chadwick, S., & Burton, N. (2011). The evolving sophistication of ambush marketing: A typology of strategies. *Thunderbird International Business Review, 53*(6), 709-719.

Constantinides, E., & Fountain, S. J. (2008). Web 2.0: Conceptual foundations and marketing issues. *Journal of direct, data and digital marketing practice, 9*(3), 231-244.

Facebook. (n.d.). Metrics for boosted posts. Retrieved 2020 from https://www.facebook.com/business/help/840929489608411?id=352109282177656

Hennig-Thurau, T., Malthouse, E.C., Friege, C., Gensler, S., Lobschat, L., Rangaswamy, A., & Skiera, B. (2010). The impact of new media on customer relationships. *Journal of Service Research, 13*(3), 311-330.

IEG. (2020). IEG Sponsorship Report. https://www.sponsorship.com/report.aspx

Kotler, P., & Keller, K. L. (2006). *Marketing management: Pearson international edition*. Pearson Prentice Hall.

McCracken, G. (1989). Who is the celebrity endorser? Cultural foundations of the endorsement process. *Journal of Consumer Research, 16*(3), 310-321.

Moran, E. (2019). NHL slides back onto TikTok, with teams following suit. Retrieved from https://frontofficesports.com/nhl-tiktok-relaunch/

Nolan, E. (2019). NHL slides back onto TiKToK, with teams following suits. https://frontofficesports.com/nhl-tiktok-relaunch/

O'Reilly, N., Pound, R., Burton, R., Séguin, B., & Brunette, M. (2015). *Global sport marketing: Sponsorship, ambush marketing, and the Olympic Games*. FIT Publishing

Rubin, J. (2019). The Raptors are now the most valuable sports franchise in Canada. www.thestar.com/business/2019/06/04/the-raptors-are-now-the-most-valuable-sports-franchise-in-canada-experts-say.html

Séguin, B., & Abeza, G. (2019). Olympic brand governance: Future research directions. In *Research handbook on sport governance*. Edward Elgar Publishing.

Uzunoğlu, E., & Kip, S.M. (2014). Brand communication through digital influencers: Leveraging blogger engagement. *International Journal of Information Management, 34*(5), 592-602.

Whiting, A., & Williams, D. (2013). Why people use social media: A uses and gratifications approach. *Qualitative Market Research, 16*(4), 362.

Chapter 13

Abratt, R., Clayton, B.C., & Pitt, L.F. (1987). Corporate objectives in sports sponsorship. *International Journal of Advertising, 6*, 299-311.

Arthur, D., Scott, D., & Woods, T. (1997). A conceptual model of the corporate decision-making process of sport sponsorship acquisition. *Journal of Sport Management, 11*, 223-333.

Bloxam, M. (1998). Brand affinity and television programme sponsorship. *International Journal of Advertising, 17*(1), 89-98.

Brooks, C.M. (1994). *Sports marketing: Competitive business strategies for sports*. Prentice Hall.

Burton, N., McKelvey, S., & Snyder, K. (2018). The evolution of media reporting of ambush marketing. *Sport Marketing Quarterly, 21*(1), 18-30.

Canadian Sponsorship Landscape Study. (2019). 13th Annual Canadian Sponsorship Landscape Study. www.sponsorshiplandscape.ca

CBC. (2017). Toronto's Air Canada Centre to be renamed Scotiabank Arena in "record-setting" deal. /www.cbc.ca/sports/scotiabank-arena-rights-deal-mlse-air-canada-centre-1.4267176

COC. (2014). Canadian Olympic Committee Report on the 2010 Vancouver Olympic Games. https://olympic.ca/press/vancouver-2010-press-release/

Cornwell, T.B., Roy, D.P., & Steinard II, E.A. (2001). Exploring managers' perceptions of the impact of sponsorship on brand equity. *Journal of Advertising, 30*(2), 41-51.

Crompton, J. (2004). Conceptualization and alternate operationalizations of the measurement of sponsorship effectiveness in sport. *Leisure Studies, 23*(3), 267-281.

Dees, W., Walsh, P., McEvoy, C., McKelvey, S., Mullin, B.J., Hardy, S., & Sutton, W.A. (2021). *Sport marketing* (5th ed.). Human Kinetics.

Faganel, A., & Bratina, D. (2013). Commercial sponsorship, brand image and WTA tournament. *International Journal of Academic Research* Part B, 156-162.

Foster, G., O'Reilly N., & Davila, A. (2020). *Sports business management: Decision-making around the globe* (2nd ed.). Routledge (Taylor & Francis), USA.

Gwinner, K. (1997). A model of image creation and image transfer in event sponsorship. *International Marketing Review, 14*(3), 145-158.

Gwinner, K.P., Larson, B.V., & Swanson, S.R. (2009). Image transfer in corporate event sponsorship: Assessing the impact of team identification and event-sponsor fit. *International Journal of Management and Marketing Research, 2*(1), 1-15.

Hanen, M. (2000). Lifestyle marketing. In B. Mullin, S. Hardy, & W. Sutton (Eds.), *Sport Marketing* (2nd ed., p. 261). Human Kinetics.

Howard, D.R., & Crompton, J.L. (Eds.). (1995). *Financing sport*. Fitness Information Technology.

IEG. (2018). IEG Sponsorship Report. www.sponsorship.com/IEG/files/f3/f3cfac41-2983-49be-8df6-3546345e27de.pdf

Irwin, R.L., & Sutton, W. (1994). Sport sponsorship objectives: An analysis of their relative importance for major corporate sponsors. *European Journal of Sport Management, 1*(2), 93-101.

Javalgi, R.G., Traylor, M.B., Gross, A.C., & Lampman, E. (1994). Awareness of sponsorship and corporate image: An empirical investigation. *Journal of Advertising, 23*(4), 47-58.

McMahon, E.A. (1996). The evolution of Olympic commercial partnerships. *Olympic Message—Sources of Financing Sports, 3,* 14-18.

Meenaghan, T. (1991). The role of sponsorship in the communications and marketing mix. *International Journal of Advertising, 10*(1), 35-47.

Meenaghan, T. (1996). Ambush marketing: A threat to corporate sponsorship? *Sloan Management Review, 38*(1), 103-113.

Meenaghan, T. (1998). Current developments and future directions in sponsorship. *International Journal of Advertising, 17*(1), 3-28.

Meenaghan, T. (2001) Understanding sponsorship effects. *Psychology and Marketing, 18*(2), 95-122.

Meenaghan, T. (2005). Evaluating sponsorship effects. In J. Amis & T. Bettina Cornwell (Eds.), *Global Sport Sponsorship* (Vol. 1, pp. 243-264). Berg.

O'Reilly, N., & Brunette, M. (2013). *Public–private partnerships in physical activity and sport.* Human Kinetics.

O'Reilly, N., & Lafrance Horning, D. (2013). Leveraging sponsorship: The activation ratio. *Sport Management Review, 16*(4), 424-437.

O'Reilly, N., & Madill, J. (2009). Methods and metrics in sponsorship evaluation. *Journal of Sponsorship, 2*(3), 215-230.

O'Reilly, N., & Madill, J. (2012). The development of a process for evaluating marketing sponsorships. *Canadian Journal of Administrative Sciences, 29*(1), 50-66.

Otker, T. (1988). Exploitation: The key to sponsorship success. *Marketing and Research Today, 16*(2), 77-86.

Sandler, D.M., & Shani, D. (1993). Sponsorship and the Olympic Games: The consumer perspective. *Sport Marketing Quarterly, 2*(3), 38-43.

Schantz, O. (1995). La présidence d'Avery Brundage (1952-1972). In R. Gafner & N. Muller (Eds.), *Un siècle du Comité International Olympique* (Vol. 2, pp. 72-200). IOC.

Séguin, B., & O'Reilly, N. (2008). The Olympic brand, ambush marketing, and clutter, *International Journal of Sport Management and Marketing. 4*(1-2), 62-84.

Shank, M., & Lyberger, M. (2014). *Sport marketing: A strategic perspective* (5th ed.). Prentice Hall.

Shanklin, W., & Kuzma, J. (1992, Spring). Buying that sporting image: What senior executives need to know about corporate sports sponsorship. *Marketing Management*, 59-64.

Sleight, S. (1989). *Sponsorship: What it is and how to use it.* McGraw-Hill.

SponsorshipX. (2020). Global COVID-19 Surveys. COVID-19 impact studies. https://sponsorshipx.com/covid-19-impact-study/

Chapter 14

Bell. (2004). Vancouver 2010 selects Bell Canada as premier national partner. http://www.bce.ca/en/news/releases/bce/2004/10/18/71721.html.

Canadian Sponsorship Landscape Study. (2019). 13th Annual Canadian Sponsorship Landscape Study. www.sponsorshiplandscape.ca

O'Reilly, N., & Lafrance Horning, D. (2013). Leveraging sponsorship: The activation ratio. *Sport Management Review, 16*(4), 424-437.

O'Reilly, N., & Madill, J. (2009). Methods and metrics in sponsorship evaluation. *Journal of Sponsorship, 2*(3), 215-230.

Séguin, B., Teed, K., & O'Reilly, N. (2005). National sport organizations and sponsorship. *International Journal of Sport Management & Marketing, 1*(1-2), 69-83.

Chapter 15

Abeza, G., Braunstein-Minkove, J., Séguin, B., O'Reilly, N., Kim, A., & Abdourazakou, Y. (2020, October 8). Ambush marketing via social media: The case of the three most recent Olympic Games. *International Journal of Sport Communication.* https://doi.org/10.1123/ijsc.2020-0266.

Burton, N., & Chadwick, S. (2018). Ambush marketing is dead, long live ambush marketing: A redefinition and typology of an increasingly prevalent phenomenon. *Journal of Advertising Research, 58*(3), 282-296.

Chadwick, S., & Burton, N. (2011). The evolving sophistication of ambush marketing: A typology of strategies. *Thunderbird International Business Review, 53*(6), 709-719.

Ellis, D., Scassa, T., & Séguin, B. (2011). Framing ambush marketing as a legal issue: An Olympic Perspective. *Sport Management Review, 14,* 297-308.

Ettore, B. (1993). Ambush marketing: Heading them off at the pass. *Management Review, 82*(3), 55.

Grady, J. (2017). Analyzing Rule 40's restrictions on using athletes in Olympic sponsorship at Rio 2016. *Entertainment and Sports Law Journal, 15*(1), 1-5.

International Olympic Committee. (2015). Charter in force as from 2 August 2015. https://stillmed.olympic.org/media/Document%20Library/OlympicOrg/Olympic-Studies-Centre/List-of-Resources/Official-Publications/Olympic-Charters/2015-Olympic-Charter.pdf

International Olympic Committee. (2020). Charter in force as from 26 June 2019. Retrieved from https://bit.ly/2YRyRWp

McCarville, R., & Copeland, R.P. (1994). Understanding sport sponsorship through exchange theory. *Journal of Sport Management, 8*(3), 102-114.

Sandler, D., & Shani, D. (1989). Olympic sponsorship vs. ambush marketing: Who gets the gold? *Journal of Advertising Research, 9*(14), 9-14.

Séguin, B., & O'Reilly, N.J. (2008). The Olympic brand, ambush marketing and clutter. *International Journal of Sport Management and Marketing, 4*(1), 62-84.

Séguin, B., Lyberger, M., O'Reilly, N., & McCarthy, L. (2005, July 1). Internationalizing ambush marketing: The Olympic brand and country of origin. *Interna-*

tional Journal of Sports Marketing and Sponsorship, 6(4). https://www.emerald.com/insight/content/doi/10.1108/IJSMS-06-04-2005-B004/full/html

Shani, D., & Sandler, D. (1998). Ambush marketing: Is confusion to blame for the flickering of the flame? *Psychology & Marketing, 15*(4), 367-383.

Chapter 16

Briggs, P. (2019, May 28). Canada digital ad spending 2019. *eMarketer*. www.emarketer.com/content/canada-digital-ad-spending-2019

Choi, W.J., & Sayedi, A. (2019). Learning in online advertising. *Marketing Science, 38*, 584-608.

Hoeber, L., & Hoeber, O. (2012). Determinants of an innovation process: A case study of technological innovation in a community sport organization. *Journal of Sport Management, 26*, 213-223.

Naraine, M.L. (2019a). The blockchain phenomenon: Conceptualizing decentralized networks and the value proposition to the sport industry. *International Journal of Sport Communication, 12*, 313-335.

Naraine, M.L. (2019b). Follower segments within and across the social media networks of major professional sport organizations. *Sport Marketing Quarterly, 28*, 222-233.

Naraine, M.L., & Karg, A. (2019). Digital media in international sport: Engaging fans via social media and fantasy sports. In E. MacIntosh, G. Bravo, & M. Li (Eds.), *International sport management* (pp. 315-331). Human Kinetics.

Naraine, M.L., O'Reilly, N., Levallet, N., & Wanless, L. (2020). If you build it, will they log on? Wi-Fi usage and behavior while attending National Basketball Association games. *Sport, Business and Management: An International Journal, 10*, 207-226.

Naraine, M.L., & Wanless, L. (2020). Going all in on AI: Examining the value proposition of and integration challenges with one branch of artificial intelligence in sport management. *Sport Innovation Journal, 1*, 49-61.

O'Reilly, N., & Rahinel, R. (2006). Forecasting the importance of media technology in sport: The case of the televised ice hockey product in Canada, *International Journal of Sport Marketing and Sponsorship, 8*(1), 82-94.

Slack, T., & Miah, A. (2021). Technology in sport organizations. In T. Slack, T. Byers, & A. Thurston (Eds.), *Understanding sport organizations* (pp. 377-394). Human Kinetics.

Chapter 17

Andreasen, A. (2002). Marketing social marketing in the social change marketplace. *Journal of Public Policy and Marketing, 21*(1), 3-13.

Andreasen, A. (2006). *Social marketing in the 21st century*. Sage Publications.

Biddle, S., Ribeiro, P.V., & Dias, T. (2020, March 16). Invisible censorship: TikTok told moderators to suppress posts by "ugly" people and the poor to attract new users. *The Intercept*. https://theintercept.com/2020/03/16/tiktok-app-moderators-users-discrimination/

Canada's Sports Hall of Fame. (n.d.). Roger Jackson. https://www.sportshall.ca/hall-of-famers/hall-of-famers-search.html?proID=627&lang=EN

Canadian Women & Sport (2020). The Rally Report: Encouraging action to improve sport for women and girls. https://womenandsport.ca/resources/research-insights/rally-report/

Hubbard, A. (2004). The major life activity of belonging. *Wake Forest Law Review, 39*, 254-264.

Kotler, P., & Levy, S. (1969). Broadening the concept of marketing. *Journal of Marketing, 33*(1), 10-15.

O'Reilly, N., & Madill, J. (2007). The World Anti-Doping Agency: The role of social marketing. *Journal of Nonprofit and Public Sector Marketing, 17*(1-2), 1-26.

Rothschild, M. (1999). Carrots, sticks, and promises: A conceptual framework for the management of public health and social issue behaviors. *Journal of Marketing, 63*(4), 24-37.

Chapter 18

Abeza, G., Seguin, B., Carton, P., & Holland, S. (2020). Measuring sponsorship effectiveness: Designing an alternative approach. *Sport Marketing Quarterly*, 1-12. http://doi.org/10.32731/SMQ.OA.092020.01

Anderson, D.R., Sweeney, D.J., Williams, T.A., Camm, J.D., & Cochran, J.J. (2018). *An introduction to management science: Quantitative approach*. Cengage Learning.

Crane, F.G. (2006). *Marketing* (6th Cnd. ed.). McGraw-Hill Ryerson.

Shank, M.D., & Lyberger, M.R. (2014). *Sports marketing: A strategic perspective*. Routledge.

Stevens, R.E., Loudon, D.L., & Wrenn, B. (2006). *Marketing planning guide*. Psychology Press.

Chapter 19

Associated Press. (1995, August 8). NBC gets Sydney, Salt Lake Games: Olympics: Network's unorthodox bid of $1.27 billion heads off competition. *Los Angeles Times*. https://www.latimes.com/archives/la-xpm-1995-08-08-sp-32589-story.html

CBC Sports. (2005, February 7). CTV wins 2010 and 2012 Olympic broadcast rights. www.cbc.ca/sports/ctv-wins-2010-and-2012-olympic-broadcast-rights-1.529023

IOC. (1998). Facts File. International Olympic Committee, 49-50.

IOC (1999). 1999 International Olympic Committee marketing fact file. IOC Library.

IOC (2001). The Olympic Marketing Guide for NOCs. IOC.

IOC (2020). 2020 International Olympic Committee marketing fact file. https://stillmed.olympic.org/media/Document%20Library/OlympicOrg/Documents/IOC

-Marketing-and-Broadcasting-General-Files/Olympic -Marketing-Fact-File.pdf

Landry, F., & Yerlès, M. (1996). *The International Olympic Committee: One hundred years: The idea—The presidents—The achievements*. Vol. 3. IOC.

Los Angeles. (1985). Official Report of the Games of the XXIIIrd Olympiad, Los Angeles, 1984.

Ludwig, J.B. (1976). Five ring circus. In A.E. Senn (Ed.), *Power, politics, and the Olympic Games*. Human Kinetics.

Martyn, S. (1996).Toward an impasse: An examination of the negotiations behind the inclusion of the United States Olympic Committee in the Olympic Programme. International Centre for Olympic Studies, *Olympic Perspectives: Third International Symposium for Olympic Research*, 107-120.

McMahon, E.A. (1996). The evolution of Olympic commercial partnerships. *Olympic Message—Sources of Financing Sports, 3*, 14-18.

Muller, N. (Dir.). (1986). *Pierre de Coubertin: Textes choisis.* Tome II: *Olympisme*. Weidmann.

Payne, M. (1998). IOC marketing policy: Marketing programmes and the broadcaster. In IOC, *Television and the Olympic Games: The New Era* (pp. 107-112).

Pound, R.W. (1986). The international Olympic marketing program. *Olympic Review, 220*, 84-86.

Preuss, H. (2000). *Economics of the Olympic Games*. Walla Walla Press.

Schantz, O. (1995). *La présidence d'Avery Brundage (1952-1972)*. In R. Gafner & N. Muller (Eds.), *Un siècle du Comité International Olympique* (Vol. 2, pp. 72-200). IOC.

Séguin, B. (2003) *Représentations d'acteurs sociaux sur les relations entre le marketing et les Jeux olympiques*. Unpub-lished doctoral dissertation, Université Marc Bloch (Strasbourg II).

Séguin, B., Richelieu, A., & O'Reilly, N. (2008). Leveraging the Olympic brand through the reconciliation of corporate and consumers' brand perceptions. *International Journal of Sport Management and Marketing, 3*(1/2), 3-22.

SportBusiness. (2020). Technogym deal adds to Tokyo 2020's $3bn in domestic revenue. www.sportbusiness .com/news/technogym-deal-adds-to-tokyo-2020s-3bn -in-domestic-revenue/

Stauble, V.B. (1994). The significance of sports marketing and the case of the Olympic Games. In P.J. Graham (Ed.), *Sport business—Operational and theoretical aspects* (pp. 14-21). WCM Brown & Benchmark.

Stotlar, D.K. (1993). Sponsorship and the Olympic Winter Games. *Sport Marketing Quarterly, 2*(1), 35-43.

Todd, J. (2016, July 6). The 40-year hangover: How the 1976 Olympics nearly broke Montreal. *The Guardian*, https:// www.theguardian.com/cities/2016/jul/06/40-year -hangover-1976-olympic-games-broke-montreal-canada

Trumpp, E. (1998). Les enjeux des Jeux: L'impact des Jeux Olympiques de 1932 sur la ville de Los Angeles. In J.-F. Loudcher & C. Vivier (Eds.), *Le sport dans la ville* (pp. 28-38). L'Harmatta.

Wenn, S. (1994). An Olympic squabble. *Journal of Sport History, 21*(3).

Wenn, S. (1995). Growing pains: The Olympic Movement and television, 1966-1972. *Olympika, 4*, 1-22.

Worldometer. (2021). Countries in the world by popula-tion 2021. https://www.worldometers.info/world -population/population-by-country/

INDEX

Note: The italicized *f* and *t* following page numbers refer to figures and tables, respectively.

A

ability 296-297
Aboriginal Peoples 96
A.C. Nielsen 49
Academic All-Canadians 30-31
accessibility 87
accomplishments 209, 211
accountability 34
activation
    commitment for 254
    definition of 245
    description of 241
    sponsorship and 225-226, 258*t*
    tactics for 258*t*
activation ratio 225
activity scheduling 309
advertising
    ambush marketing and 269-270
    clutter 233
    cost breakdown for 350*t*
    email 288
    in promotional mix 170-171
    sponsorship and 228-230, 230*t*
    thematic 270-271
advertising allowances 162
advertising inventory 269
affiliated entities or agencies 244
Afinec, Matt 162-163
AIDA (awareness, interest, desire, and action) 168
Air Canada Centre 22
Alberta Colleges Athletic Conference (ACAC) 32
Alcorn, Mike 154-155
algorithms 288
allowances 153, 160, 162, 165
"all-you-can-afford" budgeting approach 306
Alpine Canada 172
amateur sport 28, 39-41, 245
ambassador, athlete as 204
ambush marketing
    associative ambushing 206, 268
    business impact of 264
    clutter and 273
    coattail ambushing 206, 268
    counter-ambushing strategies for 206, 271-273
    definition of 205, 231, 264-265

ethics of 266
    examples of 264-265
    legislation against 272
    in Olympic Games 268, 273
    prevention of 272
    property infringement 206-207, 268
    research 266-268
    social media and 205-207, 271
    strategy of 267-271
    surveillance efforts against 272-273
    techniques 267-268
    values ambushing 206, 268
American dollar 27
American Hockey League (AHL) 22
American Marketing Association (AMA) 4, 227
American Ultimate Disc League (AUDL) 25
AMJ Campbell 81, 95
analog 115
analytics software programs 54
Andreescu, Bianca Vanessa 204
antidoping 303
Antunes, Elio 133
asset development 312-313
associative ambushing 206, 268
athlete(s)
    as ambassador 204
    description of 109-110
    endorsements by 203-204, 257
    as expert 203-204
    media representation of 122-123
    as observer 204
    as personifier 204
    social media presentation of 122-123
    as spokesperson 204
    in sponsorship 257
Athlete Assistance Program 34
athletic events. *See* sport events
athletic scholarships 32
Atlantic Colleges Athletic Association (ACAA) 32
Atlantic University Sport (AUS) 30
attachers 68*t*
attendance, at sport events
    decline in 70, 72, 72*t*
    factors that affect 68-70
attentive servicing 245

attribution 256
augmented reality (AR) 70, 132-134
Ausman, Paul 308
awareness, brand 80-81, 142-144, 202, 231

B

badminton 40
Baker, Andrew 318-319
bandwidth 282
baseball 21
bases of segmentation 88-89
basketball
    CEBL 23-24
    NBA 21-22, 116-117, 142-143
    NBL 23
B2B (business-to-business) market 88, 89*t*
BBC 321
B2C (business-to-consumer) market 88, 89*t*
BC Lions 112
Bedford, David 333-335
behaviour 293
behavioural change 293
Bell Canada 188, 259
Benoit, Krista 46-47
best practices, in sport sponsorship 259-260
Betfred Super League (BSL) 25
big data 50
BIRGing 40
blackout 321
Blockbuster Canada 129
blogs 199
boxing 26
Boynton, Darryl 103
Bradish, Cheri 287-288
brainstorming 177
brand(s). *See also* branding
    athlete endorsement of 203
    concept of 137
    definition of 141
    description of 112-113
    endorsement of 203
    perceived quality of 144, 202-203
    platforms for building of 148*f*, 148-149
brand association 138, 144-145, 202

372 Index

brand awareness 80-81, 142-144, 202, 231
brand equity 112-113, 141-145, 202
brand extensions 112-113
brand identity 141
brand image 138, 144-145
branding. *See also* brand(s)
    defined 138, 141
    process of 146f, 146-147
    purpose of 140
    social media for 202-203
brand loyalty 145, 203
brand management 147-149
brand mark 112
brand names 112, 140-141
brand positioning 81
brand strategy 147-149
Brandwatch 55t
break-even analysis 158-159, 351, 351f
break-even point 152, 158-160
Brundage, Avery 322
budget setting 51-52
business market 88, 89t

C

Calgary Flames 200
Calgary Stampede 112
Callaway Golf Canada 104, 112
Canada
    geography 16-17
    importance of sport in 15-16
    introduction to 16-17
    major events in, sport legacy of 331-332
    Olympic marketing in 330-335
    Olympic movement in 333-335
    Paralympic movement in 333-335
    population of 16
    sport events in 18t, 18-19, 109
    sport facilities in 19t, 19-20, 20t
    sport organizations in 17, 36-37
Canada Games 179-181
Canada's Teams 95
Canada West 30
Canadian Broadcasting Company (CBC) 186, 326, 332
Canadian Centre in Ethics in Sport (CCES) 299
Canadian Colleges Athletic Association (CCAA) 32-33
Canadian Cross Training Club 143
Canadian dollar, value of 27
Canadian Elite Basketball League (CEBL) 23-24, 168
Canadian Football League (CFL) 22, 40-41, 50, 110, 113, 189t, 228
Canadian Hockey League (CHL) 338

Canadian Interuniversity Athletic Union (CIAU) 27
Canadian Interuniversity Sport (CIS) 27
Canadian Olympic Committee (COC) 19, 37-39, 118-119, 141, 280, 320, 330
Canadian Paralympic Committee (CPC) 250-251, 320
Canadian Premier League (CPL) 23
Canadian Sponsorship Landscape Study (CSLS) 222, 224, 235f, 235-236, 244, 251, 260
Canadian sport. *See also* sport
    college 16, 32-33
    consumers of. *See* sport consumers
    facets of 16
    grassroot 16, 37, 39-41
    professional 16, 20-27
    provincial 37, 38t
    territorial 37, 38t
    university 27-33
Canadian Sport Centres 19
Canadian Sport Institute Ontario (CSIO) 331
Canadian Sport Policy (2002) 35-36
Canadian Tire Corporation (CTC) 103
Canadian Tire NASCAR Series 24
Canadian Women's Hockey League (CWHL) 24
car racing 25, 63
CASCAR Super Series 24
case-based reasoning 285
casters 127
causal research 53
CBC–RadioCanada 326, 332
celebrity endorser 203
census 48
CFL. *See* Canadian Football League (CFL)
chain discounts 162
change, stages of 298-299
channel management 194
Chromebooks 280
Clean and Clear B-Ball Skills Days 93
cloud 281
clubs 110-111
clutter 226, 233, 273
coattail ambushing 206, 268
COC. *See* Canadian Olympic Committee (COC)
collectors 68t
college sport 16, 27-33
commercialism 321-323
communications mix 228
community 260
community groups 210
company 8-9

company image 231-233
competition
    analysis 343-345
    description of 8-9
    global 158
    professional sport 25-26
competitive advantage 346
competitive positioning 286
complementary product price setting 154
concentrated targeting 91-92, 299
consoles 126
consumer(s). *See also* sport consumers
    description of 8-9
    needs and wants of 6, 8, 69
    perceptions of 231-233
consumer brand partnerships 80-81
consumer demand 157
consumer market 88
consumer market analysis 341-342
consumption. *See* sport consumption
content communities 199
contests 173
contingency plan 353
contribution margin 158, 159-160
control 309, 352-353
copresentational endorsement, by celebrity athletes 204
cord-cutters 129-130
CORFing 40
corporate objectives, sponsorship and 230-236
cosponsor 249
cost(s)
    controlling 158-160
    estimating 157-158
    price versus 154-155, 165
    promotional 178
    subsidization of 155
cost-oriented price setting 153
cost-volume-profit (CVP) analysis 158
Coubertin, Baron Pierre 319, 321
counter-ambushing strategies 206, 271-273
COVID-19 pandemic
    AHL season affected by 22
    Canadian Olympic Committee affected by 38
    CFL season affected by 22
    CHL and 338
    digital environment during 72
    digital sport product and 116-117, 289
    esports during 129
    NBA season affected by 22
    NHL revenue affected by 21
    remote working during 283
    revenue earning during 162-163

sponsorship during 232, 238-239
sport industry growth and 140
Tokyo 2020 Olympic Games during 184
cricket 24, 40
crisis management 192
critical path method (CPM) 309
Crosby, Sidney 110, 203
crowded markets 94
cultural entrée, 58
culture 57
Curling Canada 28-29
customer(s). *See also* consumer(s)
    loyalty of 145
    in social marketing context 298-299
customer-relationship management (CRM) 279
customized marketing messages 83

D

Dairy Farmers of Canada 94-95, 233
data
    definition of 282
    display 56
    in sport marketing 50
data analysis 56, 58-59
databases 277
data collection
    description of 56, 58-59
    social media 55*t*
    techniques for 53-54
data mining 54, 58, 285
data saturation 55
DataSift 55*t*
data warehouses 277, 285
DAZN 130
decision making 44
decision support systems (DSS) 285
decline stage, of product life cycle 102, 104, 105*t*
De Grasse, Andre 204
Delaney, John 211-212
demand 157
demand-backward price setting 153
demarketing 299
demographics 64, 69
Dennison, Sean 202
descriptive research 48, 52-53
differentiated targeting 91, 299
digital sport product
    analog sport product versus 120-124
    broadcasters of 129-130
    characteristics of 117-120
    convenience of 120-121
    discontinuous innovations 124
    dynamic continuous innovation 124-125
    dynamic selection of 121, 123

    esports. *See* esports
    extended reality 116, 132-133
    fads 125, 125*f*
    gamified 123-124
    instantaneous access of 121
    interactivity of 123
    Internet effects on 119-120
    life cycle variants of 125, 125*f*
    locating of 121
    mobile apps 119, 130-131
    NFL Canada 116-117
    over-the-top channels and services 116, 121, 123, 129-130
    overview of 115-116
    ParticipACTION 132-133
    product life cycle of 124-126
    qualities of 120-124
    rapid adoption of 125, 125*f*
    revitalization 125*f*, 125-126
    slow adoption of 125, 125*f*
    social media effects on 117
    sport consumption of 117
    sport fan of 120
    sport product versus 120
    types of 124-133
    as user-friendly 120-121
    wearables 131-132
digital watches 124
direct competitors 9, 343
direct to consumer model 188
discontinuous innovations 124
discounts 153, 160, 162, 165
DiscoverText 55*t*
discussion sites 199-200
distractive ambushing 267-268
distribution 192-194
distribution channels 193-194
distribution model 188, 189*f*
doping scandals 35
dualistic typology 67
Dubin Inquiry 35
dynamic continuous innovation 124-125

E

East Coast Hockey League (ECHL) 25
e-commerce 121
Eddy, Terry 107-108
Edmonton Oilers 106, 202
Edmonton Sport Council 41
education 296, 297*t*
Edwards, Jonathon 10-11
80/20 rule 92
elasticity of demand 157
Electronic Arts (EA) 129
Ellis, Dana Lee 310
email advertising 288
emotional attachment 112, 137-138

endemic sponsorship 223
endorsement 203-204
ensnared fan 68*t*
enterprise resource planning (ERP) system 280-282
esports
    amateur competitions in 126-127
    definition of 126
    description of 62, 116, 310
    ecosystem of 126*f*, 126-128
    game publishers 128-129
    gamers 126
    genres and titles in 127*t*
    leagues 128
    participation in 75
    revenues of 126
    teams 127-128
    tournaments 127
ethics 59, 156-157
eustress 69
evaluation framework, for sponsorship 256-257
events. *See* sport events
exchange 3
exclusivity 234-235, 235
executive summary 337, 339
expenses 352
experience curve price setting 153
experiments 54
expert, athlete as 203-204
expert interviews 54
expert systems (ES) 285
explanatory research 48, 53
explicit endorsement, by celebrity athletes 204
exploratory research 47-48
extended reality (XR) 116, 132-133. *See also* augmented reality; virtual reality
eyeballs 68*t*

F

Facebook 198, 210, 212, 215, 257
Facebook, Instagram, Twitter, and Snapchat (FITS) 288
facilities 111
fads 125, 125*f*
fan. *See* sport fan
fan cost index (FCI) 164-165
fantasy sport 62, 74*t*, 74-75, 131
Fantasy Sport Motivation Inventory (FanSMI) 74
Federal Policy for Hosting International Sports Events (2000) 36
FIFA World Cup 106, 130
"first-movers" 125
first-person shooter (FPS) games 75

374 Index

Fitness and Amateur Sport Act (1961) 35
fitness services 111
fixed costs 158, 160
focus groups 54
follow-up, after promotion 177-178
football
    CFL 22, 40-41, 50, 110, 113, 189*t*, 228
    CPL 23
    NFL 63, 116-117, 186, 189*t*
form 6
Formula One 25
four Ps, of marketing 3, 45*t*, 152-154, 227, 306, 348-351, 349*t*
full-line price setting 153-154
functional discounts 160, 162
funding 34, 36-37
future competitors 9, 344
Future of Sport Lab (FSL) 287

G

gambling 69
Game Plan (1976) 35
game publishers 128-129
gamers 126
gamification 124
Gatorade 81, 95
gender equity 294-295
geographic data 64
girls, sports for 65-66
global competition 158
Global T20 Canada 24
golf 25, 104
goods 102
Google Analytics 55*t*, 284
Google News 284
government policies 35
go viral 125
grassroots organizations 41
grassroots sport
    description of 16, 37
    participation in 39-40
    spectatorship 39-41
    volunteering importance for 40
Gretzky, Wayne 106, 203, 270
Grey Cup 40
group affiliation 70
growth stage, of product life cycle 104, 105*t*
G-Suite 281

H

hardware 278-279
Harman, Alanna 122-123
Harrison, Mark 4-5
health-related services 111
Henderson, Katherine 28-29
hierarchy of effects model 215

hierarchy of needs 9
high-definition television (HDTV) 282
hockey
    AHL 22
    Canadian culture and 57
    CHL 338
    ECHL 25
    NHL. *See* National Hockey League
    NWHL 24
Hockey Canada 138-139, 270
Hockey Night in Canada 185, 185*t*
Hoeber, Larena 84-85
hole in market 93
Hooper, Dale 80-82
hospitality 235-236
Hosting Program 34
hosting sporting events 36

I

Iceberg Principle 51
ice hockey. *See* hockey
ideas, for promotions 177
image, company 231-233
image-related similarity 232-233
IMI International 49
imperative endorsement, by celebrity athletes 204
implementation 306. *See also* marketing strategy implementation
implicit endorsement, by celebrity athletes 204
income statement 352*t*
indifferent fans 68*t*
influencers 200
information systems (IS) 278, 283-290
information technology (IT) 278
    hardware 278-279
    marketing strategy and 286, 288-290
    software 277, 279-282, 281*t*
    STP and 285-286
innovation 344-345
insiders 68*t*
Instagram 212
insurgent ambushing 267
intangible benefits, of sponsorship 256
intangible products 102
integrative sport management (ISM) system 174-175
Intel Extreme Masters (IEM) 127
International Event Group (IEG) 49, 221
International Management Group (IMG) 111
International Olympic Committee (IOC) 186, 206, 264, 271, 273, 322, 323-325, 327*t*, 329-330

international sport federations (IF) 245, 322
international sporting events, hosting of 36
Internet 119-120
interviews 54
introduction stage, of product life cycle 102, 105*t*
Ipsos Canada 49
iSPARK 49
Ispos Reid 49
ITU Toronto World Cup Triathlon 98

J

Johnson, Ben 35, 334

K

KidSport Ontario 41
Knight, Curtis 7-8
Kozinets, Robert 57-59
Kusch, Cameron 168-169
Kushari, Indivar 50

L

lacrosse 23
Ladies Professional Golf Association (LPGA) 25
language groups 97
law 296, 297*t*
leader and bait price setting 153
leagues
    description of 110
    esports 128
leveraging 13, 260*t*
LGBTQ+ community 174
licensing 113
life cycle variants (LCV) 125, 125*f*
lifestyle marketing 223
lifestyle sponsorship 223
live streaming 72
Los Angeles Olympic Games (1984) 324
Los Angeles Olympic Organizing Committee (LAOOC) 324
Low, Debbie 331-332
Lowry, Kyle 203

M

MacKenzie, Dan 338
MacLaren Advertising Agency 184
MacNab, Leah 142-143
"Mad Love" program 44
Major League Baseball (MLB) 21, 189*t*
Major League Gaming (MLG) 128
Major League Rugby (MLR) 25
Major League Soccer (MLS) 22-23, 93, 189*t*

major sponsor 249
marketing exchange 6
marketing issue, defining 51
Marketing magazine 252
marketing management 5
marketing mix 11-12, 228
marketing plan
  competition analysis 343-345
  contingency plan 353
  example 337-353
  executive summary 337, 339
  financials 351-353
  implementation and control 352-353
  marketing strategy 345-351
  market research 339-341
  product offering 344
  situation analysis 341-343
marketing strategy
  on marketing plan 345-351
  four Ps and 348-351, 349t
  STP as bridge to 80-83, 82f
  technology for 286, 288-290
marketing strategy implementation
  activities of 309
  description of 306-307
  example 353f
marketing theory
  applied sociology 8
  needs and wants 6, 8
  PEST 9, 82
  relationship marketing 8
  STP 11
  three Cs 8-9, 296
  value and utility 6
market leaders 93-94
market/marketing
  ambush. *See* ambush marketing
  B2B 88
  B2C 88
  case example of 10-11
  defined 4-5
  development of 5
  four Ps of 3, 45t, 152-154, 227, 306, 348-351, 349t
  hole in 93
  information systems and 283-290
  lifestyle 223
  Olympic. *See* Olympic marketing
  price in 152-154
  relationship to sponsorship 227-228
  as revenue generator 12
  social. *See* social marketing
  sport. *See* sport marketing
  strategic alliances in 310
  targeting 90-92, 299, 346-347
  total 87-88
  to women 84-85

market research
  causal 53
  data collection techniques 53-54
  descriptive 48, 52-53
  design of 52
  executive perspective on 46-47
  explanatory 48, 53
  exploratory 48
  netnography 57-60
  presentation of findings 56
  in presponsorship phase 248
  primary research 48, 340
  process of 49-56, 52f
  purpose of 52-53
  secondary research 48-49, 339-340
  time as key element of 44
  types of 46-48, 52-53
  uses of 44-46
market research companies 49
market segmentation
  aspects of 85-87
  bases of 88-89
  defined 83, 85
  description of 11
  feedback advantage 90
  on marketing plan 345-346
  market selection 83
  process 87-90
  scenarios 86-87
  segment-by-segment analysis 88-90, 89f
  social marketing and 299
market selection 83
Maslow, Abraham 9
Mathany, Erin 179-181
maturity stage, of product life cycle 102, 105t
Mayo, Don 237-239
McDavid, Connor 110, 134, 173
McRoberts, Scott 30-31
measurability 87
media. *See also* sport media business
  athlete representation on 122-123
  relationship building with 190
  sponsorship and 257-260
  as sport product 111-112
  traditional 122
media benefits, of sponsorship 233-234
media coverage
  media kits 191
  news releases 190-191
  press conferences 191
  sponsorship and 257-259, 268-269
  ways to get 190-192
media kits 191
media relations
  description of 171-172
  importance of 190
  management of 189-193

media rights
  agreement for 187
  fees 185-186
  revenue 186-188
mediated sports
  esports 62, 75, 116
  fantasy sport 74t, 74-75, 131
  participation in 73-75
media training 192
merchandise 112
Michelin 206
Mills Report 35
Ministry of Canadian Heritage 33
Misley, Johnny 312-313
mixed martial arts (MMA) 26
mixed reality (MR) 132, 134
mobile apps
  description of 130-131
  Team Canada 119
Montreal Olympic Games (1976) 322-323, 330, 333
motivation, opportunity, and ability (MOA) 296-297
Mox Analytics 55t
multidimensional typology 67
multiple product, multiple segments scenario 86
multisegment targeting 91
multisport/service organizations (MSOs) 33, 37, 39t, 245

N

Nadolny, Mark 118-119
NASCAR 24
National Basketball Association (NBA) 21-22, 116-117, 142-143
National Basketball League of Canada (NBL) 23
National Football League (NFL) 63, 186, 189t
National Hockey League (NHL)
  description of 20-21
  family fan zone seating 106
  fan cost index 164
  LGBTQ+ community support by 174
  national rights for 189t
  Ottawa Senators 20-21
National Lacrosse League (NLL) 23
National Olympic Committees (NOC) 322, 327, 327t
national sport organizations (NSOs) 33, 36-37, 222, 239-240
National Women's Hockey League (NWHL) 24
NBA2KL 73, 121
NCapture 55t
needs 6, 8, 69

negotiation 253-255
netnography 57-60
neural networks 285
news releases 190-191
NFL Canada 116-117
Nicorette 81, 95
NodeXL 55*t*
nonendemic sponsorship 223
nonprobability sampling 55
nonprofit governing body for sport 312-313

O

objective-based budgeting 306
objectives
  in market research 51-52
  for social media platforms 207-208
  sponsorship 230-236
observation 53-54
observer, athlete as 204
odd-even price setting 153
official language groups 97
Olympic brand
  ambush marketing and 273
  description of 329-330
  investments in 329
  sponsorship of 329
  values of 330
Olympic Games
  ambush marketing in 265, 268, 273
  ancient 226
  broadcasting of 332
  Canadian marketing of 330-335
  Canadian Olympic Committee (COC) 37-39
  commercialism of 321-323
  financing of 321
  hosting 323
  preparation for, high-performance approach to 318-319
  revenue from 186*t*, 187*t*, 327*t*
  revival of 319, 321
  sponsorship of 205, 221, 226, 229, 239-240, 259
  Sport Canada 33-36
  Sport Programs 33-34
  television coverage of 321-322
Olympic marketing
  broadcasting 325-327
  history of 319-325
  introduction to 317
  IOC and 323-325
  Los Angeles Olympic Games and 324
  TOP sponsorship program 328-329
Olympic movement 38, 317, 330, 333-335

Olympic sport 16, 33-39. *See also* Olympic Games
Olympic symbols 144, 329
one product, multiple market segments scenario 86
online communities 57-60
Ontario Colleges Athletic Association (OCAA) 32
Ontario Esports League 128
Ontario University Athletics (OUA) 30
operating systems (OSs) 279
opportunity 296-297
organizational capacity 246-247
Organizing Committee for the Olympic Games (OCOG) 321-322, 325*t*, 329
Ottawa Senators 20-21, 92
overpositioning 94
over-the-top (OTT) channels and services 116, 121, 123, 129-130, 289
Own the Podium (OTP) 19, 332-334

P

Pacific Western Athletic Association (PACWEST) 32
parallel property ambushing 268
Paralympic athletes 97
Paralympic Games 250-251
Paralympic movement 333-335
Paralympic Sport 239-240
"paralysis by analysis" 307
ParticipACTION 132-133
participants
  motivation of 73
  sport consumption as 61-62, 72-75
participation
  in esports 62, 75
  in fantasy sport 74*t*, 74-75
  in grassroot sports 39-40
  in mediated sports 73-75
  in physical sport 73
  price/cost of 154-155
  socioeconomic factors that affect 73
partnerships
  building of 295
  property–brand 80-82
Partners in Pursuit of Excellence: A National Policy on Amateur Sports 35
payment term discounts 160
perceived brand quality 202-203
perceptual mapping 95-96
performance monitoring, of social media platform 209, 211
personal digital assistant (PDA) 278
personal selling 172, 350

personifier, athlete as 204
personnel, media training for 192
PEST (political, economic, social, and technological) 9, 82
Petro-Canada 250-251
philanthropy 80-81, 227
Pirelli 206
pitch 283
place 5-6, 289, 302, 351
Play Soccer 41
point-of-purchase (POP) 174, 258
positioning
  competitive 286
  examples of 94-95
  on marketing plan 347-348
  perceptual mapping 95-96
  strategies for 93-94, 94*t*
positioning map 95
positioning partnerships 81
Pospisil, Vasek 111
possession 6
Potwarka, Luke R. 71
predatory ambushing 267
predatory pricing 156-157
premiums 173
presenting sponsor 249-250
presponsorship practices 246-253
press conferences 191
press releases 190-191
prestige price setting 153
price-demand curve 157*f*
price discrimination 156
price fixing 156
price lining 153
price/pricing
  allowances 153, 160, 162, 165
  cost versus 154, 165
  defining 152
  discounts 153, 160, 162, 165
  ethics and 156-157
  key issues 160, 162, 165
  in marketing 152-154
  four Ps of marketing and 3, 152-154
  setting 157-158
  social marketing and 301-302
  of sponsorship 251-252
  of sport participation 154-155
  strategies for 152-154, 348-349
  supply and 151
  talent and 161
  value and 156
  window 152
primary research 48, 340
probability sampling 55
product
  description of 3
  social marketing and 301
  sport. *See* sport product

product-bundling price setting 154
product distribution. *See* distribution
product endorsement 203
product life cycle (PLC)
    of digital sport product 124-126
    of sport product 102, 104-105, 105*t*, 125
product strategy 348
professionalism 259-260
professional sport. *See also* specific sport
    challenges for 26-27
    competition 25-26
    definition of 16
    public subsidy of 27
    sport entertainment 26
    tier one 20-22
    tier three 23-25
    tier two 22-23
    women's 24
profit 157-158
program evaluation review technique (PERT) 309
project calendar 309
promotion
    activating of 178-179
    activities 167-168
    advertising 170-171
    day of 178
    defined 168
    execution elements 176-179
    follow-up 177-178
    in four Ps of marketing 3
    hidden costs of 178
    ideas for 177
    in marketing mix 228
    personal sales 172
    preliminary planning 176-177
    publicity 171-172
    public relations 174-175
    sales 172-174
    social marketing and 302
    sponsorship 175-176
    strategies 349-350
    timing of 177
promotional materials 350
promotional mix 168-176, 289, 302*t*, 350-351
property–brand partnerships 80-82
property infringement 206-207, 268
provincial sport 37, 38*t*
psychography 64
psychological price setting 153
publicity 171-172, 350
public relations 174-175
public service announcements (PSAs) 171
public subsidy 27
publishers, game 128-129

push money allowances 162, 165
PuttView 70

Q
QR barcodes 289
QSSF 32
qualitative research 53, 53*f*
quality, perceived 144
Qualtrics 284
quantitative research 53
quantity discounts 160
Quebec Student Sport Federation (QSSF) 30
questionnaires 54, 284, 340-341

R
radio frequency identification (RFID) tags 289
rapid adoption, of digital sport product 125, 125*f*
real-time strategy (RTS) games 75
relationship building 259
relationship marketing 8
Report of the Commission of Inquiry into the Use of Drugs and Banned Practices Intended to Increase Athletic Performance 35
research. *See* market research
research ethics 59
resourcing strategy 308
responsiveness 87
return on investment (ROI)
    description of 87
    metrics 214-216, 215*t*
    from social media in sport 213-216, 216*f*
    from sponsorship 230
revenue
    during COVID-19 pandemic 162-163
    of esports 126
    marketing as generator of 12
    Olympic Games 186*t*, 187*t*, 327*t*
revitalization 125*f*, 125-126
rich site summary (RSS) feeding 284
rights fees 321
rivalry 107-108
Robert, François 250-251
Rogers Centre 111
Rogers Communications 186, 188
Rogers Cup 25
Roth, Gavin 242-244
Rothschild, Michael 296
Rothschild MOA framework 296-297
routine decisions 44
rugby 25
Rule 40 271
Running Room 167

S
sale price discounts 162
sales, of sponsorships 242-244
Salesforce Analytics 55*t*
sales forecasts 351-352
sales objectives 234, 257
sales promotion 172-174, 234
Samaranch, Juan Antonio 324
sampling 48, 55-56, 173-174
Sandler, Dennis 265
Sandmeyer-Graves, Allison 294-295
saturation ambushing 268
scandals 35
scholarships 32
Scott, Olan 213-214
seasonal discounts 160
secondary research 48-49, 339-340
second screen 133-134
segmentation
    market. *See* market segmentation
    of sport consumers 63-64
segmentation, targeting, and positioning (STP)
    as bridge to marketing strategy 80-83, 82*f*
    definition of 11
    as economic advantage 80
    executive perspective on 80-81
    on marketing plan 345-348
    market segmentation 83-90
    positioning 93-96
    social marketing and 299
    targeting 90-93
    technology and 285-286
segmentation grids 90, 92-93
segment of one scenario 86-87
self-actualization 9
self-esteem 70
sensitivity 88-89
Seoul Olympics (1988) 35
services 102
servicing 245
Setlur, Vijay 147-149
Shani, David 265
Shanks, Rebecca 65-66
Sharapova, Maria 204
simulated professional sports (SPS) 75
Sinclair, Christine 204
situational analysis 283-285
situation analysis 341-343
Six Degrees 198
skilled services 111
slogans 140
slow adoption, of digital sport product 125, 125*f*
SMART goal 208, 311
smartwatch 124, 131-132
Smith, Scott 138-139

Snapchat 212
soccer
    growth of 40
    MLS 22-23, 93, 189*t*
    USL 25
social marketing
    appropriateness of 296-298
    behavioural change and 293
    company in context of 298-299
    customers on context of 298-299
    defined 295
    executive perspective on 294-295
    Rothschild MOA framework 296-297
    STP and 299
    strategies 301-302
social media
    ambush marketing and 205-207
    ambush marketing initiatives on 271
    athletes' presentation on 122-123
    automated-scheduled posts 210
    balanced combination of 209
    branding uses of 202-203
    careers and 213-214
    content 209-210
    data collection tools 55*t*
    definition of 198
    digital sport product and 117
    as discontinuous innovation 124
    don'ts of 210
    endorsement and 203-204
    features of 198-201, 205
    history of 198
    interactivity of 123
    major league professional sport use of 211-212
    overview of 197-198
    profile on 210
    return on investment from 213-216, 216*f*
    sponsorship and 204-205
    sport marketing use of 201-207
    user-generated content 198
    users of 200-201
social media influencers (SMI) 200
social media platforms
    accomplishments 209, 211
    ambush marketing on 206
    automated-scheduled posts 210
    content calendar 209
    content on 209
    description of 198-200
    goal setting for 208
    information collection for 207
    managing of 207-211
    objectives for 207-208
    performance monitoring of 209, 211

    reasons for joining 200
    report 211
    return on investment metrics 214-216, 215*t*
    selection of 208-209
    target audience for 208
social media sites 198-199
Social Mention 55*t*
social networks 199
socioeconomics 64, 73
sociology 8
software 54, 277, 279-282, 281*t*
spectator(s)
    description of 61
    fans versus 62, 66-67
    ordinary 66-67
    sport consumption as 63-67
Spectator Experience and Technology (SEAT) Laboratory 71
spectatorship 39-41
spiffs 162, 165
spokesperson, athlete as 204
sponsor(s)
    categories of 249-250
    finding of 253
    fit 254
    major 249
    presenting 249-250
    research of potential 253
    supplier 250
    title 249
sponsor recognition programs 269
sponsor self-ambushing 268
sponsorship
    activation and 225-226, 258*t*
    advertising and 228-230, 230*t*
    of ancillary event activities 249
    assets that can be sponsored 249
    athletes in 257
    awareness and 231
    best practices 259-260
    business of 222
    in Canada 245-246
    competing company's media use during time of 268-269
    corporate objectives and 230-236
    COVID-19 and 232, 238-239
    definition of 221
    of digital assets 249
    effectiveness of 255
    exclusivity 235
    executive perspective on 222-224
    four-step approach to 246
    history of 226-227
    hospitality 235-236
    human resources allocated to 255
    image and 231-233
    in-kind 350

    levels of 249-251
    life of 255-259
    lifestyle 223
    marketing and 227-228
    market trends in 224-225
    media and 233-234, 257-260
    of media coverage 268-269
    model of 247*f*
    of national teams 249
    negotiation stage of 253-255
    of Olympic Games 205, 221, 226, 229, 239-240, 259
    organizational capacity 246-247
    organizational support 255-256
    of owned events 249
    philanthropy and 227
    presponsorship practices 246-253
    pricing of 251-252
    professionalism in 259-260
    of programs 249
    in promotional mix 175-176
    relationship building in 259
    researcher's view on 237-239
    return on investment 230
    sales objectives 234
    sales of 172, 242-244
    servicing of 255
    social media and 204-205
    stakeholders 225-226, 244-245
    subcategory 269
    target markets and 233-236
    termination of 259
    valuation of 251
    of women's sports 65-66
sponsorship category 246
sponsorship contract 254-255
sponsorship deal 241
sponsorship evaluation
    as best practice 260
    framework for 256-257
    goal of 256
    improvements in 245
    presponsorship benchmarks for 256
    tracking 256
Sponsorship Marketing Council of Canada 251-252
sponsorship plan 246-248
Sponsorship Report, The 252
SponsorshipX COVID-19 global studies 232
sport. *See also* specific sport
    amateur 28, 39-41, 245
    collegiate 16, 27-33
    esports 62, 75, 116
    fantasy 74*t*, 74-75, 131
    grassroots. *See* grassroots sport
    importance of, in Canada 15-16
    knowledge of 84

nonprofit governing body for 312-313
Olympic 16, 33-39
participation in 39-40
professional 16, 20-27
Sport: Everybody's Business 35
Sport: The Way Ahead 35
sport brands. *See* brand(s)
Sport Canada 33-36
sport centres 19, 20t
sport clubs 73
sport consumers. *See also* consumer(s)
attendance by 68-70, 72, 72t
demographics of 64
dualistic typology of 67
geographic influences on 64
multidimensional typology of 67
neuroscience approaches to understanding 71
as participants 61-63, 72-75
psychography of 64
socioeconomics of 64, 73
as spectators 61, 63
sport fans versus 62
tiered typologies of 67
sport consumption
digital sport product 117
factors that affect 63-64
reasons for 63
as spectators 64-67
technological developments that affect 70
types of 62t, 63
sport entertainment 26
sport equipment 105
sport events
attendance by 68-70, 72, 72t
attractiveness of 68
in Canada 18t, 18-19
competitive factors 69
demographic factors 69
description of 109
economic factors 68-69
live streaming of 72
stadium factors 69
sport facilities 19t, 19-20, 20t, 73
sport fan(s)
attendance by 68-70, 72, 72t
classifications of 67-68, 68t
clothing of 84-85
definition of 67
description of 112, 137-138
differences among 67
emotional attachment of 112, 137-138
identification of 70
motivation factors for 69-70
social media use by 213
spectators versus 62, 66-67

sport consumers versus 62
types of 68, 68t
women as 84-85
Sport Funding and Accountability Framework (SFAF) 34
sport innovation 287-288
sport involvement 69
sport marketing. *See also* marketing
data in 50
defined 12
importance of 12-13
process of 12f
professional athlete's perspective on 7-8
social media for 201-207
uniqueness of 12-13
sport market research. *See* market research
sport media business
in Canada 188-189
evolution of 185f
history of 184-185
key players in 188-189, 189t
media rights fees 185-186
media rights revenue 186-188
sport organizations 17, 36-37, 216, 247
sport packaging 113-114
sport policy 34-36
sport product
athletes 109-110
characteristics of 105-107
clubs 110-111
defined 101-102, 105
digital. *See* digital sport product
events 109
extensive nature of 103
facilities 111
forms of 107-112
leagues 110
media 111-112
merchandise 112
model of 109f
product life cycle of 102, 104-105, 105t, 125
rivalry in 107-108
skilled services 111
teams 110
varied nature of 103
Sport Programs 33-34
sport promotion. *See* promotion
sport properties
description of 245, 248
media outlets available to 252f
Sports Illustrated 106
Sportsnet 129-130, 188
Sports One 280-281
sport sponsorship. *See* sponsorship
Sport Support Program 33

stadium 69
stages of change 298-299
stakeholders, sponsorship 225-226, 244-245
Statistics Canada 48, 253
Stockholm Olympic Games (1912) 321
stocking allowances 162
STP. *See* segmentation, targeting, and positioning (STP)
St-Pierre, Georges 26, 204
strategic decisions 44
strategic marketing alliances 310
student athletes 32
subcategory sponsorship 269
subcultures 57
subscription-based video-on-demand (SVOD) service 188
substantiality 87
substitutes 9, 343
Subway 206
supplier 250
supply 151
SurveyMonkey 284
Sveinson, Katie 84-85
sweepstakes 173
SWOT analysis 342-343

T
tangible benefits, of sponsorship 256
tangible products 102
target audience
characteristics of 296-297
for social media platform 208
stages of change 298
targeting
80/20 rule 92
on marketing plan 346-347
methods of 90-92
social marketing and 299
target market
common Canadian 96-97
reaching 233-236
selection of 93
targeting of 90-92
women as 84
target-return price setting 153
task-based budgeting 306
Task Force on Sport for Canadians 35
taxation policies 27
Team Canada 118-119
teams
definition of 110
esports 127-128
technology. *See* information technology (IT)
television
commercialization and 321-322
Olympic broadcasting 325-327

television channels 111
tennis 25
territorial sport 37, 38*t*
thematic advertising 270-271
The Olympic Programme (TOP) 324, 328-329
Theory of Change 294
The Sports Network (TSN) 111, 129, 193
33Across 55*t*
Thomson, David 116-117
three Cs 8-9, 296
tier one professional sport 20-22
tier three professional sport 23-25
tier two professional sport 22-23
TikTok 202, 212
time 6
time-buy rights agreement 187
timing, of promotions 177
Tingling, Peter 161
title sponsor 249
TOP sponsorship program 328-329
Toronto Blue Jays 21, 173
Toronto Maple Leafs 12, 110, 140
Toronto Raptors 21-22, 64, 70, 110, 130-131, 202
Toronto Six 24
total market 87-88
tournaments, esports 127
trade discounts 160, 162
trade-in allowances 165
trademark 112

tree structures 286
Trudeau, Pierre 35
True Sport 41
Twitter 119, 198, 206, 212, 257

U
UFC 26
undifferentiated targeting 90-91, 299
unintentional ambushing 268
United Boxing Promotion 26
United Soccer League (USL) 25
University Cup 30
university sport 27-33
U.S. League One (USL1) 25
U.S. Television Act 226
user-generated content (UGC) 288
U SPORTS 27-32
utility 6

V
value 6, 156
values ambushing 206, 268
Vancouver Grizzlies 21
Vancouver 2010 Olympic Games 259, 320
Vancouver Organizing Committee for the Olympic and Paralympic Winter Games (VANOC) 321
Vanier Cup 30
variable costs 158, 160
Vine 198
virtual communities 57-60

virtual reality (VR) 70, 132-134
volume 157-158
volunteering 40

W
WADA. *See* World Anti-Doping Agency (WADA)
wallets 68*t*
Walling, Chris 104
wants 6, 8, 69
wearables 131-132
Wikipedia 198
William Morris Endeavor–International Management Group (WME-IMG) 111
women
  marketing to 84-85
  professional leagues for 24
  as sport fans 84-85
  sports for 65-66
  as target market 96-97
Woods, Brenda 222-224
World Anti-Doping Agency (WADA) 303, 327
World Wrestling Entertainment (WWE) 26, 188
wrestling 26

Y
YouGov Sports 49
young Canadians 97
YouTube 198, 212

ABOUT THE AUTHORS

Norm O'Reilly, PhD, MBA, CPA, is dean of the Graduate School of Business at the University of Maine and a professor of sport management in the Maine Business School. A Canadian, Dr. O'Reilly was the founding director of the International Institute for Sport Business and Leadership in the Gordon S. Lang School of Business and Economics at the University of Guelph. He has authored 16 books and more than 150 management journal articles. He was awarded the Distinguished Career Contributions Award by the American Marketing Association's Sport Marketing Special Interest Group (2015) and is a fellow of the North American Society for Sport Management. O'Reilly was assistant chef de mission (assistant mission leader) for the Canadian team at the 2016 Paralympic Games in Rio, Brazil, and has attended four Olympic Games in various capacities with Team Canada.

Benoit Séguin, PhD, is a professor of sport marketing in the School of Human Kinetics at the University of Ottawa. His research focuses mainly on sport sponsorship, ambush marketing, brand governance, and topics related to Olympic marketing. In addition to his academic work, Dr. Séguin has extensive experience in the management of Olympic sport organizations, including as marketing director of two national sport associations, past president of Diving Canada, assistant chef de mission (assistant mission leader) for the Canadian team (2003 Pan Am Games, Santo Domingo), and board member for several sport organizations.

Gashaw Abeza, PhD, is a professor at Towson University. Abeza taught graduate and undergraduate students at the University of Ottawa (Ottawa, Ontario) and Southern Methodist University (Dallas, Texas), and he guest lectured at four other universities. He has been an adjunct professor at the University of Guelph since 2019. His main research interest is marketing communications, with his specific area of expertise in digital media. He has researched and written extensively on the topic of social media in sport and is widely published. He is the coauthor of two books and coeditor of one book: *Implications and Impacts of Esports on Business and Society* (IGI Global), *Sport Sponsorship Insights* (Routledge), and *Social Media in Sport: Theory and Practice* (World Scientific). Dr. Abeza serves as an ad hoc reviewer for a number of academic journals. He currently serves on the editorial boards of eight academic journals: *International Journal of Sport Communication*; *Sport, Business, and Management*; *Journal of Relationship Marketing*; *International Journal of Esports Research*; *Journal of Global Sport Management*; *Sport Marketing Quarterly*; *International Journal of Sports Marketing and Sponsorship*; and the newly launched *Sport Management Digest*.

Michael L. Naraine, PhD, is an assistant professor in the department of sport management at Brock University and is also an honorary adjunct professor at La Trobe University in Victoria, Australia. His primary research interest is the area of digital sport management and marketing, examining the strategy, fan engagement, and analytics related to new developments in the sport business landscape, including social media, esports, business analytics, and artificial intelligence. Naraine is also a research fellow of the North American Society for Sport Management and is the current editor in chief of *Case Studies in Sport Management*. Additionally, he serves as an editorial board member for *Sport Marketing Quarterly*, *International Journal of Sport Communication*, and the newly founded *Sports Innovation Journal*.